Beginning iOS 7 Development

Exploring the iOS SDK

Jack Nutting

Fredrik Olsson

David Mark

Jeff LaMarche

Apress

Beginning iOS 7 Development: Exploring the iOS SDK

ISBN-13 (pbk): 978-1-4302-6022-6

ISBN-13 (electronic): 978-1-4302-6023-3

President and Publisher: Paul Manning
Lead Editor: Steve Anglin
Technical Reviewer: Nick Waynik
Editorial Board: Steve Anglin, Mark Beckner, Ewan Buckingham, Gary Cornell, Louise Corrigan, Jim DeWolf, Jonathan Gennick, Jonathan Hassell, Robert Hutchinson, Michelle Lowman, James Markham, Matthew Moodie, Jeff Olson, Jeffrey Pepper, Douglas Pundick, Ben Renow-Clarke, Dominic Shakeshaft, Gwenan Spearing, Matt Wade, Steve Weiss
Coordinating Editors: Anamika Panchoo and Melissa Maldonado
Copy Editor: Patrick Meader
Compositor: SPi Global
Indexer: SPi Global
Artist: SPi Global
Cover Designer: Anna Ishchenko

Distributed to the book trade worldwide by Springer Science+Business Media New York, 233 Spring Street, 6th Floor, New York, NY 10013. Phone 1-800-SPRINGER, fax (201) 348-4505, e-mail orders-ny@springer-sbm.com, or visit www.springeronline.com. Apress Media, LLC is a California LLC and the sole member (owner) is Springer Science + Business Media Finance Inc (SSBM Finance Inc). SSBM Finance Inc is a Delaware corporation.

For information on translations, please e-mail rights@apress.com, or visit www.apress.com.

Apress and friends of ED books may be purchased in bulk for academic, corporate, or promotional use. eBook versions and licenses are also available for most titles. For more information, reference our Special Bulk Sales–eBook Licensing web page at www.apress.com/bulk-sales.

Any source code or other supplementary materials referenced by the author in this text is available to readers at www.apress.com. For detailed information about how to locate your book's source code, go to www.apress.com/source-code/.

This book is dedicated to the memory of Steve Jobs.
We continue to be inspired by his spirit and his vision.

—David Mark and Jack Nutting

Dedicated to my mom and dad, who bought my first computer.

—Fredrik Olsson

Contents at a Glance

Contents

About the Authors

Jack Nutting has been using Cocoa since the olden days, long before it was even called Cocoa. He has used Cocoa and its predecessors to develop software for a wide range of industries and applications, including gaming, graphic design, online digital distribution, telecommunications, finance, publishing, and travel. Jack has written several books on iOS and Mac development, including *Beginning iOS 6 Development* (Apress, 2013), *Learn Cocoa on the Mac* (Apress, 2013), and *Beginning iPad Development for iPhone Developers* (Apress, 2010). Besides writing software and books, he also leads developer training and blogs from time to time at www.nuthole.com. He's @jacknutting on Twitter.

Fredrik Olsson has been using Cocoa since Mac OS X 10.1 and for iPhone since the unofficial toolchain. He has had a long and varied career, ranging from real-time assembly to enterprise Java. He is passionate about Objective-C for its elegance, Cocoa frameworks for its clarity, and both for creating a greater whole than their parts. When away from a keyboard, Fredrik has spoken at conferences and led developer training. You'll find Fredrik on Twitter as @peylow.

Dave Mark is a longtime Mac developer and author who has written a number of books on Mac and iOS development, including *Beginning iOS 6 Development* (Apress, 2013), *More iOS 6 Development* (Apress, 2013), *Learn C on the Mac* (Apress, 2013), *Ultimate Mac Programming* (Wiley, 1995), and the *Macintosh Programming Primer series* (Addison-Wesley, 1992). Dave was one of the founders of MartianCraft, an iOS and Android development house. Dave loves the water and spends as much time as possible on it, in it, or near it. He lives with his wife and three children in Virginia. On Twitter, he's @davemark.

Jeff LaMarche is a Mac and iOS developer with more than twenty years of programming experience. Jeff has written a number of iOS and Mac development books, including *Beginning iOS 6 Development* (Apress, 2013) and *More iOS 6 Development* (Apress, 2013). Jeff is a principal at MartianCraft, an iOS and Android development house. He has written about Cocoa and Objective-C for *MacTech* magazine, as well as articles for Apple's developer web site. Jeff also writes about iOS development for his widely read blog at www.iphonedevelopment. blogspot.com, and he can be found on Twitter as @jeff_lamarche.

About the Technical Reviewer

Nick Waynik has been working in the IT field for over fifteen years and has done everything from network administration to web development. He started writing iOS apps when the SDK was first released. Since then, he has gone on to start his own business, focusing on iOS development. He loves spending his free time with his wife, Allison, and son, Preston. He also sometimes plays golf. He blogs at nicholaswaynik.com and can be found on Twitter as @n_dubbs.

Acknowledgments

We'd like to thank all the hardworking people at Apress, whose effort and support are absolutely critical when it comes to delivering a book of this magnitude. Special thanks to Anamika Panchoo for keeping our plates full right up until the end was finally in sight, at which point her shoes were amply filled by Melissa Maldonado. Without the patience and diligence of these coordinating editors, this book would never have been completed. Patrick Meader did a terrific job of fixing faulty prose, and Nick Waynik was great at helping haphazard code. Tom Welsh, Douglas Pundick, and Matt Moodie each took a turn as development editor, and all made sure each chapter is organized and sensible. And of course, we owe a debt of gratitude to a wide range of often-overlooked people responsible for indexing, page layout, dealing with printers and retailers, and surely other things I don't know about; even though we as authors really don't interact with most of you directly, and usually don't even know your names, we know you're there and doing important things. Keep it up!

Introduction

This book is enormous. If you are reading a paper copy, you're well aware of this, but if you've got a digital copy, you might not understand the size of this thing. I mean, it's larger than most bibles I've seen. Not that I'm an expert on bibles or anything, but you know: they're big, fat books. If you asked, "Is *Beginning iOS 7 Development* bigger than a breadbox?" I'd have to say, "Almost." And yet, this book is made of smaller pieces, portioned out so that you should be able to tackle the contents of any single chapter in a delightful afternoon, learning things about iOS development that you probably never imagined. When I say "tackle," I don't mean just read each chapter. I mean you need to actually sit down in front of a Mac and work your way through it. Building all the example apps as you go through each chapter will help imprint all the usage patterns and concepts into your brain in a way that reading alone could never do. If you work your way through this book, you will come away with a great understanding of the foundations of iOS app development, and you will be more than ready to build iOS apps all on your own.

Many years ago, I met the late Torfrid Olsson, a Swedish sculptor from a rural area of northern Sweden. I expressed to him some envy and admiration about one aspect of his life, and his reply stuck with me: "Ah, that's just something you've read about in books. You have your own life that is uniquely yours. What makes you think that it's missing anything?" My hope is that you don't let the knowledge contained in these pages just be something you read in a book. Read it, of course, but also work through it, understand it, and wrestle it to the ground if you must. Make it *yours*.

—Jack Nutting

Stockholm 2014

Chapter 1

Welcome to the Jungle

So, you want to write iPhone, iPod touch, and iPad applications? Well, we can't say that we blame you. iOS, the core software of all of these devices, is an exciting platform that has been seeing explosive growth since it first came out in 2007. The rise of the mobile software platform means that people are using software everywhere they go. With the release of iOS 7, Xcode 5, and the latest incarnation of the iOS software development kit (SDK), things have only gotten better and more interesting.

What this Book Is

This book is a guide to help you get started down the path to creating your own iOS applications. Our goal is to get you past the initial difficulties, to help you understand the way iOS applications work and how they are built.

As you work your way through this book, you will create a number of small applications, each designed to highlight specific iOS features and to show you how to control or interact with those features. If you combine the foundation you'll gain through this book with your own creativity and determination, and then add in the extensive and well-written documentation provided by Apple, you'll have everything you need to build your own professional iPhone and iPad applications.

> **Tip**   Jack, Dave, Jeff, and Fredrik have set up a forum for this book. It's a great place to meet like-minded folks, get your questions answered, and even answer other people's questions. The forum is at `http://forum.learncocoa.org`. Be sure to check it out!

What You Need

Before you can begin writing software for iOS, you'll need a few items. For starters, you'll need an Intel-based Macintosh, running Mountain Lion (OS X 10.8), Mavericks (OS X 10.9) or later. Any recent Intel-based Macintosh computer—laptop or desktop—should work just fine.

To get access to the latest and greatest from Apple, you'll also really need to sign up to become a registered iOS developer. To create your developer account, just navigate to http://developer.apple.com/ios/. That will bring you to a page similar to the one shown in Figure 1-1.

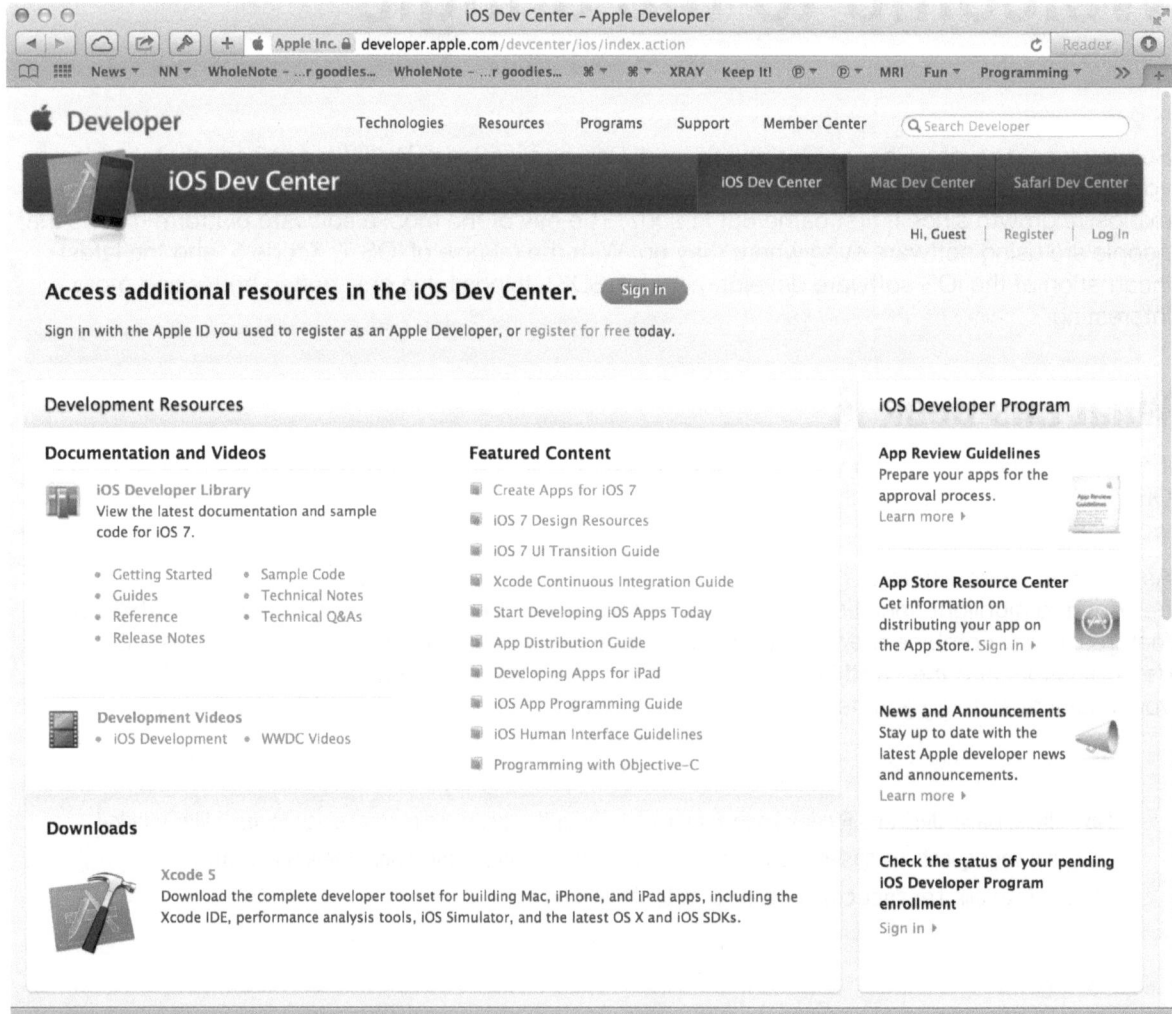

Figure 1-1. Apple's iOS Dev Center website

First, click Log in. You'll be prompted for your Apple ID. If you don't have an Apple ID, click Join now, create such an ID, and then log in. Once you are logged in, you'll be taken to the main iOS development page. You'll find links to a wealth of documentation, videos, sample code, and the like—all dedicated to teaching you the finer points of iOS application development.

The most important tool you'll be using to develop iOS applications is called Xcode. Xcode is Apple's integrated development environment (IDE). Xcode includes tools for creating and debugging source code, compiling applications, and performance tuning the applications you've written.

You can download Xcode from the Mac App Store, which you can access from your Mac's Apple menu.

SDK VERSIONS AND SOURCE CODE FOR THE EXAMPLES

As the versions of the SDK and Xcode evolve, the mechanism for downloading them will also change. For the past few years, Apple has been publishing the current "stable" version of Xcode and the iOS SDK on the Mac App Store, while simultaneously often providing developers the ability to download preview versions of upcoming releases from its developer site. Bottom line: you want to download the latest released (non-beta) version of Xcode and the iOS SDK, so use the Mac App Store.

This book has been written to work with the latest version of the SDK. In some places, we have chosen to use new functions or methods introduced with iOS 7 that may prove incompatible with earlier versions of the SDK. We'll be sure to point those situations out as they arise in this book.

Be sure to download the latest and greatest source code archives from `http://learncocoa.org` or from the book's forum at `http://forum.learncocoa.org`. We'll update the code as new versions of the SDK are released, so be sure to check the site periodically.

Developer Options

The free Xcode download includes a simulator that will allow you to build and run iPhone and iPad apps on your Mac. This is perfect for learning how to program for iOS. However, the simulator does *not* support many hardware-dependent features, such as the accelerometer and camera. Also, the free option will not allow you to install your applications onto a real iPhone or other device, and it does not give you the ability to distribute your applications on Apple's App Store. For those capabilities, you'll need to sign up for one of the other options, which aren't free:

- *The Standard program* costs $99/year. It provides a host of development tools and resources, technical support, distribution of your application via Apple's App Store, and, most importantly, the ability to test and debug your code on an iOS device, rather than just in the simulator.

- *The Enterprise program* costs $299/year. It is designed for companies developing proprietary, in-house iOS applications.

For more details on these programs, visit `http://developer.apple.com/programs/ios` and `http://developer.apple.com/programs/ios/enterprise` to compare the two.

Because iOS supports an always-connected mobile device that uses other companies' wireless infrastructure, Apple has needed to place far more restrictions on iOS developers than it ever has on Mac developers (who are able—at the moment, anyway—to write and distribute programs with absolutely no oversight or approval from Apple). Even though the iPod touch and the Wi-Fi-only versions of the iPad don't use anyone else's infrastructure, they're still subject to these same restrictions.

Apple has not added restrictions to be mean, but rather as an attempt to minimize the chances of malicious or poorly written programs being distributed that could degrade performance on the shared network. Developing for iOS may appear to present a lot of hoops to jump through, but Apple has expended quite an effort to make the process as painless as possible. And also consider that $99 is still much less expensive than buying, for example, Visual Studio, which is Microsoft's software development IDE.

This may seem obvious, but you'll also need an iPhone, iPod touch, or iPad. While much of your code can be tested using the iOS simulator, not all programs can be. And even those that can run on the simulator really need to be thoroughly tested on an actual device before you ever consider releasing your application to the public.

> **Note**   If you are going to sign up for the Standard or Enterprise program, you should do it right now. The approval process can take a while, and you'll need that approval to be able to run your applications on an actual device. Don't worry, though, because all the projects in the first several chapters and the majority of the applications in this book will run just fine on the iOS simulator.

What You Need to Know

This book assumes that you already have some programming knowledge. It assumes that you understand the fundamentals of programming in general and object-oriented programming in particular (you know what classes, objects, loops, and variables are, for example). It also assumes that you are familiar with the Objective-C programming language. Cocoa Touch, the part of the SDK that you will be working with through most of this book, uses the latest version of Objective-C, which contains several new features not present in earlier versions. But don't worry if you're not familiar with the more recent additions to the Objective-C language. We highlight any of the new language features we take advantage of, and explain how they work and why we are using them.

You should also be familiar with iOS itself, as a user. Just as you would with any platform for which you wanted to write an application, get to know the nuances and quirks of the iPhone, iPad, or iPod touch. Take the time to get familiar with the iOS interface and with the way Apple's iPhone and/or iPad applications look and feel.

NEW TO OBJECTIVE-C?

If you have not programmed in Objective-C before, here are a few resources to help you get started:

- *Learn Objective-C on the Mac: For OS X and iOS* (2nd edition, Apress, 2012): this is an excellent and approachable introduction to Objective-C by Mac-programming experts Scott Knaster, Waqar Malik, and Mark Dalrymple. You can find more information at http://www.apress.com/book/view/9781430241881.

- *Programming with Objective-C*: this is Apple's introduction to the language. You can find more information at https://developer.apple.com/library/mac/documentation/cocoa/conceptual/ProgrammingWithObjectiveC.

What's Different About Coding for iOS?

If you have never programmed in Cocoa or its predecessors NeXTSTEP or OpenStep, you may find Cocoa Touch—the application framework you'll be using to write iOS applications—a little alien. It has some fundamental differences from other common application frameworks, such as those used when building .NET or Java applications. Don't worry too much if you feel a little lost at first. Just keep plugging away at the exercises, and it will all start to fall into place after a while.

If you have written programs using Cocoa or NeXTSTEP, a lot in the iOS SDK will be familiar to you. A great many classes are unchanged from the versions that are used to develop for OS X. Even those that are different tend to follow the same basic principles and similar design patterns. However, several differences exist between Cocoa and Cocoa Touch.

Regardless of your background, you need to keep in mind some key differences between iOS development and desktop application development. These differences are discussed in the following sections.

Only One Active Application

On iOS, only one application can be active and displayed on the screen at any given time. Since iOS 4, applications have been able to run in the background after the user presses the "home" button, but even that is limited to a narrow set of situations, and you must code for it, specifically.

When your application isn't active or running in the background, it doesn't receive any attention whatsoever from the CPU, which will wreak havoc with open network connections and the like. iOS allows background processing, but making your apps play nicely in this situation will require some effort on your part.

Only One Window

Desktop and laptop operating systems allow many running programs to coexist, each with the ability to create and control multiple windows. However, iOS gives your application just one "window" to work with. All of your application's interaction with the user takes place inside this one window, and its size is fixed at the size of the screen.

Limited Access

Programs on a computer pretty much have access to everything the user who launched them does. However, iOS seriously restricts what your application can access.

You can read and write files only from the part of iOS's file system that was created for your application. This area is called your application's **sandbox**. Your sandbox is where your application will store documents, preferences, and every other kind of data it may need to retain.

Your application is also constrained in some other ways. You will not be able to access low-number network ports on iOS, for example, or do anything else that would typically require root or administrative access on a desktop computer.

Limited Response Time

Because of the way it is used, iOS needs to be snappy, and it expects the same of your application. When your program is launched, you need to get your application open, preferences and data loaded, and the main view shown on the screen as fast as possible—in no more than a few seconds.

At any time when your program is running, it may have the rug pulled out from under it. If the user presses the home button, iOS goes home, and you must quickly save everything and quit. If you take longer than five seconds to save and give up control, your application process will be killed, regardless of whether you finished saving. There is an API that allows your app to ask for additional time to work when it's about to go dark, but you've got to know how to use it.

Limited Screen Size

The iPhone's screen is really nice. When introduced, it was the highest resolution screen available on a handheld consumer device, by far.

But the iPhone display just isn't all that big, and as a result, you have a lot less room to work with than on modern computers. The screen is just 320 × 480 on the first few iPhone generations, and it was later doubled in both directions to 640 × 960 with the introduction of the iPhone 4's retina display. This was recently increased further to 640 × 1136 on the iPhone 5. That sounds like a decent number of pixels, but keep in mind that these retina displays are crammed into pretty small form factors, so you can't count on fitting more controls or anything like that. This has a big impact on the kinds of applications and interactivity you can offer on an iPhone.

The iPad increases the available space a bit by offering a 1024 × 768 display; but even today, that's not so terribly large. To give an interesting contrast, at the time of writing Apple's least expensive iMac supports 1920 × 1080 pixels, and its least expensive notebook computer, the 11-inch MacBook Air, supports 1366 × 768 pixels. On the other end of the spectrum, Apple's largest current monitor, the 27-inch LED Cinema Display, offers a whopping 2560 × 1440 pixels. Note that newer iPad models (every full-size iPad after the iPad 2, as well as the iPad Mini Retina) have retina displays that double the screen resolution in both directions. But as with the retina iPhones, that 2048 × 1536 screen is in the same physical space as the old screen was, so you can't really count on using those pixels the same way you would on a traditional screen.

Limited System Resources

Any old-time programmers who are reading this are likely laughing at the idea of a machine with at least 512MB of RAM and 16GB of storage being in any way resource-constrained, but it is true. Developing for iOS is not, perhaps, in exactly the same league as trying to write a complex spreadsheet application on a machine with 48KB of memory. But given the graphical nature of iOS and all it is capable of doing, running out of memory is very easy.

The iOS devices available right now have either 512MB (iPhone 4S, iPad 2, original iPad mini, latest iPod touch), or 1024MB of physical RAM (iPhone 5c, iPhone 5s, iPad Air, iPad mini Retina), though that will likely increase over time. Some of that memory is used for the screen buffer and by other system processes. Usually, no more than half of that memory is left for your application to use, and the amount can be considerably less, especially now that other apps can be running in the background.

Although that may sound like it leaves a pretty decent amount of memory for such a small computer, there is another factor to consider when it comes to memory on iOS. Modern computer operating systems like OS X will take chunks of memory that aren't being used and write them out to disk in something called a **swap file**. The swap file allows applications to keep running, even when they have requested more memory than is actually available on the computer. iOS, however, will not write volatile memory, such as application data, out to a swap file. As a result, the amount of memory available to your application is constrained by the amount of unused physical memory in the iOS device.

Cocoa Touch has built-in mechanisms for letting your application know that memory is getting low. When that happens, your application must free up unneeded memory or risk being forced to quit.

No Garbage Collection, but. . .

We mentioned earlier that Cocoa Touch uses Objective-C, but one of the key Objective-C features of the early 2000s is not available with iOS: Cocoa Touch does not support garbage collection. The need to do manual memory management when programming for iOS has been a bit of a stumbling block for many programmers new to the platform, especially those coming from languages that offer garbage collection.

With the version of Objective-C supported by the latest versions of iOS, however, this particular stumbling block is basically gone. This is thanks to a feature called Automatic Reference Counting (ARC), which gets rid of the need to manually manage memory for Objective-C objects. ARC not only serves as a worthy replacement to garbage collection, it's actually better in most respects. Starting in OS X 10.8, ARC became the default memory management technology for Mac apps, and garbage collection has been deprecated there in favor of ARC. And of course, it's also the default memory management mechanism in iOS as well. We'll talk about ARC in Chapter 3.

Some New Stuff

Since we've mentioned that Cocoa Touch is missing some features that Cocoa has, it seems only fair to mention that the iOS SDK contains some functionality that is not currently present in Cocoa or, at least, is not available on every Mac:

- The iOS SDK provides a way for your application to determine the iOS device's current geographic coordinates using Core Location.

- Most iOS devices have built-in cameras and photo libraries, and the SDK provides mechanisms that allow your application to access both.

- iOS devices have built-in motion sensors that let you detect how your device is being held and moved.

A Different Approach

Two things iOS devices don't have are a physical keyboard and a mouse, which means you have a fundamentally different way of interacting with the user than you do when programming for a general-purpose computer. Fortunately, most of that interaction is handled for you. For example, if you add a text field to your application, iOS knows to bring up a keyboard when the user touches that field, without you needing to write any extra code.

> **Note**   All iOS devices allow you to connect an external keyboard via Bluetooth, which gives you a nice keyboard experience and saves some screen real estate; however, it is fairly rare for users to utilize such a keyboard. Connecting a mouse is not an option.

What's in This Book

Here is a brief overview of the remaining chapters in this book:

- In Chapter 2, you'll learn how to use Xcode's partner in crime, Interface Builder, to create a simple interface, placing some text on the screen.

- In Chapter 3, you'll start interacting with the user, building a simple application that dynamically updates displayed text at runtime based on buttons the user presses.

- Chapter 4 will build on Chapter 3 by introducing you to several more of iOS's standard user-interface controls. We'll also demonstrate how to use alerts and action sheets to prompt users to make a decision or to inform them that something out of the ordinary has occurred.

- In Chapter 5, we'll look at handling autorotation and autosize attributes, the mechanisms that allow iOS applications to be used in both portrait and landscape modes.

- In Chapter 6, we'll move into more advanced user interfaces and explore creating applications that support multiple views. We'll show you how to change which view is shown to the user at runtime, which will greatly enhance the potential of your apps.

- Tab bars and pickers are part of the standard iOS user interface. In Chapter 7, we'll look at how to implement these interface elements.

- In Chapter 8, we'll cover table views, the primary way of providing lists of data to the user and the foundation of hierarchical navigation–based applications. You'll also see how to let the user search your application data.

- One of the most common iOS application interfaces is the hierarchical list that lets you drill down to see more data or more details. In Chapter 9, you'll learn what's involved in implementing this standard type of interface.

- From the beginning, all sorts of iOS applications have used table views to display dynamic, vertically scrolling lists of components. More recently, Apple introduced a new class called UICollectionView that takes this concept a few steps further, giving developers lots of new flexibility in laying out visual components. Chapter 10 will get you up and running with collection views.

- The iPad, with its different form factor from the other iOS devices, requires a different approach to displaying a GUI and provides some components to help make that happen. In Chapter 11, we'll show you how to use the iPad-specific parts of the SDK.

- In Chapter 12, we'll look at implementing application settings, which is iOS's mechanism for letting users set their application-level preferences.

- Chapter 13 covers data management on iOS. We'll talk about creating objects to hold application data and see how that data can be persisted to iOS's file system. We'll also discuss the basics of using Core Data, which allows you to save and retrieve data easily.

- In iOS 5, Apple introduced iCloud, which allows your document to store data online and sync it between different instances of the application. Chapter 14 shows you how to get started with iCloud.

- iOS developers have access to a new approach to multithreaded development using Grand Central Dispatch. They also have the ability to make their apps run in the background in certain circumstances. In Chapter 15, we'll show you how that's done.

- Everyone loves to draw, so we'll look at doing some custom drawing in Chapter 16, where we'll introduce you to the Core Graphics system.

- In iOS 7, Apple has introduced a new framework called Sprite Kit for creating 2D games. It includes a physics engine and animation systems, and works for making OS X games, too. You'll see how to make a simple game with Sprite Kit in Chapter 17.

- The multitouch screen common to all iOS devices can accept a wide variety of gestural inputs from the user. In Chapter 18, you'll learn all about detecting basic gestures, such as the pinch and swipe. We'll also look at the process of defining new gestures and talk about when new gestures are appropriate.

- iOS is capable of determining its latitude and longitude thanks to Core Location. In Chapter 19, we'll build some code that uses Core Location to figure out where in the world your device is and use that information in our quest for world dominance.

- In Chapter 20, we'll look at interfacing with iOS's accelerometer and gyroscope, which is how your device knows which way it's being held, the speed and direction in which it is moving, and where in the world it's located. We'll also explore some of the fun things your application can do with that information.

- Nearly every iOS device has a camera and a library of pictures, both of which are available to your application, if you ask nicely! In Chapter 21, we'll show you how to ask nicely.

- iOS devices are currently available in more than 90 countries. In Chapter 22, we'll show you how to write your applications in such a way that all parts can be easily translated into other languages. This helps expand the potential audience for your applications.

- By the end of this book, you'll have mastered the fundamental building blocks for creating iPhone and iPad applications. But where do you go from here? In the appendix, we'll explore the logical next steps for you to take on your journey to master the iOS SDK.

What's New in this Update?

Since the first edition of this book hit the bookstores, the growth of the iOS development community has been phenomenal. The SDK has continually evolved, with Apple releasing a steady stream of SDK updates.

Well, we've been busy, too! iOS 7 contains a lot of new enhancements and new ways of presenting content. Xcode 5 introduces a lot of enhancements too, with greatly improved support for the autolayout system in Interface Builder, new image-asset management, and an across-the-board move to storyboards instead of nib files in all project templates (note that nib files—and older projects centered around them—still work fine and will continue to do so). We've been hard at work updating the book to cover all these new technologies. We've rebuilt every project from scratch to ensure not only that the code compiles using the latest version of Xcode and the iOS SDK, but also that each one takes advantage of the latest and greatest features offered by Cocoa Touch. We've also made a ton of subtle changes throughout the book and added a good amount of substantive changes as well, including a brand-new chapter on Sprite Kit. And, of course, we've reshot every screen shown in the book.

Are You Ready?

iOS is an incredible computing platform and an exciting new frontier for your development pleasure. Programming for iOS is going to be a new experience—different from working on any other platform. For everything that looks familiar, there will be something alien—but as you work through the book's code, the concepts should all come together and start to make sense.

Keep in mind that the exercises in this book are not simply a checklist that, when completed, magically grant you iOS developer guru status. Make sure you understand what you did and why before moving on to the next project. Don't be afraid to make changes to the code. Observing the results of your experimentation is one of the best ways you can wrap your head around the complexities of coding in an environment like Cocoa Touch.

That said, if you have your iOS SDK installed, turn the page. If not, get to it! Got it? Good. Then let's go!

Chapter 2

Appeasing the Tiki Gods

As you're probably well aware, it has become something of a tradition to call the first project in any book on programming, "Hello, World." We considered breaking with this tradition, but were scared that the Tiki gods would inflict some painful retribution on us for such a gross breach of etiquette. So, let's do it by the book, shall we?

In this chapter, we're going to use Xcode to create a small iOS application that will display the text, "Hello, World!" We'll look at what's involved in creating an iOS application project in Xcode, work through the specifics of using Xcode's Interface Builder to design our application's user interface, and then run our application on the iOS simulator. After that, we'll give our application an icon to make it feel more like a real iOS application.

We have a lot to do here, so let's get going.

Setting Up Your Project in Xcode

By now, you should have Xcode and the iOS SDK installed on your machine. You should also download the book project archive from the Learn Cocoa web site (`http://www.learncocoa.org/`). While you're at it, take a look at the book forums at `http://forum.learncocoa.org/`. The book forums are a great place to discuss iOS development, get your questions answered, and meet up with like-minded people.

> **Note** Even though you have the complete set of project files at your disposal in this book's project archive, you'll get more out of the book if you create each project by hand, rather than simply running the version you downloaded. By doing that, you'll gain familiarity and expertise working with the various application development tools.
>
> There's no substitute for actually creating applications; software development is not a spectator sport.

The project we're going to build in this chapter is contained in the *02 Hello World* folder of the project archive.

Before we can start, we need to launch Xcode. Xcode is the tool that we'll use to do most of what we do in this book. After downloading it from the Mac App Store, you'll find it installed in the */Applications* folder, as with most Mac applications. You'll be using Xcode a lot, so you might want to consider dragging it to your dock, so you'll have ready access to it.

If this is your first time using Xcode, don't worry; we'll walk you through every step involved in creating a new project. If you're already an old hand but haven't worked with Xcode 5, you will find that quite a bit has changed (mostly for the better, we think).

When you first launch Xcode, you'll be presented with a welcome window like the one shown in Figure 2-1. From here, you can choose to create a new project, connect to a version-control system to check out an existing project, or select from a list of recently opened projects. The welcome window gives you a nice starting point, covering some of the most common tasks you're likely to want to do after launching Xcode. All of these actions can be accessed through the menu as well, so close the window, and we'll proceed. If you would rather not see this window in the future, just uncheck the *Show this window when Xcode launches* checkbox at the bottom of the window before closing it.

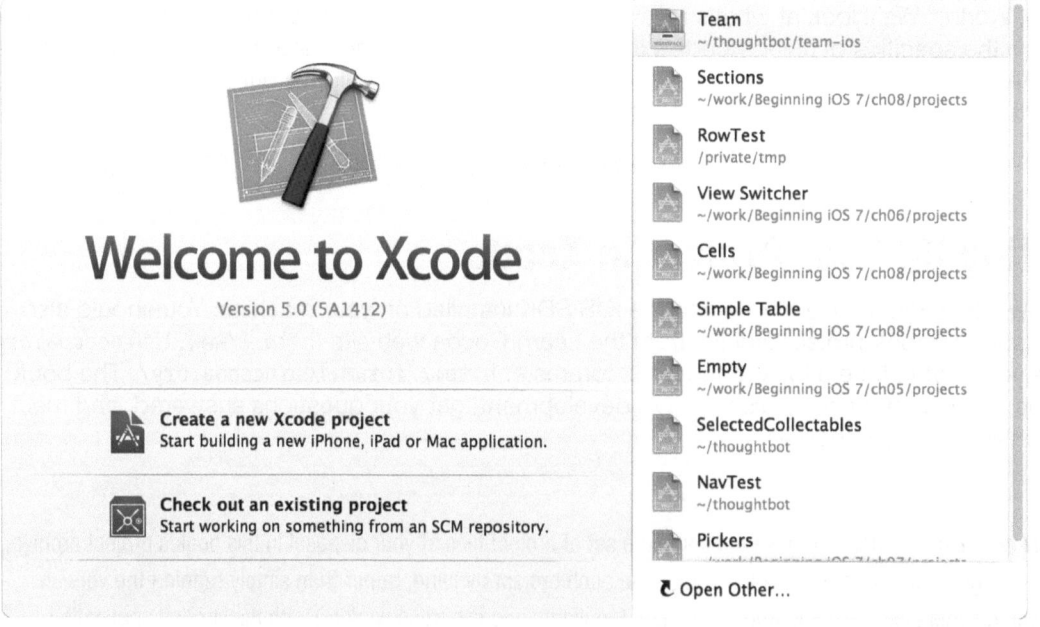

Figure 2-1. The Xcode welcome window

Note   If you have an iPhone, iPad, or IPod touch connected to your machine, you might see a message when you first launch Xcode that asks whether you want to use that device for development. For now, click the *Ignore* button. Alternatively, the *Organizer* window might appear. This window shows (among other things) the devices that have been synchronized with your computer. In that case, just close the *Organizer* window. If you choose to join the paid iOS Developer Program, you will gain access to a program portal that will tell you how to use your iOS device for development and testing.

Create a new project by selecting **New ➤ Project . . .** from the **File** menu (or by pressing ⇧⌘N). A new project window will open, showing you the project template selection sheet (see Figure 2-2). From this sheet, you'll choose a project template to use as a starting point for building your application. The pane on the left side of the sheet is divided into two main sections: *iOS* and *Mac OS X*. Since we're building an iOS application, select *Application* in the *iOS* section to reveal the iOS application templates.

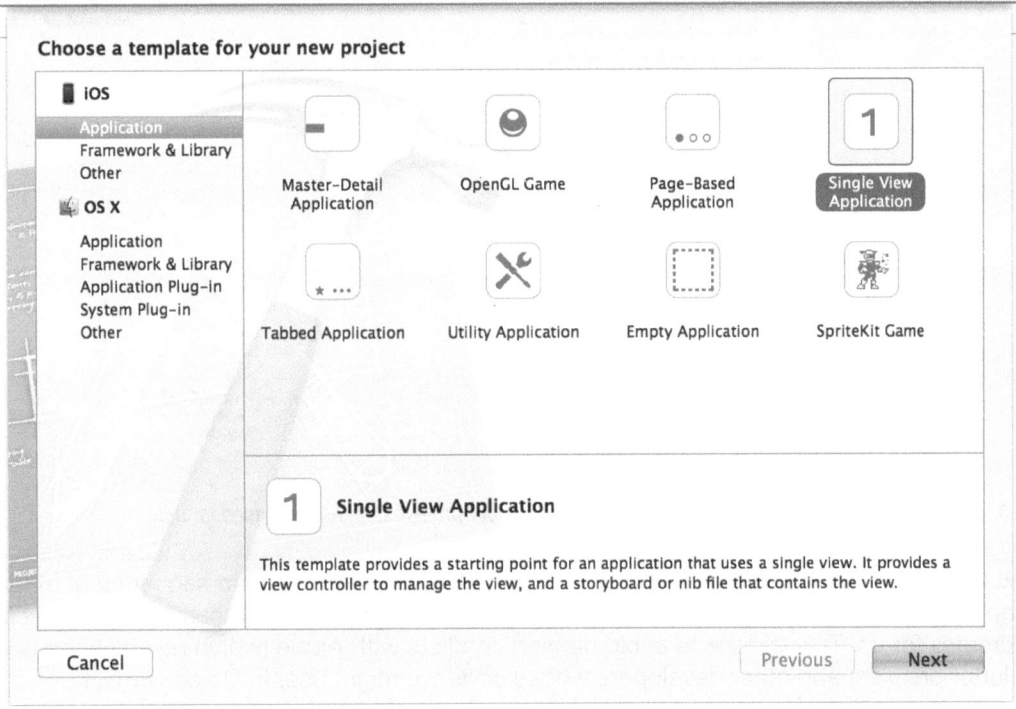

Figure 2-2. The project template selection sheet lets you select from various templates when creating a new project

Each of the icons shown in the upper-right pane in Figure 2-2 represents a separate project template that can be used as a starting point for your iOS applications. The icon labeled *Single View Application* is the simplest template and the one we'll be using for the first several chapters. The other templates provide additional code and/or resources needed to create common iPhone and iPad application interfaces, as you'll see in later chapters.

Click the *Single View Application* icon (see Figure 2-2), and then click the *Next* button. You'll see the project options sheet, which should look like Figure 2-3. On this sheet, you need to specify the *Product Name* and *Company Identifier* for your project. Xcode will combine these to generate a unique *Bundle Identifier* for your app. You'll also see a field that lets you enter an *Organization Name*, which Xcode will use to automatically insert a copyright notice into every source code file you create. Name your product *Hello World*, call your organization *Apress*, and then enter *com.apress* in the *Company Identifier* field, as shown in Figure 2-3. Later, after you've signed up for the developer program and learned about provisioning profiles, you'll want to use your own company identifier. We'll talk more about the bundle identifier later in the chapter.

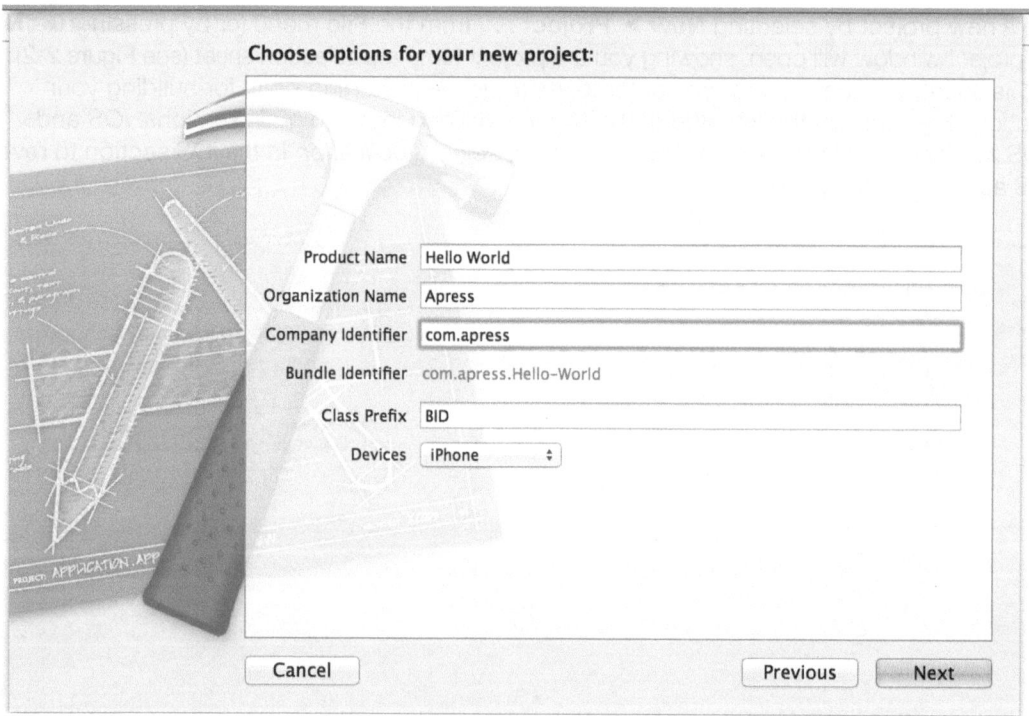

Figure 2-3. Selecting a product name and company identifier for your project. Use these settings for now

The next text box is labeled *Class Prefix*, and we should populate this with a sequence of at least three capital letters. These characters will be added to the beginning of the name of all classes that Xcode creates for us. This is done to avoid naming conflicts with Apple (which reserves the use of all two-letter prefixes) and other developers whose code we might use. In Objective-C, having more than one class with the same name will prevent your application from being built.

For the projects in the book, we're going to use the prefix *BID*, which stands for **B**eginning **i**OS **D**evelopment. While there are likely to be many classes named, for example, `MyViewController`, far fewer classes are likely to be named `BIDMyViewController`. This will significantly reduce the chance of conflicts.

We also need to specify the *Devices*. In other words, Xcode wants to know if we're building an app for the iPhone and iPod touch, if we're building an app for the iPad, or if we're building a universal application that will run on all iOS devices. Select *iPhone* for the *Devices* if it's not already selected. This tells Xcode that we'll be targeting this particular app at the iPhone and iPod touch, which have roughly the same screen size and form factor. For the first part of the book, we'll be using the iPhone device, but don't worry—we'll cover the iPad also.

Click *Next* again, and you'll be asked where to save your new project using a standard save sheet (see Figure 2-4). If you haven't already done so, jump over to the Finder, create a new master directory for these book projects, and then return to Xcode and navigate into that directory. Before you click the *Create* button, make note of the *Source Control* checkbox. We won't be talking about git in this book, but Xcode includes some support for using git and other kinds of source control management (SCM) tools. If you are already familiar with git and want to use it, leave this checkbox enabled; otherwise, feel free to turn it off.

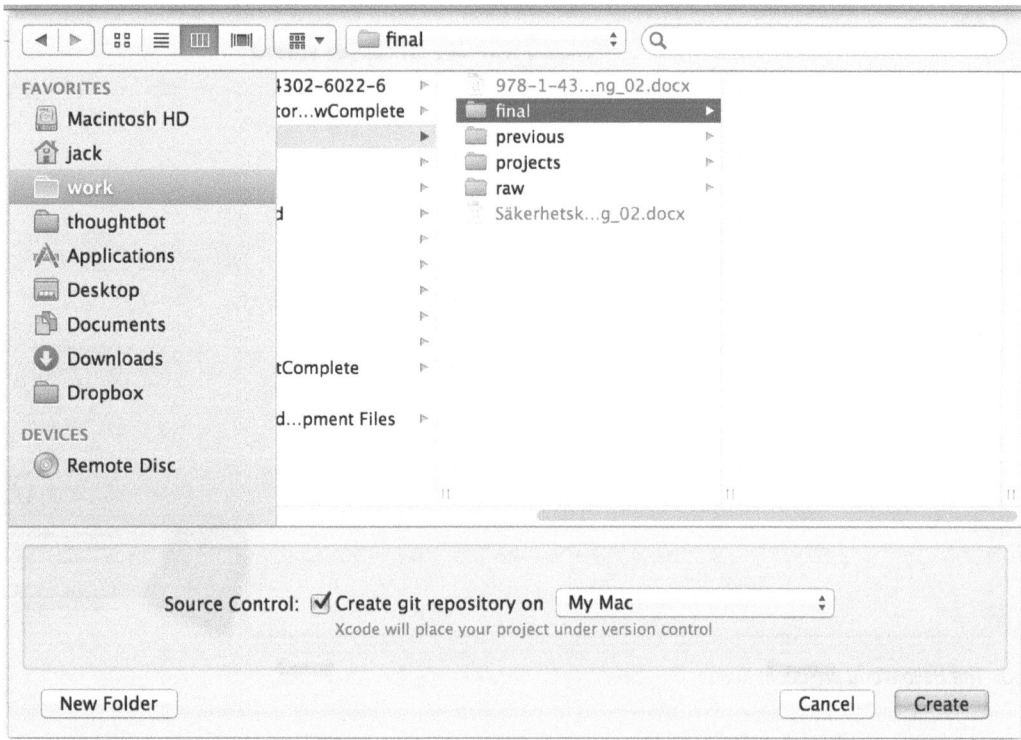

Figure 2-4. Saving your project in a project folder on your hard drive

Note   Source Control Management (SCM) is a technique for keeping track of changes made to an application's source code and resources while it's being built. It also facilitates multiple developers working on the same application at the same time by providing tools to resolve conflicts when they arise. Xcode has built-in support for git, one of the most popular SCM systems in use today. We won't be dealing with source control issues in this book, so it's up to you to enable it or disable it, whichever works for you.

After choosing whether to create a git repository, create the new project by clicking the *Create* button.

The Xcode Project Window

After you dismiss the save sheet, Xcode will create and then open your project. You will see a new **project windowx** (see Figure 2-5). There's a lot of information crammed into this window, and it's where you will be spending a lot of your iOS development time.

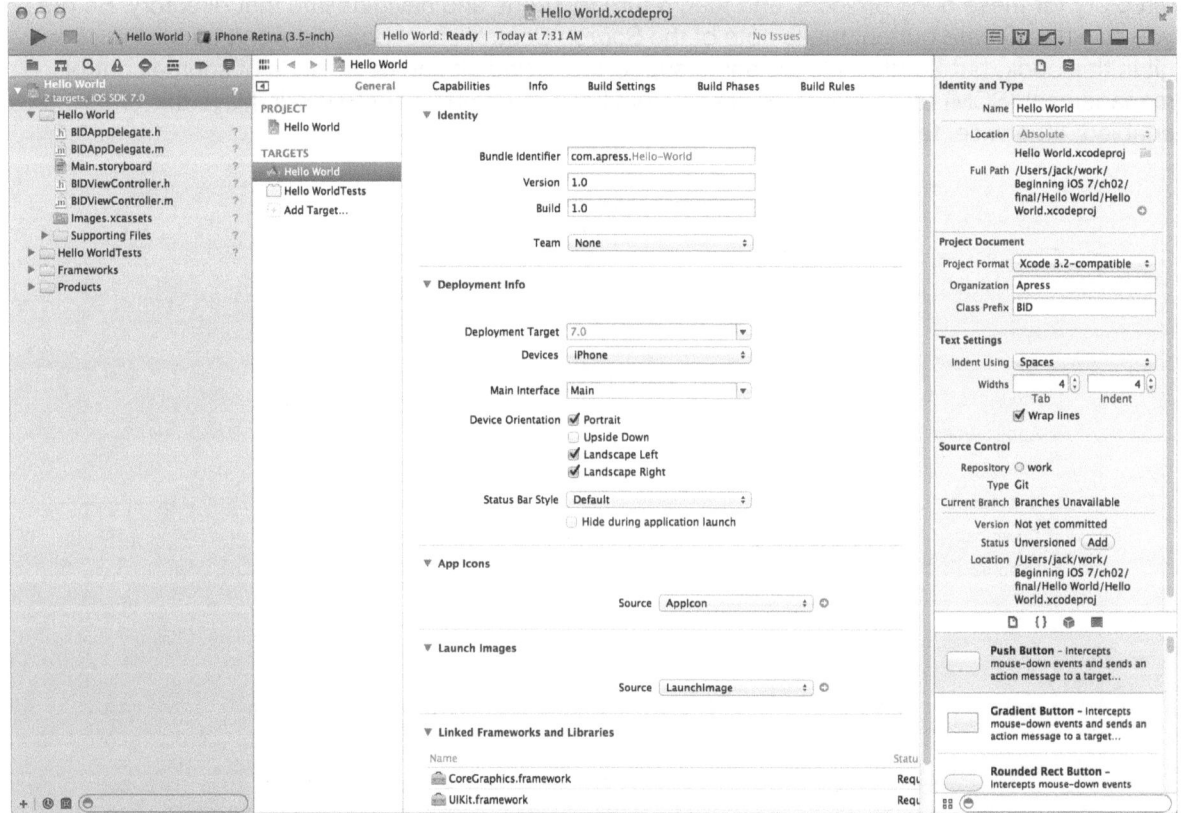

Figure 2-5. The Hello World project in Xcode

Even if you are an old hand with earlier versions of Xcode, you'll still benefit from reading through this section since it covers a lot of the new functionality in Xcode 5 (and a *whole* lot has changed since Xcode 3.*x* and Xcode 4). Let's take a quick tour.

The Toolbar

The top of the Xcode project window is called the **toolbar** (see Figure 2-6). On the left side of the toolbar are controls to start and stop running your project, as well as a pop-up menu to select the scheme you want to run. A **scheme** brings together target and build settings, and the toolbar pop-up menu lets you select a specific setup with just one click.

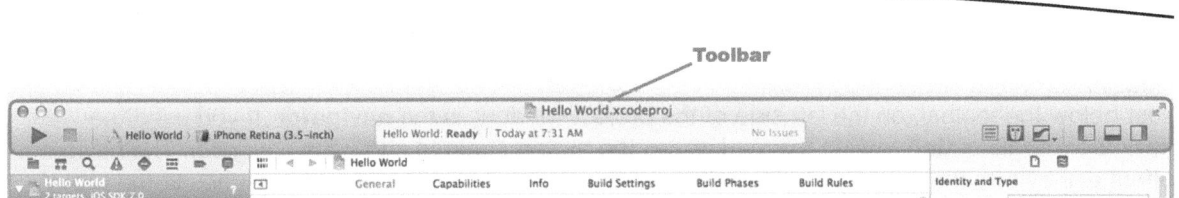

Figure 2-6. The Xcode toolbar

The big box in the middle of the toolbar is the **activity view**. As its name implies, the activity view displays any actions or processes that are currently happening. For example, when you run your project, the activity view gives you a running commentary on the various steps it's taking to build your application. If you encounter any errors or warnings, that information is displayed here, as well. If you click the warning or error, you'll go directly to the issues navigator, which provides more information about the warning or error, as described in the next section.

On the right side of the toolbar are two sets of buttons. The left set lets you switch between three different editor configurations:

- The **standard editor** gives you a single pane dedicated to editing a file or project-specific configuration values.

- The incredibly powerful **assistant editor** splits the editor pane into two panes, left and right. The pane on the right is generally used to display a file that relates to the file on the left, or that you might need to refer to while editing the file on the left. You can manually specify what goes into each pane, or you can let Xcode decide what's most appropriate for the task at hand. For example, if you're editing the implementation of an Objective-C class (the *.m* file), Xcode will automatically show you that class's header file (the *.h* file) in the right pane. If you're designing your user interface on the left, Xcode will show you the code that user interface is able to interact with on the right. You'll see the assistant editor at work throughout the book.

- The **version editor** button converts the editor pane into a time-machine-like comparison view that works with version control systems such as subversion and git. You can compare the current version of a source file with a previously committed version or compare any two earlier versions with each other.

To the right of the editor buttons is set of toggle buttons that show and hide large panes on the left and right sides of the editor view, as well as the debug area at the bottom of the window. Click each of those buttons a few times to see these panes in action. You'll learn more about how these are used soon.

The Navigator

Just below the toolbar, on the left side of the project window, is the **navigator**. If you used the navigator toggle button to hide this earlier, tap the button again to show the navigator. The navigator offers eight views that show you different aspects your project. Click one of the icons at the top of the navigator to switch among the following navigators, going from left to right:

- **Project navigator:** This view contains a list of files that are used by your project (see Figure 2-7). You can store references to everything you expect—from source code files to artwork, data models, property list (or **plist**) files (discussed in the "A Closer Look at Our Project" section later in this chapter), and even other project files. By storing multiple projects in a single workspace, multiple projects can easily share resources. If you click any file in the navigator view, that file will display in the editor pane. In addition to viewing the file, you can also edit the file (if it's a file that Xcode knows how to edit).

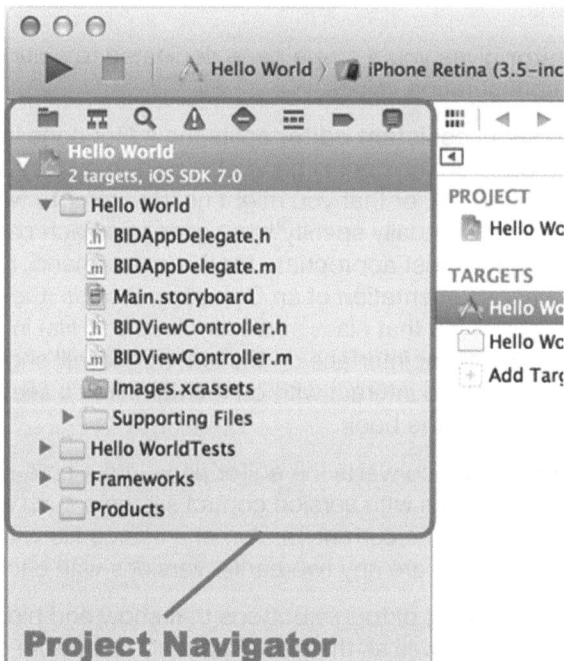

Figure 2-7. The Xcode project navigator. Click one of the seven icons at the top of the view to switch navigators

- **Symbol navigator:** As its name implies, this navigator focuses on the **symbols** defined in the workspace (see Figure 2-8). Symbols are basically the items that the compiler recognizes, such as Objective-C classes, enumerations, `structs`, and global variables.

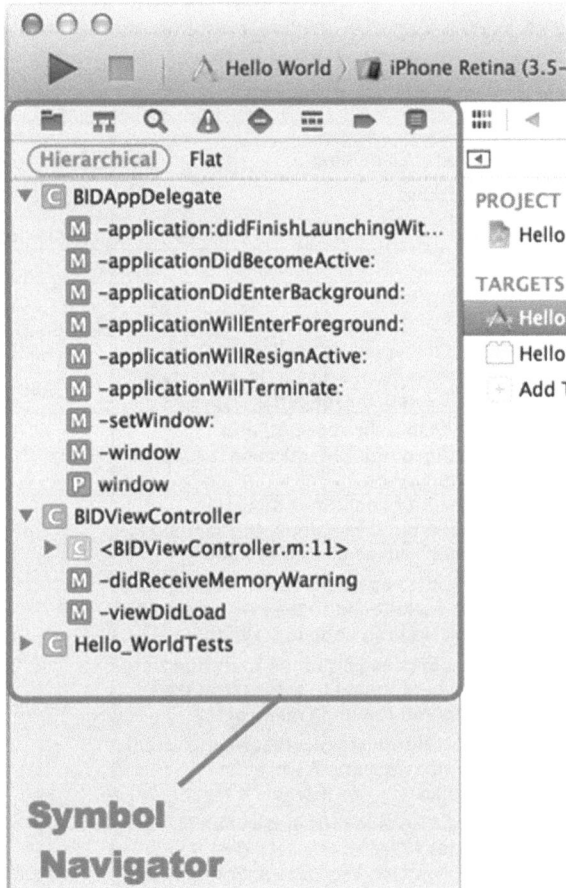

Figure 2-8. *The Xcode symbol navigator. Open the disclosure triangle to explore the classes, methods, and other symbols defined within each group*

- **Find navigator:** You'll use this navigator to perform searches on all the files in your workspace (see Figure 2-9). At the top of this pane is a multi-leveled pop-up control that lets you select *Replace* instead of *Find*, along with other options for applying search criteria to the text you enter. Below the text field, other controls let you choose to search in the entire project or just a portion of it, and specify whether searching should be case-sensitive.

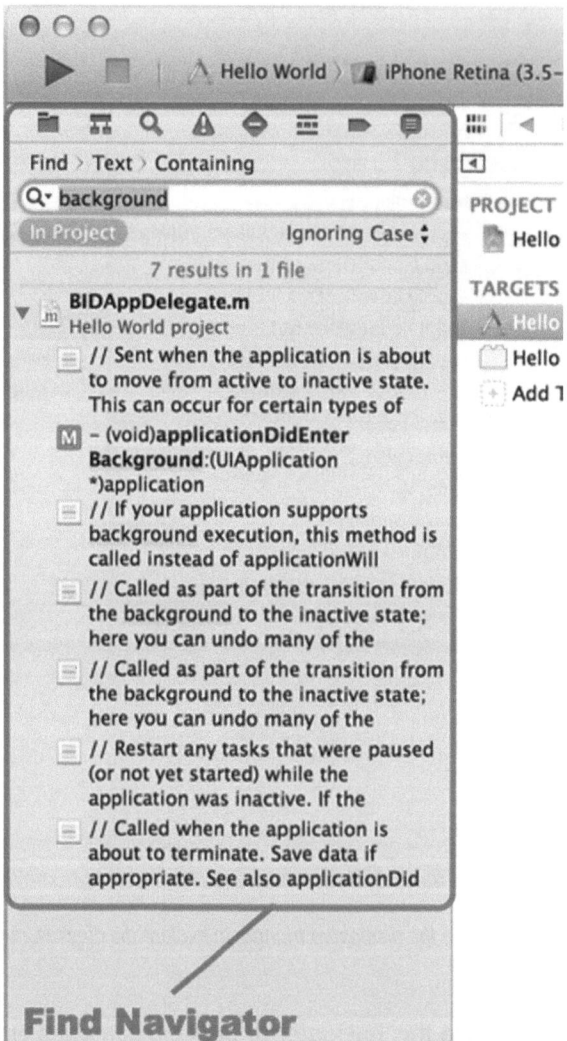

Figure 2-9. The Xcode find navigator. Be sure to check out the pop-up menus hidden under the word Find and under the buttons that are below the search field

- **Issue navigator:** When you build your project, any errors or warnings will appear in this navigator, and a message detailing the number of errors will appear in the activity view at the top of the window (see Figure 2-10). When you click an error in the issue navigator, you'll jump to the appropriate line of code in the editor.

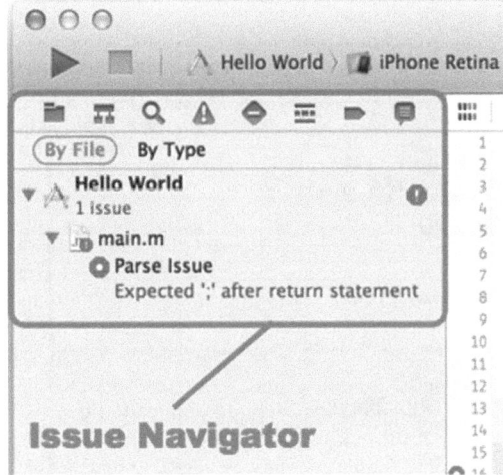

Figure 2-10. The Xcode issue navigator. This is where you'll find your compiler errors and warnings

■ **Test navigator:** If you're using Xcode's integrated unit testing capabilities (a topic which we unfortunately can't fit into this book), this is where you'll see the results of your unit tests (see Figure 2-11).

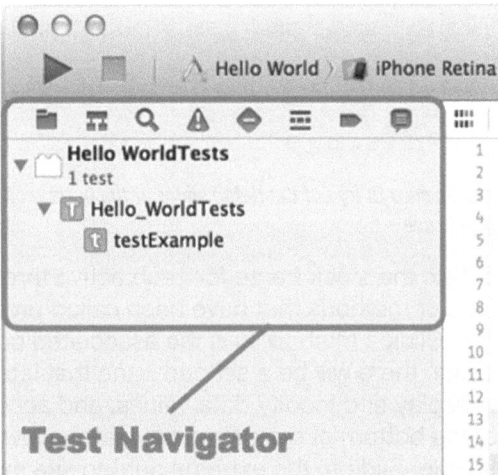

Figure 2-11. The Xcode test navigator. The output of your unit tests will appear here

■ **Debug navigator:** This navigator is your main view into the debugging process (see Figure 2-12). If you are new to debugging, you might check out this part of the Xcode 5 User Guide: http://developer.apple.com/library/mac/#documentation/ToolsLanguages/Conceptual/Xcode4UserGuide/060-Debug_Your_App/debug_app.html

Figure 2-12. The Xcode debug navigator. Be sure to try out the detail slider at the bottom of the window, which allows you to specify the level of debug detail you want to see

The debug navigator lists the stack frame for each active thread. A **stack frame** is a list of the functions or methods that have been called previously, in the order they were called. Click a method, and the associated code appears in the editor pane. In the editor, there will be a second pane that lets you control the debugging process, display and modify data values, and access the low-level debugger. A slider at the bottom of the debug navigator allows you to control the level of detail it tracks. Slide to the extreme right to see everything, including all the system calls. Slide to the extreme left to see only your calls. The default setting of right in the middle is a good place to start.

- **Breakpoint navigator:** The breakpoint navigator lets you see all the breakpoints that you've set (see Figure 2-13). Breakpoints are, as the name suggests, points in your code where the application will stop running (or **break**), so that you can look at the values in variables and do other tasks needed to debug your application. The list of breakpoints in this navigator is organized by file. Click a breakpoint in the list and that line will appear in the editor pane. Be sure to check out the pop-up at the lower-left corner of the project window when in the breakpoint navigator. The plus pop-up lets you add an exception or symbolic breakpoint, and the minus pop-up deletes any selected breakpoints.

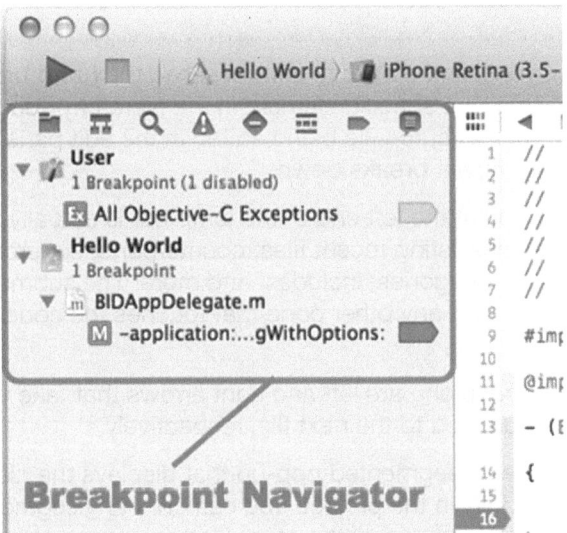

Figure 2-13. The Xcode breakpoint navigator. The list of breakpoints is organized by file

- **Log navigator:** This navigator keeps a history of your recent build results and run logs (see Figure 2-14). Click a specific log, and the build command and any build issues are displayed in the edit pane.

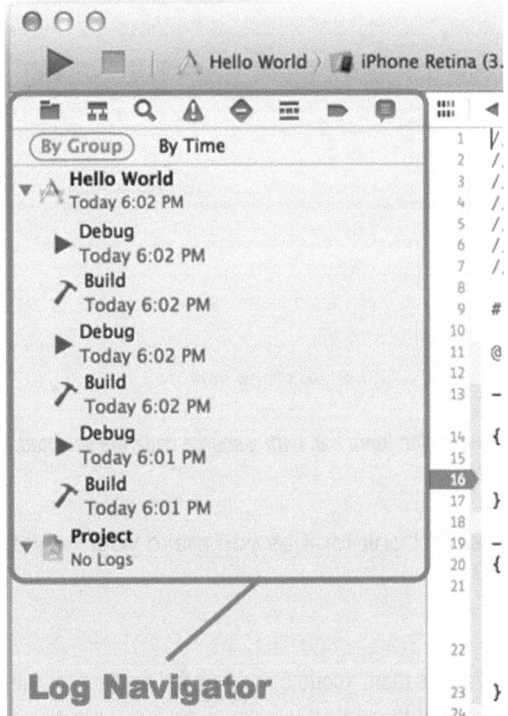

Figure 2-14. The Xcode log navigator. The log navigator displays a list of builds, with the details associated with a selected view displayed in the edit pane

The Jump Bar

Across the top of the editor, you'll find a special control called the **jump bar**. With a single click, the jump bar allows you to jump to a specific element in the hierarchy you are currently navigating. For example, Figure 2-15 shows a source file being edited in the edit pane. The jump bar is just above the source code. Here's how it breaks down:

- The funky looking icon at the left end of the jump bar is actually a pop-up menu that displays submenus listing recent files, counterparts, superclasses, and subclasses, siblings, categories, includes, and more! The submenus shown here will take you to just about any other code that touches the code currently open in the editor.

- To the right of the *über* menu are left and right arrows that take you back to the previous file and return you to the next file, respectively.

- The jump bar includes a segmented pop-up that displays the hierarchical path to reach the selected file in the project. You can click any segment showing the name of a group or a file to see all the other files and groups located at the same point in the hierarchy. The final segment shows a list of items within the selected file. In Figure 2-15, you'll see that the tail end of the jump bar is a pop-up that shows the methods and other symbols contained within the currently selected file. The jump bar shows the file *BIDAppDelegate.m*, with a submenu listing the symbols defined in that file.

Figure 2-15. The Xcode editor pane showing the jump bar, with a source code file selected. The submenu shows the list of methods in the selected file

The jump bar is incredibly powerful. Look for it as you make your way through the various interface elements that make up Xcode 5.

Tip   Like most of Apple's OS X application, Xcode 5 includes full support for full-screen mode. Just click the full-screen button in the upper right of the project window to try out distraction-free, full-screen coding!

```
XCODE KEYBOARD SHORTCUTS
```

If you prefer navigating with keyboard shortcuts instead of mousing to on-screen controls, you'll like what Xcode has to offer. Most actions that you will do regularly in Xcode have keyboard shortcuts assigned to them, such as ⌘B to build your application or ⌘N to create a new file.

You can change all of Xcode's keyboard shortcuts, as well as assign shortcuts to commands that don't already have one using Xcode's preferences, under the *Key Bindings* tab.

A really handy keyboard shortcut is ⇧⌘O, which is Xcode's Open Quickly feature. After pressing it, start typing the name of a file, setting, or symbol, and Xcode will present you with a list of options. When you narrow down the list to the file you want, hitting the **Return** key will open it in the editing pane, allowing you to switch files in just a few keystrokes.

The Utility Area

As we mentioned earlier, the second-to-last button on the right side of the Xcode toolbar opens and closes the utility area. The upper part of the utility area is a context-sensitive inspector panel, with contents that change depending on what is being displayed in the editor pane. The lower part of the utility area contains a few different kinds of resources that you can drag into your project. You'll see examples throughout the book.

Interface Builder

Earlier versions of Xcode included an interface design application called **Interface Builder**, which allowed you to build and customize your project's user interface. One of the major changes introduced in later versions of Xcode is the integration of Interface Builder into the workspace itself. Interface Builder is no longer a separate stand-alone application, which means you don't need to jump back and forth between Xcode and Interface Builder as your code and interface evolve. It's been a few years since this shift occurred, but those of us who remember the days of a separate Interface Builder application are now pretty happy with how the direct integration of Interface Builder in Xcode worked out.

We'll be working extensively with Xcode's interface-building functionality throughout the book, digging into all its nooks and crannies. In fact, we'll do our first bit of interface building a bit later in this chapter.

New Compiler and Debugger

One of the most important changes brought in by Xcode 4 lies under the hood: a brand new compiler and low-level debugger. Both are significantly faster and smarter than their predecessors.

For many years, Apple used GCC (the GNU C Compiler) as the basis for its compiler technology. But over the course of the past few years, it has shifted over completely to the LLVM (Low Level Virtual Machine) compiler. LLVM generates code that is faster by far than that generated by the traditional GCC. In addition to creating faster code, LLVM also knows more about your code, so it can generate smarter, more precise error messages and warnings.

Xcode is also tightly integrated with LLVM, which gives it some new superpowers. Xcode can offer more precise code completion, and it can make educated guesses as to the actual intent of a piece of code when it produces a warning, offering a pop-up menu of likely fixes. This makes errors like misspelled symbol names, mismatched parentheses, and missing semicolons a breeze to find and fix.

LLVM brings to the table a sophisticated **static analyzer** that can scan your code for a wide variety of potential problems, including problems with Objective-C memory management. In fact, LLVM is so smart about this that it can handle most memory management tasks for you, as long as you abide by a few simple rules when writing your code. We'll begin looking at the wonderful new ARC feature called **Automatic Reference Counting** (ARC) in the next chapter.

A Closer Look at Our Project

Now that we've explored the Xcode project window, let's take a look at the files that make up our new *Hello World* project. Switch to the project navigator by clicking the leftmost of the eight navigator icons on the left side of your workspace (as discussed in the "The Navigator View" section earlier in the chapter) or by pressing ⌘**1**.

> **Tip**   The eight navigator configurations can be accessed using the keyboard shortcuts ⌘**1** to ⌘**8**.
> The numbers correspond to the icons starting on the left, so ⌘**1** is the project navigator, ⌘**2** is the symbol navigator, and so on up to ⌘**8**, which takes you to the log navigator.

The first item in the project navigator list bears the same name as your project—in this case, *Hello World*. This item represents your entire project, and it's also where project-specific configuration can be done. If you single-click it, you'll be able to edit a number of project configuration settings in Xcode's editor. You don't need to worry about those project-specific settings now, however. At the moment, the defaults will work fine.

Flip back to Figure 2-7. Notice that the disclosure triangle to the left of *Hello World* is open, showing a number of subfolders (which are called **groups** in Xcode):

■ *Hello World*: The first folder, which is always named after your project, is where you will spend the bulk of your time. This is where most of the code that you write will go, as will the files that make up your application's user interface. You are free to create subfolders under the *Hello World* folder to help organize your code, and you're even allowed to use other groups if you prefer a different organizational approach. While we won't touch most of the files in this folder until next chapter, there is one file we will explore when we use Interface Builder in the next section:

■ Main.*storyboard* contains the user interface elements specific to your project's main view controller.

- *Supporting Files*: This folder, located inside the *Hello World* folder, contains source code files and resources that aren't Objective-C classes, but that are necessary to your project. Typically, you won't spend a lot of time in the *Supporting Files* folder. When you create a new iPhone application project, this folder contains four files:

  - *Hello World-Info.plist* Is a property list that contains information about the application. We'll look briefly at this file in the "Some iPhone Polish—Finishing Touches" section later in this chapter.

  - *InfoPlist.strings* is a text file that contains human-readable strings that may be referenced in the info property list. Unlike the info property list itself, this file can be localized, allowing you to include multiple language translations in your application (a topic we'll cover in Chapter 21).

  - *main.m* contains your application's `main()` method. You normally won't need to edit or change this file. In fact, if you don't know what you're doing, it's really a good idea not to touch it.

  - *Hello World-Prefix.pch* is a list of header files from external frameworks that are used by your project (the extension *.pch* stands for **pre**compiled **h**eader). The headers referenced in this file are typically ones that aren't part of your project and aren't likely to change very often. Xcode will precompile these headers and then continue to use that precompiled version in future builds, which will reduce the amount of time it takes to compile your project whenever you select Build or Run. It will be a while before you need to worry about this file because the most commonly used header files are already included for you.

- *Hello WorldTests*: This folder contains the initial files you'll need if you want to write some unit tests for your application code. We're not going to talk about unit testing in this book, but it's nice that Xcode sets up some of these things for you in each new project you create. Like the *Hello World* folder, this one contains its own *Supporting Files* folder with some files necessary for building and running unit test code.

- *Frameworks*: A framework is a special kind of library that can contain code as well as resources, such as image and sound files. Any framework or library that you add to the *Frameworks* folder will be linked into your application, and your code will be able to use any classes, functions, and other resources contained in that framework or library. The most commonly needed frameworks and libraries are linked into your project by default, so most of the time, you will not need to add anything to this folder. If you do need less commonly used libraries and frameworks, it's easy to add them to the *Frameworks* folder. We'll show you how to add frameworks in Chapter 7.

■ *Products*: This folder contains the application that this project produces when it is built. If you expand *Products*, you'll see an item called *Hello World.app*, which is the application that this particular project creates. It also contains an item called *Hello WorldTests.xctest*, which represents the testing code. Both of these items are called **build targets**. Because we have never built either of these, they're both red, which is Xcode's way of telling you that a file reference points to something that is not there.

Note   The "folders" in the navigator area do not necessarily correspond to folders in your Mac's file system. These are logical groupings within Xcode to help you keep everything organized and to make it faster and easier to find what you're looking for while working on your application. Often, the items contained in those two project folders are stored directly in the project's directory, but you can store them anywhere—even outside your project folder if you want. The hierarchy inside Xcode is completely independent of the file system hierarchy, so moving a file out of the *Classes* folder in Xcode, for example, will not change the file's location on your hard drive.

It is possible to configure a group to use a specific file system directory using the utility pane. However, by default, new groups added to your project are completely independent of the file system, and their contents can be contained anywhere.

Introducing Xcode's Interface Builder

In your project window's project navigator, expand the *Hello World* group, if it's not already open, and then select the file *Main.storyboard*. As soon as you do, the file will open in the editor pane, as shown in Figure 2-16. You should see something resembling an all-white iPhone screen centered on a plain white background, which makes a nice backdrop for editing interfaces. This is Xcode's Interface Builder (sometimes referred to as IB), which is where you'll design your application's user interface.

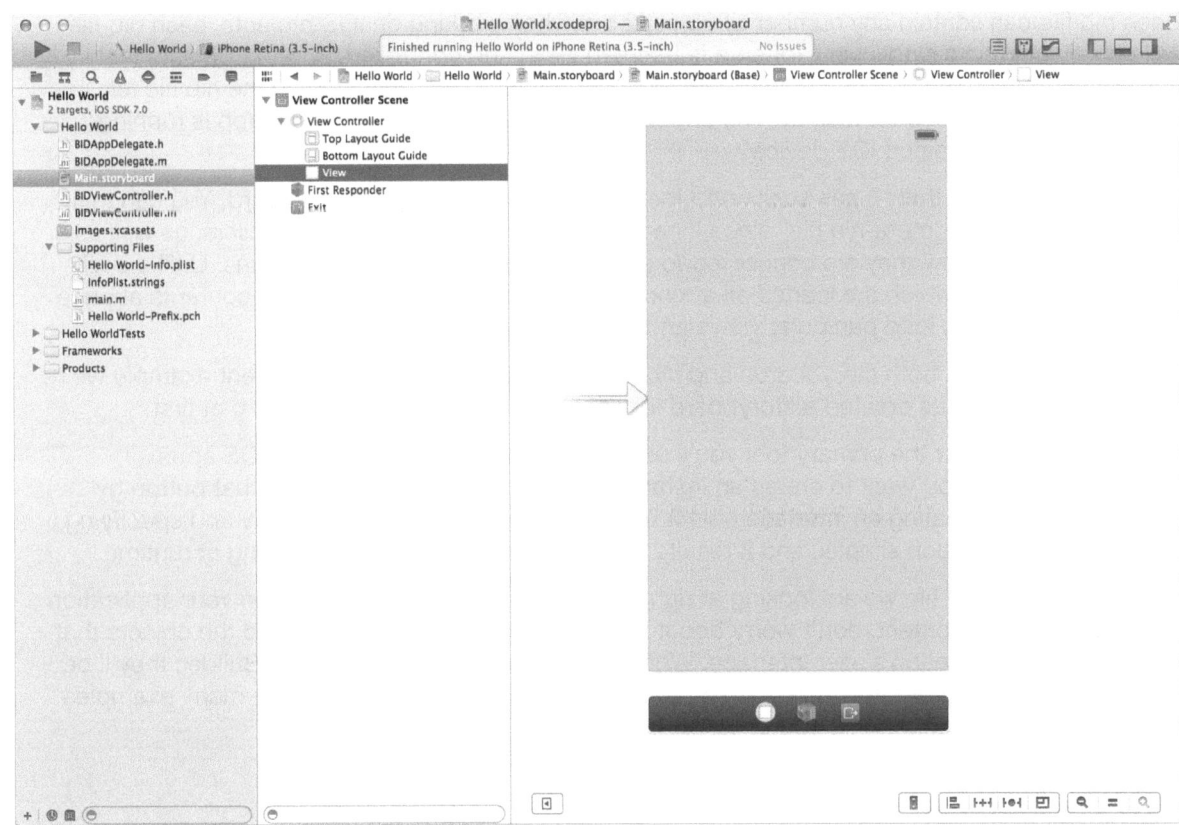

Figure 2-16. We selected Main.storyboard in the project navigator. This opened the file in Interface Builder. It looks like this

Interface Builder has a long history. It has been around since 1988 and has been used to develop applications for NeXTSTEP, OpenStep, Mac OS X, and now iOS devices such as iPhone and iPad. As we noted earlier, Interface Builder used to be a separate application that was installed along with Xcode and worked in tandem with it. Now, Interface Builder is fully integrated into Xcode.

File Formats

Interface Builder supports a few different file types. The oldest is a binary format that uses the extension *.nib*, whose newer cousin is an XML-based format that uses the extension *.xib*. Both of these formats contain exactly the same sort of document, but the *.xib* version, being a text-based format, has many advantages, especially when you're using any sort of SCM.

Note   The iOS project templates all use *.xib* files by default; but for the first 20 years Interface Builder existed, all its files had the extension, *.nib*. As a result, most developers took to calling Interface Builder files **nib files**. Interface Builder files are often called nib files, regardless of whether the extension actually used for the file is *.xib* or *.nib*. In fact, Apple still uses the terms **nib** and **nib file** throughout its documentation.

Each nib file can contain any number of objects; but when working on iOS projects, each nib file will usually contain a single view (often a full-screen view) and controllers or other objects that it is connected to. This lets us compartmentalize our applications, only loading the nib file for a view when it's needed for display. The end result: We save memory when our app is running on a memory-constrained iOS device.

The other file format that IB has supported for the past few years is the storyboard. You can think of a storyboard as a "meta-nib file" since it can contain several views and controllers, as well as information about how they are connected to each other when the application runs. Unlike a nib file, the contents of which are loaded all at once, a storyboard never loads all its contents at once. Instead, you ask it to load particular views and controllers when you need them.

We'll be dealing with both storyboards and nibs throughout the book. In the current example we're working on, Xcode has created a storyboard for us, so that's what we'll be looking at first.

You're now looking at the primary tool you'll use for building user interfaces for iOS apps. Now, let's say that you want to create an instance of a button. You could create that button by writing code, but creating an interface object by dragging a button out of a library and specifying its attributes is so much simpler, and it results in exactly the same thing happening at runtime.

The *Main.storyboard* file we are looking at right now is loaded automatically when your application launches—for the moment, don't worry about how—so it is the right place to add the objects that make up your application's user interface. When you create objects in Interface Builder, they'll be instantiated in your program when that storyboard or nib file is loaded. You'll see many examples of this process throughout this book.

The Storyboard

Every storyboard is compartmentalized into one or more pairs of views and controllers. The view is the part you can see graphically and edit in Interface Builder, while the controller is application code you will write to make things happen when a user interacts with your app. The controllers are where the real action of your application happens.

In IB, you often see a view represented by an iPhone-sized rectangle (though other sizes are possible), and our current example is no exception. Click anywhere in this rectangle, and you'll see a row of three icons shown below it. Drag your mouse over each of them, and you'll see tooltips pop up with their names: *View Controller*, *First Responder*, and *Exit*. Forget about *Exit* for now, and focus instead on the two that are really important.

- *View Controller* represents the controller that is loaded from file storage along with its associated view.

- *First Responder* is, in very basic terms, the object with which the user is currently interacting. If, for example, the user is currently entering data into a text field, that field is the current first responder. The first responder changes as the user interacts with the user interface, and the *First Responder* icon gives you a convenient way to communicate with whatever control or other object is the current first responder, without needing to write code to determine which control or view that might be.

We'll talk more about these objects starting in the next chapter, so don't worry if you're a bit fuzzy right now on when you would use *First Responder* or how a *View Controller* gets loaded.

Apart from those icons, the rest of what you see in the editing area is the space where you can place graphical objects. But before we get to that, there's one more thing you should see about IB's editor area: its hierarchy view. Click the little button in the lower-left corner of the editing area, and you'll see the hierarchy view slide in from the left. This shows all the contents of the storyboard, split up into **scenes** containing chunks of related content. In our case, we have just one scene, called View Controller Scene. You'll see that it contains an item called View Controller, which in turn contains an item called View (along with some other things you'll learn about later). This is a pretty handy way of getting an overview of your content. Everything you see in the main editing area is mirrored here.

The *View* icon represents an instance of the UIView class. A UIView object is an area that a user can see and interact with. In this application, we will have only one view, so this icon represents everything that the user can see in our application. Later, we'll build more complex applications that have more than one view. For now, just think of this as what the user can see when using your application.

> **Note**   Technically speaking, our application will actually have more than one view. All user interface elements that can be displayed on the screen—including buttons, text fields, and labels—are descendants of UIView. When you see the term *view* used in this book, however, we will generally be referring only to actual instances of UIView, and this application has only one of those.

If you click the *View* icon, Xcode will automatically highlight the iPhone-sized screen rectangle that we were talking about earlier. This is where you can design your user interface graphically.

The Library

The utility view, which makes up the right side of the workspace, is divided into two sections (see Figure 2-17). If you're not currently seeing the utility view, click the rightmost of the three *View* buttons in the toolbar, select **View ➤ Utilities ➤ Show Utilities**, or press ⌥⌘0 (**Option-Command-Zero**).

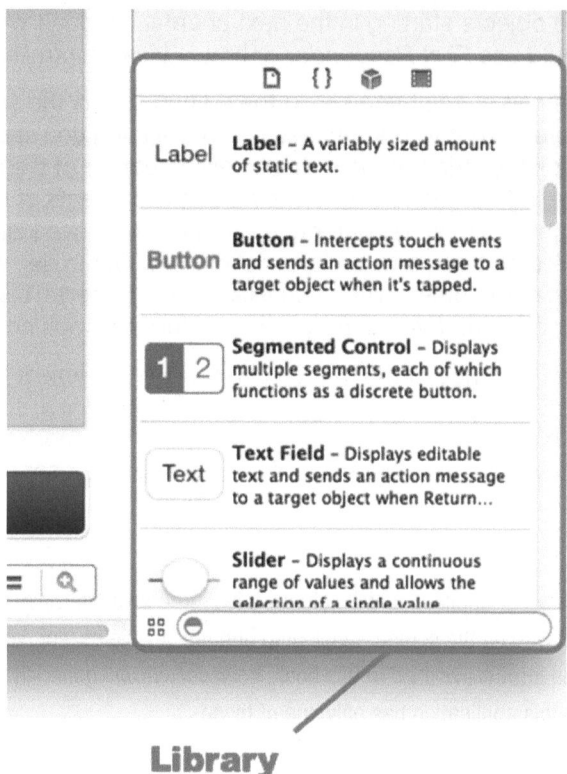

Library

Figure 2-17. *The library is where you'll find stock objects from the UIKit that are available for use in Interface Builder. Everything above the library but below the toolbar is known collectively as the inspector*

The bottom half of the utility view is called the **library pane**, or just plain **library**. The library is a collection of reusable items you can use in your own programs. The four icons in the bar at the top of the library pane divide the library into four sections:

- **File template library:** This section contains a collection of file templates you can use when you need to add a new file to your project. For example, if you want to add a new Objective-C class to your project, drag an Objective-C class file from the file template library.

- **Code snippet library:** This section features a collection of code snippets you can drag into your source code files. Can't remember the syntax for Objective-C fast enumeration? That's fine—just drag that particular snippet out of the library, and you don't need to look it up. Have you written something you think you'll want to use again later? Select it in your text editor and drag it to the code snippet library.

- **Object library:** This section is filled with reusable objects, such as text fields, labels, sliders, buttons, and just about any object you would ever need to design your iOS interface. We'll use the object library extensively in this book to build the interfaces for our sample programs.

- **Media library:** As its name implies, this section is for all your media, including pictures, sounds, and movies.

Note   The items in the object library are primarily from the iOS UIKit, which is a framework of objects used to create an app's user interface. UIKit fulfills the same role in Cocoa Touch as AppKit does in Cocoa. The two frameworks are similar conceptually; however, because of differences in the platforms, there are obviously many differences between them. On the other hand, the Foundation framework classes, such as NSString and NSArray, are shared between Cocoa and Cocoa Touch.

Note the search field at the bottom of the library. Do you want to find a button? Type **button** in the search field, and the current library will show only items with "button" in the name. Don't forget to clear the search field when you are finished searching.

Adding a Label to the View

Let's give Interface Builder a try. Click the *Object Library* icon (it looks like a cube) at the top of the library to bring up the object library. Just for fun, scroll through the library to find a *Table View*. That's it—keep scrolling, and you'll find it. Or wait! There's a better way: just type the words *Table View* in the search field. Isn't that so much easier?

Tip   Here's a nifty shortcut: press ^⌥⌘3 to jump to the search field and highlight its contents. Next, you can just type what you want to search for.

Now find a *Label* in the library. It is likely on or near the top of the list. Next, drag the label onto the view we saw earlier. (If you don't see the view in your editor pane, click the *View* icon in the Interface Builder dock.) As your cursor appears over the view, it will turn into the standard, "I'm making a copy of something" green plus sign you know from the Finder. Drag the label to the center of the view. A pair of blue guidelines—one vertical and one horizontal—will appear when your label is centered. It's not vital that the label be centered, but it's good to know those guidelines are there. Figure 2-18 shows what our workspace looked like just before we released our drag.

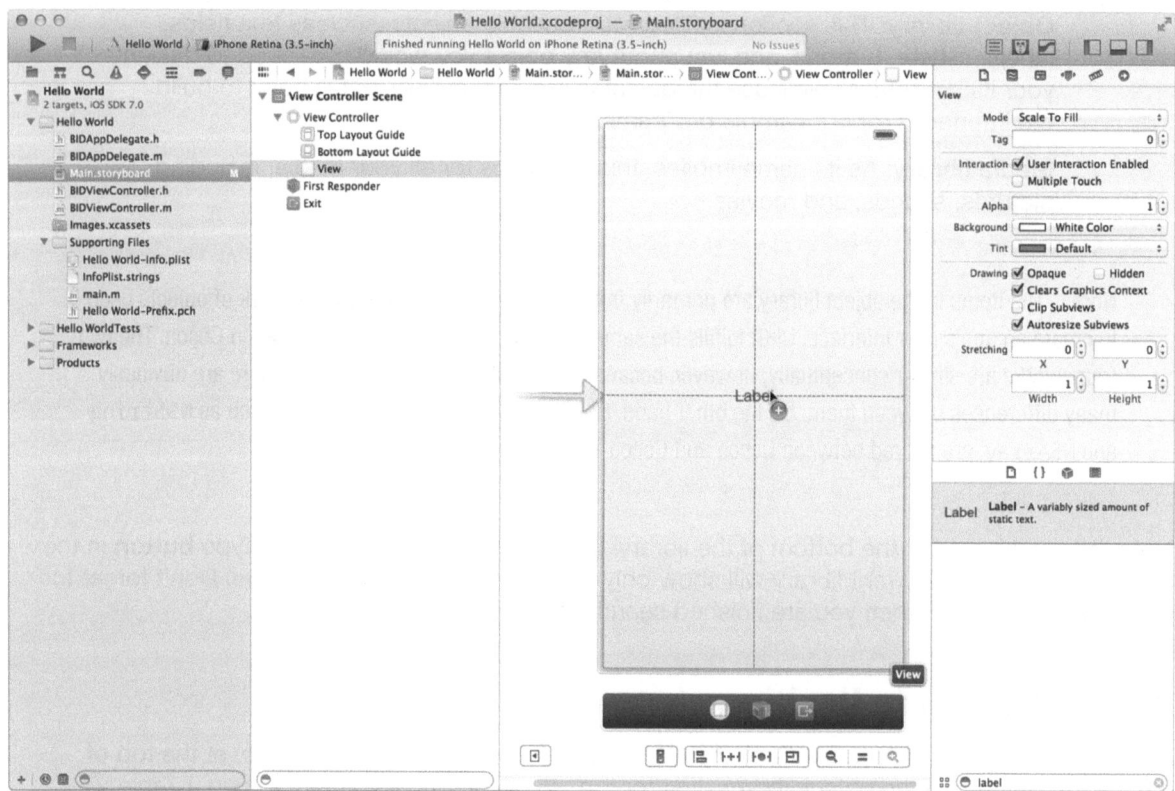

Figure 2-18. We've found a label in our library and dragged it onto our view. Note that we typed Label into the library search field to limit our object list to those containing the word Label

User interface items are stored in a hierarchy. Most views can contain **subviews**; however, there are some, like buttons and most other controls, that can't. Interface Builder is smart. If an object does not accept subviews, you will not be able to drag other objects onto it.

By dragging a label directly to the view we're editing, we add it as a subview of that main view (the view named *View*), which will cause it to show up automatically when that view is displayed to the user. Dragging a *Label* from the library to the view called *View* adds an instance of UILabel as a subview of our application's main view.

Let's edit the label so it says something profound. Double-click the label you just created, and type the text, **Hello, World!** Next, click off the label, and then reselect it and drag the label to recenter it or position it wherever you want it to appear on the screen.

Guess what? Once we save, we're finished. Select **File ➤ Save**, or press ⌘S. Now check out the pop-up menu at the upper left of the Xcode project window. This is actually a multi-segment pop-up control. The left side lets you choose a different compilation target and do a few other things, but we're interested in the right side, which lets you pick which device you want to run on. Click the right side and you'll see a list of available devices. At the top, if you have any iOS device plugged in and ready to go, you'll see it listed. Otherwise, you'll just see a generic *iOS Device* entry. Below that, you'll see a whole section, headed by *iOS Simulator*, listing all the kinds of devices that can be used with the iOS Simulator. From that lower section, choose *iPhone Retina (4-inch)*, so that our app will run in the simulator, configured as if it were an iPhone 5. If you are a member of Apple's paid iOS Developer Program, you can try running your app on your phone. In this book, we'll stick with the simulator as much as possible, since running in the simulator doesn't require any paid membership.

Ready to run? Select **Product ➤ Run** or press ⌘R. Xcode will compile your app and launch it in the iOS simulator (see Figure 2-19).

Figure 2-19. Here's the Hello, World program in its full iPhone glory!

Note   If your iOS device is connected to your Mac when you build and run, things might not go quite as planned. In a nutshell, in order to be able to build and run your applications on your iPhone, iPad, or iPod touch, you must sign up and pay for one of Apple's iOS Developer Programs, and then go through the process of configuring Xcode appropriately. When you join the program, Apple will send you the information you'll need to get this done. In the meantime, most of the programs in this book will run just fine using the iPhone or iPad simulator.

When you are finished admiring your handiwork, you can head back over to Xcode. Xcode and the simulator are separate applications.

Tip   You are welcome to quit the simulator once you finish examining your app, but you'll just be restarting it in a moment. If you leave the simulator running and ask Xcode to run your application again, Xcode will ask you to confirm that you want to stop your existing app before starting a new instance of it. If this seems confusing, feel free to quit the simulator each time you finish testing your app. No one will know!

Wait a second! That's it? But we didn't write any code. That's right.

Pretty neat, huh?

Well, how about if we wanted to change some of the properties of the label, like the text size or color? We would need to write code to do that, right? Nope. Let's see just how easy it is to make changes.

Changing Attributes

Head back to Xcode and single-click the *Hello, World* label to select it. Now turn your attention to the area above the library pane. This part of the utility pane is called the **inspector**. Like the library, the inspector pane is topped by a series of icons, each of which changes the inspector to view a specific type of data. To change the attributes of the label, we'll need the fourth icon from the left, which brings up the object attributes inspector (see Figure 2-20).

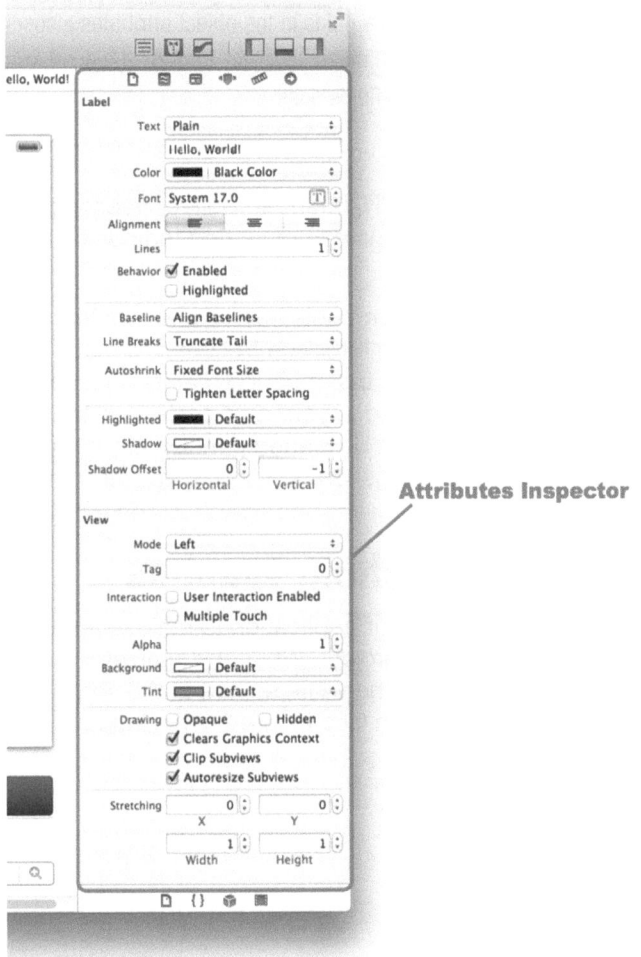

Figure 2-20. The object attributes inspector showing our label's attributes

TIP   The inspector, like the project navigator, has keyboard shortcuts corresponding to each of its icons. The inspector's keyboard shortcuts start with ⌥⌘1 for the leftmost icon, ⌥⌘2 for the next icon, and so on. Unlike the project navigator, the number of icons in the inspector is context-sensitive and changes depending on which object is selected in the navigator and/or editor.

Go ahead and change the label's appearance to your heart's delight. Feel free to play around with the font, size, and color of the text. Note that if you increase the font size, you may need to resize the label itself to make room for larger text. Once you're finished playing, save the file and select **Run** again. The changes you made should show up in your application, once again without writing any code.

> **Note**   Don't worry too much about what all of the fields in the object attributes inspector mean, or fret if you can't get one of your changes to show up. As you make your way through the book, you'll learn a lot about the object attributes inspector and what each of the fields does.

By letting you design your interface graphically, Interface Builder frees you to spend time writing the code that is specific to your application, instead of writing tedious code to construct your user interface.

Most modern application development environments have some tool that lets you build your user interface graphically. One distinction between Interface Builder and many of these other tools is that Interface Builder does not generate any code that must be maintained. Instead, Interface Builder creates Objective-C objects, just as you would in your own code, and then serializes those objects into the storyboard or nib file so that they can be loaded directly into memory at runtime. This avoids many of the problems associated with code generation and is, overall, a more powerful approach.

Some iPhone Polish—Finishing Touches

Now let's put a last bit of spit and polish on our application to make it feel a little more like an authentic iPhone application. First, run your project. When the simulator window appears, click the iPhone's home button (the black button with the white square at the very bottom of the window). That will bring you back to the iPhone home screen (see Figure 2-21). Notice anything a bit, well, boring?

Figure 2-21.   The AppIcon boxes on your project's assets catalog. This is where you can set your application's icon

Take a look at the *Hello, World* icon at the top of the screen. Yeah, that icon will never do, will it? To fix it, you need to create an icon and save it as a portable network graphic (*.png*) file. Actually, for best results you should create three icons. One needs to be 120 × 120 pixels in size, another 80 × 80, and yet another needs to be 58 × 58 pixels. Why three icons? The first one is the icon that will be used for displaying your app on the iPhone home screen. The second one will be shown if your app shows up in the results list from a Spotlight search on the phone. The third icon will be displayed in the Settings app. If you don't supply either of the smaller ones, the larger one will be scaled down appropriately; but for best results, you (or a graphic artist on your team) should probably scale it in advance.

> **Note**   The issue of icon sizes is even more complex than this. Before iOS 7, the side dimension of an icon for all modern iPhones was 114 × 114 pixels. But if you still wanted to support older, non-Retina iPhones, you needed to include an icon at half that resolution too, 57 × 57. Then there's the issue of the iPad, which has still other icons sizes, both Retina and non-Retina, for both iOS 7 and for earlier versions of iOS! For now, we'll avoid diving further down this particular rabbit hole, and just provide icons for an iPhone running iOS 7.

Do not try to match the style of the buttons that are already on the phone when you create the icons; your iPhone will automatically round the edges. Just create normal, square images. We have provided a set of icon images in the project archive *02 - Hello World - icons* folder. These images are called *icon-120.png*, *icon-80*, and *icon-58.png*; feel free to use them if you don't want to create your own.

> **Note**   For your application's icon, you must use *.png* images; in fact, you should actually use that format for all images in your iOS projects. Xcode automatically optimizes *.png* images at build time, which makes them the fastest and most efficient image type for use in iOS apps. Even though most common image formats will display correctly, you should use *.png* files unless you have a compelling reason to use another format.

After you've designed your app icon, press ⌘1 to open the project navigator, and look inside the Hello World group for an item called *Images.xcassets*. This is something called an **asset catalog**, and it is new to Xcode 5. By default, each new Xcode project is created with an asset catalog, ready to hold your app icon and other images. Select *Images.xcassets* and turn your attention to the editing pane.

On the left side of the editing pane, you'll see a white column with list entries labeled *AppIcon* and *LaunchImage*. Make sure that the *AppIcon* item is selected. To the right of that column, you'll see a white space with the text "AppIcon" in the upper-left corner, as well as dashed-line squares corresponding to the three icons we just talked about (see Figure 2-21). This is where we'll drag our app icons.

You'll see that beneath each icon is a bit of text explaining where that version of the icon will be used. It also tells you what size the icon should be. But here's the tricky part: Xcode shows you the size in points, not pixels. In this context, a **point** is a particular size on a screen. It's the size of a single pixel on the earliest iPhones (everything earlier than the iPhone 4), as well as on the iPad 1, iPad 2, and iPad Mini. On other devices, those with a Retina display, a single point is actually a 2 × 2 pixel square. The items shown in the asset catalog hint at this with their *2x* labels, but those are really just labels. To figure out what size an item really expects, select one of them and press ⌥⌘4 to open the attributes inspector on the right side of the window. This will show you both the size (again in points) and the scale, which for each of these icons is 2x. Multiply the size by the scale, and you'll get the actual pixel size that's required. Check each of the items in the AppIcon box, and the inspector will give you the details. They should match up with what we described earlier, but you never know what Apple has up its sleeve. Between the time this book goes to print and the time you read this, Apple may have some fantastic new devices that require still more icons!

From the Finder, drag *icon-120.png* to the item labeled "iPhone App"– this should be the one on the right. This will copy *icon-120.png* into your project and set it as your application's icon. Next, drag *icon-80.png* from the Finder to the middle square, which will set that as your application's *Spotlight* icon. Finally, drag *icon-58*.png to the left square, setting the icon to be used for Settings in iOS 7.

Now compile and run your app. When the simulator has finished launching, press the button with the white square to go home, and check out your snazzy new icon. Ours is shown in Figure 2-22. To see one of the smaller icons in use, swipe down inside the home screen to bring up the spotlight search field, and start typing the word, **Hello**–you'll see your new app's icon appear immediately.

Figure 2-22. Your application now has a snazzy icon!

Note   If you want to clear out old applications from the iOS simulator's home screen, you can choose iOS Simulator ➤ **Reset Content and Settings. . .** from the iOS simulator's application menu.

Bring It on Home

Pat yourself on the back. Although it may not seem like you accomplished all that much in this chapter, we actually covered a lot of ground. You learned about the iOS project templates, created an application, learned a ton about Xcode 5, started using Interface Builder, and learned how to set your application icon.

The Hello, World program, however, is a strictly one-way application. We show some information to the users, but we never get any input from them. When you're ready to see how to go about getting input from the user of an iOS device and taking actions based on that input, take a deep breath and turn the page.

Chapter 3

Handling Basic Interaction

Our Hello, World application was a good introduction to iOS development using Cocoa Touch, but it was missing a crucial capability—the ability to interact with the user. Without that, our application is severely limited in terms of what it can accomplish.

In this chapter, we're going to write a slightly more complex application—one that will feature two buttons as well as a label (see Figure 3-1). When the user taps either of the buttons, the label's text will change. This may seem like a rather simplistic example, but it demonstrates the key concepts involved in creating interactive iOS apps. Just for fun, we're also going to introduce you to the NSAttributedString class, which lets you use styled text with many CocoaTouch GUI elements.

Figure 3-1. The simple two-button application we will build in this chapter

The Model-View-Controller Paradigm

Before diving in, a bit of theory is in order. The designers of Cocoa Touch were guided by a concept called **Model-View-Controller** (MVC), which is a very logical way of dividing the code that makes up a GUI-based application. These days, almost all object-oriented frameworks pay a certain amount of homage to MVC, but few are as true to the MVC model as Cocoa Touch.

The MVC pattern divides all functionality into three distinct categories:

- **Model**: The classes that hold your application's data.

- **View**: Made up of the windows, controls, and other elements that the user can see and interact with.

- **Controller**: The code that binds together the model and view. It contains the application logic that decides how to handle the user's inputs.

The goal in MVC is to make the objects that implement these three types of code as distinct from one another as possible. Any object you create should be readily identifiable as belonging in one of the three categories, with little or no functionality that could be classified as being either of the other two. An object that implements a button, for example, shouldn't contain code to process data when that button is tapped, and an implementation of a bank account shouldn't contain code to draw a table to display its transactions.

MVC helps ensure maximum reusability. A class that implements a generic button can be used in any application. A class that implements a button that does some particular calculation when it is clicked can be used only in the application for which it was originally written.

When you write Cocoa Touch applications, you will primarily create your view components using a visual editor within Xcode called **Interface Builder**, although you will also modify, and sometimes even create, your user interfaces from code.

Your model will be created by writing Objective-C classes to hold your application's data or by building a data model using something called Core Data, which you'll learn about in Chapter 13. We won't be creating any model objects in this chapter's application because we do not need to store or preserve data. However, we will introduce model objects as our applications get more complex in future chapters.

Your controller component will typically be composed of classes that you create and that are specific to your application. Controllers can be completely custom classes (NSObject subclasses), but more often they will be subclasses of one of several existing generic controller classes from the UIKit framework, such as UIViewController (as you'll see shortly). By subclassing one of these existing classes, you will get a lot of functionality for free and won't need to spend time recoding the wheel, so to speak.

As we get deeper into Cocoa Touch, you will quickly start to see how the classes of the UIKit framework follow the principles of MVC. If you keep this concept in the back of your mind as you develop, you will end up creating cleaner, more easily maintained code.

Creating Our Project

It's time to create our next Xcode project. We're going to use the same template that we used in the previous chapter: *Single View Application*. By starting with this simple template again, it will be easier for you to see how the view and controller objects work together in an iOS application. We'll use some of the other templates in later chapters.

Launch Xcode and select **File ➤ New ➤ Project...** or press ⇧⌘N. Select the *Single View Application* template, and then click *Next*.

You'll be presented with the same options sheet that you saw in the previous chapter. In the *Product Name* field, type the name of our new application, *Button Fun*. The *Organization Name*, *Company Identifier,* and *Class Prefix* fields should still have the values you used in the previous chapter (*Apress*, *com.apress*, and *BID*), so you can leave those alone. Just as we did with Hello, World, we're going to write an iPhone application, so select *iPhone* for *Device*s. Figure 3-2 shows the completed options sheet.

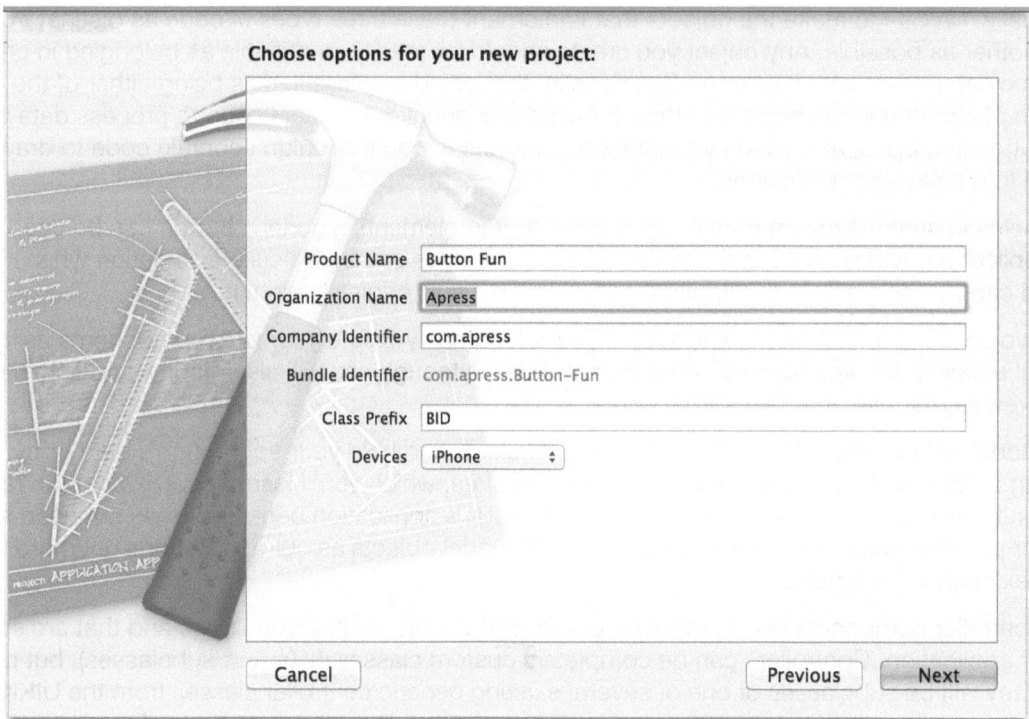

Figure 3-2. Naming your project and selecting options

Hit *Next*, and you'll be prompted for a location for your project. You can leave the *Create git repository* checkbox checked or unchecked, whichever you prefer. Save the project with the rest of your book projects.

Looking at the View Controller

A little later in this chapter, we'll design a view (or user interface) for our application using Interface Builder, just as we did in the previous chapter. Before we do that, we're going to look at and make some changes to the source code files that were created for us. Yes, Virginia, we're actually going to write some code in this chapter.

Before we make any changes, let's look at the files that were created for us. In the project navigator, the *Button Fun* group should already be expanded; but if it's not, click the disclosure triangle next to it (see Figure 3-3).

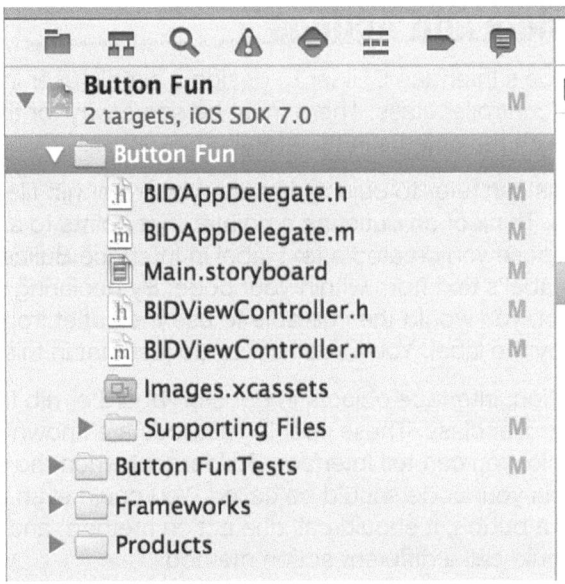

Figure 3-3. The project navigator showing the class files that were created for us by the project template. Note that our class prefix was automatically incorporated into the class file names

The *Button Fun* folder should contain four source code files (the ones that end in *.h* or *.m*) along with a storyboard file and an asset catalog for containing any images our app needs. The four source code files implement two classes that our application needs: our application delegate and the view controller for our application's only view. Notice that Xcode automatically added the prefix we specified to all of our class names.

We'll look at the application delegate a little later in the chapter. First, we'll work with the view controller class that was created for us.

The controller class called BIDViewController is responsible for managing our application's view. The BID part of the name is derived automatically from the class prefix we specified, and the ViewController part of the name identifies that this class is, well, a view controller. Click *BIDViewController.h* in the *Groups & Files* pane, and take a look at the contents of the class's header file:

```
#import <UIKit/UIKit.h>

@interface BIDViewController : UIViewController

@end
```

Not much to it, is there? BIDViewController is a subclass of UIViewController, which is one of those generic controller classes we mentioned earlier. It is part of the UIKit framework, and by subclassing this class, we get a bunch of functionality for free. Xcode doesn't know what our application-specific functionality is going to be, but it does know that we're going to have some, so it has created this class for us to write that application-specific functionality.

Understanding Outlets and Actions

In Chapter 2, you used Xcode's Interface Builder to design a simple user interface. A moment ago, you saw the shell of a view controller class. There must be some way for the code in this view controller class to interact with the objects in the storyboard, right?

Absolutely! A controller class can refer to objects in a storyboard or nib file by using a special kind of property called an **outlet**. Think of an outlet as a pointer that points to an object within the user interface. For example, suppose you created a text label in Interface Builder (as we did in Chapter 2) and wanted to change the label's text from within your code. By declaring an outlet and connecting that outlet to the label object, you would then be able to use the outlet from within your code to change the text displayed by the label. You'll see how to do just that in this chapter.

Going in the opposite direction, interface objects in our storyboard or nib file can be set up to trigger special methods in our controller class. These special methods are known as **action methods** (or just **actions**). For example, you can tell Interface Builder that when the user taps a button, a specific action method within your code should be called. You could even tell Interface Builder that when the user first touches a button, it should call one action method; and then later, when the finger is lifted off the button, it should call a different action method.

Xcode supports multiple ways of creating outlets and actions. One way is to specify them in our source code before using Interface Builder to connect them with our code. Xcode's assistant view gives us a much faster and more intuitive approach that lets us create and connect outlets and actions in a single step, a process we're going to look at shortly. But before we start making connections, let's talk about outlets and actions in a little more detail. Outlets and actions are two of the most basic building blocks you'll use to create iOS apps, so it's important that you understand what they are and how they work.

Outlets

Outlets are special Objective-C class properties that are declared using the keyword IBOutlet. Declaring an outlet is done either in your controller's class header file or in a special section (called the **class extension**) of your controller's implementation file. It might look something like this:

```
@property (weak, nonatomic) IBOutlet UIButton *myButton;
```

This example is an outlet called *myButton*, which can be set to point to any button in Interface Builder.

The IBOutlet keyword isn't built into the Objective-C language. It's a simple C preprocessor definition in a system header file, where it looks something like this:

```
#ifndef IBOutlet
#define IBOutlet
#endif
```

Confused? IBOutlet does absolutely nothing as far as the compiler is concerned. Its sole purpose is to act as a hint to tell Xcode that this is a property that we're going to want to connect to an object in a nib file. Any property that you create and want to connect to an object in a nib file must be preceded by the IBOutlet keyword. Fortunately, Xcode will now create outlets for us automatically.

OUTLET CHANGES

Over time, Apple has changed the way that outlets are declared and used. Since you are likely to run across older code at some point, let's look at how outlets have changed.

In the first version of this book, we declared both a property and its underlying instance variable for our outlets. At that time, properties were a new construct in the Objective-C language, and they required you to declare a corresponding instance variable:

```
@interface MyViewController : UIViewController
{
    UIButton *myButton;
}
@property (weak, nonatomic) UIButton *myButton;
@end
```

Back then, we placed the IBOutlet keyword before the instance variable declaration:

```
IBOutlet UIButton *myButton;
```

This was how Apple's sample code was written at the time. It was also how the IBOutlet keyword had traditionally been used in Cocoa and NeXTSTEP.

By the time we wrote the second edition of the book, Apple had moved away from placing the IBOutlet keyword in front of the instance variable, and it became standard to place it within the property declaration:

```
@property (weak, nonatomic) IBOutlet UIButton *myButton;
```

Even though both approaches continued to work (and still do), we followed Apple's lead and changed the book code so that the IBOutlet keyword was in the property declaration rather than in the instance variable declaration.

When Apple switched the default compiler from the GNU C Compiler (GCC) to the Low Level Virtual Machine (LLVM) recently, it stopped being necessary to declare instance variables for properties. If LLVM finds a property without a matching instance variable, it will create one automatically. As a result, in this edition of the book, we've stopped declaring instance variables for our outlets altogether.

All of these approaches do exactly the same thing, which is to tell Interface Builder about the existence of an outlet. Placing the IBOutlet keyword on the property declaration is Apple's current recommendation, so that's what we're going to use. But we wanted to make you aware of the history in case you come across older code that has the IBOutlet keyword on the instance variable.

You can read more about Objective-C properties in the book *Learn Objective-C on the Mac* by Scott Knaster, Waqar Malik, and Mark Dalrymple (Apress, 2012) and in the document called *Introduction to the Objective-C Programming Language*, available from Apple's Developer web site at http://developer.apple.com/library/ios/#documentation/Cocoa/Conceptual/ProgrammingWithObjectiveC.

Actions

In a nutshell, actions are methods that are declared with a special return type, `IBAction`, which tells Interface Builder that this method can be triggered by a control in a nib file. The declaration for an action method will usually look like this:

```
- (IBAction)doSomething:(id)sender;
```

It might also look like this:

```
- (IBAction)doSomething;
```

The actual name of the method can be anything you want, but it must have a return type of `IBAction`, which is the same as declaring a return type of `void`. A `void` return type is how you specify that a method does not return a value. Also, the method must either take no arguments or take a single argument, usually called `sender`. When the action method is called, `sender` will contain a pointer to the object that called it. For example, if this action method was triggered when the user tapped a button, `sender` would point to the button that was tapped. The `sender` argument exists so that you can respond to multiple controls using a single action method. It gives you a way to identify which control called the action method.

Tip There's actually a third, less frequently used type of `IBAction` declaration that looks like this:

```
- (IBAction)doSomething:(id)sender
                forEvent:(UIEvent *)event;
```

We'll begin talking about control events in the next chapter.

It won't hurt anything if you declare an action method with a `sender` argument and then ignore it. You will likely see a lot of code that does just that. Action methods in Cocoa and NeXTSTEP needed to accept `sender` whether they used it or not, so a lot of iOS code, especially early iOS code, was written that way.

Now that you understand what actions and outlets are, you'll see how they work as we design our user interface. Before we start doing that, however, we have one quick piece of housekeeping to do to keep everything neat and orderly.

Cleaning Up the View Controller

Single-click *BIDViewController.m* in the project navigator to open the implementation file. As you can see, there's a small amount of boilerplate code in the form of `viewDidLoad` and `didReceiveMemoryWarning` methods that were provided for us by the project template we chose. These methods are commonly used in `UIViewController` subclasses, so Xcode gave us stub implementations of them. If we need to use them, we can just add our code there. However, we don't need any of these stub implementations for this project, so all they're doing is taking up space and making our code harder to read. We're going to do our future selves a favor and clear away methods that we don't need, so go ahead and delete those methods.

At the top of the file, you'll also see an empty class extension ready for us to use. A class extension is a special kind of Objective-C category declaration that lets you declare methods and properties that will only be usable within a class's primary implementation block, within the same file. We'll use class extensions later in the book but not here, so delete the empty @implementation...@end pair as well. When you're finished, your implementation should look like this:

```
#import "BIDViewController.h"

@implementation BIDViewController

@end
```

That's much simpler, huh? Don't worry about those methods you just deleted. You'll be introduced to most of them throughout the course of the book.

Designing the User Interface

Make sure you save the changes you just made, and then single-click *Main.storyboard* to open your application's view in Xcode's Interface Builder (see Figure 3-4). As you'll remember from the previous chapter, the white window that shows up in the editor represents your application's one and only view. If you look back at Figure 3-1, you can see that we need to add two buttons and a label to this view.

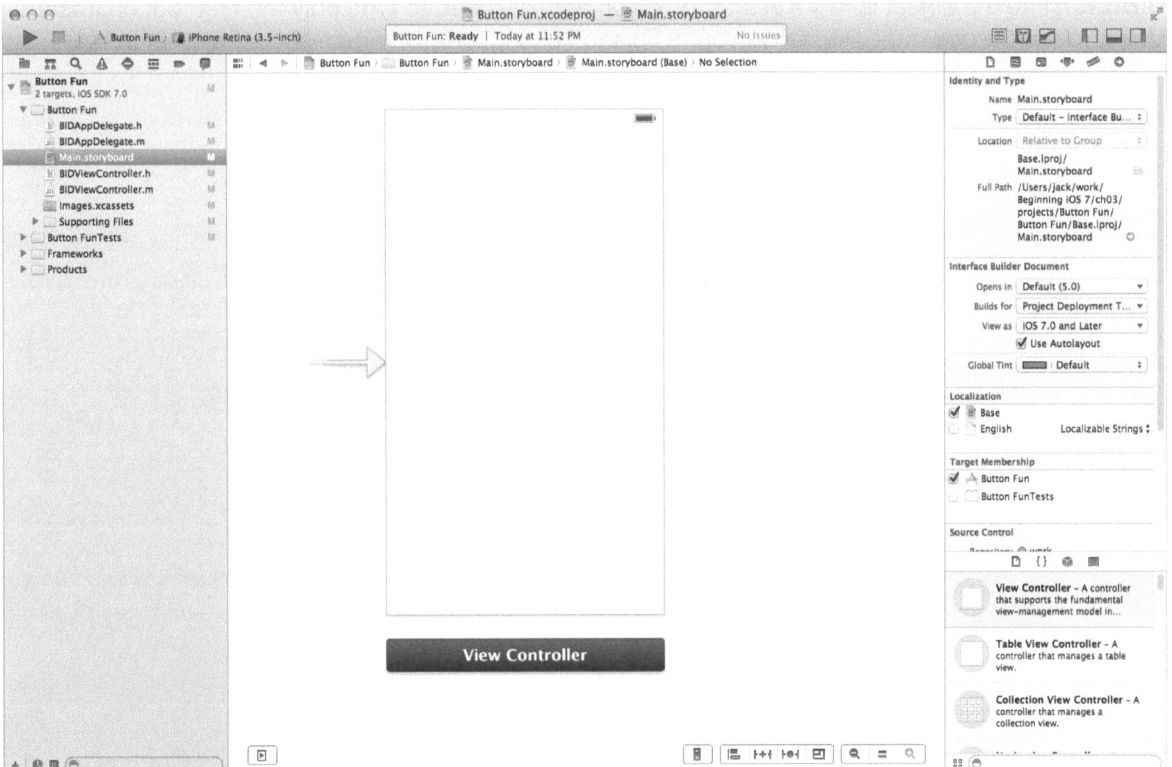

Figure 3-4. Main.storyboard open for editing in Xcode's Interface Builder

Let's take a second to think about our application. We're going to add two buttons and a label to our user interface, and that process is very similar to what we did in the previous chapter. However, we're also going to need outlets and actions to make our application interactive.

The buttons will need to each trigger an action method on our controller. We could choose to make each button call a different action method; but since they're going to do essentially the same task (update the label's text), we will need to call the same action method. We'll differentiate between the two buttons using that sender argument we discussed earlier in the section on actions. In addition to the action method, we'll also need an outlet connected to the label, so that we can change the text that the label displays.

Let's add the buttons first and then place the label. We'll create the corresponding actions and outlets as we design our interface. We could also manually declare our actions and outlets and then connect our user interface items to them, but why do extra work when Xcode will do it for us?

Adding the Buttons and Action Method

Our first order of business is to add two buttons to our user interface. We'll then have Xcode create an empty action method for us, and we can connect both buttons to that action method. This will cause the buttons, when tapped by the user, to call that action method. Any code we place in that action method will be executed when the user taps the button.

Select **View ➤ Utilities ➤ Show Object Library** or press ^⌥⌘3 to open the object library. Type **UIButton** into the object library's search box (you actually need to type only the first four characters, **UIBu**, to narrow down the list). Once you're finished typing, only one item should appear in the object library: *Button* (see Figure 3-5).

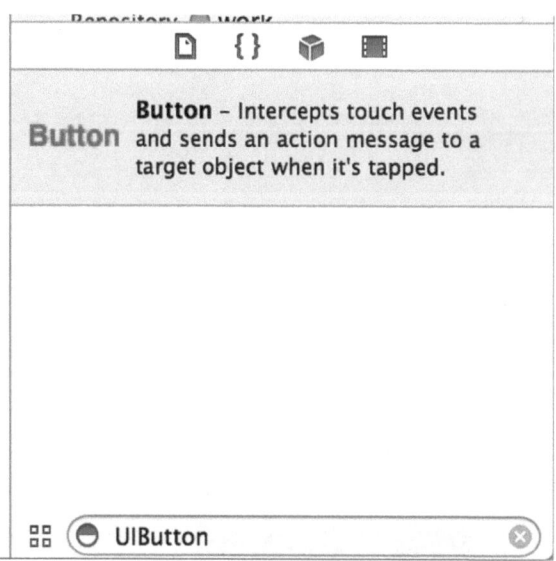

Figure 3-5. The Button as it appears in the object library

Drag *Button* from the library and drop it on the white window inside the editing area. This will add a button to your application's view. Place the button along the left side of the view the appropriate distance from the left edge by using the blue guidelines that appear to place it. For vertical placement, use the blue guidelines to place the button halfway down in the view. You can use Figure 3-1 as a placement guide, if that helps.

> **Note**   The little, blue guidelines that appear as you move objects around in Interface Builder are there to help you stick to the *iOS Human Interface Guidelines* (usually referred to as **the HIG**). Apple provides the HIG for people designing iPhone and iPad applications. The HIG tells you how you should—and shouldn't—design your user interface. You really should read it because it contains valuable information that every iOS developer needs to know. You'll find it at `http://developer.apple.com/library/ios/documentation/ UserExperience/Conceptual/MobileHIG/`.

Double-click the newly added button. This will allow you to edit the button's title. Give this button a title of *Left*.

Now, it's time for some Xcode magic. Select **View ➤ Assistant Editor ➤ Show Assistant Editor**, or press ⌥⌘↩ to open the assistant editor. You can also show and hide the assistant editor by clicking the middle editor button in the collection of seven buttons on the upper-right side of the project window (see Figure 3-6).

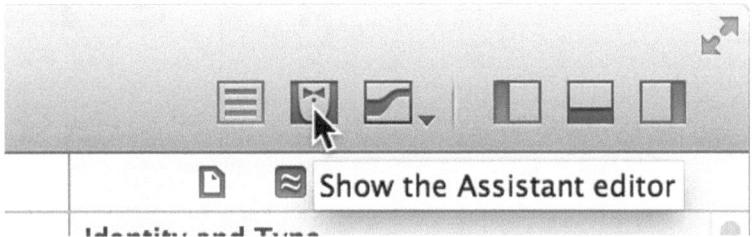

Figure 3-6. The Show the Assistant editor toggle button

Unless you specifically request otherwise (see the options in the **Assistant Editor** menu), the assistant editor will appear to the right of the editing pane. The left side will continue to show Interface Builder, but the right will display either *BIDViewController.h* or *BIDViewController.m*, which are the header and implementation files for the view controller that "owns" the view you're looking at.

> **Tip**   After opening the assistant editor, you may need to resize your window to have enough room to work. If you're on a smaller screen, like the one on a MacBook Air, you might need to close the utility view and/or project navigator to give yourself enough room to use the assistant editor effectively. You can do this easily using the three view buttons in the upper right of the project window (see Figure 3-6).

Remember the *View Controller* icon we discussed in the previous chapter? This is the same thing all over again. Xcode knows that our view controller class is responsible for displaying this view, and so the assistant editor knows to show us the header and/or implementation of the view controller class, which are the most likely places we'll want to create to connect actions and outlets.

As you saw earlier, there's really not much in the BIDViewController class. It's just an empty UIViewController subclass. But it won't be an empty subclass for long!

We're now going to ask Xcode to automatically create a new action method for us and associate that action with the button we just created. We're going to add these definitions to the header file. If that's not currently shown in the assistant view, use the jump bar above it to select *BIDViewController.h*.

To do this, begin by clicking your new button so it is selected. Now, hold down the control key on your keyboard, and then click-and-drag from the button over to the source code in the assistant editor. You should see a blue line running from the button to your cursor (see Figure 3-7). This blue line is how we connect objects in IB to code or other objects.

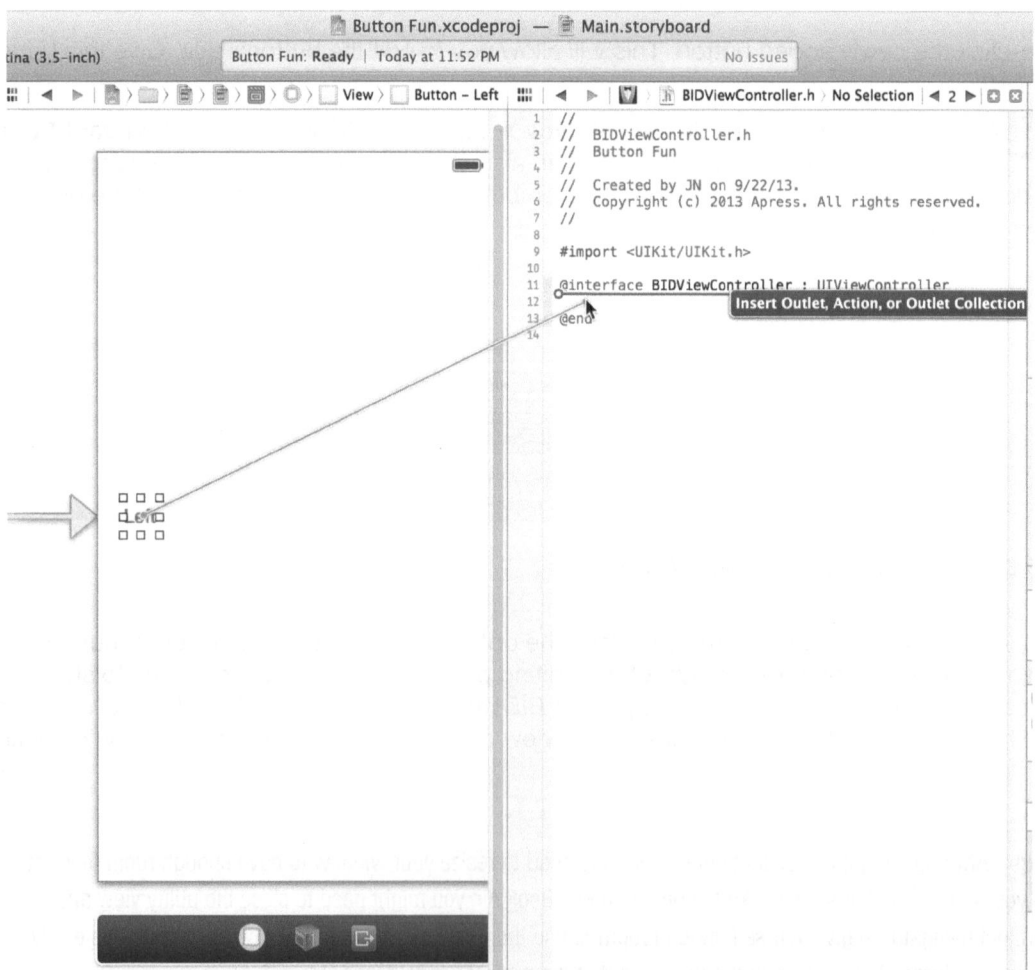

Figure 3-7. Control-dragging to source code will give you the option to create an outlet, action, or outlet collection

Tip   You can drag that blue line to anything you want to connect to your button: to the header file in the assistant editor, to the *File's Owner* icon, to any of the other icons on the left side of the editing pane, or even to other objects in the editing area.

If you move your cursor so it's between the `@interface` and `@end` keywords (see Figure 3-7), a gray box will appear, letting you know that releasing the mouse button will insert an outlet, an action, or an outlet collection for you.

Note   We use actions and outlets in this book, but we do not use outlet collections. Outlet collections allow you to connect multiple objects of the same kind to a single `NSArray` property, rather than creating a separate property for each object.

To finish this connection, release your mouse button, and a floating pop-up will appear, like the one shown in Figure 3-8. This window lets you customize your new action. In the window, click the pop-up menu labeled *Connection* and change the selection from *Outlet* to *Action*. This tells Xcode that we want to create an action instead of an outlet.

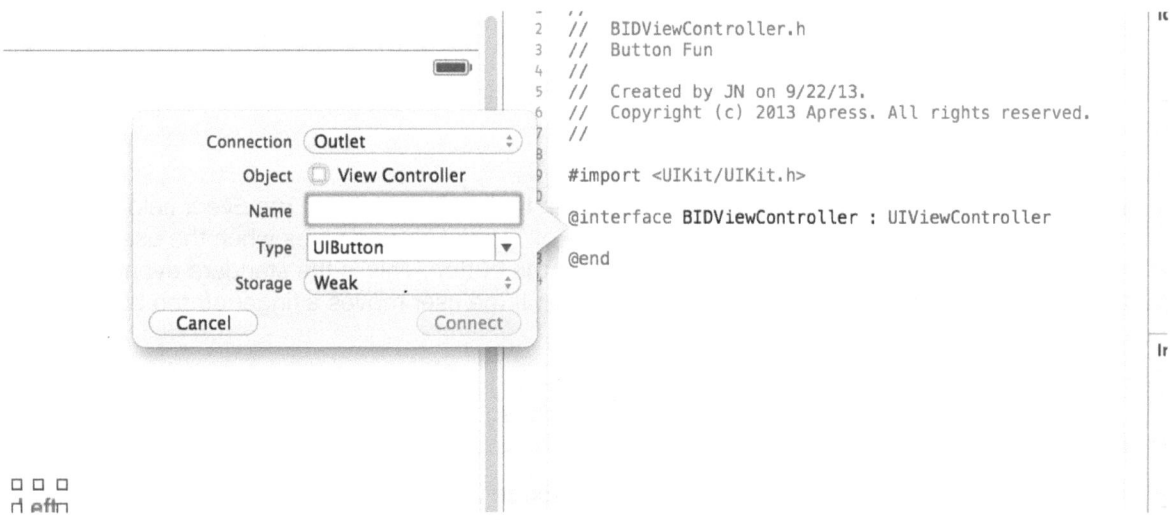

Figure 3-8. The floating pop-up that appears after you control-drag to source code

The pop-up will change to look like Figure 3-9. In the *Name* field, type *buttonPressed*. When you're finished, do *not* hit the **Return** key. Pressing **Return** would finalize our outlet, and we're not quite ready to do that. Instead, press the **Tab** key to move to the *Type* field and type in *UIButton*, replacing the default value of *id*.

```
2  //  BIDViewController.h
3  //  Button Fun
4  //
5  //  Created by JN on 9/22/13.
6  //  Copyright (c) 2013 Apress. All rights reserved.
7  //

   #import <UIKit/UIKit.h>

   @interface BIDViewController : UIViewController

   @end
```

Figure 3-9. Changing the connection type to Action changes the appearance of the pop-up

Note   As you probably remember, an *id* is a generic pointer that can point to any Objective-C object. We could leave this as *id*, and it would work fine; but if we change it to the class we expect to call the method, the compiler can warn us if we try to do this from the wrong type of object. There are times when you'll want the flexibility to be able to call the same action method from different types of controls; and in those cases, you would want to leave this set to *id*. In our case, we're only going to call this method from buttons, so we're letting Xcode and LLVM know that. Now, it can warn us if we unintentionally try to connect something else to it.

There are two fields below *Type*, which we will leave at their default values. The *Event* field lets you specify when the method is called. The default value of *Touch Up Inside* fires when the user lifts a finger off the screen if–and only if–the finger is still on the button. This is the standard event to use for buttons. This gives the user a chance to reconsider. If the user moves a finger off the button before lifting it off the screen, the method won't fire.

The *Arguments* field lets you choose between the three different method signatures that can be used for action methods. We want the sender argument, so that we can tell which button called the method. That's the default, so we just leave it as is.

Hit the **Return** key or click the *Connect* button, and Xcode will insert the action method for you. Your *BIDViewController.h* file should now look like this:

```
#import <UIKit/UIKit.h>

@interface BIDViewController : UIViewController
- (IBAction)buttonPressed:(UIButton *)sender;

@end
```

Xcode has now added a method declaration to your class's header file for you. Use the jump bar above the assistant editor to switch over to *BIDViewController.m*, and you'll see that it has also added a method stub for you.

```
- (IBAction)buttonPressed:(UIButton *)sender {
}
```

In a few moments, we'll come back here to write the code that needs to run when the user taps either button. In addition to creating the method declaration and implementation, Xcode has also connected that button to this action method and stored that information in the storyboard. That means we don't need to do anything else to make that button call this method when our application runs.

Go back to *Main.storyboard* and drag out another button, this time placing the button on the right side of the screen. After placing it, double-click it and change its name to *Right*. The blue lines will pop up to help you align it with the right margin, as you saw before, and they will also help you align the button vertically with the other button.

> **Tip** Instead of dragging a new object out from the library, you could hold down the ⌥ key (the **Option** key) and drag the original object (the *Left* button in this example) over. Holding down the ⌥ key tells Interface Builder to drag out a copy of the original object.

This time, we don't want to create a new action method. Instead, we want to connect this button to the existing one that Xcode created for us a moment ago. How do we do that? We do it pretty much the same way as we did for the first button.

After changing the name of the button, control-click the new button and drag toward your code in the assistant editor. It doesn't matter if you're looking at the *.h* or the *.m* file—just drag towards the declaration of the buttonPressed: method. This time, as your cursor gets near buttonPressed:, that method should highlight, and you'll get a gray pop-up saying *Connect Action* (see Figure 3-10). When you see that pop-up, release the mouse button, and Xcode will connect this button to the existing action method. That will cause this button, when tapped, to trigger the same action method as the other button.

Figure 3-10. Dragging to an existing action will connect the button to an existing action

Again, note that this will work even if you control-drag to connect your button to a method in your implementation file. In other words, you can control-drag from your new button to the buttonPressed declaration in *BIDViewController.h* or to the buttonPressed method implementation in *BIDViewController.m*. Xcode sure am smart!

Adding the Label and Outlet

In the object library, type *Label* into the search field to find the *Label* user interface item (*see* Figure 3-11). Drag the *Label* to your user interface, somewhere above the two buttons you placed earlier. After placing it, use the resize handles to stretch the label from the left margin to the right margin. That should give it plenty of room for the text we'll be displaying to the user.

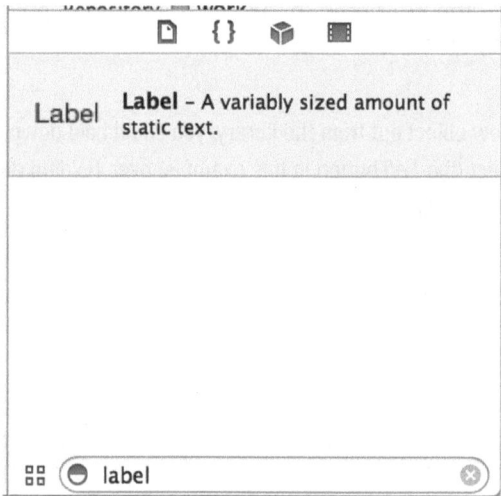

Figure 3-11. The label as it appears in the object library

Labels, by default, are left-aligned, but we want this one to be centered. Select **View ➤ Utilities ➤ Show Attributes Inspector** (or press ⌥⌘4) to bring up the attributes inspector (see Figure 3-12). Make sure the label is selected, and then look in the attributes inspector for the *Alignment* buttons. Select the middle *Alignment* button to center the label's text.

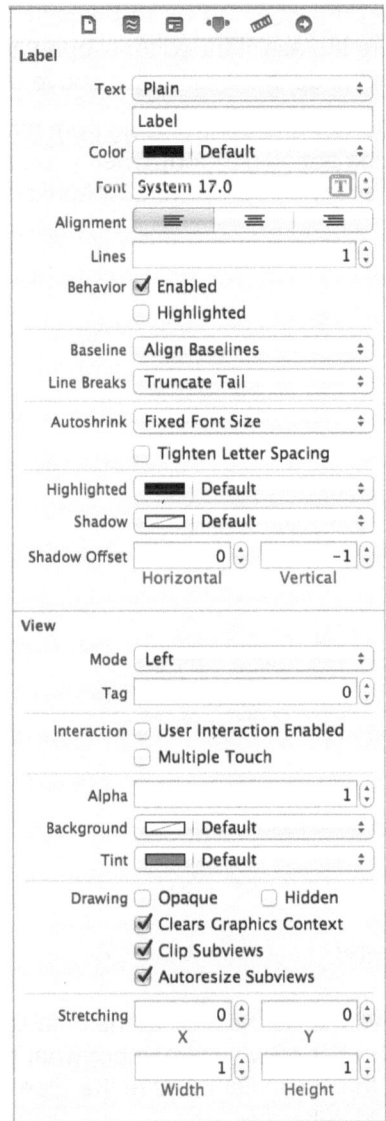

Figure 3-12. *The attribute inspector for the label*

Before the user taps a button, we don't want the label to say anything, so double-click the label (so the text is selected) and press the **Delete** button on your keyboard. That will delete the text currently assigned to the label. Hit **Return** to commit your changes. Even though you won't be able to see the label when it's not selected, don't worry—it's still there.

Tip If you have invisible user interface elements, like empty labels, and want to be able to see where they are, select *Canvas* from the *Editor* menu. Next, from the submenu that pops up, turn on *Show Bounds Rectangles*.

All that's left is to create an outlet for the label. We do this exactly the way we created and connected actions earlier. Make sure the assistant editor is open and displaying *BIDViewController.h*. If you need to switch files, use the pop-up in the jump bar above the assistant editor.

Next, select the label in Interface Builder and control-drag from the label to the header file. Drag until your cursor is right above the existing action method. When you see something like Figure 3-13, let go of the mouse button, and you'll see the pop-up window again (shown earlier in Figure 3-8).

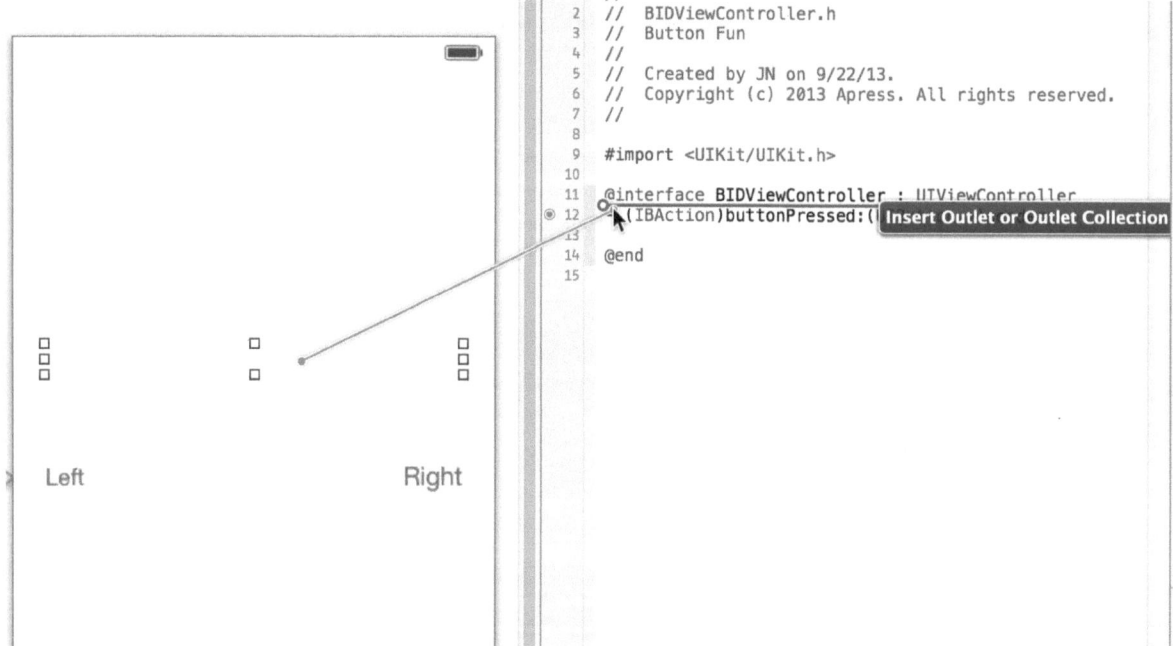

Figure 3-13. Control-dragging to create an outlet

We want to create an outlet, so leave the *Connection* at the default type of *Outlet*. We want to choose a descriptive name for this outlet so we'll remember what it is used for when we're working on our code. Type *statusLabel* into the *Name* field. Leave the *Type* field set to *UILabel*. The final field, labeled *Storage*, can be left at the default value.

Hit **Return** to commit your changes, and Xcode will insert the outlet property into your code. Your controller class's header file should now look like this:

```
#import <UIKit/UIKit.h>

@interface BIDViewController : UIViewController
@property (weak, nonatomic) IBOutlet UILabel *statusLabel;
- (IBAction)buttonPressed:(UIButton *)sender;
@end
```

Now we have an outlet, and Xcode has automagically connected the label to our outlet. This means that if we make any changes to statusLabel in code, those changes will affect the label on our user interface. If we set the text property on statusLabel, for example, it will change what text is displayed to the user.

AUTOMATIC REFERENCE COUNTING

If you're already familiar with Objective-C, or if you've read earlier versions of this book, you might have noticed that we don't have a dealloc method. We're not releasing our instance variables!

Warning! Warning! Danger, Will Robinson!

Actually, Will, you can relax. We're quite OK. There's no danger at all—really.

It's no longer necessary to release objects. Well, that's not entirely true. It is necessary, but the LLVM compiler that Apple includes with Xcode these days is so smart that it will release objects for us, using a new feature called **Automatic Reference Counting**, or ARC, to do the heavy lifting. That means less frequent use of dealloc methods and no more worrying about calling release or autorelease. ARC is such a big improvement that we're using it for all examples in this book. ARC has been an option in Xcode for the past couple of years, but now it's enabled by default for each new project you create.

ARC applies to only Objective-C objects, not to Core Foundation objects or to memory allocated with malloc() and the like, and there are some caveats and gotchas that can trip you up. But for the most part, worrying about memory management is a thing of the past.

To learn more about ARC, check out the ARC release notes at this URL:

http://developer.apple.com/library/ios/#releasenotes/ObjectiveC/RN-TransitioningToARC/

ARC is very cool, but it's not magic. You should still understand the basic rules of memory management in Objective-C to avoid getting in trouble with ARC. To brush up on the Objective-C memory management contract, read Apple's *Memory Management Programming Guide* at this URL:

http://developer.apple.com/library/ios/#documentation/Cocoa/Conceptual/MemoryMgmt/

Writing the Action Method

So far, we've designed our user interface and wired up both outlets and actions to our user interface. All that's left to do is to use those actions and outlets to set the text of the label when a button is pressed. Single-click *BIDViewController.m* in the project navigator to open it in the editor. Find the empty buttonPressed: method that Xcode created for us earlier.

To differentiate between the two buttons, we're going to use the sender parameter. We'll retrieve the title of the button that was pressed using sender, and then create a new string based on that title and assign that as the label's text. Add the bold code below to your empty method:

```
- (IBAction)buttonPressed:(UIButton *)sender {
    NSString *title = [sender titleForState:UIControlStateNormal];
    NSString *plainText = [NSString stringWithFormat:@"%@ button pressed.", title];
    _statusLabel.text = plainText;
}
```

This is pretty straightforward. The first line retrieves the tapped button's title using sender. Since buttons can have different titles depending on their current state, we use the UIControlStateNormal parameter to specify that we want the title when the button is in its normal, untapped state. This is usually the state you want to specify when asking a control (a button is a type of control) for its title. We'll look at control states in more detail in Chapter 4.

The next line creates a new string by appending this text to the title we retrieved in the previous line: "button pressed." So, if the left button, which has a title of *Left*, is tapped, this line will create a string that says, "Left button pressed." The final line assigns the new string to the label's text property, which is how we change the text that the label is displaying.

MESSAGE NESTING

Objective-C messages are often nested by some developers. You may come across code like this in your travels:

```
NSString *plainText = [NSString stringWithFormat:@"%@ button
  pressed.",
  [sender titleForState:UIControlStateNormal]];
```

This one line of code will function exactly the same as the first two lines of our buttonPressed: method. This is because Objective-C methods can be nested, which essentially substitutes the return value from the nested method call.

For the sake of clarity, we won't generally nest Objective-C messages in the code examples in this book, with the exception of calls to alloc and init, which, by long-standing convention, are almost always nested.

Trying It Out

Guess what? We're basically finished. Are you ready to try out our app? Let's do it!

Select **Product ➤ Run**. If you run into any compile or link errors, go back and compare your code changes to those shown in this chapter. Once your code builds properly, Xcode will launch the iOS simulator and run your application. When you tap the right button, this text should appear: "Right button pressed." (See Figure 3-1 again). If you then tap the left button, the label will change to say, "Left button pressed."

So far, so good. But if you look back at Figure 3-1, you'll see that one thing is missing. The screenshot we showed you for our end result displays the name of the chosen button in bold text; however, what we've made just shows a plain string. We'll bring on the boldness using an NSAttributedString class.

Adding Some style

The NSAttributedString class lets you attach formatting information, such as fonts and paragraph alignment to a string. This metadata can be applied to an entire string, or different attributes can be applied to different parts. If you think about the ways that formatting can be applied to pieces of text in a word processor, that's basically the model for how NSAttributedString works.

However, until recently, none of the Apple-provided UIKit classes have been able to do anything with attributed strings. If you wanted to present a label containing both bold text and normal text, you'd have to either use two labels or draw the text directly into a view on your own. Those approaches aren't insurmountable hurdles, but they're tricky enough that most developers would rather not follow those paths too often. iOS 6 brought many improvements for anyone who wants to display styled text, since most of the main UIKit controls now let you use attributed strings. In the case of a UILabel such as the one we have here, it's as simple as creating an attributed string, then passing it to the label via its attributedText property.

So, update the buttonPressed: method by deleting the crossed-out line and adding the bold lines shown in this snippet:

```
- (IBAction)buttonPressed:(UIButton *)sender {
    NSString *title = [sender titleForState:UIControlStateNormal];
    NSString *plainText = [NSString stringWithFormat:@"%@ button pressed.", title];
    _statusLabel.text = plainText;

    NSMutableAttributedString *styledText = [[NSMutableAttributedString alloc]
                                             initWithString:plainText];
    NSDictionary *attributes =
    @{
      NSFontAttributeName : [UIFont boldSystemFontOfSize:_statusLabel.font.pointSize]
      };

    NSRange nameRange = [plainText rangeOfString:title];

    [styledText setAttributes:attributes range:nameRange];
    _statusLabel.attributedText = styledText;
}
```

The first thing that new code does is create an attributed string—specifically, an NSMutableAttributedString instance—based on the string we want to display. We need a mutable attributed string here because we want to change its attributes.

Next, we create a dictionary to hold the attributes we want to apply to our string. Really, we have just one attribute right now, so this dictionary contains a single key-value pair. The key, NSFontAttributeName, lets you specify a font for a portion of an attributed string. The value we pass in is something called the **bold system font**, which is specified to be the same size as the font currently used by the label. Specifying the font this way is more flexible in the long run than specifying a font by name, since we know that the system will always have a reasonable idea of what to use for a bold font.

> **Tip**   If you've been using Objective-C for a while, you may not be familiar with this new dictionary syntax—but it's pretty simple. Instead of requiring an explicit call to a class method on NSDictionary, the version of LLVM included with Xcode now provides a shorthand form, which is nicer to use. It basically looks like this:
>
> ```
> @{
>   key1 : value1,
>   key2 : value2
> }
> ```
>
> Apart from eliminating the need to type the same lengthy class name and method name every time you want to make a dictionary, it also puts the keys and values in the "right order"—at least according to anyone who's ever used a language with built-in dictionaries, such as Ruby, Python, Perl, or JavaScript.
>
> This new dictionary syntax was introduced in 2012, along with similar syntax for arrays and numbers. We'll be using these new pieces of syntax throughout the book.

Next, we ask our plainText string to give us the range (consisting of a start index and a length) of the substring where our title is found. We apply the attributes to the attributed string and pass it off to the label.

Now you can hit the *Run* button, and you'll see that the app now shows the name of the clicked button in bold text.

Looking at the Application Delegate

Well, cool! Your application works! Before we move on to our next topic, let's take a minute to look through the two source code files we have not yet examined, *BIDAppDelegate.h* and *BIDAppDelegate.m*. These files implement our **application delegate**.

Cocoa Touch makes extensive use of **delegates**, which are objects that take responsibility for doing certain tasks on behalf of another object. The application delegate lets us do things at certain predefined times on behalf of the UIApplication class. Every iOS application has exactly one instance of UIApplication, which is responsible for the application's run loop and handles application-level functionality, such as routing input to the appropriate controller class. UIApplication is a standard part of the UIKit, and it does its job mostly behind the scenes, so you generally don't need to worry about it.

At certain well-defined times during an application's execution, UIApplication will call specific methods on its delegate, if there is a delegate and that delegate implements the method. For example, if you have code that needs to fire just before your program quits, you would implement the method applicationWillTerminate: in your application delegate and put your termination code there. This type of delegation allows your application to implement common application-wide behavior without needing to subclass UIApplication or, indeed, without needing to know anything about the inner workings of UIApplication.

Click *BIDAppDelegate.h* in the project navigator to see the application delegate's header file. It should look similar to this:

```
#import <UIKit/UIKit.h>

@interface BIDAppDelegate : UIResponder <UIApplicationDelegate>

@property (strong, nonatomic) UIWindow *window;

@end
```

One thing worth pointing out is this line of code:

```
@interface BIDAppDelegate : UIResponder <UIApplicationDelegate>
```

Do you see that value between the angle brackets? This indicates that this class conforms to a protocol called UIApplicationDelegate. Hold down the ⌥ key. Your cursor should turn into crosshairs. Move your cursor so that it is over the word, UIApplicationDelegate. Your cursor should turn into a question mark, and the word UIApplicationDelegate should be highlighted, as if it were a link in a browser (see Figure 3-14).

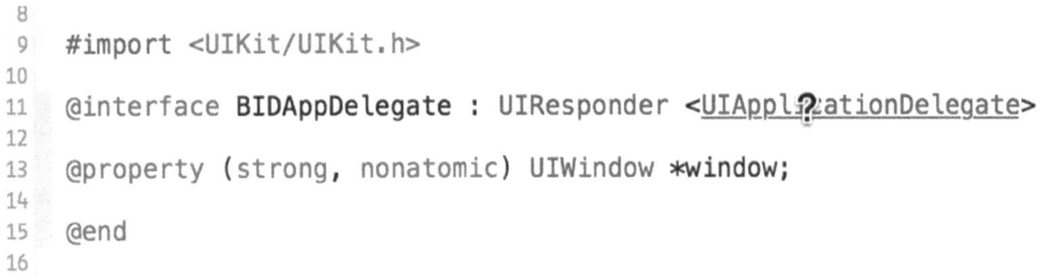

```
 8
 9   #import <UIKit/UIKit.h>
10
11   @interface BIDAppDelegate : UIResponder <UIApplicationDelegate>
12
13   @property (strong, nonatomic) UIWindow *window;
14
15   @end
16
```

Figure 3-14. When you hold down the ⌥ key (the Option key) in Xcode and point at a symbol in your code, the symbol is highlighted and your cursor changes into a pointing hand with a question mark

With the ⌥ key still held down, click this link. This will open a small pop-up window showing a brief overview of the UIApplicationDelegate protocol (see Figure 3-15).

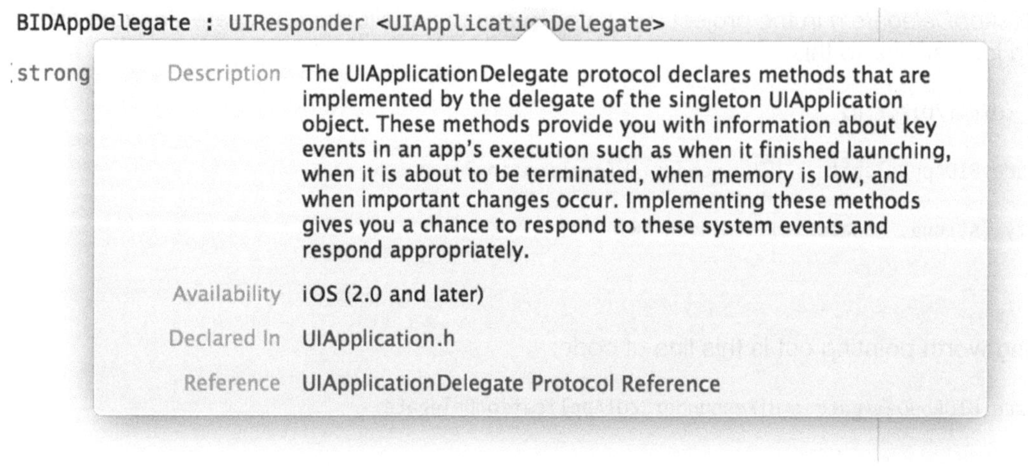

```
BIDAppDelegate : UIResponder <UIApplicationDelegate>
```

strong	Description	The UIApplicationDelegate protocol declares methods that are implemented by the delegate of the singleton UIApplication object. These methods provide you with information about key events in an app's execution such as when it finished launching, when it is about to be terminated, when memory is low, and when important changes occur. Implementing these methods gives you a chance to respond to these system events and respond appropriately.
Availability	iOS (2.0 and later)
Declared In	UIApplication.h
Reference	UIApplicationDelegate Protocol Reference

Figure 3-15. When we option-clicked <UIApplicationDelegate> from within our source code, Xcode popped up this window, called the Quick Help panel, which describes the protocol

Notice the two links at the bottom of this new pop-up documentation window (see Figure 3-15). Click the *Reference* link to view the full documentation for this symbol or click the *Declared In* link to view the symbol's definition in a header file. This same trick works with class, protocol, and category names, as well as method names displayed in the editor pane. Just option-click a word, and Xcode will search for that word in the documentation browser.

Knowing how to look up things quickly in the documentation is definitely worthwhile, but looking at the definition of this protocol is perhaps more important. Here's where you'll find which methods the application delegate can implement and when those methods will be called. It's probably worth your time to read over the descriptions of these methods.

> **Note** If you've worked with Objective-C before but not with Objective-C 2.0, you should be aware that protocols can now specify optional methods. UIApplicationDelegate contains many optional methods. However, you do not need to implement any of the optional methods in your application delegate unless you have a reason to do so.

Back in the project navigator, click *BIDAppDelegate.m* to see the implementation of the application delegate. It should look something like this:

```
#import "BIDAppDelegate.h"

@implementation BIDAppDelegate

- (BOOL)application:(UIApplication *)application didFinishLaunchingWithOptions:
    (NSDictionary *)launchOptions
{
    // Override point for customization after application launch.
    return YES;
}
```

```
- (void)applicationWillResignActive:(UIApplication *)application
{
    // Sent when the application is about to move from active to inactive state.
        This can occur for certain types of temporary interruptions (such as an
        incoming phone call or SMS message) or when the user quits the
        application and it begins the transition to the background state.
    // Use this method to pause ongoing tasks, disable timers, and throttle down
        OpenGL ES frame rates. Games should use this method to pause the game.

}

- (void)applicationDidEnterBackground:(UIApplication *)application
{
    // Use this method to release shared resources, save user data, invalidate
        timers, and store enough application state information to restore your
        application to its current state in case it is terminated later.
    // If your application supports background execution, this method is called
        instead of applicationWillTerminate: when the user quits.

}

- (void)applicationWillEnterForeground:(UIApplication *)application
{
    // Called as part of the transition from the background to the inactive
        state; here you can undo many of the changes made on entering the
        background.

}

- (void)applicationDidBecomeActive:(UIApplication *)application
{
    // Restart any tasks that were paused (or not yet started) while the
        application was inactive. If the application was previously in the
        background, optionally refresh the user interface.

}

- (void)applicationWillTerminate:(UIApplication *)application
{
    // Called when the application is about to terminate. Save data if
        appropriate. See also applicationDidEnterBackground:.

}

@end
```

At the top of the file, you can see that our application delegate has implemented one of those protocol methods covered in the documentation, called `application:didFinishLaunchingWithOptions:`. As you can probably guess, this method fires as soon as the application has finished all the setup work and is ready to start interacting with the user. This method is often used to create any objects that need to exist for the entire lifetime of the running app.

You'll see more of this later in the book. We just wanted to give you a bit of background on application delegates and show how this all ties together before closing this chapter.

Bring It on Home

This chapter's simple application introduced you to MVC, creating and connecting outlets and actions, implementing view controllers, and using application delegates. You learned how to trigger action methods when a button is tapped and saw how to change the text of a label at runtime. Although we built a simple application, the basic concepts we used are the same as those that underlie the use of all controls under iOS, not just buttons. In fact, the way we used buttons and labels in this chapter is pretty much the way that we will implement and interact with most of the standard controls under iOS.

It's critical that you understand everything we did in this chapter and why we did it. If you don't, go back and review the parts that you don't fully understand. This is important stuff! If you don't make sure you understand everything now, you will only get more confused as we get into creating more complex interfaces later in this book.

In the next chapter, we'll take a look at some of the other standard iOS controls. You'll also learn how to use alerts to notify the user of important happenings and how to use action sheets to indicate that the user needs to make a choice before proceeding. When you feel you're ready to proceed, give yourself a pat on the back for being such an awesome student and head on over to the next chapter.

Chapter 4

More User Interface Fun

In Chapter 3, we discussed MVC and built an application using it. You learned about outlets and actions, and you used them to tie a button control to a text label. In this chapter, we're going to build an application that will take your knowledge of controls to a whole new level.

We'll implement an image view, a slider, two different text fields, a segmented control, a couple of switches, and an iOS button that looks more like, well, an iOS button. You'll see how to set and retrieve the values of various controls. You'll learn how to use action sheets to force the user to make a choice, and how to use alerts to give the user important feedback. You'll also learn about control states and the use of stretchable images to make buttons look the way they should.

Because this chapter's application uses so many different user interface items, we're going to work a little differently than we did in the previous two chapters. We'll break our application into pieces, implementing one piece at a time. Bouncing back and forth between Xcode and the iOS simulator, we'll test each piece before we move on to the next. Dividing the process of building a complex interface into smaller chunks makes it much less intimidating, as well as more like the actual process you'll go through when building your own applications. This code-compile-debug cycle makes up a large part of a software developer's typical day.

A Screen Full of Controls

As we mentioned, the application we're going to build in this chapter is a bit more complex than the one we created in Chapter 3. We'll still use only a single view and controller; but as you can see in Figure 4-1, there's a lot more going on in this one view.

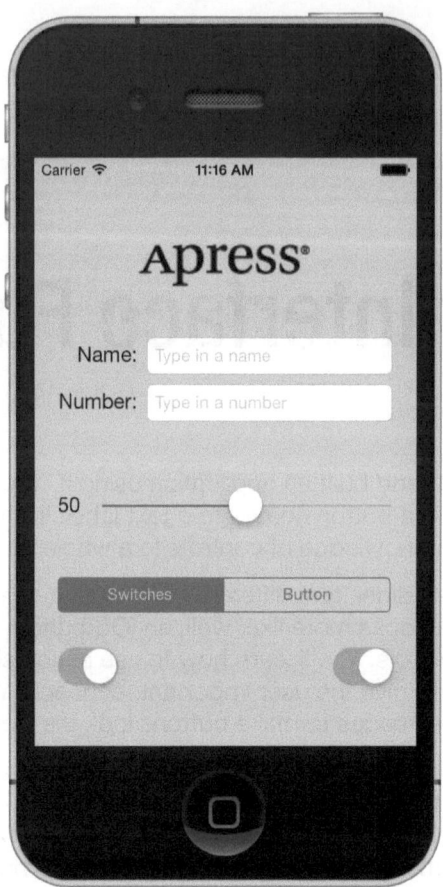

Figure 4-1. *The Control Fun application features text fields, labels, a slider, and several other stock iPhone controls*

The logo at the top of the iPhone screen is an **image view**; and in this application, it does nothing more than display a static image. Below the logo are two **text fields**: one that allows the entry of alphanumeric text and one that allows only numbers. Below the text fields is a **slider**. As the user moves the slider, the value of the label next to it will change so that it always reflects the slider's current value.

Below the slider are a **segmented control** and two **switches**. The segmented control will toggle between two different types of controls in the space below it. When the application first launches, two switches will appear below the segmented control. Changing the value of either switch will cause the other one to change its value to match. Now, this isn't something you would likely do in a real application, but it does demonstrate how to change the value of a control programmatically and how Cocoa Touch animates certain actions without you needing to do any work.

Figure 4-2 shows what happens when the user taps the segmented control. The switches disappear and are replaced by a button. When the *Do Something* button is pressed, an action sheet pops up, asking if the user really meant to tap the button (see Figure 4-3). This is the standard way of responding to input that is potentially dangerous or that could have significant repercussions, and it gives the user a chance to stop potential badness from happening. If *Yes, I'm Sure!* is selected, the application will put up an alert, letting the user know that everything is OK (see Figure 4-4).

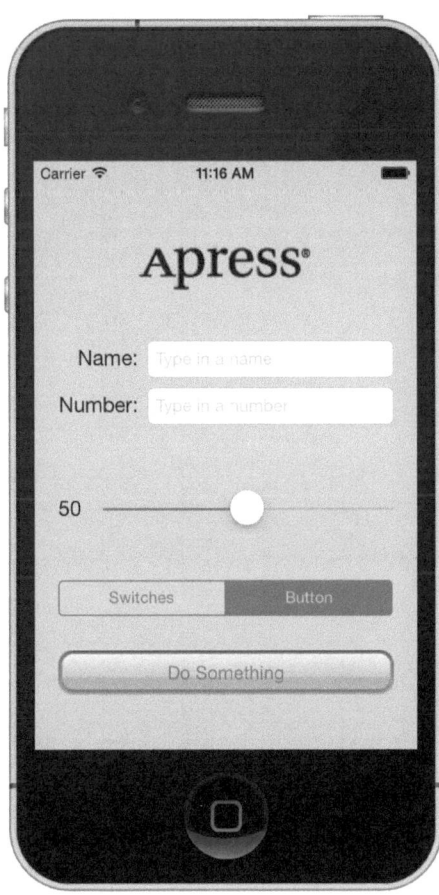

Figure 4-2. *Tapping the segmented controller on the left side causes a pair of switches to be displayed. Tapping the right side causes a button to be displayed*

Figure 4-3. Our application uses an action sheet to solicit a response from the user

Figure 4-4. Alerts are used to notify the user when important things happen. We use one here to confirm that everything went OK

Active, Static, and Passive Controls

Interface controls are used in three basic modes: active, static (or inactive), and passive. The buttons that we used in the previous chapter are classic examples of active controls. You push them, and something happens—usually, a piece of code that you wrote fires.

Although many of the controls that you will use will directly trigger action methods, not all controls will. The image view that we'll be implementing in this chapter is a good example of a control being used statically. A UIImageView can be configured to trigger action methods, but in our application the image view is passive—the user cannot do anything with it. Labels and image controls are often used in this manner.

Some controls can work in a passive mode, simply holding on to a value that the user has entered until you're ready for it. These controls don't trigger action methods, but the user can interact with them and change their values. A classic example of a passive control is a text field on a web page. Although it's possible to create validation code that fires when the user tabs out of a field, the vast majority of web page text fields are simply containers for data that's submitted to the server when the user clicks the submit button. The text fields themselves usually don't cause any code to fire, but when the submit button is clicked, the text field's data goes along for the ride.

On an iOS device, most of the available controls can be used in all three modes, and nearly all of them can function in more than one mode, depending on your needs. All iOS controls are subclasses of UIControl, so they are capable of triggering action methods. Many controls can be used passively, and all of them can be made inactive or invisible. For example, using one control might trigger another inactive control to become active. However, some controls, such as buttons, really don't serve much purpose unless they are used in an active manner to trigger code.

There are some behavioral differences between controls on iOS and those on your Mac. Here are a few examples:

■ Because of the multitouch interface, all iOS controls can trigger multiple actions, depending on how they are touched. The user might trigger a different action with a finger swipe across the control than with just a tap.

■ You could have one action fire when the user presses down on a button and a separate action fire when the finger is lifted off the button.

■ You could have a single control call multiple action methods on a single event. For example, you could have two different action methods fire on the *Touch Up*Inside event when the user's finger is lifted after touching that button.

> **Note**   Although controls can trigger multiple methods on iOS, the vast majority of the time, you're probably better off implementing a single action method that does what you need for a particular use of a control. You won't usually need this capability, but it's good to keep it in mind when working in Interface Builder. Connecting an event to an action in Interface Builder does *not* disconnect a previously connected action from the same control! This can lead to surprising misbehaviors in your app, where a control will trigger multiple action methods. Keep an eye open when retargeting an event in Interface Builder, and make sure you remove old actions before connecting to new ones.

Another major difference between iOS and the Mac stems from the fact that, normally, iOS devices do not have a physical keyboard. The standard iOS software keyboard is actually just a view filled with a series of button controls that are managed for you by the system. Your code will likely never directly interact with the iOS keyboard.

Creating the Application

Let's get started. Fire up Xcode if it's not already open, and create a new project called *Control Fun*. We're going to use the Single View Application template again, so create your project just as you did in the previous two chapters.

Now that you've created your project, let's get the image we'll use in our image view. The image must be imported into Xcode before it will be available for use inside Interface Builder, so we'll import it now. You can use the image named *apress_logo.png* in the project archives in the *04 - Control Fun* folder in the project archives. You'll find two images in the folder, named *apress_logo_344.png* and *apress_logo_172.png*; these are the retina and non-retina versions of the same image. We're going to add both of these to the new project's image resource catalog and let the app decide which of them to use at runtime. If you'd rather use an image-pair of your own choosing, make sure that they are *.png* images sized correctly for the space available. The larger version should be less than 200 pixels tall and a maximum of 600 pixels wide, so that it can fit comfortably at the top of the view without being resized. The smaller one should be half the size in both dimensions.

In Xcode, select the *Images.xcassets* item and click the plus button in the lower-left corner of the editing area. This brings up a small menu of choices, from which you should select **New Image Set**. This creates a new spot for adding your actual image files. Right now it's just called *Image*, but we want to give it a unique name, so we can refer to it elsewhere in the project. Select the *Image* item, bring up the attributes inspector (**⌥⌘3, or Opt-Cmd-3**), and use it to change the image's name to *apress_logo*.

Now add the images themselves to the *apress_logo* image item by dragging each image from the Finder to the image detail box. Drag the smaller image to the spot labeled *1x* and the larger to the spot labeled *2x*.

Implementing the Image View and Text Fields

With the image added to your project, your next step is to implement the five interface elements at the top of the application's screen: the image view, the two text fields, and the two labels (see Figure 4-5).

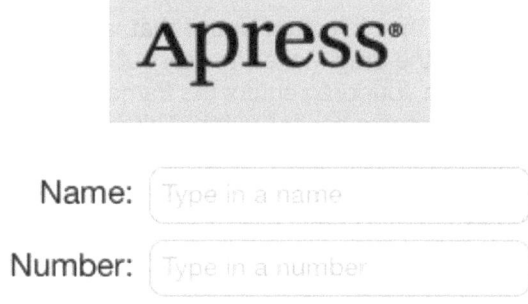

Figure 4-5. *The image view, labels, and text fields we will implement first*

Adding the Image View

In the project navigator, click *Main.storyboard* to open the file in Interface Builder. You'll see the familiar white background and a single iPhone-sized view where you can lay out your application's interface.

If the object library is not open, select **View ➤ Utilities ➤ Show Object Library** to open it. Scroll about one-fourth of the way through the list until you find *Image View* (see Figure 4-6) or just type "image view" in the search field. Remember that the object library is the third icon on top of the library pane. You won't find *Image View* under any of the other icons.

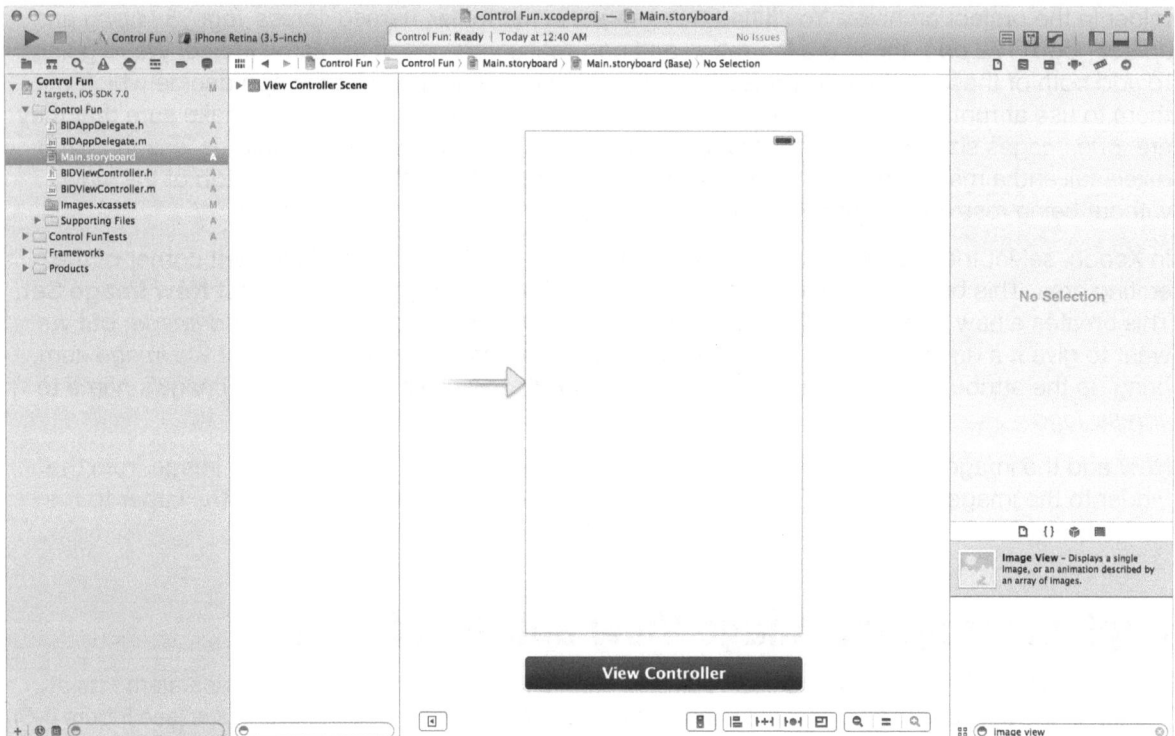

Figure 4-6. The Image View element in Interface Builder's library

Drag an image view onto the view in the nib editor. Notice that, as you drag your image view out of the library, it changes size twice. As the drag makes its way out of the library pane, it takes the shape of a horizontal rectangle. Then, when your drag enters the frame of the view, the image view resizes to be the size of the view, minus the status bar at the top. This behavior is normal. Indeed, in many cases it is exactly what you want because the first image you place in a view is often a background image. Release the drag inside the view, taking care that the new UIImageView snaps to the sides and bottom of the surrounding view. In this particular case, we actually don't want our image view to take the entire space, so we use the drag handles to resize the image view to the approximate size of the image previously imported into Xcode. Don't worry about getting it exactly right yet; we'll take care of that in the next section. Figure 4-7 shows our resized UIImageView.

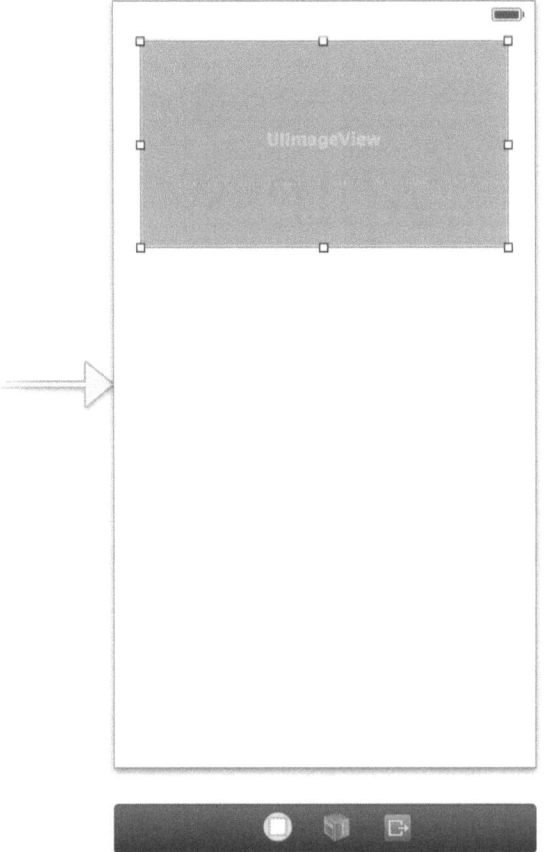

Figure 4-7. Our resized UIImageView, sized to accommodate the image we will place here

Remember that, if you ever encounter difficulty selecting an item in the editing area, you can bring up the editor's list view by clicking the small triangle icon in the lower-left corner. Now, click the item you want selected in the list and, sure enough, that item will be selected in the editor.

To get at an object that is nested inside another object, click the disclosure triangle to the left of the enclosing object to reveal the nested object. In this case, to select the image view, first click the disclosure triangle to the left of the view. Then, when the image view appears in the dock, click it, and the corresponding image view in the nib editor will be selected.

With the image view selected, bring up the object attributes inspector by pressing ⌥⌘4, and you should see the editable options of the UIImageView class (see Figure 4-8).

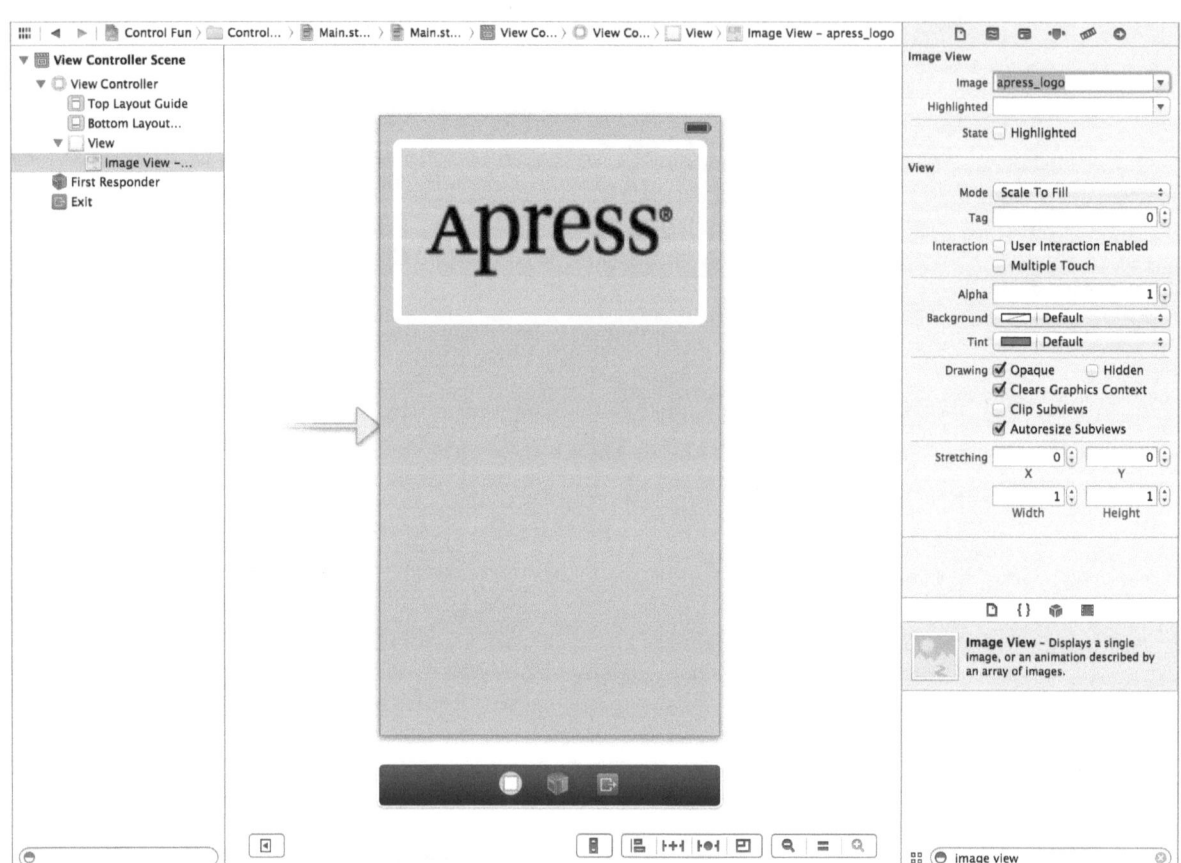

Figure 4-8. The image view attributes inspector. We selected our image from the Image pop-up at the top of the inspector, and this populated the image view with our image

The most important setting for our image view is the topmost item in the inspector, labeled *Image*. Click the little arrow to the right of the field to see a pop-up menu that lists the available images. This list should include any images you added to your project's image assets catalog. Select the image you added earlier. Your image should now appear in your image view.

Resizing the Image View

As it turns out, the image we used is a fair amount smaller than the image view in which it was placed. If you take another look at Figure 4-8, you'll notice that the image we used was scaled to completely fill the image view. A big clue that this is so is the *Mode* setting in the attributes inspector, which is set to *Scale To Fill*.

Though we could keep our app this way, it's generally a good idea to do any image scaling before runtime, as image scaling takes time and processor cycles. Let's resize our image view to the exact size of our image.

Make sure the image view is selected and that you can see the resize handles. Now select the image view one more time. You should see the outline of the image view replaced by a thick, gray border. Finally, press ⌘= or select **Editor ➤ Size to Fit Content**. This will resize the image view to match the size of its contents.

Now that the image view is resized, move it into its final position. You'll need to click off it, and then click it again to reselect it. Now drag the Image view so the top hits the blue guideline toward the top of your view and it is centered according to the blue guideline. Note that you can also center an item in its containing view by choosing **Editor ➤ Align ➤ Horizontal Center in Container**, which also does an extra trick: it establishes a **constraint** that makes the image view always want to remain centered within the view that contains it, even if that view changes size. You may have noticed the way Interface Builder shows some solid lines running from an edge of one view to an edge of its superview, in contrast to the dashed blue lines that are shown while you're dragging things around. These solid lines represent constraints, which give you a way of expressing layout rules directly in Interface Builder. The new constraint you just created is also represented by a solid orange line, this one running the entire height of the main view (see Figure 4-9). This specifies that the center of the image view will remain horizontally centered within its parent view, even if the parent view's geometry changes (as it may, for example, when the device is rotated). We'll talk more about constraints throughout the book.

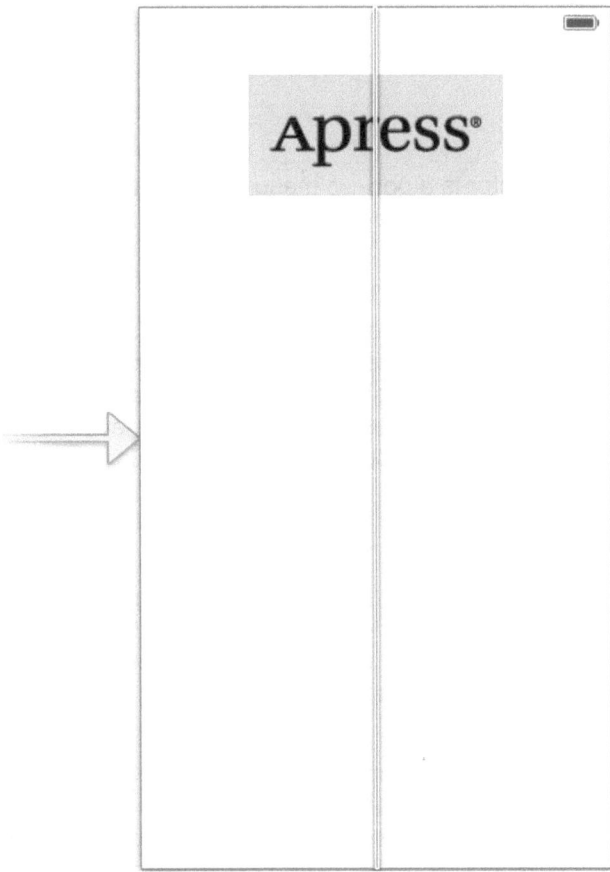

Figure 4-9. Once we have resized our image view to fit the size of its image, we drag it into position using the view's blue guidelines, and create a constraint to keep it centered

> **Tip**   Dragging and resizing views in Interface Builder can be tricky. Don't forget about the hierarchical list
> mode, activated by clicking the small triangle icon at the bottom of the nib editor's dock. When it comes to
> resizing, hold down the ⌥ key, and Interface Builder will draw some helpful red lines on the screen
> that make it much easier to get a sense of the image view's size. This trick won't work with dragging since
> the ⌥ key will prompt Interface Builder to make a copy of the dragged object. However, if you select
> **Editor ➤ Canvas ➤ Show Bounds Rectangles**, Interface Builder will draw a line around all of your interface
> items, making them easier to see. You can turn off those lines by selecting Show Bounds Rectangles a second time.

Setting View Attributes

Select your image view, and then switch your attention back over to the attributes inspector. Below
the *Image View* section of the inspector is the *View* section. As you may have deduced, the pattern
here is that the attributes that are specific to the selected object are shown at the top, followed by
more general attributes that apply to the selected object's parent class. In this case, the parent class
of UIImageView is UIView, so the next section is simply labeled *View*, and it contains attributes that
any view class will have.

The Mode Attribute

The first option in the view inspector is a pop-up menu labeled **Mode**. The **Mode** menu defines
how the view will display its content. This determines how the image will be aligned inside the view
and whether it will be scaled to fit. Feel free to play with the various options, but the default value of
Scale To Fill will work fine for now.

Keep in mind that choosing any option that causes the image to scale will potentially add processing
overhead, so it's best to avoid those and size your images correctly before you import them. If you
want to display the same image at multiple sizes, generally it's better to have multiple copies of the
image at different sizes in your project, rather than force the iOS device to do scaling at runtime. Of
course, there are times when scaling at runtime is appropriate; this is a guideline, not a rule.

Tag

The next item, *Tag*, is worth mentioning, though we won't be using it in this chapter. All subclasses
of UIView, including all views and controls, have a property called tag, which is just a numeric
value that you can set here or in code. The tag is designed for your use; the system will never set
or change its value. If you assign a tag value to a control or view, you can be sure that the tag will
always have that value unless you change it.

Tags provide an easy, language-independent way of identifying objects on your interface. Let's
say you have five different buttons, each with a different label, and you want to use a single action
method to handle all five buttons. In that case, you probably need some way to differentiate among
the buttons when your action method is called. Sure, you could look at the button's title, but code
that does that probably won't work when your application is translated into Swahili or Sanskrit.

Unlike labels, tags will never change, so if you set a tag value here in Interface Builder, you can then use that as a fast and reliable way to check which control was passed into an action method in the sender argument.

Interaction Checkboxes

The two checkboxes in the *Interaction* section have to do with user interaction. The first checkbox, *User Interaction Enabled*, specifies whether the user can do anything at all with this object. For most controls, this box will be checked because, if it's not, the control will never be able to trigger action methods. However, image views default to unchecked because they are often used just for the display of static information. Since all we're doing here is displaying a picture on the screen, there is no need to turn this on.

The second checkbox is *Multiple Touch*, and it determines whether this control is capable of receiving multitouch events. Multitouch events allow complex gestures like the pinch gesture used to zoom in in many iOS applications. We'll talk more about gestures and multitouch events in Chapter 13. Since this image view doesn't accept user interaction at all, there's no reason to turn on multitouch events; leave the checkbox unchecked.

The Alpha Value

The next item in the inspector is *Alpha*. Be careful with this one. Alpha defines how transparent your image is—how much of what's beneath it shows through. It's defined as a floating-point number between 0.0 and 1.0, where 0.0 is fully transparent and 1.0 is completely opaque. If you use any value less than 1.0, your iOS device will draw this view with some amount of transparency, so that any objects behind it show through. With a value of less than 1.0, even if there's nothing interesting behind your image, you will cause your application to spend processor cycles compositing your partially-transparent view over the emptiness behind it. Therefore, don't set *Alpha* to anything other than 1.0 unless you have a very good reason for doing so.

Background

The next item down, *Background*, is a property inherited from UIView, and it determines the color of the background for the view. For image views, this matters only when an image doesn't fill its view and is letterboxed, or when parts of the image are transparent. Since we've sized our view to perfectly match our image, this setting will have no visible effect, so we can leave it alone.

Tint

The next control lets you specify a tint color for the selected view. This is a color that can be used to show a highlight or selected state in a GUI component. UIImageView doesn't use the tint color, so just ignore this for now. Later on we will encounter other GUI components that actually do use the tint color.

Drawing Checkboxes

Below *Tint* is a series of *Drawing* checkboxes. The first one is labeled *Opaque*. That should be checked by default; if not, click to check that checkbox. This tells iOS that nothing behind your view needs to be drawn and allows iOS's drawing methods to do some optimizations that speed up drawing.

You might be wondering why we need to select the *Opaque* checkbox when we've already set the value of *Alpha* to 1.0 to indicate no transparency. The alpha value applies to the parts of the image to be drawn; but if an image doesn't completely fill the image view, or there are holes in the image thanks to an alpha channel, the objects below will still show through, regardless of the value set in *Alpha*. By selecting *Opaque*, we are telling iOS that nothing behind this view ever needs to be drawn, no matter what, so it does not need to waste processing time with anything behind our object. We can safely select the *Opaque* checkbox because we selected *Size To Fit* earlier, which caused the image view to match the size of the image it contains.

The *Hidden* checkbox does exactly what you think it does. If it's checked, the user can't see this object. Hiding an object can be useful at times, as you'll see later in this chapter when we hide our switches and button; however, the vast majority of the time—including now—you want this to remain unchecked.

The next checkbox, *Clears Graphics Context*, will rarely need to be checked. When it is checked, iOS will draw the entire area covered by the object in transparent black before it actually draws the object. Again, it should be turned off for the sake of performance and because it's rarely needed. Make sure this checkbox is unchecked (it is likely checked by default).

Clip Subviews is an interesting option. If your view contains subviews, and those subviews are not completely contained within the bounds of its parent view, this checkbox determines how the subviews will be drawn. If *Clip Subviews* is checked, only the portions of subviews that lie within the bounds of the parent will be drawn. If *Clip Subviews* is unchecked, subviews will be drawn completely, even if they lie outside the bounds of the parent.

Clip Subviews is unchecked by default. It might seem that the default behavior should be the opposite of what it actually is, so that child views won't be able to draw all over the place. However, calculating the clipping area and displaying only part of the subviews is a somewhat costly operation, mathematically speaking; most of the time, a subview won't lie outside the bounds of its superview. You can turn on *Clip Subviews* if you really need it for some reason, but it is off by default for the sake of performance.

The last checkbox in this section, *Autoresize Subviews*, tells iOS to resize any subviews if this view is resized. Leave this checked (since we don't allow our view to be resized, it really does not matter whether it's checked).

Stretching

Next up is a section simply labeled *Stretching*. You can leave your yoga mat in the closet, though, because the only stretching going on here is in the form of rectangular views being redrawn as they're resized on the screen. The idea is that, rather than the entire content of a view being stretched uniformly, you can keep the outer edges of a view, such as the beveled edge of a button, looking the same even as the center portion stretches.

The four floating-point values set here let you declare which portion of the rectangle is stretchable by specifying a point at the upper-left corner of the view and the size of the stretchable area, all in the form of a number between 0.0 and 1.0 that represents a portion of the overall view size. For example, if you wanted to keep 10% of each edge not stretchable, you would specify 0.1 for both *X* and *Y*, and 0.8 for both *Width* and *Height*. In this case, we're going to leave the default values of 0.0 for *X* and *Y*, and 1.0 for *Width* and *Height*. Most of the time, you will not change these values.

Adding the Text Fields

With your image view finished, it's time to bring on the text fields. Grab a text field from the library, and drag it into the *View*, underneath the image view. Use the blue guidelines to align it with the right margin and make it snug, just under your image view (see Figure 4-10).

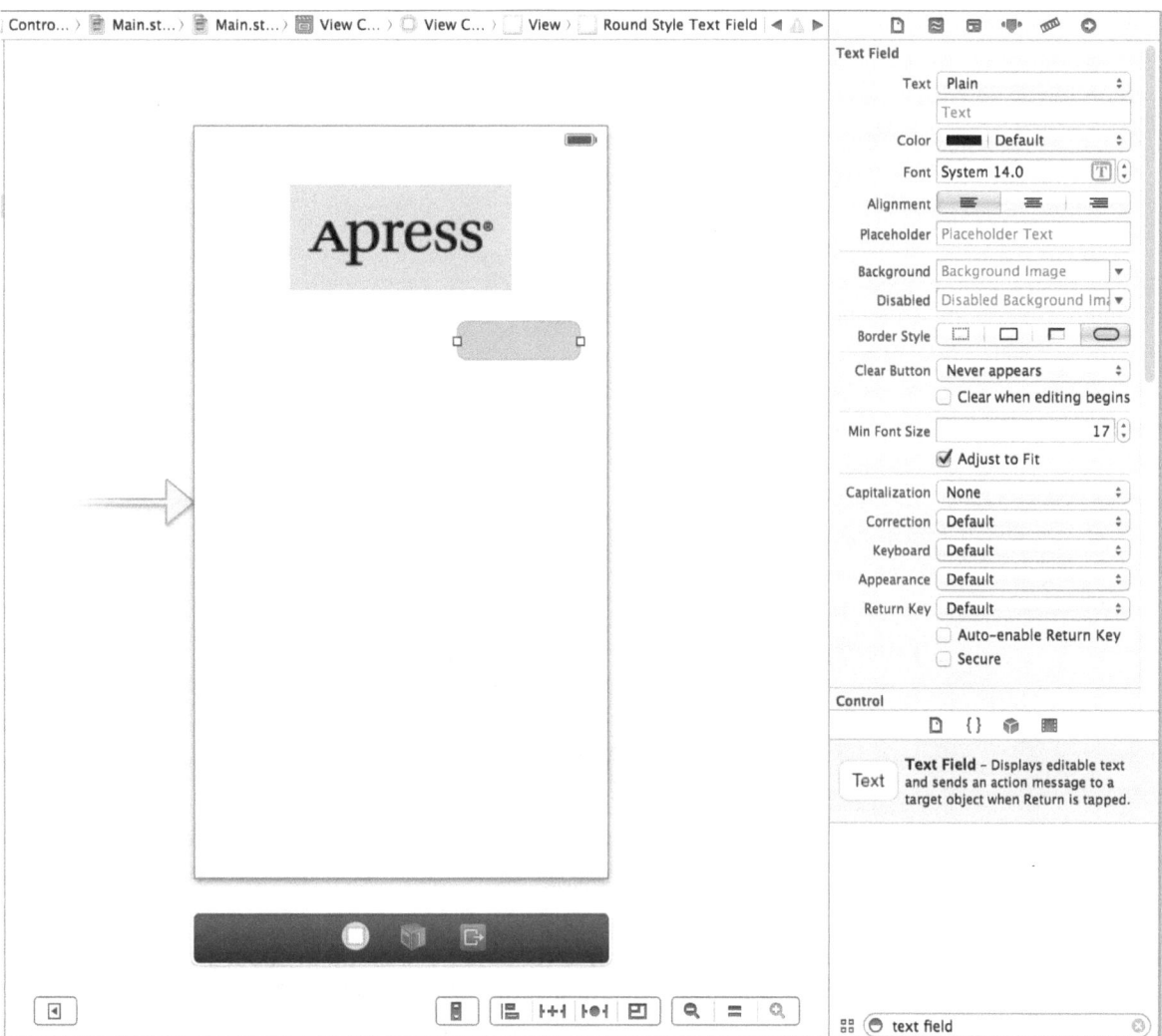

Figure 4-10. *We dragged a text field out of the library and dropped it onto the view, just below our image view and touching the right-hand side's blue guideline*

A horizontal blue guideline will appear just above the text field when you move it very close to the bottom of your image view. That guideline tells you when the object you are dragging is the minimum reasonable distance from an adjacent object. You can leave your text field there for now; but to give it a balanced appearance, consider moving the text field just a little farther down. Remember that you can always use Interface Builder to edit your GUI again in order to change the position and size of interface elements—without needing to change code or reestablish connections.

After you drop the text field, grab a label from the library, and then drag that over so it is aligned with the left margin of the view and vertically with the text field you placed earlier. Notice that multiple blue guidelines will pop up as you move the label around, making it easy to align the label to the text field using the top, bottom, or middle of the label. We're going to align the label and the text field using the baseline, which shows up as you're dragging around the middle of those guidelines (see Figure 4-11).

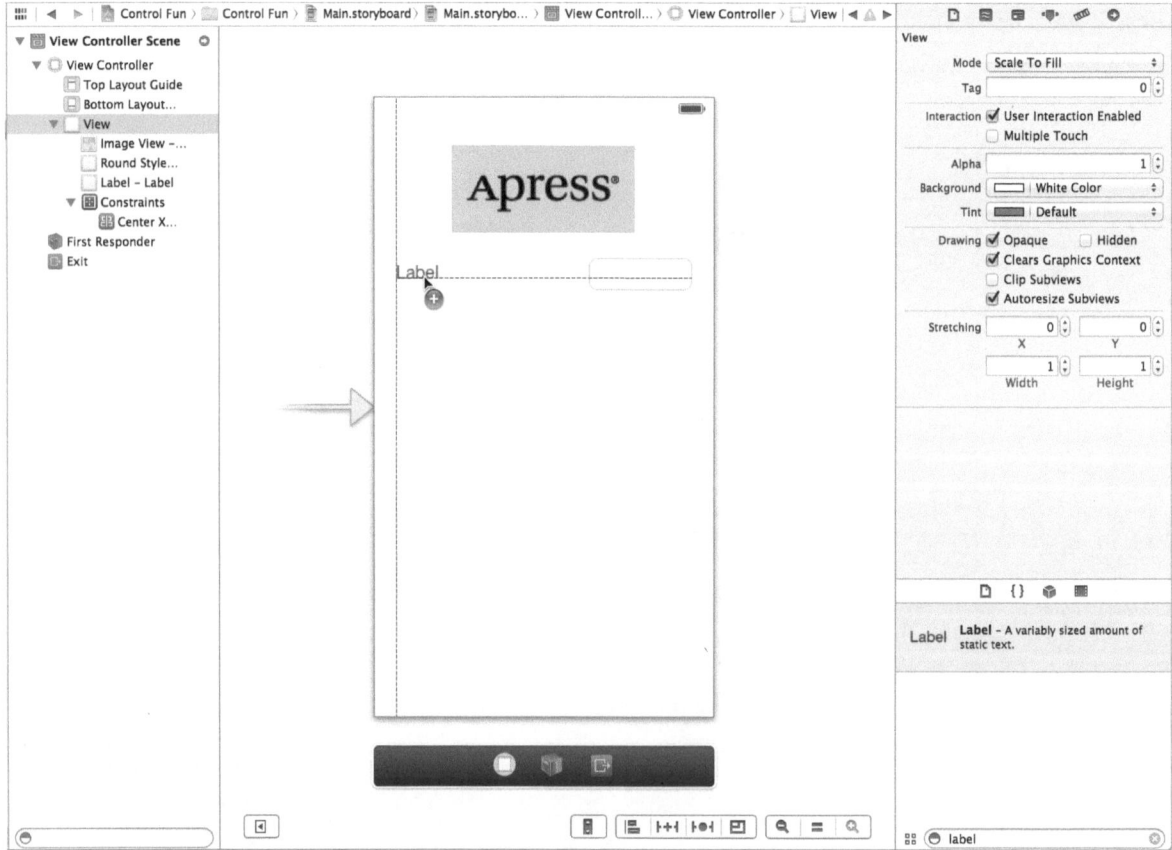

Figure 4-11. Aligning the label and text field using the baseline guide

Double-click the label you just dropped, change it to read *Name:* instead of *Label* (note the colon character at the end of the label), and press the **Return** key to commit your changes.

Next, drag another text field from the library to the view and use the guidelines to place it below the first text field (see Figure 4-12).

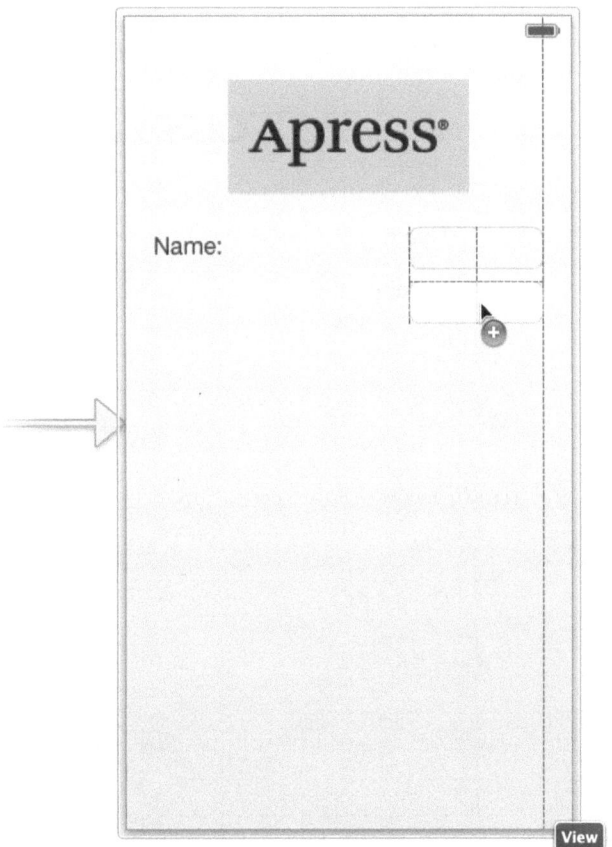

Figure 4-12. Adding the second text field

Once you've added the second text field, grab another label from the library and place it on the left side, below the existing label. Again, use the middle blue guideline to align your new label with the second text field. Double-click the new label and change it to read *Number:* (again, don't forget the colon).

Now, let's expand the size of the bottom text field to the left, so it is snug up against the right side of the label. Why start with the bottom text field? We want the two text fields to be the same size, and the bottom label is longer.

Single-click the bottom text field and drag the left resize dot to the left until a blue guideline appears to tell you that you are as close as you should ever be to the label (see Figure 4-13). This particular guideline is somewhat subtle—it's only as tall as the text field itself, so keep your eyes peeled.

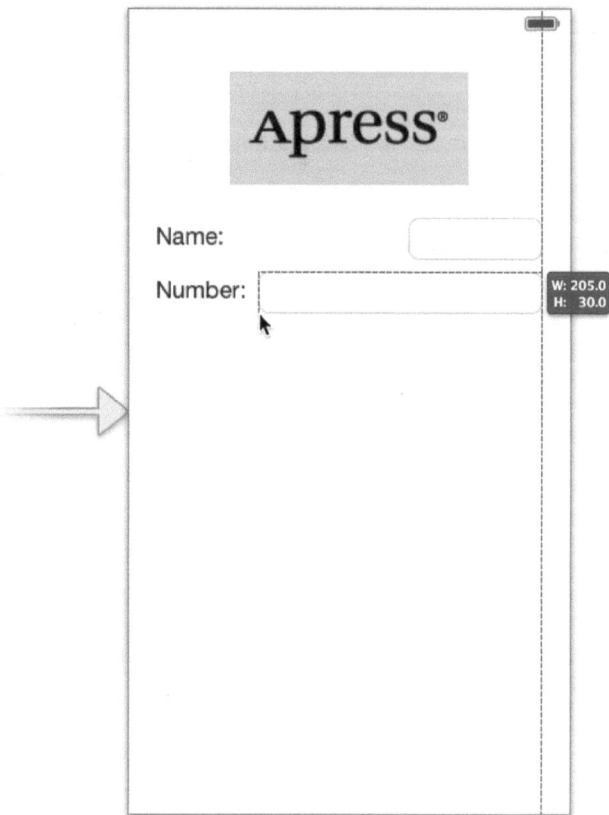

Figure 4-13. Expanding the size of the bottom text field

Now, expand the top text field in the same way, so that it matches the bottom one in size. Once again, a blue guideline provides some help, and this one extends all the way down to the other text field, making it easier to spot.

We're basically finished with the text fields, except for one small detail. Look back at Figure 4-5. Do you see how the *Name:* and *Number:* are right-aligned? Right now, ours are both against the left margin. To align the right sides of the two labels, click the *Name:* label, hold down the ⇧ **(Shift)** key, and click the *Number:* label, so both labels are selected. Next, press ⌥⌘4 to bring up the attributes inspector and make sure the *Label* section is expanded, so you can see the label-specific attributes. Just click the *Label* section header to expand and compact it. Now use the *Alignment* control in the inspector to make the content of these labels right-justified, and then make a constraint to make sure these two fields are always the same width by selecting **Editor ➤ Pin ➤ Widths Equally**.

When you are finished, the interface should look very much like the one shown in Figure 4-5. The only difference is the light-gray text in each text field. We'll add that now.

Select the top text field (the one next to the *Name:* label) and press ⌥⌘4 to bring up the attributes inspector (see Figure 4-14). The text field is one of the most complex iOS controls, as well as one of the most commonly used. Let's take a walk through the settings, beginning from the top of the inspector.

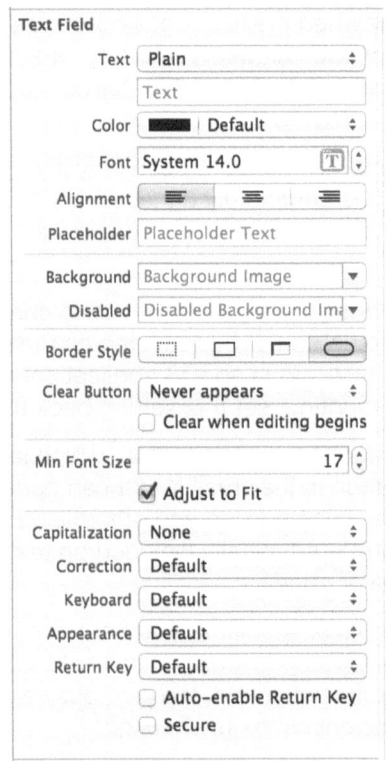

Figure 4-14. The inspector for a text field showing the default values

Text Field Inspector Settings

In the first section, the *Text* label points out two controls that give you some control over the text that will appear in the text field. The upper one is a pop-up button that lets you choose between plain text and attributed text, which can contain a variety of fonts and other attributes. Let's leave that pop-up button set to *Plain* for now. Immediately below that, you can set a default value for the text field. Whatever you type here will show up in the text field when your application launches, instead of just a blank space.

After that comes a series of controls that let you set the font and font color. We'll leave the *Color* at the default value of black. Note that the *Color* pop-up is divided into two parts. The right side allows you to select from a set of preselected colors, and the left side gives you access to a color well to more precisely specify your color.

The *Font* setting is divided into three parts. On the right side is a control that lets you increment or decrement the text size, one point at a time. The left side allows you to manually edit the font name and size. Finally, click the *T-in-a-box* icon to bring up a pop-up window that lets you set the various font attributes. We'll leave the *Font* at its default setting of *System 14.0*.

Below these fields are three buttons for controlling the alignment of the text displayed in the field. We'll leave this setting at the default value of left-aligned (the leftmost button).

Rounding out this first section, *Placeholder* allows you to specify a bit of text that will be displayed in gray inside the text field, but only when the field does not have a value. You can use a placeholder instead of a label if space is tight, or you can use it to clarify what the user should type into this text field. Type in the text *Type in a name* as the placeholder for our currently selected text field, and then hit **Return** to commit the change.

The next two fields, *Background* and *Disabled*, are used only if you need to customize the appearance of your text field, which is completely unnecessary and actually ill-advised the vast majority of the time. Users expect text fields to look a certain way. We're going to skip over these fields, leaving them set to their defaults.

Next are four buttons labeled *Border Style*. These allow you to change the way the text field's edge will be drawn. The default value (the rightmost button) creates the text field style that users are most accustomed to seeing for normal text fields in an iOS application. Feel free to try all four different styles. When you're finished experimenting, set this setting back to the rightmost button.

Below the border setting is a *Clear Button* pop-up button, which lets you choose when the *clear button* should appear. The clear button is the small *X* that can appear at the right end of a text field. Clear buttons are typically used with search fields and other fields where you would be likely to change the value frequently. They are not typically included on text fields used to persist data, so leave this at the default value of *Never appears*.

The *Clear when editing begins* checkbox specifies what happens when the user touches this field. If this box is checked, any value that was previously in this field will be deleted, and the user will start with an empty field. If this box is unchecked, the previous value will remain in the field, and the user will be able to edit it. Leave this checkbox unchecked.

The next section starts with a control that lets you set the minimum font size that the text field will use for displaying its text. Leave that at its default value for now.

The *Adjust to Fit* checkbox specifies whether the size of the text should shrink if the text field is reduced in size. Adjusting to fit will keep the entire text visible in the view, even if the text would normally be too big to fit in the allotted space. This checkbox works in conjunction with the minimum font size setting. No matter the size of the field, the text will not be resized below that minimum size. Specifying a minimum size allows you to make sure that the text doesn't get too small to be readable.

The next section defines how the keyboard will look and behave when this text field is being used. Since we're expecting a name, let's change the *Capitalization* pop-up to *Words*. This causes every word to be automatically capitalized, which is what you typically want with names.

The next three pop-ups—*Correction*, *Keyboard*, and *Appearance*—can be left at their default values. Take a minute to look at each to get a sense of what these settings do.

Next is the *Return Key* pop-up. The **Return** key is the key on the lower right of the keyboard, and its label changes based on what you're doing. If you are entering text into Safari's search field, for example, then it says *Search*. In an application like ours, where the text fields share the screen with other controls, *Done* is the right choice. Make that change here.

If the *Auto-enable Return Key* checkbox is checked, the **Return** key is disabled until at least one character is typed into the text field. Leave this unchecked because we want to allow the text field to remain empty if the user prefers not to enter anything.

The *Secure* checkbox specifies whether the characters being typed are displayed in the text field. You would check this checkbox if the text field was being used as a password field. Leave it unchecked for our app.

The next section allows you to set control attributes inherited from UIControl; however, these generally don't apply to text fields and, with the exception of the *Enabled* checkbox, won't affect the field's appearance. We want to leave these text fields enabled, so that the user can interact with them. Leave the default settings in this section.

The last section on the inspector, *View*, should look familiar. It's identical to the section of the same name on the image view inspector we looked at earlier. These are attributes inherited from the UIView class; since all controls are subclasses of UIView, they all share this section of attributes. As you did earlier for the image view, check the *Opaque* checkbox and uncheck *Clears Graphics Context* and *Clip Subviews*—for the reasons we discussed earlier.

Setting the Attributes for the Second Text Field

Next, single-click the lower text field (the one next to the *Number:* label) in the *View* window and return to the inspector. In the *Placeholder* field, type *Type in a number*, and make sure *Clear When Editing Begins* is unchecked. A little farther down, click the *Keyboard* pop-up menu. Since we want the user to enter only numbers, not letters, select *Number Pad*. This ensures that the users will be presented with a keyboard containing only numbers, meaning they won't be able to enter alphabetical characters, symbols, or anything other than numbers. We don't need to set the *Return Key* value for the numeric keypad because that style of keyboard doesn't have a **Return** key; therefore, all of the other inspector settings can stay at the default values. As you did earlier, check the *Opaque* checkbox and uncheck *Clears Graphics Context* and *Clip Subviews*.

Creating and Connecting Outlets

We are almost ready to take our app for its first test drive. For this first part of the interface, all that's left is creating and connecting our outlets. The image view and labels on our interface do not need outlets because we don't need to change them at runtime. The two text fields, however, are passive controls that hold data we'll need to use in our code, so we need outlets pointing to each of them.

As you probably remember from the previous chapter, Xcode allows us to create and connect outlets at the same time using the assistant editor. Go into the assistant editor now by selecting the middle toolbar button labeled *Editor* or by selecting **View ➤ Assistant Editor ➤ Show Assistant Editor**.

Make sure your nib file is selected in the project navigator. If you don't have a large amount of screen real estate, you might also want to select **View ➤ Utilities ➤ Hide Utilities** to hide the utility pane during this step. When you bring up the assistant editor, the nib editing pane will be split in two, with Interface Builder in one half and either *BIDViewController.h* or *BIDViewController.m* in the other (see Figure 4-15). This new editing area—the one on the right—is the assistant.

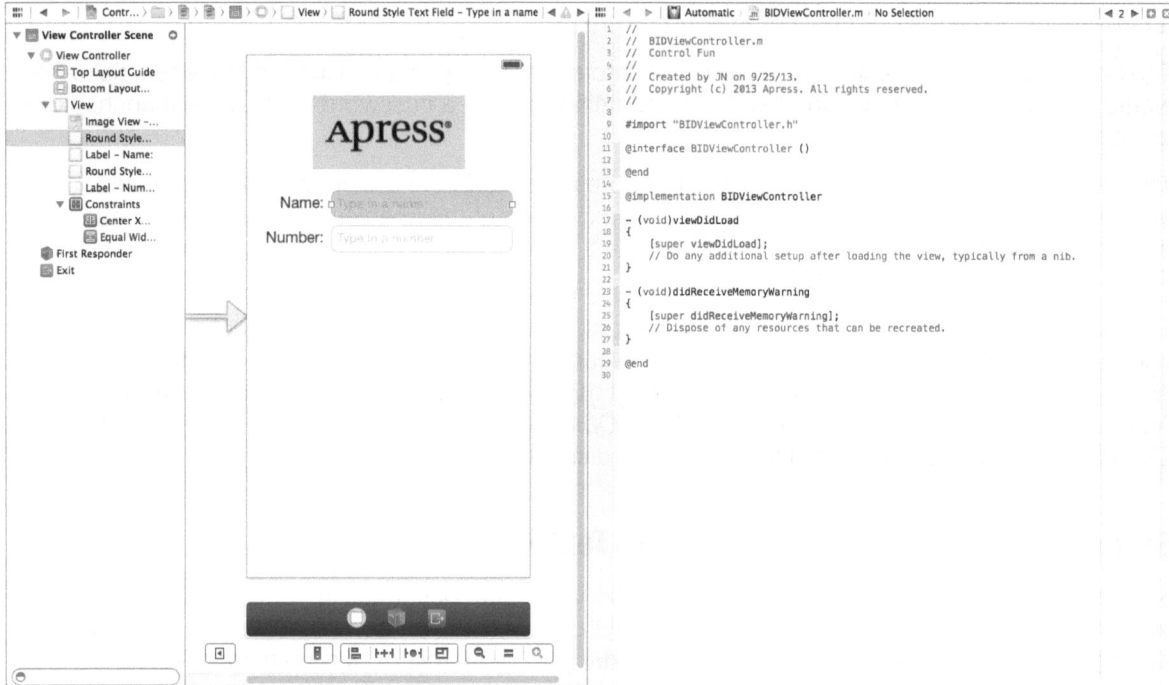

Figure 4-15. The nib editing area with the assistant turned on. You can see the assistant area on the right, showing the code from BIDViewController.m

You'll see that the upper boundary of the assistant includes a jump bar, much like the normal editor pane. One important feature of the assistant's jump bar is a set of "smart" selections, which let you switch between a variety of files that Xcode believes are relevant, based on what appears in the main view. By default, it shows a group of files labeled *Automatic*. These include any *.h* and *.m* files relevant to the current selection in the editor. In this case, that includes both source code files for the controller class. Take a few minutes to click around the jump bar at the top of the assistant, just to get a feel for what's what. Once you have a sense of the jump bar and files represented there, move on.

Now comes the fun part. Make sure *BIDViewController.m* is showing in the assistant (use the jump bar to return there if necessary). Next, control-drag from the top text field in the view over to the *BIDViewController.m* source code, right below the @interface line. You should see a gray pop-up that reads *Insert Outlet, Action, or Outlet Collection* (see Figure 4-16). Release the mouse button, and you'll get the same pop-up you saw in the previous chapter. We want to create an outlet called nameField, so type *nameField* into the *Name* field (say that five times fast!), and then hit **Return** or click the *Connect* button.

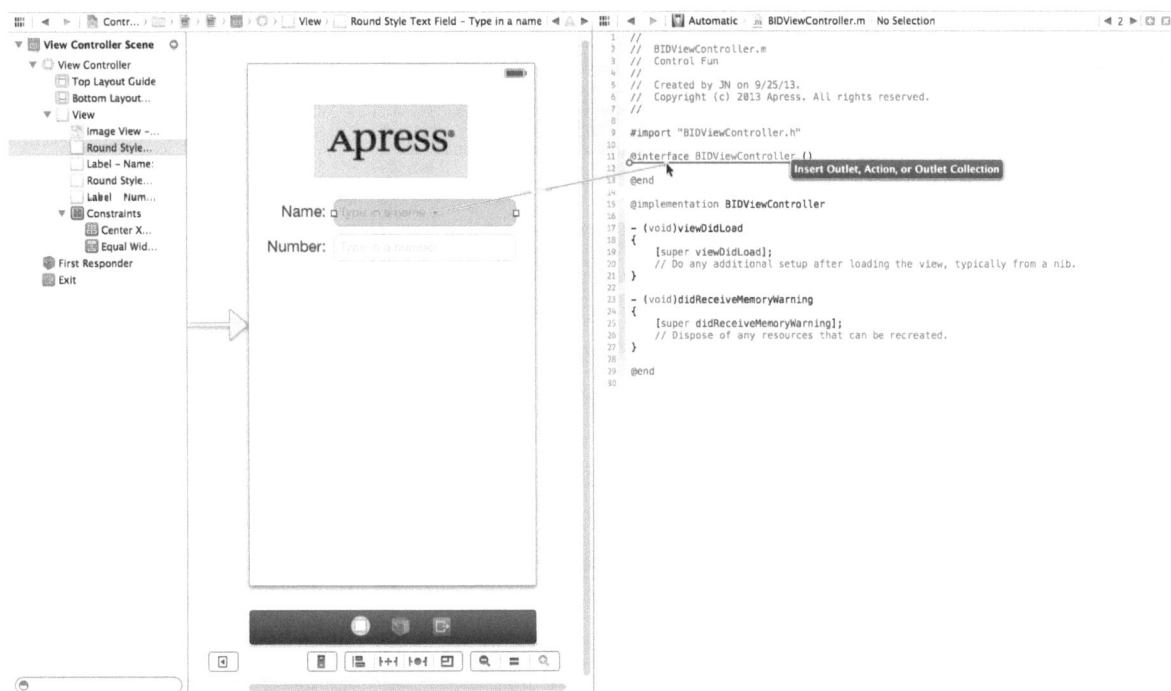

Figure 4-16. *With the assistant turned on, we control-drag over to the source code in order to simultaneously create the nameField outlet and connect it to the appropriate text field*

You now have a property called nameField in BIDViewController, and it has been connected to the top text field. Do the same for the second text field, creating and connecting it to a property called *numberField*.

Closing the Keyboard

Let's see how our app works, shall we? Select **Product ➤ Run**. Your application should come up in the iOS simulator. Click the *Name* text field, and the traditional keyboard should appear. Type in a name, and then tap the *Number* field. The numeric keypad should appear (see Figure 4-17). Cocoa Touch gives us all this functionality for free just by adding text fields to our interface.

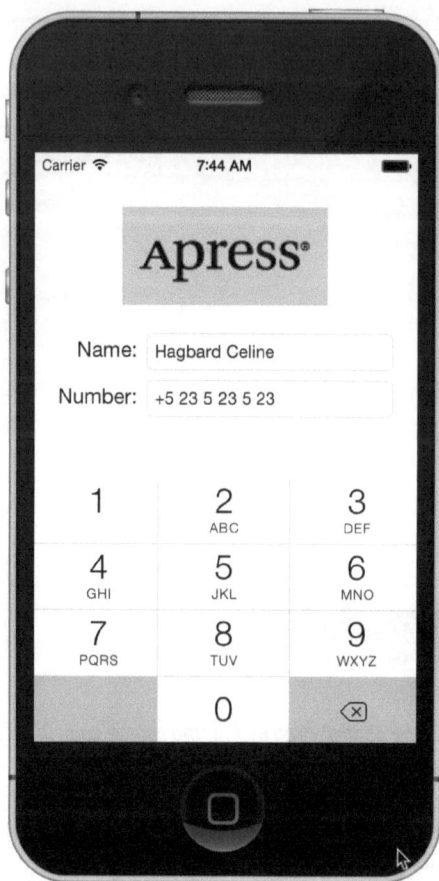

Figure 4-17. *The keyboard comes up automatically when you touch either the text field or the number field*

Woo-hoo! But there's a little problem. How do you get the keyboard to go away? Go ahead and try. We'll wait right here while you do.

Closing the Keyboard When *Done* Is Tapped

Because the keyboard is software-based rather than a physical keyboard, we need to take a few extra steps to make sure the keyboard goes away when the user is finished with it. When the user taps the *Done* button on the text keyboard, a *Did End On Exit* event will be generated; at that time, we need to tell the text field to give up control, so that the keyboard will go away. In order to do that, we need to add an action method to our controller class.

Select *BIDViewController.h* in the project navigator, and add the following line of code, shown in bold:

```
#import <UIKit/UIKit.h>

@interface BIDViewController : UIViewController

- (IBAction)textFieldDoneEditing:(id)sender;
@end
```

When you selected the header file in the project navigator, you probably noticed that the assistant we opened earlier has adapted to having a source code file selected in the main editor pane, and it now automatically shows the selected file's counterpart. If you select a *.h* file, the assistant will automatically show the matching *.m* file, and vice versa. This is a remarkably handy Xcode capability! As a result of this behavior, *BIDViewController.m* is now shown in the assistant view, ready for us to implement this method.

Add this action method at the bottom of *BIDViewController.m*, just before the @end:

```
- (IBAction)textFieldDoneEditing:(id)sender {
    [sender resignFirstResponder];
}
```

As you learned in Chapter 2, the first responder is the control with which the user is currently interacting. In our new method, we tell our control to resign as a first responder, giving up that role to the previous control the user worked with. When a text field yields first responder status, the keyboard associated with it goes away.

Save both of the files you just edited. Let's hop back to the storyboard and trigger this action from both of our text fields.

Select *Main.storyboard* in the project navigator, single-click the *Name* text field, and press ⌥⌘6 to bring up the connections inspector. This time, we don't want the *Touch Up Inside* event that we used in the previous chapter. Instead, we want *Did End On Exit* since that event will fire when the user taps the *Done* button on the text keyboard.

Drag from the circle next to *Did End On Exit* to the yellow *View Controller* icon, shown just below the view you've been configuring, and let go. A small pop-up menu will appear containing the name of a single action, the one we just added. Click the *textFieldDoneEditing:* action to select it. You can also do this by dragging to the textFieldDoneEditing: method in the assistant view. Repeat this procedure with the other text field, save your changes, and then press ⌘R to run the app again.

When the simulator appears, click the *Name* field, type in something, and then tap the *Done* button. Sure enough, the keyboard drops away, just as you expected. All right! What about the *Number* field, though? Um, where's the *Done* button on that one (see Figure 4-17)?

Well, crud! Not all keyboard layouts feature a *Done* button. We could force the user to tap the *Name* field and then tap *Done*, but that's not very user-friendly, is it? And we most definitely want our application to be user-friendly. Let's see how to handle this situation.

Touching the Background to Close the Keyboard

Can you recall what Apple's iPhone applications do in this situation? Well, in most places where there are text fields, tapping anywhere in the view where there's no active control will cause the keyboard to go away. How do we implement that?

The answer is probably going to surprise you because of its simplicity. Our view controller has a property called view that it inherited from UIViewController. This view property corresponds to the *View* in the storyboard. The view property points to an instance of UIView that acts as a container for all the items in our user interface. It has no appearance in the user interface, but it covers the entire iPhone window, sitting "below" all of the other user interface objects. It is sometimes referred to as a

container view because its main purpose is to simply hold other views and controls. For all intents and purposes, the container view is the background of our user interface.

Using Interface Builder, we can change the class of the object that view points to so that its underlying class is UIControl instead of UIView. Because UIControl is a subclass of UIView, it is perfectly appropriate for us to connect our view property to an instance of UIControl. Remember that when a class subclasses another object, it is just a more specialized version of that class, so a UIControl is a UIView. If we simply change the instance that is created from UIView to UIControl, we gain the ability to trigger action methods. Before we do that, though, we need to create an action method that will be called when the background is tapped.

We need to add one more action to our controller class. Add the following method to your *BIDViewController.m* file, just before @end:

```
- (IBAction)backgroundTap:(id)sender {
    [self.nameField resignFirstResponder];
    [self.numberField resignFirstResponder];
}
```

This method simply tells both text fields to yield first responder status if they have it. It is perfectly safe to call resignFirstResponder on a control that is not the first responder, so we can call it on both text fields without needing to check whether either is the first responder. Note that, unlike the last time we added an action method, when we included the method in both the header and the implementation, this time we're just putting it in the implementation. Xcode is smart enough these days to let us skip the redundant declaration in the header file just for purposes of connecting our GUI to our code. If we wanted to make this method available for other classes to use, we'd still need to include the method declaration in the header file, too.

> **Tip** You'll be switching between header and implementation files a lot as you code. Fortunately, in addition to the convenience provided by the assistant, Xcode also has a key combination that will switch between counterparts quickly. The default key combination is ^⌘↑, although you can change it to anything you want using Xcode's preferences.

Save this file. Now, select the storyboard again. Make sure your document outline is expanded (click the triangle icon at the bottom left of the editing area to toggle this), and then single-click *View* so it is selected. Do *not* select one of your view's subitems; we want the container view itself.

Next, press ⌥⌘3 to bring up the **identity inspector** (see Figure 4-18). This is where you can change the underlying class of any object instance in your nib file.

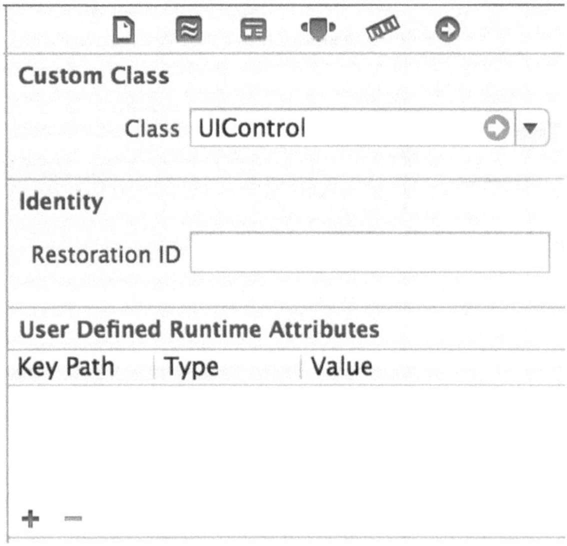

Figure 4-18. *We switched Interface Builder to list view and selected our view. We then switched to the identity inspector, which allows us to change the underlying class of any object instance in our nib*

The field labeled *Class* should currently say *UIView*. If not, you likely don't have the container view selected. Now, change that setting to *UIControl* and press **Return** to commit the change. All controls that are capable of triggering action methods are subclasses of UIControl; by changing the underlying class, we have just given this view the ability to trigger action methods. You can verify this by pressing ⌥⌘6 to bring up the connections inspector. You should now see all the events that you saw when you were connecting buttons to actions in the previous chapter.

Drag from the *Touch Down* event to the *View Controller* icon (see Figure 4-19), and choose the *backgroundTap:* action. Now, touches anywhere in the view without an active control will trigger our new action method, which will cause the keyboard to retract. Connecting to *View Controller* like this is exactly the same as connecting to the method in the code. Inside the storyboard, the *View Controller* is simply an instance of the view controller class, so that was just a slightly different way of achieving the exact same result.

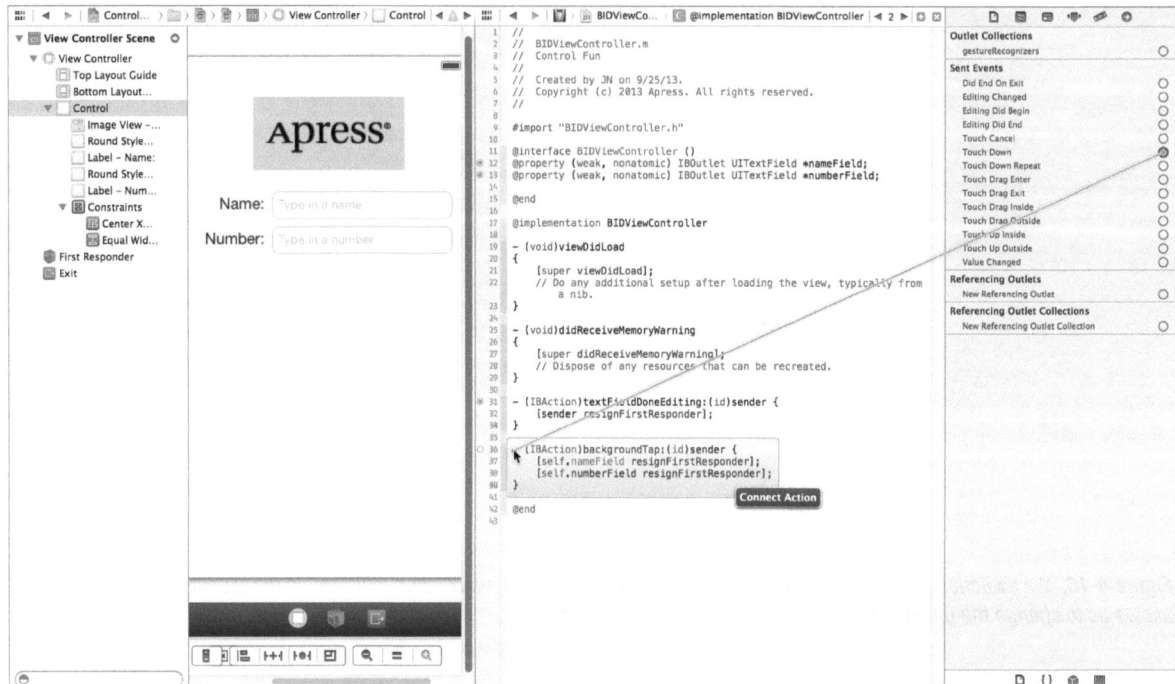

Figure 4-19. By changing the class of our view from UIView to UIControl, we gain the ability to trigger action methods on any of the standard events. We'll connect the view's Touch Down event to the backgroundTap: action

Note   You might be wondering why we selected *Touch Down* instead of *Touch Up Inside*, as we did in the previous chapter. The answer is that the background isn't a button. It's not a control in the eyes of the user, so it wouldn't occur to most users to try to drag their finger somewhere to cancel the action.

Save the storyboard, and then compile and run your application again. This time, the keyboard should disappear not only when the *Done* button is tapped, but also when you tap anywhere that's not an active control, which is the behavior that your users will expect.

Excellent! Now that we have this section all squared away, are you ready to move on to the next group of controls?

Adding the Slider and Label

Now it's time to add the slider and accompanying label. Remember that the value in the label will change as the slider is used. Select *Main.storyboard* in the project navigator, so we can add more items to our application's user interface.

Before we place the slider, let's add a bit of breathing room to our design. The blue guidelines we used to determine the spacing between the top text field and the image above it are really suggestions for minimum proximity. In other words, the blue guidelines tell you, "Don't get any closer than this." Drag the two text fields and their labels down a bit, using Figure 4-1 as a guide. Now let's add the slider.

From the object library, bring over a slider and arrange it below the *Number* text field, using the right-hand side's blue guideline as a stopping point and leaving a little breathing room below the bottom text field. Our slider ended up about halfway down the view. Single-click the newly added slider to select it, and then press ⌥⌘4 to go back to the object attributes inspector if it's not already visible (see Figure 4-20).

Figure 4-20. The inspector showing default attributes for a slider

A slider lets you choose a number in a given range. Use the inspector to set the *Minimum* value to *1*, the *Maximum* value to *100*, and the *Current* value to *50*. Leave the *Update Events, Continuous* checkbox checked. This ensures a continuous flow of events as the slider's value changes. That's all we need to worry about for now.

Bring over a label and place it next to the slider, using the blue guidelines to align it vertically with the slider and to align its left edge with the left margin of the view (see Figure 4-21).

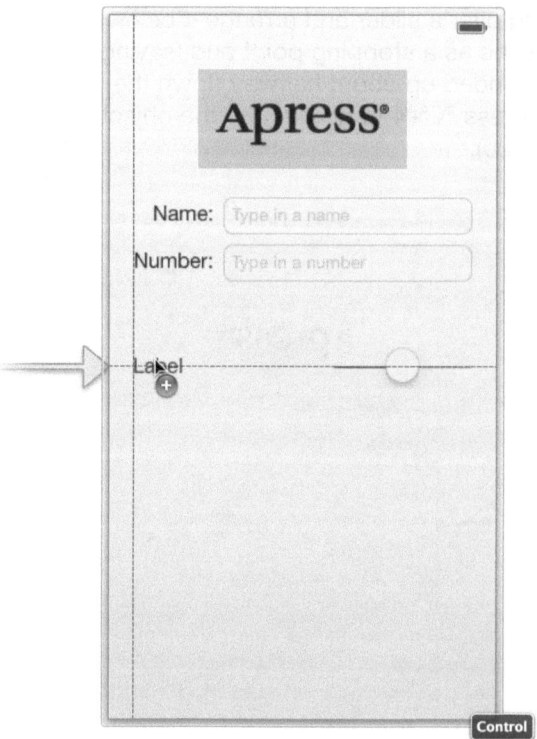

Figure 4-21. Placing the slider's label

Double-click the newly placed label, and change its text from *Label* to *100*. This is the largest value that the slider can hold, and we can use that to determine the correct width of the slider. Since "100" is shorter than "Label," Interface Builder automatically makes the label smaller for you, as if you had dragged the right-middle resize dot to the edge. Despite this automatic behavior, you're still free to resize the label however you want, of course. If you later decide you want the tool to pick the optimum size for you again, just press ⌘= or select **Editor ➤ Size to Fit Content**.

Next, resize the slider by single-clicking the slider to select it and dragging the left resize dot to the left until the blue guidelines indicate that you're getting close to the label's right-side edge.

Adding Constraints

Before we go on, we need to adjust some constraints for this layout. When you drag a view into another view in Interface Builder (as we just did), Xcode doesn't create any constraints for it automatically. The layout system requires a complete set of constraints, so when it's time to compile your app, Xcode will make a set of default constraints describing the layout. Which sort of constraints are created depends on each object's position within its superview. Depending on whether it's nearer the left or right edge, it will be pinned to the left of the right. Similarly, depending on whether it's nearer the top or the bottom edge, it will be pinned to the top or the bottom. If it's centered in either direction, it will typically get a constraint pinning it to the center.

To complicate matters further, Xcode may also apply automatic constraints pinning each new object to one or more of its "sibling" objects within the same superview. This automatic behavior may or may not be what you want, so normally you're better off creating a complete set of constraints within Interface Builder before your app is compiled.

Let's start poking around what we have so far. To see all the constraints that are in play for any particular view, try selecting it and opening the size inspector. If you select any of the labels, text fields, or the slider, you'll see that the size inspector shows a message claiming that there are no constraints for the selected view. In fact, this GUI we've been building has only one constraint: binding the horizontal centers of the image view and the container view. Click either the container view or the image view to see this constraint in the inspector.

What we really want is a full set of constraints to tell the layout system precisely how to handle all our views and controls, just as it would get at compile time. Fortunately, this is pretty simple to accomplish. Select all the views and controls by click-dragging a box around them, from inside the upper-left corner of our container view down toward the lower right. When all items are selected, use the menu to execute the **Editor ➤ Resolve Auto Layout Issues ➤ Add Missing Constraints command**. After doing that, you'll see that all our views and controls now have some little blue sticks connecting them to one another and to the container view. Each of those sticks represents a constraint. The big advantage to creating these now instead of letting Xcode create them at compile time is that we now have a chance to modify each constraint if we need to. We'll explore more of what we can do with constraints throughout the book.

Normally, the layout we've created here wouldn't require any particular modification of these constraints to make sure it works fine on all devices. However, it's important to know that things changed a bit with the release of the iPhone 5. iPhones and iPod touches now come in two distinct screen sizes. This means that when the system is loading a set of GUI components from a storyboard or nib file, it may have to adjust the content to a different screen size than what the nib file contains, and then reapply all the constraints in the process. User interfaces created in Xcode now start off at the iPhone 5 size, also called "iPhone Retina 4" (since it's a 4-inch screen) by default. So, if some of your views are bound to the top of the superview, and some are bound to the bottom or the center, you're likely to be in for a surprise when running on an iPhone 4 (its screen size is now referred to as "iPhone Retina 3.5") because some of the controls are vertically squashed together.

For our current GUI, this isn't a problem, however, which we can verify by doing the following. At the bottom-right corner of the editing area, you'll see a row of buttons for performing some common actions when editing your user interface. The leftmost of these buttons shows an Apply Retina 3.5-inch Form Factor tooltip when you let your mouse pointer hover there. Click there, and you'll see that the size of the container view changes, but all the views and controls remain positioned as expected. Click again to switch back to the Retina 4-inch form factor, and you'll see that everything remains OK. Later in the book, we'll deal with some GUIs that need a bit of adjustment in this area.

Creating and Connecting the Actions and Outlets

All that's left to do with these two controls is to connect the outlet and action. We will need an outlet that points to the label, so that we can update the label's value when the slider is used. We're also going to need an action method for the slider to call as it's changed.

Make sure you're using the assistant editor and editing *BIDViewController.m*, and then control-drag from the slider to just above the @end declaration in the assistant editor. When the pop-up window appears, change the *Connection* pop-up menu to *Action*, and then type *sliderChanged* in the *name* field. Set the *Type* to UISlider, then hit **Return** to create and connect the action.

Next, control-drag from the newly added label (the one showing "100") over to the assistant editor. This time, drag to just below the last property declaration, in between the @interface and @end at the top. When the pop-up comes up, type *sliderLabel* into the *Name* text field, and then hit **Return** to create and connect the outlet.

Implementing the Action Method

Though Xcode has created and connected our action method, it's still up to us to actually write the code that makes up the action method so it does what it's supposed to do. Save your work, and then, in the project navigator, single-click *BIDViewController.m* and look for the sliderChanged: method, which should be empty. Add this code to that method:

```
- (IBAction)sliderChanged:(UISlider *)sender {
    int progress = lroundf(sender.value);
    self.sliderLabel.text = [NSString stringWithFormat:@"%d", progress];
}
```

The first line in the method retrieves the current value of the slider, rounds it to the nearest integer, and assigns it to an integer variable. The second line of code creates a string containing that number and assigns it to the label.

That takes care of our controller's response to the movements of the slider; but in order to be really consistent, we need to make sure that the label shows the correct slider value before the user even touches it. Add this line to the viewDidLoad method:

```
- (void)viewDidLoad
{
    [super viewDidLoad];
    // Do any additional setup after loading the view, typically from a nib.
    self.sliderLabel.text = @"50";
}
```

The preceding method will be executed immediately after the running app loads the view from the storyboard file, but before it's displayed on the screen. The line we added makes sure that the user sees the correct starting value right away.

Save the file. Next, press ⌘R to build and launch your app in the iOS simulator, and try out the slider. As you move it, you should see the label's text change in real time. Another piece falls into place.

But if you drag the slider toward the left (bringing the value below 10) or all the way to the right (setting the value to 100), you'll see an odd thing happen. The label to the left will shrink horizontally when it drops down to showing a single digit, and will grow horizontally when showing three. Now, apart from the text it contains, you don't actually see the label itself, so you can't see its size changing, but what you will see is that the slider actually changes its size along with the label, getting smaller or larger. It's maintaining a size relationship with the label, making sure the gap between the two is always the same.

This isn't anything we've asked for, is it? Not really. It's simply a side effect of the way Interface Builder works, helping you create GUIs that are responsive and fluid. We created some default constraints previously, and here you're seeing one in action. One of the constraints created by Interface Builder keeps the horizontal distance between these elements constant.

Fortunately, you can override this behavior by making your own constraint. Back in Xcode, select the slider in your nib, and select **Editor ➤ Pin ➤ Width** from the menu. This makes a new high-priority constraint that tells the layout system, "Don't mess with the width of this slider." If you now press **⌘R** to build and run again, you'll see that the slider no longer expands and contracts as you drag back and forth across it.

We'll see more examples of constraints and their uses throughout the book. But for now, let's look at implementing the switches.

Implementing the Switches, Button, and Segmented Control

Back to Xcode we go once again. Getting dizzy, yet? This back and forth may seem a bit strange, but it's fairly common to bounce around between source code, storyboards, and nib files in Xcode, testing your app in the iOS simulator while you're developing.

Our application will have two switches, which are small controls that can have only two states: on and off. We'll also add a segmented control to hide and show the switches. Along with that control, we'll add a button that is revealed when the segmented control's right side is tapped. Let's implement those next.

Back in the storyboard, drag a segmented control from the object library (see Figure 4-22) and place it on the *View* window, a little below the slider.

Figure 4-22. Here's what we see when dragging a segmented control from the library to the left side of the parent view. Next, we'll resize the segmented control, so it stretches to the right side of the view

> **Tip** To give you a sense of the spacing we're going for, take a look at the image view with the Apress logo. We tried to leave about the same amount of space above and below the image view. We did the same thing with the slider: we tried to leave about the same amount of space above and below the slider.

Expand the width of the segmented control, so that it stretches from the view's left margin to its right margin. Double-click the word *First* on the segmented control and change the title from *First* to *Switches*. After doing that, repeat the process with the *Second* segment, renaming it *Button* (see Figure 4-23).

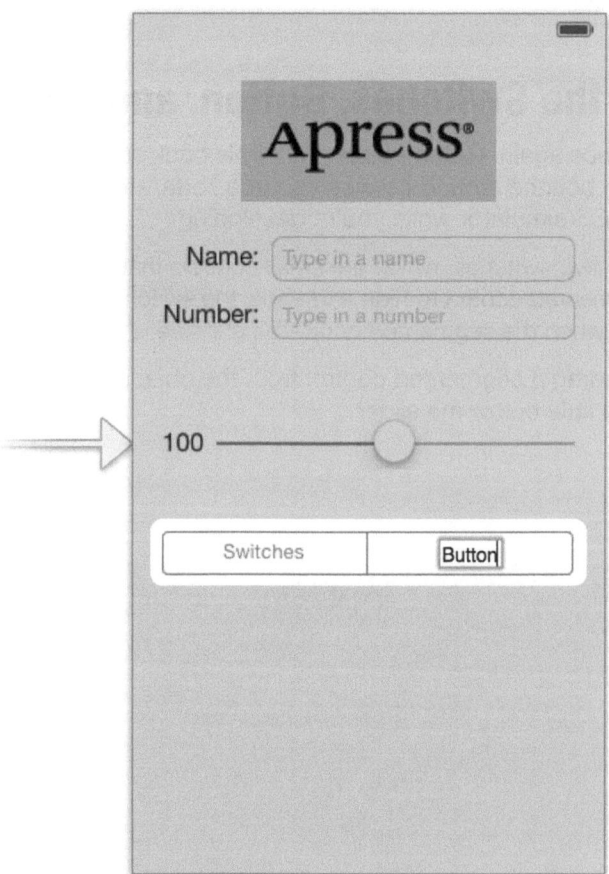

Figure 4-23. Renaming the segments in the segmented control

Adding Two Labeled Switches

Next, grab a switch from the library and place it on the view, below the segmented control and against the left margin. Now drag a second switch and place it against the right margin, aligned vertically with the first switch (see Figure 4-24).

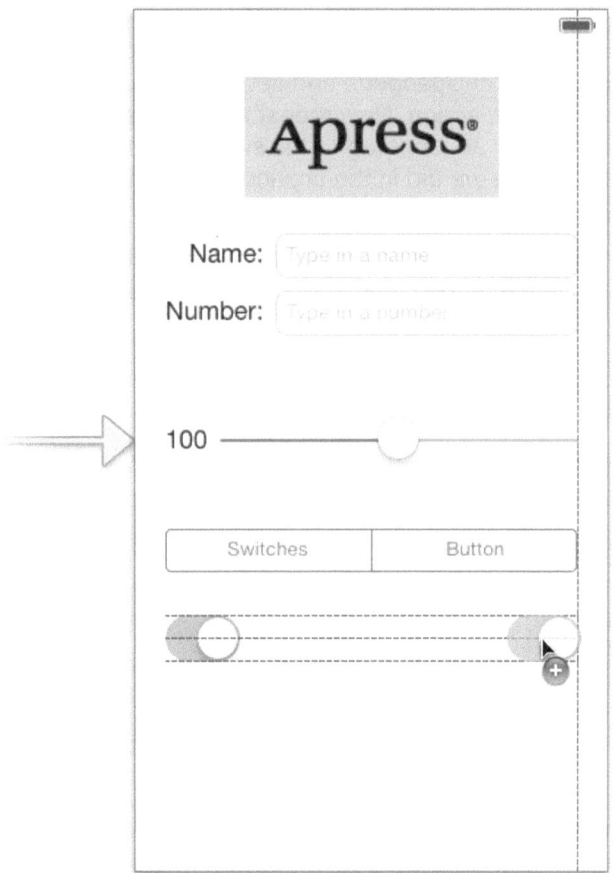

Figure 4-24. Adding the switches to the view

> **Tip**   Holding down the ⌥ key and dragging an object in Interface Builder will create a copy of that item. When you have many instances of the same object to create, it can be faster to drag only one object from the library, and then option-drag as many copies as you need.

Connecting and Creating Outlets and Actions

Before we add the button, we'll create outlets for the two switches and connect them. The button that we'll be adding next will actually sit on top of the switches, making it harder to control-drag to and from them, so we want to take care of the switch connections before we add the button. Since the button and the switches will never be visible at the same time, having them in the same physical location won't be a problem.

Using the assistant editor, control-drag from the switch on the left to just below the last outlet in *BIDViewController.m*. When the pop-up appears, name the outlet *leftSwitch* and hit **Return**. Repeat this process with the other switch, naming its outlet *rightSwitch*.

Now, select the left switch again by single-clicking it. Control-drag once more to the assistant editor. This time, drag to right above the @end declaration before letting go. When the pop-up appears, name the new action method *switchChanged:*, and set the *Type* of its sender argument to UISwitch. Next, hit **Return** to create the new action. Now repeat this process with the right switch, with one change: instead of creating a new action, drag to the *switchChanged:* action that was just created and connect to it, instead. Just as we did in the previous chapter, we're going to use a single method to handle both switches.

Finally, control-drag from the segmented control to the assistant editor, right above the @end declaration. Insert a new action method called *toggleControls:*, just as you've done before. This time, set the *Type* of its sender parameter to UISegmentedControl.

Implementing the Switch Actions

Save the storyboard and divert your attention to *BIDViewController.m*, which is already open in the assistant view. Look for the switchChanged: method that was added for you automatically and add this code to it:

```
- (IBAction)switchChanged:(UISwitch *)sender {
    BOOL setting = sender.isOn;
    [self.leftSwitch setOn:setting animated:YES];
    [self.rightSwitch setOn:setting animated:YES];

}
```

The switchChanged: method is called whenever one of the two switches is tapped. In this method, we simply grab the isOn value of sender (which represents the switch that was pressed) and use that value to set both switches. The idea here is that setting the value of one switch will change the other switch at the other time, keeping them in sync at all times.

Now, sender is always going to be either leftSwitch or rightSwitch, so you might be wondering why we're setting them both. The reason is one of practicality. It's less work to set the value of both switches every time than to determine which switch made the call and set only the other one. Whichever switch called this method will already be set to the correct value, and setting it again to that same value won't have any effect.

Adding the Button

Next, go back to Interface Builder and drag a *Button* from the library to your view. Add this button directly on top of the leftmost switch, aligning it with the left margin and vertically aligning its top edge with the top edge of the two switches (see Figure 4-25).

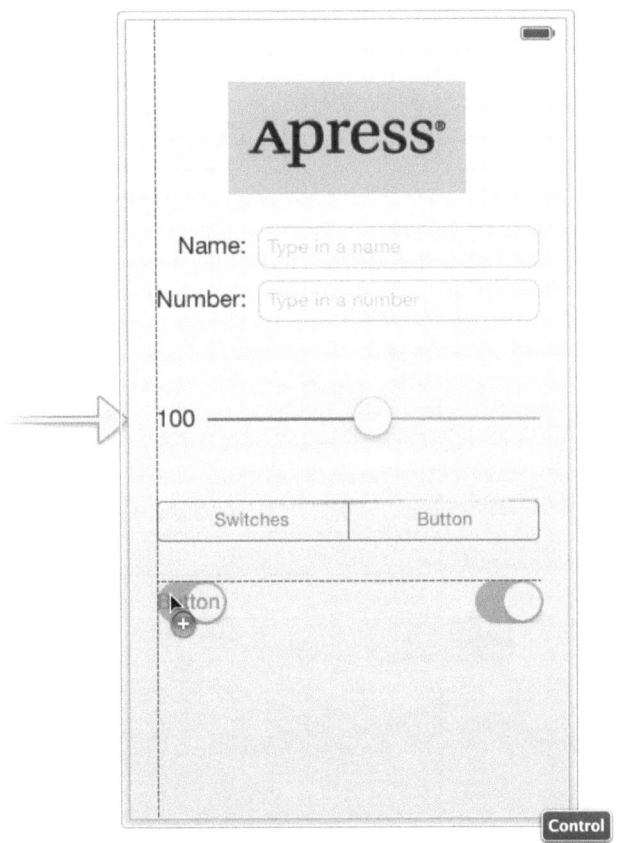

Figure 4-25. Adding a button on top of the existing switches

Now, grab the right-center resize handle and drag all the way to the right until you reach the blue guideline that indicates the right-side margin. The button should completely overlay the space occupied by the two switches, but because the default button is transparent, you will still see the switches (see Figure 4-26).

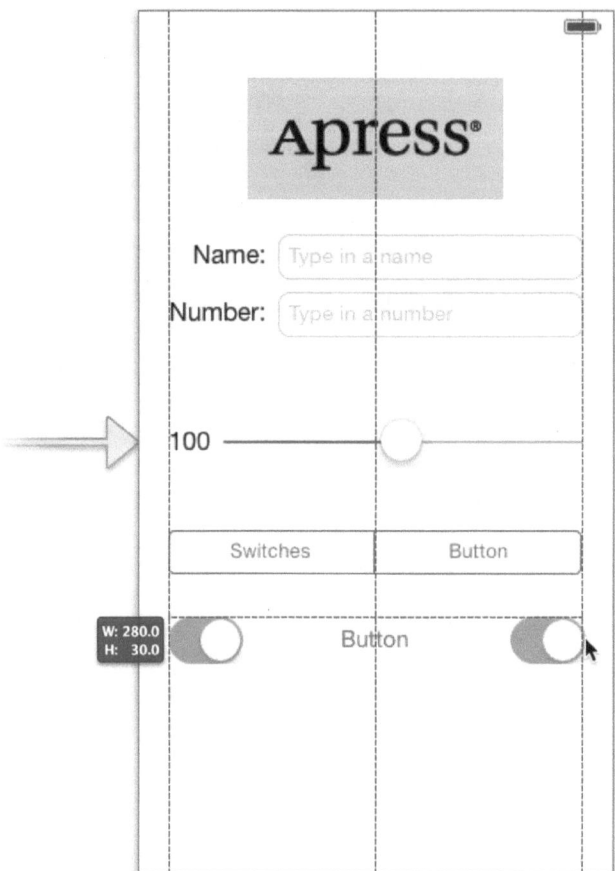

Figure 4-26. The round rect button, once placed and resized, will fill the space occupied by the two switches

Double-click the newly added button and give it a title of *Do Something.*

Spiffing Up the Button

If you compare your running application to Figure 4-2, you might notice an interesting difference. Your *Do Something* button doesn't look like the one in the figure. That's because the default button in iOS 7 has a very simple appearance: it's just a piece of plain text with no outline, border, background color, or other decorative features. That conforms nicely to Apple's new design guidelines for iOS 7, but there are still cases where you'll want to use custom buttons, so we're going to show you how it's done.

Many of the buttons you see on your iOS device are drawn using images. Don't worry; you don't need to create images in an image editor for every button. All you need to do is specify a kind of template image that iOS will use when drawing your buttons.

It's important to keep in mind that your application is sandboxed. You can't get to the template images that are used in other applications on your iOS device or the ones used by iOS itself, so you must make sure that any images you need are in your application's bundle. So, where can you get these image templates?

Fortunately, Apple has provided a bunch for you. You can get them from the iPhone sample application called UICatalog, available from the iOS Developer Library:

`http://developer.apple.com/library/ios/#samplecode/UICatalog/index.html`

Alternatively, you can simply copy the images from the *04 - Control Fun* folder from this book's project archive. Yes, it is OK to use these images in your own applications because Apple's sample code license specifically allows you to use and distribute them.

So, from either the *04 - Control Fun* folder or the *images* subfolder of the UICatalog project's folder, find the two images named *blueButton.png* and *whiteButton.png*. In Xcode, select *Images.xcassets* (the same assets catalog that we used earlier when we added images for the Apress logo), then just drag both images from the Finder straight into the editing area in your Xcode window. The images are added to your project and will be immediately available through your app.

Stretchable Images

Now, if you look at the two button images we just added, you'll probably be struck by the size of them. They're very small, and seem much too narrow to fill out the button you added to the storyboard. That's because these graphics are meant to be stretchable. It so happens that UIKit can stretch graphics to nicely fill just about any size you want. Stretchable images are an interesting concept. A stretchable image is a resizable image that knows how to resize itself intelligently, so that it maintains the correct appearance. For these button templates, we don't want the edges to stretch evenly with the rest of the image. **Edge insets** are the parts of an image, measured in pixels, that should not be resized. We want the bevel around the edges to stay the same, no matter what size we make the button, so we need to specify how much non-stretchable space makes up each edge.

In the past, this could only be accomplished in code. You'd have to use a graphics program to measure pixel boundaries of your images, then use those number to set edge insets in your code. Xcode 5 eliminates the need for this however, by letting you visually "slice" any image you have in an assets catalog! That's what we're going to do next.

Select the *Images.xcassets* asset catalog in Xcode, and inside that select *whiteButton*. At the bottom of the editing area, you'll see a button labeled *Show Slicing*. Click that to initiate the slicing process, which begins by simply putting a *Start Slicing* button right on top of your image. That's where the magic begins, so click it! You'll see three new buttons that let you choose whether you want the image to be sliced (and therefore stretchable) vertically, horizontally, or both. Choose the button in the middle to slice both ways. Xcode does a quick analysis of your image, and then finds the sections that seem to have unique pixels around the edges, and vertical and horizontal slices in the middle that should be repeatable. You'll see these boundaries represented by dashed lines, as shown in Figure 4-27. If you have a tricky image, you may need to adjust these (it's easy to do, just drag them with the mouse); but for this image, the automatic edge insets will work fine.

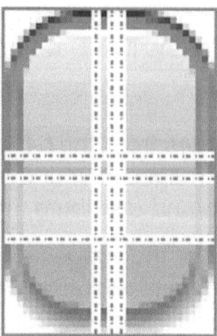

whit...- 1x

Figure 4-27. This is what the default slicing for the white button looks like

Next, select *blueButton* and do the same automatic slicing for it. All done! Now it's time to put these graphics to use.

Go back to the storyboard you've been working on and single-click the *Do Something* button. Yeah, we know, the button is now invisible because we marked it as hidden; however, you should have no problem seeing the ghost image. In addition, you can also click the button in the hierarchical view at the left side, if you have it open.

With the button selected, press ⌥⌘4 to open the attributes inspector. In the inspector, first go down to the View section and turn off the Hidden checkbox, just so we can see what we're doing. Next, go back up to the top and use the first pop-up menu to change the type from *System* to *Custom*. You'll see in the inspector that you can specify an *Image* and a *Background* for your button. We're going to use the *Background* to show our resizable graphic, so click in the *Background* pop-up and select *whiteButton*. You'll see that the button now shows the white graphic, perfectly stretched to cover the entire button frame. Nice!

Now we want to use the blue button to define the look of this button's highlighted state, which is what you see while the button is pressed. We'll talk more about control states in the next section of this chapter; but for now, just take a look at the second pop-up from the top, labeled *State Config*. A UIButton can have multiple states, each with its own text and images. Right now we've been configuring the default state, so switch this pop-up to *Highlighted*, so that we can configure that state. You'll see that the *Background* popup has been cleared; click it to select *blueButton*, and you're done!

There's just one problem with this new button appearance: The default UIButton size isn't tall enough to properly show the gradient buttons we imported. Use the resizing control at the bottom edge of the button, dragging it down to make the button a little taller. It will actually snap into position when it reaches the appropriate height, just a few pixels larger than it started out.

Configuring this button introduces two new concepts: **stretchable images** and **control states**. We already talked about the former, so now let's tackle the latter.

Control States

Every iOS control has four possible control states and is always in one, and only one, of these states at any given moment:

- **Normal:** The most common state is the normal control state, which is the default state. It's the state that controls are in when not in any of the other states.

- **Highlighted:** The highlighted state is the state a control is in when it's currently being used. For a button, this would be while the user has a finger on the button.

- **Disabled:** Controls are in the disabled state when they have been turned off, which can be done by unchecking the *Enabled* checkbox in Interface Builder or setting the control's enabled property to NO.

- **Selected:** Only some controls support the selected state. It is usually used to indicate that the control is turned on or selected. Selected is similar to highlighted, but a control can continue to be selected when the user is no longer directly using that control.

Certain iOS controls have attributes that can take on different values depending on their state. For example, by specifying one image for UIControlStateNormal and a different image for UIControlStateHighlighted, we are telling iOS to use one image when the user has a finger on the button and a different image the rest of the time. That's essentially what we did when we configured two different background states for the button in the storyboard.

Connecting and Creating the Button Outlets and Actions

Control-drag from the new button to the assistant editor, just below the last outlet already in the section at the top of the file. When the pop-up appears, create a new outlet called *doSomethingButton*. After you've done that, control-drag from the button a second time to just above the @end declaration at the bottom of the file. There, create an action called *buttonPressed:*. We don't need to set the *Type* to anything in particular because the method we'll write soon won't use it, anyway.

If you save your work and take the application for a test drive, you'll see that the segmented control will be live, but it won't do anything particularly useful yet. We need to add some logic to make the button and switches hide and unhide.

We also need to mark our button as hidden from the start. We didn't want to do that before because it would have made it harder to connect the outlets and actions. Now that we've done that, however, let's hide the button. We'll show the button when the user taps the right side of the segmented control; but when the application starts, we want the button hidden. Press ⌥⌘4 to bring up the attributes inspector, scroll down to the *View* section, and click the *Hidden* checkbox. The button will still be visible in Interface Builder, but will look faded out and transparent, to indicate its hidden status.

Implementing the Segmented Control Action

Save the storyboard and focus once again on *BIDViewController.m*. Look for the `toggleControls:` method that Xcode created for us and add the code in bold to it:

```
- (IBAction)toggleControls:(UISegmentedControl *)sender {
    // 0 == switches index
    if (sender.selectedSegmentIndex == 0) {
        self.leftSwitch.hidden = NO;
        self.rightSwitch.hidden = NO;
        self.doSomethingButton.hidden = YES;
    }
    else {
        self.leftSwitch.hidden = YES;
        self.rightSwitch.hidden = YES;
        self.doSomethingButton.hidden = NO;
    }
}
```

This code looks at the `selectedSegmentIndex` property of sender, which tells us which of the sections is currently selected. The first section, called `switches`, has an index of 0. We've noted this fact in a comment, so that when we revisit the code later, we will know what's going on. Depending on which segment is selected, we hide or show the appropriate controls.

At this point, save and try running the application in the iOS simulator. If you've typed everything correctly, you should be able to switch between the button and the pair of switches using the segmented control. And if you tap either switch, the other one will change its value as well. The button, however, still doesn't do anything. Before we implement it, we need to talk about action sheets and alerts.

Implementing the Action Sheet and Alert

Action sheets and **alerts** are both used to provide the user with feedback:

- Action sheets are used to force the user to make a choice between two or more items. The action sheet comes up from the bottom of the screen and displays a series of buttons (see Figure 4-3). Users are unable to continue using the application until they have tapped one of the buttons. Action sheets are often used to confirm a potentially dangerous or irreversible action such as deleting an object.

- Alerts appear as a rounded rectangle in the middle of the screen (see Figure 4-4). Like action sheets, alerts force users to respond before they are allowed to continue using the application. Alerts are usually used to inform the user that something important or out of the ordinary has occurred. Unlike action sheets, alerts may be presented with only a single button, although you have the option of presenting multiple buttons if more than one response is appropriate.

Note   A view that forces users to make a choice before they are allowed to continue using their application is known as a **modal view**.

Conforming to the Action Sheet Delegate Method

Remember back in Chapter 3 when we talked about the application delegate? Well, `UIApplication` is not the only class in Cocoa Touch that uses delegates. In fact, delegation is a common design pattern in Cocoa Touch. Action sheets and alerts both use delegates, so that they know which object to notify when they're dismissed. In our application, we'll need to be notified when the action sheet is dismissed. We don't need to know when the alert is dismissed because we're just using it to notify the user of something, not to solicit a choice.

In order for our controller class to act as the delegate for an action sheet, it needs to conform to a protocol called `UIActionSheetDelegate`. We do that by adding the name of the protocol in angle brackets after the superclass in our class declaration. Add this protocol declaration to *BIDViewController.h*:

```
#import <UIKit/UIKit.h>

@interface BIDViewController : UIViewController <UIActionSheetDelegate>
. . .
```

Showing the Action Sheet

Let's switch over to *BIDViewController.m* and implement the button's action method. We actually need to implement another method in addition to our existing action method: the `UIActionSheetDelegate` method that the action sheet will use to notify us that it has been dismissed.

Begin by looking for the empty `buttonPressed:` method that Xcode created for you, and then add the code in bold to that method to create and show the action sheet:

```
- (IBAction)buttonPressed:(id)sender {
    UIActionSheet *actionSheet = [[UIActionSheet alloc]
                                  initWithTitle:@"Are you sure?"
                                  delegate:self
                                  cancelButtonTitle:@"No Way!"
                                  destructiveButtonTitle:@"Yes, I'm Sure!"
                                  otherButtonTitles:nil];
    [actionSheet showInView:self.view];
}
```

Next, add a new method just after the existing `buttonPressed:` method:

```
- (void)actionSheet:(UIActionSheet *)actionSheet
    didDismissWithButtonIndex:(NSInteger)buttonIndex
{
    if (buttonIndex != [actionSheet cancelButtonIndex]) {
        NSString *msg = nil;

        if ([self.nameField.text length] > 0) {
            msg = [NSString stringWithFormat:
                    @"You can breathe easy, %@, everything went OK.",
                    self.nameField.text];
```

```
        } else {
            msg = @"You can breathe easy, everything went OK.";
        }

        UIAlertView *alert = [[UIAlertView alloc]
                                initWithTitle:@"Something was done"
                                message:msg
                                delegate:self
                                cancelButtonTitle:@"Phew!"
                                otherButtonTitles:nil];
        [alert show];
    }
}
```

What exactly did we do there? Well, first, in the doSomething: action method, we allocated and initialized a UIActionSheet object, which is the object that represents an action sheet (in case you couldn't puzzle that one out for yourself):

```
UIActionSheet *actionSheet = [[UIActionSheet alloc]
                                initWithTitle:@"Are you sure?"
                                delegate:self
                                cancelButtonTitle:@"No Way!"
                                destructiveButtonTitle:@"Yes, I'm Sure!"
                                otherButtonTitles:nil];
```

The initializer method takes a number of parameters. Let's look at each of them in turn.

The first parameter is the title to be displayed. Refer back to Figure 4-3 to see how the title we're supplying will be displayed at the top of the action sheet.

The second parameter is the delegate for the action sheet. The action sheet's delegate will be notified when a button on that sheet has been tapped. More specifically, the delegate's actionSheet:didDismissWithButtonIndex: method will be called. By passing self as the delegate parameter, we ensure that our version of actionSheet:didDismissWithButtonIndex: will be called.

Next, we pass in the title for the button that users will tap to indicate they do not want to proceed. All action sheets should have a cancel button, though you can give it any title that is appropriate to your situation. You do not want to use an action sheet if there is no choice to be made. In situations where you want to notify the user without giving a choice of options, an alert view is more appropriate.

The next parameter is the destructive button, and you can think of this as the "yes, please go ahead" button; again, though, you can assign it any title.

The last parameter allows you to specify any number of other buttons that you may want shown on the sheet. This final argument can take a variable number of values, which is one of the nice features of the Objective-C language. If we had wanted two more buttons on our action sheet, we could have done it like this:

```
UIActionSheet *actionSheet = [[UIActionSheet alloc]
                                initWithTitle:@"Are you sure?"
                                delegate:self
                                cancelButtonTitle:@"No Way!"
                                destructiveButtonTitle:@"Yes, I'm Sure!"
                                otherButtonTitles:@"Foo", @"Bar", nil];
```

This code would have resulted in an action sheet with four buttons. You can pass as many arguments as you want in the otherButtonTitles parameter, as long as you pass nil as the last one. Of course, there is a practical limitation on how many buttons you can have, based on the amount of screen space available.

After we create the action sheet, we tell it to show itself:

```
[actionSheet showInView:self.view];
```

Action sheets always have a parent, which must be a view that is currently visible to the user. In our case, we want the view that we designed in Interface Builder to be the parent, so we use self.view. Note the use of Objective-C dot notation. self.view is equivalent to saying [self view], using the accessor to return the value of our view property.

Why didn't we just use view, instead of self.view? Our parent class UIViewController may have an instance variable called view, but it doesn't expose it, not even to a subclass like ours. This means we can't access it directly, but instead must use an accessor method.

Well, that wasn't so hard, was it? In just a few lines of code, we showed an action sheet and required the user to make a decision. iOS will even animate the sheet for us without requiring us to do any additional work. Now, we just need to find out which button the user tapped. The other method that we just implemented, actionSheet:didDismissWithButtonIndex, is one of the UIActionSheetDelegate methods; and since we specified self as our action sheet's delegate, this method will automatically be called by the action sheet when a button is tapped.

The argument buttonIndex will tell us which button was actually tapped. But how do we know which button index refers to the cancel button and which one refers to the destructive button? Fortunately, the delegate method receives a pointer to the UIActionSheet object that represents the sheet, and that action sheet object knows which button is the cancel button. We just need look at one of its properties, cancelButtonIndex:

```
if (buttonIndex != [actionSheet cancelButtonIndex])
```

This line of code makes sure the user didn't tap the cancel button. Since we gave the user only two options, we know that if the cancel button wasn't tapped, the destructive button must have been tapped, and it's OK to proceed. Once we know the user didn't cancel, the first thing we do is create a new string that will be displayed to the user. In a real application, this is where you would do whatever processing the user requested. We're just going to pretend we did something, and notify the user by using an alert.

If the user has entered a name in the top text field, we'll grab that, and we'll use it in the message that we'll display in the alert. Otherwise, we'll just craft a generic message to show:

```
NSString *msg = nil;

if ([self.nameField.text length] > 0) {
    msg = [NSString stringWithFormat:
            @"You can breathe easy, %@, everything went OK.",
            self.nameField.text];
}
else {
    msg = @"You can breathe easy, everything went OK.";
}
```

The next few lines of code are going to look kind of familiar. Alert views and action sheets are created and used in a very similar manner:

```
UIAlertView *alert = [[UIAlertView alloc]
                      initWithTitle:@"Something was done"
                      message:msg
                      delegate:nil
                      cancelButtonTitle:@"Phew!"
                      otherButtonTitles:nil];
```

Again, we pass a title to be displayed. We also pass a more detailed message, which is that string we just created. Alert views have delegates, too; and if we needed to know when the user had dismissed the alert view or which button was tapped, we could specify self as the delegate here, just as we did with the action sheet. If we had done that, we would now need to conform our class to the UIAlertViewDelegate protocol, and implement one or more of the methods from that protocol. In this case, we're just informing the user of something and giving the user only one button. We don't really care when the button is tapped, and we already know which button will be tapped, so we just specify nil here to indicate that we don't need to be pinged when the user is finished with the alert view.

Alert views, unlike action sheets, are not tied to a particular view, so we just tell the alert view to show itself without specifying a parent view. After that, we're finished. Save the file, then build, run, and try out the completed application.

One Last Tweak

With iOS 7, Apple has introduced some new GUI paradigms. One of these is that the status bar at the top of the screen is transparent in iOS 7 apps, so that your content shines right through it. Right now, that yellow Apress icon really sticks out like a sore thumb against our app's white background, so let's extend that yellow color to cover our entire view. In *Main.storyboard*, select the main content view, and press ⌥⌘4 to bring up the attributes inspector. Click the color swatch labeled *Background* to open the standard OS X color picker. One feature of this color picker is that it lets you choose any color you see on the screen. Just click the icon showing magnifying glass at the upper left, then click anywhere in the yellow part of the Apress icon to set that color as the background for the entire view. When you're done, close the color picker.

On your screen, you may find that the background and the Apress image seem to have slightly different colors, but when run in the simulator or on a device they will be the same. These colors appear to be different in Interface Builder because OS X automatically adapts colors depending on the display you're using. On an iOS device, and in the simulator, that doesn't happen.

Now run your app, and you'll see that the yellow color fills the entire screen, with no visible distinction between the status bar and your app's content. If you don' t have full-screen scrolling content, or other content that requires the use of a navigation bar or other controls at the top of the screen, this can be a nice way to show full-screen content that isn't interrupted by the status bar quite as much.

Crossing the Finish Line

This was a big chapter. Conceptually, we didn't hit you with too much new stuff, but we took you through the use of a good number of controls and showed you many different implementation details. You got a lot more practice with outlets and actions, saw how to use the hierarchical nature of views to your advantage, and cut your teeth on some constraints. You learned about control states and stretchable images, and you also learned how to use both action sheets and alerts.

There's a lot going on in this little application. Feel free to go back and play with it. Change values, experiment by adding and modifying code, and see what different settings in Interface Builder do. There's no way we could take you through every permutation of every control available in iOS, but the application you just put together is a good starting point and covers a lot of the basics.

In the next chapter, we're going to look at what happens when the user rotates an iOS device from portrait to landscape orientation or vice versa. You're probably well aware that many apps change their displays based on the way the user is holding the device, and we're going to show you how to do that in your own applications.

Chapter 5

Autorotation and Autosizing

The iPhone and iPad are amazing pieces of engineering. Apple engineers found all kinds of ways to squeeze maximum functionality into a pretty darn small package. One example of this is how these devices can be used in either portrait (tall and skinny) or landscape (short and wide) mode, and how that orientation can be changed at runtime simply by rotating the device. You can see an example of this behavior, which is called **autorotation**, in iOS's web browser, Mobile Safari (see Figure 5-1).

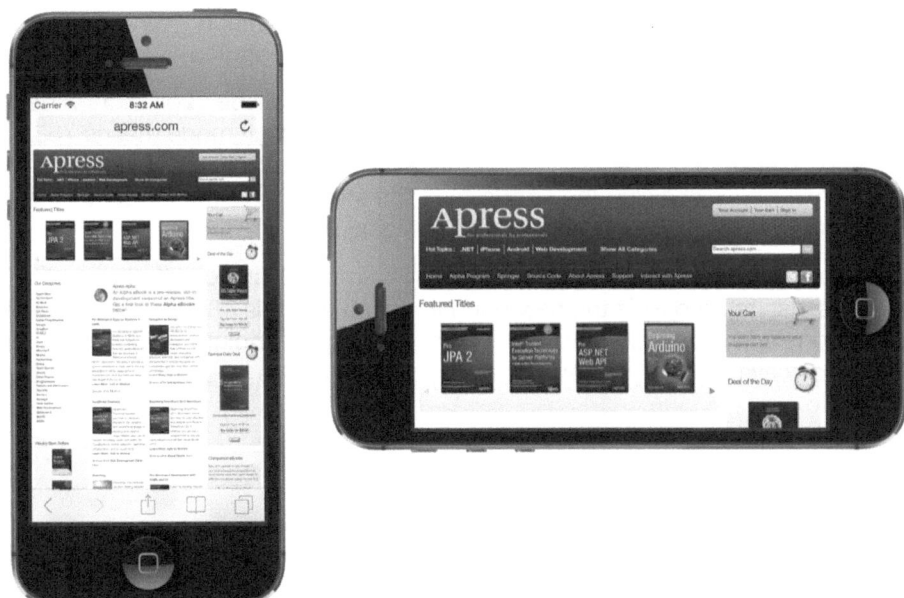

Figure 5-1. *Like many iOS applications, Mobile Safari changes its display based on how it is held, making the most of the available screen space*

In this chapter, we'll cover autorotation in detail. We'll start with an overview of the ins and outs of autorotation, and then move on to different ways of implementing that functionality in your apps.

The Mechanics of Autorotation

Autorotation might not be right for every application. Several of Apple's iPhone applications support only a single orientation. Contacts can be edited only in portrait mode, for example. However, iPad applications are different. Apple recommends that most applications (with the exception of immersive apps like games that are inherently designed around a particular layout) should support every orientation when running on an iPad.

In fact, most of Apple's own iPad apps work fine in both orientations. Many of them use the orientations to show different views of your data. For example, the Mail and Notes apps use landscape orientation to display a list of items (folders, messages, or notes) on the left and the selected item on the right. In portrait orientation, however, these apps let you focus on the details of just the selected item.

For iPhone apps, the base rule is that, if autorotation enhances the user experience, you should add it to your application. For iPad apps, the rule is you should add autorotation unless you have a compelling reason not to. Fortunately, Apple did a great job of hiding the complexities of autorotation in iOS and in the UIKit, so implementing this behavior in your own iOS applications is actually quite easy.

Autorotation is specified in the view controller. If the user rotates the device, the active view controller will be asked if it's okay to rotate to the new orientation (which you'll see how to do in this chapter). If the view controller responds in the affirmative, the application's window and views will be rotated, and the window and view will be resized to fit the new orientation.

On the iPhone and iPod touch, a view that starts in portrait mode will be 320 points wide and 480 points tall (568 points tall on the iPhone 5 series). On the iPad, portrait mode means 768 points wide and 1024 points tall. The amount of screen real estate available for your app will be decreased by 20 points vertically if your app is showing the **status bar**. The status bar is the 20-point strip at the top of the screen (see Figure 5-1) that shows information like signal strength, time, and battery charge.

When the device is switched to landscape mode, the view rotates, along with the application's window. The app is also resized to fit the new orientation, so that it is 480 (or 568) points wide by 320 points tall (iPhone and iPod touch) or 1024 points wide by 768 points tall (iPad). As before, the vertical space actually available to your app is reduced by 20 points if you're showing the status bar, which most apps do.

Points, Pixels, and the Retina Display

You might be wondering why we're talking about "points" instead of pixels. Earlier versions of this book did, in fact, refer to screen sizes in pixels rather than points. The reason for this change is Apple's introduction of the **retina display**.

The retina display is Apple's marketing term for the high-resolution screen on the iPhone 4, iPhone 4s, iPhone 5, and later-generation iPod touches, as well as the Retina iPad. It doubles the iPhone screen resolution from the original 320 × 480 pixels to 640 × 960 pixels (now up to 640 × 1136 on iPhone 5), and the iPad screen resolution from 1024 × 768 to 2048 × 1536.

Fortunately, you don't need to do a thing in most situations to account for this. When we work with on-screen elements, we specify dimensions and distances in *points*, not in pixels. For older iPhones, iPad 1 , iPad 2, and iPad Mini 1, points and pixels are equivalent. One point is one pixel. On more recent model iPhones and iPod touches, however, a point equates to a 4-pixel square (2 pixels wide and 2 pixels high) and the screen is still 320 points wide, even though it's actually 640 pixels across. Likewise, the latest iPads still have a screen geometry of 1024 × 768 points, although they actually have 2048 × 1536 pixels. Think of it as a "virtual resolution," with iOS automatically mapping points to the physical pixels of your screen. We'll talk more about this in Chapter 16.

In typical applications, most of the work in actually moving the pixels around the screen is managed by iOS. Your application's main job in all this is making sure everything fits nicely and looks proper in the resized window.

Autorotation Approaches

Your application can take three general approaches when managing rotation. Which one you use depends on the complexity of your interface. We'll look at all three approaches in this chapter.

With simpler interfaces, you can specify the correct **constraints** for all of the objects that make up your interface. Constraints tell the iOS device how your controls should behave when their enclosing view is resized. If you've worked with Cocoa on OS X, you may already be familiar with the basic process because it is the same one used to specify how Cocoa controls behave when the user resizes the window in which they are contained. This system is also known as Cocoa Autolayout, but we'll be describing things in terms of constraints, which are the parts of Cocoa Autolayout that we can most directly interact with and configure.

The simplest way of using constraints is to configure them in Interface Builder (IB). Interface Builder lets you define constraints that describe how your GUI components will be repositioned and resized as their parent view changes or as other views move around. You did a little bit of this in Chapter 4 and will delve further into this subject in this chapter. You can think of constraints as equations that make statements about view geometry and the iOS view system itself as a "solver" that will rearrange things as necessary to make those statements true.

Constraints were added to iOS 6, but have been present on the Mac for a bit longer than that. On both iOS and OS X, constraints can be used in place of the old "springs and struts" system that came before. Constraints can do everything the old technology could do, and a whole lot more.

Configuring constraints in Interface Builder is quick and easy, but this approach isn't appropriate for all applications. More complex interfaces must handle autorotation in a different manner. For more complex views, you will need to override methods from `UIViewController` in your view's controller class. This will enable you to lay out your views the way you want. We'll show you this approach at the end of this chapter.

Let's get started, shall we? Before we get into the different ways you can configure your GUI to shuffle its views around, we'll show you how to specify which orientations your app will allow.

Choosing Your View Orientations

We'll create a simple app to show you how to pick which orientations you want your app to work with. Start a new *Single View Application* project in Xcode, and call it *Orientations*. Choose *iPhone* from the *Devices* pop-up, and save it along with your other projects.

Before we lay out our GUI in the storyboard, we need to tell iOS that our view supports autorotation. There are actually two ways of doing this. You can create an app-wide setting that will be the default for all view controllers, and you can further tweak things for each individual view controller. We'll do both of these things, starting with the app-wide setting.

Supported Orientations at the App Level

First, we need to specify which orientations our application supports. When your new Xcode project window appeared, it should have opened to your project settings. If not, click the top line in the project navigator (the one named after your project), and then make sure you're on the *General* tab. Among the options available in the summary, you should see a section called *Deployment Info* and, within that, a section called *Device Orientation* (see Figure 5-2) with a list of checkboxes.

Figure 5-2. The General tab for our project shows, among other things, the supported device orientations

This is how you identify which orientations your application supports. It doesn't necessarily mean that every view in your application will use all of the selected orientations; but if you're going to support an orientation in any of your application's views, that orientation must be selected here.

> **Note** The four checkboxes shown in Figure 5-2 are actually just a shortcut to adding and deleting entries in your application's *Info.plist* file. If you single-click *Orientations-Info.plist* in the *Supporting Files* folder in the project navigator, you should see an entry called *Supported interface orientations*, with three subentries for the three orientations currently selected. Selecting and deselecting those checkboxes in the project summary simply adds and removes items from this array. Using the checkboxes is easier and less prone to error, so we definitely recommend using the checkboxes. However, we thought you should know what they do.

Have you noticed that the *Upside Down* orientation is off by default? That's because, if the phone rings while it is being held upside down, the phone is likely to remain upside down when you answer it. iPad app projects default to all four orientations being supported because the iPad is meant to be used in any orientation. Since our project is an iPhone project, we can leave the checkboxes the way they are.

Now, select *Main.storyboard*, find a *Label* in the object library, and drag it into your view, dropping it somewhere just above the center, as shown in Figure 5-3. Select the label's text and change it to *This way up*. Changing the text may shift the label's position, so drag it to make it horizontally centered again.

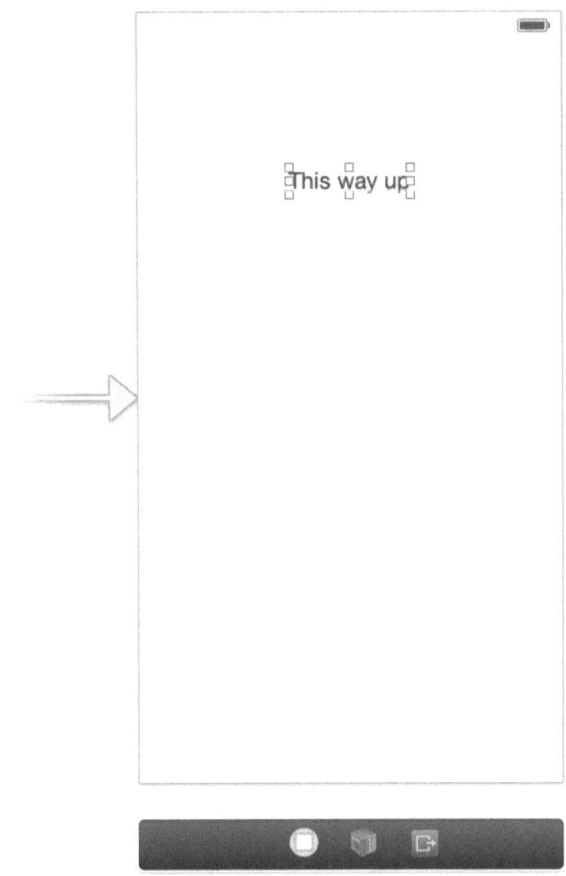

Figure 5-3. A useful reminder in case you lose your sense of gravity

Now, press ⌘R to build and run this simple app. When it comes up in the simulator, try rotating the device a few times by pressing ⌘-**Left-Arrow** or ⌘-**Right-Arrow**. You'll see that the entire view (including the label you added) rotates to every orientation except upside-down, just as we configured it to do.

We've identified the orientations our app will support, but that's not all we need to do. We can also specify a set of accepted orientations for each view controller, giving us some more fine-grained control over which orientations will work in different parts of our apps.

Per-Controller Rotation Support

Let's configure our view controller to allow a different, smaller set of accepted orientations. Note that the global configuration for the app specifies a sort of absolute upper limit for allowed orientations. If the global configuration doesn't include upside-down orientation, for example, there's no way that any individual view controller can force the system to rotate the display to upside-down. All we can do in the view controller is place further limits on what is acceptable.

Single-click *BIDViewController.m*. Here we're going to implement a method, defined in the UIViewController superclass, that lets us specify which orientations we'll accept.

```
- (NSUInteger)supportedInterfaceOrientations {
    return (UIInterfaceOrientationMaskPortrait |
            UIInterfaceOrientationMaskLandscapeLeft);
}
```

This method lets us return a C-style mask of acceptable orientations. This is iOS's way of asking a view controller if it's okay to rotate to a specific orientation. In this case, we're returning a value that indicates that we'll accept two orientations: the default portrait orientation and the orientation you get when you turn your phone 90° clockwise, so that the phone's left edge is at the top. We use the Boolean OR operator (the vertical bar symbol) to combine these two orientation masks and return the combined value.

UIApplication.h defines the following orientation masks, which you can combine in any way you like using the OR operator, as previously discussed:

- UIInterfaceOrientationMaskPortrait

- UIInterfaceOrientationMaskLandscapeLeft

- UIInterfaceOrientationMaskLandscapeRight

- UIInterfaceOrientationMaskPortraitUpsideDown

In addition, there are some predefined combinations of these for common use cases. These are functionally equivalent to OR'ing them together on your own, but can save you some typing and make your code more readable:

- UIInterfaceOrientationMaskLandscape

- UIInterfaceOrientationMaskAll

- UIInterfaceOrientationMaskAllButUpsideDown

When the iOS device is changed to a new orientation, the supportedInterfaceOrientations method is called on the active view controller. Depending on whether the return value includes the new orientation, the application determines whether it should rotate the view. Because every view controller subclass can implement this differently, it is possible for one application to support autorotation with some of its views but not with others, or for one view controller to support certain orientations under certain conditions.

CODE COMPLETION IN ACTION

Have you noticed that the defined system constants on the iPhone are always designed so that values that work together start with the same letters? One reason why UIInterfaceOrientationMaskPortrait, UIInterfaceOrientationMaskPortraitUpsideDown, UIInterfaceOrientationMaskLandscapeLeft, and UIInterfaceOrientationMaskLandscapeRight all begin with UIInterfaceOrientationMask is to let you take advantage of Xcode's **code completion** feature.

You've probably noticed that as you type, Xcode frequently tries to complete the word you are typing. That's code completion in action.

Developers cannot possibly remember all the various defined constants in the system, but you can remember the common beginning for the groups you use frequently. When you need to specify an orientation, simply type *UIInterfaceOrientationMask* (or even *UIInterf*), and you'll see a list of all matches pop up. (In Xcode's preferences, you can configure the list to pop up only when you press the **Esc** key.) You can use the arrow keys to navigate the list that appears and make a selection by pressing the **Tab** or **Return** key. This is much faster than needing to look up the values in the documentation or header files.

Feel free to play around with this method by returning different orientation mask combinations. You can force the system to constrict your view's display to whichever orientations make sense for your app, but don't forget the global configuration we talked about earlier! Remember that if you haven't enabled upside-down there (for example), none of your views will ever appear upside-down, no matter what their views say.

> **Note**   iOS actually has two different types of orientations. The one we're discussing here is the **interface orientation**. There's also a separate but related concept of **device orientation**. Device orientation specifies how the device is currently being held. Interface orientation is which way the views on the screen are rotated. If you turn a standard iPhone upside down, the device orientation will be upside down, but the interface orientation will almost always be one of the other three, since iPhone apps typically don't support portrait upside down.

Designing an Interface Using Constraints

In Xcode, make another new project based on the *Single View Application* template and name it *Autosize*. Select *Main.storyboard* to edit the interface file in Interface Builder. One nice thing about using constraints is that they accomplish quite a lot using very little code. We do need to specify which orientations we support in code, but the rest of the autoresize implementation can be done right here in Interface Builder.

To see how this works, drag four *Labels* from the library over to your view, and place them as shown in Figure 5-4. Use the dashed blue guidelines to help you line up each one near its respective corner. In this example, we're using instances of the UILabel class to show how to use constraints with your GUI layout, but the same rules apply to all kinds of GUI objects.

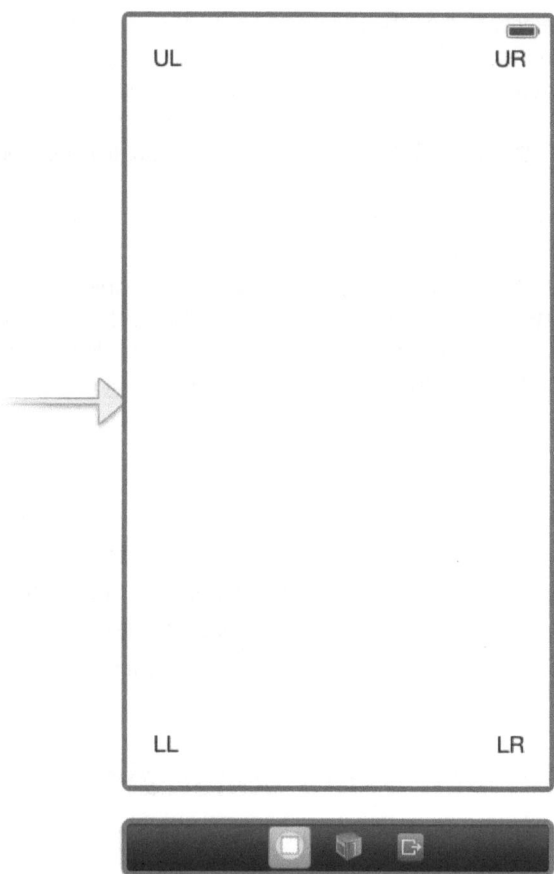

Figure 5-4. Adding four labels to the interface

Double-click each label, and assign a title to each one so you can tell them apart later. We've used *UL* for the upper-left label, *UR* for the upper-right label, *LL* for the lower-left label, and *LR* for the lower-right label. After setting the text for each label, drag all of them into position so that they are lined up evenly with respect to the container view's corners (see Figure 5-4).

Let's see what happens now that we've specified that we support autorotation, but haven't set any autosize attributes. Build and run the app. Once the iOS simulator comes up, select **Hardware ➤ Rotate Left**, which will simulate turning the iPhone to landscape mode. Take a look at Figure 5-5.

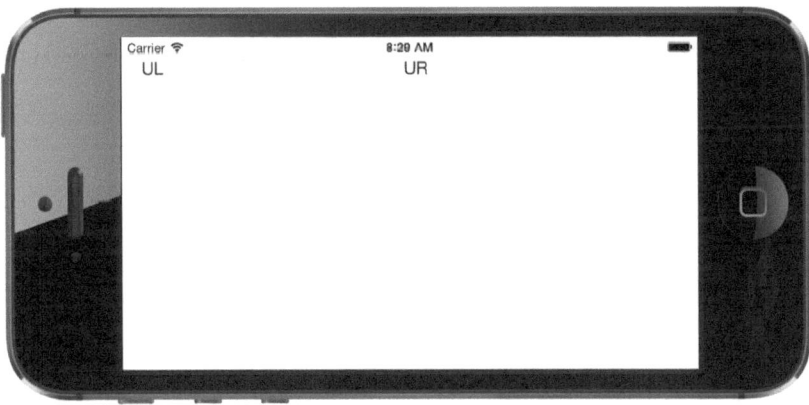

Figure 5-5. So far, not so good. What happened?

As you can see, things aren't looking so good. The top left label is in the right spot after rotating, but the upper right label is floating somewhere around the middle, and the bottom labels aren't visible at all! What's happened is that every object has maintained its distance relative to the upper-left corner of the view.

What we really want is to have each label sticking tightly to its nearest corner after rotating. The labels on the right should shift out to the right to match the view's new width, and the labels on the bottom should be pulled up to match the new height instead of disappearing off the bottom edge. Fortunately, we can easily set up constraints in Interface Builder to make these changes happen for us.

In fact, Interface Builder is smart enough to examine this set of objects and create a set of default constraints that will do exactly what we want. It uses some rules of thumb to figure out that if we have objects near edges, we probably want to keep them there. To make it apply these rules, first select all four labels. You can do this by clicking one, and then holding down the ⌘ key while clicking each of the other three. With all of them selected, choose **Editor ➤ Resolve Auto Layout Issues ➤ Add Missing Constraints** from the menu. Next, just press the *Run* button to launch the app in the simulator, and verify that it works.

Knowing that this works is one thing, but to use constraints like this most effectively, it's pretty important to understand how it works, too. So, let's dig into this a bit. Back in Xcode, click the upper-left label to select it. You'll notice that you can see four solid blue lines attached to the label: one leading to the left edge of the container view, one to the top edge, and two leading to other labels. These blue lines are different from the dashed blue guidelines you see when dragging objects around the screen (see Figure 5-6).

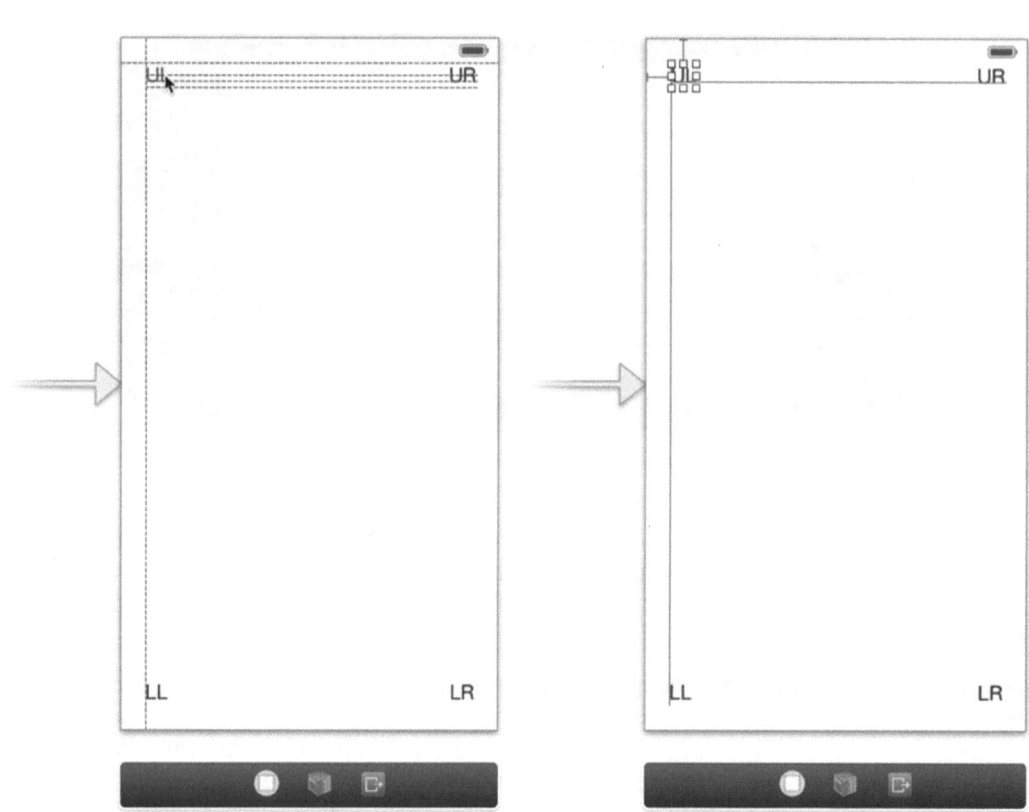

Figure 5-6. On the left, the dashed blue lines help you line up objects while you're dragging. On the right, the solid blue lines show constraints that are configured for the chosen object

Each of those solid blue lines represents a constraint. If you now press ⌥⌘5 to open the **size inspector**, you'll see that it contains a list of four constraints. Two of them deal with this label's position relative to its superview, the container view: one controlling the space between the top of this view and the top of its superview, and one controlling the **leading space**, which generally means the space to the left. These constraints cause the label to maintain the same distance to the top and left edges of its superview when the superview's size changes. The other two constraints are attached to two of the other labels and work to keep them lined up with this label.

Note that in languages where text is written and read from right to left, "leading space" is on the right, so a leading constraint may cause a GUI to be laid out in the opposite direction if the user has picked a language such as Arabic for their phone. For now, let's just act as if "leading space" means "left space."

Now, select the label which you placed in the upper right of your view, and you'll see that things look a little different. This one has its solid lines extending to the right edge of its superview and to two of the other labels. A look at the Constraints section in the size inspector shows constraints controlling the baseline, which is the vertical position, and the trailing space, which for our purposes means "space to the right" (the same caveat mentioned earlier applies here, as well). This set of constraints makes this label stick to the upper-right corner of its superview when the superview's size changes. Examine each of the remaining labels to see what constraints they have.

Overriding Default Constraints

Grab another label from the library and drag it over to the layout area. This time, instead of moving toward a corner, drag it toward the left edge of your view, lining up the label's left edge with the left edges of the other labels on the left side, and centering it vertically in the view. Dashed lines will appear to help you out. Figure 5-7 shows you what this looks like.

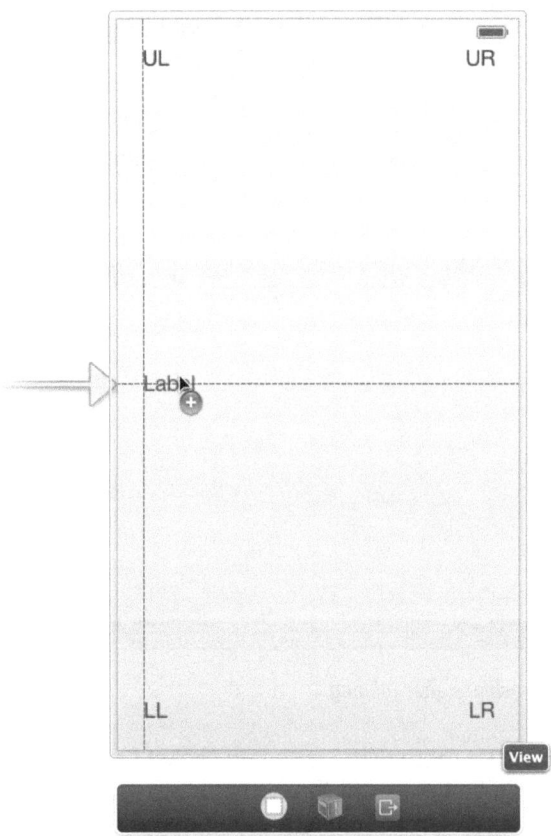

Figure 5-7. Placing the Left label

After placing the left label, give it a title like "Left." Press ⌘R to run your app in the simulator, rotate it to landscape mode, and you'll see that the left label maintains its distance from the top (again, just like the upper-left label), placing it a fair bit below center. Oops!

We need to create a new constraint to make this work, so go back to Xcode and select the left label in your nib. Adding a constraint to force this label to stay vertically centered is really easy—just select **Editor ➤ Align ➤ Vertical Center in Container**. When you do this, Xcode creates a new constraint and immediately selects the new constraint itself in the editor view. This is slightly confusing, but don't worry! Just click the label again to select it. Make sure the size inspector is on display by pressing ⌥⌘5, and you'll see that this label now has a constraint aligning its center Y value to that of its superview. Press ⌘R to run the app again, do some rotating, and you'll see that all the labels now move perfectly into their expected places. Nice!

Now, let's complete our ring of labels by dragging out a new one to the right side of the view, lining up its right edge with the other labels on the right, and aligning it vertically with the *Left* label. Change this label's title to *Right*, and then drag it a bit to make sure its right edge is vertically aligned with the right edges of the other two labels, using the dashed blue line as your guide. We want to use the automatic constraints that Xcode can provide us with, so select **Editor ➤ Resolve Auto Layout Issues ➤ Add Missing Constraints** to generate them.

With the label selected, take a peek at the constraints that Xcode has created for us. You should see two of them, one tying the label's right edge to the right edge of the UR label above it, and another one aligning its baseline (i.e., the imaginary bottom line of the text in the label) to the *Left* label. Xcode actually made a perfect guess! Build and run again, do some rotating again, and you'll see that all the labels stay on the screen and are correctly positioned relative to each other (see Figure 5-8). If you rotate back, they should return to their original positions. This technique will work for a great many applications.

Figure 5-8. The labels in their new positions after rotating

That's all fine, but we can do a lot more with just a few clicks! Let's say that we've been struck by a great visionary idea and decide that we want the two uppermost labels, UL and UR, to form a sort of header, filling the entire width of the screen. With a bit of resizing and some constraints, we'll sort that out in no time.

Full-Width Labels

We're going to create some constraints that make sure that our labels stay the same width as each other, with tight spacing to keep them stretched across the top of the view even when the device rotates. Figure 5-9 shows what we're shooting for.

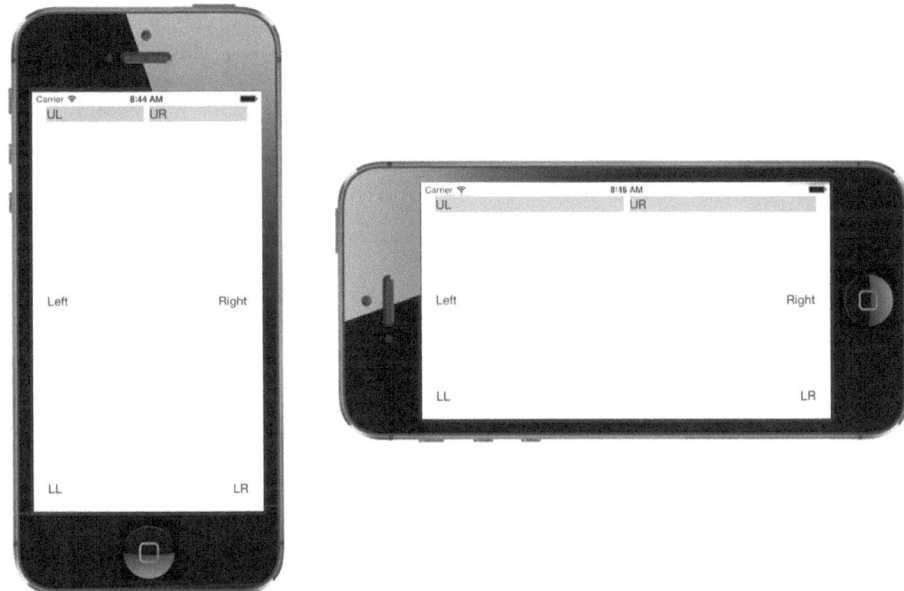

Figure 5-9. *The top labels, spread across the entire width of the display, in both portrait and landscape orientations*

The hardest part about this is being able to visually verify that we've got the result we want, where each label is precisely centered within its half of the screen. In order to make it easier to see whether we've got it right, let's temporarily set a background color for the labels. Select both the *UL* and *UR* labels, open the attributes inspector, and scroll down to the View section. Use the *Background* control to select a nice, bright color. You'll see that the entire frame of each label fills with the color you chose.

Now, direct your attention to the UL label and drag the resizing control on its right edge, pulling it almost to the horizontal midpoint of the view. You don't have to be exact here, for reasons that will become clear soon. After doing this, resize the UR label by dragging its left-edge resizing control to the left until you see the dashed blue guideline appear, which tells you that it's the recommended width from the label to its left. Now we'll add a constraint to make these labels fill the whole width of their superview. Select both the UL and UR labels, and select **Editor ➤ Pin ➤ Horizontal Spacing** from the menu. That constraint tells the layout system to hold these labels beside one another with the same horizontal space they have right now. Build and run to see what happens. Rotate the device, and you'll probably see something like Figure 5-10.

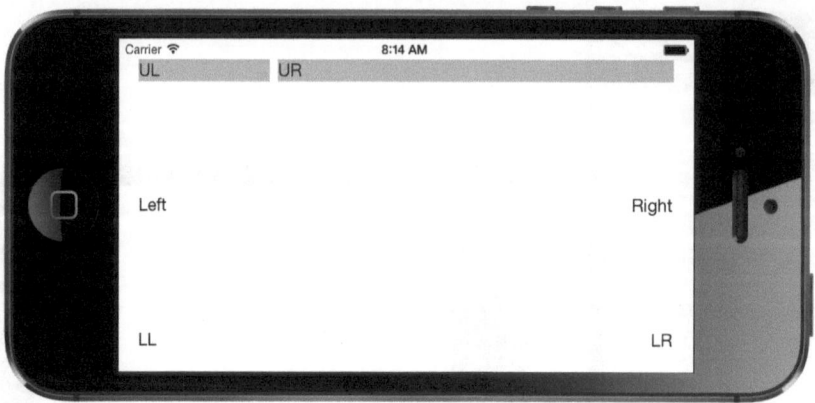

Figure 5-10. The labels are stretched across the display, but not evenly

That's pretty close, but not really what we had in mind. So what's missing? We've defined constraints that control each label's position relative to its superview and the allowed distance between the two labels, but we haven't said anything about the size of the labels. This leaves the layout system free to size them in whatever way it wants (which, as we've just seen, can be quite wrong). To remedy this, we need to add one more constraint.

Make sure the *UL* label is selected, then hold down the **Shift** key (⇧) and click the *UR* label. With both labels selected, you can make a constraint that affects both of them. From the menu, select **Editor ➤ Pin ➤ Widths Equally** to make the new constraint. You'll now see a new constraint appear, and just like before, it's automatically selected. Whenever a constraint is selected, the affected views are highlighted with a yellow color, so here you'll see that both of the top labels have a yellow highlight, as shown in Figure 5-11. You may also note that if the two labels weren't exactly the same width before you created this constraint, they certainly are now, as the existence of this new constraint snaps them into place.

Figure 5-11. The top labels are now made equal in width by a constraint

If you run again at this point, you should now be able to rotate the device and see the labels spread across the entire screen (see Figure 5-9).

In this example, all of our labels are visible and correctly laid out in multiple orientations; however, there is a lot of unused space on the screen. Perhaps it would be better if we also set up the other two rows of labels to fill the width of the view or allowed the height of our labels to change so that there will be less empty space on the interface? Feel free to experiment with the constraints of these six labels and perhaps even add some others. Apart from what we've covered so far, you'll find more actions that create constraints in the **Editor ➤ Pin** menu. And if you end up making a constraint that doesn't do what you want, you can delete it by selecting it and pressing the **Backspace** key, or try configuring it in the attributes inspector. Play around until you feel comfortable with the basics of how constraints work. We'll use them now and then throughout the book; but if you want the full details, just search for "auto layout" in Xcode's documentation window.

In the course of your experimentation, you're bound to notice that sometimes no combination of constraints will give you exactly what you want. In some cases, you'll need to rearrange your interface more drastically than can be handled with this technique. For those situations, a little more code is in order. Let's take a look at that next.

Restructuring a View When Rotated

Back in Xcode, make a new Single-View project like you've done before, naming this one *Restructure*. We're going to show you how to construct a layout that changes quite a bit between portrait and landscape by manually specifying frame rectangles for each component. We'll still use Interface Builder to configure our GUI and make connections between objects, but we'll use code to place each part of the GUI exactly where we want it.

We're going to construct a GUI that consists of one large content area and a small set of buttons that perform various actions. If the device is in portrait orientation, the buttons should be ordered in a small grid at the bottom of the screen; but in landscape orientation, they should be in a single column on the right. Figure 5-12 shows both alternatives.

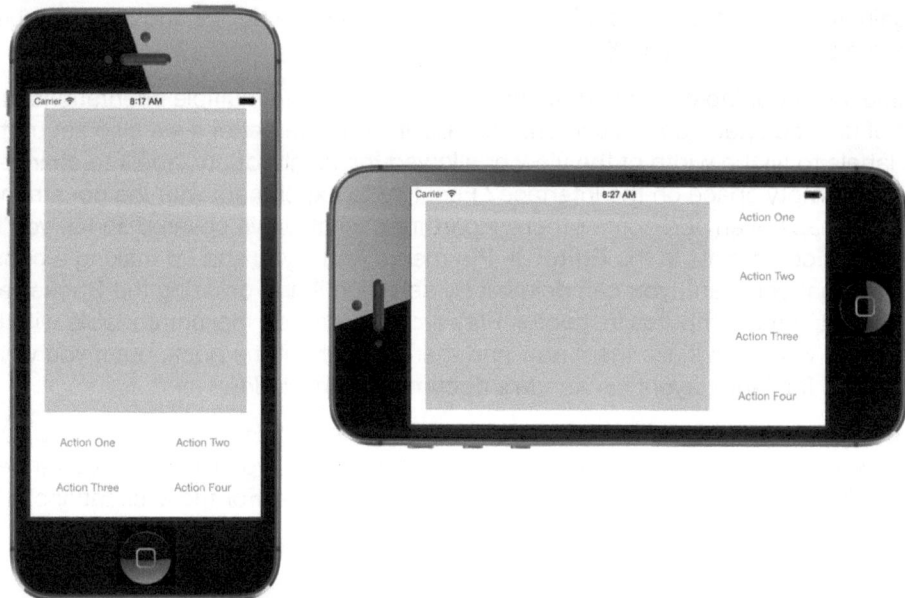

Figure 5-12. The final GUI of the Restructure app, shown in both orientations

Select *Main.storyboard* to start editing the GUI. Since we don't really have an interesting content view we want to display, we'll just use a large colored rectangle. Drag a single UIView from the object library into your container view. You'll notice as you do so that it expands to fill your container view completely, which is really not what we want. While it's still selected, use the size inspector to change the new view's width and height to 280 each. Next, switch over to the attributes inspector and use the *Background* pop-up to pick some other background color. You can choose anything you like, as long as it's not white, so that the view stands out from the background. Finally drag the view into the upper center of its superview (see Figure 5-13).

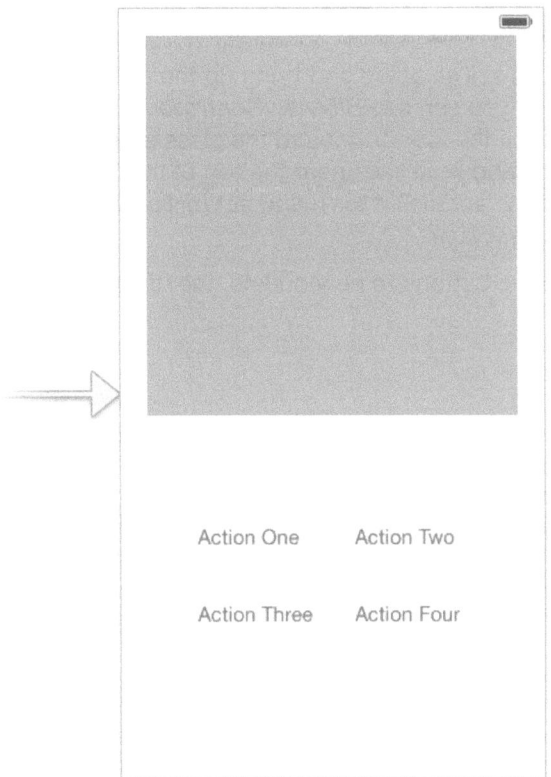

Figure 5-13. The basic portrait layout for the Restructure view

Now drag a button from the object library and place it in the lower part of the view. Double-click to select the text in its label, and change it to *Action One*. Now alt-drag three copies of this button and place them in a grid (see Figure 5-13). You don't have to line them up perfectly because we're going to adjust all their positions in code. Adjust the titles of three of them to *Action Two*, *Action Three*, and *Action Four*.

Can you guess what's going to happen now when we rotate the screen? Go ahead and run the app in the simulator to find out. Chances are, you won't be pleased. As usual, each view's position is based on keeping the same distance from the upper-left corner, which means the small views probably disappear off the bottom again.

There's really no way we can get the result we want here using constraints, so we'll fix this layout in our code instead. Before we write any layout code, we first need to disable the constraint system for the content of this nib file. Otherwise, the automatic constraints created by Xcode when our app is compiled would kick in during our view's layout, which would defeat the purpose of manually specifying the geometry of our GUI in code.

Press ⌥⌘1 to open the file inspector. In the middle of the Interface Builder Document section, you'll see a checkbox labeled *Use Autolayout*. Click to turn it off, which will make Interface Builder forget about constraints for this nib file. Now the layout of the view in this nib file is completely in your control.

Creating and Connecting Outlets

Make sure *Main.storyboard* is still selected and bring up the assistant editor (as you did in the previous chapter). Make sure you can see *BIDViewController.m* next to the GUI layout area, and then control-drag from each of the four buttons to the class extension in your code (the section between the first @interface and @end lines near the top of the file) to create four outlets called actionButton1, actionButton2, actionButton3, and actionButton4. Now do the same for the large view, naming this outlet contentView.

Once you've connected all five buttons to new outlets, the upper part of *BIDViewController.m* should look like this:

```
#import "BIDViewController.h"

@interface BIDViewController ()
@property (weak, nonatomic) IBOutlet UIButton *actionButton1;
@property (weak, nonatomic) IBOutlet UIButton *actionButton2;
@property (weak, nonatomic) IBOutlet UIButton *actionButton3;
@property (weak, nonatomic) IBOutlet UIButton *actionButton4;
@property (weak, nonatomic) IBOutlet UIView *contentView;

@end
```

Moving the Views on Rotation

To move these views around and make the best use of space, we need to override the method willAnimateRotationToInterfaceOrientation:duration: in *BIDViewController.m*. This method is called automatically after the device has been rotated into a new orientation, but before the final rotation animations have occurred.

Add the following method at the bottom of *BIDViewController.m*, just above the @end:

```
- (void)willAnimateRotationToInterfaceOrientation:(UIInterfaceOrientation)
            toInterfaceOrientation duration:(NSTimeInterval)duration {
  [self doLayoutForOrientation:toInterfaceOrientation];
}
```

As you can see, this method just passes the new orientation along to another method, one which you haven't written yet. We put this functionality into a new method for reasons that will become clear soon. Here's the new method:

```
- (void)doLayoutForOrientation:(UIInterfaceOrientation)orientation {
   if (UIInterfaceOrientationIsPortrait(orientation)) {
      [self layoutPortrait];
   } else {
      [self layoutLandscape];
   }
}
```

The doLayoutForOrientation: method simply passes control off to one of two other methods, which individually set up the views in the correct positions. We haven't defined those yet either, so here they are, along with some constant values we're going to use for some of our layout geometry:

```objc
static const CGFloat buttonHeight = 40;
static const CGFloat buttonWidth = 120;
static const CGFloat spacing = 20;

- (void)layoutPortrait {
    CGRect b = self.view.bounds;

    CGFloat contentWidth = CGRectGetWidth(b) - (2 * spacing);
    CGFloat contentHeight = CGRectGetHeight(b) - (4 * spacing) -
                            (2 * buttonHeight);

    self.contentView.frame = CGRectMake(spacing, spacing,
                                        contentWidth, contentHeight);

    CGFloat buttonRow1y = contentHeight + (2 * spacing);
    CGFloat buttonRow2y = buttonRow1y + buttonHeight +  spacing;

    CGFloat buttonCol1x = spacing;
    CGFloat buttonCol2x = CGRectGetWidth(b) - buttonWidth - spacing;

    self.actionButton1.frame = CGRectMake(buttonCol1x, buttonRow1y,
                                          buttonWidth, buttonHeight);

    self.actionButton2.frame = CGRectMake(buttonCol2x, buttonRow1y,
                                          buttonWidth, buttonHeight);

    self.actionButton3.frame = CGRectMake(buttonCol1x, buttonRow2y,
                                          buttonWidth, buttonHeight);

    self.actionButton4.frame = CGRectMake(buttonCol2x, buttonRow2y,
                                          buttonWidth, buttonHeight);
}

- (void)layoutLandscape {
    CGRect b = self.view.bounds;

    CGFloat contentWidth = CGRectGetWidth(b) - buttonWidth - (3 * spacing);
    CGFloat contentHeight = CGRectGetHeight(b) - (2 * spacing);

    self.contentView.frame = CGRectMake(spacing, spacing,
                                        contentWidth, contentHeight);

    CGFloat buttonX = CGRectGetWidth(b) - buttonWidth - spacing;
    CGFloat buttonRow1y = spacing;
    CGFloat buttonRow4y = CGRectGetHeight(b) - buttonHeight - spacing;
    CGFloat buttonRow2y = buttonRow1y + floor((buttonRow4y - buttonRow1y)
                                        * 0.333);
```

```
CGFloat buttonRow3y = buttonRow1y + floor((buttonRow4y - buttonRow1y)
                                          * 0.667);

self.actionButton1.frame = CGRectMake(buttonX, buttonRow1y,
                                      buttonWidth, buttonHeight);

self.actionButton2.frame = CGRectMake(buttonX, buttonRow2y,
                                      buttonWidth, buttonHeight);

self.actionButton3.frame = CGRectMake(buttonX, buttonRow3y,
                                      buttonWidth, buttonHeight);

self.actionButton4.frame = CGRectMake(buttonX, buttonRow4y,
                                      buttonWidth, buttonHeight);
}
```

Each of those methods functions in a similar way, but they achieve different results. They first store the superview's bounds rectangle in a local variable for the sake of convenience. Next, they use that rectangle's size and our geometry constants to figure out a good position for the big content view, and then set that view's frame so that it ends up in the right spot. After that, some button positions are calculated, and each button's frame is adjusted so that they all end up in the right places, too.

That's the 10,000-foot view, but there are lots of interesting details here. The size and position of all views, including controls such as buttons, are specified in properties called frame and bounds, both of which are structs of type CGRect. The difference between the two is this. A view's frame describes its location within its parent view's coordinate system, while a view's bounds describe its own coordinate system, which is useful in case you want to figure out where subviews belong. There are many ways of using these values, but one of the most typical uses is the kind of thing we're doing here: using the position of one or more objects to decide the position of another. As a rule, if you want to calculate a view's position, you are likely to read a parent view's bounds or a sibling view's frame to base things on—you end up setting the target view's frame to put it in its place. We'll see more of this throughout the book.

Apart from that, the Apple-provided CGRectMake() function lets you easily create a CGRect by specifying the x and y positions along with the width and height. We also use the CGRectGetHeight() and CGRectGetWidth() functions here, which simply tell you the height and width, respectively, of a given CGRect.

> **Note**   You may have noticed something in this code that you haven't seen before. Remember when we created properties for all those buttons using Interface Builder's drag-to-code feature? Those properties declare the existence of methods for each button, allowing us to access their values by calling the methods or by using Objective-C's dot notation (e.g., `[self contentView]` or `self.contentView`). In the past, you were required to create those methods in your *.m* file, either by really implementing them with code or by using the `@synthesize` declaration to have them made for you. If you did any Objective-C development before 2012 or so, you probably remember doing this sort of thing a lot.
>
> Over the past few years, this behavior has been tweaked a bit. If you leave out the `@synthesize` declaration, as the click-to-code feature now does, the compiler just creates those methods for you, anyway. At the same time, it creates an instance variable, the name of which is established by putting an underscore in front of the method name. In concrete terms, take a look at this line of code:
>
> `@synthesize bigButton = _bigButton;`
>
> In modern versions of Xcode (4.4 and up), that line of code is now completely redundant. If your property declarations look just like that, you can leave them out entirely. Unless you really want to use a different naming convention for your instance variables, you should be able to skip the step of explicitly synthesizing accessors entirely.

There's one more thing to do here before we're done. Since we've gone to all the trouble of setting exact positions for all our GUI elements in code, we should use that code for all of our GUI layout, including the moment when the view objects have just been loaded from the storyboard or nib file. Add the bold lines shown here to the viewDidLoad method to make this happen:

```
- (void)viewDidLoad
{
    [super viewDidLoad];
    // Do any additional setup after loading the view, typically from a nib.
    UIApplication *app = [UIApplication sharedApplication];
    UIInterfaceOrientation currentOrientation = app.statusBarOrientation;
    [self doLayoutForOrientation:currentOrientation];
}
```

Here we're grabbing the shared instance of the UIApplication class and asking it for its statusBarOrientation. This tells us in which direction the screen is oriented when the view loads. We pass that along to the doLayoutForOrientation: method that we wrote earlier, so that it will position all of our GUI elements properly.

Save this code. Now build and run the application to see it in action. Try rotating and watch how the buttons slide over to new positions, nicely lined up along the right side of the screen. Rotate back, and they go right back to where they started from. Smooth! You should also try running in different simulated devices. Xcode lets you choose whether you want to run as a 3.5-inch or 4-inch iPhone. Both should work equally well.

Rotating Out of Here

In this chapter, you tried out a few different approaches to supporting autorotation in your applications. You learned about using constraints to define view layout; and you also saw how to restructure your views, in code, when the iOS device rotates.

In the next chapter, we're going to start looking at true multiview applications. Every application we've written so far has used a single view controller and a single content view. A lot of complex iOS applications, such as Mail and Contacts, are made possible only by the use of multiple views and view controllers, and we're going to look at exactly how that works in Chapter 6.

Multiview Applications

Up until this point, we've written applications with a single view controller. While there certainly is a lot you can do with a single view, the real power of the iOS platform emerges when you can switch out views based on user input. Multiview applications come in several different flavors, but the underlying mechanism is the same, regardless of how the app may appear on the screen.

In this chapter, we're going to focus on the structure of multiview applications and the basics of swapping content views by building our own multiview application from scratch. We will write our own custom controller class that switches between two different content views, establishing a strong foundation for taking advantage of the various multiview controllers that Apple provides.

But before we start building our application, let's see how multiple-view applications can be useful.

Common Types of Multiview Apps

Strictly speaking, we have worked with multiple views in our previous applications since buttons, labels, and other controls are all subclasses of UIView, and they can all go into the view hierarchy. But when Apple uses the term **view** in documentation, it is generally referring to a UIView or one of its subclasses that has a corresponding view controller. These types of views are also sometimes referred to as **content views** because they are the primary container for the content of your application.

The simplest example of a multiview application is a utility application. A utility application focuses primarily on a single view, but offers a second view that can be used to configure the application or to provide more detail than the primary view. The Stocks application that ships with iPhone is a good example (see Figure 6-1). If you click the button in the lower-right corner, the view transitions to a configuration view that lets you configure the list of stocks tracked by the application.

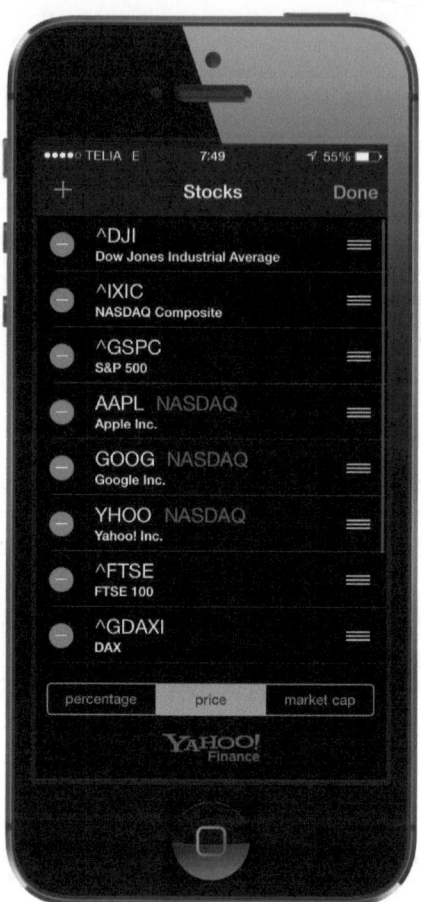

Figure 6-1. *The Stocks application that ships with iPhone has two views: one to display the data and another to configure the stock list*

There are also several tab bar applications that ship with the iPhone, including the Phone application (see Figure 6-2) and the Clock application. A tab bar application is a multiview application that displays a row of buttons, called the **tab bar**, at the bottom of the screen. Tapping one of the buttons causes a new view controller to become active and a new view to be shown. In the Phone application, for example, tapping *Contacts* shows a different view than the one shown when you tap *Keypad*.

Figure 6-2. The Phone application is an example of a multiview application using a tab bar

Another common kind of multiview iPhone application is the navigation-based application, which features a navigation controller that uses a **navigation bar** to control a hierarchical series of views. The Settings application is a good example. In Settings, the first view you get is a series of rows, each row corresponding to a cluster of settings or a specific app. Touching one of those rows takes you to a new view where you can customize one particular set of settings. Some views present a list that allows you to dive even deeper. The navigation controller keeps track of how deep you go and gives you a control to let you make your way back to the previous view.

For example, if you select the *Sounds* preference, you'll be presented a view with a list of sound-related options. At the top of that view is a navigation bar with a left arrow labeled *Settings* that takes you back to the previous view if you tap it. Within the sound options is a row labeled *Ringtone*. Tap *Ringtone*, and you're taken to a new view featuring a list of ringtones and a navigation bar that takes you back to the main *Sounds* preference view (see Figure 6-3). A navigation-based application is useful when you want to present a hierarchy of views.

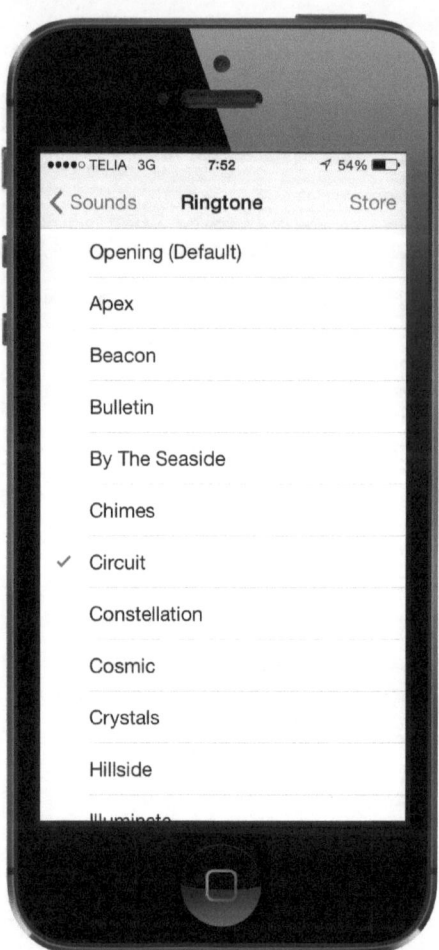

Figure 6-3. The iPhone Settings application is an example of a multiview application using a navigation bar

On the iPad, most navigation-based applications, such as Mail, are implemented using a **split view**, where the navigation elements appear on the left side of the screen, and the item you select to view or edit appears on the right. You'll learn more about split views and other iPad-specific GUI elements in Chapter 10.

Because views are themselves hierarchical in nature, it's even possible to combine different mechanisms for swapping views within a single application. For example, the iPhone's Music application uses a tab bar to switch between different methods of organizing your music, and a navigation controller and its associated navigation bar to allow you to browse your music based on that selection. In Figure 6-4, the tab bar is at the bottom of the screen, and the navigation bar is at the top of the screen.

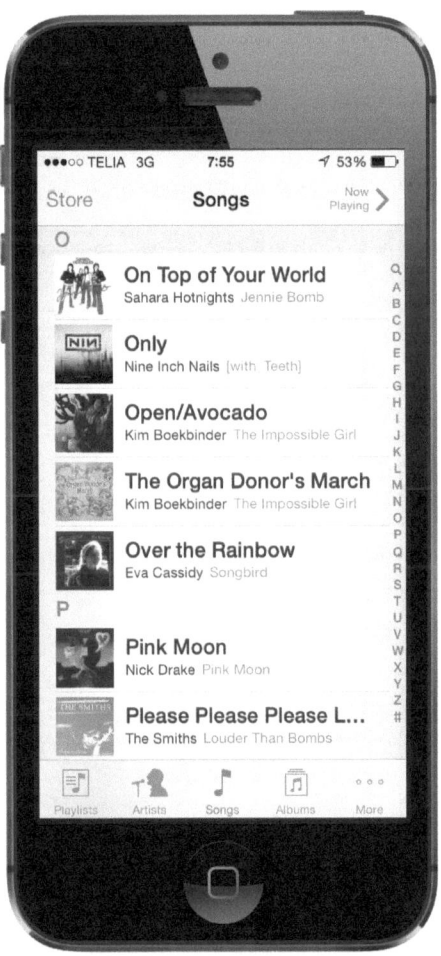

Figure 6-4. The Music application uses both a navigation bar and a tab bar

Some applications use a **toolbar**, which is often confused with a tab bar. A tab bar is used for selecting one and only one option from among two or more options. A toolbar can hold buttons and certain other controls, but those items are not mutually exclusive. A perfect example of a toolbar is at the bottom of the main Safari view (see Figure 6-5). If you compare the toolbar at the bottom of the Safari view with the tab bar at the bottom of the Phone or Music application, you'll find the two pretty easy to tell apart. The tab bar has multiple segments, exactly one of which (the selected one) is highlighted with a tint color; but on a toolbar, normally every enabled button is highlighted.

Figure 6-5. *Mobile Safari features a toolbar at the bottom. The toolbar is like a free-form bar that allows you to include a variety of controls*

Each of these multiview application types uses a specific controller class from the UIKit. Tab bar interfaces are implemented using the class UITabBarController, and navigation interfaces are implemented using UINavigationController. We'll describe their use in detail in the next few chapters.

The Architecture of a Multiview Application

The application we're going to build in this chapter, View Switcher, is fairly simple in appearance; however, in terms of the code we're going to write, it's by far the most complex application we've yet tackled. View Switcher will consist of three different controllers, a storyboard, and an application delegate.

When first launched, View Switcher will look like Figure 6-6, with a toolbar at the bottom containing a single button. The rest of the view will contain a blue background and a button yearning to be pressed.

Figure 6-6. *When you first launch the View Switcher application, you'll see a blue view with a button and a toolbar with its own button*

When the *Switch Views* button is pressed, the background will turn yellow, and the button's title will change (see Figure 6-7).

Figure 6-7. *When you press the Switch Views button, the blue view flips over to reveal the yellow view*

If either the *Press Me* or *Press Me, Too* button is pressed, an alert will pop up indicating which view's button was pressed (see Figure 6-8).

Figure 6-8. *When the Press Me or Press Me, Too button is pressed, an alert is displayed*

Although we could achieve this same functionality by writing a single-view application, we're taking this more complex approach to demonstrate the mechanics of a multiview application. There are actually three view controllers interacting in this simple application: one that controls the blue view, one that controls the yellow view, and a third special controller that swaps the other two in and out when the *Switch Views* button is pressed.

Before we start building our application, let's talk about the way iPhone multiview applications are put together. Most multiview applications use the same basic pattern.

The Root Controller

The storyboard is a key player here since it will contain all the views and view controllers for our application. We're going to make an empty storyboard, and then we'll add an instance of a controller class that is responsible for managing which other view is currently being shown to the user. We call this controller the **root controller** (as in "the root of the tree" or "the root of all evil") because it is the first controller the user sees and the controller that is loaded when the application loads. This root controller is often an instance of `UINavigationController` or `UITabBarController`, although it can also be a custom subclass of `UIViewController`.

In a multiview application, the job of the root controller is to take two or more other views and present them to the user as appropriate, based on the user's input. A tab bar controller, for example, will swap in different views and view controllers based on which tab bar item was last tapped. A navigation controller will do the same thing as the user drills down and backs up through hierarchical data.

> **Note**   The root controller is the primary view controller for the application; and, as such, it is the view that specifies whether it is OK to automatically rotate to a new orientation. However, the root controller can pass responsibility for tasks like that to the currently active controller.

In multiview applications, most of the screen will be taken up by a content view, and each content view will have its own controller with its own outlets and actions. In a tab bar application, for example, taps on the tab bar will go to the tab bar controller, but taps anywhere else on the screen will go to the controller that corresponds to the content view currently being displayed.

Anatomy of a Content View

In a multiview application, each view controller controls a content view, and these content views are where the bulk of your application's user interface is built. Taken together, each of these pairings is called a **scene** within a storyboard. Each scene consists of a view controller and a content view, which may be an instance of `UIView` or one of its subclasses. Unless you are doing something really unusual, your content view will always have an associated view controller and will sometimes subclass `UIView`. Although you can create your interface in code rather than using Interface Builder, few people choose that route because it is more time-consuming and the code is difficult to maintain.

In this project, we'll be creating a new controller class for each content view. Our root controller controls a content view that consists of a toolbar that occupies the bottom of the screen. The root controller then loads a blue view controller, placing the blue content view as a subview to the root controller view. When the root controller's *Switch Views* button (the button is in the toolbar) is pressed, the root controller swaps out the blue view controller and swaps in a yellow view controller, instantiating that controller if it needs to do so. Confused? If so, don't worry because this will become clearer as we walk through the code.

Building View Switcher

Enough theory! Let's go ahead and build our project. Select **File ➤ New ➤ Project...** or press ⇧⌘N. When the template selection sheet opens, select *Empty Application* (see Figure 6-9), and then click *Next*. On the next page of the assistant, enter *View Switcher* as the *Product Name*, leave *BID* as the *Class Prefix*, and set the *Device Family* pop-up button to *iPhone*. Also make sure the checkbox labeled *Use Core Data* is unchecked. When everything is set up correctly, click *Next* to continue. On the next screen, navigate to wherever you're saving your projects on disk and click the *Create* button to create a new project directory.

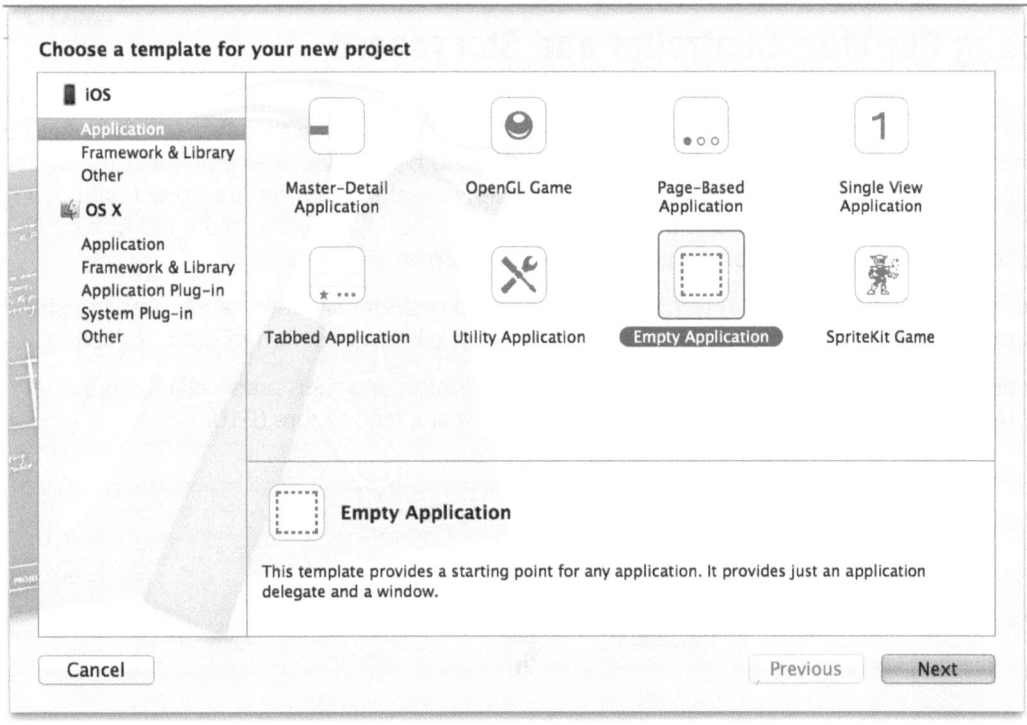

Figure 6-9. *Creating a new project using the Empty Application project template*

The template we just selected is actually even simpler than the *Single View Application* template we've been using up to now. This template will give us an application delegate that creates its own window, an asset catalog, and nothing else—no views, no controllers, no nothing.

> **Note**   The **window** is the most basic container in iOS. Each app has exactly one window that belongs to it, though it is possible to see more than one window on the screen at a time. For example, if your app is running and your device receives an SMS or iMessage, you'll see the message displayed in its own window, in front of your app's window. Your app can't access that overlaid window because it belongs to the Messages app.

You won't use the *Empty Application* template very often when you're creating applications; but by starting from nothing in this example, you'll really get a feel for the way multiview applications are put together.

If they're not expanded already, take a second to expand the *View Switcher* folder in the project navigator, as well as the *Supporting Files* folder it contains. Inside the *View Switcher* folder, you'll find the two files that implement the application delegate. Within the *Supporting Files* folder, you'll find the *View Switcher-Info.plist* file, the *InfoPlist.strings* file (which contains the localized versions of your *Info.plist* file), the standard *main.m*, and the precompiled header file (*View Switcher-Prefix.pch*). Everything else we need for our application, we must create.

Creating Our View Controller and Storyboard

One of the more daunting aspects of building a multiview application from scratch is that we need to create several interconnected objects. We're going to create all the files that will make up our application before we do anything in Interface Builder and before we write any code. By creating all the files first, we'll be able to use Xcode's Code Sense feature to write our code faster. If a class hasn't been declared, Code Sense has no way to know about it, so we would need to type its name in full every time, which takes longer and is more error-prone.

Fortunately, in addition to project templates, Xcode also provides file templates for many standard file types, which helps simplify the process of creating the basic skeleton of our application.

Single-click the *View Switcher* folder in the project navigator, and then press ⌘**N** or select **File ➤ New ➤ File....** Take a look at the window that opens (see Figure 6-10).

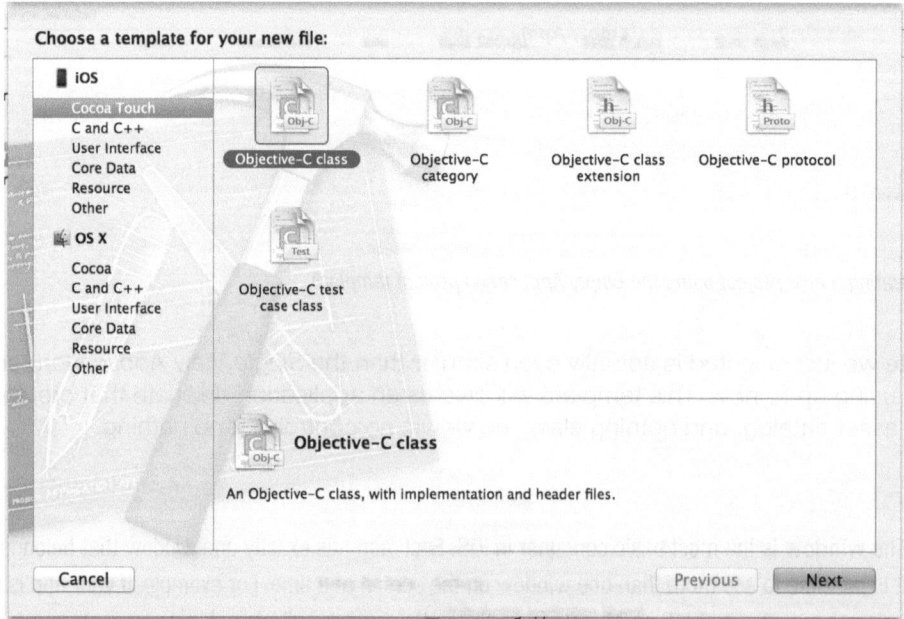

Figure 6-10. The template we'll use to create a new view controller subclass

If you select *Cocoa Touch* from the left pane, you will be given templates for a number of common Objective-C constructs, such as classes, categories, and so on. Select *Objective-C Class* and click *Next*. On the next page of the assistant, you'll see two fields labeled *Class* and *Subclass of*. In the *Subclass of* field, enter *UIViewController* to tell Xcode which existing class should be the parent of our new class. You'll see that Xcode starts to fill in a value in the *Class* text field. Change that value to *BIDSwitchViewController*, and then direct your attention to the other controls that let you configure the subclass:

- The second is a checkbox labeled *Targeted for iPad*. If it's checked by default, you should uncheck it now (since we're not making an iPad GUI).

- The third is another checkbox, labeled *With XIB for user interface*. If that box is checked, uncheck it as well. If you left that checkbox checked, Xcode would create a nib file that corresponds to this controller class. We're going to define our entire GUI in one storyboard file instead, so leave this unchecked.

Click *Next*. A window appears that lets you choose a particular directory in which to save the files and pick a group and target for your files. By default, this window will show the directory most relevant to the folder you selected in the project navigator. For the sake of consistency, you'll want to save the new class into the *View Switcher* folder, which Xcode set up when you created this project; it should already contain the BIDAppDelegate class. That's where Xcode puts all of the Objective-C classes that are created as part of the project, and it's as good a place as any for you to put your own classes.

About halfway down the window, you'll find the *Group* pop-up list. You'll want to add the new files to the *View Switcher* group. Finally, make sure the *View Switcher* target is selected in the *Targets* list before clicking the *Create* button.

Xcode should add two files to your *View Switcher* folder: *BIDSwitchViewController.h* and *BIDSwitchViewController.m*. BIDSwitchViewController will be your root controller—the controller that swaps the other views in and out. Now, we need to create the controllers for the two content views that will be swapped in and out. Repeat the same steps two more times to create *BIDBlueViewController.m*, *BIDYellowViewController.m*, and their *.h* counterparts, adding them to the same spot in the project hierarchy.

> **Caution**   Make sure you check your spelling, as a typo here will create classes that don't match the source code later in the chapter.

Our next step is to create a storyboard, where we'll later configure a scene for each of the content views we just created. Single-click the *View Switcher* folder in the project navigator, and then press ⌘ **N** or select **File ➤ New ➤ File....** again. This time, select *User Interface* under the *iOS* heading in the left pane (see Figure 6-11). Next, select the icon for the *Storyboard* template, which will create an empty storyboard. Click *Next*. On the next screen, select *iPhone* from the *Device Family* pop-up, and then click the *Next* button.

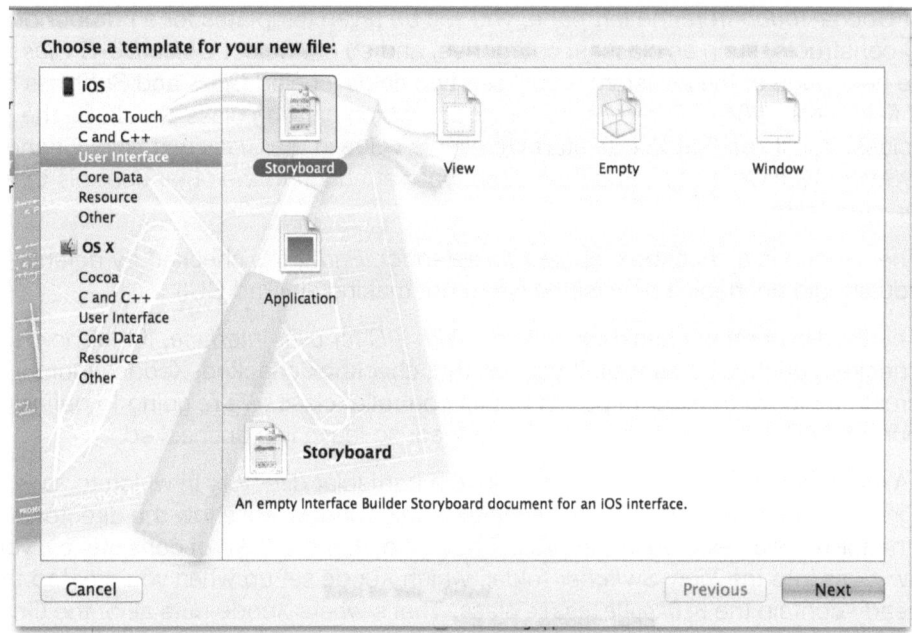

Figure 6-11. We're creating a new storyboard, using the View template in the User Interface section

When prompted for a file name, type *Main.storyboard*. Just as you did earlier, you should choose the *View Switcher* folder as the save location next to the *Where* pop-up menu. Make sure that *View Switcher* is selected from the *Group* pop-up menu and that the *View Switcher* target is checked, and then click *Create*. You'll know you succeeded when the file *Main.storyboard* appears in the *View Switcher* group in the project navigator.

After you've done that, you have all the files you need. It's time to start hooking everything together. The first step in doing so is letting Xcode know that it should use the storyboard you just created as the starting point from which it should bootstrap the app's GUI. To do this, select the uppermost *View Switcher* item in the project navigator, and then switch to the *General* tab in the editing area. This brings up a multi-section configuration view. In the *Deployment Info* section, use the *Main Interface* pop-up menu to choose *Main.storyboard*. With that in place, the app will automatically create its initial interface from the contents of the storyboard when it launches. We haven't gone over this before, but every project we've created before this one had the exact same configuration from the start, thanks to Xcode's *Single View Application* project template.

Modifying the App Delegate

Our first stop on the multiview express is the application delegate. Single-click the file *BIDAppDelegate.m* in the project navigator (make sure it's the app delegate and not *BIDSwitchViewController.m*) and make the following changes to that file:

```
- (BOOL)application:(UIApplication *)application
didFinishLaunchingWithOptions:(NSDictionary *)launchOptions
{
```

```
———  self.window = [[UIWindow alloc] initWithFrame:
———                    [[UIScreen mainScreen] bounds]];
———  // Override point for customization after application launch.
———  self.window.backgroundColor = [UIColor whiteColor];
———  [self.window makeKeyAndVisible];
    return YES;
}
```

What you want to do is delete the lines shown with a line drawn through them. In a completely empty application like the one we started off with, it's necessary to manually create the application window in code. Since we're going to load our GUI from the storyboard, that code is unnecessary and can be deleted.

Modifying BIDSwitchViewController.m

Because we're going to be setting up an instance of BIDSwitchViewController in *Main.storyboard*, now is the time to add any needed outlets or actions to the *BIDSwitchViewController.m* file.

We'll need one action method to toggle between the blue and yellow views. We won't create any outlets, but we will need two other pointers: one to each of the view controllers that we'll be swapping in and out. These don't need to be outlets because we're going to create them in code rather than in the storyboard. Add the following code to the upper part of *BIDSwitchViewController.m*:

```
#import "BIDSwitchViewController.h"

#import "BIDYellowViewController.h"
#import "BIDBlueViewController.h"

@interface BIDSwitchViewController ()

@property (strong, nonatomic) BIDYellowViewController *yellowViewController;
@property (strong, nonatomic) BIDBlueViewController *blueViewController;

@end
```

Next, add the following empty action method toward the end of the file, just before the final @end line:

```
- (IBAction)switchViews:(id)sender
{

}

@end
```

In the past, we've added action methods directly within Interface Builder, but here you'll see that we can work the other way around just as well, since IB can see what outlets and actions are already defined in our source code. Now that we've declared the action we need, we can set this controller up in our storyboard.

Adding a View Controller

Save your source code and click *Main.storyboard* to edit the GUI for this app. You'll see a completely blank editing area, with no views or controllers in sight. Use the object library to find a View Controller and drag it into the editing area. You'll now see the familiar view of an iPhone-sized rectangle with a row of icons below it.

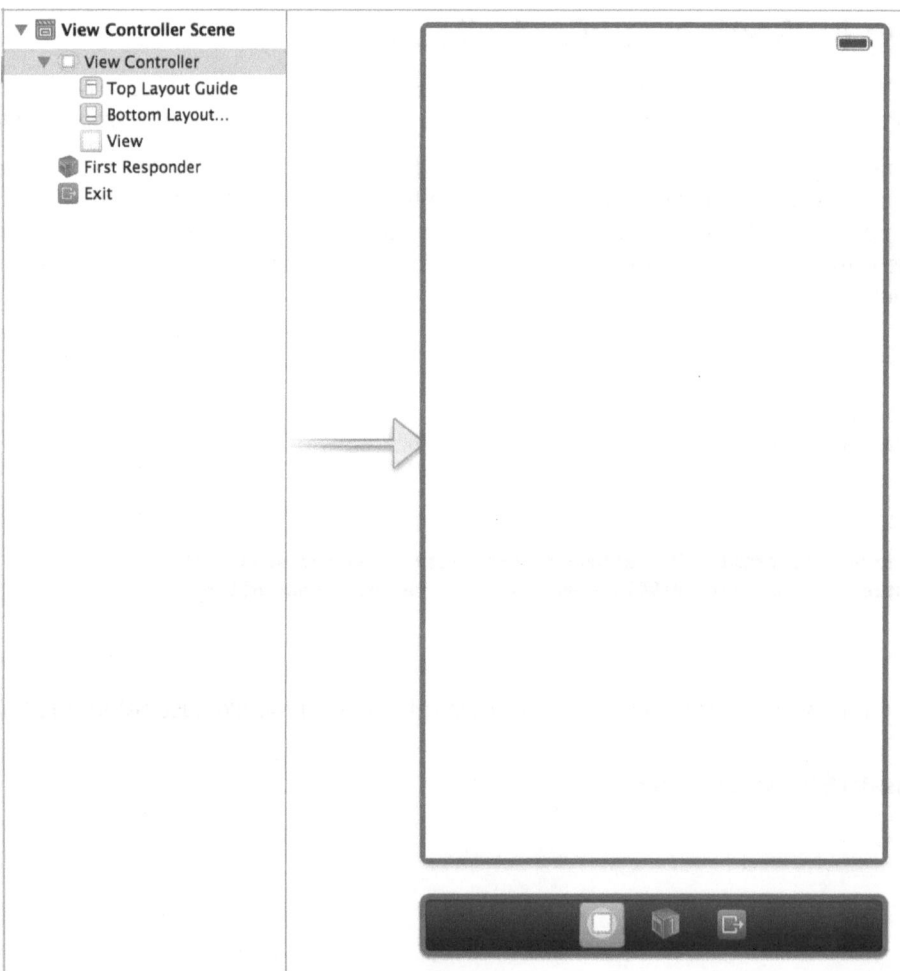

Figure 6-12. Main.storyboard, showing the first scene this app will use

By default, the view controller in this scene is configured to be an instance of UIViewController. We'll need to change that to BIDSwitchViewController so that Interface Builder allows us to build connections to the BIDSwitchViewController outlets and actions. Single-click the *View Controller* icon at the bottom of the scene and press ⌥⌘3 to open the identity inspector (see Figure 6-13).

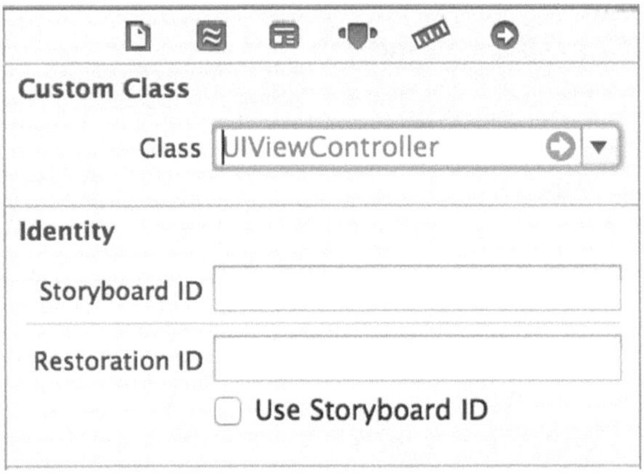

Figure 6-13. Notice that the Custom Class field is currently set to UIViewController in the identity inspector. We're about to change that to BIDSwitchViewController

The identity inspector allows you to specify the class of the currently selected object. Our view controller is currently specified as a *UIViewController*, and it has no actions defined. Click inside the combo box labeled *Class* in the *Custom Class* section, which is at the top of the inspector and currently reads *UIViewController*. Change this to *BIDSwitchViewController*.

Once you make that change, press ⌥⌘6 to switch to the connections inspector, where you will see that the switchViews: action method now appears in the section labeled *Received Actions* (see Figure 6-14). The connection inspector's *Received Actions* section shows all the actions defined for the current class. When we changed our view controller to a BIDSwitchViewController, the BIDSwitchViewController action switchViews: became available for connection. You'll see how to use this action in the next section.

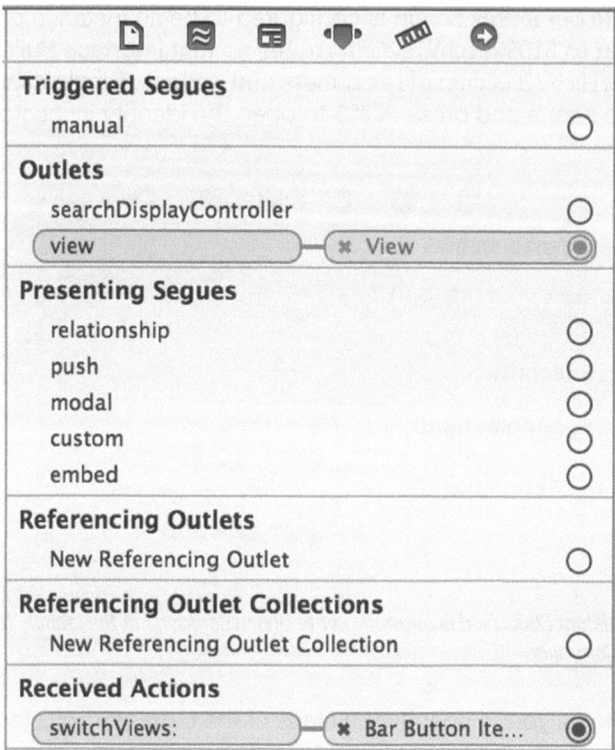

Figure 6-14. The connections inspector showing that the switchViews: action has been added to the Received Actions section

Caution   If you don't see the switchViews: action as shown in Figure 6-14, check the spelling of your class file names. If you don't get the name exactly right, things won't match up. Watch your spelling!

Save your storyboard and move to the next step.

Building a View with a Toolbar

We now need to set up the view for BIDSwitchViewController. As a reminder, this new view controller will be our root view controller—the controller that is in play when our application is launched. BIDSwitchViewController's content view will consist of a toolbar that occupies the bottom of the screen. Its job is to switch between the blue view and the yellow view, so it will need a way for the user to change the views. For that, we're going to use a toolbar with a button. Let's build the toolbar view now.

In the IB editor view, click the view for the scene you just added. The view is an instance of UIView, and as you can see in Figure 6-15, it's currently empty and quite dull. This is where we'll start building our GUI.

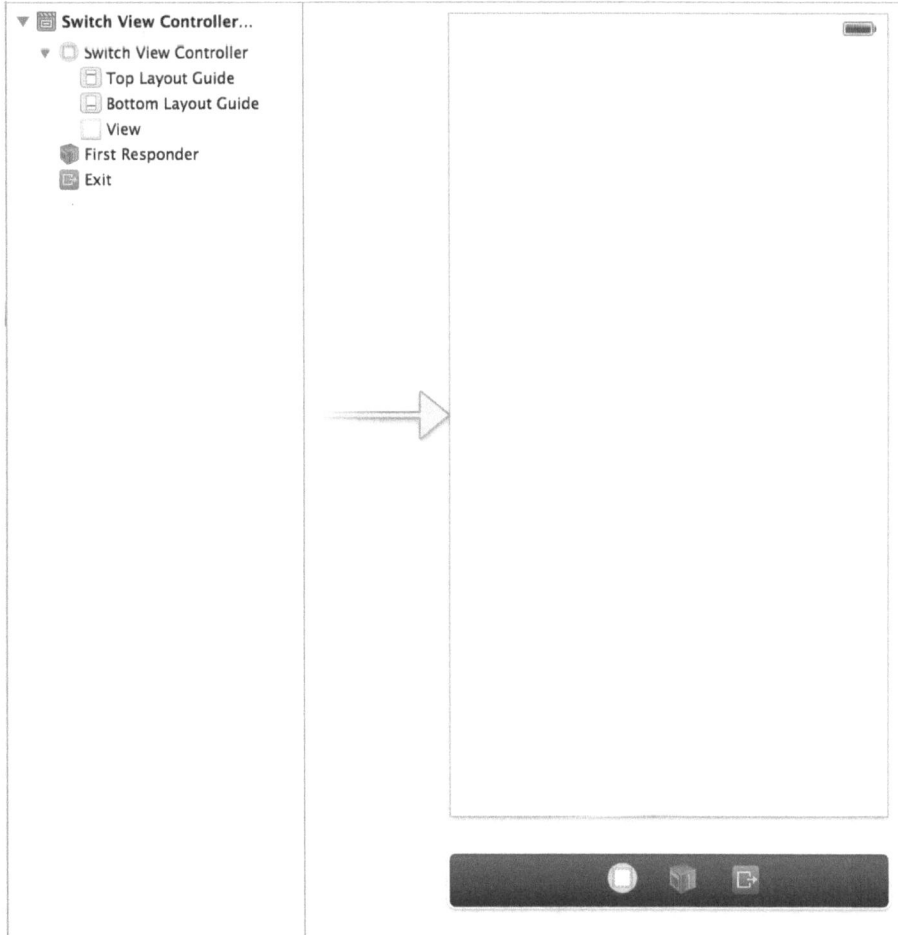

Figure 6-15. The new empty view contained within our storyboard, just waiting to be filled with interesting stuff

Now, let's add a toolbar to the bottom of the view. Grab a *Toolbar* from the library, drag it onto your view, and place it at the bottom, so that it looks like Figure 6-16. We want to keep this toolbar at the bottom of the view no matter what size the view has. To do so, select **Editor ➤ Pin ➤ Bottom Space to Superview**. This creates a constraint that makes that happen.

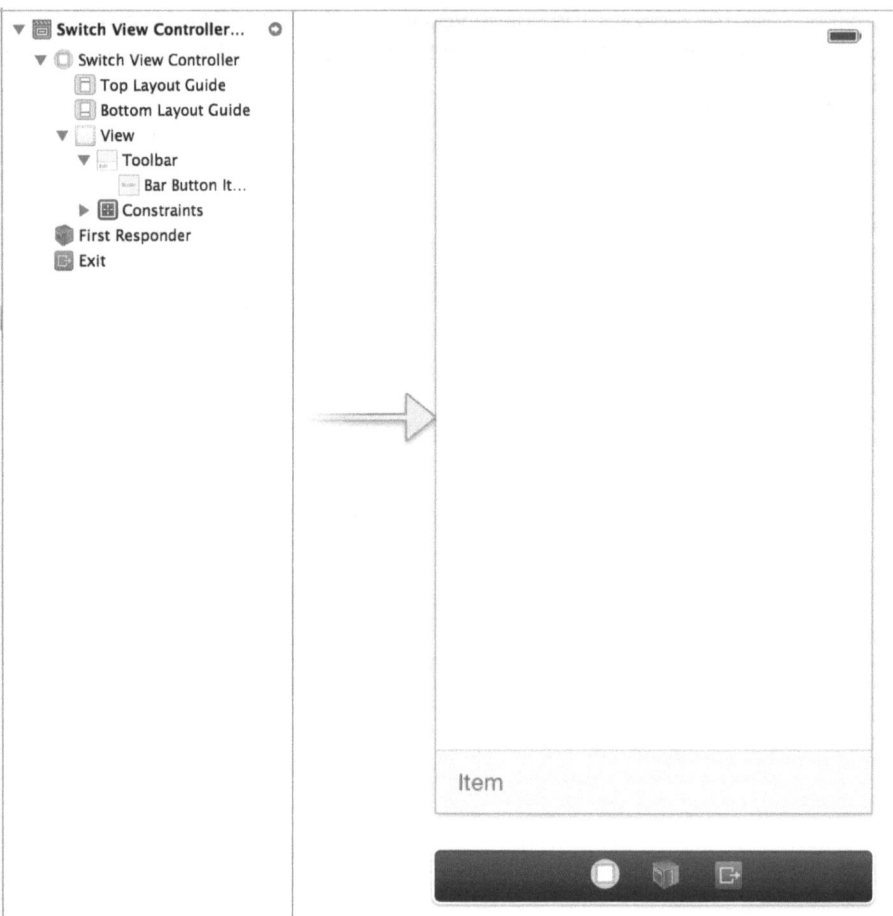

Figure 6-16. We dragged a toolbar onto our view. Notice that the toolbar features a single button, labeled Item

Now, to make sure you're on the right track, click the Run button to make this app launch in the iOS Simulator. You should see a plain white app start up, with a pale gray toolbar at the bottom containing a lone button. If not, go back and retrace your steps to see what you missed.

The toolbar features a single button. We'll use that button to let the user switch between the different content views. Double-click the button and change its title to *Switch Views*. Press the **Return** key to commit your change.

Now we can link the toolbar button to our action method. Before doing that, though, you should be aware that toolbar buttons aren't like other iOS controls. They support only a single target action, and they trigger that action only at one well-defined moment—the equivalent of a touch up inside event on other iOS controls.

Selecting a toolbar button in Interface Builder can be tricky. Click the view so we are all starting in the same place. Now single-click the toolbar button. Notice that this selects the toolbar, not the button. Click the button a second time. This should select the button itself. You can confirm you have the button selected by switching to the object attributes inspector (⌥⌘4) and making sure the top group name is *Bar Button Item*.

Once you have the *Switch Views* button selected, control-drag from it over to the *Switch View Controller* icon at the bottom of the scene, and select the *switchViews:* action. If the *switchViews:* action doesn't pop up, and instead you see an outlet called *delegate*, you've most likely control-dragged from the toolbar rather than the button. To fix it, just make sure you have the button rather than the toolbar selected, and then redo your control-drag.

> **Tip**   Remember that you can always view the document outline by clicking the button in the lower-left corner of IB's editor area or by selecting **Editor ➤ Show Document Outline** from the menu. In the document outline, you can use the disclosure triangles to drill down through the hierarchy to get to any element in the view hierarchy.

We have one more thing to point out in this scene, which is BIDSwitchViewController's view outlet. This outlet is already connected to the view in the scene. The view outlet is inherited from the parent class, UIViewController and gives the controller access to the view it controls. When we dragged out a View Controller scene from the object library, IB created both the controller and the view, and hooked them up for us. Nice.

That's all we need to do here, so save your work. Next, let's get started implementing BIDSwitchViewController.

Writing the Root View Controller

It's time to write our root view controller. Its job is to switch between the blue view and the yellow view whenever the user clicks the *Switch Views* button.

In the project navigator, select *BIDSwitchViewController.m* and modify the viewDidLoad method to set some things up by adding the lines shown here in bold:

```
- (void)viewDidLoad
{
    [super viewDidLoad];
    // Do any additional setup after loading the view.
    self.blueViewController = [self.storyboard
                              instantiateViewControllerWithIdentifier:
                              @"Blue"];
    [self.view insertSubview:self.blueViewController.view atIndex:0];

}
```

Now fill in the switchViews: method you created earlier by adding the cold shown in bold:

```
- (IBAction)switchViews:(id)sender
{
    if (!self.yellowViewController.view.superview) {
        if (!self.yellowViewController) {
            self.yellowViewController = [self.storyboard
                instantiateViewControllerWithIdentifier:@"Yellow"];
        }
```

```
        [self.blueViewController.view removeFromSuperview];
        [self.view insertSubview:self.yellowViewController.view atIndex:0];
    } else {
        if (!self.blueViewController) {
            self.blueViewController = [self.storyboard
                instantiateViewControllerWithIdentifier:@"Blue"];
        }
        [self.yellowViewController.view removeFromSuperview];
        [self.view insertSubview:self.blueViewController.view atIndex:0];
    }
}
```

Also, add this code to the existing didReceiveMemoryWarning method:

```
- (void)didReceiveMemoryWarning {
    [super didReceiveMemoryWarning];
    // Dispose of any resources that can be recreated.
    if (!self.blueViewController.view.superview) {
        self.blueViewController = nil;
    } else {
        self.yellowViewController = nil;
    }
}
```

The first method we modified, viewDidLoad, overrides a UIViewController method that is called when the storyboard is loaded. How could we tell? Hold down the ⌥ key (the **Option** key) and single-click the method name viewDidLoad. A documentation pop-up window will appear (see Figure 6-17). Alternatively, you can select **View ➤ Utilities ➤ Show Quick Help Inspector** to view similar information in the Quick Help panel. viewDidLoad is defined in our superclass, UIViewController, and is intended to be overridden by classes that need to be notified when the view has finished loading.

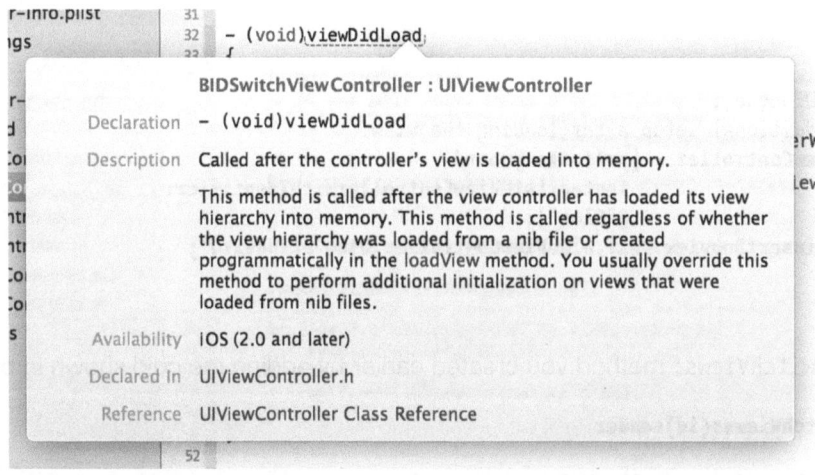

Figure 6-17. This documentation window appears when you option-click the viewDidLoad method name

This version of viewDidLoad creates an instance of BIDBlueViewController. We use the instantiateViewControllerWithIdentifier: method to load the BIDBlueViewController instance from the same storyboard that contains our root view controller. To access a particular view controller from a storyboard, we use a string as an identifier—in this case "Blue" —which we'll set up when we configure our storyboard a little more. Once the BIDBlueViewController is created, we assign this new instance to our blueViewController property:

```
self.blueViewController = [self.storyboard
                             instantiateViewControllerWithIdentifier:@"Blue"];
```

Next, we insert the blue view as a subview of the root view. We insert it at index zero, which tells iOS to put this view behind everything else. Sending the view to the back ensures that the toolbar we created in Interface Builder a moment ago will always be visible on the screen, since we're inserting the content views behind it:

```
[self.view insertSubview:self.blueViewController.view atIndex:0];
```

Now, why didn't we load the yellow view here also? We're going to need to load it at some point, so why not do it now? Good question. The answer is that the user may never tap the *Switch Views* button. The user might just use the view that's visible when the application launches, and then quit. In that case, why use resources to load the yellow view and its controller?

Instead, we'll load the yellow view the first time we actually need it. This is called **lazy loading**, and it's a standard way of keeping memory overhead down. The actual loading of the yellow view happens in the switchViews: method, so let's take a look at that.

switchViews: first checks which view is being swapped in by seeing whether yellowViewController's view's superview is nil. This will return true if one of two things is true:

- ▪ If yellowViewController exists but its view is not being shown to the user, that view will not have a superview because it's not presently in the view hierarchy, and the expression will evaluate to true.

- ▪ If yellowViewController doesn't exist because it hasn't been created yet or was flushed from memory, it will also return true.

We then check to see whether yellowViewController exists:

```
if (!self.yellowViewController.view.superview) {
```

If it's a nil pointer, that means there is no instance of yellowViewController, and we need to create one. This could happen because it's the first time the button has been pressed or because the system ran low on memory and it was flushed. In this case, we need to create an instance of BIDYellowViewController, as we did for the BIDBlueViewController in the viewDidLoad method:

```
if (!self.yellowViewController) {
    self.yellowViewController = [self.storyboard
                                  instantiateViewControllerWithIdentifier:@"Yellow"];
}
```

At this point, we know that we have a yellowViewController instance because either we already had one or we just created it. We then remove blueViewController's view from the view hierarchy and add the yellowViewController's view:

```
[self.blueViewController.view removeFromSuperview];
[self.view insertSubview:self.yellowViewController.view atIndex:0];
```

If self.yellowViewController.view.superview is not nil, then we need to do the same thing, but for blueViewController. Although we create an instance of BIDBlueViewController in viewDidLoad, it is still possible that the instance has been flushed because memory got low. Now, in this application, the chances of memory running out are slim, but we're still going to be good memory citizens and make sure we have an instance before proceeding:

```
} else {
    if (!self.blueViewController) {
        self.blueViewController = [self.storyboard
                                   instantiateViewControllerWithIdentifier:@"Blue"];
    }
    [self.yellowViewController.view removeFromSuperview];
    [self.view insertSubview:self.blueViewController.view atIndex:0];
}
```

In addition to not using resources for the yellow view and controller if the *Switch Views* button is never tapped, lazy loading also gives us the ability to release whichever view is not being shown to free up its memory. iOS will call the UIViewController method didReceiveMemoryWarning, which is inherited by every view controller, when memory drops below a system-determined level.

Since we know that either view will be reloaded the next time it is shown to the user, we can safely release either controller. We do this by adding a few lines to the existing didReceiveMemoryWarning method:

```
- (void)didReceiveMemoryWarning {
    [super didReceiveMemoryWarning];

    // Release any cached data, images, etc, that aren't in use
    if (!self.blueViewController.view.superview) {
        self.blueViewController = nil;
    } else {
        self.yellowViewController = nil;
    }
}
```

This newly added code checks to see which view is currently being shown to the user and releases the controller for the other view by assigning nil to its property. This will cause the controller, along with the view it controls, to be deallocated, freeing up its memory.

> **Tip** Lazy loading is a key component of resource management on iOS, and you should implement it anywhere you can. In a complex, multiview application, being responsible and flushing unused objects from memory can be the difference between an application that works well and one that crashes periodically because it runs out of memory.

Implementing the Content Views

The two content views that we are creating in this application are extremely simple. They each have one action method that is triggered by a button, and neither one needs any outlets. The two views are also nearly identical. In fact, they are so similar that they could have been represented by the same class. We chose to make them two separate classes because that's how most multiview applications are constructed.

The two action methods we're going to implement do nothing more than show an alert (as we did in Chapter 4's Control Fun application), so go ahead and add this code to *BIDBlueViewController.m*:

```
#import "BIDBlueViewController.h"

@implementation BIDBlueViewController

- (IBAction)blueButtonPressed {
    UIAlertView *alert = [[UIAlertView alloc]
                            initWithTitle:@"Blue View Button Pressed"
                            message:@"You pressed the button on the blue view"
                            delegate:nil
                            cancelButtonTitle:@"Yep, I did."
                            otherButtonTitles:nil];
    [alert show];
}
...
```

Save the file. Next, switch over to *BIDYellowViewController.m* and add this very similar code to that file:

```
#import "BIDYellowViewController.h"

@implementation BIDYellowViewController

- (IBAction)yellowButtonPressed {
    UIAlertView *alert = [[UIAlertView alloc]
                            initWithTitle:@"Yellow View Button Pressed"
                            message:@"You pressed the button on the yellow view"
                            delegate:nil
                            cancelButtonTitle:@"Yep, I did."
                            otherButtonTitles:nil];
    [alert show];
}
```

Save this file, as well.

Next, select *Main.storyboard* to open it in Interface Builder, so we can make a few changes. First, we need to add a new scene for `BIDBlueViewController`. Up until now, each storyboard we've dealt with contained just a single controller-view pairing, but the storyboard has more tricks up its sleeve, and holding multiple scenes is one of them. From the object library, drag out another *View Controller* and drop it in the editing area next to the existing one. Now your storyboard has two scenes, each of which can be loaded dynamically and independently while your application is running. In the row of icons at the bottom of the new scene, single-click the *View Controller* icon and press ⌥⌘3 to bring up the identity inspector. In the *Custom Class* section, *Class* defaults to *UIViewController*; change it to *BIDBlueViewController.*

We also need to create an identifier for this new view controller, so that our code can find it inside the storyboard. Just below the Custom Class in the identity inspector, you'll see a Storyboard ID field. Click there and type *Blue* to match what we used in our code.

So now you have two scenes. We showed you earlier how to configure your app to load this storyboard at launch time, but we didn't mention anything about scenes there. How will the app know which of these two views to show? The answer lies in the big arrow pointing at the first scene, as shown in Figure 6-18. That arrow points out the storyboard's default scene, which is what the app shows when it starts up. If you want to choose a different default scene, all you have to do is drag the arrow to point at the scene you want.

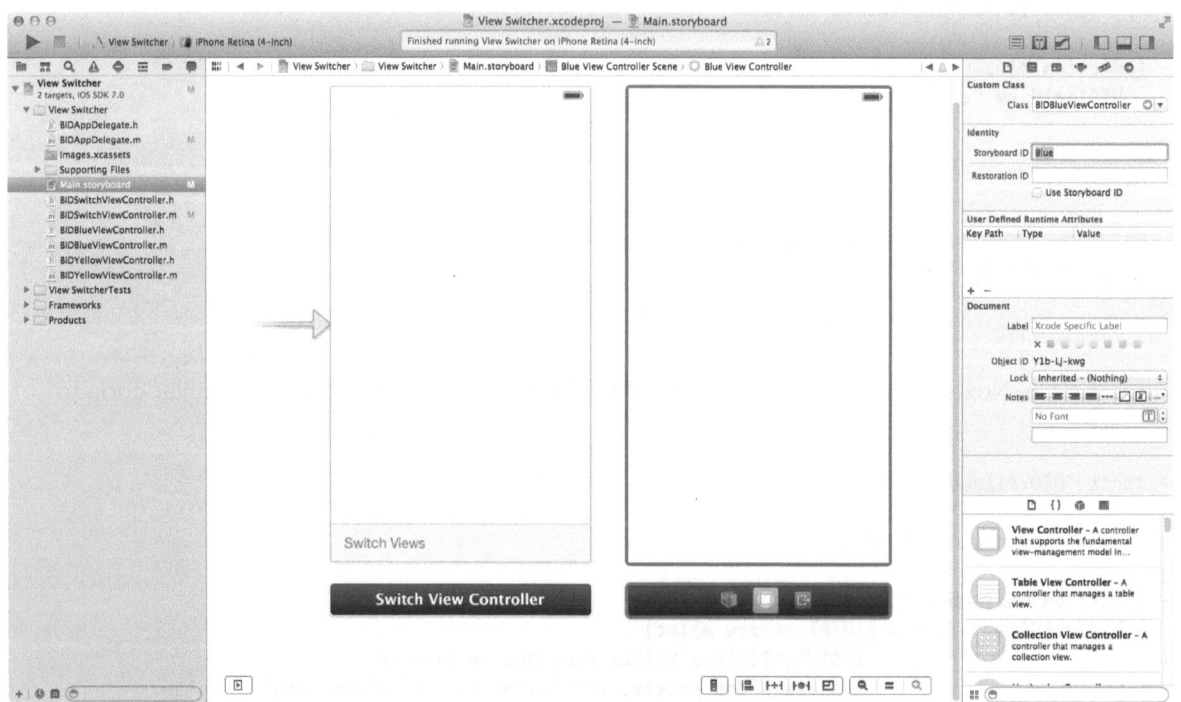

Figure 6-18. We just added a second scene to our storyboard. The big arrow points at the default scene

Single-click the big rectangular view in the new scene you just added, and then press ⌥⌘4 to bring up the object attributes inspector. In the inspector's *View* section, click the color well that's labeled *Background*, and use the pop-up color picker to change the background color of this view to a nice shade of blue. Once you are happy with your blue, close the color picker.

Drag a *Button* from the library over to the view, using the guidelines to center the button in the view, both vertically and horizontally. We want to make sure that the button stays centered no matter what, so make two constraints to that effect. First select **Editor ➤ Align ➤ Horizontal Center in Container** from the menu. Then click the new button again, and select **Editor ➤ Align ➤ Vertical Center in Container** from the menu.

Double-click the button and change its title to *Press Me*. Next, with the button still selected, switch to the connections inspector (by pressing ⌥⌘6), drag from the *Touch Up Inside* event to the *File's Owner* icon, and connect to the *blueButtonPressed* action method. You'll notice that the text of the button is a blue color by default. Since our background is also blue, there's a pretty big risk that this button's text will be hard to see! Switch to the attributes inspector with ⌥⌘4, and then use the combined color-picker/pop-up button to change the Text Color value to something else. Depending on how dark your background color is, you might want to choose either white or black.

Now it's time to do pretty much the same set of things for BIDYellowViewController. Grab yet another *View Controller* from the object library and drag it into the editor area. Don't worry if things are getting crowded; you can stack those scenes on top of each other, and no one will mind! Click the *View Controller* icon in the dock and use the identity inspector to change its class to *BIDYellowViewController* and its *Storyboard ID* to *Yellow*.

Next, select the view and switch to the object attributes inspector. There, click the *Background* color well, select a bright yellow, and then close the color picker.

Next, drag out a *Button* from the library and use the guidelines to center it in the view. Use the menu actions to create constraints aligning its horizontal and vertical center, just like for the last button. Now change its title to *Press Me, Too*. With the button still selected, use the connections inspector to drag from the *Touch Up Inside* event to the *View Controller* icon, and connect to the *yellowButtonPressed* action method.

When you're finished, save the storyboard and get ready to take this bad boy for a spin. Hit the *Run* button in Xcode, and your app should start up and present you with a full screen of blue.

When our application launches, it shows the blue view we built. When you tap the *Switch Views* button, it will change to show the yellow view that we built. Tap it again, and it goes back to the blue view. If you tap the button centered on the blue or yellow view, you'll get an alert view with a message indicating which button was pressed. This alert shows that the correct controller class is being called for the view that is being shown.

The transition between the two views is kind of abrupt, though. Gosh, if only there were some way to make the transition look nicer.

Of course, there is a way to make the transition look nicer! We can animate the transition to give the user visual feedback of the change.

Animating the Transition

UIView has several class methods we can call to indicate that the transition between views should be animated, to indicate the type of transition that should be used, and to specify how long the transition should take.

Go back to *BIDSwitchViewController.m* and enhance your switchViews: method by adding the lines shown here in bold:

```
- (IBAction)switchViews:(id)sender
{
    [UIView beginAnimations:@"View Flip" context:NULL];
    [UIView setAnimationDuration:0.4];
    [UIView setAnimationCurve:UIViewAnimationCurveEaseInOut];
    if (!self.yellowViewController.view.superview) {
        if (!self.yellowViewController) {
            self.yellowViewController = [self.storyboard
                                    instantiateViewControllerWithIdentifier:@"Yellow"];
        }
        [UIView setAnimationTransition:UIViewAnimationTransitionFlipFromRight
                            forView:self.view cache:YES];
        [self.blueViewController.view removeFromSuperview];
        [self.view insertSubview:self.yellowViewController.view atIndex:0];
    } else {
        if (!self.blueViewController) {
            self.blueViewController = [self.storyboard
                                    instantiateViewControllerWithIdentifier:@"Blue"];
        }
        [UIView setAnimationTransition:UIViewAnimationTransitionFlipFromLeft
                            forView:self.view cache:YES];
        [self.yellowViewController.view removeFromSuperview];
        [self.view insertSubview:self.blueViewController.view atIndex:0];
    }
    [UIView commitAnimations];
}
```

Compile this new version and run your application. When you tap the *Switch Views* button, instead of the new view just snapping into place, the old view will flip over to reveal the new view, as shown in Figure 6-19.

Figure 6-19. One view transitioning to another, using the flip style of animation

To tell iOS that we want a change animated, we need to declare an **animation block** and specify how long the animation should take. Animation blocks are declared by using the UIView class method beginAnimations:context:, like so:

```
[UIView beginAnimations:@"View Flip" context:NULL];
[UIView setAnimationDuration:0.4];
```

beginAnimations:context: takes two parameters. The first is an animation block title. This title comes into play only if you take more direct advantage of Core Animation, the framework behind this animation. For our purposes, we could have used nil. The second parameter is a (void *) that allows you to specify an object (or any other C data type) whose pointer you would like associated with this animation block. We used NULL here, since we don't need to do that. We also set the duration of the animation, which tells UIView how long (in seconds) the animation should last.

After that, we set the **animation curve**, which determines the timing of the animation. The default, which is a linear curve, causes the animation to happen at a constant speed. The option we set here, `UIViewAnimationCurveEaseInOut`, specifies that the animation should start slow but speed up in the middle, and then slow down again at the end. This gives the animation a more natural, less mechanical appearance:

```
[UIView setAnimationCurve:UIViewAnimationCurveEaseInOut];
```

Next, we need to specify the transition to use. At the time of this writing, four iOS view transitions are available:

- `UIViewAnimationTransitionFlipFromLeft`
- `UIViewAnimationTransitionFlipFromRight`
- `UIViewAnimationTransitionCurlUp`
- `UIViewAnimationTransitionCurlDown`

We chose to use two different effects, depending on which view was being swapped in. Using a left flip for one transition and a right flip for the other makes the view seem to flip back and forth.

The cache option speeds up drawing by taking a snapshot of the view when the animation begins and using that image, rather than redrawing the view at each step of the animation. You should always cache the animation unless the appearance of the view may need to change during the animation:

```
[UIView setAnimationTransition:UIViewAnimationTransitionFlipFromRight
                    forView:self.view cache:YES];
```

Next, we remove the currently shown view from our controller's view and instead add the other view.

When we're finished specifying the changes to be animated, we call `commitAnimations` on `UIView`. Everything between the start of the animation block and the call to `commitAnimations` will be animated together.

Thanks to Cocoa Touch's use of Core Animation under the hood, we're able to do fairly sophisticated animation with only a handful of code.

Switching Off

Whoo-boy! Creating our own multiview controller was a lot of work, wasn't it? You should have a very good grasp on how multiview applications are put together, now that you've built one from scratch.

Although Xcode contains project templates for the most common types of multiview applications, you need to understand the overall structure of these types of applications, so you can build them yourself from the ground up. The delivered templates are incredible time-savers; but at times, they simply won't meet your needs.

In the next few chapters, we're going to continue building multiview applications to reinforce the concepts from this chapter and to give you a feel for how more complex applications are put together. In Chapter 7, we'll construct a tab bar application. Let's get going!

Tab Bars and Pickers

In the previous chapter, you built your first multiview application. In this chapter, you're going to build a full tab bar application with five different tabs and five different content views. Building this application will reinforce a lot of what you learned in Chapter 6. Now, you're too smart to spend a whole chapter doing stuff you already sort of know how to do, so we're going to use those five content views to demonstrate a type of iOS control that we have not yet covered. The control is called a **picker view**, or just a **picker**.

You may not be familiar with the name, but you've almost certainly used a picker if you've owned an iPhone or iPod touch for more than, say, 10 minutes. Pickers are the controls with dials that spin. You use them to input dates in the Calendar application or to set a timer in the Clock application (see Figure 7-1). On the iPad, the picker view isn't quite as common since the larger display lets you present other ways of choosing among multiple items; but even there, it's used in the Calendar application.

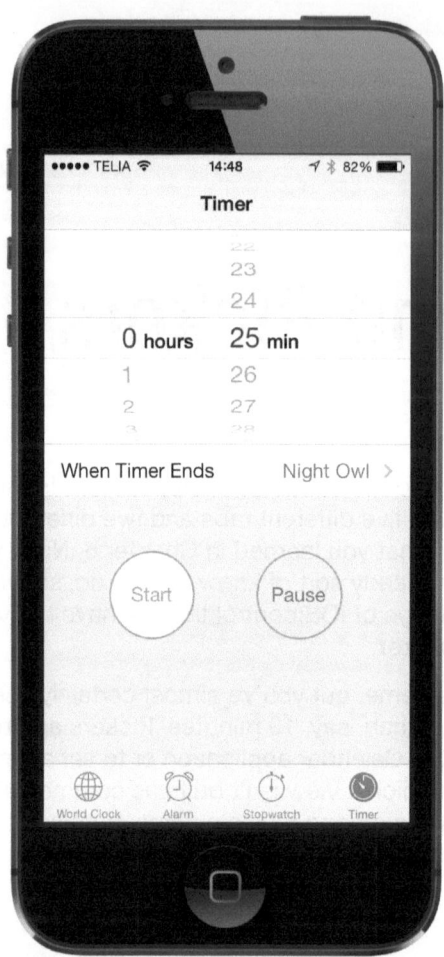

Figure 7-1. A picker in the Clock application

Pickers are a bit more complex than the iOS controls you've seen so far; and as such, they deserve a little more attention. Pickers can be configured to display one dial or many. By default, pickers display lists of text, but they can also be made to display images.

The Pickers Application

This chapter's application, Pickers, will feature a tab bar. As you build Pickers, you'll change the default tab bar so that it has five tabs, add an icon to each of the tab bar items, and then create a series of content views and connect each view to a tab.

The application's content views will feature five different pickers:

- **Date picker:** The first content view we'll build will have a date picker, which is the easiest type of picker to implement (see Figure 7-2). The view will also have a button that, when tapped, will display an alert that shows the date that was picked.

Figure 7-2. *The first tab will show a date picker*

■ **Single-component picker:** The second tab will feature a picker with a single list of values (see Figure 7-3). This picker is a little more work to implement than a date picker. You'll learn how to specify the values to be displayed in the picker by using a delegate and a data source.

Figure 7-3. A picker displaying a single list of values

■ **Multicomponent picker:** In the third tab, we're going to create a picker with two separate wheels. The technical term for each of these wheels is a **picker component**, so here we are creating a picker with two components. You'll see how to use the data source and delegate to provide two independent lists of data to the picker (see Figure 7-4). Each of this picker's components can be changed without impacting the other one.

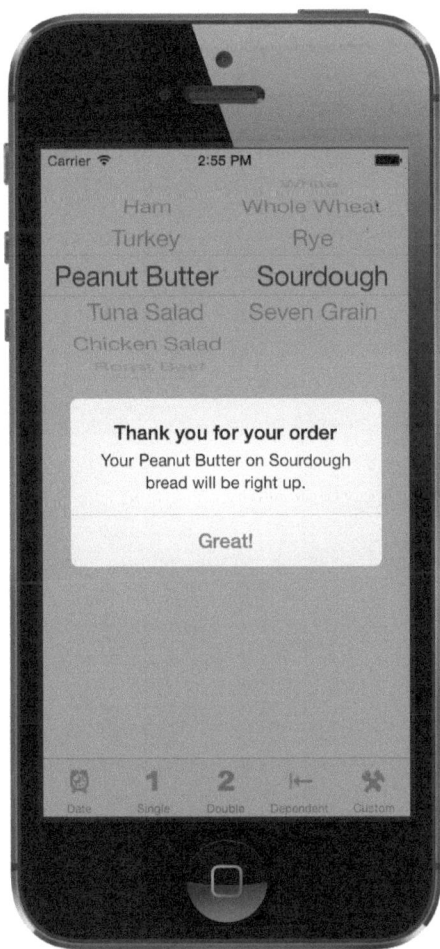

Figure 7-4. A two-component picker, showing an alert that reflects our selection

▪ **Picker with dependent components:** In the fourth content view, we'll build another picker with two components. But this time, the values displayed in the component on the right will change based on the value selected in the component on the left. In our example, we're going to display a list of states in the left component and a list of that state's ZIP codes in the right component (see Figure 7-5).

Figure 7-5. In this picker, one component is dependent on the other. As you select a state in the left component, the right component changes to a list of ZIP codes in that state

- **Custom picker with images:** Last but most certainly not least, we're going to have some fun with the fifth content view. We'll demonstrate how to add image data to a picker, and we're going to do it by writing a little game that uses a picker with five components. In several places in Apple's documentation, the picker's appearance is described as looking a bit like a slot machine. Well then, what could be more fitting than writing a little slot machine game (see Figure 7-6)? For this picker, the user won't be able to manually change the values of the components, but will be able to select the *Spin* button to make the five wheels spin to a new, randomly selected value. If three copies of the same image appear in a row, the user wins.

Figure 7-6. Our fifth component picker. Note that we do not condone using your iPhone as a tiny casino

Delegates and Data Sources

Before we dive in and start building our application, let's look at what makes pickers more complex than the other controls you've used so far. With the exception of the date picker, you can't use a picker by just grabbing one in the object library, dropping it on your content view, and configuring it. You also need to provide each picker with both a picker **delegate** and a picker **data source**.

By this point, you should be comfortable using delegates. We've already used application delegates and action sheet delegates, and the basic idea is the same here. The picker defers several jobs to its delegate. The most important of these is the task of determining what to actually draw for each of the rows in each of its components. The picker asks the delegate for either a string or a view that will be drawn at a given spot on a given component. The picker gets its data from the delegate.

In addition to the delegate, pickers need to have a data source. In this instance, the name *data source* is a bit of a misnomer. The data source tells the picker how many components it will be working with and how many rows make up each component. The data source works like the delegate in that its methods are called at certain, prespecified times. Without a data source and a delegate, pickers cannot do their job; in fact, they won't even be drawn.

It's very common for the data source and the delegate to be the same object. And it's just as common for that object to be the view controller for the picker's enclosing view, which is the approach we'll be using in this application. The view controllers for each of our application's content panes will be the data source and the delegate for their picker.

> **Note**   Here's a pop quiz: is the picker data source part of the model, view, or controller portion of the application? It's a trick question. A data source sounds like it must be part of the model, but it's actually part of the controller. The data source isn't usually an object designed to hold data. In simple applications, the data source might hold data, but its true job is to retrieve data from the model and pass it along to the picker.

Let's fire up Xcode and get to it.

Creating the Pickers Application

Although Xcode provides a template for tab bar applications, we're going to build ours from scratch. It's not much extra work, and it's good practice.

Create a new project, select the *Empty Application* template again, and choose *Next* to go to the next screen. In the *Product Name* field, type *Pickers*. Make sure the checkbox that says *Use Core Data* is unchecked, and set the *Devices* pop-up to *iPhone*. Then choose *Next* again, and Xcode will let you select the folder where you want to save your project.

We're going to walk you through the process of building the whole application; but at any step of the way, if you feel like challenging yourself by moving ahead, by all means do so. If you get stumped, you can always come back. If you don't feel like skipping ahead, that's just fine. We love the company.

Creating the View Controllers

In the previous chapter, we created a root view controller ("root controller" for short) to manage the process of swapping our application's other views. We'll be doing that again this time, but we won't need to create our own root view controller class. Apple provides a very good class for managing tab bar views, so we're just going to use an instance of UITabBarController as our root controller.

First, we need to create five new classes in Xcode: the five view controllers that the root controller will swap in and out.

Expand the *Pickers* folder in the Project Navigator. There, you'll see the source code files that Xcode created to start off the project. Single-click the *Pickers* folder, and press ⌘N or select **File ➤ New ➤ File....**

Select *Cocoa Touch* in the left pane of the new file assistant, and then select the icon for *Objective-C class* and click *Next* to continue. The next screen lets you give your new class a name. Enter *BIDDatePickerViewController* in the *Class* field. As always when naming a new class file, carefully check your spelling. A typo here will cause your new class to be named incorrectly. You'll also see a control that lets you select or enter a superclass for your new class; you should ensure this is *UIViewController*. Below that, you should see a pair of checkboxes labeled *Targeted for iPad* and *With XIB for user interface*. Make sure that both of them are unchecked before clicking *Next*.

Finally, you'll be shown a folder selection window, which lets you choose where the class should be saved. Choose the *Pickers* directory, which already contains the *BIDAppDelegate* class and a few other files. Make sure also that the *Group* pop-up has the *Pickers* folder selected and that the target checkbox for *Pickers* is checked.

After you click the *Create* button, two new files will appear in your *Pickers* folder: *BIDDatePickerViewController.h* and *BIDDatePickerViewController.m*.

Repeat those steps four more times, using the names *BIDSingleComponentPickerViewController*, *BIDDoubleComponentPickerViewController*, *BIDDependentComponentPickerViewController*, and *BIDCustomPickerViewController*. At the end of all this, the *Pickers* folder should contain all the fresh files, nicely bunched together (see Figure 7-7).

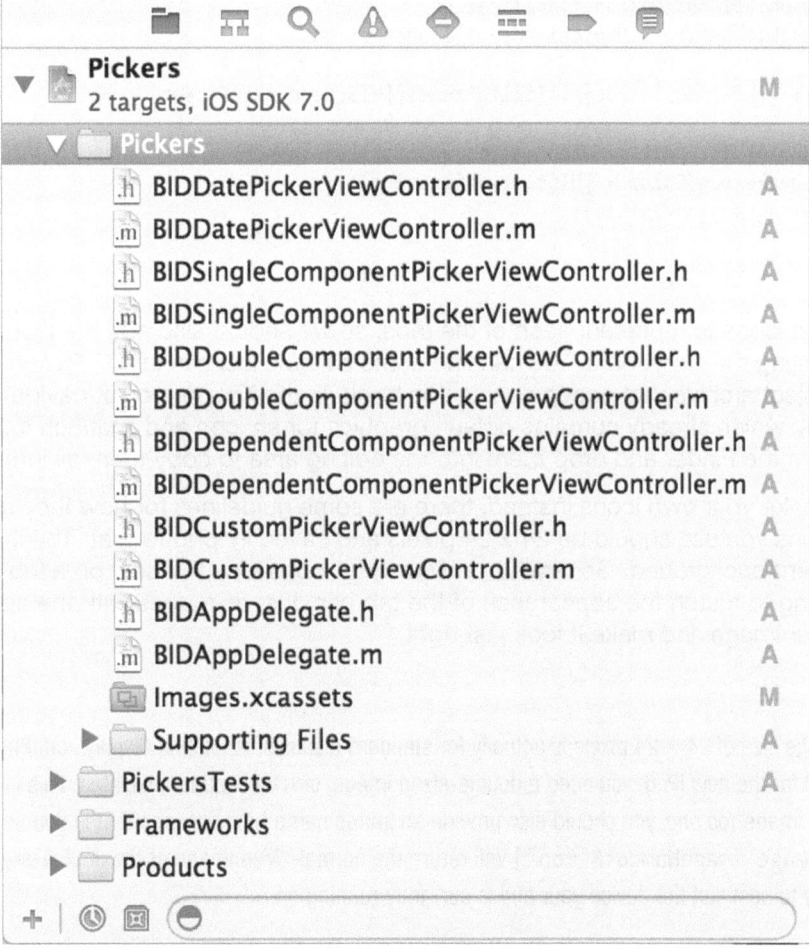

Figure 7-7. The Project Navigator should contain all these files after creating the five view controller classes

Adding the Storyboard

We're going to create our root view controller, which will be an instance of *UITabBarController*, in Interface Builder. Start by pressing ⌘**N** to create a new storyboard, which you'll find in the User Interface section of the file creation assistant. Set its *Device Family* to *iPhone*, name it *Main.storyboard*, and be sure to click the checkbox to add it to the *Pickers* target.

Now that we've created a storyboard, we need to tell Xcode that this is what should define the app's GUI at launch. So, click the uppermost *Pickers* folder in the project navigator, switch to the *General* tab in the editing area, and use the *Main Interface* pop-up in the *Deployment Info* section to choose *Main.storyboard*.

Since we created this project using the *Empty Application* template, it was created without any storyboard. Instead, there is some code in its application delegate that creates a basic empty view. Our next step is delete that code so that our storyboard will load instead. Select *BIDAppDelegate.m* in the project navigator and delete all but the final line of code in the application:didFinishLaunchingWithOptions: method:

```
- (BOOL)application:(UIApplication *)application
didFinishLaunchingWithOptions:(NSDictionary *)launchOptions
{
    self.window = [[UIWindow alloc] initWithFrame:[[UIScreen mainScreen]
                                               bounds]];
    // Override point for customization after application launch.
    self.window.backgroundColor = [UIColor whiteColor];
    [self.window makeKeyAndVisible];
    return YES;
}
```

Tab bars can use icons to represent each of the tabs, so we should also add the icons we're going to use before editing the storyboard. You can find some suitable icons in the *07 Pickers/Tab Bar Icons/* folder of the project archive that accompanies this book. In the Xcode project navigator, select *Images.xcassets*, which already contains default graphics for an icon and a launch image. Next, drag all five icons from the Finder and drop them into the editing area to copy them all into the project.

If you want to make your own icons instead, there are some guidelines for how they should be created. The icons you use should be 24 × 24 pixels and saved in *.png* format. The icon file should have a transparent background. Generally, medium-gray icons look the best on a tab bar. Don't worry about trying to match the appearance of the tab bar. Just as it does with the application icon, iOS will take your image and make it look just right.

> **Tip**   An image size of 24 × 24 pixels is actually for standard displays; for Retina displays on iPhone 4 and later and for the new iPad, you need a double-sized image, or it will appear pixelated. This is very easy: for any image *foo.png*, you should also provide an image named *foo@2x.png* that is doubled in size. Calling [UIImage imageNamed:@"foo"] will return the normal-sized image or the double-sized image automatically to best suit the device your app is currently running on.

Creating the Tab Bar Controller

Now, let's create our tab bar controller. Go back to *Main.storyboard* and drag *a Tab Bar Controller* from the object library (see Figure 7-8) over to the editing area.

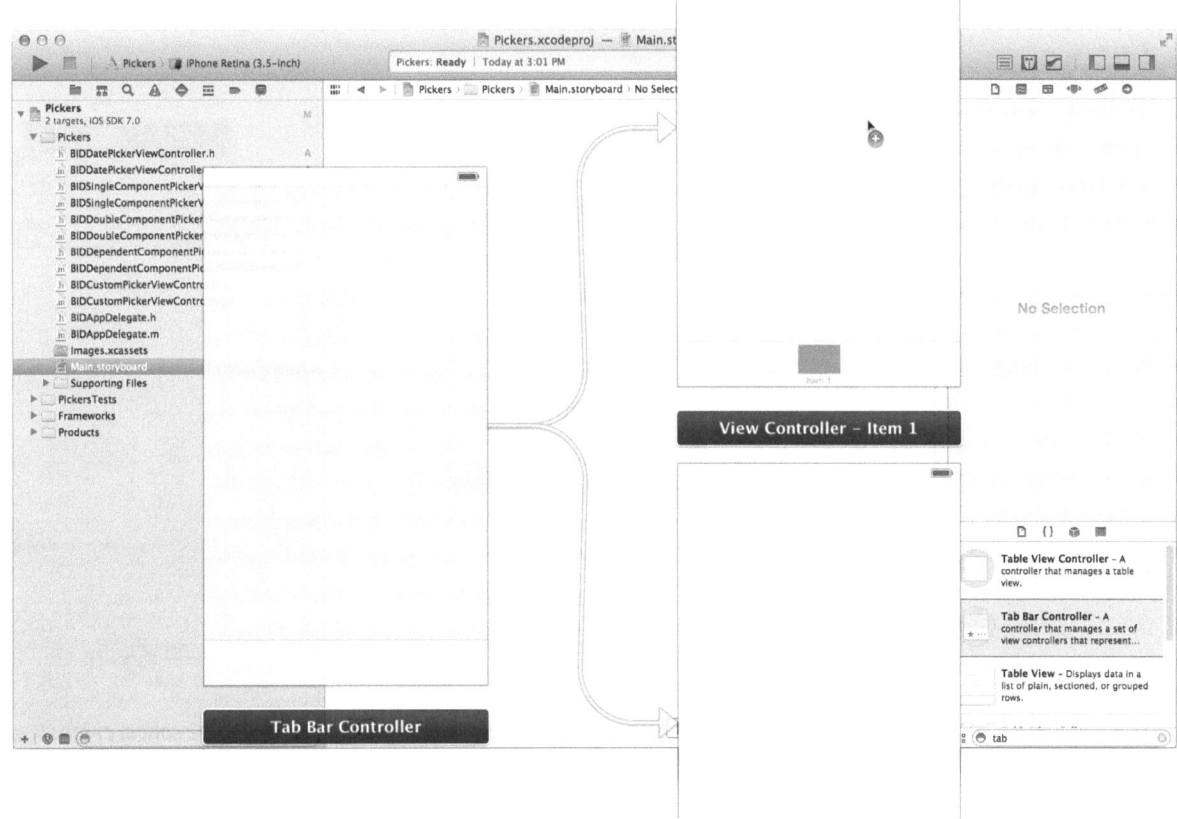

Figure 7-8. Dragging a tab bar controller from the library into the editor area. That's one heck of a big thing you're dragging around there

While you're dragging, you'll see that, unlike the other controllers we've been asking you to drag out from the object library, this one actually pulls out three complete view-controller pairs at once, all of which are connected to each other with curved lines. This is actually more than just a tab bar controller; it's also two child controllers, already connected and ready to use.

Once you drop the tab bar controller onto the editing area, three new scenes are added to the storyboard. If you expand the document view on the left, you will see a nice overview of all the scenes contained in the storyboard (see Figure 7-9). You'll also see the curvy lines still in place connected the tab bar controller with each of its children. Those lines will always adjust themselves to stay connected if you move the scenes around, which you are always free to do. The on-screen position of each scene within a storyboard has no impact on your app's appearance when it runs.

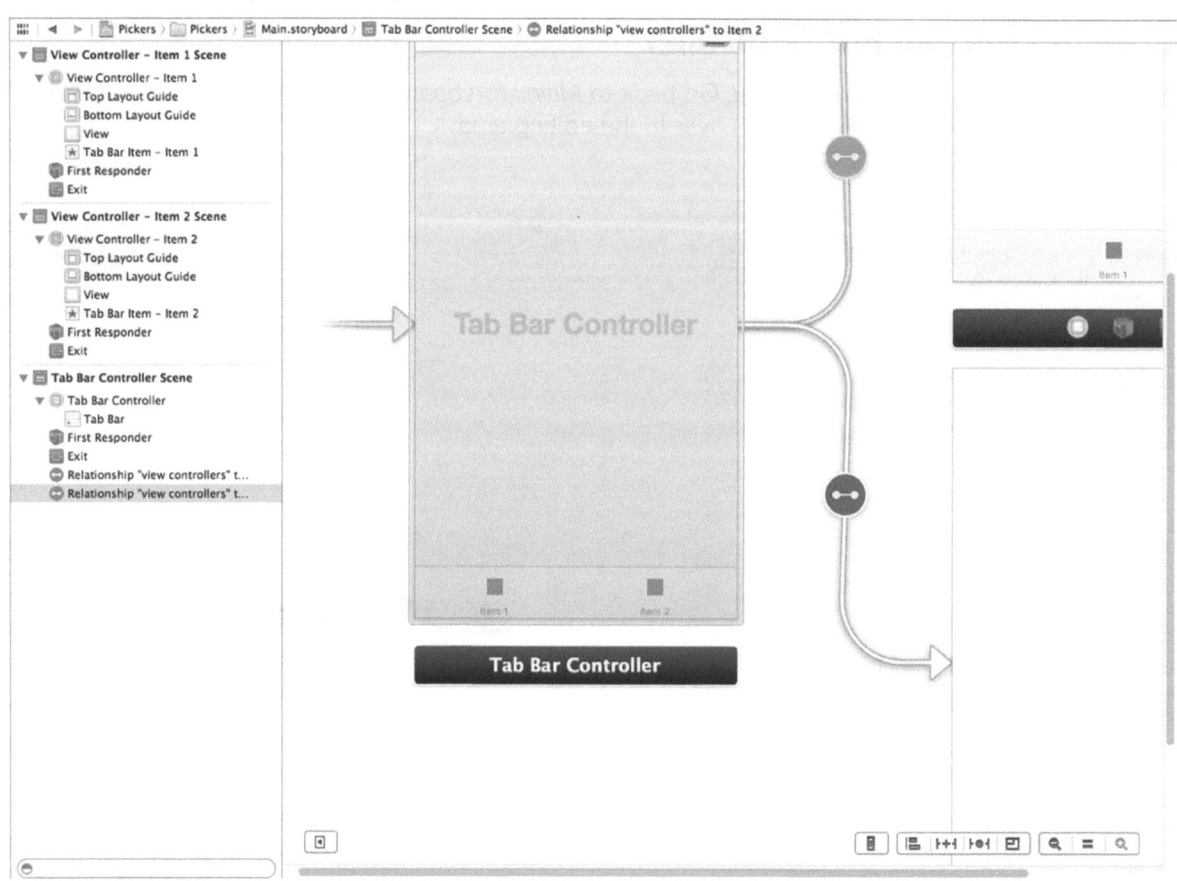

Figure 7-9. The tab bar controller's scene, and two child scenes. Notice the tab bar containing two tabs at the bottom of the view, and the curved lines connected to each of the child view controllers

This tab bar controller will be our root controller. As a reminder, the root controller controls the very first view that the user will see when your program runs. It is responsible for switching the other views in and out. Since we'll connect each of our views to one of the tabs in the tab bar, the tab bar controller makes a logical choice as a root controller.

You can see that each of the child view controllers shows a name like "View Controller – Item 1" at the bottom, and each shows a single bar item at the bottom of its view, with a simple label matching what is present in the tab bar. We might as well set these two up so that they have the right names from the start, so select the *Item 1* view controller, then click the tab bar item that is shown at its bottom end. Open the attributes inspector, and you'll see a text field for setting the *Title* of the *Bar Item*. Type in *Date* and press the **Enter** key. This immediately changes the text of the bar item at the bottom of this view controller, as well as the corresponding tab bar item in the parent. While you're still in the inspector, click the *Image* pop-up and select *clockicon* to set the icon, too. Couldn't be simpler!

Now repeat the same steps for the second child view controller, but name this one "Single" and use the *singleicon* image for its bar item.

Our next step is to complete our tab bar so it reflects the five tabs shown in Figure 7-2. Each of those five tabs represents one of our five pickers. The way we're going to do this is by simply adding three more view controllers to the storyboard (in addition to the two that were added along with the tab bar controller), and then connecting each of them up so that the tab bar controller can activate them. Get started by dragging out a normal *View Controller* from the object library. Next, ctrl-drag from the tab bar controller to your new view controller, release the mouse button, and select *view controllers* from the small pop-up window that appears. This tells the tab bar controller that it has a new child to maintain, so the tab bar immediately acquires a new item, and your new view controller gets a bar item in the bottom of its view, just like the others already had. Now do the same steps outlined previously to give this latest view controller's bar item "Double" as a title and *doubleicon* for its image.

Now we are really getting somewhere. Drag out two more view controllers and connect each of them to the tab bar controller as described previously. One at a time, select each of their bar items, naming one of them Dependent with *dependenticon* as its image, and the other Custom with *toolicon* as its image.

Now that all our view controllers are in place, it's time to set up each of them with the correct controller class. This will let us have different functionality in each of these views. Select the view controller associated with the leftmost tab and bring up the Identity Inspector. In the *Custom Class* section of the inspector, change the class to *BIDDatePickerViewController*, and press **Return** or tab to set it. You'll see that the name of the selected control in the dock changes to *Date Picker View Controller – Item 1,* mirroring the change you made.

Now repeat this same process for the next four view controllers. In the Identity Inspector for each, enter the class names *BIDSingleComponentPickerViewController*, *BIDDoubleComponentPickerViewController*, *BIDDependentComponentPickerViewController*, and *BIDCustomPickerViewController*, respectively.

Before moving on to the next bit of GUI editing, save your storyboard file.

The Initial Test Run

At this point, the tab bar and the content views should all be hooked up and working. Compile and run, and your application should launch with a tab bar that functions (see Figure 7-10). Click each of the tabs in turn. Each tab should be selectable.

Figure 7-10. The application with five empty but selectable tabs

There's nothing in the content views now, so the changes won't be very dramatic. In fact, you won't see any difference at all, except for the highlighting tab bar items. But if everything went OK, the basic framework for your multiview application is now set up and working, and we can start designing the individual content views.

> **Tip**   If your simulator bursts into flames when you click one of the tabs, don't panic! Most likely, you've either missed a step or made a typo. Go back and make sure the connections are right and the class names are all set correctly.

If you want to make doubly sure everything is working, you can add a different label or some other object to each of the content views, and then relaunch the application. At this point, you should see the content of the different views change as you select different tabs.

Implementing the Date Picker

To implement the date picker, we'll need a single outlet and a single action. The outlet will be used to grab the value from the date picker. The action will be triggered by a button and will put up an alert to show the date value pulled from the picker. We'll add both of these from inside Interface Builder while editing the *Main.storyboard* file, so select it in the project navigator if it's not already front-and-center.

The first thing we need to do is find a *Date Picker* in the library and drag it over to *Date Picker View Controller* in the editing area. Place the date picker at the top of the view, right up against the top of the display. It's OK if it overlaps the status bar because, in OS 7, this control has so much built-in vertical padding at the top that no one will notice. It should take up the entire width of your content view and a good portion of the height (see Figure 7-11).

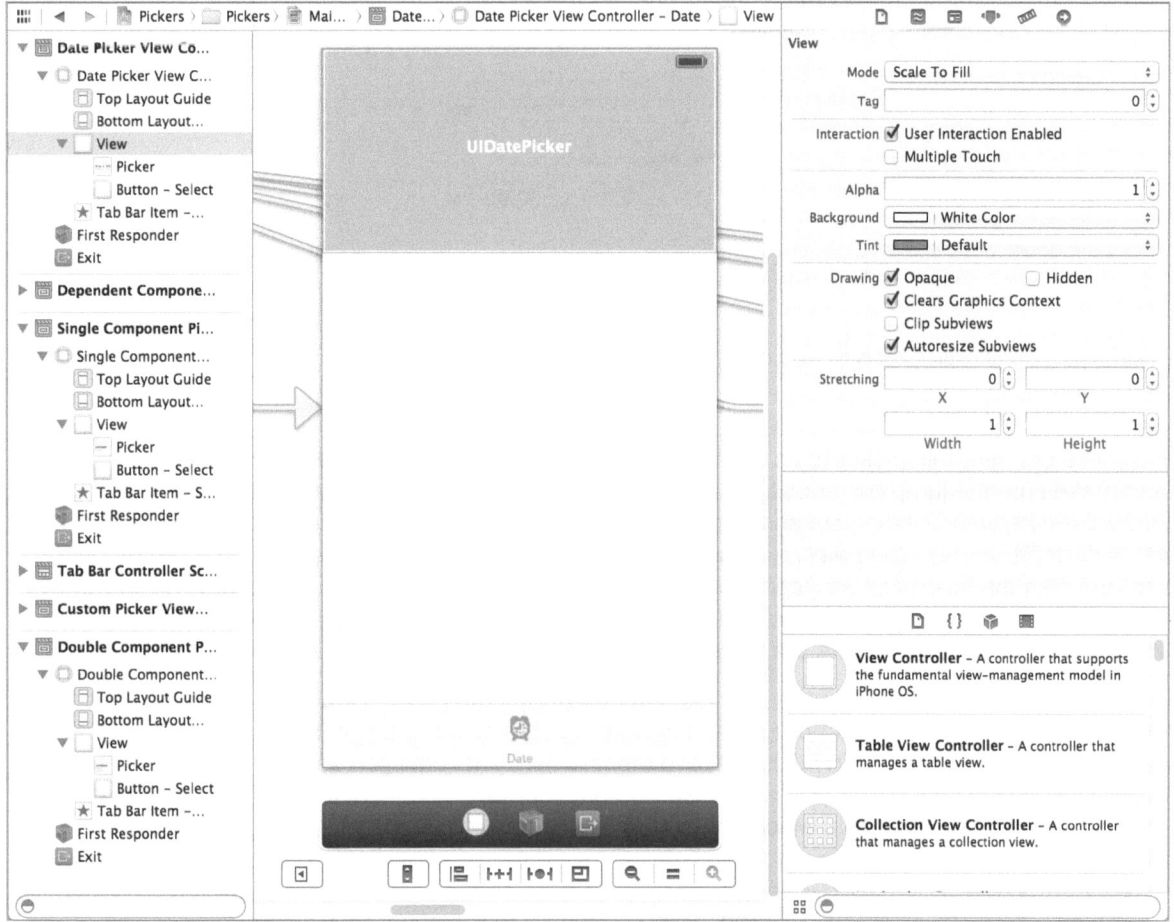

Figure 7-11. We dragged a date picker from the library. Notice that it takes up the entire width of the view, and that we placed it at the top of the view, overlapping the status bar

Single-click the date picker if it's not already selected and go back to the attributes inspector. As you can see in Figure 7-12, a number of attributes can be configured for a date picker. We're going to leave most of the values at their defaults (but feel free to play with the options when we're finished, to see what they do). The one thing we will do is limit the range of the picker to reasonable dates. Look for the heading that says *Constraints* and check the box that reads *Minimum Date.* Leave the value at the default of *1/1/1970.* Also check the box that reads *Maximum Date* and set that value *to 12/31/2200.*

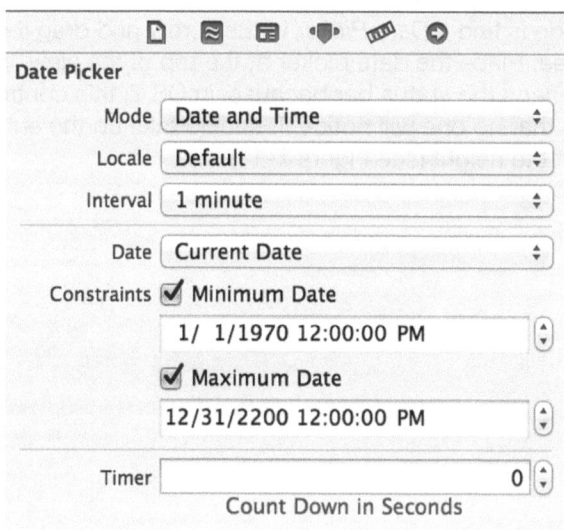

Figure 7-12. The attributes inspector for a date picker. Set the maximum date, but leave the rest of the settings at their default values

Now let's connect this picker to its controller. Press ⌥⌘**Enter** to open the assistant editor and make sure the jump bar above the assistant editor is set to *Automatic*. That should make *BIDDatePickerViewController.m* show up there. Next, ctrl-drag from the picker to the upper portion of *BIDDatePickerViewController.m*, between the @interface and @end lines, releasing the mouse button when the *Insert Outlet, Action, or Outlet Collection* tooltip appears. In the pop-up window that appears after you let go, make sure the *Connection* is set to *Outlet*, enter *datePicker* as the *Name*, and then press **Enter** to create the outlet and connect it to the picker.

Next, grab a *Button* from the library and place it below the date picker. Double-click the button and give it a title of *Select*. Now ctrl-drag from the button to the source code in the assistant view, this time dragging it down near the bottom, just above the final @end line, until you see the *Insert Action* tooltip appear. Name the new action *buttonPressed* and press **Enter** to connect it. Doing so creates an empty method called buttonPressed:, which you should now complete with the following bold lines:

```
- (IBAction)buttonPressed:(id)sender {
    NSDate *selected = [self.datePicker date];
    NSString *message = [[NSString alloc] initWithFormat:
                         @"The date and time you selected is: %@", selected];
    UIAlertView *alert = [[UIAlertView alloc]
                         initWithTitle:@"Date and Time Selected"
                         message:message
```

```
                        delegate:nil
                        cancelButtonTitle:@"That's so true!"
                        otherButtonTitles:nil];

    [alert show];
}
```

Next, add a bit of setup code to the viewDidLoad: method to finish this controller class:

```
- (void)viewDidLoad
{
    [super viewDidLoad];
    // Do any additional setup after loading the view.
    NSDate *now = [NSDate date];
    [self.datePicker setDate:now animated:NO];
}
```

Here, we first add the implementation of buttonPressed and then override viewDidLoad. In buttonPressed, we use our datePicker outlet to get the current date value from the date picker, and then we construct a string based on that date and use it to show an alert sheet.

In viewDidLoad, we create a new NSDate object. An NSDate object created this way will hold the current date and time. We then set datePicker to that date, which ensures that every time this view is loaded from the storyboard, the picker will reset to the current date and time.

Go ahead and build and run to make sure your date picker checks out. If everything went OK, your application should look like Figure 7-2 when it runs. If you choose the *Select* button, an alert sheet will pop up, telling you the date and time currently selected in the date picker.

Note   The date picker does not allow you to specify seconds or a time zone. The alert displays the time with seconds and in Greenwich Mean Time (GMT). We could have added some code to simplify the string displayed in the alert, but isn't this chapter long enough already? If you're interested in customizing the formatting of the date, take a look at the NSDateFormatter class.

Implementing the Single-Component Picker

Our next picker lets the user select from a list of values. In this example, we're going to create an NSArray to hold the values we want to display in the picker.

Pickers don't hold any data themselves. Instead, they call methods on their data source and delegate to get the data they need to display. The picker doesn't really care where the underlying data lives. It asks for the data when it needs it, and the data source and delegate (which are often, in practice, the same object) work together to supply that data. As a result, the data could be coming from a static list, as we'll do in this section. It also could be loaded from a file or a URL, or even made up or calculated on the fly.

For the picker class to ask its controller for data, we must ensure that the controller implements the right methods. One part of doing that is declaring in the controller's interface that it will implement a couple of protocols. In the Project Navigator, single-click *BIDSingleComponentPickerViewController.h*.

This controller class will act as both the data source and the delegate for its picker, so we need to make sure it conforms to the protocols for those two roles. Add the following code:

```
#import <UIKit/UIKit.h>

@interface BIDSingleComponentPickerViewController : UIViewController
  <UIPickerViewDelegate, UIPickerViewDataSource>

@end
```

Building the View

Now select *Main.storyboard* again, since it's time to edit the content view for the second tab in our tab bar. In the document outline, click the *Single Component Picker View* scene. If you can't see what's inside it, click the disclosure triangle, and then click the small yellow icon inside that to bring the view itself into focus. Next, bring over a *Picker View* from the library (see Figure 7-13), and add it to your view, placing it snugly into the top of the view, as you did with the date picker view.

Figure 7-13. Dragging a picker view from the library onto your second view

Now let's connect this picker to its controller. The procedure here is just like for the previous picker view: open the assistant editor, set the jump bar to show the *.m* file, ctrl-drag from the picker to the @interface section at the top of *BIDDatePickerViewController.m*, and create an outlet named *singlePicker*.

Next, with the picker selected, press ⌥⌘6 to bring up the connections inspector. If you look at the connections available for the picker view, you'll see that the first two items are *dataSource* and *delegate*. If you don't see those outlets, make sure you have the picker selected, rather than the UIView that contains it! Drag from the circle next to *dataSource* to the *View Controller* icon, and then drag from the circle next to *delegate* to the *View Controller* icon. Now this picker knows that the instance of the *BIDSingleComponentPickerViewController* class in the storyboard is its data source and delegate, and the picker will ask it to supply the data to be displayed. In other words, when the picker needs information about the data it is going to display, it asks the *BIDSingleComponentPickerViewController* instance that controls this view for that information.

Drag a *Button* to the view, double-click it, and give it a title of *Select.* Press **Return** to commit the change. In the Connections Inspector, drag from the circle next to *Touch Up Inside* to code in the assistant view, releasing it just above the @end at the bottom to make a new action method. Name this action buttonPressed, and you'll see that Xcode fills in an empty method. Now you've finished building the GUI for the second tab. Save the storyboard and let's get back to some coding.

Implementing the Controller as a Data Source and Delegate

To make our controller work properly as the picker's data source and delegate, we'll start with some code you should feel comfortable with, and then add a few methods that you've never seen before.

Single-click *BIDSingleComponentPickerViewController.m* and add the following property to the @interface section at the top. This will let us keep a pointer to an array with the names of several well-known movie characters:

```
@interface BIDSingleComponentPickerViewController ()

@property (weak, nonatomic) IBOutlet UIPickerView *singlePicker;
@property (strong, nonatomic) NSArray *characterNames;

@end
```

Next, add this initialization code to the viewDidLoad method to set up the contents of the character name array:

```
- (void)viewDidLoad
{
    [super viewDidLoad];
    // Do any additional setup after loading the view.
    self.characterNames = @[@"Luke", @"Leia", @"Han", @"Chewbacca",
                            @"Artoo", @"Threepio", @"Lando"];
}
```

And then, add the following code to the buttonPressed method:

```
- (IBAction)buttonPressed:(id)sender {
    NSInteger row = [self.singlePicker selectedRowInComponent:0];
    NSString *selected = self.characterNames[row];
    NSString *title = [[NSString alloc] initWithFormat:
                        @"You selected %@!", selected];
    UIAlertView *alert = [[UIAlertView alloc] initWithTitle:title
                                    message:@"Thank you for choosing."
                                    delegate:nil
                            cancelButtonTitle:@"You're Welcome"
                            otherButtonTitles:nil];
    [alert show];
}
```

These two methods should be familiar to you by now. The buttonPressed method is nearly identical to the one we used with the date picker.

Unlike the date picker, a regular picker can't tell us what data it holds because it doesn't maintain the data. It hands off that job to the delegate and data source. Instead, the buttonPressed: method needs to ask the picker which row is selected and then grab the corresponding data from your pickerData array. Here is how we ask it for the selected row:

```
NSInteger row = [self.singlePicker selectedRowInComponent:0];
```

Notice that we needed to specify which component we want to know about. We have only one component in this picker, so we simply pass in 0, which is the index of the first component.

Note   Did you notice that there is no asterisk between NSInteger and row in our request for the selected row? Throughout most of the iOS SDK, the prefix NS often indicates an Objective-C class from the Foundation framework, but this is one of the exceptions to that general rule. NSInteger is always defined as an integer datatype, either an int or a long. We use NSInteger rather than int or long because, with NSInteger, the compiler automatically chooses whichever size is best for the platform for which we are compiling. It will create a 32-bit int when compiling for a 32-bit processor and a longer 64-bit long when compiling for a 64-bit architecture. Now that Apple has begun releasing 64-bit iOS devices, using these types makes a lot of sense. You might also write classes for your iOS applications that you'll later want to recycle and use in Cocoa applications for OS X, which has been running on both 32- and 64-bit machines for several years.

In viewDidLoad, we assign an array with several objects to the *characterNames* property so that we have data to feed the picker. Usually, your data will come from other sources, like a property list in your project's *Resources* folder or a web service query. By embedding a list of items in our code the way we've done here, we are making it much harder on ourselves if we need to update this list or if we want to have our application translated into other languages. But this approach is the quickest and easiest way to get data into an array for demonstration purposes. Even though you won't usually create your arrays like this, you will almost always configure some form of access to your application's model objects here in the viewDidLoad method, so that you're not constantly going to disk or to the network every time the picker asks you for data.

> **Tip**   If you're not supposed to create arrays from lists of objects in your code, as we just did in viewDidLoad,
> how should you do it? Embed the lists in property list files and add those files to the *Resources* folder of
> your project. Property list files can be changed without recompiling your source code, which means there
> is little risk of introducing new bugs when you do so. You can also provide different versions of the list
> for different languages, as you'll see in Chapter 20. Property lists can be created directly in Xcode, which
> offers a template for creating a property list in the *Resource* section of the new file assistant and supports
> the editing of property lists in the editor pane. Both NSArray and NSDictionary offer a method called
> initWithContentsOfFile: to allow you to initialize instances from a property list file, as we'll do later in
> this chapter when we implement the Dependent tab.

Finally, insert the following new code at the end of the file:

```
#pragma mark -
#pragma mark Picker Data Source Methods
- (NSInteger)numberOfComponentsInPickerView:(UIPickerView *)pickerView
{
    return 1;
}

- (NSInteger)pickerView:(UIPickerView *)pickerView
numberOfRowsInComponent:(NSInteger)component
{
    return [self.characterNames count];
}

#pragma mark Picker Delegate Methods
- (NSString *)pickerView:(UIPickerView *)pickerView
            titleForRow:(NSInteger)row
          forComponent:(NSInteger)component
{
    return self.characterNames[row];
}

@end
```

At the bottom of the file, we get into the new methods required to implement the picker. The first two
methods are from the UIPickerViewDataSource protocol, and they are both required for all pickers
(except date pickers). Here's the first one:

```
- (NSInteger)numberOfComponentsInPickerView:(UIPickerView *)pickerView
{
    return 1;
}
```

Pickers can have more than one spinning wheel, or component, and this is how the picker asks how many components it should display. We want to display only one list this time, so we return a value of 1. Notice that a `UIPickerView` is passed in as a parameter. This parameter points to the picker view that is asking us the question, which makes it possible to have multiple pickers being controlled by the same data source. In our case, we know that we have only one picker, so we can safely ignore this argument because we already know which picker is calling us.

The second data source method is used by the picker to ask how many rows of data there are for a given component:

```
- (NSInteger)pickerView:(UIPickerView *)pickerView
numberOfRowsInComponent:(NSInteger)component
{
    return [self.characterNames count];
}
```

Once again, we are told which picker view is asking and which component that picker is asking about. Since we know that we have only one picker and one component, we don't bother with either of the arguments and simply return the count of objects from our sole data array.

#PRAGMA WHAT?

Did you notice the following lines of code from *BIDSingleComponentPickerViewController.m*?

```
#pragma mark -
#pragma mark Picker Data Source Methods
```

Any line of code that begins with `#pragma` is technically a compiler directive. More specifically, a `#pragma` marks a **pragmatic**, or compiler-specific, directive that won't necessarily work with other compilers or in other environments. If the compiler doesn't recognize the directive, it ignores it, though it may generate a warning. In this case, the `#pragma` directives are actually directives to the IDE, not the compiler, and they tell Xcode's editor to put a break in the pop-up menu of methods and functions at the top of the editor pane. The first one puts the break in the menu. The second creates a text entry containing whatever the rest of the line holds, which you can use as a sort of descriptive header for groups of methods in your source code.

Some of your classes, especially some of your controller classes, are likely to get rather long, and the methods and functions pop-up menu makes navigating around your code much easier. Putting in `#pragma` directives and logically organizing your code will make that pop-up more efficient to use.

After the two data source methods, we implement one delegate method. Unlike the data source methods, all of the delegate methods are optional. The term *optional* is a bit deceiving because you do need to implement at least one delegate method. You will usually implement the method that we are implementing here. However, if you want to display something other than text in the picker, you must implement a different method instead, as you'll see when we get to the custom picker later in this chapter:

```
#pragma mark Picker Delegate Methods
- (NSString *)pickerView:(UIPickerView *)pickerView
              titleForRow:(NSInteger)row
              forComponent:(NSInteger)component
{
    return self.characterNames[row];
}
```

In this method, the picker is asking us to provide the data for a specific row in a specific component. We are provided with a pointer to the picker that is asking, along with the component and row that it is asking about. Since our view has one picker with one component, we simply ignore everything except the row argument and use that to return the appropriate item from our data array.

Go ahead and compile and run again. When the simulator comes up, switch to the second tab—the one labeled *Single*—and check out your new custom picker, which should look like Figure 7-3.

When you're done reliving all those *Star Wars* memories, come on back to Xcode and we'll show you how to implement a picker with two components. If you feel up to a challenge, this next content view is actually a good one for you to attempt on your own. You've already seen all the methods you'll need for this picker, so go ahead and take a crack at it. We'll wait here. You might want to start with a good look at Figure 7-4, just to refresh your memory. When you're finished, read on and you'll see how we tackled this problem.

Implementing a Multicomponent Picker

The next content pane will have a picker with two components, or wheels, each independent of the other. The left wheel will have a list of sandwich fillings and the right wheel will have a selection of bread types. We'll write the same data source and delegate methods that we did for the single-component picker. We'll just need to write a little additional code in some of those methods to make sure we're returning the correct value and row count for each component.

Declaring Outlets and Actions

Single-click *BIDDoubleComponentPickerViewController.h* and add the following code:

```
#import <UIKit/UIKit.h>

@interface BIDDoubleComponentPickerViewController : UIViewController
<UIPickerViewDelegate, UIPickerViewDataSource>

@end
```

Here, we simply conform our controller class to both the delegate and data source. Save this and click *Main.storyboard* to work on the GUI.

Building the View

Add a picker view and a button to the view, change the button label to *Select*, and then make the necessary connections. We're not going to walk you through it this time, but you can refer to the previous section if you need a step-by-step guide, since the two view controllers are identical in terms of connections in the storyboard. Here's a summary of what you need to do:

1. Create an outlet called doublePicker to connect the *View Controller* to the picker.

2. Connect the *DataSource* and *Delegate* connections on the picker view to *View Controller* (use the Connections Inspector).

3. Connect the *Touch Up Inside* event of the button to a new action called buttonPressed on the *View Controller* (use the Connections Inspector).

Make sure you save your storyboard and close it before you dive back into the code. Oh, and dog-ear this page (or use a bookmark, if you prefer). You'll be referring to it in a bit.

Implementing the Controller

Select *BIDDoubleComponentPickerViewController.m* and add the following code at the top of the file:

```
#import "BIDDoubleComponentPickerViewController.h"

#define kFillingComponent 0
#define kBreadComponent   1

@interface BIDDoubleComponentPickerViewController ()

@property (weak, nonatomic) IBOutlet UIPickerView *doublePicker;
@property (strong, nonatomic) NSArray *fillingTypes;
@property (strong, nonatomic) NSArray *breadTypes;

@end
```

As you can see, we start out by defining two constants that will represent the two components, which is just to make our code easier to read. Components are assigned numbers, with the leftmost component being assigned zero and increasing by one each move to the right. Next, we declare properties for two arrays to hold the data for our two picker components.

Now implement the *buttonPressed:* button, as shown here:

```
- (IBAction)buttonPressed:(id)sender {
    NSInteger fillingRow = [self.doublePicker selectedRowInComponent:
                                kFillingComponent];
    NSInteger breadRow = [self.doublePicker selectedRowInComponent:
                                kBreadComponent];

    NSString *filling = self.fillingTypes[fillingRow];
    NSString *bread = self.breadTypes[breadRow];
```

```
    NSString *message = [[NSString alloc] initWithFormat:
                            @"Your %@ on %@ bread will be right up.", filling, bread];

    UIAlertView *alert = [[UIAlertView alloc] initWithTitle:
                            @"Thank you for your order"
                                                message:message
                                                delegate:nil
                                        cancelButtonTitle:@"Great!"
                                        otherButtonTitles:nil];
    [alert show];
}
```

Next, add the following lines of code to the viewDidload method:

```
- (void)viewDidLoad
{
    [super viewDidLoad];
    // Do any additional setup after loading the view.
    self.fillingTypes = @[@"Ham", @"Turkey", @"Peanut Butter", @"Tuna Salad",
                            @"Chicken Salad", @"Roast Beef", @"Vegemite"];
    self.breadTypes = @[@"White", @"Whole Wheat", @"Rye", @"Sourdough",
                            @"Seven Grain"];
}
```

Also, add the delegate and data source methods at the bottom, before the final @end line:

```
#pragma mark -
#pragma mark Picker Data Source Methods
- (NSInteger)numberOfComponentsInPickerView:(UIPickerView *)pickerView
{
    return 2;
}

- (NSInteger)pickerView:(UIPickerView *)pickerView
numberOfRowsInComponent:(NSInteger)component
{
    if (component == kBreadComponent) {
        return [self.breadTypes count];
    } else {
        return [self.fillingTypes count];
    }
}
```

```
#pragma mark Picker Delegate Methods
- (NSString *)pickerView:(UIPickerView *)pickerView
            titleForRow:(NSInteger)row
            forComponent:(NSInteger)component
{
    if (component == kBreadComponent) {
        return self.breadTypes[row];
    } else {
        return self.fillingTypes[row];
    }
}
```

@end

The buttonPressed method is a bit more involved this time, but there's very little there that's new to you. We just need to specify which component we are talking about when we request the selected row using those constants we defined earlier, kBreadComponent and kFillingComponent:

```
NSInteger fillingRow = [self.doublePicker selectedRowInComponent:
                        kFillingComponent];
NSInteger breadRow = [self.doublePicker selectedRowInComponent:
                      kBreadComponent];
```

You can see here that using the two constants instead of 0 and 1 makes our code considerably more readable. From this point on, the buttonPressed method is fundamentally the same as the last one we wrote.

viewDidLoad: is also very similar to the version we wrote for the previous picker. The only difference is that we are loading two arrays with data rather than just one array. Again, we're just creating arrays from a hard-coded list of strings—something you generally won't do in your own applications.

When we get down to the data source methods, that's where things start to change a bit. In the first method, we specify that our picker should have two components rather than just one:

```
- (NSInteger)numberOfComponentsInPickerView:(UIPickerView *)pickerView
{
    return 2;
}
```

This time, when we are asked for the number of rows, we need to check which component the picker is asking about and return the correct row count for the corresponding array:

```
- (NSInteger)pickerView:(UIPickerView *)pickerView
numberOfRowsInComponent:(NSInteger)component
{
    if (component == kBreadComponent) {
        return [self.breadTypes count];
    } else {
        return [self.fillingTypes count];
    }
}
```

Next, in our delegate method, we do the same thing. We check the component and use the correct array for the requested component to fetch and return the correct value:

```
- (NSString *)pickerView:(UIPickerView *)pickerView
            titleForRow:(NSInteger)row
          forComponent:(NSInteger)component
{
    if (component == kBreadComponent) {
        return self.breadTypes[row];
    } else {
        return self.fillingTypes[row];
    }
}
```

That wasn't so hard, was it? Compile and run your application, and make sure the *Double* content pane looks like Figure 7-4.

Notice that the wheels are completely independent of each other. Turning one has no effect on the other. That's appropriate in this case, but there will be times when one component is dependent on another. A good example of this is in the date picker. When you change the month, the dial that shows the number of days in the month may need to change because not all months have the same number of days. Implementing this isn't really hard once you know how, but it's not the easiest thing to figure out on your own, so let's do that next.

Implementing Dependent Components

We're picking up steam now. For this next section, we're not going to hold your hand quite as much when it comes to material we've already covered. Instead, we'll focus on the new stuff. Our new picker will display a list of US states in the left component and a list of corresponding ZIP codes in the right component.

We'll need a separate list of ZIP code values for each item in the left-hand component. We'll declare two arrays, one for each component, as we did last time. We'll also need an NSDictionary. In the dictionary, we're going to store an NSArray for each state (see Figure 7-14). Later, we'll implement a delegate method that will notify us when the picker's selection changes. If the value on the left changes, we will grab the correct array out of the dictionary and assign it to the array being used for the right-hand component. Don't worry if you didn't catch all that; we'll talk about it more as we get into the code.

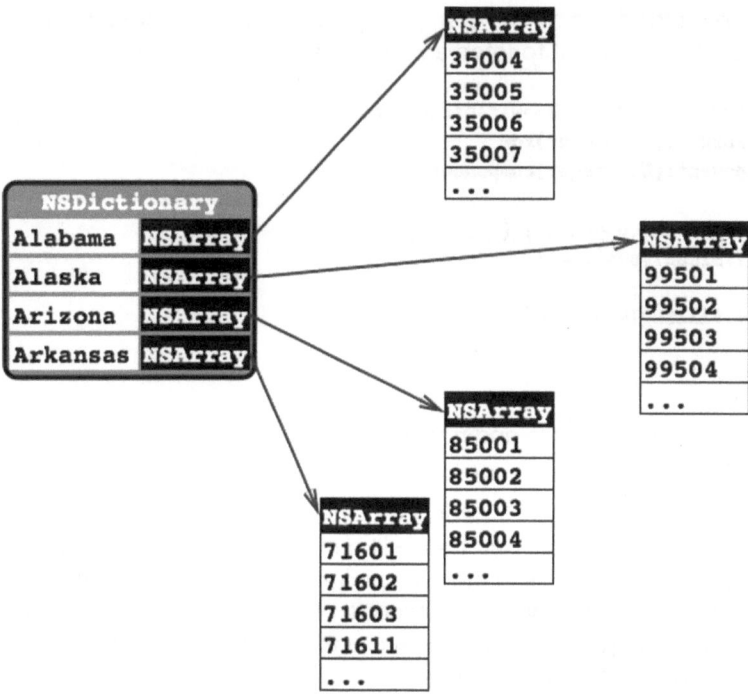

Figure 7-14. Our application's data. For each state, there will be one entry in a dictionary with the name of the state as the key. Stored under that key will be an NSArray instance containing all the ZIP codes from that state

Add the following code to your *BIDDependentComponentPickerViewController.h* file:

```
#import <UIKit/UIKit.h>

@interface BIDDependentComponentPickerViewController : UIViewController
<UIPickerViewDelegate, UIPickerViewDataSource>

@end
```

Next, add the following to *BIDDependentComponentPickerViewController.m*:

```
#import "BIDDependentComponentPickerViewController.h"

#define kStateComponent 0
#define kZipComponent   1

@interface BIDDependentComponentPickerViewController ()

@property (strong, nonatomic) NSDictionary *stateZips;
@property (strong, nonatomic) NSArray *states;
@property (strong, nonatomic) NSArray *zips;

@end
```

Now it's time to build the content view. That process will be almost identical to the previous two component views we built. If you get lost, flip back to the Building the View section for the single-component picker and follow those step-by-step instructions. Here's a hint: start off by opening *Main.storyboard*, find the view for the BIDDependentComponentPickerViewController class, and then repeat the same basic steps you've done for all the other content views in this chapter. You should end up with a property called dependentPicker connected to a picker, an empty buttonPressed: method connected to a button, and both the delegate and dataSource outlets of the picker connected to the view controller. When you're finished, save the storyboard.

OK, take a deep breath. Let's implement this controller class. This implementation may seem a little gnarly at first. By making one component dependent on the other, we have added a whole new level of complexity to our controller class. Although the picker displays only two lists at a time, our controller class must know about and manage 51 lists. The technique we're going to use here actually simplifies that process. The data source methods look almost identical to the one we implemented for the *DoublePicker* view. All of the additional complexity is handled elsewhere, between viewDidLoad and a new delegate method called pickerView:didSelectRow:inComponent:.

Before we write the code, we need some data to display. Up to now, we've created arrays in code by specifying a list of strings. Because we didn't want you to need to type in several thousand values, and because we figured we should show you the correct way to do this, we're going to load the data from a property list. As we've mentioned, both NSArray and NSDictionary objects can be created from property lists. We've included a property list called *statedictionary.plist* in the project archive, under the *07 Pickers* folder.

Copy that file into the *Pickers* folder in your Xcode project. If you single-click the plist file in the project window, you can see and even edit the data that it contains (see Figure 7-15).

Key	Type	Value
▼ Root	Dictionary	(50 items)
▶ Alabama	Array	(657 items)
▶ Alaska	Array	(251 items)
▶ Arizona	Array	(376 items)
▶ Arkansas	Array	(618 items)
▶ California	Array	(1757 items)
▶ Colorado	Array	(501 items)
▶ Connecticut	Array	(276 items)
▶ Delaware	Array	(68 items)
▶ Florida	Array	(972 items)
▶ Georgia	Array	(736 items)
▶ Hawaii	Array	(92 items)
▶ Idaho	Array	(292 items)
▶ Illinois	Array	(1375 items)
▶ Indiana	Array	(780 items)
▶ Iowa	Array	(972 items)
▶ Kansas	Array	(721 items)
▶ Kentucky	Array	(799 items)
▶ Louisiana	Array	(542 items)
▶ Maine	Array	(415 items)
▶ Maryland	Array	(466 items)
▶ Massachusetts	Array	(519 items)
▶ Michigan	Array	(987 items)
▶ Minnesota	Array	(892 items)
▶ Mississippi	Array	(447 items)
▶ Missouri	Array	(1040 items)
▶ Montana	Array	(364 items)
▶ Nebraska	Array	(590 items)
▶ Nevada	Array	(158 items)
▶ New Hampshire	Array	(238 items)
▶ New Jersey	Array	(604 items)
▶ New Mexico	Array	(366 items)
▶ New York	Array	(1677 items)
▶ North Carolina	Array	(809 items)
▶ North Dakota	Array	(392 items)
▶ Ohio	Array	(1189 items)
▶ Oklahoma	Array	(680 items)
▶ Oregon	Array	(428 items)

Figure 7-15. The statedictionary.plist file, showing our list of states. Within Hawaii, you can see the start of a list of ZIP codes

Now, let's write some code. In *BIDDependentComponentPickerViewController.m,* we're going to first show you some whole methods to implement, and then we'll break it down into more digestible chunks. Start with the implementation of buttonPressed:

```
- (IBAction)buttonPressed:(id)sender {
    NSInteger stateRow = [self.dependentPicker
                          selectedRowInComponent:kStateComponent];
    NSInteger zipRow = [self.dependentPicker
                        selectedRowInComponent:kZipComponent];

    NSString *state = self.states[stateRow];
    NSString *zip = self.zips[zipRow];
```

```
    NSString *title = [[NSString alloc] initWithFormat:
                        @"You selected zip code %@.", zip];
    NSString *message = [[NSString alloc] initWithFormat:
                         @"%@ is in %@", zip, state];

    UIAlertView *alert = [[UIAlertView alloc] initWithTitle:title
                                               message:message
                                               delegate:nil
                                        cancelButtonTitle:@"OK"
                                        otherButtonTitles:nil];
    [alert show];
}
```

Next, add the following code to the existing viewDidLoad method:

```
- (void)viewDidLoad
{
    [super viewDidLoad];
    // Do any additional setup after loading the view from its nib.
    NSBundle *bundle = [NSBundle mainBundle];
    NSURL *plistURL = [bundle URLForResource:@"statedictionary"
                              withExtension:@"plist"];

    self.stateZips = [NSDictionary
                      dictionaryWithContentsOfURL:plistURL];

    NSArray *allStates = [self.stateZips allKeys];
    NSArray *sortedStates = [allStates sortedArrayUsingSelector:
                             @selector(compare:)];
    self.states = sortedStates;

    NSString *selectedState = self.states[0];
    self.zips = self.stateZips[selectedState];
}
```

And, finally, add the delegate and data source methods at the bottom of the file:

```
#pragma mark -
#pragma mark Picker Data Source Methods
- (NSInteger)numberOfComponentsInPickerView:(UIPickerView *)pickerView
{
    return 2;
}

- (NSInteger)pickerView:(UIPickerView *)pickerView
numberOfRowsInComponent:(NSInteger)component {
    if (component == kStateComponent) {
        return [self.states count];
    } else {
        return [self.zips count];
    }
}
```

```
#pragma mark Picker Delegate Methods
- (NSString *)pickerView:(UIPickerView *)pickerView
            titleForRow:(NSInteger)row
          forComponent:(NSInteger)component
{
    if (component == kStateComponent) {
        return self.states[row];
    } else {
        return self.zips[row];
    }
}

- (void)pickerView:(UIPickerView *)pickerView
      didSelectRow:(NSInteger)row
       inComponent:(NSInteger)component
{
    if (component == kStateComponent) {
        NSString *selectedState = self.states[row];
        self.zips = self.stateZips[selectedState];
        [self.dependentPicker reloadComponent:kZipComponent];
        [self.dependentPicker selectRow:0
                            inComponent:kZipComponent
                               animated:YES];
    }
}
```

@end

There's no need to talk about the buttonPressed: method since it's fundamentally the same as the previous one. We should talk about the viewDidLoad method, though. There's some stuff going on there that you need to understand, so pull up a chair and let's chat.

The first thing we do in this new viewDidLoad method is grab a reference to our application's main bundle:

```
NSBundle *bundle = [NSBundle mainBundle];
```

What is a bundle, you ask? Well, a **bundle** is just a special type of folder, the contents of which follow a specific structure. Applications and frameworks are both bundles, and this call returns a bundle object that represents our application.

One of the primary uses of NSBundle is to get to resources that you added to the *Resources* folder of your project. Those files will be copied into your application's bundle when you build your application. We've added resources like images to our projects; but up to now, we've used those only in Interface Builder. If we want to get to those resources in our code, we usually need to use NSBundle. We use the main bundle to retrieve the URL of the resource in which we're interested:

```
NSURL *plistURL = [bundle URLForResource:@"statedictionary"
                             withExtension:@"plist"];
```

This will return a URL containing the location of the *statedictionary.plist* file. We can then use that URL to create an NSDictionary object. Once we do that, the entire contents of that property list will be loaded into the newly created NSDictionary object; that is, it is assigned to stateZips:

```
self.stateZips = [NSDictionary
                  dictionaryWithContentsOfURL:plistURL];;
```

The dictionary we just loaded uses the names of the states as the keys and contains an NSArray with all the ZIP codes for that state as the values. To populate the array for the left-hand component, we get the list of all keys from our dictionary and assign those to the states array. Before we assign it, though, we sort it alphabetically:

```
NSArray *allStates = [self.stateZips allKeys];
NSArray *sortedStates = [allStates sortedArrayUsingSelector:
                  @selector(compare:)];
self.states = sortedStates;
```

Unless we specifically set the selection to another value, pickers start with the first row (row 0) selected. To get the zips array that corresponds to the first row in the states array, we grab the object from the states array that's at index 0. That will return the name of the state that will be selected at launch time. We then use that state name to grab the array of ZIP codes for that state, which we assign to the zips array that will be used to feed data to the right-hand component:

```
NSString *selectedState = self.states[0];
self.zips = self.stateZips[selectedState];
```

The two data source methods are practically identical to the previous version. We return the number of rows in the appropriate array. The same is true for the first delegate method we implemented. The second delegate method is the new one, and it's where the magic happens:

```
- (void)pickerView:(UIPickerView *)pickerView
     didSelectRow:(NSInteger)row
      inComponent:(NSInteger)component
{
    if (component == kStateComponent) {
        NSString *selectedState = self.states[row];
        self.zips = self.stateZips[selectedState];
        [self.dependentPicker reloadComponent:kZipComponent];
        [self.dependentPicker selectRow:0
                          inComponent:kZipComponent
                             animated:YES];
    }
}
```

In this method, which is called any time the picker's selection changes, we look at the component and see whether the left-hand component changed. If it did, we grab the array that corresponds to the new selection and assign it to the zips array. Next, we set the right-hand component back to the first row and tell it to reload itself. By swapping the zips array whenever the state changes, the rest of the code remains pretty much the same as it was in the *DoublePicker* example.

We're not quite finished yet. Compile and run your application, and then check out the *Dependent* tab (see Figure 7-16). Do you see anything there you don't like?

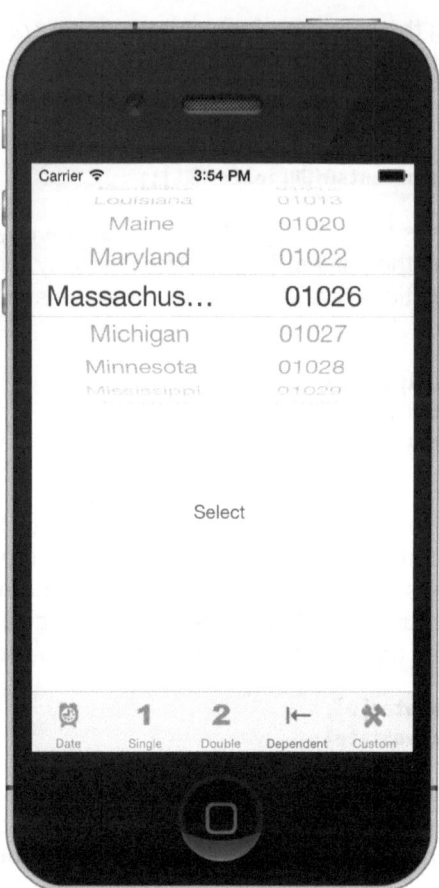

Figure 7-16. Do we really want the two components to be of equal size? Notice the clipping of a long state name

The two components are equal in size. Even though the ZIP code will never be more than five characters long, it has been given equal billing with the state. Since state names like Mississippi and Massachusetts won't fit in half of the picker, this seems less than ideal. Fortunately, there's another delegate method we can implement to indicate how wide each component should be. We have about 295 points available to the picker components in portrait orientation; but for every additional component we add, we lose a little space to drawing the edges of the new component. You might need to experiment a bit with the values to get it to look right. Add the following method to the delegate section of *BIDDependentComponentPickerViewController.m*:

```
- (CGFloat)pickerView:(UIPickerView *)pickerView
    widthForComponent:(NSInteger)component
{
    if (component == kZipComponent) {
        return 90;
    } else {
        return 200;
    }
}
```

In this method, we return a number that represents how many pixels wide each component should be, and the picker will do its best to accommodate this. Save, compile, and run, and the picker on the *Dependent* tab will look more like the one shown in Figure 7-5.

By this point, you should be pretty darn comfortable with both pickers and tab bar applications. We have one more thing to show you about pickers, and we plan to have a little fun while doing it. Let's create a simple slot machine game.

Creating a Simple Game with a Custom Picker

Next up, we're going to create an actual working slot machine. Well, OK, it won't dispense silver dollars, but it does look pretty cool. Take a look back at Figure 7-6 before proceeding, so you know what we're building.

Writing the Controller Header File

Begin by adding the following code to *BIDCustomPickerViewController.h*:

```
#import <UIKit/UIKit.h>

@interface BIDCustomPickerViewController : UIViewController
<UIPickerViewDataSource, UIPickerViewDelegate>

@end
```

Next, switch to *BIDCustomerPickerViewController.m* and add the following property to the class extension near the top of the file:

```
#import "BIDCustomPickerViewController.h"

@interface BIDCustomPickerViewController ()

@property (strong, nonatomic) NSArray *images;

@end
```

At this point, all we've added to the class is a property for an NSArray object that will hold the images to use for these symbols. The rest will come a little later.

Building the View

Even though the picker in Figure 7-6 looks quite a bit fancier than the other ones we've built, there's actually very little difference in the way we'll design our nib. All the extra work is done in the delegate methods of our controller.

Make sure you've saved your new source code, and then select *Main.storyboard* in the project navigator and select the *Custom Picker View Controller* to edit the GUI. Add a picker view, a label below that, and a button below that. Center the label and button horizontally, and give the button the title *Spin*.

Now, move your label so it lines up with the view's left guideline and touches the guideline below the bottom of the picker view. Next, resize the label so it goes all the way to the right guideline and down to the guideline above the top of the button.

With the label selected, bring up the attributes inspector. Set the *Alignment* to centered. Then click *Text Color* and set the color to something festive, like a bright fuchsia (we don't actually know what color that is, but it does sound festive).

Next, let's make the text a little bigger. Look for the *Font* setting in the inspector, and click the icon inside it (it looks like the letter "T" inside a little box) to pop up the font selector. This control lets you switch from the device's standard system font to another if you like, or simply change the size. For now, just change the size to 48. After getting the text the way you want it, delete the word "Label," since we don't want any text displayed until the first time the user wins.

After that, make all the connections to outlets and actions. Create a new outlet called `picker` to connect the *View Controller* to the picker view, another called `winLabel` to connect the *View Controller* to the label, and connect the button's *Touch Up Inside* event to a new action called `spin`. After that, just make sure to specify the *delegate* and *data source* for the picker.

Oh, and there's one additional thing that you need to do. Select the picker and bring up the attributes inspector. You need to uncheck the checkbox labeled *User Interaction Enabled* within the *View* settings, so that the user can't manually change the dial and cheat. Once you've done all that, save the changes you've made to the storyboard.

FONTS SUPPORTED BY IOS DEVICES

Be careful when using the fonts palette in Interface Builder for designing iOS interfaces. The attribute inspector's font selector will let you assign from a wide range of fonts, but not all iOS devices have the same set of fonts available. At the time of writing, for instance, there are several fonts that are available on the iPad, but not on the iPhone or iPod touch. You should limit your font selections to one of the font families found on the iOS device you are targeting. This post on Jeff LaMarche's excellent iOS blog shows you how to grab this list programmatically: http://iphonedevelopment.blogspot.com/2010/08/fonts-and-font-families.html.

In a nutshell, create a view-based application and add this code to the method application:didFinishLaunchingWithOptions: in the application delegate:

```
for (NSString *family in [UIFont familyNames]) {
    NSLog(@"%@", family);
    for (NSString *font in [UIFont fontNamesForFamilyName:family]) {
        NSLog(@"\t%@", font);
    }
}
```

Run the project in the appropriate simulator, and your fonts will be displayed in the project's console log.

Adding Image Resources

Now we need to add the images that we'll be using in our game. We've included six pairs of image files (*seven.png*, *bar.png*, *crown.png*, *cherry.png*, *lemon.png*, *apple.png* and the "@2x" variants for each of them) for you in the project archive under the *07 Pickers/Custom Picker Images* folder. Add all of those files to your project by dragging them into the *Images.xcassets* item in Xcode, just as you did for the tab bar icons.

Implementing the Controller

We have a bunch of new stuff to cover in the implementation of this controller. Select *BIDCustomPickerViewController.m* and get started by filling in the contents of the spin: method:

```
- (IBAction)spin:(id)sender {
    BOOL win = NO;
    int numInRow = 1;
    int lastVal = -1;
    for (int i = 0; i < 5; i++) {
        int newValue = random() % [self.images count];

        if (newValue == lastVal) {
            numInRow++;
        } else {
            numInRow = 1;
        }
        lastVal = newValue;

        [self.picker selectRow:newValue inComponent:i animated:YES];
        [self.picker reloadComponent:i];
        if (numInRow >= 3) {
            win = YES;
        }
    }
    if (win) {
        self.winLabel.text = @"WIN!";
    } else {
        self.winLabel.text = @"";
    }
}
```

Next, insert the following code into the viewDidLoad method:

```
- (void)viewDidLoad
{
    [super viewDidLoad];
    // Do any additional setup after loading the view.
    self.images = @[[UIImage imageNamed:@"seven"],
                    [UIImage imageNamed:@"bar"],
                    [UIImage imageNamed:@"crown"],
                    [UIImage imageNamed:@"cherry"],
```

```
            [UIImage imageNamed:@"lemon"],
            [UIImage imageNamed:@"apple"]];

    srandom(time(NULL));
}
```

Finally, add the following code to the end of the file, before the final @end line:

```
#pragma mark -
#pragma mark Picker Data Source Methods
- (NSInteger)numberOfComponentsInPickerView:(UIPickerView *)pickerView
{
    return 5;
}

- (NSInteger)pickerView:(UIPickerView *)pickerView
numberOfRowsInComponent:(NSInteger)component
{
    return [self.images count];
}

#pragma mark Picker Delegate Methods
- (UIView *)pickerView:(UIPickerView *)pickerView
            viewForRow:(NSInteger)row
         forComponent:(NSInteger)component reusingView:(UIView *)view
{
    UIImage *image = self.images[row];
    UIImageView *imageView = [[UIImageView alloc] initWithImage:image];
    return imageView;
}

@end
```

There's a lot going on here, huh? Let's take the new stuff, method by method.

The spin Method

The spin method fires when the user touches the *Spin* button. In it, we first declare a few variables that will help us keep track of whether the user has won. We'll use win to keep track of whether we've found three in a row by setting it to YES if we have. We'll use numInRow to keep track of how many of the same value we have in a row so far, and we will keep track of the previous component's value in lastVal, so that we have a way to compare the current value to the previous value. We initialize lastVal to -1 because we know that value won't match any of the real values:

```
BOOL win = NO;
int numInRow = 1;
int lastVal = -1;
```

Next, we loop through all five components and set each one to a new, randomly generated row selection. We get the count from the column1 array to do that, which is a shortcut we can use because we know that all five columns have the same number of values:

```
for (int i = 0; i < 5; i++) {
    int newValue = random() % [self.images count];
```

We compare the new value to the previous value and increment numInRow if it matches. If the value didn't match, we reset numInRow back to 1. We then assign the new value to lastVal, so we'll have it to compare the next time through the loop:

```
if (newValue == lastVal) {
    numInRow++;
} else {
    numInRow = 1;
}
lastVal = newValue;
```

After that, we set the corresponding component to the new value, telling it to animate the change, and we tell the picker to reload that component:

```
[self.picker selectRow:newValue inComponent:i animated:YES];
[self.picker reloadComponent:i];
```

The last thing we do each time through the loop is check whether we have three in a row, and then set win to YES if we do:

```
if (numInRow >= 3) {
    win = YES;
}
```

Once we're finished with the loop, we set the label to say whether the spin was a win:

```
if (win) {
    self.winLabel.text = @"WIN!";
} else {
    self.winLabel.text = @"";
}
```

The viewDidLoad Method

Looking back at what we added here, the first thing was to load six different images. We did this using the imageNamed: convenience method on the UIImage class:

```
self.images = @[[UIImage imageNamed:@"seven"],
[UIImage imageNamed:@"bar"], [UIImage imageNamed:@"crown"],
[UIImage imageNamed:@"cherry"], [UIImage imageNamed:@"lemon"],
[UIImage imageNamed:@"apple"]];
```

The last thing we did in this method was to seed the random number generator. If we don't do that, the game will play the same way every time, which gets kind of boring:

```
srandom(time(NULL));
```

That was really simple, wasn't it? But, um, what do we do with those five images? If you scroll down through the code you just typed, you'll see that two data source methods look pretty much the same as before; however, if you look further into the delegate methods, you'll see that we're using a completely different delegate method to provide data to the picker. The one that we've used up to now returned an NSString *, but this one returns a UIView *.

Using this method instead, we can supply the picker with anything that can be drawn into a UIView. Of course, there are limitations on what will work here and look good at the same time, given the small size of the picker. But this method gives us a lot more freedom in what we display, although it is a bit more work:

```
- (UIView *)pickerView:(UIPickerView *)pickerView
          viewForRow:(NSInteger)row
        forComponent:(NSInteger)component reusingView:(UIView *)view
{
    UIImage *image = self.images[row];
    UIImageView *imageView = [[UIImageView alloc] initWithImage:image];
    return imageView;
}
```

This method returns one UIImageView object initialized with one of the images for the symbols. To do that, we first get the image for the symbol for the row. Next, create and return an image view with that symbol. For views more complex than a single image, it can be beneficial to create all needed views first (e.g., in viewDidLoad:), and then return these precreated views to the picker view when requested. But for our simple case, creating the needed views on the fly works well.

Wow, take a deep breath. You got through all of it in one piece, and now you get to take it for a spin.

Final Details

Our game is rather fun, especially when you think about how little effort it took to build it. Now let's improve it with a couple more tweaks. There are two things about this game right now that really bug us:

- It's so darn quiet. Slot machines aren't quiet!

- It tells us that we've won before the dials have finished spinning, which is a minor thing, but it does tend to eliminate the anticipation. To see this in action, run your application again. It is subtle, but the label really does appear before the wheels finish spinning.

The *07 Pickers/Custom Picker Sounds* folder in the project archive that accompanies the book contains two sound files: *crunch.wav* and *win.wav*. Add this folder to your project's *Pickers* folder. These are the sounds we'll play when the users tap the *Spin* button and when they win, respectively.

To work with sounds, we'll need access to the iOS Audio Toolbox classes. Insert this line at the top of *BIDCustomPickerViewController.m*:

```
#import <AudioToolbox/AudioToolbox.h>
```

Next, we need to add an outlet that will point to the button. While the wheels are spinning, we're going to hide the button. We don't want users tapping the button again until the current spin is all done. Add the following code to *BIDCustomPickerViewController.m*:

```
@interface BIDCustomPickerViewController ()

@property (strong, nonatomic) NSArray *images;
@property (weak, nonatomic) IBOutlet UIPickerView *picker;
@property (weak, nonatomic) IBOutlet UILabel *winLabel;
@property (weak, nonatomic) IBOutlet UIButton *button;

@end
```

After you type that and save the file, click *Main.storyboard* to edit the GUI. Once it's open, control-drag from *View Controller* to the *Spin* button and connect it to the new `button` outlet we just created. Save the storyboard.

Now, we need to do a few things in the implementation of our controller class. First, we need an instance variable to hold a reference to the loaded sounds. Open *BIDCustomPickerViewController.m* and add the following lines:

```
@implementation BIDCustomPickerViewController {
    SystemSoundID winSoundID;
    SystemSoundID crunchSoundID;

}
.
.
.
```

We also need a couple of methods added to our controller class. Add the following two methods to *BIDCustomPickerViewController.m* as the first two methods in the class:

```
- (void)showButton
{
    self.button.hidden = NO;
}

- (void)playWinSound
{
    if (winSoundID == 0) {
        NSURL *soundURL = [[NSBundle mainBundle] URLForResource:@"win"
                                               withExtension:@"wav"];
        AudioServicesCreateSystemSoundID((__bridge CFURLRef)soundURL,
                                          &winSoundID);
    }
```

```
AudioServicesPlaySystemSound(winSoundID);
self.winLabel.text = @"WINNING!";
[self performSelector:@selector(showButton)
            withObject:nil
            afterDelay:1.5];
}
```

The first method is used to show the button. As noted previously, we're going to hide the button when the user taps it because, if the wheels are already spinning, there's no point in letting them spin again until they've stopped.

The second method will be called when the user wins. First, we check if we have already loaded the winning sound. Instance variables are initialized as zero and valid identifiers for loaded sounds are not zero, so we can check whether the sound is loaded yet by comparing the identifier to zero. To load a sound, we first ask the main bundle for the path to the sound called *win.wav*, just as we did when we loaded the property list for the Dependent picker view. Once we have the path to that resource, the next three lines of code load the sound file in and play it. Next, we set the label to "WINNING!" and call the showButton method; however, we call the showButton method in a special way using a method called performSelector:withObject:afterDelay:. This is a very handy method available to all objects. It lets you call the method sometime in the future—in this case, one and a half seconds in the future, which will give the dials time to spin to their final locations before telling the user the result.

> **Note**   You may have noticed something a bit odd about the way we called the AudioServicesCreateSystemSoundID function. That function takes a URL as its first parameter, but it doesn't want an instance of NSURL. Instead, it wants a CFURLRef structure. Apple provides C interfaces to many common components—such as URLs, arrays, strings, and much more—via the Core Foundation framework. This allows even applications written entirely in C some access to the functionality that we normally use from Objective-C. The interesting thing is that these C components are "bridged" to their Objective-C counterparts, so that a CFURLRef is functionally equivalent to an NSURL pointer, for example. That means that certain kinds of objects created in Objective-C can be pushed over the bridge to use C APIs, and vice versa. This is accomplished by using a C language cast, putting the type you want your variable to be interpreted as inside parentheses before the variable name. Starting in iOS 5, with the use of ARC, the type name itself must be preceded by the keyword __bridge, which gives ARC a hint about how it should handle this Objective-C object as it passes into a C API call.

We also need to make some changes to the spin: method. We will write code to play a sound and to call the playerWon method if the player won. Make the following changes to the spin: method now:

```objc
- (IBAction)spin:(id)sender {
    BOOL win = NO;
    int numInRow = 1;
    int lastVal = -1;
    for (int i = 0; i < 5; i++) {
        int newValue = random() % [self.images count];

        if (newValue == lastVal) {
            numInRow++;
        } else {
            numInRow = 1;
        }
        lastVal = newValue;

        [self.picker selectRow:newValue inComponent:i animated:YES];
        [self.picker reloadComponent:i];
        if (numInRow >= 3) {
            win = YES;
        }
    }
    if (crunchSoundID == 0) {
        NSString *path = [[NSBundle mainBundle] pathForResource:@"crunch"
                                                         ofType:@"wav"];
        NSURL *soundURL = [NSURL fileURLWithPath:path];
        AudioServicesCreateSystemSoundID((__bridge CFURLRef)soundURL,
                                         &crunchSoundID);
    }
    AudioServicesPlaySystemSound(crunchSoundID);

    if (win) {
        [self performSelector:@selector(playWinSound)
                   withObject:nil
                   afterDelay:.5];
    } else {
        [self performSelector:@selector(showButton)
                   withObject:nil
                   afterDelay:.5];
    }
    self.button.hidden = YES;
    self.winLabel.text = @"";

    if (win) {
        self.winLabel.text = @"WIN!";
    } else {
        self.winLabel.text = @"";
    }
}
```

First, we load the crunch sound if needed, just as we did with the win sound before. Now play the crunch sound to let the player know the wheels have been spun. Next, instead of setting the label to "WINNING?" as soon as we know the user has won, we do something tricky. We call one of the two methods we just created, but we do it after a delay using `performSelector:afterDelay:`. If the user won, we call our `playerWon` method half a second into the future, which will give time for the dials to spin into place; otherwise, we just wait a half a second and reenable the *Spin* button. While waiting for the result, we hide the button and clear the label's text.

Now you're done! Hit the *Run* button and click the final tab to see and hear this slot machine in action. Tapping the *Spin* button should play a little cranking sound, and a win should produce a winning sound. Hooray!

Final Spin

By now, you should be comfortable with tab bar applications and pickers. In this chapter, we built a full-fledged tab bar application containing five different content views from scratch. You learned how to use pickers in a number of different configurations, how to create pickers with multiple components, and even how to make the values in one component dependent on the value selected in another component. You also saw how to make the picker display images rather than just text.

Along the way, you learned about picker delegates and data sources, and saw how to load images, play sounds, and create dictionaries from property lists. It was a long chapter, so congratulations on making it through! When you're ready to tackle table views, turn the page and we'll keep going.

Chapter 8

Introduction to Table Views

In this chapter, we're going to build a hierarchical navigation-based application similar to the Mail application that ships on iOS devices. Our application will allow the user to drill down into nested lists of data and edit that data. But before we can build that application, you need to master the concept of table views. And that's the goal of this chapter.

Table views are the most common mechanism used to display lists of data to the user. They are highly configurable objects that can be made to look practically any way you want them to look. Mail uses table views to show lists of accounts, folders, and messages; however, table views are not limited to just the display of textual data. Table views are also used in the Settings, Music, and Clock applications, even though those applications have very different appearances (see Figure 8-1).

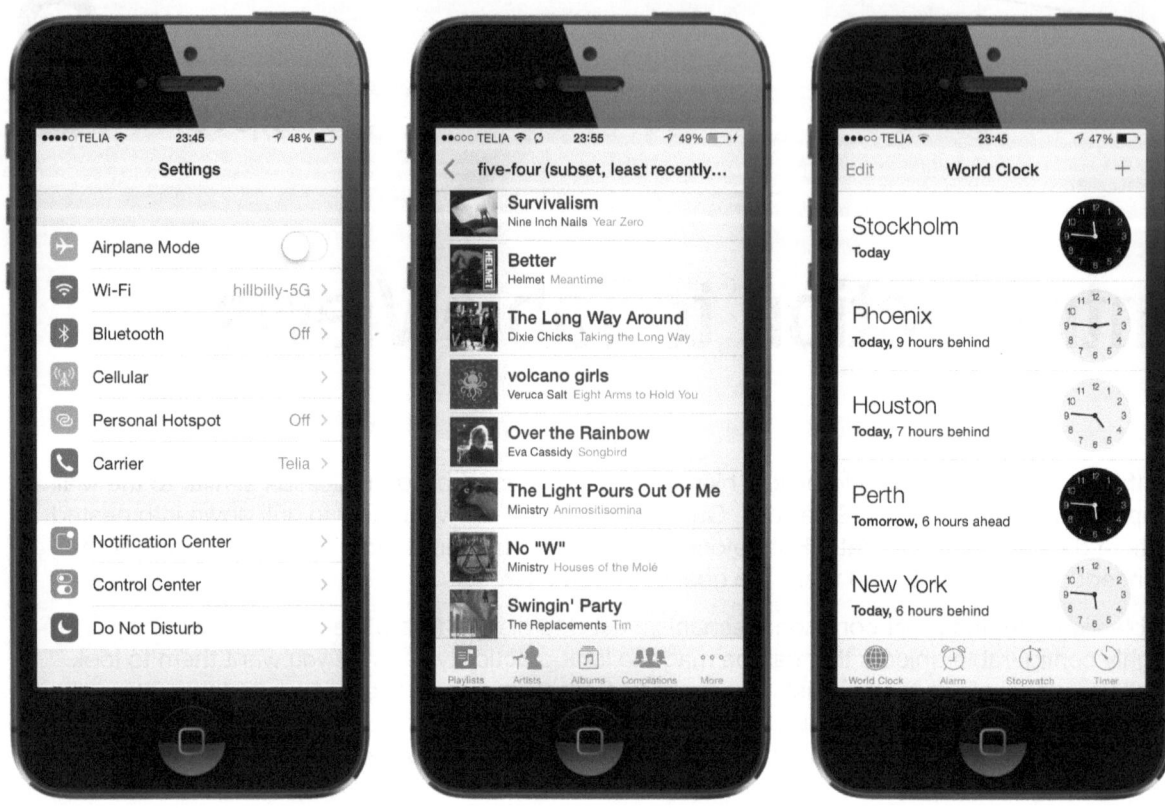

Figure 8-1. *Though they all look different, the Settings, Music, and Clock applications use table views to display their data*

Table View Basics

Tables display lists of data. Each item in a table's list is a row. iOS tables can have an unlimited number of rows, constrained only by the amount of available memory. iOS tables can be only one column wide.

Table Views and Table View Cells

A table view is the view object that displays a table's data and is an instance of the class `UITableView`. Each visible row of the table is implemented by the class `UITableViewCell`. So, a table view is the object that displays the visible part of a table, and a table view cell is responsible for displaying a single row of the table (see Figure 8-2).

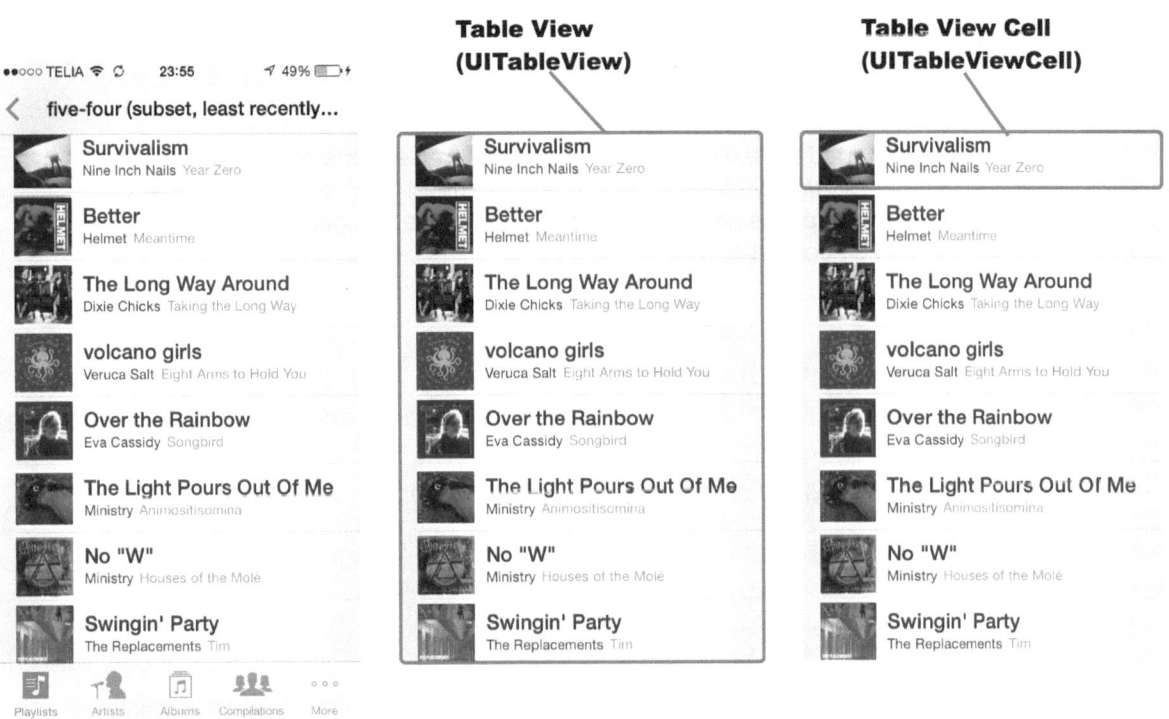

Figure 8-2. Each table view is an instance of UITableView, and each visible row is an instance of UITableViewCell

Table views are not responsible for storing your table's data. They store only enough data to draw the rows that are currently visible. Table views get their configuration data from an object that conforms to the UITableViewDelegate protocol and their row data from an object that conforms to the UITableViewDataSource protocol. You'll see how all this works when we get into our sample programs later in the chapter.

As mentioned, all tables are implemented as a single column. The Clock application, shown on the right side of Figure 8-1, does give the appearance of having at least two columns, perhaps even three if you count the clock faces. But no, each row in the table is represented by a single UITableViewCell. By default, each UITableViewCell object can be configured with an image, some text, and an optional accessory icon, which is a small icon on the right side (we'll cover accessory icons in detail in the next chapter).

You can put even more data in a cell if you need to by adding subviews to UITableViewCell. You do this using one of two basic techniques: by adding subviews programmatically when creating the cell or by loading them from a storyboard or nib file. You can lay out the table view cell out in any way you like and include any subviews you desire. So, the single-column limitation is far less limiting than it probably sounds at first. If this is confusing, don't worry—we'll show you how to use both of these techniques in this chapter.

Grouped and Plain Tables

Table views come in two basic styles:

> **Grouped**: A grouped table view contains one or more sections of rows. Within each section, all rows sit tightly together in a nice little group; but between sections, there are clearly visible gaps, as shown in the leftmost picture in Figure 8-3. Note that a grouped table can consist of a single group.

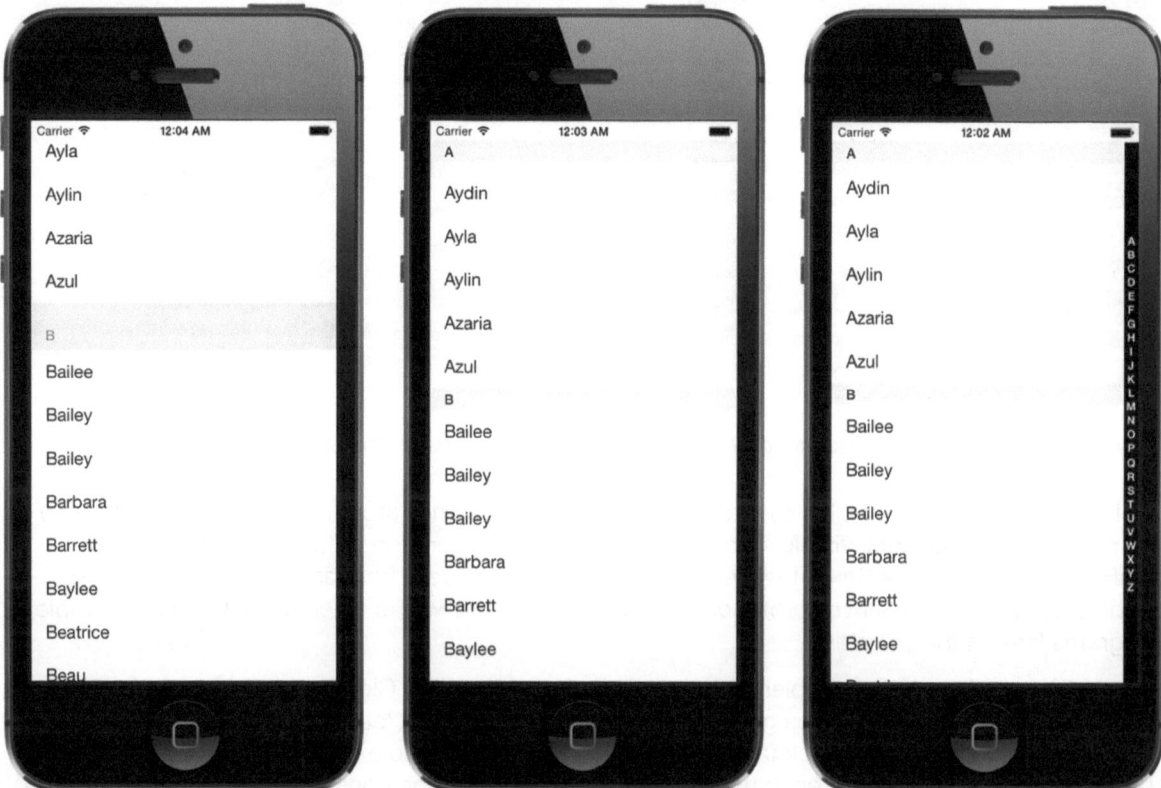

Figure 8-3. The same table view displayed as a grouped table (left); a plain table without an index (middle); and a plain table with an index, which is also called an indexed table (right)

> **Plain**: Plain is the default style. In this style, the sections are slightly closer together, and each section's header can optionally be styled in a custom manner. When an index is used, this style is also referred to as **indexed** (Figure 8-3, right).

If your data source provides the necessary information, the table view will let the user navigate your list using an index that is displayed down the right side.

Each division of your table is known to your data source as a **section**. In a grouped table, each group is a section. In an indexed table, each indexed grouping of data is a section. For example, in the indexed table shown in Figure 8-3, all the names beginning with *A* would be one section, those beginning with *B* would be another, and so on.

Sections have two primary purposes. In a grouped table, each section represents one group. In an indexed table, each section corresponds to one index entry. For example, if you wanted to display a list indexed alphabetically with an index entry for every letter, you would have 26 sections, each containing all the values that begin with a particular letter.

> **Caution**   Even though it is technically possible to create a grouped table with an index, you should not do so. The *iPhone Human Interface Guidelines* specifically state that grouped tables should not provide indexes.

Implementing a Simple Table

Let's look at the simplest possible example of a table view to get a feel for how it works. In this example, we're just going to display a list of text values.

Create a new project in Xcode. For this chapter, we're going back to the *Single View Application* template, so select that one. Call your project *Simple Table*, enter *BID* as the *Class Prefix*, and set the *Device Family* to *iPhone*.

Designing the View

In the project navigator, expand the top-level *Simple Table* project and the *Simple Table* folder. This is such a simple application that we're not going to need any outlets or actions. Go ahead and select *Main.storyboard* to edit the GUI. If the *View* window isn't visible in the layout area, single-click its icon in the document outline to open it. Next, look in the object library for a *Table View* (see Figure 8-4) and drag that over to the *View* window.

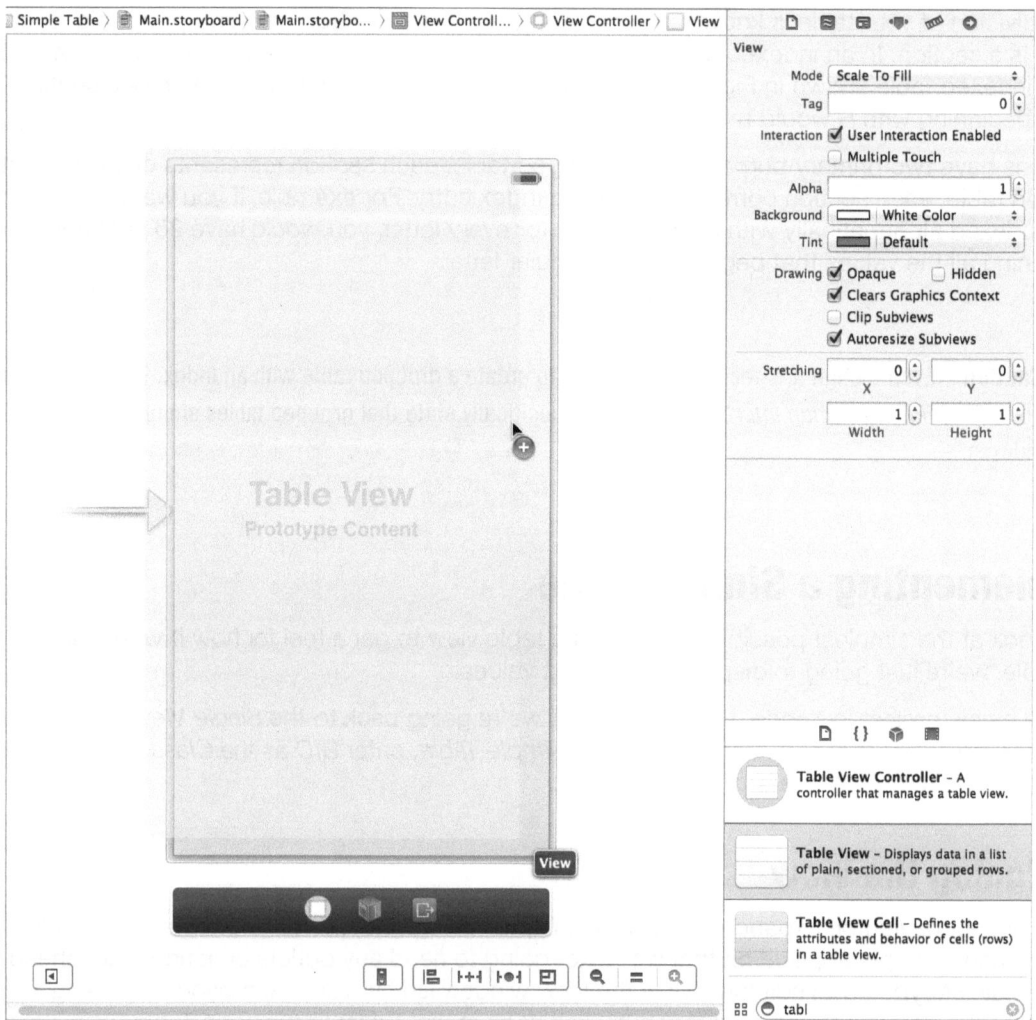

Figure 8-4. *Dragging a table view from the library onto our main view. Notice that the table view automatically resizes to the full size of the view*

The table view should automatically size itself to the height and width of the view. This is exactly what we want. Table views are designed to fill the entire width of the screen and most of the height as well—whatever isn't taken up by your application's navigation bars, toolbars, and tab bars. Drop the table view onto the *View* window and line it up to be centered in its parent view.

Before we go on, there's one problem that we should fix. Right now, this view has a fixed size, matching that of its parent view. But, what happens if the parent view changes its size? This happens when launching the app on a device with a different screen size than what is configured in the storyboard. For example, let's say you've configured this view as a Retina 4-inch sized screen in Interface Builder. If you run the app on an iPhone 4 or with the simulator in Retina 3.5-inch mode, then the table view will keep its original size, which means it will be too large for the screen and will stick part way off the bottom.

Fortunately, we can fix this easily by using constraints. In earlier chapters, we've added constraints using various items from the **Editor** menu, but now we're going to show you another way. As you may have seen, at the bottom of Interface Builder's editing area there's a row of floating buttons. One section of these is all about constraints. With the new table view still selected, move your mouse over each of the buttons at the bottom and see what comes up. We want to pin the edges of our table view to its parent's edges, so look for the button that shows *Pin* in a hovering tooltip and click it. Figure 8-5 shows what comes up.

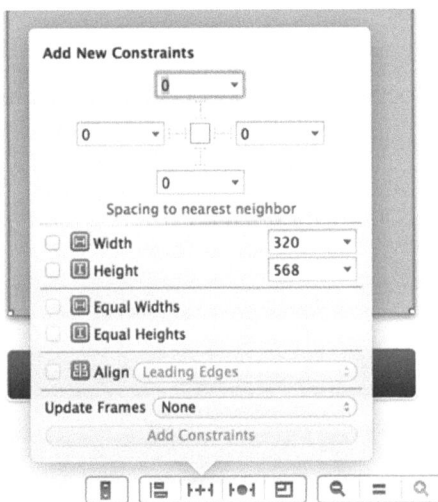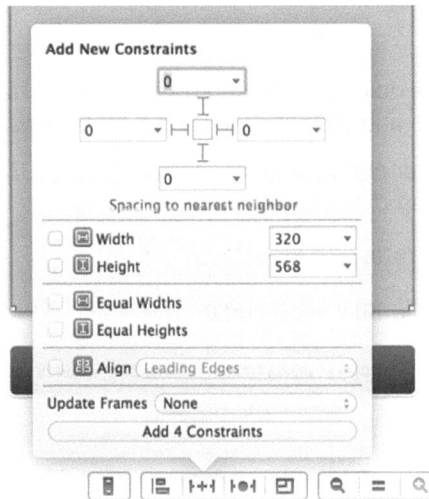

Figure 8-5. The Add New Constraints panel, before and after setting up some constraints

This panel lets you set up new constraints for the chosen view. In our case, we want to make new constraints pinning all the edges of our view to its parent. This is as simple as clicking each of the dotted-line connector symbols surrounding the little square in the upper part of the panel. Each one becomes solid as you click it, and the button at the bottom updates its number to tell you how many constraints you're about to add. When all four are enabled, click the *Add 4 Constraints* button to put them in place.

With the table view still selected, press ⌥⌘6 to bring up the Connections Inspector. You'll notice that the first two available connections for the table view are the same as the first two for the picker view: *dataSource* and *delegate*. Drag from the circle next to each of those connections over to the *View Controller* icon. By doing this, we are making our controller class both the data source and delegate for this table.

With the table view still selected, open the Attributes Inspector (⌥⌘4), and then enter *1* for the Tag value in the View section. If we give unique tag values to views, then these values can later be used to retrieve them in code. We will need to do this later for the table view.

After setting the connections, save your storyboard and get ready to dig into some UITableView code.

Writing the Controller

The next stop is our controller class's header file. Single-click *BIDViewController.h* and add the following code:

```
#import <UIKit/UIKit.h>

@interface BIDViewController : UIViewController
<UITableViewDataSource, UITableViewDelegate>

@end
```

All we're doing here is conforming our class to the two protocols that are needed for it to act as the delegate and data source for the table view.

Save your changes. Next, switch over to *BIDViewController.m* and add the following code at the beginning of the file:

```
#import "BIDViewController.h"

@interface BIDViewController ()

@property (copy, nonatomic) NSArray *dwarves;

@end

@implementation BIDViewController

- (void)viewDidLoad
{
    [super viewDidLoad];
    // Do any additional setup after loading the view, typically from a nib.
    self.dwarves = @[@"Sleepy", @"Sneezy", @"Bashful", @"Happy",
                     @"Doc", @"Grumpy", @"Dopey",
                     @"Thorin", @"Dorin", @"Nori", @"Ori",
                     @"Balin", @"Dwalin", @"Fili", @"Kili",
                     @"Oin", @"Gloin", @"Bifur", @"Bofur",
                     @"Bombur"];

    UITableView *tableView = (id)[self.view viewWithTag:1];
    UIEdgeInsets contentInset = tableView.contentInset;
    contentInset.top = 20;
    [tableView setContentInset:contentInset];
}
```

Finally, add the following code at the end of the file:

```
- (NSInteger)tableView:(UITableView *)tableView
 numberOfRowsInSection:(NSInteger)section
{
    return [self.dwarves count];
}
```

```
- (UITableViewCell *)tableView:(UITableView *)tableView
        cellForRowAtIndexPath:(NSIndexPath *)indexPath
{
    static NSString *SimpleTableIdentifier = @"SimpleTableIdentifier";

    UITableViewCell *cell = [tableView dequeueReusableCellWithIdentifier:
                                        SimpleTableIdentifier];
    if (cell == nil) {
        cell = [[UITableViewCell alloc]
                initWithStyle:UITableViewCellStyleDefault
                reuseIdentifier:SimpleTableIdentifier];
    }

    cell.textLabel.text = self.dwarves[indexPath.row];
    return cell;
}
```

`@end`

First, we declared an array that will hold the data to be displayed. And finally, we added three methods to the controller. You should be comfortable with the first one, viewDidLoad, since we've done similar things in the past. We're simply creating an array of data to display in the table. In a real application, this array would likely come from another source, such as a text file, property list, or a web service. Here we're doing one new thing, however: we're adjusting the top edge inset value for the table view, so that the initial display won't interfere with the transparent status bar. Here's where we make use of the tag value we set in the storyboard to access the table view.

If you scroll down to the end, you can see we added two data source methods. The first one, tableView:numberOfRowsInSection:, is used by the table to ask how many rows are in a particular section. As you might expect, the default number of sections is one, and this method will be called to get the number of rows in the one section that makes up the list. We just return the number of items in our array.

The next method probably requires a little explanation, so let's look at it more closely:

```
- (UITableViewCell *)tableView:(UITableView *)tableView
        cellForRowAtIndexPath:(NSIndexPath *)indexPath
```

This method is called by the table view when it needs to draw one of its rows. Notice that the second argument to this method is an NSIndexPath instance. This is the mechanism that table views use to wrap the section and row indexes into a single object. To get the row index or the section index out of an NSIndexPath, you just access its row property or its section property, both of which return an integer value.

The first parameter, tableView, is a reference to the table doing the asking. This allows us to create classes that act as a data source for multiple tables.

Next, we declare a static string instance:

```
static NSString *SimpleTableIdentifier = @"SimpleTableIdentifier";
```

This string will be used as a key to represent the type of our table cell. Our table will use only a single type of cell.

A table view can display only a few rows at a time on the iPhone's small screen, but the table itself can conceivably hold considerably more. Remember that each row in the table is represented by an instance of UITableViewCell, a subclass of UIView, which means each row can contain subviews. With a large table, this could represent a huge amount of overhead if the table were to try to keep one table view cell instance for every row in the table, regardless of whether that row was currently being displayed. Fortunately, tables don't work that way.

Instead, as table view cells scroll off the screen, they are placed into a queue of cells available to be reused. If the system runs low on memory, the table view will get rid of the cells in the queue. But as long as the system has some memory available for those cells, it will hold on to them in case you want to use them again.

Every time a table view cell rolls off the screen, there's a pretty good chance that another one just rolled onto the screen on the other side. If that new row can just reuse one of the cells that has already rolled off the screen, the system can avoid the overhead associated with constantly creating and releasing those views. To take advantage of this mechanism, we'll ask the table view to give us a previously used cell of the specified type. Note that we're using the NSString identifier we declared earlier. In effect, we're asking for a reusable cell of type SimpleTableIdentifier:

```
UITableViewCell *cell = [tableView dequeueReusableCellWithIdentifier:
                         SimpleTableIdentifier];
```

Now, it's completely possible that the table view won't have any spare cells (e.g., when it's being initially populated), so we check the cell after the call to see whether it's nil. If it is, we manually create a new table view cell using that identifier string. At some point, we'll inevitably reuse one of the cells we create here, so we need to make sure that we create it using SimpleTableIdentifier:

```
if (cell == nil) {
    cell = [[UITableViewCell alloc]
            initWithStyle:UITableViewCellStyleDefault
            reuseIdentifier:SimpleTableIdentifier];
}
```

Curious about UITableViewCellStyleDefault? Hold that thought. We'll get to it when we look at the table view cell styles.

We now have a table view cell that we can return for the table view to use. So, all we need to do is place whatever information we want displayed in this cell. Displaying text in a row of a table is a very common task, so the table view cell provides a UILabel property called textLabel that we can set to display strings. That just requires getting the correct string from our listData array and using it to set the cell's textLabel.

To get the correct value, however, we need to know which row the table view is asking for. We get that information from the indexPath's row property. We use the row number of the table to get the corresponding string from the array, assign it to the cell's textLabel.text property, and then return the cell:

```
cell.textLabel.text = self.dwarves[indexPath.row];
return cell;
```

That wasn't so bad, was it?

Compile and run your application, and you should see the array values displayed in a table view (see Figure 8-6).

Figure 8-6. *The Simple Table application, in all its dwarven glory*

Adding an Image

It would be nice if we could add an image to each row. Guess we would need to create a subclass of UITableViewCell or add subviews to do that, huh? Actually, no, not if you can live with the image being on the left side of each row. The default table view cell can handle that situation just fine. Let's check it out.

In the project archive, in the *08 - Simple Table folder*, grab the file called *star.png* and add it to your project's *Images.assets*. *star.png* is a small icon that was prepared just for this project.

Next, let's get to the code. In the file *BIDViewController.m*, add the following code to the `tableView:c ellForRowAtIndexPath:` method:

```
- (UITableViewCell *)tableView:(UITableView *)tableView
        cellForRowAtIndexPath:(NSIndexPath *)indexPath
{
    static NSString *SimpleTableIdentifier = @"SimpleTableIdentifier";

    UITableViewCell *cell = [tableView dequeueReusableCellWithIdentifier:
                                     SimpleTableIdentifier];
    if (cell == nil) {
        cell = [[UITableViewCell alloc]
                initWithStyle:UITableViewCellStyleDefault
                reuseIdentifier:SimpleTableIdentifier];
    }

    UIImage *image = [UIImage imageNamed:@"star"];
    cell.imageView.image = image;

    cell.textLabel.text = self.dwarves[indexPath.row];
    return cell;
}
```

Yep, that's it. Each cell has an `imageView` property. Each `imageView` has an `image` property, as well as a `highlightedImage` property. The image appears to the left of the cell's text and is replaced by the `highlightedImage`, if one is provided, when the cell is selected. You just set the cell's `imageView.image` property to whatever image you want to display.

If you compile and run your application now, you should get a list with a bunch of nice little star icons to the left of each row (see Figure 8-7). Of course, we could have included a different image for each row in the table. Or, with very little effort, we could have used one icon for all of Mr. Disney's dwarves and a different one for Mr. Tolkien's.

Figure 8-7. We used the cell's image property to add an image to each of the table view's cells

If you like, make a copy of *star.png* and use your favorite graphics application to colorize it a bit. Next, add it to the project, load it with imageNamed:, and use it to set imageView.highlightedImage. Now if you click a cell, your new image will be drawn. If you don't feel like coloring, use the *star2.png* icon we provided in the project archive.

Note   UIImage uses a caching mechanism based on the file name, so it won't load a new image property each time imageNamed: is called. Instead, it will use the already cached version.

Using Table View Cell Styles

The work you've done with the table view so far has used the default cell style shown in Figure 8-7, represented by the constant UITableViewCellStyleDefault. But the UITableViewCell class includes several other predefined cell styles that let you easily add a bit more variety to your table views. These cell styles use three different cell elements:

> **Image**: If an image is part of the specified style, the image is displayed to the left of the cell's text.

> **Text label**: This is the cell's primary text. In the UITableViewCellStyleDefault style we used earlier, the text label is the only text shown in the cell.

> **Detail text label**: This is the cell's secondary text, usually used as an explanatory note or label.

To see what these new style additions look like, add the following code to tableView:cellForRowAtIndexPath: in *BIDViewController.m*:

```
- (UITableViewCell *)tableView:(UITableView *)tableView
        cellForRowAtIndexPath:(NSIndexPath *)indexPath
{
    static NSString *SimpleTableIdentifier = @"SimpleTableIdentifier";

    UITableViewCell *cell = [tableView dequeueReusableCellWithIdentifier:
                                        SimpleTableIdentifier];
    if (cell == nil) {
        cell = [[UITableViewCell alloc]
                initWithStyle:UITableViewCellStyleDefault
                reuseIdentifier:SimpleTableIdentifier];
    }

    UIImage *image = [UIImage imageNamed:@"star.png"];
    cell.imageView.image = image;

    cell.textLabel.text = self.dwarves[indexPath.row];
    if (indexPath.row < 7) {
        cell.detailTextLabel.text = @"Mr. Disney";
    } else {
        cell.detailTextLabel.text = @"Mr. Tolkien";
    }
    return cell;
}
```

All we've done here is set the cell's detail text. We use the string @"Mr. Disney" for the first seven rows and the string @"Mr. Tolkien" for the rest. When you run this code, each cell will look just as it did before (see Figure 8-8). That's because we are using the style UITableViewCellStyleDefault, which does not use the detail text.

Figure 8-8. *The default cell style shows the image and text label in a straight row*

Now change `UITableViewCellStyleDefault` to `UITableViewCellStyleSubtitle` and run the app again. With the subtitle style, both text elements are shown, one below the other (see Figure 8-9).

Sneezy
Mr. Disney

Figure 8-9. *The subtitle style shows the detail text in smaller gray letters below the text label*

Change `UITableViewCellStyleSubtitle` to `UITableViewCellStyleValue1`, and then build and run. This style places the text label and detail text label on the same line, but on opposite sides of the cell (see Figure 8-10).

Sneezy   Mr. Disney

Figure 8-10. *The style value 1 will place the text label on the left side in black letters and the detail text right-justified on the right side in blue letters*

Finally, change `UITableViewCellStyleValue1` to `UITableViewCellStyleValue2`. This format is often used to display information along with a descriptive label. It doesn't show the cell's icon, but places the detail text label to the left of the text label (see Figure 8-11). In this layout, the detail text label acts as a label describing the type of data held in the text label.

Sneezy Mr. Disney

Figure 8-11. *The style value 2 does not display the image and places the detail text label in blue letters to the left of the text label*

Now that you've seen the cell styles that are available, go ahead and change back to the `UITableViewCellStyleDefault` style before continuing. Later in this chapter, you'll see how to customize the appearance of your table. But before you decide to do that, make sure you consider the available styles to see whether one of them will suit your needs.

You may have noticed that we made our controller both the data source and delegate for this table view; but up to now, we haven't actually implemented any of the methods from `UITableViewDelegate`. Unlike picker views, simpler table views don't require the use of a delegate to do their thing. The data source provides all the data needed to draw the table. The purpose of the delegate is to configure the appearance of the table view and to handle certain user interactions. Let's take a look at a few of the configuration options now. We'll discuss a few more in the next chapter.

Setting the Indent Level

The delegate can be used to specify that some rows should be indented. In the file *BIDViewController.m*, add the following method to your code, just above the @end declaration:

```
- (NSInteger)tableView:(UITableView *)tableView
indentationLevelForRowAtIndexPath:(NSIndexPath *)indexPath
{
    return indexPath.row;
}
```

This method sets the **indent level** for each row to its row number, so row 0 will have an indent level of 0, row 1 will have an indent level of 1, and so on. An indent level is simply an integer that tells the table view to move that row a little to the right. The higher the number, the further to the right the row will be indented. You might use this technique, for example, to indicate that one row is subordinate to another row, as Mail does when representing subfolders.

When you run the application again, you can see that each row is now drawn a little further to the right than the last one (see Figure 8-12).

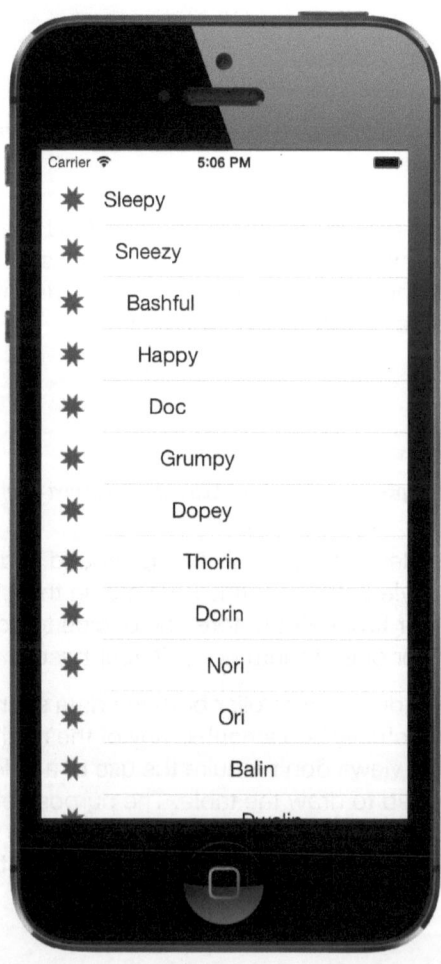

Figure 8-12. Each row of the table is drawn with an indent level higher than the row before it

Handling Row Selection

The table's delegate can use two methods to determine if the user has selected a particular row. One method is called before the row is selected, and it can be used to prevent the row from being selected or even to change which row gets selected. Let's implement that method and specify that the first row is not selectable. Add the following method to the end of *BIDViewController.m*, just before the @end declaration:

```
- (NSIndexPath *)tableView:(UITableView *)tableView
  willSelectRowAtIndexPath:(NSIndexPath *)indexPath
{
    if (indexPath.row == 0) {
        return nil;
    } else {
        return indexPath;
    }
}
```

This method is passed indexPath, which represents the item that's about to be selected. Our code looks at which row is about to be selected. If the row is the first row, which is always index zero, then it returns nil, which indicates that no row should actually be selected. Otherwise, it returns indexPath, which is how we indicate that it's OK for the selection to proceed.

Before you compile and run, you should also implement the delegate method that is called after a row has been selected, which is typically where you'll actually handle the selection. This is where you take whatever action is appropriate when the user selects a row. In the next chapter, we'll use this method to handle the drill-downs; but in this chapter, we'll just put up an alert to show that the row was selected. Add the following method to the bottom of *BIDViewController.m*, just before the @ end declaration again:

```
- (void)tableView:(UITableView *)tableView
didSelectRowAtIndexPath:(NSIndexPath *)indexPath
{
    NSString *rowValue = self.dwarves[indexPath.row];
    NSString *message = [[NSString alloc] initWithFormat:
                        @"You selected %@", rowValue];
    UIAlertView *alert = [[UIAlertView alloc]
                        initWithTitle:@"Row Selected!"
                        message:message
                        delegate:nil
                        cancelButtonTitle:@"Yes I Did"
                        otherButtonTitles:nil];
    [alert show];

    [tableView deselectRowAtIndexPath:indexPath animated:YES];
}
```

Once you've added this method, compile and run the app, and then take it for a spin. For example, see whether you can select the first row (you shouldn't be able to), and then select one of the other rows. The selected row should be highlighted and your alert should pop up, telling you which row you selected while the selected row fades in the background (see Figure 8-13).

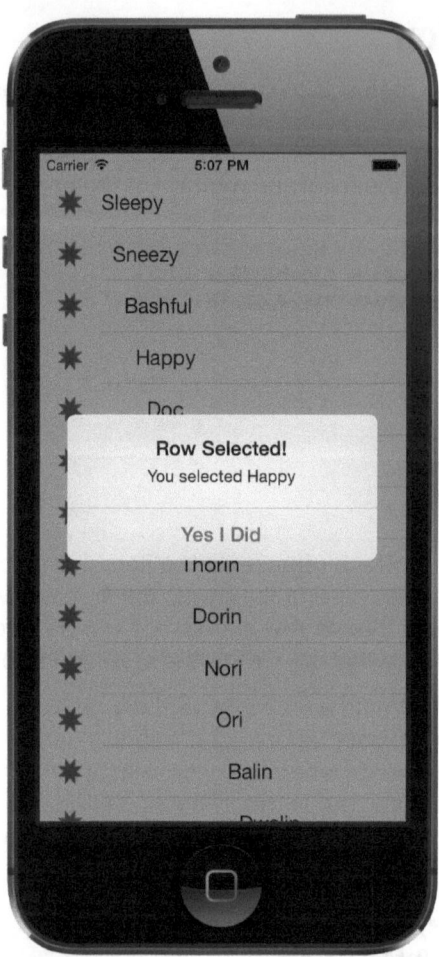

Figure 8-13. In this example, the first row is not selectable, and an alert is displayed when any other row is selected. This was done using the delegate methods

Note that you can also modify the index path before you pass it back, which would cause a different row and/or section to be selected. You won't do that very often, as you should have a very good reason for changing the user's selection. In the vast majority of cases where you use this method, you will either return indexPath unmodified to allow the selection or return nil to disallow it.

Changing the Font Size and Row Height

Let's say that we want to change the size of the font being used in the table view. In most situations, you shouldn't override the default font; it's what users expect to see. But sometimes there are valid reasons to change the font. Add the following line of code to your `tableView:cellForRowAtIndexPath:` method:

```
- (UITableViewCell *)tableView:(UITableView *)tableView
        cellForRowAtIndexPath:(NSIndexPath *)indexPath
{
    static NSString *SimpleTableIdentifier = @"SimpleTableIdentifier";

    UITableViewCell *cell = [tableView dequeueReusableCellWithIdentifier:
                                    SimpleTableIdentifier];
    if (cell == nil) {
        cell = [[UITableViewCell alloc]
                initWithStyle:UITableViewCellStyleDefault
                reuseIdentifier:SimpleTableIdentifier];
    }

    UIImage *image = [UIImage imageNamed:@"star.png"];
    cell.imageView.image = image;

    cell.textLabel.text = self.dwarves[indexPath.row];
    cell.textLabel.font = [UIFont boldSystemFontOfSize:50];

    if (indexPath.row < 7) {
        cell.detailTextLabel.text = @"Mr. Disney";
    } else {
        cell.detailTextLabel.text = @"Mr. Tolkien";
    }
    return cell;
}
```

When you run the application now, the values in your list are drawn in a really large font size, but they don't exactly fit in the row (see Figure 8-14).

Figure 8-14. Look how nice and big! But, um, it would be even nicer if we could see everything

Well, here comes the table view delegate to the rescue! The table view delegate can specify the height of the table view's rows. In fact, it can specify unique values for each row if you find that necessary. Go ahead and add this method to your controller class, just before @end:

```
- (CGFloat)tableView:(UITableView *)tableView
heightForRowAtIndexPath:(NSIndexPath *)indexPath
{
    return 70;
}
```

We've just told the table view to set the row height for all rows to 70 pixels tall. Compile and run, and your table's rows should be much taller now (see Figure 8-15).

Figure 8-15. Changing the row size using the delegate

There are more tasks that the delegate handles, but most of the remaining ones come into play when you start working with hierarchical data, which we'll do in the next chapter. To learn more, use the documentation browser to explore the UITableViewDelegate protocol and see what other methods are available.

Customizing Table View Cells

You can do a lot with table views right out of the box; but often, you will want to format the data for each row in ways that simply aren't supported by UITableViewCell directly. In those cases, there are two basic approaches: one that involves adding subviews to UITableViewCell programmatically when creating the cell, and a second that involves loading a set of subviews from a nib file. Let's look at both techniques.

Adding Subviews to the Table View Cell

To show how to use custom cells, we're going to create a new application with another table view. In each row, we'll display two lines of information along with two labels (see Figure 8-16). Our application will display the name and color of a series of potentially familiar computer models, and we'll show both of those pieces of information in the same table cell by adding subviews to the table view cell.

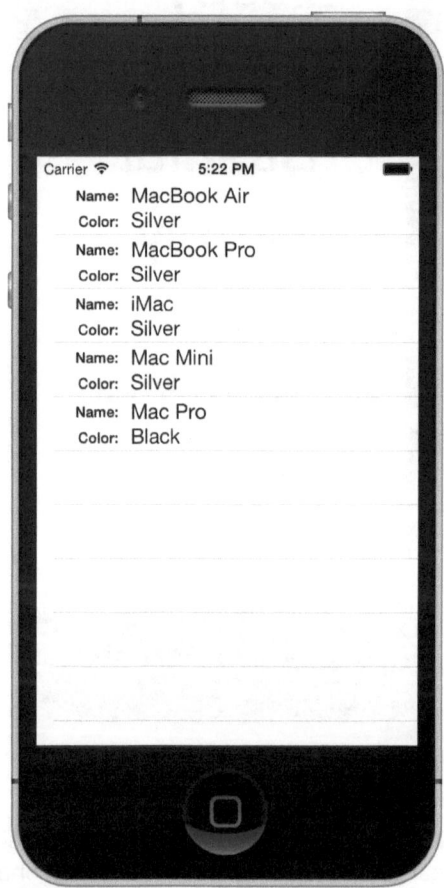

Figure 8-16. Adding subviews to the table view cell can give you multiline rows

Create a new Xcode project using the *Single View Application* template. Name the project *Cells* and use the same settings as your last project. Click *Main.storyboard* to edit the GUI in Interface Builder.

Add a *Table View* to the main view, and then use the Connections Inspector to set its delegate and data source to *File's Owner*, as we did for the Simple Table application. Select the table view and show the Attributes Inspector (⌥⌘4), then enter *1* for the Tag value in the View section. This lets us access the table view from our code without needing to add a specific property for it, just as we did last time. Also, use the *Pin* button at the bottom of the window to create constraints between the table view's edges and those of its parent view, just like last time. Finally, save the storyboard.

Creating a UITableViewCell Subclass

Until this point, the standard table view cells we've been using have taken care of all the details of cell layout for us. Our controller code has been kept clear of the messy details about where to place labels and images, and it has been able to just pass off the display values to the cell. This keeps presentation logic out of the controller, and that's a really good design to stick to. For this project, we're going to make a new cell subclass of our own that takes care of the details for the new layout, which will keep our controller as simple as possible.

Adding New Cells

Select the *Cells* folder in the Project Navigator, and press ⌘N to create a new file. In the assistant that pops up, choose *Objective-C class* from the *Cocoa Touch* section and click *Next*. On the following screen, enter *BIDNameAndColorCell* as the name of the new class, select *UITableViewCell* in the *Subclass of* popup list, and click *Next* again. On the final screen, select the *Cells* folder that already contains your other source code, make sure *Cells* is chosen both in the *Group* and *Target* controls at the bottom, and click *Create*.

Now select *BIDNameAndColorCell.h* and add the following code:

```objectivec
#import <UIKit/UIKit.h>

@interface BIDNameAndColorCell : UITableViewCell

@property (copy, nonatomic) NSString *name;
@property (copy, nonatomic) NSString *color;

@end
```

Here, we've added two properties to our cell's interface that our controller will use to pass values to each cell. Note that instead of declaring the NSString properties with strong semantics, we're using copy. Doing so with NSString values is always a good idea because there's a risk that the string value passed into a property setter may actually be an NSMutableString, which the sender can modify later on, leading to problems. Copying each string that's passed in to a property gives us a stable, unchangeable snapshot of what the string contains at the moment the setter is called.

Now switch over to *BIDNameAndColorCell.m* and add the following code:

```objectivec
#import "BIDNameAndColorCell.h"

@interface BIDNameAndColorCell ()

@property (strong, nonatomic) UILabel *nameLabel;
@property (strong, nonatomic) UILabel *colorLabel;

@end
```

Here, we've added a class extension defining two properties that we'll use to access some of the subviews we'll be adding to our cell. Our cell will contain four subviews, two of which are labels where the content will be changed for every row, so we created a pair of properties to attach to those labels.

Those are all the properties we need to add, so let's move onto the @implementation section. We're going to add some code to the initWithStyle:reuseIdentifier: method to create the views that we'll need to display:

```objc
- (id)initWithStyle:(UITableViewCellStyle)style reuseIdentifier:(NSString *)reuseIdentifier
{
    self = [super initWithStyle:style reuseIdentifier:reuseIdentifier];
    if (self) {
        // Initialization code
        CGRect nameLabelRect = CGRectMake(0, 5, 70, 15);
        UILabel *nameMarker = [[UILabel alloc] initWithFrame:nameLabelRect];
        nameMarker.textAlignment = NSTextAlignmentRight;
        nameMarker.text = @"Name:";
        nameMarker.font = [UIFont boldSystemFontOfSize:12];
        [self.contentView addSubview:nameMarker];

        CGRect colorLabelRect = CGRectMake(0, 26, 70, 15);
        UILabel *colorMarker = [[UILabel alloc] initWithFrame:colorLabelRect];
        colorMarker.textAlignment = NSTextAlignmentRight;
        colorMarker.text = @"Color:";
        colorMarker.font = [UIFont boldSystemFontOfSize:12];
        [self.contentView addSubview:colorMarker];

        CGRect nameValueRect = CGRectMake(80, 5, 200, 15);
        _nameLabel = [[UILabel alloc] initWithFrame:
                            nameValueRect];
        [self.contentView addSubview:_nameLabel];

        CGRect colorValueRect = CGRectMake(80, 25, 200, 15);
        _colorLabel = [[UILabel alloc] initWithFrame:
                            colorValueRect];
        [self.contentView addSubview:_colorLabel];
    }
    return self;
}
```

That should be pretty straightforward. We create four UILabels and add them to the table view cell. The table view cell already has a UIView subview called contentView, which it uses to group all of its subviews, much as we grouped those two switches inside a UIView back in Chapter 4. As a result, we don't add the labels as subviews directly to the table view cell, but rather to its contentView.

Two of these labels contain static text. The label nameMarker contains the text *Name:*, and the label colorMarker contains the text *Color:*. Those are just labels that we won't change. Both these labels have right-aligned text using NSTextAlignmentRight.

We'll use the other two labels to display our row-specific data. Remember that we need some way of retrieving these fields later, so we keep references to both of them in the properties that we declared earlier.

Now let's put the finishing touches on the BIDNameAndColorCell class by adding these two setter methods just before the @end:

```
- (void)setName:(NSString *)n
{
    if (![n isEqualToString:_name]) {
        _name = [n copy];
        self.nameLabel.text = _name;
    }
}

- (void)setColor:(NSString *)c
{
    if (![c isEqualToString:_color]) {
        _color = [c copy];
        self.colorLabel.text = _color;
    }
}
```

You already know that using @property, as we did in the header file, implicitly creates getter and setter methods for each property. Yet, here we're defining our own setters for both name and color! As it turns out, this is just fine. Any time a class defines its own getters or setters, those will be used instead of the default methods. In this class, we're using the default, synthesized getters, but defining our own setters. Whenever we are passed new values for the name or color properties, we update the labels we created earlier.

Implementing the Controller's Code

Now, let's set up the simple controller to display values in our nice new cells. Start off by selecting *BIDViewController.h*, where you need to add the following code:

```
#import <UIKit/UIKit.h>

@interface BIDViewController : UIViewController
    <UITableViewDataSource, UITableViewDelegate>

@end
```

In our controller, we need to set up some data to use, and then implement the table data source methods to feed that data to the table. Switch to *BIDViewController.m* and add the following code at the beginning of the file:

```
#import "BIDViewController.h"
#import "BIDNameAndColorCell.h"

static NSString *CellTableIdentifier = @"CellTableIdentifier";
```

```objc
@interface BIDViewController ()

@property (copy, nonatomic) NSArray *computers;

@end

@implementation BIDViewController

- (void)viewDidLoad
{
    [super viewDidLoad];
    // Do any additional setup after loading the view, typically from a nib.

    self.computers = @[@{@"Name" : @"MacBook Air", @"Color" : @"Silver"},
                       @{@"Name" : @"MacBook Pro", @"Color" : @"Silver"},
                       @{@"Name" : @"iMac", @"Color" : @"Silver"},
                       @{@"Name" : @"Mac Mini", @"Color" : @"Silver"},
                       @{@"Name" : @"Mac Pro", @"Color" : @"Black"}];

    UITableView *tableView = (id)[self.view viewWithTag:1];
    [tableView registerClass:[BIDNameAndColorCell class]
      forCellReuseIdentifier:CellTableIdentifier];

    UIEdgeInsets contentInset = tableView.contentInset;
    contentInset.top = 20;
    [tableView setContentInset:contentInset];

}
```

This version of viewDidLoad assigns an array of dictionaries to the computers property. Each dictionary contains the name and color information for one row in the table. The name for that row is held in the dictionary under the key Name, and the color is held under the key Color. At the end, it also uses a tag number to find the tableView, and then registers our cell class for future reuse. More on that, soon!

> **Note**   Remember when Macs came in different colors, like beige, platinum, black, and white? And that's not to mention the original iMac and iBook series, with their beautiful assortment of rainbow hues. Now, except for the newest Mac Pro, there's just one color: silver. Harrumph. Well, at least we can now comfort ourselves with colorful iPhones.

Now add this code at the end of the file, above the @end declaration:

```objc
- (NSInteger)tableView:(UITableView *)tableView
 numberOfRowsInSection:(NSInteger)section
{
    return [self.computers count];
}
```

```
- (UITableViewCell *)tableView:(UITableView *)tableView
        cellForRowAtIndexPath:(NSIndexPath *)indexPath
{
    BIDNameAndColorCell *cell = [tableView dequeueReusableCellWithIdentifier:
                                    CellTableIdentifier
                                                    forIndexPath:indexPath];

    NSDictionary *rowData = self.computers[indexPath.row];

    cell.name = rowData[@"Name"];
    cell.color = rowData[@"Color"];

    return cell;
}
```

`@end`

Let's focus on `tableView:cellForRowWithIndexPath:` since that's where we're really getting into some new stuff. Here we're using an interesting feature: a table view can use a sort of registry to create a new cell when needed. That means that as long as we've registered all the reuse identifiers we're going to use for a table view, we can always get access to an available cell. In our previous example, we did something similar using the `dequeueReusableCellWithIdentifier:` method, which also uses the registry but returns `nil` if the identifier isn't already in the registry. Now, with the `dequeueReusableCellWithIdentifier:forIndexPath:` method, things are a little bit different because this method never returns `nil`. If we happen to pass it an identifier that isn't registered, the method crashes instead of returning nil. Crashing sounds bad; but in this case, it's the result of a small bug that you'll discover right away during development. Therefore, we can remove the lines that check for a `nil` cell value since that will never happen.

Once we've got our new cell, we use the `indexPath` argument that was passed in to determine which row the table is requesting a cell for, and then use that row value to grab the correct dictionary for the requested row. Remember that the dictionary has two key/value pairs: one with name and another with color:

```
NSDictionary *rowData = self.computers[indexPath.row];
```

Now, all that's left to do is populate the cell with data from the chosen row, using the properties we defined in our subclass:

```
cell.name = rowData[@"Name"];
cell.color = rowData[@"Color"];
```

Compile and run your application. You should see a table of rows, each with two lines of data, as shown earlier in Figure 8-16.

Being able to add views to a table view cell provides a lot more flexibility than using the standard table view cell alone, but it can get a little tedious creating, positioning, and adding all the subviews programmatically. Gosh, it sure would be nice if we could design the table view cell graphically, using Xcode's GUI editing tools. Well, we're in luck. As we mentioned earlier, you can use Interface Builder to design your table view cells, and then simply load the views from a nib file when you create a new cell.

Loading a UITableViewCell from a Nib

We're going to re-create that same two-line interface we just built in code using the visual layout capabilities that Xcode provides in Interface Builder. To do this, we'll create a new nib file that will contain the table view cell and lay out its views using Interface Builder. Then, when we need a table view cell to represent a row, instead of creating a standard table view cell, we'll just load the nib file and use the properties we already defined in our cell class to set the name and color. In addition to using Interface Builder's visual layout, we'll also simplify our code in a few other places.

First, we'll make a few changes to the BIDNameAndColorCell class, inside *BIDNameAndColorCell.m*. The first step is to mark up our properties as outlets, so we can use them in Interface Builder. Make these changes in the class extension near the top:

```
@interface BIDNameAndColorCell ()

@property (strong, nonatomic) IBOutlet UILabel *nameLabel;
@property (strong, nonatomic) IBOutlet UILabel *colorLabel;

@end
```

Now, remember that setup we did in initWithStyle:reuseIdentifier:, where we created our labels? All that can go. In fact, you should just delete the entire method since all that setup will now be done in Interface Builder!

After all that, you're left with a cell class that's even smaller and cleaner than before. Its only real function now is to shuffle data to the labels. Now we need to re-create the labels in Interface Builder.

Right-click the *Cells* folder in Xcode and select **New File...** from the contextual menu. In the left pane of the new file assistant, click *User Interface* (making sure to pick it in the *iOS* section, rather than the *Mac OS X* section). From the upper-right pane, select *Empty*, and then click *Next*. On the following screen, leave the *Device Family* pop-up set to *iPhone* and click *Next* once again. When prompted for a name, type *BIDNameAndColorCell.xib*. Make sure that the main project directory is selected in the file browser and that the *Cells* group is selected in the *Group* pop-up.

Designing the Table View Cell in Interface Builder

Next, select *BIDNameAndColorCell.xib* in the Project Navigator to open the file for editing. Until now, we've been doing all our GUI editing inside of storyboards, but now we're using a nib file instead. Most things are similar and will look very familiar to you, but there are a few differences. One of the main differences is that, while a storyboard file is centered around scenes that pair up a view controller and a view, inside a nib file there's no such forced pairing. In fact, a nib file often doesn't contain a real controller object at all, just a proxy that is called *File's Owner*. If you open up the document outline you'll see it there, right above *First Responder*.

Before we do anything else, the first thing we're going to do is turn off autolayout for this nib file. Autolayout, as you recall, is the system of constraints that determine at runtime just how a view's position and size should change as a result of other geometry changes in its parent or sibling views. Since we're going to define a fixed layout for this view, we can do without it. Just bring up the File Inspector (⌥⌘**1**) and turn off the *Use Autolayout* checkbox in the *Interface Builder Document* section.

Look in the library for a *Table View Cell* (see Figure 8-17) and drag one of those over to the GUI layout area.

Figure 8-17. We dragged a table view cell from the library into the nib editor's GUI layout area

Make sure the table view cell is selected; press ⌥⌘5 to bring up the Size Inspector; and, in the *View* section, change the cell's height from *44* to *65*. That will give us a little more room to play with.

Next, press ⌥⌘4 to go to the Attributes Inspector (see Figure 8-18). One of the first fields you'll see there is *Identifier*. That's the reuse identifier that we've been using in our code. If this does not ring a bell, scan back through the chapter and look for CellTableIdentifier. Set the *Identifier* value to *CellTableIdentifier*.

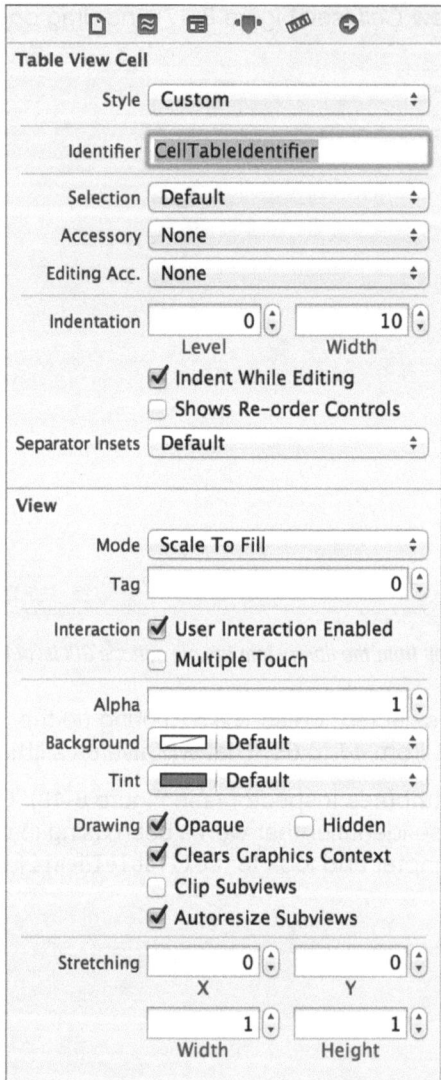

Figure 8-18. The Attributes Inspector for a table view cell

The idea here is that, when we retrieve a cell for reuse, perhaps because of scrolling a new cell into view, we want to make sure we get the correct cell type. When this particular cell is instantiated from the nib file, its reuse identifier instance variable will be prepopulated with the NSString you entered in the *Identifier* field of the Attributes Inspector—*CellTableIdentifier*, in this case.

Imagine a scenario where you created a table with a header and then a series of "middle" cells. If you scroll a middle cell into view, it's important that you retrieve a middle cell to reuse and not a header cell. The *Identifier* field lets you tag the cells appropriately.

Our next step is to edit our table cell's content view. Go to the library, drag out four *Label* controls, and place them in the content view, using Figure 8-19 as a guide. The labels will be too close to the top and bottom for those guidelines to be of much help, but the left guideline and the alignment guidelines should serve their purpose. Note that you can drag out one label, and then option-drag to create copies, if that approach makes things easier for you.

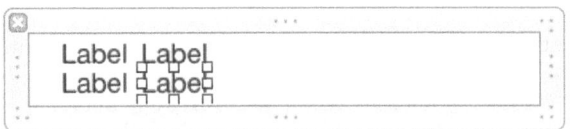

Figure 8-19. The table view cell's content view, with four labels dragged in

Next, double-click the upper-left label and change it to *Name:*, and then change the lower-left label to *Color:*.

Now, select both the *Name:* and *Color:* labels and press the small *T* button in the Attribute Inspector's *Font* field. This will open a small panel containing a *Font* pop-up button. Click that and choose *System Bold* as the typeface. If needed, select the two unchanged label fields on the right and drag them a little more to the right to give the design a bit of breathing room.

Finally, resize the two right-side labels so they stretch all the way to the right guideline. Figure 8-20 should give you a sense of our final cell content view.

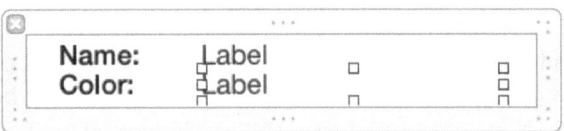

Figure 8-20. The table view cell's content view with the left label names changed and set to bold, and with the right labels slightly moved and resized

Now, we need to let Interface Builder know that this table view cell isn't just a normal cell, but our special subclass. Otherwise, we wouldn't be able to connect our outlets to the relevant labels. Select the table view cell, bring up the Identity Inspector by pressing ⌥⌘3, and choose *BIDNameAndColorCell* from the *Class* control.

Next, switch to the Connections Inspector (⌥⌘6), where you'll see the *colorLabel* and *nameLabel* outlets. Drag each of them to its corresponding label in the GUI.

Using the New Table View Cell

To use the cell we designed, we just need to make a few pretty simple changes to the viewDidLoad: method in *BIDViewController.m*:

```
- (void)viewDidLoad
{
    [super viewDidLoad];
    // Do any additional setup after loading the view, typically from a nib.

    self.computers = @[@{@"Name" : @"MacBook Air", @"Color" : @"Silver"},
                       @{@"Name" : @"MacBook Pro", @"Color" : @"Silver"},
                       @{@"Name" : @"iMac", @"Color" : @"Silver"},
                       @{@"Name" : @"Mac Mini", @"Color" : @"Silver"},
                       @{@"Name" : @"Mac Pro", @"Color" : @"Black"}];

    UITableView *tableView = (id)[self.view viewWithTag:1];
    [tableView registerClass:[BIDNameAndColorCell class]
         forCellReuseIdentifier:CellTableIdentifier];
    tableView.rowHeight = 65;
    UINib *nib = [UINib nibWithNibName:@"BIDNameAndColorCell" bundle:nil];
    [tableView registerNib:nib forCellReuseIdentifier:CellTableIdentifier];

    UIEdgeInsets contentInset = tableView.contentInset;
    contentInset.top = 20;
    [tableView setContentInset:contentInset];
}
```

The first change you see is that we tell the table view to use a row height of 65. We already changed the height of our table view cell from the default value in *CustomCell.xib*, but that's not quite enough. We also need to inform the table view of that fact; otherwise, it won't leave enough space for the cell to display properly. The value of the rowHeight property is used for all rows unless you implement the tableView:heightForRowAtIndexPath: delegate method. The delegate method allows individual heights for each row, but that's not what we're interested in right now, so we use the rowHeight property to quickly change all row heights.

Just as it can associate a class with a reuse identifier, a table view can keep track of which nib files are meant to be associated with particular reuse identifiers. This allows you to register cells for each row type you have using classes or nib files once, and dequeueReusableCellWithIdentifier:forIndexPath: will always provide a cell ready for use.

That's it. Build and run. Now your two-line table cells are based on your mad Interface Builder design skillz.

So, now that you've seen a couple of approaches, what do you think? Many people who delve into iOS development are somewhat confused at first by the focus on Interface Builder; but as you've seen, it has a lot going for it. Besides having the obvious appeal of letting you visually design your GUI, this approach promotes the proper use of nib files, which helps you stick to the MVC architecture pattern. Also, you can make your application code simpler, more modular, and just plain easier to write. As our good buddy Mark Dalrymple says, "No code is the best code!"

Grouped and Indexed Sections

Our next project will explore another fundamental aspect of tables. We're still going to use a single table view—no hierarchies yet—but we'll divide data into sections. Create a new Xcode project using the *Single View Application* template again, this time calling it *Sections*.

Building the View

Open the *Sections* folders, and click *Main.storyboard* to edit the file. Drop a table view onto the *View* window, as we did before. Then press ⌥⌘6 and connect the *dataSource* and *delegate* connections to the *File's Owner* icon.

Next, make sure the table view is selected and press ⌥⌘4 to bring up the Attributes Inspector. Change the table view's *Style* from *Plain* to *Grouped* (see Figure 8-21). Also, set the table view's Tag property to the unique value *1* so we can retrieve it later. Finally, use the *Pin* button to once again set up the constraints for this new table view, just like the previous two. Save the storyboard and move along. (We discussed the difference between indexed and grouped styles at the beginning of the chapter.)

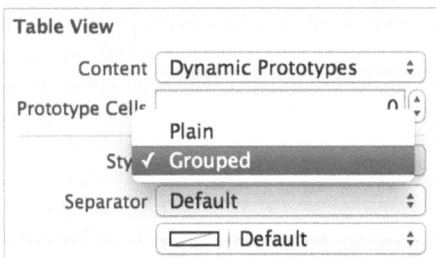

Figure 8-21. The Attributes Inspector for the table view, showing the Style popup with Grouped selected

Importing the Data

This project needs a fair amount of data to do its thing. To save you a few hours of typing, we've provided another property list for your tabling pleasure. Grab the file named *sortednames.plist* from the *08 Sections/Sections* subfolder in this book's project archive and add it to your project's *Sections* folder.

Once *sortednames.plist* is added to your project, single-click it just to get a sense of what it looks like (see Figure 8-22). It's a property list that contains a dictionary, with one entry for each letter of the alphabet. Underneath each letter is a list of names that start with that letter.

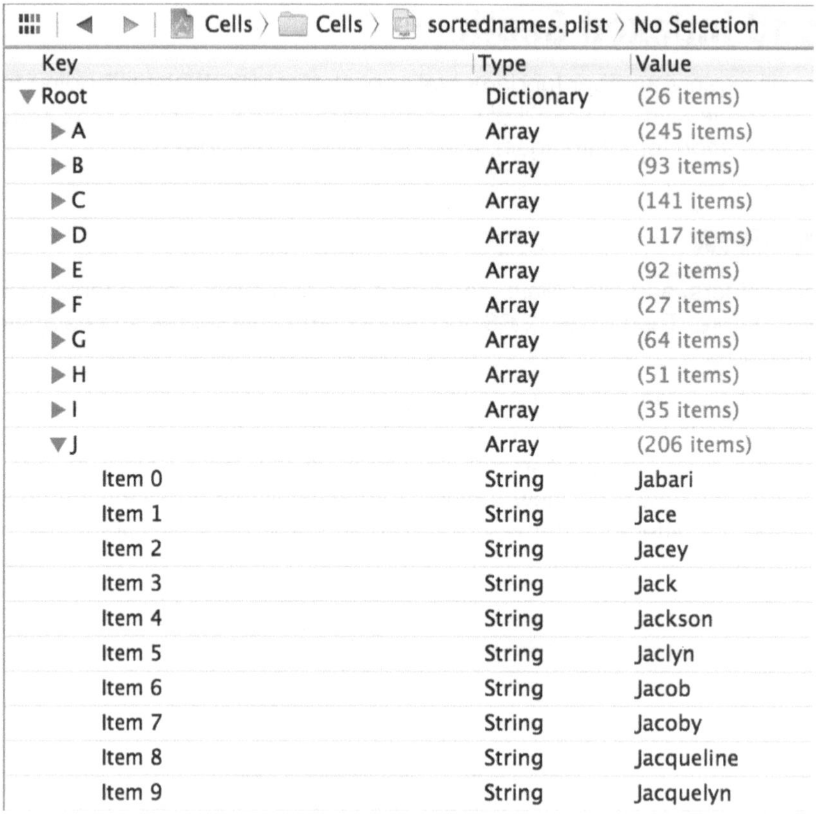

Key	Type	Value
▼ Root	Dictionary	(26 items)
▶ A	Array	(245 items)
▶ B	Array	(93 items)
▶ C	Array	(141 items)
▶ D	Array	(117 items)
▶ E	Array	(92 items)
▶ F	Array	(27 items)
▶ G	Array	(64 items)
▶ H	Array	(51 items)
▶ I	Array	(35 items)
▼ J	Array	(206 items)
Item 0	String	Jabari
Item 1	String	Jace
Item 2	String	Jacey
Item 3	String	Jack
Item 4	String	Jackson
Item 5	String	Jaclyn
Item 6	String	Jacob
Item 7	String	Jacoby
Item 8	String	Jacqueline
Item 9	String	Jacquelyn

Figure 8-22. The sortednames.plist property list file. We opened the letter J to give you a sense of one of the dictionaries

We'll use the data from this property list to feed the table view, creating a section for each letter.

Implementing the Controller

Single-click the *BIDViewController.h* file and make the class conform to the UITableViewDataSource and UITableViewDelegate protocols by adding the following code in bold:

```
#import <UIKit/UIKit.h>

@interface BIDViewController : UIViewController
    <UITableViewDataSource, UITableViewDelegate>

@end
```

Now, switch over to *BIDViewController.m*, and add the following code to the beginning of that file:

```
#import "BIDViewController.h"

static NSString *SectionsTableIdentifier = @"SectionsTableIdentifier";
```

```objc
@interface BIDViewController ()

@property (copy, nonatomic) NSDictionary *names;
@property (copy, nonatomic) NSArray *keys;

@end

@implementation BIDViewController

- (void)viewDidLoad
{
    [super viewDidLoad];
    // Do any additional setup after loading the view, typically from a nib.

    UITableView *tableView = (id)[self.view viewWithTag:1];
    [tableView registerClass:[UITableViewCell class]
      forCellReuseIdentifier:SectionsTableIdentifier];

    NSString *path = [[NSBundle mainBundle] pathForResource:@"sortednames"
                                                     ofType:@"plist"];
    self.names = [NSDictionary dictionaryWithContentsOfFile:path];

    self.keys = [[self.names allKeys] sortedArrayUsingSelector:
                   @selector(compare:)];
}
```

Now add the following code at the end of the file, just above the @end declaration:

```objc
#pragma mark -
#pragma mark Table View Data Source Methods
- (NSInteger)numberOfSectionsInTableView:(UITableView *)tableView
{
    return [self.keys count];
}

- (NSInteger)tableView:(UITableView *)tableView
 numberOfRowsInSection:(NSInteger)section
{
    NSString *key = self.keys[section];
    NSArray *nameSection = self.names[key];
    return [nameSection count];
}

- (NSString *)tableView:(UITableView *)tableView
titleForHeaderInSection:(NSInteger)section
{
    return self.keys[section];
}

- (UITableViewCell *)tableView:(UITableView *)tableView
        cellForRowAtIndexPath:(NSIndexPath *)indexPath
{
    UITableViewCell *cell =
    [tableView dequeueReusableCellWithIdentifier:SectionsTableIdentifier
                                    forIndexPath:indexPath];
```

```
    NSString *key = self.keys[indexPath.section];
    NSArray *nameSection = self.names[key];

    cell.textLabel.text = nameSection[indexPath.row];
    return cell;
}
```

@end

Most of this isn't too different from what you've seen before. In the class extension at the top, we added property declarations for both an NSDictionary and an NSArray. The dictionary will hold all of our data, while the array will hold the sections sorted in alphabetical order. In the viewDidLoad method, we registered the default table view cell class that should be displayed for each row, using our declared identifier. After that, we created an NSDictionary instance from the property list we added to our project and assigned it to the names property. Next we grabbed all the keys from that dictionary and sorted them to give us an ordered NSArray with all the key values in the dictionary in alphabetical order. Remember that the NSDictionary uses the letters of the alphabet as its keys, so this array will have 26 letters sorted from A to Z, and we'll use the array to help us keep track of the sections.

You might notice one thing we didn't do this time that we did for the previous table view examples: we didn't set a special offset for the top edge of the table. That's because, when you're using a grouped table view (as we are), Apple automatically shifts everything down a little bit, so you don't need to worry about the initial table view contents interfering with the status bar.

Scroll down to the data source methods. The first one we added to our class specifies the number of sections. We didn't implement this method in the earlier examples because we were happy with the default setting of 1. This time, we're telling the table view that we have one section for each key in our dictionary:

```
- (NSInteger)numberOfSectionsInTableView:(UITableView *)tableView
{
    return [self.keys count];
}
```

The next method calculates the number of rows in a specific section. In the previous example, we had only one section, so we just returned the number of rows in our array. This time, we need to break it down by section. We can do this by retrieving the array that corresponds to the section in question and returning the count from that array:

```
- (NSInteger)tableView:(UITableView *)tableView
 numberOfRowsInSection:(NSInteger)section
{
    NSString *key = self.keys[section];
    NSArray *nameSection = self.names[key];
    return [nameSection count];
}
```

The method `tableView:titleForHeaderInSection` allows you to specify an optional header value for each section, and we simply return the letter for this group:

```
- (NSString *)tableView:(UITableView *)tableView
titleForHeaderInSection:(NSInteger)section
{
    return self.keys[section];
}
```

In our `tableView:cellForRowAtIndexPath:` method, we need to extract both the section key and the names array using the section and row properties from the index path, and then use those to determine which value to use. The section will tell us which array to pull out of the `names` dictionary, and then we can use the row to figure out which value from that array to use. Everything else in that method is basically the same as the version in the Cells application we built earlier in the chapter.

Compile and run the project, and revel in its grooviness. Remember that we changed the table's *Style* to *Grouped*, so we ended up with a grouped table with 26 sections, which should look like Figure 8-23.

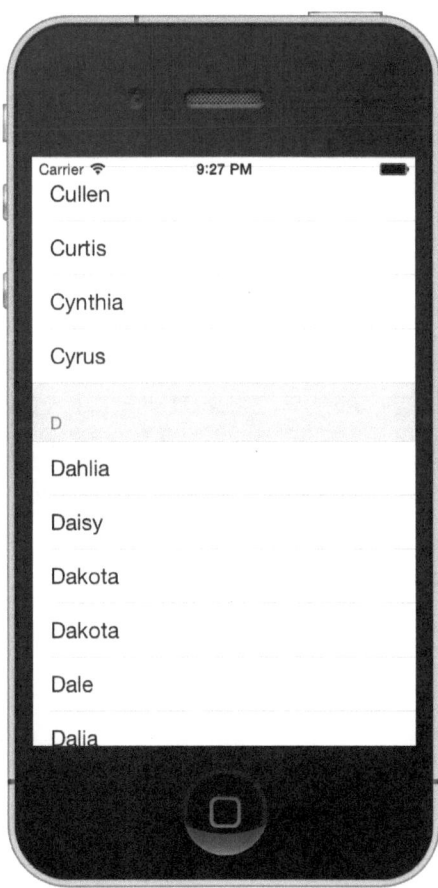

Figure 8-23. A grouped table with multiple sections

As a contrast, let's change our table view back to the plain style and see what a plain table view with multiple sections looks like. Select *Main.storyboard* to edit the file in Interface Builder again. Select the table view and use the Attributes Inspector to switch the view to *Plain*. Save the project, and then build and run it—same data, different grooviness (see Figure 8-24). You'll also see how the lack of a top edge offset makes the plain tableview interfere with the status bar right off the bat. We'll deal with that in a little while.

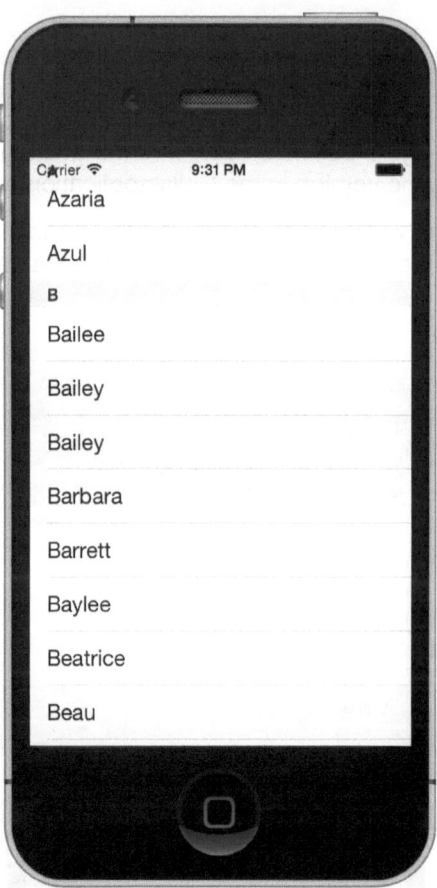

Figure 8-24. A plain table with sections and no index

Adding an Index

One problem with our current table is the sheer number of rows. There are 2,000 names in this list. Your finger will get awfully tired looking for Zachariah or Zayne, not to mention Zoie.

One solution to this problem is to add an index down the right side of the table view. Now that we've set our table view style back to *Plain*, that's relatively easy to do. Add the following method to the bottom of *BIDViewController.m*, just above the @end:

```
- (NSArray *)sectionIndexTitlesForTableView:(UITableView *)tableView
{
    return self.keys;
}
```

Yep, that's it. In this method, the delegate is asking for an array of the values to display in the index. You must have more than one section in your table view to use the index, and the entries in this array must correspond to those sections. The returned array must have the same number of entries as you have sections, and the values must correspond to the appropriate section. In other words, the first item in this array will take the user to the first section, which is section 0.

Since we've switched over to a plain table view, let's fix the top edge offset, too, by adding some code to the viewDidLoad method. This time, we'll even be a little extra smart about this. Since we know that we want to change this offset on a plain table view, but not a grouped table view, we'll make our code check which kind of table view we're dealing with:

```
- (void)viewDidLoad
{
    [super viewDidLoad];
    // Do any additional setup after loading the view, typically from a nib.
    UITableView *tableView = (id)[self.view viewWithTag:1];
    [tableView registerClass:[UITableViewCell class]
       forCellReuseIdentifier:SectionsTableIdentifier];

    NSString *path = [[NSBundle mainBundle] pathForResource:@"sortednames"
                                                     ofType:@"plist"];
    self.names = [NSDictionary dictionaryWithContentsOfFile:path];

    self.keys = [[self.names allKeys] sortedArrayUsingSelector:
                @selector(compare:)];

    if (tableView.style == UITableViewStylePlain) {
        UIEdgeInsets contentInset = tableView.contentInset;
        contentInset.top = 20;
        [tableView setContentInset:contentInset];
    }

}
```

Compile and run the app again, and you'll have yourself a nice index (see Figure 8-25).

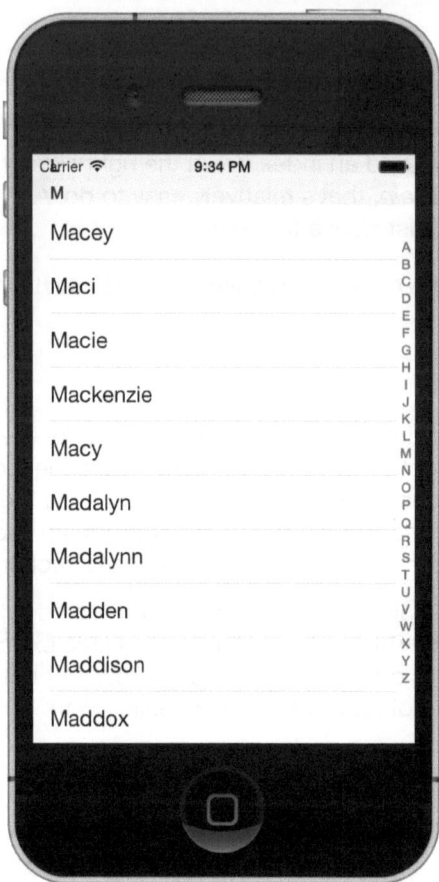

Figure 8-25. The table view with an index

Reducing Status Bar Interference

When trying this out, you're bound to notice one glaring problem: even though the table view's top edge is offset, as soon as you start scrolling, the contents of the table view start interfering with the status bar. This has actually been a problem with all the table view apps we've built so far. But now that there's an opaque section header always stuck to the top of the display, it's even more jarring. As soon as you start scrolling, text starts rolling past the section header and sliding up behind the status bar. This is really ugly!

In the next chapter, you'll see how Apple deals with this situation in a nice, automatic way using something called a *Navigation Controller*; but for the moment we're doing without, so we're going to look at a simple way to make this a little easier on the eyes. The following addition to viewDidLoad will create a simple UIView instance the same size as the status bar, make it white but mostly transparent, and add it to our view. Since we only want to do this for a non-grouped table view, we put it inside the if section we added recently:

```
if (tableView.style == UITableViewStylePlain) {
    UIEdgeInsets contentInset = tableView.contentInset;
    contentInset.top = 20;
    [tableView setContentInset:contentInset];

    UIView *barBackground = [[UIView alloc] initWithFrame:CGRectMake(0, 0, 320, 20)];
    barBackground.backgroundColor = [UIColor colorWithWhite:1.0 alpha:0.9];
    [self.view addSubview:barBackground];
}
```

If you run the app now, you'll see that the text is nearly, but not quite, invisible after it slides up past the table view's section header. If you want to try different opacity values, change the alpha level and see what happens. If you set it to 1.0, the view you added will be completely opaque, and you won't see the scrolling text. A value of 0.0 will make it completely transparent.

Implementing a Search Bar

The index is helpful, but even so, we still have a whole lot of names here. If we want to see whether the name Arabella is in the list, for example, we'll need to scroll for a while even after using the index. It would be nice if we could let the user pare down the list by specifying a search term, wouldn't it? That would be darn user-friendly. Well, it's a bit of extra work, but it's not too bad. We're going to implement a standard iOS search bar using a search display controller, like the one shown in Figure 8-26.

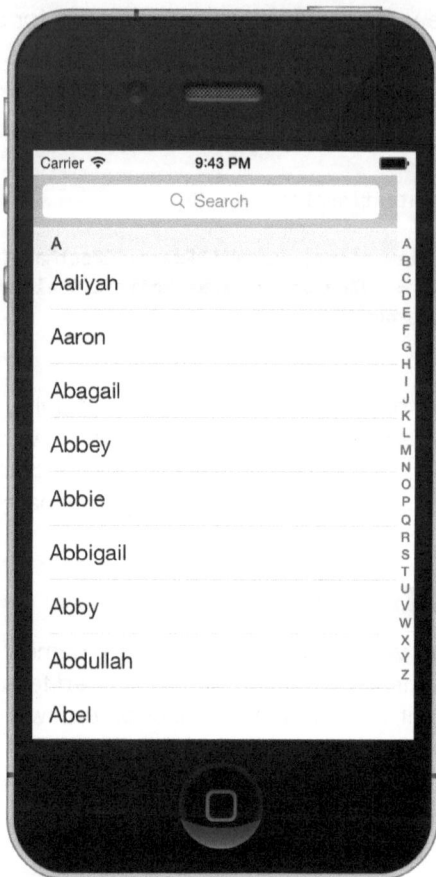

Figure 8-26. *The application with a search bar added to the table*

First we need to update the *BIDViewController.h* file so that our view controller conforms to the UISearchDisplayDelegate protocol:

```
#import <UIKit/UIKit.h>

@interface BIDViewController : UIViewController
    <UITableViewDataSource, UITableViewDelegate, UISearchDisplayDelegate>

@end
```

Next, we need to add two instance variables to our view controller, one to hold a list of only the names matching our filtered search and one for the UISearchDisplayController. Add this code to *BIDViewController.m*:

```
@implementation BIDViewController {
    NSMutableArray *filteredNames;
    UISearchDisplayController *searchController;
}
```

Next, we need to make another set of changes at the end of viewDidLoad, as shown here:

```
- (void)viewDidLoad
{
    [super viewDidLoad];
    // Do any additional setup after loading the view, typically from a nib.
    UITableView *tableView = (id)[self.view viewWithTag:1];
    [tableView registerClass:[UITableViewCell class]
      forCellReuseIdentifier:SectionsTableIdentifier];

    NSString *path = [[NSBundle mainBundle] pathForResource:@"sortednames"
                                                      ofType:@"plist"];
    self.names = [NSDictionary dictionaryWithContentsOfFile:path];

    self.keys = [[self.names allKeys] sortedArrayUsingSelector:
                    @selector(compare:)];

    if (tableView.style == UITableViewStylePlain) {
        UIEdgeInsets contentInset = tableView.contentInset;
        contentInset.top = 20;
        [tableView setContentInset:contentInset];

        UIView *barBackground = [[UIView alloc] initWithFrame:CGRectMake(0, 0, 320, 20)];
        barBackground.backgroundColor = [UIColor colorWithWhite:1.0 alpha:0.9];
        [self.view addSubview:barBackground];
    }

    filteredNames = [NSMutableArray array];
    UISearchBar *searchBar = [[UISearchBar alloc]
                                initWithFrame:CGRectMake(0, 0, 320, 44)];
    tableView.tableHeaderView = searchBar;
    searchController = [[UISearchDisplayController alloc]
                           initWithSearchBar:searchBar
                           contentsController:self];
    searchController.delegate = self;
    searchController.searchResultsDataSource = self;
}
```

First, we initialize our filteredNames to an empty array. Later, that variable will be used to contain the filtered results based on the user's search criteria. After that, we create a UISearchBar and add it as a header view to the table. The header view acts as a special row that is always displayed at the top of the table. Next we create a search display controller for showing the contents of a search. We initialize it using the search bar for input and the view controller itself as owner. We also set our view controller as the delegate for the search display controller to act on changes to the search criteria. Finally, we display the search results by setting our view controller as the data source for the search results.

The search display controller will provide its own table, but we are responsible for providing it with table view cells to display. We need to register a table view cell class to create in the searchDisplayController:didLoadSearchResultsTableView: delegate method. Add this code just above the @end declaration:

```
- (void)searchDisplayController:(UISearchDisplayController *)controller
  didLoadSearchResultsTableView:(UITableView *)tableView
{
    [tableView registerClass:[UITableViewCell class]
      forCellReuseIdentifier:SectionsTableIdentifier];
}
```

Both the search display controller and our own table will use our view controller as the data source to populate a table view, calling on the same data source methods. If the caller is our own table we should act just as we do now; and if the caller is the table for the search display controllers, we should instead display the filtered names. We need to use the table's tag property to determine which table is calling us, and then do the right thing. Update all data source methods like this:

```
- (NSInteger)numberOfSectionsInTableView:(UITableView *)tableView
{
    if (tableView.tag == 1) {
        return [self.keys count];
    } else {
        return 1;
    }
}

- (NSInteger)tableView:(UITableView *)tableView
 numberOfRowsInSection:(NSInteger)section
{
    if (tableView.tag == 1) {
        NSString *key = self.keys[section];
        NSArray *nameSection = self.names[key];
        return [nameSection count];
    } else {
        return [filteredNames count];
    }
}

- (NSString *)tableView:(UITableView *)tableView
titleForHeaderInSection:(NSInteger)section
{
    if (tableView.tag == 1) {
        return self.keys[section];
    } else {
        return nil;
    }
}
```

```
- (UITableViewCell *)tableView:(UITableView *)tableView
        cellForRowAtIndexPath:(NSIndexPath *)indexPath
{
    UITableViewCell *cell = [tableView dequeueReusableCellWithIdentifier:
                                    SectionsTableIdentifier
                                                forIndexPath:indexPath];

    if (tableView.tag == 1) {
        NSString *key = self.keys[indexPath.section];
        NSArray *nameSection = self.names[key];

        cell.textLabel.text = nameSection[indexPath.row];
    } else {
        cell.textLabel.text = filteredNames[indexPath.row];
    }
    return cell;
}

- (NSArray *)sectionIndexTitlesForTableView:(UITableView *)tableView
{
    if (tableView.tag == 1) {
        return self.keys;
    } else {
        return nil;
    }
}
```

As the last piece of the puzzle, we must respond to changes to the search criteria made by the user by implementing the searchDisplayController:shouldReloadTableForSearchString: delegate method. Add this code just before the @end declaration:

```
- (BOOL)searchDisplayController:(UISearchDisplayController *)controller
shouldReloadTableForSearchString:(NSString *)searchString
{
    [filteredNames removeAllObjects];
    if (searchString.length > 0) {
        NSPredicate *predicate =
        [NSPredicate
         predicateWithBlock:^BOOL(NSString *name, NSDictionary *b) {
            NSRange range = [name rangeOfString:searchString
                                        options:NSCaseInsensitiveSearch];
            return range.location != NSNotFound;
        }];
        for (NSString *key in self.keys) {
            NSArray *matches = [self.names[key]
                                    filteredArrayUsingPredicate: predicate];
            [filteredNames addObjectsFromArray:matches];
        }
    }
    return YES;
}
```

This delegate method is called whenever the user edits the search criteria in the search bar to ask if the display of matching results should be reloaded. We always return "yes" to reload for now, but we could add more logic to reload the result table only if the new search criteria results in an actual change.

First, we clear any previous search result:

```
[filteredNames removeAllObjects];
```

Next, we check that the search criteria string is not empty. Do not display any matching results for an empty search string:

```
if (searchString.length > 0) {
```

Now we define a predicate for matching names against the search string. A predicate is an object that tests an input value, returning "yes" if the value matches and "no" if there's no match. Our test is to search for the range of the search string in a name. If the start of the search string is found, we have a match:

```
NSPredicate *predicate =
[NSPredicate
 predicateWithBlock:^BOOL(NSString *name, NSDictionary *b) {
    NSRange range = [name rangeOfString:searchString
                         options:NSCaseInsensitiveSearch];
    return range.location != NSNotFound;
}];
```

Finally, we iterate over all the keys. For each key, we use the predicate to get a filtered array of matching names that we add to the filtered names array:

```
for (NSString *key in self.keys) {
    NSArray *matches = [self.names[key]
                    filteredArrayUsingPredicate:predicate];
    [filteredNames addObjectsFromArray:matches];
}
```

You can now run the app and try to filter the names with a result like the one shown in Figure 8-27.

Figure 8-27. The application with a search bar added to the table. Note that before tapping the search bar, it appears truncated on the right side of the screen

As you can see, there is on visual "glitch" here: the search bar seems to be mysteriously chopped off near the right edge. In fact, what you're seeing is the upper end of the vertical section index bar on the right. Our search bar is a part of the table view (since we set it up to be the header view). When a table view shows a section index, it automatically squashes all its other views in from the right. Since the default section index background color is white, it pretty much blends in with the rows of the table view, which makes its appearance next to the search bar stick out like a sore thumb!

To remedy this, let's set some colors on the section index. We'll use a contrasting color to make it stick out like a sore thumb the whole way up and down the table, so that users can see what's going on more clearly. Just add these lines to the bottom of the `viewDidLoad` method:

```
tableView.sectionIndexBackgroundColor = [UIColor blackColor];
tableView.sectionIndexTrackingBackgroundColor = [UIColor darkGrayColor];
tableView.sectionIndexColor = [UIColor whiteColor];
```

First, we set the main background color for the section index, which is what the user sees when they're not touching it. Then we set the tracking background color, to let the entire column light up a bit when the user touches it and drags up and down the edge. Finally, we set the text color for the index items themselves. Figure 8-28 shows the final result.

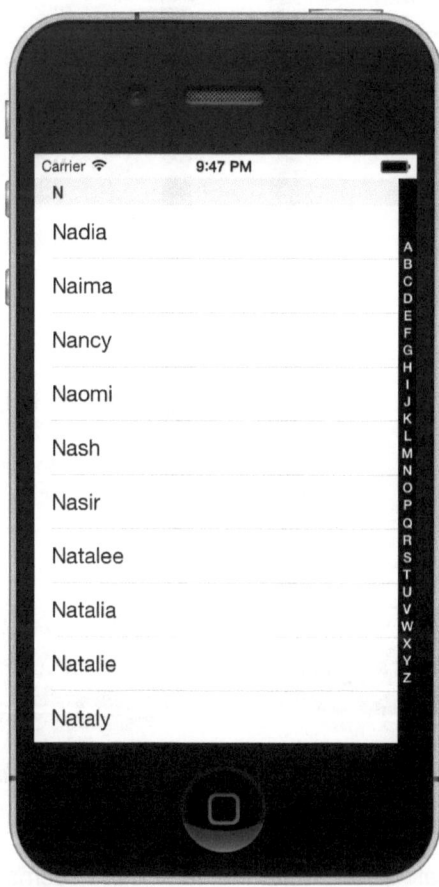

Figure 8-28. With a more visually pronounced section index, it's more clear to the user that this is actually a control surface

Putting It All on the Table

Well, how are you doing? This was a pretty hefty chapter, and you've learned a ton! You should have a very solid understanding of the way that flat tables work. You should know how to customize tables and table view cells, as well as how to configure table views. You also saw how to implement a search bar, which is a vital tool in any iOS application that presents large volumes of data. Make sure you understand everything we did in this chapter because we're going to build on it.

We're going to continue working with table views in the next chapter. For example, you'll learn how to use them to present hierarchical data. And you'll see how to create content views that allow the user to edit data selected in a table view, as well as how to present checklists in tables, embed controls in table rows, and delete rows.

Chapter 9

Navigation Controllers and Table Views

In the previous chapter, you mastered the basics of working with table views. In this chapter, you'll get a whole lot more practice because we're going to explore **navigation controllers**.

Table views and navigation controllers work hand in hand. Strictly speaking, a navigation controller doesn't need a table view to do its thing. As a practical matter, however, when you implement a navigation controller, you almost always implement at least one table, and usually several, because the strength of the navigation controller lies in the ease with which it handles complex hierarchical data. On the iPhone's small screen, hierarchical data is best presented using a succession of table views.

In this chapter, we're going to build an application progressively, just as we did with the Pickers application back in Chapter 7. We'll get the navigation controller and the root view controller working, and then we'll start adding more controllers and layers to the hierarchy. Each view controller we create will reinforce some aspect of table use or configuration:

- How to drill down from table views into child table views
- How to drill down from table views into content views, where detailed data can be viewed and even edited
- How to use multiple sections within a table view
- How to use edit mode to allow rows to be deleted from a table view
- How to use edit mode to let the user reorder rows within a table view

That's a lot, isn't it? Well, let's get started with an introduction to navigation controllers.

Navigation Controller Basics

The main tool you'll use to build hierarchical applications is UINavigationController. UINavigationController is similar to UITabBarController in that it manages, and swaps in and out, multiple content views. The main difference between the two is that UINavigationController is implemented as a stack, which makes it well suited to working with hierarchies.

Do you already know everything there is to know about stacks? If so, scan through the following subsection (or skip it altogether), and we'll meet you at the beginning of the next subsection, "A Stack of Controllers." If you're new to stacks, continue reading. Fortunately, stacks are a pretty easy concept to grasp.

Stacky Goodness

A **stack** is a commonly used data structure that works on the principle of "last in, first out." Believe it or not, a Pez dispenser is a great example of a stack. Ever try to load one? According to the little instruction sheet that comes with each and every Pez dispenser, there are a few easy steps. First, unwrap the pack of Pez candy. Second, open the dispenser by tipping its head straight back. Third, grab the stack (notice the clever way we inserted the word "stack" in there!) of candy, holding it firmly between your pointer finger and thumb, and insert the column into the open dispenser. Fourth, pick up all the little pieces of candy that flew all over the place because these instructions just never work.

OK, so far this example has not been particularly useful. But what happens next is. As you pick up the pieces and jam them, one at a time, into the dispenser, you are working with a stack. Remember that we said a stack was last in, first out? That also means first in, last out. The first piece of Pez you push into the dispenser will be the last piece that pops out. The last piece of Pez you push in will be the first piece you pop out. A computer stack follows the same rules:

- When you add an object to a stack, it's called a **push**. You push an object onto the stack.

- The first object you push onto the stack is called the **base** of the stack.

- The last object you pushed onto the stack is called the **top** of the stack (at least until it is replaced by the next object you push onto the stack).

- When you remove an object from the stack, it's called a **pop**. When you pop an object off the stack, it's always the last one you pushed onto the stack. Conversely, the first object you push onto the stack will always be the last one you pop off the stack.

A Stack of Controllers

A navigation controller maintains a stack of view controllers. When you design your navigation controller, you'll need to specify the very first view the user sees. As we've discussed in previous chapters, that view's controller is called the **root view controller**, or just **root controller**, and is the base of the navigation controller's stack of view controllers. As the user selects the next view to display, a new view controller is pushed onto the stack, and the view it controls appears. We refer to these new view controllers as **subcontrollers.** As you'll see, this chapter's application, Fonts, is made up of a navigation controller and several subcontrollers.

Take a look at Figure 9-1. Notice the **title** centered in the navigation bar and the **back button** on the left side of the navigation bar. The title of the navigation bar is populated with the title property of the top view controller in the navigation controller's stack, and the title of the back button is populated with the title of the previous view controller. The back button acts similar to a web browser's back button. When the user taps that button, the current view controller is popped off the stack, and the previous view becomes the current view.

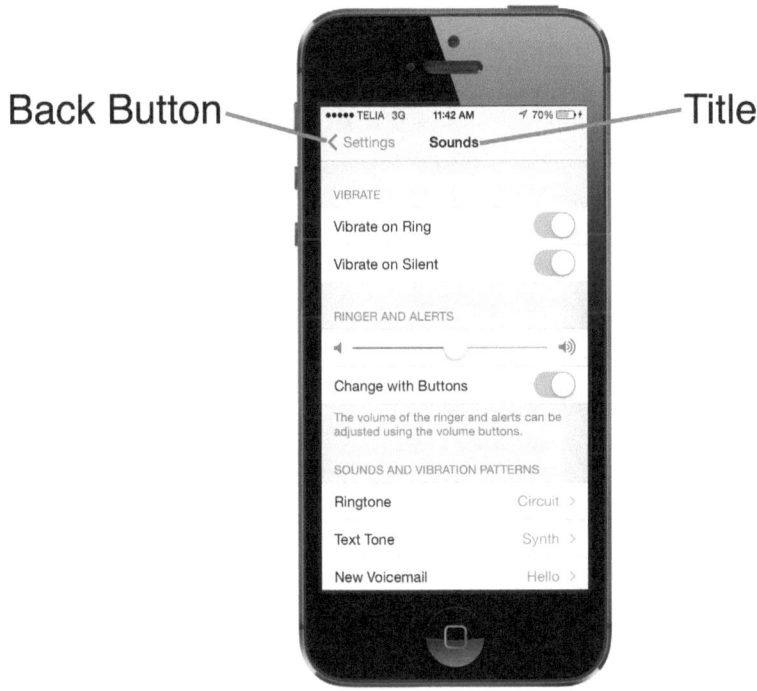

Figure 9-1. *The Settings application uses a navigation controller. The back button at the upper left pops the current view controller off the stack, returning you to the previous level of the hierarchy. The title of the current content view controller is also displayed*

We love this design pattern. It allows us to build complex hierarchical applications iteratively. We don't need to know the entire hierarchy to get things up and running. Each controller only needs to know about its child controllers, so it can push the appropriate new controller object onto the stack when the user makes a selection. You can build up a large application from many small pieces this way, which is exactly what we're going to do in this chapter.

The navigation controller is really the heart and soul of many iPhone apps; however, when it comes to iPad apps, the navigation controller plays a more marginal role. A typical example of this is the Mail app, which features a hierarchical navigation controller to let users navigate among all their mail servers, folders, and messages. In the iPad version of Mail, the navigation controller never fills the screen, but appears either as a sidebar or a temporary view covering part of the main view. We'll dig into that usage a little later, when we cover iPad–specific GUI functionality in Chapter 11.

Fonts, a Simple Font Browser

The application we're about to build will show you how to do most of the common tasks associated with displaying a hierarchy of data. When the application launches, you'll be presented with a list of all the **font families** that are included with iOS, as shown in Figure 9-2. A font family is a group of closely related fonts, or fonts that are stylistic variations on one another. For example, Helvetica, Helvetica-Bold, Helvetic-Oblique, and other variations are all included in the Helvetica font family.

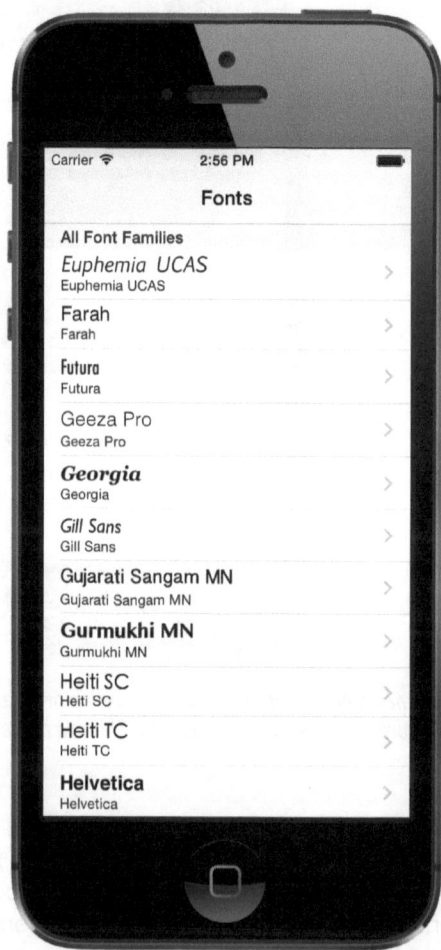

Figure 9-2. This chapter application's root view. Note the accessory icons on the right side of the view. This particular type of accessory icon is called a disclosure indicator. It tells the user that touching that row drills down to another table view

Selecting any row in this top-level view will push a view controller onto the navigation controller's stack. The icons on the right side of each row are called **accessory icons**. This particular accessory icon (the gray arrow) is called a **disclosure indicator**, and its presence lets the user know that touching that row drills down to another table view.

Meet the Subcontrollers

Before we start building the Fonts application, let's take a quick look at each of the views displayed by our subcontrollers.

The Font List Controller

Touching any row of the table shown in Figure 9-2 will bring up the child view shown in Figure 9-3.

Figure 9-3. The first of the Fonts application's subcontrollers implements a table in which each row contains a detail disclosure button

The accessory icon to the right of each row in Figure 9-3 is a bit different. This accessory is known as a **detail disclosure button**. Unlike the disclosure indicator, the detail disclosure button is not just an icon—it's a control that the user can tap. This means that you can have two different options available for a given row: one action is triggered when the user selects the row, and another action is triggered when the user taps the button. Tapping the small info button within this accessory should allow the user to view, and perhaps edit, more detailed information about the current row. Meanwhile, the presence of the right-pointing arrow should indicate to the user that there is some deeper navigation to be found by tapping elsewhere in the row.

The Font Sizes View Controller

Touching any row of the table shown in Figure 9-3 will bring up the child view shown in Figure 9-4.

Figure 9-4. Located one layer deeper than the Font List View Controller, the Font Sizes View Controller shows multiple sizes of the chosen font, one per row

Here's a recap of when to use disclosure indicators and detail disclosure buttons:

- If you want to offer a single choice for a row tap, don't use an accessory icon if a row tap will *only* lead to a more detailed view of that row.

- Mark the row with a disclosure indicator (right-pointing arrow) if a row tap will lead to a new view listing more items (*not* a detail view).

- If you want to offer two choices for a row, mark the row with either a detail disclosure indicator or a detail button. This allows the user to tap the row for a new view or the disclosure button for more details.

The Font Info View Controller

The final of our application's subcontrollers, and the only one that is not a table view, is shown in Figure 9-5. This is the view that appears when you tap on the info icon for any row in the Font List Controller shown in Figure 9-2.

Figure 9-5. The final view controller in the Fonts application allows you to view the chosen font at any size you want

This view lets the user drag a slider to adjust the size of the displayed font. It also includes a switch that lets the user specify whether this font should be listed among the user's favorites. If any fonts are set as favorites, they'll appear within a separate group in the root view controller.

The Fonts Application's Skeleton

Xcode offers a perfectly good template for creating navigation-based applications, and you will likely use it much of the time when you need to create hierarchical applications. However, we're not going to use that template today. Instead, we'll construct our navigation-based application from the ground up, so we get a feel for how everything fits together. We'll also walk through it one piece at a time, so it should be easy to keep up.

In Xcode, press ⌘⇧N to create a new project, select *Empty Application* from the iOS *Application* template list, and then click *Next* to continue. Set *Fonts* as the *Product Name*, *Apress* as the *Organization Name*, *com.apress* as the *Company Identifier*, and *BID* as the *Class Prefix*. Also, make sure that *Use Core Data* is not checked, that *Devices* is set to *iPhone*, and then click Next and choose the location to save your project.

As you'll see if you select the project navigator and look inside the *Fonts* folder, this template gives you an application delegate and not much else. At this point, there are no view controllers or navigation controllers.

To make this app run, we'll need to add a navigation controller, which includes a navigation bar. We'll also need to add a series of views and view controllers for the navigation controller to show. The first of these views is the top-level view shown in Figure 9-2.

Creating the Storyboard

Our app's GUI is going to be contained in a single storyboard. This is the best, most compact way to manage a predetermined hierarchy of view controllers. Press ⌘N to open the file creation assistant and choose *Storyboard* from the *User Interface* section. On the next screen, set the *Device Family* to *iPhone*; and on the screen after that, name the file *Main.storyboard* and save it in your project.

Now you need to make sure the app loads its GUI configuration from this storyboard, so select the top-level *Fonts* item in the project navigator. In the editing area, select the *Fonts* item from the *Targets* section on the left. Next, look for the *Deployment Info* section under the *General* tab, where you'll find a combo box for *Main Interface*. Select *Main.storyboard* to finish that piece of configuration.

Apart from that, you'll need to remove the code from the application delegate that sets up a basic GUI when there's no storyboard or nib file to load, so select *BIDAppDelegate.m*. The first method is the familiar `application:didFinishLaunchingWithOptions:` method that we've dealt with before. Delete all but the last line in that method, leaving just `return YES;`

Setting Up the Navigation Controller

We now need to create the basic navigation structure for our application. At the core of this will be a `UINavigationController`, which manages the stack of view controllers that a user can navigate between, and a `UITableViewController` that shows the top-level list of rows we're going to display. As it turns out, Interface Builder makes this remarkably easy to do.

Select *Main.storyboard* and use the object library to search for *UINavigationController*. Drag one of those into the editing area, and you'll see that you actually get two scenes instead of one, similar to what you saw when creating a tab view controller in Chapter 7. On the left is a `UINavigationController`, which has a connection wired to the second scene, which contains a `UITableViewController`. You'll see that the table has the title *Root View Controller*. Click that title, open the attributes inspector, and then set the title to *Fonts*.

It's worth taking a moment to think about this. What exactly do we get by configuring our application to load the initial scene from this storyboard? First, we get the view created by the navigation controller, a composite view that contains a combination of two things: the navigation bar at the top of the screen (which usually contains some sort of title and often a back button of some kind on the left) and the content of whatever the navigation controller's current view controller wants to display. In our case, the lower part of the display will be filled with the table view that was created alongside the navigation controller.

You'll learn more about how to control what the navigation controller shows in the navigation bar as we go forward. You'll also gain an understanding of how the navigation controller shifts focus from one subordinate view controller to another. For now, you've laid enough groundwork that you can start defining what your custom view controllers are going to do.

At this point, the application skeleton is essentially complete. Save all your files, and then build and run the app. If all is well, the application should launch, and a navigation bar with the title *Fonts* should appear. You haven't given the table view any information about what to show yet, so no rows will display at this point (see Figure 9-6).

Figure 9-6. *The application skeleton in action*

Keeping Track of Favorites

At several points in this application, we're going to let the user maintain a list of favorite fonts by letting them add chosen fonts, view a whole list of already-chosen favorites, and remove fonts from the list. In order to manage this list in a consistent way, we're going to make a new class that will hang onto an array of favorites and store them in the user's preferences settings for this application. You'll learn a lot more about user preferences in chapter 12, but here we'll just touch on some basics.

Start by creating a new class. Select the Fonts folder in the project navigator and press ⌘N to bring up the new file assistant. Select *Cocoa Touch* in the left pane, select *Objective-C class,* and then click *Next*. On the following screen, choose *NSObject* to subclass from and name the new class

BIDFavoritesList. After creating the files for this class, select *BIDFavoritesList.h* and add the bold code shown here:

```
#import <Foundation/Foundation.h>

@interface BIDFavoritesList : NSObject

+ (instancetype)sharedFavoritesList;

- (NSArray *)favorites;

- (void)addFavorite:(id)item;
- (void)removeFavorite:(id)item;

@end
```

In the preceding snippet, we declared the API for our new class. For starters, we declared a factory method called `sharedFavoritesList` that returns an instance of this class. No matter how many times this method is called, the same instance will always be returned. The idea is that `BIDFavoritesList` should work as a singleton; instead of using multiple instances, we'll just use one instance throughout the application.

> **Note**   The declaration for `sharedFavoritesList` has a return type that you may not recognize: `instancetype`. This is a fairly recent addition to Objective-C. It's now recommended that all factory methods and `init` methods that would have otherwise used `id` as their return type should now use `instancetype` instead. The problem with using `id` is the lack of type safety. In the past, you could easily write wrong-headed code like "NSString *s = [NSArray array];" and the compiler wouldn't complain (though your program would crash later, when you tried to send one of `NSString`'s methods to the `NSArray` you created). Using `instancetype` lets you keep a level of genericness, while still telling the compiler that the return value should really be limited to the type of the message recipient (or one of its subclasses).
>
> `instancetype` is not being used by all of Apple's code yet, but some classes in the iOS 7 SDK have been updated to use it. In fact, the bad array assignment shown in the previous paragraph now generates a compiler warning, since `NSArray`'s `array` class method now has `instancetype` as its return type. This will probably be used more and more in the future, so it's worth getting started with.

Next, we defined methods for accessing the array, as well as adding and deleting items.

Now we want to switch over to *BIDFavoritesList.m*, so we can start implementing it. For starters, let's add this property to the class extension at the top:

```
#import "BIDFavoritesList.h"

@interface BIDFavoritesList ()

@property (strong, nonatomic) NSMutableArray *favorites;

@end
```

Note that we're declaring a property named favorites, of type NSMutableArray. In our header file, we just declared a method called favorites that returns an NSArray. Since declaring a property also typically declares the existence of a getter and a setter, won't this lead to a conflict? Fortunately, no. Since our property's type is a subclass of what we are using in the header, it will work just fine. This means that internally, within our class, we can use a mutable array; however, what we expose through our API seems to be an immutable NSArray. The API that this class provides should be considered a contract by any users of this code. If another piece of code digs deep, discovers that this class is actually returning an NSMutableArray, and uses it directly as such, then that code is effectively breaking the contract, and that is Not Our Problem.

Moving on, here's the sharedFavoritesList factory method:

```
+ (instancetype)sharedFavoritesList {
    static BIDFavoritesList *shared = nil;
    static dispatch_once_t onceToken;
    dispatch_once(&onceToken, ^{
        shared = [[self alloc] init];
    });
    return shared;
}
```

This may look complicated, but it really just does one thing: it creates a new instance of the class, and returns it. The creation part is tucked inside a block of code which is passed off to the dispatch_once() function, which makes sure that the code in question runs exactly one time. Every time this method is called after the first time, the instance has already been created, so it is simply returned.

Now, it's time for the init method:

```
- (instancetype)init {
    self = [super init];
    if (self) {
        NSUserDefaults *defaults = [NSUserDefaults standardUserDefaults];
        NSArray *storedFavorites = [defaults objectForKey:@"favorites"];
        if (storedFavorites) {
            self.favorites = [storedFavorites mutableCopy];
        } else {
            self.favorites = [NSMutableArray array];
        }
    }
    return self;
}
```

This method uses the NSUserDefaults class (more about that in Chapter 12) to see if there are any favorites stored in preferences. If so, it puts a mutable copy of the favorites into the favorites property; otherwise, it puts a new, empty mutable array in there instead.

Let's finish up by implementing the two methods for adding and removing favorites, as well as a method they will both call to immediately save their changes:

```
- (void)addFavorite:(id)item {
    [_favorites insertObject:item atIndex:0];
    [self saveFavorites];
}

- (void)removeFavorite:(id)item {
    [_favorites removeObject:item];
    [self saveFavorites];
}

- (void)saveFavorites {
    NSUserDefaults *defaults = [NSUserDefaults standardUserDefaults];
    [defaults setObject:self.favorites forKey:@"favorites"];
    [defaults synchronize];
}
```

Both addFavorite: and removeFavorite: are very straightforward. The only thing worth noting here is the fact that, instead of accessing the array through self.favorites (the preferred style through most of this book), we're accessing the underlying instance variable _favorites instead. The reason for this is subtle: Even though we've defined the property in the class extension as an NSMutableArray, the compiler will find what we declared in the @interface in the header file when trying to resolve self.favorites, and that's an immutable NSArray! This workaround diverges from our normal style, but it will work just fine.

Each of those methods calls the saveFavorites method, which uses the NSUserDefaults class to save the array in the user's preferences. You'll learn more about how this works in Chapter 12; but for now, it's enough to know that the defaults object we grab here acts like a sort of persistent dictionary, and anything that we put in there will be available the next time we ask for it, even if the application has been stopped and restarted.

Creating the Root View Controller

Now we're ready to start working on our first view controller. In the previous chapter, we used simple arrays of strings to populate our table rows. We're going to do something similar here, but this time we'll use the UIFont class to get a list of font families, and then use the names of those font families to populate each row. We'll also use the fonts themselves to display the font names, so that each row will contain a small preview of what the font family contains.

It's time to create the first controller class for this application. Select the *Fonts* folder in the project navigator and press ⌘N to bring up the new file assistant. Select *Cocoa Touch* in the left pane, select *Objective-C class,* and then click *Next*. On the following screen, enter *UITableViewController* for *Subclass of*, and then name the new class *BIDRootViewController*. Click *Next*, and then click *Create* to create the new class. Finally, select *BIDRootViewController.m* and add the bold lines in the snippet that follows to import the header for our favorites list and add a few properties:

```
#import "BIDRootViewController.h"
#import "BIDFavoritesList.h"

@interface BIDRootViewController ()

@property (copy, nonatomic) NSArray *familyNames;
@property (assign, nonatomic) CGFloat cellPointSize;
@property (strong, nonatomic) BIDFavoritesList *favoritesList;

@end
```

We'll assign values to each of those properties from the outset, and then use them at various times while this class is in use. The `familyNames` array will contain a list of all the font families we're going to display; the `cellPointSize` will contain the font size that we want to use in all of our table view cells; and `favoritesList` will contain a pointer to the `BIDFavoritesList` singleton.

Note   You may notice that the `familyNames` property is declared using the `copy` keyword instead of `strong`. What's up with that? Why should we be copying arrays willy-nilly? The reason is the potential existence of mutable arrays.

Imagine if we had declared the property using `strong`, and an outside piece of code passed in an instance of `NSMutableArray` to set the value of the `familyNames` property. If that original caller later decides to change the contents of that array, the `BIDRootViewController` instance will end up in an inconsistent state, where the contents of `familyNames` is no longer in sync with what's on the screen! Using `copy` eliminates that risk, since calling `copy` on any `NSArray` (including any mutable subclasses) always gives us an immutable copy. Also, we don't need to worry about the performance impact too much. As it turns out, sending `copy` to any immutable object doesn't actually copy the object. Instead, it returns the same object after increasing its reference count. In effect, calling `copy` on an immutable object is the same as calling `retain`, which is what ARC might do behind the scenes anytime you set a `strong` property. So, it works out just fine for everyone, since the object can never change.

This situation applies to all **value classes** where the base class is immutable, but mutable subclasses exist. These value classes include `NSArray`, `NSDictionary`, `NSSet`, `NSString`, `NSData`, and a few more. Any time you want to hang onto an instance of one of these in a property, you should probably declare the property's storage with `copy` instead of `strong` to avoid any problems.

Set up all of this class's properties by adding the bold code shown here to the `viewDidLoad` method:

```
- (void)viewDidLoad
{
    [super viewDidLoad];

    self.familyNames = [[UIFont familyNames]
                           sortedArrayUsingSelector:@selector(compare:)];
    UIFont *preferredTableViewFont = [UIFont preferredFontForTextStyle:
                                      UIFontTextStyleHeadline];
    self.cellPointSize = preferredTableViewFont.pointSize;
    self.favoritesList = [BIDFavoritesList sharedFavoritesList];
}
```

In the preceding snippet, we populated `familyNames` by asking the `UIFont` class for all known family names, and then sorting the resulting array. We then used `UIFont` once again to ask for the preferred font for use in a headline. We did this using a new piece of functionality in iOS 7, which builds on the new font size setting that can be specified in the Settings app. This dynamic font sizing lets the user set an overall font scaling for system-wide use. Here, we used that font's `pointSize` to establish a baseline font size that we'll use elsewhere in this view controller. Finally, we grabbed the singleton favorites list.

Before we go on, let's delete the `initWithStyle:` and `didReceiveMemoryWarning` methods, as well as any table view delegate or data source methods that are commented out (typically `tableView:canEditRowAtIndexPath:`, `tableView:commitEditingStyle:`, `tableView:moveRowAtIndexPath:toIndexPath:`, and `tableView:canMoveRowAtIndexPath:`)—we're not going to use any of them in this class.

The idea behind this view controller is to show two sections. The first section is a list of all available font families, each of which leads to a list of all the fonts in the family. The second selection is for favorites, and it contains just a single entry that will lead the user to a list of their favorite fonts. However, if the user has no favorites (for example when the app is launched for the first time), we'd rather not show that second section at all, since it would just lead the user to an empty list. So, we'll have to do a few things throughout the rest of this class to compensate for this eventuality. The first of these is to implement this method:

```
- (void)viewWillAppear:(BOOL)animated {
    [self.tableView reloadData];
}
```

The reason for this is that there may be times when the set of things we're going to display might change from one viewing to the next. For example, the user may start with no favorites, but then drill down, view a font, set it as a favorite, and then come back out to the root view. At that time, we need to reload the table view, so that the second section will appear.

Next, we're going to implement a sort of utility method for use within this class. At a couple of points, while configuring the table view via its data source methods, we'll need to be able to figure out which font we want to display in a cell. We put that functionality into a method of its own:

```
- (UIFont *)fontForDisplayAtIndexPath:(NSIndexPath *)indexPath {
    if (indexPath.section == 0) {
        NSString *familyName = self.familyNames[indexPath.row];
```

```
        NSString *fontName = [[UIFont fontNamesForFamilyName:familyName]
                            firstObject];
        return [UIFont fontWithName:fontName size:self.cellPointSize];
    } else {
        return nil;
    }
}
```

The preceding method uses the UIFont class, first to find all the font names for the given family name, and then later to grab the first font name within that family. We don't necessarily know that the first named font in a family is the best one to represent the whole family, but it's as good a guess as any.

Now, let's move on to the meat of this view controller: the table view datasource methods. First up, let's look at the number of sections:

```
- (NSInteger)numberOfSectionsInTableView:(UITableView *)tableView {
#warning Potentially incomplete method implementation.
    // Return the number of sections.
    if ([self.favoritesList.favorites count] > 0) {
        return 2;
    } else {
        return 1;
    }
    return 0;
}
```

We use the favorites list to determine whether we want to show the second section. Next, we tackle the number of sections in each row:

```
- (NSInteger)tableView:(UITableView *)tableView
 numberOfRowsInSection:(NSInteger)section
{
#warning Incomplete method implementation.
    // Return the number of rows in the section.
    if (section == 0) {
        return [self.familyNames count];
    } else {
        return 1;
    }
    return 0;
}
```

That one's also pretty simple. We just use the section number to determine whether the section is showing all family names, or a single cell linking to the list of favorites. Now let's define one other method, an optional method in the UITableViewDataSource protocol that lets us specify the title for each of our sections:

```
- (NSString *)tableView:(UITableView *)tableView
titleForHeaderInSection:(NSInteger)section {
    if (section == 0) {
        return @"All Font Families";
```

```
    } else {
        return @"My Favorite Fonts";
    }
}
```

The preceding snippet implements another simple method. It uses the section number to determine which header title to use. The final core method that every table view data source must implement is the one for configuring each cell, and ours looks like this:

```
- (UITableViewCell *)tableView:(UITableView *)tableView
        cellForRowAtIndexPath:(NSIndexPath *)indexPath
{
    static NSString *CellIdentifier = @"Cell";
    UITableViewCell *cell = [tableView dequeueReusableCellWithIdentifier:CellIdentifier
                                                           forIndexPath:indexPath];

    static NSString *FamilyNameCell = @"FamilyName";
    static NSString *FavoritesCell = @"Favorites";
    UITableViewCell *cell = nil;

    // Configure the cell...
    if (indexPath.section == 0) {
        cell = [tableView dequeueReusableCellWithIdentifier:FamilyNameCell
                                               forIndexPath:indexPath];
        cell.textLabel.font = [self fontForDisplayAtIndexPath:indexPath];
        cell.textLabel.text = self.familyNames[indexPath.row];
        cell.detailTextLabel.text = self.familyNames[indexPath.row];
    } else {
        cell = [tableView dequeueReusableCellWithIdentifier:FavoritesCell
                                               forIndexPath:indexPath];
    }

    return cell;
}
```

In the preceding snippet, we define two different cell identifiers that we will use to point out two different cells from the storyboard. We haven't configured those yet, but we will soon! Next, we use the section number to determine which of those cells we want to show for the current indexPath. If the cell is meant to contain a font family name, then we put the family name into both its label and its detailLabel. We also use a font from the family (the one we get from the fontForDisplayAtIndexPath: method) within the text label, so that we'll see the font family name shown in the font itself, as well as a smaller version in the standard system font.

Initial Storyboard Setup

Now that we have a view controller that we think should show something, let's configure the storyboard to make things happen. Select *Main.storyboard* in the project navigator. You'll see the navigation controller and the table view controller that we added earlier. The first thing we need to configure is the table view controller. By default, the controller's class is set to UITableViewController. We need to change that and connect some outlets so that our table view will load successfully.

Select the Table View Controller by selecting the scene, and then selecting the small yellow icon that represents the view controller. Use the identity inspector to change the view controller's *Class* to BIDRootViewController. After that, **Ctrl**-drag from the table view to the controller icon, select *dataSource* from the popup, and then do the same gesture and choose *delegate*. At this point, you've connected both of the table view's outlets to the controller, so it knows which object to ask for information about its cells.

The other configuration we'll need to do right now is to set up a pair of prototype cells to match the cell identifiers we used in our code. From the start, the table view has a single prototype cell. Select it and press **Cmd-D** to duplicate it, and you'll see that you now have two cells. Select the first one, and then use the attributes inspector to set its *Style* to *Subtitle* and its *Identifier* to *FamilyName*. Next, select the second prototype cell, and then set its *Style* to *Basic* and its *Identifier* to *Favorites*. Also, double-click the title shown in the cell itself and change the text from *Title* to *Favorites*.

Now build and run this app on your device or the simulator, and you should see a nice list of fonts. But there is a problem! You might spot it as soon as you scroll down to the *Damascus* font; but to see the full extent of the problem, go all the way to the bottom and look at the *Zapfino* font. You'll probably see something like what's shown in Figure 9-7.

Figure 9-7. Some fonts are bigger than others

It turns out that *Zapfino*, and a few other fonts in the list, are way too tall to display this way. Even though we're specifying the same point size for each font we use, the fact is that every font can have characters that extend outside the area we might expect it would take.

If you look at the lowercase letters in all the fonts you see in the list, you can see that the lowercase characters all have roughly the same height. However, you might also notice that some fonts have tall letters that go much higher than others or parts of characters that extend much further down than others. In typographical terms, these vertical distances are called **ascenders** and **descenders**. Fortunately, the UIFont class gives us a way to examine these heights for any given font. And the UITableViewDelegate protocol includes a method we can implement to specify a different height for each cell, so we can calculate a good height for each cell. Add this method to *BIDRootViewController.m*:

```
- (CGFloat)tableView:(UITableView *)tableView
heightForRowAtIndexPath:(NSIndexPath *)indexPath {
    if (indexPath.section == 0) {
        UIFont *font = [self fontForDisplayAtIndexPath:indexPath];
        return 25 + font.ascender - font.descender;
    } else {
        return tableView.rowHeight;
    }
}
```

This method calculates a height for each cell in the table view's first section by calculating the difference between the font's ascender and descender attributes. We add 25 to this number to make space for the detail text label shown below. In this case, 25 is simply a number that was arrived at by trial and error. Since the detail text label is always the same height, this will work just fine.

With that method in place, you can build and run, and you will see that each row is now perfectly adapted to the size of the font it contains. Nice!

First Subcontroller: The Font List View

Our app currently just shows a list of font families, and nothing more. We want to add the ability for a user to touch a font family and see all the fonts it contains, so let's make a new view controller that can manage a list of fonts. Use Xcode's new file assistant to create a new Objective-C class called BIDFontListViewController as a subclass of UITableViewController. After creating the class, select its header file and add the following properties:

```
#import <UIKit/UIKit.h>

@interface BIDFontListViewController : UITableViewController

@property (copy, nonatomic) NSArray *fontNames;
@property (assign, nonatomic) BOOL showsFavorites;

@end
```

The fontNames property is what we'll use to tell this view controller what to display. We also created a showsFavorites property that we'll use to let this view controller know if it's showing the list of favorites instead of just a list of fonts in a family, since this will be useful later on.

Now switch over to BIDFontListController.m and start by deleting the initWithStyle: and didReceiveMemoryWarning methods—we're not going to do anything with them here, either. Next, go to the top of the file, where you'll need to import a header and declare a property:

```
#import "BIDFontListViewController.h"
#import "BIDFavoritesList.h"

@interface BIDFontListViewController ()

@property (assign, nonatomic) CGFloat cellPointSize;

@end
```

We'll use the cellPointSize property to hold the preferred display size for displaying each font, once again using UIFont to find the preferred size. We do this by implementing viewDidLoad as follows:

```
- (void)viewDidLoad
{
    [super viewDidLoad];

    // Uncomment the following line to preserve selection between presentations.
    // self.clearsSelectionOnViewWillAppear = NO;

    // Uncomment the following line to display an Edit button in the navigation
    // bar for this view controller.
    // self.navigationItem.rightBarButtonItem = self.editButtonItem;

    UIFont *preferredTableViewFont = [UIFont preferredFontForTextStyle:
                                      UIFontTextStyleHeadline];
    self.cellPointSize = preferredTableViewFont.pointSize;
}
```

Now the first thing we want to do is create a little utility method for choosing the font to be shown in each row, similar to what we have in BIDRootViewController. Here it's a bit different, though. Instead of holding onto a list of font families, in this view controller we're holding onto a list of font names, and we'll use the UIFont class to get each named font, like this:

```
- (UIFont *)fontForDisplayAtIndexPath:(NSIndexPath *)indexPath {
    NSString *fontName = self.fontNames[indexPath.row];
    return [UIFont fontWithName:fontName size:self.cellPointSize];
}
```

Now it's time for a small addition in the form of a viewWillAppear: implementation. Remember how, in BIDRootViewController, we implemented this method in case the list of favorites might change, requiring a refresh? Well, the same applies here. This view controller might be showing the list of favorites, and the user might switch to another view controller, change a favorite (we'll get there later), and then come back here. We need to reload the table view then, and this method takes care of that:

```
- (void)viewWillAppear:(BOOL)animated {
    if (self.showsFavorites) {
        self.fontNames = [BIDFavoritesList sharedFavoritesList].favorites;
        [self.tableView reloadData];
    }
}
```

The basic idea is that this view controller, in normal operation, is passed a list of font names before it displays, and that the list stays the same the whole time this view controller is around. In one particular case, however, this view controller is responsible for reloading its list now and then.

Moving on, we delete the numberOfSectionsInTableView: method entirely. We'll only have one section here, and just skipping that method is the equivalent of implementing it and returning 1. Next, we implement the two other main data source methods, like this:

```
- (NSInteger)tableView:(UITableView *)tableView
  numberOfRowsInSection:(NSInteger)section
{
#warning Incomplete method implementation.
    // Return the number of rows in the section.
    return [self.fontNames count];
    return 0;
}

- (UITableViewCell *)tableView:(UITableView *)tableView
         cellForRowAtIndexPath:(NSIndexPath *)indexPath
{
    static NSString *CellIdentifier = @"Cell";
    static NSString *CellIdentifier = @"FontName";
    UITableViewCell *cell = [tableView
                               dequeueReusableCellWithIdentifier:CellIdentifier
                               forIndexPath:indexPath];

    // Configure the cell...
    cell.textLabel.font = [self fontForDisplayAtIndexPath:indexPath];
    cell.textLabel.text = self.fontNames[indexPath.row];
    cell.detailTextLabel.text = self.fontNames[indexPath.row];

    return cell;
}
```

The first of these needs no explanation, and maybe not the second one, either. It's similar to what we used in BIDRootViewController, but even simpler.

As you'll recall, different fonts can have different visible heights. To make each table view cell the correct height, implement this delegate method that is identical to the one in BIDRootViewController:

```
- (CGFloat)tableView:(UITableView *)tableView
heightForRowAtIndexPath:(NSIndexPath *)indexPath {
    UIFont *font = [self fontForDisplayAtIndexPath:indexPath];
    return 25 + font.ascender - font.descender;
}
```

We'll add some more to this class later, but first we want to see it in action. To make this happen, we'll need to configure the storyboard some more, and then make some modifications to BIDRootViewController. Switch over to *Main.storyboard* to get started.

Storyboarding the Font List

The storyboard currently has one table view controller, embedded inside a navigation controller. You need to add one new layer of depth to display a list of fonts, so find *Table View Controller* in the object library and drag one out into the editing area, probably to the right of the existing table view controller. Select the new table view controller and use the identity inspector to set its class to *BIDFontListViewController*. Make sure the *delegate* and *dataSource* connections from the table view to the controller are in place. Select the prototype cell in the table view and open the attributes inspector to make some adjustments. Change its *Style* to *Subtitle*, its *Identifier* to *FontName*, and its *Accessory* to *Detail Disclosure*. Using the detail disclosure accessory will let rows of this type respond to two kinds of taps, so that the user can trigger two different actions, depending on whether they tap the accessory or any other part of the row.

One way to make a user action in one view controller cause the instantiation and display of another view controller is to create a **segue** connecting the two of them. This is probably an unfamiliar word for many people, so let's get this out of the way: Segue means essentially "transition," and it is sometimes used by writers and filmmakers to describe making a smooth movement from one paragraph or scene to the next. Apple could have been a little straightforward and just called it a transition; but since that word appears elsewhere in the UIKit APIs, maybe Apple decided to use a distinct term to avoid confusion. We should also mention here that the word "segue" is pronounced exactly the same as the name of the Segway personal transportation product (and now you know why the Segway is called that).

Often, segues are created entirely within Interface Builder. The idea is that an action in one scene can trigger a segue to load and display another scene. If you're using a navigation controller, the segue can push the next controller onto the navigation stack automatically. We'll be using this functionality in our app, starting right now!

In order for the cells in the root view controller to make the font list view controller appear, you need to create a couple of segues connecting the two scenes. This is done simply by **Ctrl**-dragging from the first prototype cell over to the new scene; you'll see the entire scene highlight when you drag over it, indicating it's ready to connect. Release the mouse button and select *push* from the *Selection Segue* section of the floating menu that appears. Now do the same for the other prototype cell. Creating these segues means that, as soon as the user taps any of these cells, the view controller at the other end of the connection will be allocated and made ready.

Making the Root View Controller Prepare for Segues

Save your changes and switch back to *BIDRootViewController.m*. Note that we're not talking about our latest class, BIDFontListViewController, but instead its "parent" controller. This is the place where you'll need to respond to the user's touches in the root table view by preparing the new BIDFontListViewController (specified by one of the segues you just created) for display, by passing it the values it needs to display. Start by importing the header for the new class:

```
#import "BIDRootViewController.h"
#import "BIDFavoritesList.h"
#import "BIDFontListViewController.h"
```

The actual preparation of the new view controller is done using the prepareForSegue:sender: method. You'll find this method at the bottom of the @implementation section, which is commented out when this file is first created. Remove the comment marks and fill in the method's implementation as shown here:

```
/*
#pragma mark - Navigation

// In a story board-based application, you will often want to do a little
// preparation before navigation
- (void)prepareForSegue:(UIStoryboardSegue *)segue sender:(id)sender
{
    // Get the new view controller using [segue destinationViewController].
    // Pass the selected object to the new view controller.
    NSIndexPath *indexPath = [self.tableView indexPathForCell:sender];
    BIDFontListViewController *listVC = segue.destinationViewController;

    if (indexPath.section == 0) {
        NSString *familyName = self.familyNames[indexPath.row];
        listVC.fontNames = [[UIFont fontNamesForFamilyName:familyName]
                            sortedArrayUsingSelector:@selector(compare:)];
        listVC.navigationItem.title = familyName;
        listVC.showsFavorites = NO;
    } else {
        listVC.fontNames = self.favoritesList.favorites;
        listVC.navigationItem.title = @"Favorites";
        listVC.showsFavorites = YES;
    }
}
*/
```

This method uses the sender (which is the UITableViewCell that was tapped) to determine which row was tapped and asks the segue for its destinationViewController, which is the BIDFontListViewController instance that is about to be displayed. We then pass some values along to the new view controller, depending on whether the user tapped a font family (section 0) or the favorites cell (section 1). Not only do we set our custom properties for our specific view controller classes, we also access each controller's navigationItem property in order to set a title.

The navigationItem property is an instance of UINavigationItem, which is a UIKit class that contains information about what should be displayed in the navigation bar for any given view controller.

Now run the app, and you'll see that touching the name of any font family shows you a list of all the individual fonts it contains, as seen in Figure 9-3.

Creating the Font Sizes View Controller

What you'll notice, however, is that the app currently doesn't let you go any further. Figures 9-4 and 9-5 show additional screens that let you view a chosen font in various ways, and we're not there yet. But soon, we will be! Let's create the view shown in Figure 9-4, which shows multiple font sizes at once. Use Xcode's new file assistant to create a new Objective-C class that subclasses UITableViewController, and name it BIDFontSizesViewController. The only parameter this class will need from its parent controller is a font, which you should add to *BIDFontSizesViewController.h*, like this:

```
#import <UIKit/UIKit.h>

@interface BIDFontSizesViewController : UITableViewController

@property (strong, nonatomic) UIFont *font;

@end
```

Now switch over the *BIDFontSizesViewController.m*. This is going to be a pretty simple table view controller that just implements some standard table view delegate and data source methods, plus a few private internal methods. For starters, go ahead and delete the initWithStyle:, viewDidLoad, didReceiveMemoryWarning, and numberOfSectionsInTableView: methods, along with all of the commented-out methods at the bottom. Again, you're not going to need any of those.

What you will need, instead, are a couple of internal, private methods. One will return a list of point sizes to define all the sizes that the chosen font will be displayed in. The other will return a font corresponding to an index path, similar to those used for each of our other view controllers:

```
- (NSArray *)pointSizes {
    static NSArray *pointSizes = nil;
    static dispatch_once_t onceToken;
    dispatch_once(&onceToken, ^{
        pointSizes = @[@9,
                       @10,
                       @11,
                       @12,
                       @13,
                       @14,
                       @18,
                       @24,
                       @36,
                       @48,
                       @64,
```

```
                        @72,
                        @96,
                        @144];
    });
    return pointSizes;
}

- (UIFont *)fontForDisplayAtIndexPath:(NSIndexPath *)indexPath {
    NSNumber *pointSize = self.pointSizes[indexPath.row];
    return [self.font fontWithSize:pointSize.floatValue];
}
```

Note that the pointSizes method uses the same dispatch_once() function we used earlier, to ensure that a piece of code is run exactly once. In this case, it initializes a list of numbers that will be used to specify fonts for each row in the table.

For this view controller, we're going to skip the method that lets us specify the number of sections to display, since we're going to just use the default number (1). However, we must implement the methods for specifying the number of rows and the content of each cell. We'll also implement the method to determine the height for each row, as we have in the past. Here are those three methods:

```
- (NSInteger)tableView:(UITableView *)tableView
 numberOfRowsInSection:(NSInteger)section
{
#warning Incomplete method implementation.
    // Return the number of rows in the section.
    return [self.pointSizes count];
    return 0;
}

- (UITableViewCell *)tableView:(UITableView *)tableView
         cellForRowAtIndexPath:(NSIndexPath *)indexPath
{
    static NSString *CellIdentifier = @"Cell";
    static NSString *CellIdentifier = @"FontNameAndSize";
    UITableViewCell *cell = [tableView
                             dequeueReusableCellWithIdentifier:CellIdentifier
                             forIndexPath:indexPath];

    // Configure the cell...
    cell.textLabel.font = [self fontForDisplayAtIndexPath:indexPath];
    cell.textLabel.text = self.font.fontName;
    cell.detailTextLabel.text = [NSString stringWithFormat:@"%@ point",
                                 self.pointSizes[indexPath.row]];

    return cell;
}

- (CGFloat)tableView:(UITableView *)tableView
heightForRowAtIndexPath:(NSIndexPath *)indexPath {
    UIFont *font = [self fontForDisplayAtIndexPath:indexPath];
    return 25 + font.ascender - font.descender;
}
```

There's really nothing in any of these methods we haven't seen before, so let's move on to setting up the GUI for this.

Storyboarding the Font Sizes View Controller

Go back to *Main.storyboard* and drag another *Table View Controller* into the editing area. Use the identity inspector to set its class to *BIDFontSizesViewController*. You'll need to make a segue connection from its parent, the *Font List View Controller*. So find that controller and **Ctrl**-drag from its prototype cell to the newest view controller, and then select *push* from the *Selection Segue* section of the context menu that appears. Next, select the prototype cell in the new scene you just added, and then use the attributes inspector to set its *Style* to *Subtitle* and its *Identifier* to *FontNameAndSize*.

Making the Font List View Controller Prepare for Segues

Now, just like the last time we extended our storyboard's navigation hierarchy, we need to jump up to the parent controller so it can configure its child. That means we need to go to *BIDFontListViewController.m* and import the header for the new child controller:

```
#import "BIDFontListViewController.h"
#import "BIDFavoritesList.h"
#import "BIDFontSizesViewController.h"
```

Next, down at the bottom of the @implementation section, remove the comment marks around the prepareForSegue:sender: method and implement it like this:

```
/*
#pragma mark - Navigation

// In a story board-based application, you will often want to do a little
// preparation before navigation
- (void)prepareForSegue:(UIStoryboardSegue *)segue sender:(id)sender
{
    // Get the new view controller using [segue destinationViewController].
    // Pass the selected object to the new view controller.
    NSIndexPath *indexPath = [self.tableView indexPathForCell:sender];
    UIFont *font = [self fontForDisplayAtIndexPath:indexPath];
    [segue.destinationViewController navigationItem].title = font.fontName;

    BIDFontSizesViewController *sizesVC = segue.destinationViewController;
    sizesVC.font = font;
}
*/
```

That probably all looks pretty familiar by now, so we won't dwell on it further.

Run the app, select a font family, select a font (by tapping a row anywhere except the accessory on the right), and you'll now see the multi-size listing shown in Figure 9-4.

Creating the Font Info View Controller

The final view controller we're going to create is the one shown in Figure 9-6. This one isn't based on a table view. Instead, it features a large text label, a slider for setting text size, and a switch for toggling whether this font should be included in the list of favorites. Create a new Objective-C class in your project using UIViewController as the superclass, and then name it BIDFontInfoViewController. Like most of the other controllers in this app, this one needs to have a couple of parameters passed in by its parent controller. Enable this by defining these properties in *BIDFontInfoViewController.h*:

```
#import <UIKit/UIKit.h>

@interface BIDFontInfoViewController : UIViewController

@property (strong, nonatomic) UIFont *font;
@property (assign, nonatomic) BOOL favorite;

@end
```

Now switch over to *BIDFontInfoViewController.m* and add a single import and a handful of IBOutlet properties at the top:

```
#import "BIDFontInfoViewController.h"
#import "BIDFavoritesList.h"

@interface BIDFontInfoViewController ()

@property (weak, nonatomic) IBOutlet UILabel *fontSampleLabel;
@property (weak, nonatomic) IBOutlet UISlider *fontSizeSlider;
@property (weak, nonatomic) IBOutlet UILabel *fontSizeLabel;
@property (weak, nonatomic) IBOutlet UISwitch *favoriteSwitch;

@end
```

Next, delete the boilerplate initWithNibName:bundle: and didReceiveMemoryWarning methods, since you're not going to need them. In their place, implement viewDidLoad, as well as a pair of action methods that will be triggered by the slider and switch, respectively:

```
- (void)viewDidLoad
{
    [super viewDidLoad];
    // Do any additional setup after loading the view.

    self.fontSampleLabel.font = self.font;
    self.fontSampleLabel.text = @"AaBbCcDdEeFfGgHhIiJjKkLlMmNnOoPpQqRrSsTtUuVv"
                                "WwXxYyZz 0123456789";
    self.fontSizeSlider.value = self.font.pointSize;
    self.fontSizeLabel.text = [NSString stringWithFormat:@"%.0f",
                                self.font.pointSize];
    self.favoriteSwitch.on = self.favorite;
}
```

```
- (IBAction)slideFontSize:(UISlider *)slider {
    float newSize = roundf(slider.value);
    self.fontSampleLabel.font = [self.font fontWithSize:newSize];
    self.fontSizeLabel.text = [NSString stringWithFormat:@"%.0f", newSize];
}

- (IBAction)toggleFavorite:(UISwitch *)sender {
    BIDFavoritesList *favoritesList = [BIDFavoritesList sharedFavoritesList];
    if (sender.on) {
        [favoritesList addFavorite:self.font.fontName];
    } else {
        [favoritesList removeFavorite:self.font.fontName];
    }
}
```

These methods are all pretty straightforward. The viewDidLoad method sets up the display based on the chosen font; slideFontSize: changes the size of the font in the fontSampleLabel label based on the value of the slider; and toggleFavorite: either adds the current font to the favorites list or removes it from the favorites list, depending on the value of the switch.

Storyboarding the Font Info View Controller

Now head back over to *Main.storyboard* to build the GUI for this app's final view controller. Use the object library to find a plain *View Controller*. Drag it into the editing area, and use the identity inspector to set its class to *BIDFontInfoViewController*. Next, use the object library to find some more objects and drag them into your new scene. You need three labels, a switch, and a slider. Lay them out roughly as shown in Figure 9-8.

Figure 9-8. Each of the labels here has been given a light gray background color, just for purposes of this illustration. Yours should have white backgrounds

Notice that we left some space above the upper label, since we're going to end up having a navigation bar up there. Also, we want the upper label to be able to display long pieces of text across multiple lines, but by default the label is set to show only one line. To change that, select the label, open the attributes inspector, and set the number in the *Lines* field to *0*.

Figure 9-8 also shows changed text in the lower two labels. Go ahead and make the same changes yourself. What you can't see here is that the attributes inspector was used to right-align both of them. You should do the same, since they both have layouts that essentially tie them to their right edges. Also, select the slider at the bottom, and then use the attributes inspector to set its *Minimum* to *1* and its *Maximum* to *200*.

Now it's time to wire up all the connections for this GUI. Start by selecting the view controller and opening the connections inspector. When we have so many connections to make, the overview shown by that inspector is pretty nice. Make connections for each of the outlets by dragging from the small circles next to *favoriteSwitch*, *fontSampleLabel*, *fontSizeLabel*, and *fontSizeSlider* to the appropriate objects in the scene. In case it's not obvious, *fontSampleLabel* should be connected to the label at the top, *fontSizeLabel* to the label at the bottom right, and the *favoriteSwitch* and *fontSizeSlider* outlets to the only places they can go. To connect the actions to the controls, you can continue to use the connections inspector. Drag from the little circle next to *slideFontSize:* over to the slider, release the mouse button, and select *Value Changed* from the context menu that appears. Next, drag from the little circle next to *toggleFavorite:* over to the switch and again select *Value Changed*.

One more thing we need to do here is to create a segue, so that this view can be shown. Remember that this view is going to be displayed whenever a user taps the detail accessory (the little blue "i" in a circle) when the *Font List View Controller* is displayed. So, find that controller, **Ctrl**-drag from its prototype cell to the new font info view controller you've been working on, and select *push* from the *Accessory Action* section of the context menu that appears. Note that we just said "Accessory Action," not "Selection Segue." The accessory action is the segue that is triggered when the user taps the detail accessory, while the selection segue is the segue that is triggered by a tap anywhere else in the row. We already set this cell's selection segue to open a BIDFontSizesViewController.

Now we have two different segues that can be triggered by touches in different parts of a row. Since these will present different view controllers, with different properties, we need to have a way to differentiate them. Fortunately, the UIStoryboardSegue class, which represents a segue, has a way to accomplish this: we can use an identifier, just as we do with table view cells!

All you have to do is select a segue in the editing area and use the attributes inspector to set its *Identifier*. You may need to shift your scenes around a bit, so that you can see both of the segues that are snaking their way out of the right-hand side of the *Font List View Controller*. Select the one that's pointing at the *Font Sizes View Controller* and set its *Identifier* to *ShowFontSizes*. Next, select the one that's pointing at the *Font Info View Controller* and set its *Identifier* to *ShowFontInfo*.

Setting up Constraints

Setting up that segue lets Interface Builder know that our new scene will be used within the context of the navigation controller like everything else, so that scene automatically receives a blank navigation bar at the top. Now that the real confines of our view are in place, it's a good time to set up the constraints. This is a fairly complex view with several subviews, especially near the bottom, so we can't quite rely on the system's automatic constraints to do the right thing for us. We'll use the *Pin* button at the bottom of the editing area and the pop-up window it triggers to build most of the constraints we'll need.

Start with the uppermost label. Click *Pin*, and then, in the pop-up window, select the little red bars above, to the left, and to the right of the little square—but not the one below it. Now click the *Add 3 Constraints* button at the bottom.

Next, select the slider at the bottom and click the *Pin* button. This time, select the red bars below, to the left, and to the right of the little square—but not the one above it. Again, click *Add 3 Constraints* to put them in place.

For each of the two remaining labels and for the switch, follow this procedure: select the object, click *Pin*, select the red bars below and to the right of the little square, turn on the checkboxes for *Width* and *Height*, and finally, click *Add 4 Constraints*. Setting those constraints for all three of those objects will bind them to the lower right corner.

There's just one more constraint to make. We want the top label to grow to contain its text, but to never grow so large that it overlaps the views at the bottom. We can accomplish this with a single constraint! **Ctrl**-drag from the upper label to the *Include in Favorites* label, release the mouse button, and select *Vertical Spacing* from the context menu that appears. Next, click the new constraint to select it and open the attributes inspector, where you'll see some configurable attributes for the constraint. Change the *Relation* popup to *Greater Than or Equal*, and then set the *Constant* value to *10*. That ensures that the expanding upper label won't push past the other views at the bottom.

Adapting Font List View Controller for Multiple Segues

Now head back over to good old *BIDFontListViewController.m*. Since this class will now be able to trigger segues to two different child view controllers, it now needs to import the header for the latest view controller:

```
#import "BIDFontListViewController.h"
#import "BIDFavoritesList.h"
#import "BIDFontSizesViewController.h"
#import "BIDFontInfoViewController.h"
```

You also need to adapt the prepareForSegue:sender: method, as shown here:

```
- (void)prepareForSegue:(UIStoryboardSegue *)segue sender:(id)sender
{
    // Get the new view controller using [segue destinationViewController].
    // Pass the selected object to the new view controller.
    NSIndexPath *indexPath = [self.tableView indexPathForCell:sender];
    UIFont *font = [self fontForDisplayAtIndexPath:indexPath];
    [segue.destinationViewController navigationItem].title = font.fontName;

    if ([segue.identifier isEqualToString:@"ShowFontSizes"]) {
        BIDFontSizesViewController *sizesVC = segue.destinationViewController;
        sizesVC.font = font;
    } else if ([segue.identifier isEqualToString:@"ShowFontInfo"]) {
        BIDFontInfoViewController *infoVC = segue.destinationViewController;
        infoVC.font = font;
        infoVC.favorite = [[BIDFavoritesList sharedFavoritesList].favorites
                            containsObject:font.fontName];

    }
}
```

Now run the app and let's see where we are! Select a font family that contains many fonts (for example, Gill Sans), and then tap the middle of the row for any font. You'll be taken to the same list you saw earlier, which shows the font in multiple sizes. Press the navigation button at the upper left to go back, and then tap another row; however, this time tap on the right-hand side where the detail accessory is shown. This should bring up the final view controller, which shows a sample of the font with a slider at the bottom that lets you pick whatever size you want.

Also, you can now use the *Include in favorites* switch to mark this font as a favorite. Do that, then hit the navigation button at the top-left corner a couple of times to get back to the root controller view.

My Favorite Fonts

Scroll down to the bottom of the root view controller, and you'll see something new: the second section is now there, as you can see in Figure 9-9.

Figure 9-9. *Now that we've picked at least one favorite font, we can see a list of them by tapping the new row that appears at the bottom of the root view controller*

Tap the *Favorites* row, and you'll see a listing of any fonts you've chosen as favorites. From there, you can do the same things you could do with the other font listing: you can tap a row to see a list of multiple font sizes, or you can tap a detail accessory to see the slider-adjustable font view and the favorites switch. You can even try turning off that switch and hitting the back button, and you'll see that the font you were just looking at is no longer listed.

Table View Niceties

Now the basic functionality of our app is complete. But before we can really call it a day, there are a couple more features we should implement. If you've been using iOS for a while, you're probably aware that you can often delete a row from a table view by swiping from right to left. For example, in Mail you can use this technique to delete a message in a list of messages. Performing this gesture brings up a small GUI, right inside the table view row. This GUI asks you to confirm the deletion, and then the row disappears and the remaining rows slide up to fill the gap. That whole interaction—including handling the swipe, showing the confirmation GUI, and animating any affected rows—is taken care of by the table view itself. All you need to do is implement two methods in your controller to make it happen.

Also, the table view provides easy functionality for letting the user reorder rows within a table view by dragging them up and down. As with swipe-to-delete, the table view takes care of the entire user interaction for us. All we have to do is one line of setup (to create a button that activates the reordering GUI), and then implement a single method that is called when the user has finished dragging. The table view gives us so much for free, it would be criminal not to use it!

Implementing Swipe-to-Delete

In this app, the BIDFontListViewController class is a typical example of where this feature should be used. Whenever the app is showing the list of favorites, we should let the user delete a favorite with a swipe, saving them the step of tapping the detail accessory and then turning off the switch. Select *BIDFontListController.m* in Xcode to get started. Both of the methods we need to implement are already included in each view controller source file by default, but they are commented out. We're going to un-comment each of them and provide them with real implementations.

Start by removing the comment marks around tableView:canEditRowAtIndexPath: and providing this implementation:

```
/*
// Override to support conditional editing of the table view.
- (BOOL)tableView:(UITableView *)tableView
canEditRowAtIndexPath:(NSIndexPath *)indexPath
{
    // Return NO if you do not want the specified item to be editable.
    return self.showsFavorites;
    return YES;
}
*/
```

That method will return YES if it's showing the list of favorites, and NO otherwise. This means that the editing functionality that lets you delete rows is only enabled while displaying favorites. If you were to try to run the app and delete rows with just this change, you wouldn't see any difference. The table view won't bother to deal with the swipe gesture because it sees that we haven't implemented the other method that is required to complete a deletion. So, let's put that in place, too. Delete the comment marks around the tableView:commitEditingStyle:forRowAtIndexPath: method and make the other changes shown inside the method that follows:

```
/*
// Override to support editing the table view.
- (void)tableView:(UITableView *)tableView
commitEditingStyle:(UITableViewCellEditingStyle)editingStyle
forRowAtIndexPath:(NSIndexPath *)indexPath
```

```
{
    if (!self.showsFavorites) return;

    if (editingStyle == UITableViewCellEditingStyleDelete) {
        // Delete the row from the data source
        NSString *favorite = self.fontNames[indexPath.row];
        [[BIDFavoritesList sharedFavoritesList] removeFavorite:favorite];
        self.fontNames = [BIDFavoritesList sharedFavoritesList].favorites;

        [tableView deleteRowsAtIndexPaths:@[indexPath]
                          withRowAnimation:UITableViewRowAnimationFade];
    }
    else if (editingStyle == UITableViewCellEditingStyleInsert) {
        // Create a new instance of the appropriate class, insert it into the
        // array, and add a new row to the table view
    }
}
*/
```

This method is pretty straightforward, but there are some subtle things going on. The first thing we do is check to make sure we're showing the favorites list; and if not, we just bail. Normally, this should never happen, since we specified with the previous method that only the favorites list should be editable. Nevertheless, we're doing a bit of defensive programming here. After that, we check the editing style to make sure that the particular edit operation we're going to conclude really was a deletion. It's possible to do insertion edits in a table view, but not without additional setup that we're not doing here, so we don't need to worry about other cases. Next, we determine which font should be deleted, remove it from the BIDFavoritesList singleton, and update our local copy of the favorites list.

Finally, we tell the table view to delete the row and make it disappear with a visual fade animation. It's important to understand what happens when you tell the table view to delete a row. Intuitively, you might think that calling that method would delete some data, but that's not what happened. In fact, we've already deleted the data! That final method call is really our way of telling the table view, "Hey, I've made a change, and I want you to animate away this row. Ask me if you need anything more." When that happens, the table view will start animating any rows that are below the deleted row by moving them up, which means that it's possible that one or more rows that were previously off-screen will now come on-screen, at which time it will indeed ask the controller for cell data via the usual methods. For that reason, it's important that our implementation of the tableView:commitEditingStyle:forRowAtIndexPath: method makes necessary changes to the data model (in this case, the BIDFavoritesList singleton) before telling the table view to delete a row.

Now run the app again, make sure you have some favorite fonts set up, and then go into the *Favorites* list and delete a row by swiping from right to left. The row slides partly off-screen, and a *Delete* button appears on the right. Tap the *Delete* button, and the row goes away.

Implementing Drag-to-Reorder

The final feature we're going to add to the font list will let users rearrange their favorites just by dragging them up and down. In order to accomplish this, we're going to add one method to the BIDFavoritesList class, which will let us reorder its items however we want. Open up *BIDFavoritesList.h* and add the following declaration to the @interface section:

```
- (void)moveItemAtIndex:(NSInteger)from toIndex:(NSInteger)to;
```

Next, switch over to *BIDFavoritesList.m* and add this method to the @implementation section:

```
- (void)moveItemAtIndex:(NSInteger)from toIndex:(NSInteger)to {
    id item = _favorites[from];
    [_favorites removeObjectAtIndex:from];
    [_favorites insertObject:item atIndex:to];
    [self saveFavorites];
}
```

That provides the underpinnings for what we're going to do. Now select *BIDFontListViewController.m* and add the following lines at the end of the viewDidLoad method:

```
if (self.showsFavorites) {
    self.navigationItem.rightBarButtonItem = self.editButtonItem;
}
```

We've mentioned the navigation item previously. It's an object that holds the information about what should appear in the navigation bar for a view controller. It has a property called rightBarButtonItem that can hold an instance of UIBarButtonItem, a special sort of button meant only for navigation bars and tool bars. Here, we're pointing that at editButtonItem, a property of UIViewController that gives us a special button item that's preconfigured to activate the table view's editing/reordering GUI.

With that in place, try running the app again and go into the Favorites list. You'll see that there's now an *Edit* button in the upper-right corner. Pressing that button toggles the table view's editing GUI, which right now means that each row acquires a delete button on the left, while its content slides a bit to the right to make room. This enables yet another way that users can delete rows, using the same methods we already implemented.

But our main interest here is in adding reordering functionality. For that, all we need to do is implement this method. Be sure to take away the comment marks that are there by default, and then add the bold code:

```
/*
// Override to support rearranging the table view.
- (void)tableView:(UITableView *)tableView
moveRowAtIndexPath:(NSIndexPath *)fromIndexPath
     toIndexPath:(NSIndexPath *)toIndexPath
{
    [[BIDFavoritesList sharedFavoritesList] moveItemAtIndex:fromIndexPath.row
                                    toIndex:toIndexPath.row];
    self.fontNames = [BIDFavoritesList sharedFavoritesList].favorites;
}
*/
```

This method is called as soon as the user finishes dragging a row. All we do here is tell the BIDFavoritesList singleton to do the reordering, and then refresh our list of font names, just as we did after deleting an item. To see this in action, run the app, go into the *Favorites*, and tap the *Edit* button. You'll see that the edit mode now includes little "dragger" icons on the right side of each row, and you can use the draggers to rearrange items.

With that, our app is complete! At least, it's complete as far as this book is concerned. If you can think of more useful things to do with these fonts, have at it!

Breaking the Tape

This chapter was a marathon. And if you're still standing, you should feel pretty darn good about yourself. Dwelling on these mystical table view and navigation controller objects is important because they are the backbone of a great many iOS applications, and their complexity can definitely get you into trouble if you don't truly understand them.

As you start building your own tables, refer back to this chapter and the previous one, and don't be afraid of Apple's documentation, either. Table views are extraordinarily complex, and it would be impossible to cover every conceivable permutation; however, you should now have a very good set of table view building blocks you can use as you design and build your own applications. As always, feel free to reuse this code in your own applications. It's a gift from the authors to you. Enjoy!

Chapter 10

Collection View

In this chapter, we're going to look at a fairly recent addition to UIKit: the UICollectionView class. You'll see how it relates to the familiar UITableView, how it differs, and how it can be extended to do things that UITableView can't even dream about.

For years, iOS developers have used the UITableView component to create a huge variety of interfaces. With its ability to let you define multiple cell types, create them on the fly as needed, and handily scroll them vertically, UITableView has become a key component of thousands of apps. And Apple has truly given its table view class lots of API love over the years, adding new and better ways to supply it with content in each major new iOS release.

However, it's still not the ultimate solution for all large sets of data. If you want to present data in multiple columns, for example, you need to combine all the columns for each row of data into a single cell. There's also no way to make a UITableView scroll its content horizontally. In general, much of the power of UITableView has come with a particular trade-off: developers have no control of the overall layout of a table view. You can define the look of each individual cell all you want; but at the end of the day, the cells are just going to be stacked on top of each other in one big scrolling list!

Well, apparently Apple realized this, too. In iOS 6, it introduced a new class called UICollectionView that addresses these shortcomings. Like a table view, this class lets you display a bunch of "cells" of data and handles things like queuing up unused cells for later use. But unlike a table view, UICollectionView doesn't lay these cells out in a vertical stack for you. In fact, UICollectionView doesn't lay them out at all! Instead, it uses a helper class to do layout, as you'll see soon.

Creating the DialogViewer Project

To show some of the capabilities of UICollectionView, we're going to use it to lay out some paragraphs of text. Each word will be placed in a cell of its own, and all the cells for each paragraph will be clustered together in a section. Each section will also have its own header. This may not seem too exciting, considering that UIKit already contains other perfectly good ways of laying out text. However, this process will be instructive anyway, since you'll get a feel for just how flexible this thing is. You certainly wouldn't get very far doing something like Figure 10-1 with a table view!

Figure 10-1. *Each word is a separate cell. All of this is laid out using a single UICollectionView, and no explicit geometry calculations of our own*

In order to make this work, we'll define a couple of custom cell classes; we'll use `UICollectionViewFlowLayout` (the one and only layout helper class included in UIKit at this time); and, as usual, we'll use our view controller class to glue it all together. Let's get started!

Use Xcode to create a new *Single View Application*, as you've done many times by now. Name your project *DialogViewer* and use the standard settings we've used throughout the book (leaving *Class Prefix* set to *BID*, choosing *iPhone* in the *Devices* popup, etc).

Fixing the View Controller's Class

There's nothing in particular we need to do with the app delegate in this app, so let's jump straight into *BIDViewController.h* and make just one simple change, switching our super class to UICollectionView:

```
@interface BIDViewController : UIViewController
@interface BIDViewController : UICollectionViewController
```

Next, open up *Main.storyboard*. We need to set up the view here to match what we just specified in the header. Select the one and only *View Controller Scene* in the editing area and delete it. Now use the object library to locate a *Collection View Controller* and drag it into the editing area. Select the icon for the *View Controller* you just dragged out and use the Identity Inspector to change its class to *BIDViewController*.

Defining Custom Cells

Next, let's define some cell classes. As you saw in Figure 10-1, we're displaying two basic kinds of cells: a "normal" one containing a word and another that is used as a sort of header. Any cell you're going to create for use in a UICollectionView needs to be a subclass of the system-supplied UICollectionViewCell, which provides basic functionality similar to UITableViewCell. This functionality includes a backgroundView, a contentView, and so on. Because our two cells will have some shared functionality, we'll actually make one a subclass of the other and use the subclass to override some functionality.

Start by creating a new Objective-C class in Xcode. Name the new class BIDContentCell and make it a subclass of UICollectionViewCell. Select the new class's header file and add declarations for a couple of properties and one class method:

```
#import <UIKit/UIKit.h>

@interface BIDContentCell : UICollectionViewCell

@property (strong, nonatomic) UILabel *label;
@property (copy, nonatomic) NSString *text;

+ (CGSize)sizeForContentString:(NSString *)s;

@end
```

The label property will point at a UILabel used for display. We'll use the text property to tell this cell what to display, and we'll use the sizeForContentString: method to ask a class how big the cell needs to be to display a given string. This will come in handy when creating and configuring instances of our cell classes.

Now switch over to BIDContentCell.m, where several pieces of work await us. Let's start by filling out the initWithFrame: method, as shown here:

```
- (id)initWithFrame:(CGRect)frame
{
    self = [super initWithFrame:frame];
    if (self) {
        // Initialization code
        self.label = [[UILabel alloc] initWithFrame:self.contentView.bounds];
        self.label.opaque = NO;
        self.label.backgroundColor = [UIColor colorWithRed:0.8
                                                     green:0.9
                                                      blue:1.0
                                                     alpha:1.0];
        self.label.textColor = [UIColor blackColor];

        self.label.textAlignment = NSTextAlignmentCenter;
        self.label.font = [[self class] defaultFont];
        [self.contentView addSubview:self.label];
    }
    return self;
}
```

That code is pretty simple. It just creates a label, sets its display properties, and adds the label to the cell's contentView. The only mysterious thing here is that it uses the class method defaultFont to get a font, which is used to set the label's font. The idea is that this class should define which font will be used for displaying content, while also allowing any subclasses to declare their own display font by overriding the defaultFont method. But we haven't created this method yet, so let's do so:

```
+ (UIFont *)defaultFont {
    return [UIFont preferredFontForTextStyle:UIFontTextStyleBody];
}
```

Pretty straighforward. This uses a new piece of iOS 7 functionality that lets the user determine, in the Settings app, what their preferred font sizes are. By using this instead of hard-coding a font size, we make our apps a bit more user friendly.

To finish off this class, let's add the method we mentioned in the header, the one that computes an appropriate size for the cell:

```
+ (CGSize)sizeForContentString:(NSString *)string {
    CGSize maxSize = CGSizeMake(300, 1000);

    NSStringDrawingOptions opts = NSStringDrawingUsesLineFragmentOrigin |
                                  NSStringDrawingUsesFontLeading;

    NSMutableParagraphStyle *style = [[NSMutableParagraphStyle alloc] init];
    [style setLineBreakMode:NSLineBreakByCharWrapping];

    NSDictionary *attributes = @{ NSFontAttributeName : [self defaultFont],
                                  NSParagraphStyleAttributeName : style };
```

```
CGRect rect = [string boundingRectWithSize:maxSize
                                   options:opts
                                attributes:attributes
                                   context:nil];

    return rect.size;
}
```

That method does a lot of things, so it's worth walking through it. First, we declare a maximum size; no word will be allowed to be wider than the screen space we want to use. Next, we define some options that will help the system calculate the right dimensions for the string we're dealing with. We also create a paragraph style that allows for character wrapping, so in case our string is too big to fit in the minimum width we presented early, so it can wrap around to a subsequent line. We also create an attributes dictionary that contains the default font we defined for this class and the paragraph style we just created. Finally, we use some NSString functionality provided in UIKit that lets us calculate screen sizes for a string. We pass in an absolute maximum size and the other options and attributes we set up, and we get back a size.

All that's left for this class is some special handling of the text property. Instead of letting this use an implicit instance variable as we normally do, we're going to define methods that get and set the value based on the UILabel we created earlier, basically using the UILabel as storage for the displayed value. By doing so, we can also use the setter to recalculate the cell's geometry when the text changes. Here's what this looks like:

```
- (NSString *)text {
    return self.label.text;
}

- (void)setText:(NSString *)text {
    self.label.text = text;
    CGRect newLabelFrame = self.label.frame;
    CGRect newContentFrame = self.contentView.frame;
    CGSize textSize = [[self class] sizeForContentString:text];
    newLabelFrame.size = textSize;
    newContentFrame.size = textSize;
    self.label.frame = newLabelFrame;
    self.contentView.frame = newContentFrame;
}
```

The getter is nothing special; but the setter is doing some extra work. Basically, it's modifying the frame for both the label and the content view, based on the size needed for displaying the current string.

That's all we need for our base cell class. Now let's make a cell class to use for a header. Use Xcode to make another new Objective-C class, naming this one *BIDHeaderCell* and making it a subclass of *BIDContentCell*. We don't need to touch the header file at all, so jump straight to *BIDHeaderCell.m* to make some changes. All we're going to do in this class is override a few methods to change the cell's appearance, making it look different from the normal content cell:

```
- (id)initWithFrame:(CGRect)frame
{
    self = [super initWithFrame:frame];
    if (self) {
```

```
        // Initialization code
        self.label.backgroundColor = [UIColor colorWithRed:0.9
                                                    green:0.9
                                                     blue:0.8
                                                    alpha:1.0];
        self.label.textColor = [UIColor blackColor];

    }
    return self;
}

+ (UIFont *)defaultFont {
    return [UIFont preferredFontForTextStyle:UIFontTextStyleHeadline];
}
```

That's all we need to do to give the header cell a distinct look, with its own colors and font.

Configuring the View Controller

Now let's focus our attention on our view controller. Select *BIDViewController.m* and start by importing the headers for our custom cells and declaring an array to contain the content we want to display:

```
#import "BIDViewController.h"
#import "BIDContentCell.h"
#import "BIDHeaderCell.h"

@interface BIDViewController ()
@property (copy, nonatomic) NSArray *sections;
@end
```

Next, we'll use viewDidLoad to define that data. The sections array will contain a list of dictionaries, each of which will have two keys: *header* and *content*. We'll use the values associated with those keys to define our display content. The actual content we're using is adapted from a well-known play:

```
- (void)viewDidLoad
{
    [super viewDidLoad];
    // Do any additional setup after loading the view, typically from a nib.
    self.sections =
    @[
      @{ @"header" : @"First Witch",
         @"content" : @"Hey, when will the three of us meet up later?" },
      @{ @"header" : @"Second Witch",
         @"content" : @"When everything's straightened out." },
      @{ @"header" : @"Third Witch",
         @"content" : @"That'll be just before sunset." },
```

```
        @{ @"header" : @"First Witch",
            @"content" : @"Where?" },
        @{ @"header" : @"Second Witch",
            @"content" : @"The dirt patch." },
        @{ @"header" : @"Third Witch",
            @"content" : @"I guess we'll see Mac there." },
    ];

}
```

Much like UITableView, UICollectionView lets us register the class of a reusable cell based on an identifier. Doing this lets us call a dequeuing method later on, when we're going to provide a cell. If no cell is available, the collection view will create one for us. Just like UITableView! Add this line to the end of viewDidLoad to make this happen:

```
[self.collectionView registerClass:[BIDContentCell class]
        forCellWithReuseIdentifier:@"CONTENT"];
```

By default, UICollectionView has a black background. We want a lighter look in this app, so let's make it white instead:

```
self.collectionView.backgroundColor = [UIColor whiteColor];
```

We'll make just one more change to viewDidLoad. Since this application has no navigation bar, the main view will once again interfere with the status bar. To prevent that, add the following lines to the end of viewDidLoad (we've done something very similar with some other views in past chapters):

```
UIEdgeInsets contentInset = self.collectionView.contentInset;
contentInset.top = 20;
[self.collectionView setContentInset:contentInset];
```

That's enough configuration in viewDidLoad, at least for now. Before we get to the code that will populate the collection view, we need to write one little helper method. All of our content is contained in lengthy strings, but we're going to need to deal with them one word at a time to be able to put each word into a cell. So let's create an internal method of our own to split those strings apart. This method takes a section number, pulls the relevant content string from our section data, and splits it into words:

```
- (NSArray *)wordsInSection:(NSInteger)section {
    NSString *content = self.sections[section][@"content"];
    NSCharacterSet *space = [NSCharacterSet whitespaceAndNewlineCharacterSet];
    NSArray *words = [content componentsSeparatedByCharactersInSet:space];
    return words;
}
```

Providing Content Cells

Now it's time for the group of methods that will actually populate the collection view. These next three methods are remarkably similar to their UITableView correspondents. First, we need a method to let the collection view know how many sections to display:

```
- (NSInteger)numberOfSectionsInCollectionView:(UICollectionView *)collectionView {
    return [self.sections count];
}
```

Next, we have a method to tell the collection how many items each section should contain. This uses the wordsInSection: method we defined earlier:

```
- (NSInteger)collectionView:(UICollectionView *)collectionView
    numberOfItemsInSection:(NSInteger)section {
    NSArray *words = [self wordsInSection:section];
    return [words count];
}
```

And here's the method that actually returns a single cell, configured to contain a single word. This method uses our wordsInSection: method. As you can see, it uses a dequeuing method on UICollectionView, similar to UITableView. Since we've registered a cell class for the identifier we're using here, we know that the dequeuing method always returns an instance:

```
- (UICollectionViewCell *)collectionView:(UICollectionView *)collectionView
                 cellForItemAtIndexPath:(NSIndexPath *)indexPath {
    NSArray *words = [self wordsInSection:indexPath.section];

    BIDContentCell *cell = [self.collectionView
                            dequeueReusableCellWithReuseIdentifier:@"CONTENT"
                            forIndexPath:indexPath];
    cell.text = words[indexPath.row];
    return cell;
}
```

Judging by the way that UITableView works, you might think that at this point we'd have something that works, in at least a minimal way. Build and run your app, and you'll see that we're not really at a useful point yet.

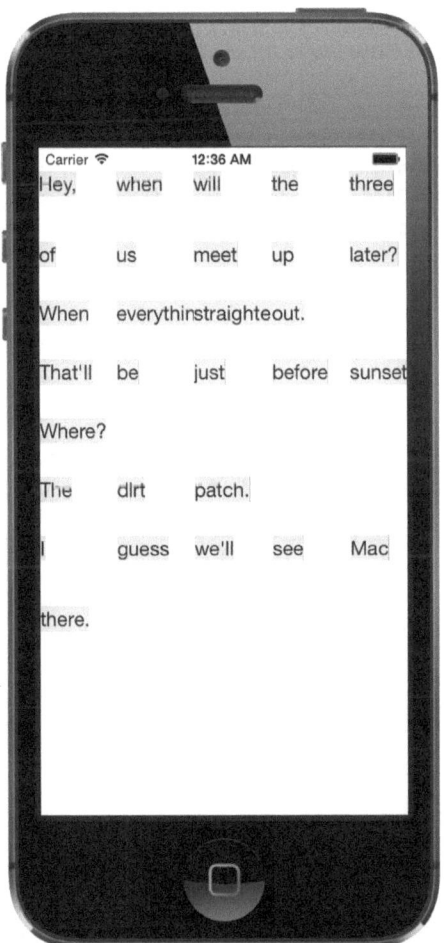

Figure 10-2. This isn't very useful

We can see some of the words, but there's no "flow" going on here. Each cell is the same size, and everything is all jammed together. The reason for this is that we have more delegate responsibilities we have to take care of to make things work.

Making the Layout Flow

Until now, we've been dealing with the UICollectionView; but as we mentioned earlier, this class has a sidekick that takes care of the actual layout. UICollectionViewFlowLayout, which is the default layout helper for UICollectionView, has some delegate methods of its own that it will use to try to pull more information out of us. We're going to implement one of these right now. The layout object calls this method for each cell to find out how large it should be. Here we're once again using our wordsInSection: method to get access to the word in question, and then using a method we defined in the BIDContentCell class to see how large it needs to be:

```
- (CGSize)collectionView:(UICollectionView *)collectionView
             layout:(UICollectionViewLayout*)collectionViewLayout
  sizeForItemAtIndexPath:(NSIndexPath *)indexPath {
    NSArray *words = [self wordsInSection:indexPath.section];
    CGSize size = [BIDContentCell sizeForContentString:words[indexPath.row]];
    return size;
}
```

Now build and run the app again, and you'll see that we've taken a pretty large step forward.

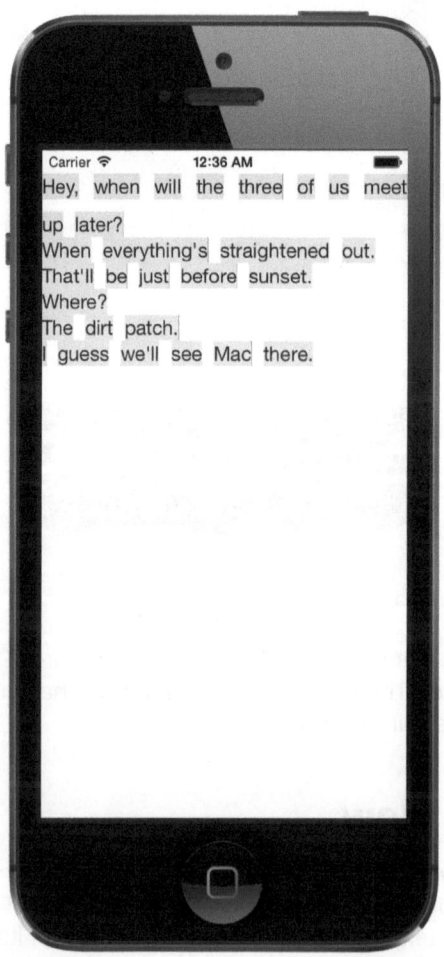

Figure 10-3. Paragraph flow is starting to take shape

You can see that the cells are now flowing and wrapping around so that the text is readable, and that the beginning of each section drops down a bit. But each section is jammed really tightly against the ones before and after it. They're also pressing all the way out to the sides, which doesn't look too nice. Let's fix that by adding a bit more configuration. Add these lines to the end of the viewDidLoad method:

```
UICollectionViewLayout *layout = self.collectionView.collectionViewLayout;
UICollectionViewFlowLayout *flow = (UICollectionViewFlowLayout *)layout;
flow.sectionInset = UIEdgeInsetsMake(10, 20, 30, 20);
```

Here we're grabbing the layout object from our collection view. We assign this first to a temporary UICollectionViewLayout pointer, primarily to highlight a point: UICollectionView only really seems to "know" about this generic layout class, which cannot in fact be used directly at runtime. In practice, unless we specify something else, it's really using a UICollectionFlowLayout instance. Knowing the true type of the layout object, we can use a typecast to assign it to another variable, enabling us to access methods that only that subclass has.

Build and run again, and you'll see that our text cells have gained some much-needed breathing room.

Figure 10-4. Now 14% less cramped

Providing Header Views

The only thing missing now is the display of our header objects, so it's time to fix that. You will recall that UITableView has a system of header and footer views, and it asks for those specifically for each section. UICollectionView has made this concept a bit more generic, allowing for more flexibility in the layout. The way this works is that, along with the system of accessing normal cells from the delegate, there is a parellel system for accessing additional views that can be used as headers, footers, or anything else. Add this bit of code to the end of viewDidLoad to let the collection view know about our header cell class:

```
[self.collectionView registerClass:[BIDHeaderCell class]
        forSupplementaryViewOfKind:UICollectionElementKindSectionHeader
            withReuseIdentifier:@"HEADER"];
```

As you can see, in this case we're not only specifying a cell class and an identifer, but we're also specifying a "kind." The idea is that different layouts may define different kinds of supplementary views and may ask the delegate to supply views for them. UICollectionFlowLayout is going to ask for one section header for each section in the collection view, and we'll apply them like this:

```
- (UICollectionReusableView *)collectionView:(UICollectionView *)collectionView
          viewForSupplementaryElementOfKind:(NSString *)kind
                            atIndexPath:(NSIndexPath *)indexPath {
    if ([kind isEqual:UICollectionElementKindSectionHeader]) {
        BIDHeaderCell *cell = [self.collectionView
                          dequeueReusableSupplementaryViewOfKind:kind
                          withReuseIdentifier:@"HEADER"
                          forIndexPath:indexPath];

        cell.text = self.sections[indexPath.section][@"header"];
        return cell;
    }
    return nil;
}
```

Build and run, and you'll see . . . wait! Where are those headers? As it turns out, UICollectionFlowLayout won't give the headers any space in the layout unless we tell it exactly how large they should be. So go back to viewDidLoad and add the following line at the end:

```
flow.headerReferenceSize = CGSizeMake(100, 25);
```

Build and run once more, and now you'll see the headers in place, as Figure 10-1 showed earlier and Figure 10-5 shows again.

Figure 10-5. *The completed DialogViewer app*

In this chapter, we've really just dipped our toes into `UICollectionView` and what can be accomplished with the default `UICollectionFlowLayout` class. You can get even fancier with it by defining your own layout classes, but that is a topic for another book.

Now that you've gotten familiar with all the major big-picture components, it's time to learn how to use them in whole new ways and whole new screen sizes. We're talking about iPad, and Chapter 11 is where we get started.

iPad Considerations

From a technical standpoint, programming for the iPad is pretty much the same as programming for any other iOS platform. Apart from the screen size, there's very little that differentiates a 3G iPad from an iPhone, or a Wi-Fi iPad from an iPod touch. In spite of the fundamental similarities between the iPhone and iPad, from the user's point of view these devices are really quite different. Fortunately, Apple had the good sense to recognize this fact from the outset and to equip the iPad with additional UIKit components that help developers create applications that better utilize the iPad's screen size and usage patterns. In this chapter, you'll learn how to use these components. Let's get started!

Split Views and Popovers

In Chapter 9, you spent a lot of time dealing with app navigation based on selections in table views, where each selection causes the top-level view, which fills the entire screen, to slide to the left and bring in the next view in the hierarchy (or perhaps yet another table view). Plenty of iPhone and iPod touch apps work this way, both among Apple's own apps and third-party apps.

One typical example is Mail, which lets you drill down through servers and folders until you finally make your way to a message. Technically, this approach can work on the iPad as well, but it leads to a user interaction problem.

On a screen the size of the iPhone or iPod touch, having a screen-sized view slide away to reveal another screen-sized view works well. On a screen the size of the iPad, however, that same interaction feels a little wrong, a little exaggerated, and even a little overwhelming. In addition, consuming such a large display with a single table view is inefficient in most cases. As a result, you'll see that the built-in iPad apps do not actually behave that way. Instead, any drill-down navigation functionality, like that used in Mail, is relegated to a narrow column whose contents slide left or right as the user drills down or backs out. With the iPad in landscape mode, the navigation column is in a fixed position on the left, with the content of the selected item displayed on the right. This is what's called, in the iPad world, a **split view** (see Figure 11-1).

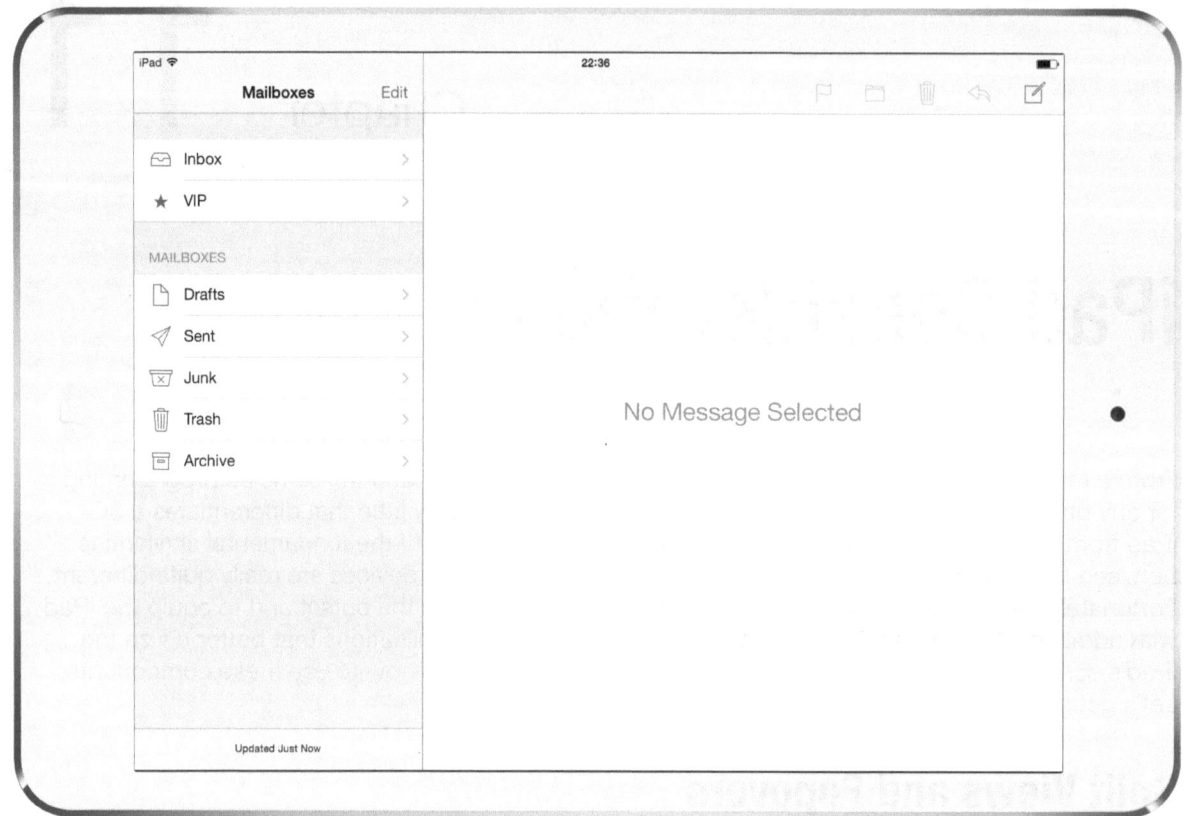

Figure 11-1. This iPad, in landscape mode, is showing a split view. The navigation column is on the left. Tap an item in the navigation column—in this case, a specific mail account—and that item's content is displayed in the area on the right

The left side of the split view is always 320 points wide (the same width as an iPhone in its vertical position). The split view itself, with navigation and content side by side, typically appears only in landscape mode. If you turn the device to a portrait orientation, the split view is still in play, but it's no longer visible in the same way. The navigation view loses its permanent location and can be activated only by pressing a toolbar button, which causes the navigation view to pop up in a view that floats in front of everything else on the screen (see Figure 11-2). This is what's called a **popover**.

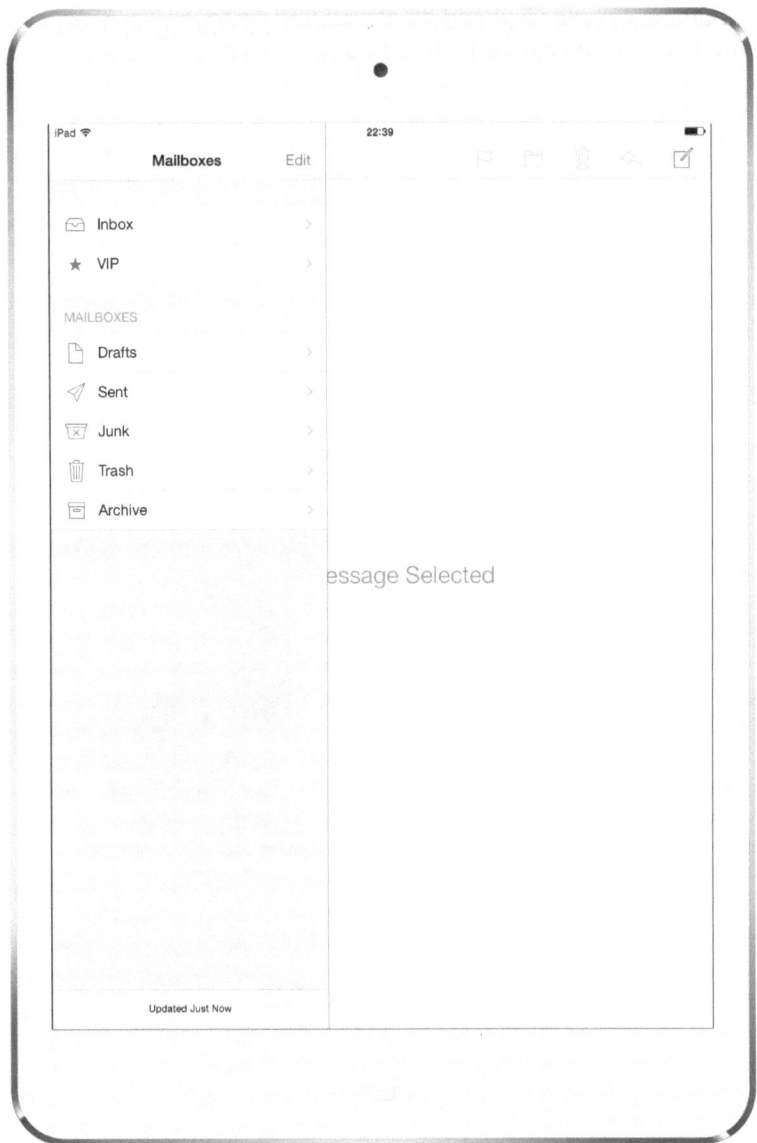

Figure 11-2. This iPad, in portrait mode, does not show the same split view as seen in landscape mode. Instead, the information that made up the left side of the split view in landscape mode is embedded in a popover. Mmmm, popovers

Some applications don't follow this rule strictly, though. The iPad Settings app, for instance, uses a split view that is visible all the time, and the left side neither disappears nor covers the content view on the right. In this chapter, however, we'll stick to the standard usage pattern.

The popover displayed by a split view is visually different from some popovers you may have seen before. This popover always fills the screen and appears at the left edge, but that's not the case for all popovers. They can be configured for different sizes and positioned anywhere on the screen. For example, by the time you're through with this chapter you'll be displaying a small popover hanging off a button in a toolbar (see Figure 11-3). In this chapter's example project, you'll see how to create an iPad application that uses a split view and its associated popover. You'll also learn how to create and display your own popover that isn't attached to any split view.

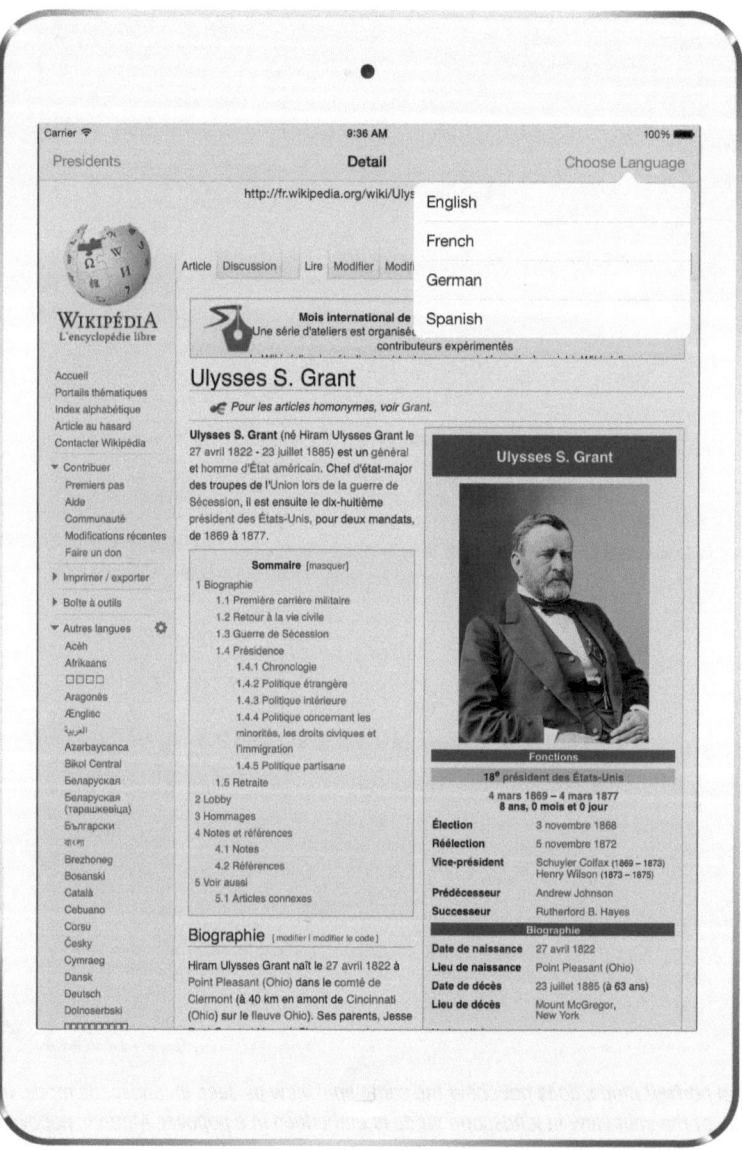

Figure 11-3. A traditional popover, which visually seems to sprout from the button that triggered its appearance

Creating a Split View Project

We're going to start off with an easy task: taking advantage of one of Xcode's predefined templates to create a split view project. We'll build an app that presents a slightly different take on Chapter 9's presidential app, listing all the US presidents and showing the Wikipedia entry for whichever one you select.

Go to Xcode and select **File ➤ New ➤ Project...**. From the iOS *Application* group, select *Master-Detail Application* and click *Next*. On the next screen, name the new project *Presidents*, set the *Class Prefix* to *BID*, and switch *Devices* to *iPad*. Make sure the *Use Core Data* checkbox is unchecked. Click *Next*, choose the location for your project, and then click *Create*. Xcode will do its usual thing, creating a handful of classes and a storyboard file for you, and then showing the project. If it's not already open, expand the *Presidents* folder and take a look at what it contains.

From the start, the project contains an app delegate (as usual), a class called `BIDMasterViewController`, and a class called `BIDDetailViewController`. Those two view controllers represent, respectively, the views that will appear on the left and right sides of the split view. `BIDMasterViewController` defines the top level of a navigation structure and `BIDDetailViewController` defines what's displayed in the larger area when a navigation element is selected. When the app launches, both of these are contained inside a split view, which, as you may recall, does a bit of shape-shifting as the device is rotated.

To see what this particular application template gives you in terms of functionality, build the app and run it in the simulator. Switch between landscape mode (see Figure 11-4) and portrait mode (see Figure 11-5), and you'll see the split view in action. In landscape mode, the split view works by showing the navigation view on the left and the detail view on the right. In portrait mode, the detail view occupies most of the picture, with the navigation elements confined to the popover, which is brought into view with the press of the button in the top left of the view.

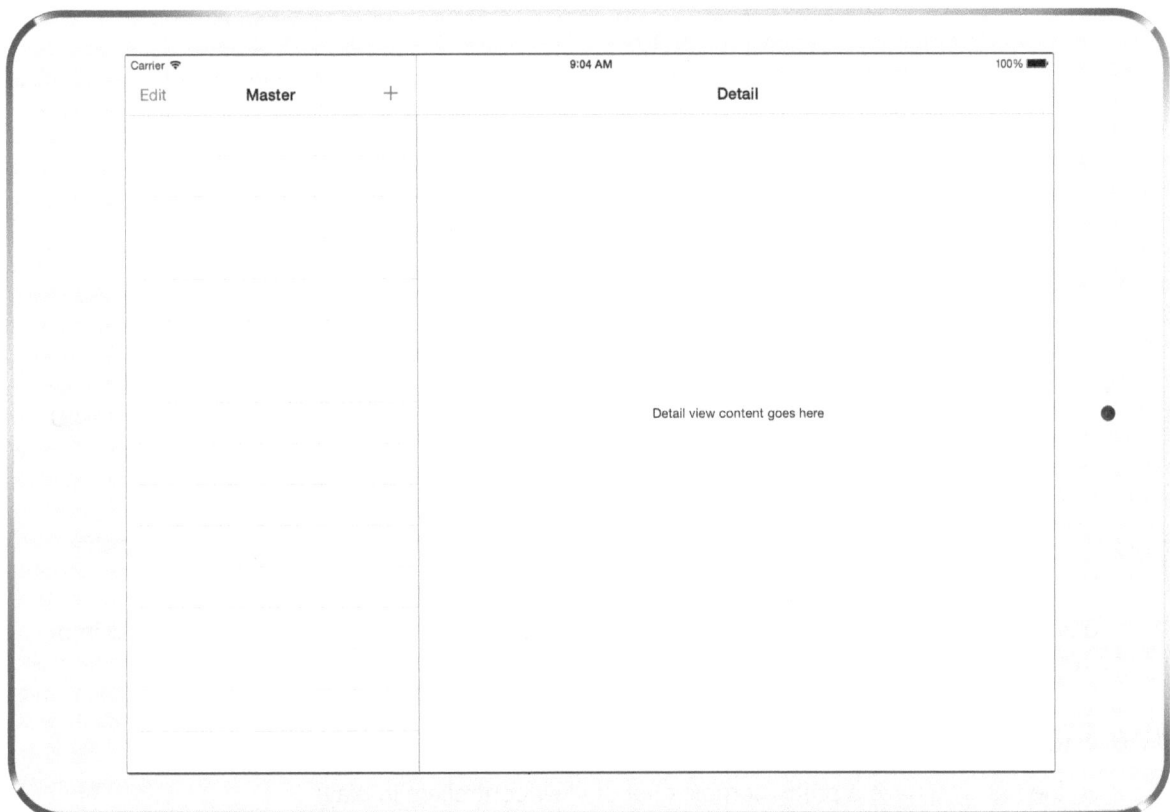

Figure 11-4. The default Master-Detail Application template in landscape mode. Note the similar layouts shown in this figure and Figure 11-1

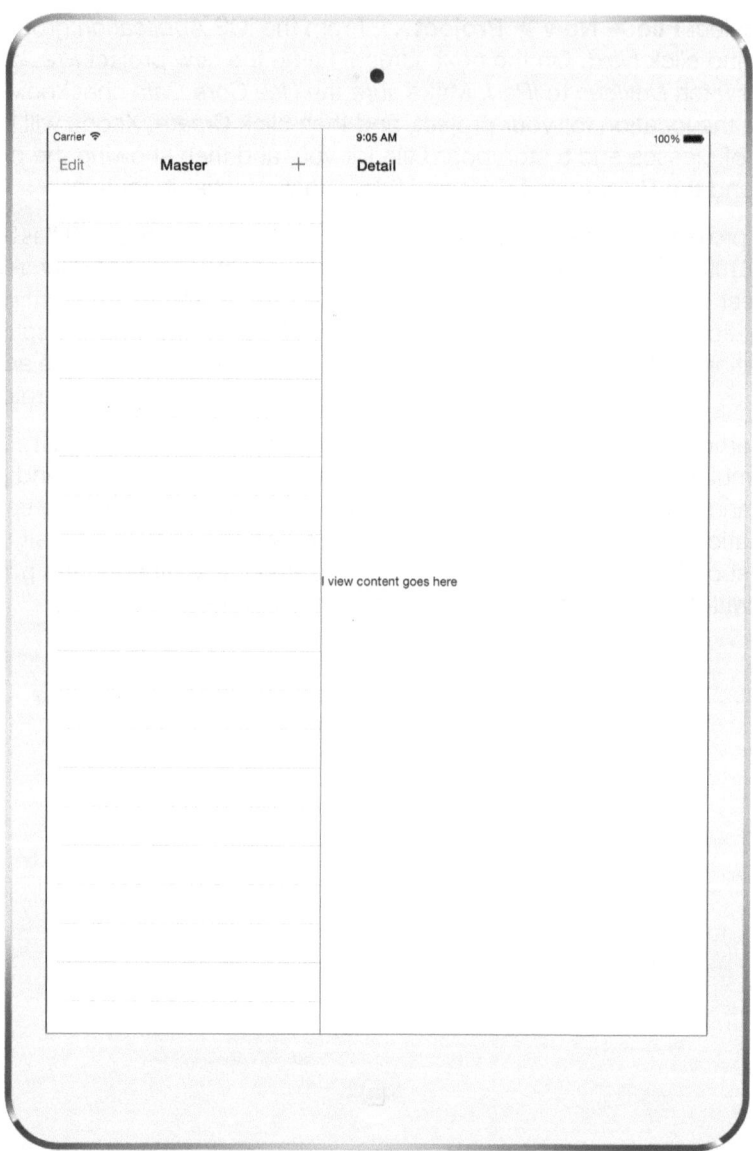

Figure 11-5. The default Master-Detail Application template in portrait mode with the popover showing. Note the similarity between this figure and Figure 11-2

We're going to build on this to make the president-presenting app we want, but first let's dig into what's already there.

The Storyboard Defines the Structure

Right off the bat, you have a pretty complex set of view controllers in play:

- A split view controller that contains all the elements
- A navigation controller to handle what's happening on the left side of the split

- A master view controller (displaying a master list of items) inside the navigation controller

- A detail view controller on the right

- Another navigation controller as a container for the detail view controller on the right

In the default Master-Detail Application template that we used, these view controllers are set up and interconnected primarily in the main storyboard file, rather than in code. Apart from doing GUI layout, Interface Builder really shines as a way of letting you connect different components without writing a bunch of code just to establish relationships. Let's dig into the project's storyboard to see how things are set up.

Select *MainStoryboard.storyboard* to open it in Interface Builder. This storyboard really has a lot of stuff going on. You'll definitely want to open the document outline for the best results (see Figure 11-6). Zooming out, by using the controls at the lower right corner of the editor, can also help you see the big picture.

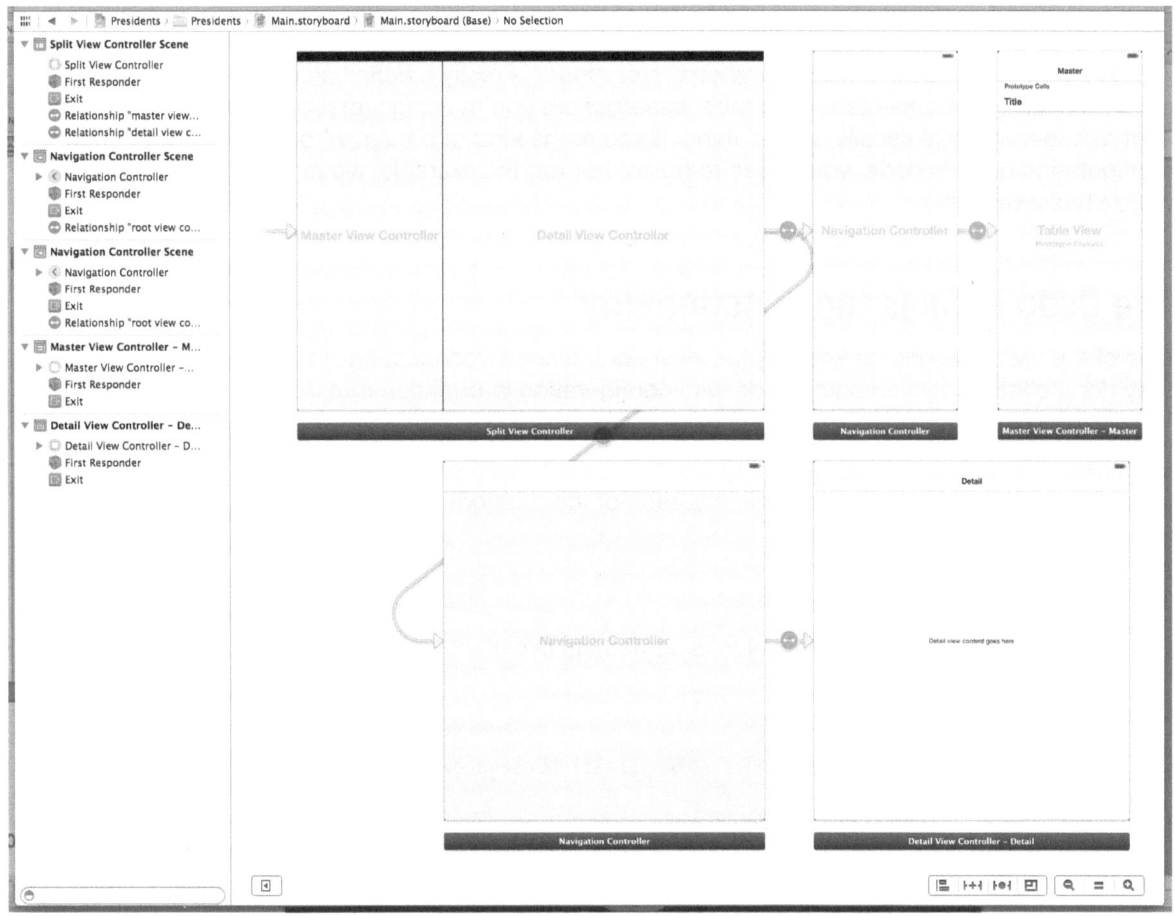

Figure 11-6. MainStoryboard.storyboard open in Interface Builder. This complex object hierarchy is best viewed in list mode

To get a better sense of how these controllers relate to one another, open the Connections Inspector, and then spend some time clicking each of the view controllers in turn.

The split view controller and the two navigation controller objects each have one or more connections to other controllers from the start, as shown in the *Storyboard Segues* section of the Connections Inspector. In Chapter 9, you gained some familiarity with these sorts of connections, including the rootViewController relationship that each UINavigationController has. Here, you'll find that the UISplitViewController actually has two relationships connected to other controllers: masterViewController and detailViewController. These are used to tell the UISplitViewController what it should use for the narrow strip it displays on the left or in a popup (the masterViewController), as well as what it should use for the larger display area (the detailViewController). Note that the masterViewController and detailViewController are instances of UINavigationController, rather than the specific classes that will contain our application's GUI. Each navigation controller in turn has a rootViewController connection to another view controller, which will display the actual content. Using a navigation controller this way is pretty common, even in apps like this one that don't really much use of the navigation controller's central feature. That's because, apart from the ability to push and pop view controllers from its stack, the navigation controller provides a built-in navigation bar at the top, which is nice for displaying a title and, in our case, a few buttons. This navigation bar also gives us the fuzzy, transparent background effect that is a hallmark of iOS 7.

At this point, the content of *MainStoryboard.storyboard* is really a definition of how the app's various controllers are interconnected. As in most cases where you're using storyboards, this eliminates a lot of code, which is usually a good thing. If you're the kind of person who likes to see all such configuration done in code, you're free to do so; but for this example, we're going to stick with what Xcode has provided.

The Code Defines the Functionality

One of the main reasons for keeping the view controller interconnections in a storyboard is that they don't clutter up your source code with configuration information that doesn't need to be there. What's left is just the code that defines the actual functionality.

Let's look at what we have as a starting point. Xcode defined several classes for us when the project was created, and we're going to peek into each of them before we start making any changes.

The App Delegate

First up is *BIDAppDelegate.h*, which looks something like this:

```
#import <UIKit/UIKit.h>

@interface BIDAppDelegate : UIResponder <UIApplicationDelegate>

@property (strong, nonatomic) UIWindow *window;

@end
```

This is pretty similar to several other application delegates you've seen in this book so far.

Switch over to the implementation in *BIDAppDelegate.m*, which looks something like the following (we've deleted most comments and empty methods here for the sake of brevity):

```
#import "BIDAppDelegate.h"

@implementation BIDAppDelegate

- (BOOL)application:(UIApplication *)application
didFinishLaunchingWithOptions:(NSDictionary *)launchOptions
{
    // Override point for customization after application launch.
    UISplitViewController *splitViewController =
        (UISplitViewController *)self.window.rootViewController;
    UINavigationController *navigationController =
        [splitViewController.viewControllers lastObject];
    splitViewController.delegate =
        (id)navigationController.topViewController;
    return YES;
}

@end
```

This code really does just one thing: it sets the UISplitViewController's delegate property, pointing it at the controller for the main part of the display (the view labeled *Detail* in Figure 11-6). Later in this chapter, when we dig into split views, we'll explore the logic behind that UISplitViewController delegate connection. But why make this connection here in code, instead of having it hooked up directly in the storyboard? After all, just a few paragraphs ago, you were told that elimination of boring code—"connect this thing to that thing"—is one of the main benefits of both nibs and storyboards. And you've seen us hook up delegates in interface builder plenty of times, so why can't we do that here?

To understand why using a storyboard to make the connections can't really work here, you need to consider how a storyboard differs from a nib file. We've only used nib files a little bit in this book, since storyboards are preferable for most use cases now, but they're still around and have a few differences that you should be aware of.

A nib file is really a frozen object graph. When you load a nib into a running application, the objects it contains all "thaw out" and spring into existence, including all interconnections specified in the nib file. The system creates a fresh instance of every single object in the nib file, one after another, and connects all the outlets and connections between objects.

A storyboard, however, is something more than that. You could say that each scene in a storyboard corresponds roughly to a nib file. When you add in the metadata describing how the scenes are connected via segues, you end up with a storyboard. Unlike a single nib, a complex storyboard is not normally loaded all at once. Instead, any activity that causes a new scene to come into focus will end up loading that particular scene's frozen object graph from the storyboard. This means that the objects you see when looking at a storyboard won't necessarily all exist at the same time.

Since Interface Builder has no way of knowing which scenes will coexist, it actually forbids you from making any outlet or target/action connections from an object in one scene to an object in another scene. In fact, the only connections it allows you to make from one scene to another are segues.

But don't take our word for it, try it out yourself! First, select the *Split View Controller* in the storyboard (you'll find it within the dock in the *Split View Controller Scene*). Now bring up the Connections Inspector and try to drag a connection from the *delegate* outlet to another view controller or object. You can drag all over the layout view and the list view, and you won't find any spot that highlights (which would indicate it was ready to accept a drag).

So, we'll need to connect the delegate outlet from our UISplitViewController to its destination in code. Referring back to *BIDAppDelegate.m*, that sequence starts like this:

```
UISplitViewController *splitViewController =
    (UISplitViewController *)self.window.rootViewController;
```

This lets us grab the window's rootViewController, which you may recall is pointed out in the storyboard by the free-floating arrow directed at our UISplitViewController instance. This code comes next:

```
UINavigationController *navigationController =
    [splitViewController.viewControllers lastObject];
```

On this line, we dig into the UISplitViewController's viewControllers array. We happen to know that it always has exactly two view controllers: one for the left side and one for the right (more on that later). So, we grab the one for the right side, which will contain our detail view. Finally, we see this:

```
splitViewController.delegate =
    (id)navigationController.topViewController;
```

This last line simply assigns the detail view controller as the UISplitViewController's delegate.

All in all, this extra bit of code is a small price to pay, considering how much other code is eliminated by our use of storyboards.

The Master View Controller

Now, let's take a look at BIDMasterViewController, which controls the setup of the table view containing the app's navigation. *BIDMasterViewController.h* looks like this:

```
#import <UIKit/UIKit.h>

@class BIDDetailViewController;

@interface BIDMasterViewController : UITableViewController

@property (strong, nonatomic) BIDDetailViewController *detailViewController;

@end
```

Its corresponding *BIDMasterViewController.m* file starts off like this (we're just looking at the first few methods now and will deal with the rest later):

```
#import "BIDMasterViewController.h"

#import "BIDDetailViewController.h"

@interface BIDMasterViewController () {
    NSMutableArray *_objects;
}
@end

@implementation BIDMasterViewController

- (void)awakeFromNib
{
    self.clearsSelectionOnViewWillAppear = NO;
    self.preferredContentSize = CGSizeMake(320.0, 600.0);
    [super awakeFromNib];
}

- (void)viewDidLoad
{
    [super viewDidLoad];
    // Do any additional setup after loading the view, typically from a nib.
    self.navigationItem.leftBarButtonItem = self.editButtonItem;

    UIBarButtonItem *addButton =
        [[UIBarButtonItem alloc]
            initWithBarButtonSystemItem:UIBarButtonSystemItemAdd
                                 target:self
                                 action:@selector(insertNewObject:)];
    self.navigationItem.rightBarButtonItem = addButton;
    self.detailViewController =
        (BIDDetailViewController *)[[self.splitViewController.viewControllers
                                 lastObject] topViewController];
}
.
.
.
@end
```

A fair amount of configuration is happening here. Fortunately, Xcode provides it as part of the split view template. This code contains a few things that are relevant to the iPad that you may not have come across before.

First, the awakeFromNib method starts like this:

```
self.clearsSelectionOnViewWillAppear = NO;
```

The clearsSelectionOnViewWillAppear property is defined in the UITableViewController class (our superclass) and lets us tweak the controller's behavior a bit. By default, UITableViewController is set up to deselect all rows each time it's displayed. That may be OK in an iPhone app, where each table view is usually displayed on its own; however, in an iPad app featuring a split view, you probably don't want that selection to disappear. To revisit an earlier example, consider the Mail app. The user selects a message on the left side and expects that selection to remain there, even if the message list disappears (due to rotating the iPad or closing the popover containing the list). This line fixes that.

The awakeFromNib method also includes a line that sets the view's preferredContentSize property. That property sets the size of the view if this view controller should happen to be used to provide the display for some other view controller that allows a variable size. In this case, it's for the popover controller that will contain our master view controller when it's displayed in portrait mode. This rectangle must be at least 320 pixels wide. Apart from that, you can set the size pretty much however you like. We'll talk more about popover issues later in this chapter.

The final point of interest here is the viewDidLoad method. In previous chapters, when you implemented a table view controller that responds to a user row selection, you typically responded to the user selecting a row by creating a new view controller and pushing it onto the navigation controller's stack. In this app, however, the view controller we want to show is already in place, and it will be reused each time the user makes a selection on the left. It's the instance of BIDDetailViewController contained in the storyboard file. Here, we're grabbing that BIDDetailViewController instance and hanging onto it with a property, anticipating that we'll want to use it later, when we have some content to display.

There are several more methods included in the template for this class, but don't worry about those right now. We're going to delete some of those and rewrite the others, but only after taking a detour through the detail view controller.

The Detail View Controller

The final class created for us by Xcode is BIDDetailViewController, which takes care of the actual display of the item the user chooses. Here's what *BIDDetailViewController.h* looks like:

```
#import <UIKit/UIKit.h>

@interface BIDDetailViewController : UIViewController <UISplitViewControllerDelegate>

@property (strong, nonatomic) id detailItem;

@property (weak, nonatomic) IBOutlet UILabel *detailDescriptionLabel;
@end
```

Apart from the detailItem property that we've seen referenced before (in the BIDMasterViewController class), BIDDetailViewController also has an outlet for connecting to a label in the storyboard (detailDescriptionLabel).

Switch over to *BIDDetailViewController.m*, where you'll find the following (once again, this is somewhat abridged):

```objc
#import "BIDDetailViewController.h"

@interface BIDDetailViewController ()
@property (strong, nonatomic) UIPopoverController *masterPopoverController;
- (void)configureView;
@end

@implementation BIDDetailViewController

#pragma mark - Managing the detail item

- (void)setDetailItem:(id)newDetailItem
{
    if (_detailItem != newDetailItem) {
        _detailItem = newDetailItem;
        [self configureView];
    }
    if (self.masterPopoverController != nil) {
        [self.masterPopoverController dismissPopoverAnimated:YES];
    }
}

- (void)configureView
{
    if (self.detailItem) {
        self.detailDescriptionLabel.text = [self.detailItem description];
    }
}

- (void)viewDidLoad
{
    [super viewDidLoad];
    [self configureView];
}

#pragma mark - Split view

- (void)splitViewController:(UISplitViewController *)splitController
     willHideViewController:(UIViewController *)viewController
          withBarButtonItem:(UIBarButtonItem *)barButtonItem
       forPopoverController:(UIPopoverController *)popoverController
{
    barButtonItem.title = NSLocalizedString(@"Master", @"Master");
    [self.navigationItem setLeftBarButtonItem:barButtonItem animated:YES];
    self.masterPopoverController = popoverController;
}
```

```
- (void)splitViewController:(UISplitViewController *)splitController
      willShowViewController:(UIViewController *)viewController
   invalidatingBarButtonItem:(UIBarButtonItem *)barButtonItem
{
    [self.navigationItem setLeftBarButtonItem:nil animated:YES];
    self.masterPopoverController = nil;
}

@end
```

Much of this should look familiar to you, but this class contains a few items worth going over. The first of these is something called a **class extension**, which is declared near the top of the file:

```
@interface BIDDetailViewController ()
@property (strong, nonatomic) UIPopoverController *masterPopoverController;
- (void)configureView;
@end
```

We've talked a bit about class extensions before, but their purpose is worth mentioning again. Creating a class extension lets you define some methods and properties that are going to be used within your class, but that you don't want to expose to other classes in a header file. Here, we've declared a masterPopoverController property and a utility method which will be called whenever we need to update the display. We still haven't told you what the masterPopoverController property is meant to be used for, but we're getting there!

Just a bit further down, you'll see this method:

```
- (void)setDetailItem:(id)newDetailItem
{
    if (_detailItem != newDetailItem) {
        _detailItem = newDetailItem;
        [self configureView];
    }
    if (self.masterPopoverController != nil) {
        [self.masterPopoverController dismissPopoverAnimated:YES];
    }
}
```

The setDetailItem: method may seem surprising to you. We did, after all, define detailItem as a property, and it is automatically synthesized to create the getter and setter for us, so why create a setter in code? In this case, we need to be able to react whenever the user calls the setter (by selecting a row in the master list on the left), so that we can update the display. This is a good way to do that. The first part of the method seems pretty straightforward, but at the end it diverges into a call to dismiss the current masterPopoverController, if there is one. Where in the world is that hypothetical masterPopupController coming from? Scroll down a bit, and you'll see that this method contains the answer:

```
- (void)splitViewController:(UISplitViewController *)splitController
      willHideViewController:(UIViewController *)viewController
           withBarButtonItem:(UIBarButtonItem *)barButtonItem
          forPopoverController:(UIPopoverController *)popoverController
```

```
{
    barButtonItem.title = NSLocalizedString(@"Master", @"Master");
    [self.navigationItem setLeftBarButtonItem:barButtonItem animated:YES];
    self.masterPopoverController = popoverController;
}
```

This is a delegate method for UISplitViewController. It's called when the split view controller is no longer going to show the left side of the split view as a permanent fixture (that is, when the iPad is rotated to portrait orientation). The first thing this method does is configure the title displayed in barButtonItem's title using the NSLocalizedString function, which gives you a chance to use text strings in other languages, if you've prepared any. We'll talk more about localization issues in Chapter 21; but for now, all you need to know is that one parameter is basically a key that the function uses to retrieve a localized string from a dictionary, and the other is simply a comment.

The split view controller calls this method in the delegate when the left side of the split is about to disappear, and then passes in a couple of interesting items: a UIBarButtonItem and a UIPopoverController. The UIPopoverController is already preconfigured to contain whatever was in the left side of the split view, and the UIBarButtonItem is set up to display that very same popover. This means that if our GUI contains a UIToolBar or a UINavigationItem (the standard toolbar presented by UINavigationController), we just need to add the button item to it to let the user bring up the navigation view (wrapped inside a popover) with a single tap on the button item.

In this case, since this controller is itself wrapped inside a UINavigationController, we have immediate access to a UINavigationItem where we can place the button item. If our GUI didn't contain a UINavigationItem or a UIToolbar, we would still have the popover controller passed in, which we could assign to some other element of our GUI so it could pop open the popover for us. We're also handed the wrapped UIViewController itself (BIDMasterViewController, in this example) in case we would rather present its contents in some other way.

So, that's where the popover controller comes from. You may not be too surprised to learn that the next method effectively takes it away:

```
- (void)splitViewController:(UISplitViewController *)splitController
      willShowViewController:(UIViewController *)viewController
   invalidatingBarButtonItem:(UIBarButtonItem *)barButtonItem
{
    [self.navigationItem setLeftBarButtonItem:nil animated:YES];
    self.masterPopoverController = nil;
}
```

This method is called when the user switches back to landscape orientation. At that point, the split view controller wants to draw the left-side view in a permanent position again, so it tells us to get rid of the UIBarButtonItem we were given previously.

That concludes our overview of what Xcode's Master-Detail Application template gives you. It might be a lot to absorb at a glance, but, ideally, by presenting it a piece at a time, we've helped you understand how all the pieces fit together.

Here Come the Presidents

Now that you've seen the basic layout of our project, it's time to fill in the blanks and turn this autogenerated app into something all your own. Start by looking in the book's source code archive, where the folder *11 – Presidents* contains a file called *PresidentList.plist*. Drag that file into your project's *Presidents* folder in Xcode to add it to the project, making sure that the checkbox telling Xcode to copy the file itself is in the *on* state. This plist file contains information about all the US presidents so far, consisting of just the name and Wikipedia entry URL for each of them.

Now, let's look at the `BIDMasterViewController` class and see how we need to modify it to handle the presidential data properly. It's going to be a simple matter of loading the list of presidents, presenting them in the table view, and passing a URL to the detail view for display. In *BIDMasterViewController.m*, start off by adding the bold line shown here to the class extension and removing the crossed-out portion:

```
#import "BIDMasterViewController.h"

#import "BIDDetailViewController.h"

@interface BIDMasterViewController () {
    NSMutableArray *_objects;
}
@property (copy, nonatomic) NSArray *presidents;
@end
```

Instead of holding our list of presidents in the mutable array that was created by Xcode, we'll create our own array and store it as a property.

Now divert your attention to the `viewDidLoad` method, where the changes are a little more involved (but still not too bad). You're going to add a few lines to load the list of presidents, and then remove a few other lines that set up edit and insertion buttons in the toolbar:

```
- (void)viewDidLoad
{
    [super viewDidLoad];
    // Do any additional setup after loading the view, typically from a nib.
    self.navigationItem.leftBarButtonItem = self.editButtonItem;

    NSString *path = [[NSBundle mainBundle] pathForResource:@"PresidentList"
                                                     ofType:@"plist"];
    NSDictionary *presidentInfo = [NSDictionary
        dictionaryWithContentsOfFile:path];
    self.presidents = [presidentInfo objectForKey:@"presidents"];

    UIBarButtonItem *addButton =
    [[UIBarButtonItem alloc] initWithBarButtonSystemItem:UIBarButtonSystemItemAdd
                                                  target:self
                                                  action:@selector(insertNewObject:)];
    self.navigationItem.rightBarButtonItem = addButton;
    self.detailViewController =
    (BIDDetailViewController *)[[self.splitViewController.viewControllers
                                lastObject] topViewController];
}
```

This template-generated class also includes a method called insertNewObject: for adding items to the _objects array. We don't even have that array anymore, so we delete the entire method:

```
- (void)insertNewObject:(id)sender
{
    if (!_objects) {
        _objects = [[NSMutableArray alloc] init];
    }
    [_objects insertObject:[NSDate date] atIndex:0];
    NSIndexPath *indexPath = [NSIndexPath indexPathForRow:0 inSection:0];
    [self.tableView insertRowsAtIndexPaths:@[indexPath]
withRowAnimation:UITableViewRowAnimationAutomatic];
}
```

Also, we have a couple of data source methods that deal with letting users edit rows in the table view. We're not going to allow any editing of rows in this app, so let's just remove this code before adding our own:

```
- (BOOL)tableView:(UITableView *)tableView
canEditRowAtIndexPath:(NSIndexPath *)indexPath
{
    // Return NO if you do not want the specified item to be editable.
    return YES;
}

- (void)tableView:(UITableView *)tableView commitEditingStyle:(UITableViewCellEditingStyle)editingStyle
forRowAtIndexPath:(NSIndexPath *)indexPath
{
    if (editingStyle == UITableViewCellEditingStyleDelete) {
        [_objects removeObjectAtIndex:indexPath.row];
        [tableView deleteRowsAtIndexPaths:@[indexPath]
                        withRowAnimation:UITableViewRowAnimationFade];
    } else if (editingStyle == UITableViewCellEditingStyleInsert) {
    }
}
```

Now it's time to get to the main table view data source methods, adapting them for our purposes. Let's start by editing the method that tells the table view how many rows to display:

```
- (NSInteger)tableView:(UITableView *)tableView
    numberOfRowsInSection:(NSInteger)section
{
    return [_objects count];
    return [self.presidents count];
}
```

After that, edit the `tableView:cellForRowAtIndexPath:` method to make each cell display a president's name:

```
- (UITableViewCell *)tableView:(UITableView *)tableView
         cellForRowAtIndexPath:(NSIndexPath *)indexPath
{
    UITableViewCell *cell = [tableView
        dequeueReusableCellWithIdentifier:@"Cell"
                            forIndexPath:indexPath];
    NSDate *object = _objects[indexPath.row];
    cell.textLabel.text = [object description];

    NSDictionary *president = self.presidents[indexPath.row];
    cell.textLabel.text = president[@"name"];
    return cell;
}
```

Finally, it's time to edit `tableView:didSelectRowAtIndexPath:` to pass the URL to the detail view controller, as follows:

```
- (void)tableView:(UITableView *)tableView
    didSelectRowAtIndexPath:(NSIndexPath *)indexPath
{
    NSDate *object = _objects[indexPath.row];
    self.detailViewController.detailItem = object;
    NSDictionary *president = self.presidents[indexPath.row];
    NSString *urlString = president[@"url"];
    self.detailViewController.detailItem = urlString;
}
```

That's all we need to do for `BIDMasterViewController`. At this point, you can build and run the app. Use landscape mode, or tap the *Master* button in the upper-left corner to bring up a popover with a list of presidents (see Figure 11-7). Tap a president's name to display that president's Wikipedia page URL in the detail view.

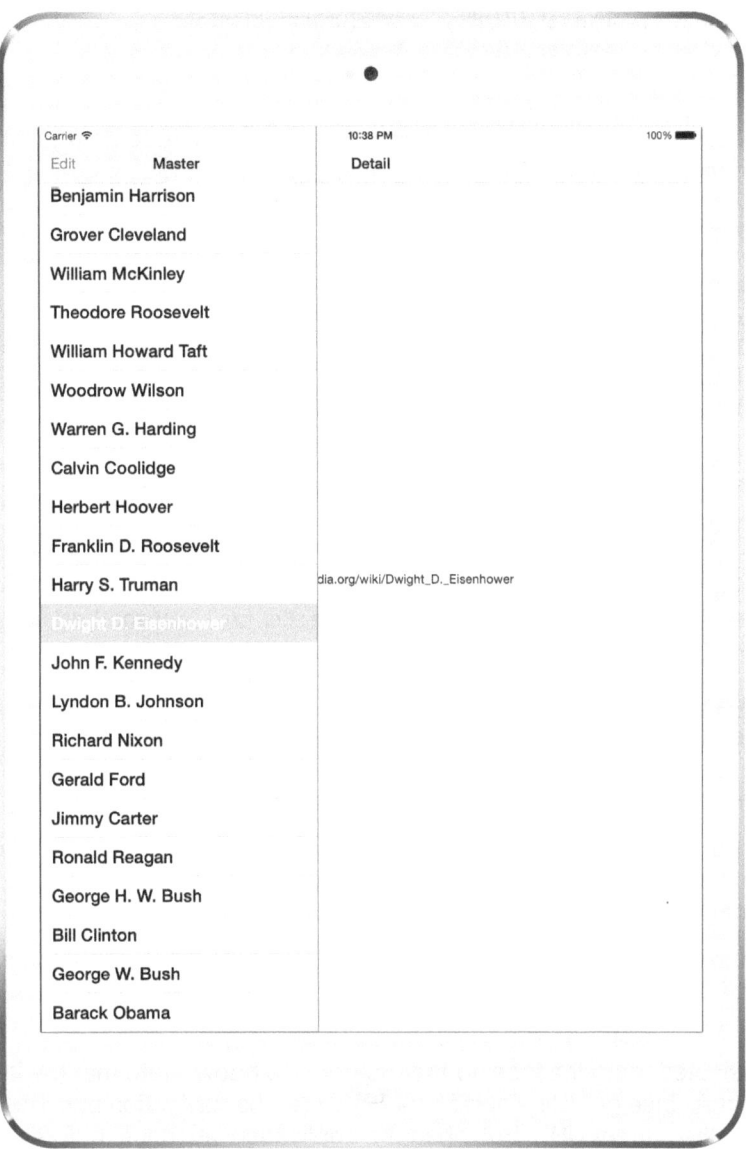

Figure 11-7. *Our first run of the Presidents app. Note that we tapped the Master button to bring up the popover. Tap a president's name, and the link to that president's Wikipedia entry will be displayed*

Let's finish this section by making the detail view do something a little more useful with the URL. Start with *BIDDetailViewContoller.h*, where we'll add an outlet for a web view to display the Wikipedia page for the selected president. Add the bold line shown here:

```
#import <UIKit/UIKit.h>

@interface BIDDetailViewController : UIViewController <UISplitViewControllerDelegate>

@property (strong, nonatomic) id detailItem;
```

```
@property (weak, nonatomic) IBOutlet UILabel *detailDescriptionLabel;
@property (weak, nonatomic) IBOutlet UIWebView *webView;
@end
```

Next, switch to *BIDDetailViewController.m*, where we have a bit more to do (though really, not too much). Scroll down to the `configureView` method and add the methods shown in bold here:

```
- (void)configureView
{
    NSURL *url = [NSURL URLWithString:self.detailItem];
    NSURLRequest *request = [NSURLRequest requestWithURL:url];
    [self.webView loadRequest:request];
    if (self.detailItem) {
        self.detailDescriptionLabel.text = [self.detailItem description];
    }
}
```

These new lines are all we need to get our web view to load the requested page.

Next, move on to the `splitViewController: willHideViewController:withBarButtonItem:forPopoverController:` method, where we're simply going to give the `UIBarButtonItem` a more relevant title:

```
barButtonItem.title = NSLocalizedString(@"Master", @"Master");
barButtonItem.title = NSLocalizedString(@"Presidents", @"Presidents");
```

Believe it or not, these few edits are all the code we need to write at this point.

The final changes we need to make are in *MainStoryboard.storyboard*. Open it for editing, find the detail view at the lower right, and start by taking care of the label in the GUI (the text of which reads, "Detail view content goes here").

Start by selecting the label. You might find it easiest to select the label in the document outline, in the section labeled *Detail View Controller – Detail Scene*. You can find it quickly by typing *label* in the document outline's search field.

Once the label is selected, drag the label to the top of the window. Note that the label should run from the left to right blue guideline and fit snugly under the navigation bar. This label is being repurposed to show the current URL. But when the application launches, before the user has chosen a president, we want this field to give the user a hint about what to do.

Double-click the label and change it to *Select a President*. You should also use the Size Inspector to make sure that the label's position is constrained to both the left and right sides of its superview, as well as the top edge (see Figure 11-8). If you need to adjust these constraints, use the methods described previously to set them up. You can probably get almost exactly what you want by selecting **Editor ➤ Resolve Auto Layout Issues ➤ Reset to Suggested Constraints** from the menu.

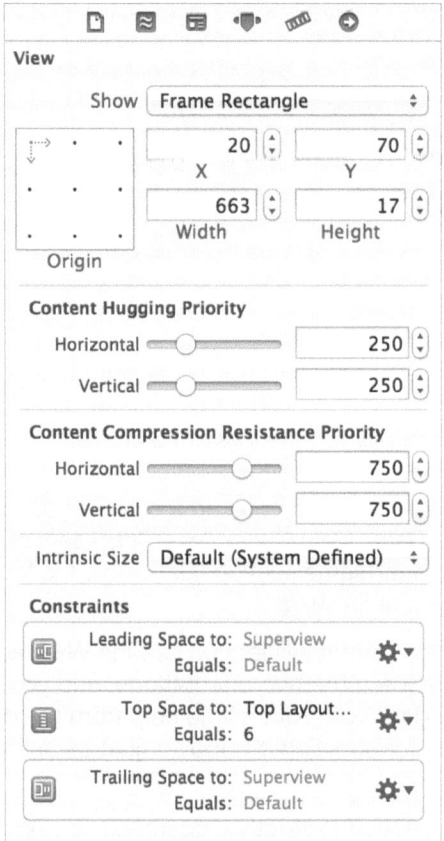

Figure 11-8. The Size Inspector, showing the constraints settings for the "Select a President" label at the bottom

Next, use the library to find a *UIWebView* and drag it into the space below the label you just moved. After dropping the web view there, use the resize handles to make it fill the rest of the view below the label. Make it go from the left edge to the right edge, and from the blue guideline just below the bottom of the label all the way to the very bottom of the window. Now use the Size Inspector to constrain the web view to the left, bottom, and right edges of the superview, as well as to the label for the top edge (see Figure 11-9). Once again, you can probably get exactly what you need by selecting **Editor ➤ Resolve Auto Layout Issues ➤ Reset to Suggested Constraints** from the menu.

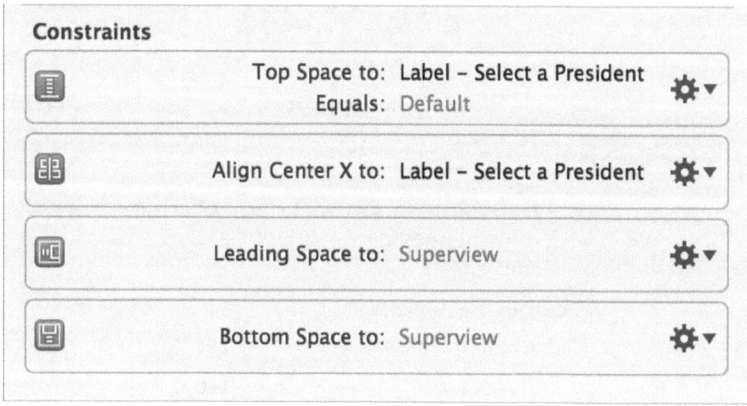

Figure 11-9. The Size Inspector, showing the constraints settings for the web view

We have one last bit of trickery to perform. To hook up the outlet you created, control-drag from the *Detail View Controller* icon (in the *Detail View Controller – Detail* section in the dock, just below the *First Responder* icon) to our new web view (same section, just below the label), and connect the *webView* outlet. Save your changes, and you're finished!

Now you can build and run the app, and it will let you see the Wikipedia entries for each of the presidents. Rotate the display between the two orientations, and you'll see how the split view controller takes care of everything for you, with a little help from the detail view controller. The latter handles the toolbar item required for showing a popover (just as in the original app before we made our changes).

The final change to make in this section is strictly a cosmetic one. When you run this app in landscape orientation, the heading above the navigation view on the left is still *Master*. Switch to portrait orientation, tap the *Presidents* toolbar button, and you'll see the same heading.

To fix the heading, open *MainStoryboard.storyboard*, double-click the navigation bar above the table view at the upper right, double-click the text shown there, and change it to *Presidents* (see Figure 11-10). Save the storyboard, build and run the app, and you should see your change in place.

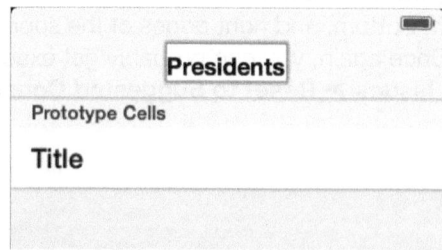

Figure 11-10. The current state of MainStoryboard.storyboard. We've changed the title of the master detail view's table view to Presidents

Creating Your Own Popover

There's still one piece of iPad GUI technology that we haven't dealt with in quite enough detail yet: the creation and display of your own popover. So far, we've had a UIPopoverController handed to us from a UISplitView delegate method, which let us keep track of it in an instance variable so we could force it to go away. However, popovers really come in handy when we want to present our own view controllers.

To see how this works, we're going to add a popover to be activated by a permanent toolbar item (unlike the one that the UISplitView delegate method gives us, which is meant to come and go). This popover will display a table view containing a list of languages. If the user picks a language from the list, the web view will load (in the new language) whatever Wikipedia entry was already showing. This will be simple enough to do, since switching from one language to another in Wikipedia is just a matter of changing a small piece of the URL that contains an embedded country code.

> **Note**   Both uses of popovers in this example are in the service of showing a UITableView, but don't let that mislead you—UIPopoverController can be used to handle the display of any view controller content you like! We're sticking with table views for this example because it's a common use case, it's easy to show in a relatively small amount of code, and it's something with which you should already be quite familiar.

Start by right-clicking the *Presidents* folder in Xcode and selecting **New File...** from the contextual menu. When the assistant appears, select *Cocoa Touch*, select *Objective-C class*, and then click *Next*. On the next screen, name the new class *BIDLanguageListController* and select *UITableViewController* from the *Subclass of* field. Turn on the checkbox next to *Targeted for iPad* and turn off the checkbox next to *With XIB for user interface*. Click *Next*, double-check the location where you're saving the file, and click *Create*.

The BIDLanguageListController is going to be a pretty standard table view controller class. It will display a list of items and let the detail view controller know when a choice is made by using a pointer back to the detail view controller. Edit *BIDLanguageListController.h*, adding the bold lines shown here:

```objective-c
#import <UIKit/UIKit.h>

@class BIDDetailViewController;

@interface BIDLanguageListController : UITableViewController

@property (weak, nonatomic) BIDDetailViewController *detailViewController;
@property (copy, nonatomic) NSArray *languageNames;
@property (copy, nonatomic) NSArray *languageCodes;

@end
```

These additions define a pointer back to the detail view controller (which we'll set from code in the detail view controller itself when we're about to display the language list), as well as a pair of arrays for containing the values that will be displayed (English, French, etc.) and the underlying values that will be used to build an URL from the chosen language (en, fr, and so on). Note that we've declared these arrays to have copy storage semantics instead of strong. This means that whenever some piece of code calls one of these setters, the parameter is sent a copy message instead of just being held as a strong pointer. This is done to prevent a situation where another class might send in an NSMutableArray instead of an NSArray, and then make changes to the array without our knowledge. Sending copy to an NSMutableArray instance always returns an immutable NSArray, so we know that the array we're using can't be changed by someone else. At the same time, sending copy to an NSArray, which is already immutable, doesn't actually make a new copy, it just returns a strong pointer to self, so sending it a copy message isn't wasteful in any way.

If you copied and pasted this code from the book's source archive (or e-book) into your own project or typed it yourself a little sloppily, you may not have noticed an important difference in how the detailViewController property was declared earlier. Unlike most properties that reference an object pointer, we declared this one using weak instead of strong. This is something that we must do to avoid a **retain cycle**.

What's a retain cycle? It's a situation where a set of two or more objects have retained one another in a circular fashion. Each object has a retain counter of one or higher and will therefore never release the pointers it contains. Thus, objects in a retain cycle will never be deallocated, either. Most potential retain cycles can be avoided by carefully considering the creation of your objects, often by trying to figure out which object "owns" which. In this sense, an instance of BIDDetailViewController owns an instance of BIDLanguageListController because it's the BIDDetailViewController that actually creates the BIDLanguageListController to get a piece of work done. Whenever you have a pair of objects that need to refer to one another, you'll usually want the owner object to retain the other object, while the other object should specifically not retain its owner. Since we're using the ARC feature that Apple introduced in Xcode 4.2, the compiler does most of the work for us. Instead of paying attention to the details about releasing and retaining objects, all we need to do is declare a property with the weak keyword instead of strong. ARC will do the rest!

Now, switch over to *BIDLanguageListController.m* to implement the following changes. At the top of the file, start by importing the header for BIDDetailViewController:

```
#import "BIDLanguageListController.h"
#import "BIDDetailViewController.h"
.
.
.
```

Next, scroll down a bit to the viewDidLoad method and add a bit of setup code:

```
- (void)viewDidLoad
{
    [super viewDidLoad];

    self.languageNames = @[@"English", @"French", @"German", @"Spanish"];
    self.languageCodes = @[@"en", @"fr", @"de", @"es"];
```

```
    self.clearsSelectionOnViewWillAppear = NO;
    self.preferredContentSize = CGSizeMake(320.0,
                                [self.languageCodes count] * 44.0);

    [self.tableView registerClass:[UITableViewCell class]
        forCellReuseIdentifier:@"Cell"];

}
```

This sets up the language arrays and also defines the size that this view will use if shown in a popover (which, as we know, it will be). Without defining the size, we would end up with a popover stretching vertically to fill nearly the whole screen, even if it can be displayed in full with a much smaller view. And finally, we register a default table view cell class to use, as explained previously in Chapter 8.

Further down, we have a few methods generated by Xcode's template that don't contain particularly useful code—just a warning and some placeholder text. Let's replace those with something real:

```
- (NSInteger)numberOfSectionsInTableView:(UITableView *)tableView
{
#warning Potentially incomplete method implementation.
    return 0;
    return 1;
}

- (NSInteger)tableView:(UITableView *)tableView
    numberOfRowsInSection:(NSInteger)section
{
#warning Incomplete method implementation.
    // Return the number of rows in the section.
    return 0;
    return [self.languageCodes count];
}
```

Now add a line near the end of tableView:cellForRowAtIndexPath: to put a language name into a cell:

```
// Configure the cell...
cell.textLabel.text = self.languageNames[indexPath.row];
return cell;
```

Next, implement tableView:didSelectRowAtIndexPath:: so that you can respond to a user's touch by passing the language selection back to the detail view controller:

```
- (void)tableView:(UITableView *)tableView
didSelectRowAtIndexPath:(NSIndexPath *)indexPath
{
    self.detailViewController.languageString =
        self.languageCodes[indexPath.row];
}
```

> **Note** BIDDetailViewController doesn't actually have a languageString property, so you will see a compiler error. We'll take care of that in just a bit.

Now it's time to make the changes required for BIDDetailViewController to handle the popover, as well as to generate the correct URL whenever the user either changes the display language or picks a different president. Start by making the following changes in *BIDDetailViewController.h*:

```
#import <UIKit/UIKit.h>

@interface BIDDetailViewController : UIViewController <UISplitViewControllerDelegate,
 UIPopoverControllerDelegate>

@property (strong, nonatomic) id detailItem;

@property (weak, nonatomic) IBOutlet UILabel *detailDescriptionLabel;
@property (weak, nonatomic) IBOutlet UIWebView *webView;
@property (strong, nonatomic) UIBarButtonItem *languageButton;
@property (strong, nonatomic) UIPopoverController *languagePopoverController;
@property (copy, nonatomic) NSString *languageString;

@end
```

Here, we declared that this class conforms to the UIPopoverControllerDelegate protocol (to handle a notification from the popover controller later) and added some properties to keep track of the GUI components required for the popover and the user's selected language. All we need to do now is fix *BIDDetailViewController.m* so that it can handle the language popover and the URL construction. Start by adding this import somewhere at the top:

```
#import "BIDLanguageListController.h"
```

The next thing we're going to add is a function that takes as arguments a URL pointing to a Wikipedia page and a two-letter language code, and then returns a URL that combines the two. We'll use this at appropriate spots in our controller code later. You can place this function just about anywhere, including within the class's implementation. The compiler is smart enough to always treat a function as just a function. Place it just after the setDetailItem: method:

```
static NSString * modifyUrlForLanguage(NSString *url, NSString *lang) {
    if (!lang) {
        return url;
    }

    // We're relying on a particular Wikipedia URL format here. This
    // is a bit fragile!
    NSRange codeRange = NSMakeRange(7, 2);
```

```
        if ([[url substringWithRange:codeRange] isEqualToString:lang]) {
            return url;
        } else {
            NSString *newUrl = [url stringByReplacingCharactersInRange:codeRange
                                                            withString:lang];
            return newUrl;
        }
    }
```

Why make this a function instead of a method? There are a couple of reasons. First, instance methods in a class are typically meant to do something involving one or more instance variables, or accessing an object's internal state either through getters and setters or through direct instance variable access. This function does not use any instance variables. It simply performs an operation on two strings and returns another. We could have made it a class method, but even that feels a bit wrong, since what the method does isn't really related specifically to the controller class. Sometimes, a function is just what you need.

Our next move is to update the setDetailItem: method. This method will use the function we just defined to combine the URL that's passed in with the chosen languageString to generate the correct URL. It also makes sure that our second popover, if present, disappears just like the first popover (the one that was defined for us) does:

```
- (void)setDetailItem:(id)newDetailItem
{
    if (self.detailItem != newDetailItem) {
        _detailItem = newDetailItem;
        _detailItem = modifyUrlForLanguage(newDetailItem, self.languageString);

        // Update the view.
        [self configureView];
    }

    if (self.masterPopoverController != nil) {
        [self.masterPopoverController dismissPopoverAnimated:YES];
    }
}
```

Now let's update the viewDidLoad method. Here, we're going to create a UIBarButtonItem and put it into the UINavigationItem at the top of the screen:

```
- (void)viewDidLoad
{
    [super viewDidLoad];
    self.languageButton =
     [[UIBarButtonItem alloc] initWithTitle:@"Choose Language"
                                      style:UIBarButtonItemStyleBordered
                                     target:self
                                     action:@selector(toggleLanguagePopover)];
    self.navigationItem.rightBarButtonItem = self.languageButton;
    [self configureView];
}
```

Next, we implement setLanguageString:. This also calls our modifyUrlForLanguage() function so that the URL can be regenerated (and the new page loaded) immediately. Add this method to the bottom of the file, just above the @end:

```
- (void)setLanguageString:(NSString *)newString {
    if (![newString isEqualToString:self.languageString]) {
        _languageString = [newString copy];
        self.detailItem = modifyUrlForLanguage(_detailItem, self.languageString);
    }
    if (self.languagePopoverController != nil) {
        [self.languagePopoverController dismissPopoverAnimated:YES];
        self.languagePopoverController = nil;
    }
}
```

Now, let's define what will happen when the user taps the *Choose Language* button. Simply put, we create a BIDLanguageListController, wrap it in a UIPopoverController, and display it. Place this method after the viewDidLoad method:

```
- (void)toggleLanguagePopover
{
    if (self.languagePopoverController == nil) {
        BIDLanguageListController *languageListController =
            [[BIDLanguageListController alloc] init];
        languageListController.detailViewController = self;
        UIPopoverController *poc =
            [[UIPopoverController alloc]
                    initWithContentViewController:languageListController];
        [poc presentPopoverFromBarButtonItem:self.languageButton
                    permittedArrowDirections:UIPopoverArrowDirectionAny
                                    animated:YES];
        self.languagePopoverController = poc;
    } else {
        if (self.languagePopoverController != nil) {
            [self.languagePopoverController dismissPopoverAnimated:YES];
            self.languagePopoverController = nil;
        }
    }
}
```

Finally, we need to implement one more method to handle the situation where the user taps to open our Languages popover, and then taps somewhere outside the popover to make it go away. In that case, our toggleLanguagePopover method isn't called. However, we can implement a method declared in UIPopoverControllerDelegate to be notified when that happens, and then remove the language popover:

```
- (void)popoverControllerDidDismissPopover:
    (UIPopoverController *)popoverController
{
    if (popoverController == self.languagePopoverController) {
        self.languagePopoverController = nil;
    }
}
```

And that's all! You should now be able to run the app in all its glory, switching willy-nilly between presidents and languages. Switching from one language to another should always leave the chosen president intact; likewise, switching from one president to another should leave the language intact.

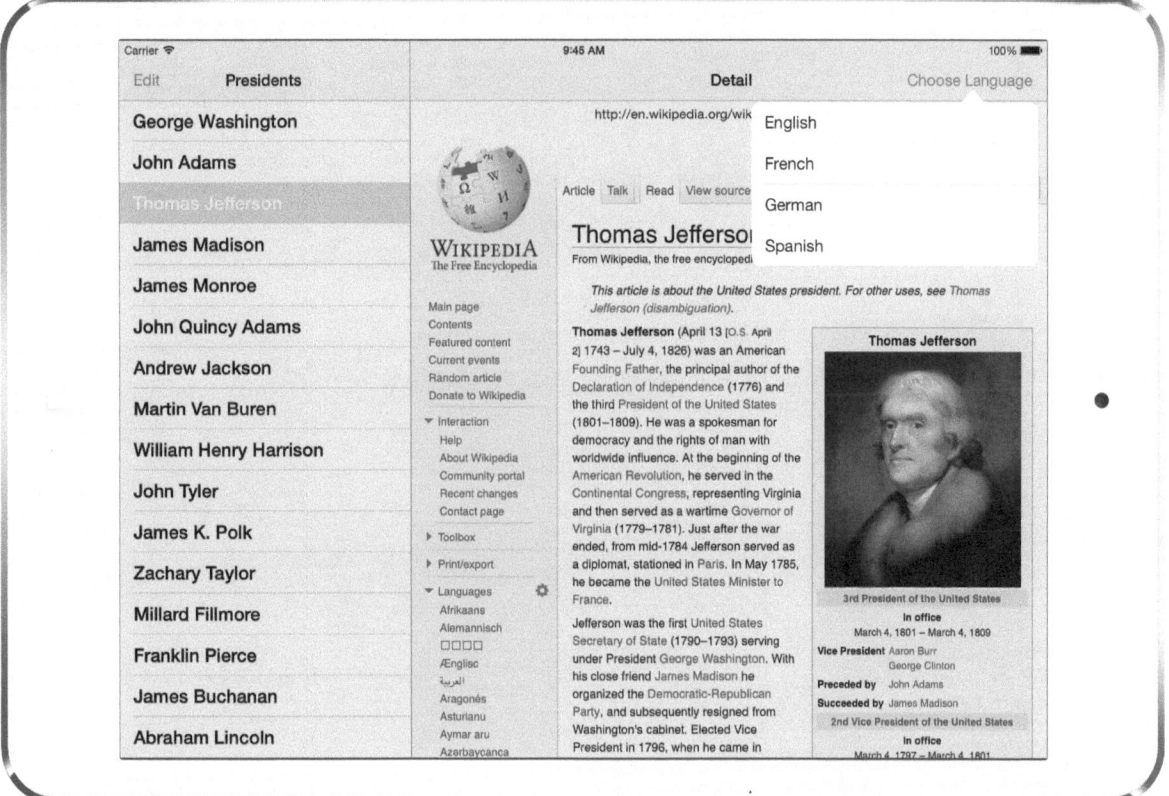

Figure 11-11. *The Abraham Lincoln Wikipedia entry shown in the details view, along with a language list popover*

iPad Wrap-Up

In this chapter, you learned about the main GUI components that are available only on the iPad: popovers and split views. You've also seen an example of how a complex iPad application with several interconnected view controllers can be configured entirely within Interface Builder. With this hard-won knowledge, you should be well on your way to building your first great iPad app.

If you want to dig even further into the particulars of iPad development, you may want to take a look at *Beginning iPad Development for iPhone Developers* by David Mark, Jack Nutting, and Dave Wooldridge (Apress, 2010).

Next up, it's time to visit application settings and user defaults.

Chapter 12

Application Settings and User Defaults

All but the simplest computer programs today have a preferences window where the user can set application-specific options. On Mac OS X, the **Preferences. . .** menu item is usually found in the application menu. Selecting it brings up a window where the user can enter and change various options. The iPhone and other iOS devices have a dedicated application called Settings, which you no doubt have played with any number of times. In this chapter, we'll show you how to add settings for your application to the Settings application and how to access those settings from within your application.

Getting to Know Your Settings Bundle

The Settings application lets the user enter and change preferences for any application that has a settings bundle. A **settings bundle** is a group of files built in to an application that tells the Settings application which preferences the application wishes to collect from the user.

Pick up your iOS device and locate your Settings icon. Touch the icon to launch the Settings app. Ours is shown in Figure 12-1.

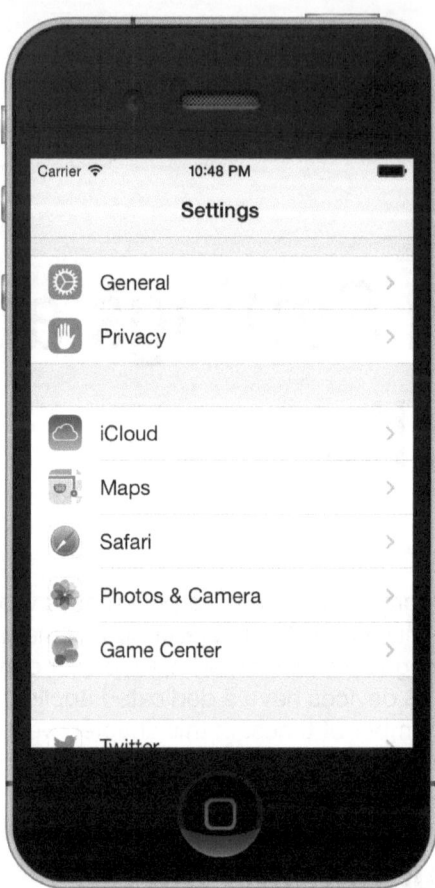

Figure 12-1. The Settings application

The Settings application acts as a common user interface for the iOS User Defaults mechanism. User Defaults is the part of the system that stores and retrieves preferences.

In an iOS application, User Defaults is implemented by the NSUserDefaults class. If you've done Cocoa programming on the Mac, you're probably already familiar with NSUserDefaults because it is the same class that is used to store and read preferences on the Mac. You will have your applications use NSUserDefaults to read and store preference data using pairs of keys and values, just as you would access keyed data from an NSDictionary. The difference is that NSUserDefaults data is persisted to the file system rather than stored in an object instance in memory.

In this chapter, we're going to create an application, add and configure a settings bundle, and then access and edit those preferences from within our application.

One nice thing about the Settings application is that it provides a solution, so you don't need to design your own user interface for your preferences. You create a property list describing your application's available settings, and the Settings application creates the interface for you.

Immersive applications, such as games, generally should provide their own preferences view so that the user doesn't need to quit to make a change. Even utility and productivity applications might, at times, have preferences that a user should be able to change without leaving the application. We'll also show you to how to collect preferences from the user directly in your application and store those in iOS's User Defaults.

One additional complication is that the user can actually switch to the Settings application, change a preference, and then switch back to your still-running application. We'll show you how to handle that situation at the end of this chapter.

The Bridge Control Application

In this chapter, we're going to build a simple application that keeps track of some aspects of managing the bridge of a starship, which I'm sure you'll agree is a useful enterprise. Our first step will be to create a settings bundle so that, when the user launches the Settings application, there will be an entry for our application, Bridge Control (see Figure 12-2).

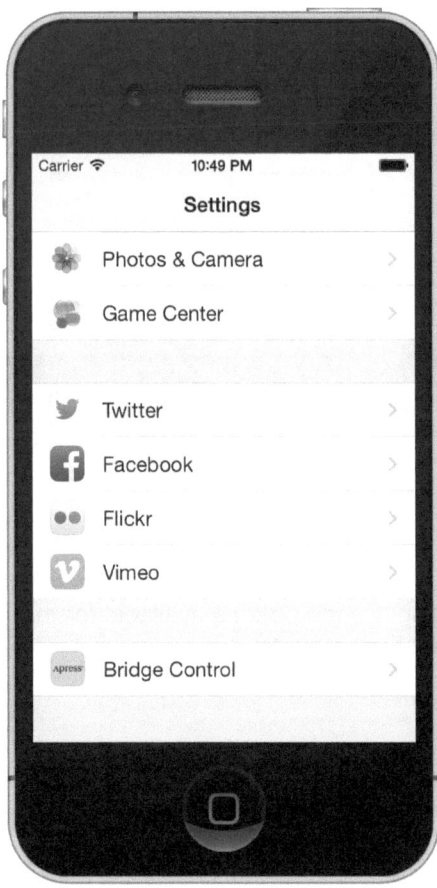

Figure 12-2. The Settings application, which shows an entry for our Bridge Control application in the simulator

If the user selects our application, Settings will drill down into a view that shows the preferences relevant to our application. As you can see in Figure 12-3, the Settings application uses text fields, secure text fields, switches, and sliders to coax values out of our intrepid user.

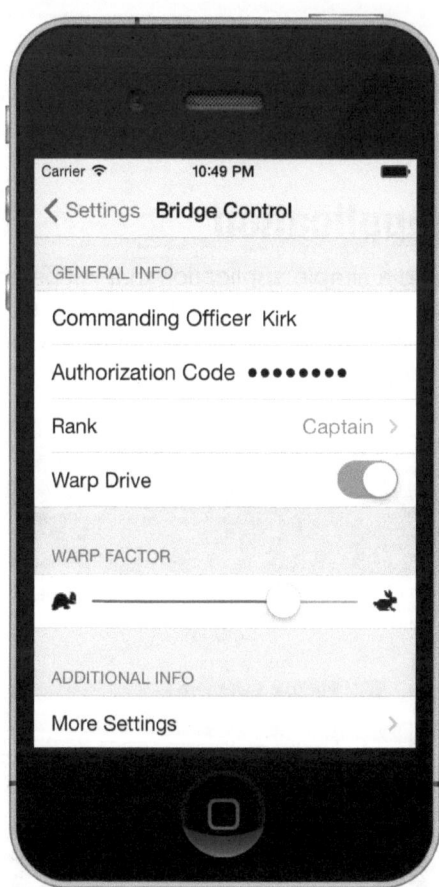

Figure 12-3. Our application's primary settings view

Also notice the two items in the view that have disclosure indicators. The first one, *Rank*, takes the user to another table view that displays the options available for that item. From that table view, the user can select a single value (see Figure 12-4).

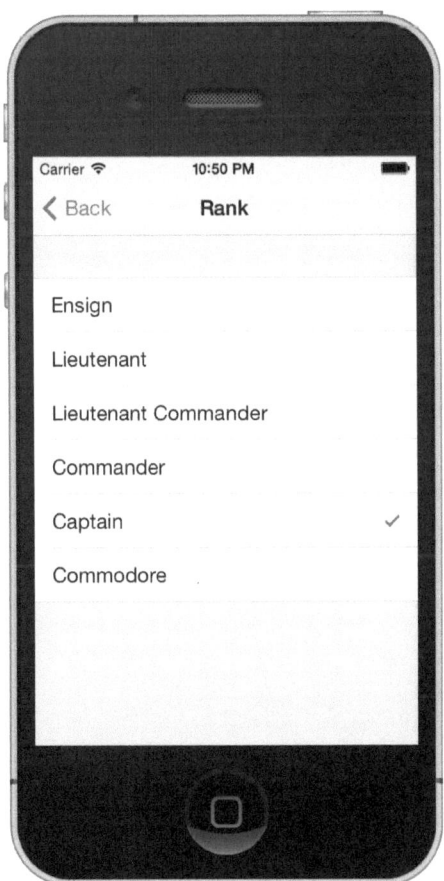

Figure 12-4. Selecting a single preference item from a list

The *More Settings* disclosure indicator allows the user to drill down to another set of preferences (see Figure 12-5). This child view can have the same kinds of controls as the main settings view and can even have its own child views. You may have noticed that the Settings application uses a navigation controller, which it needs because it supports the construction of hierarchical preference views.

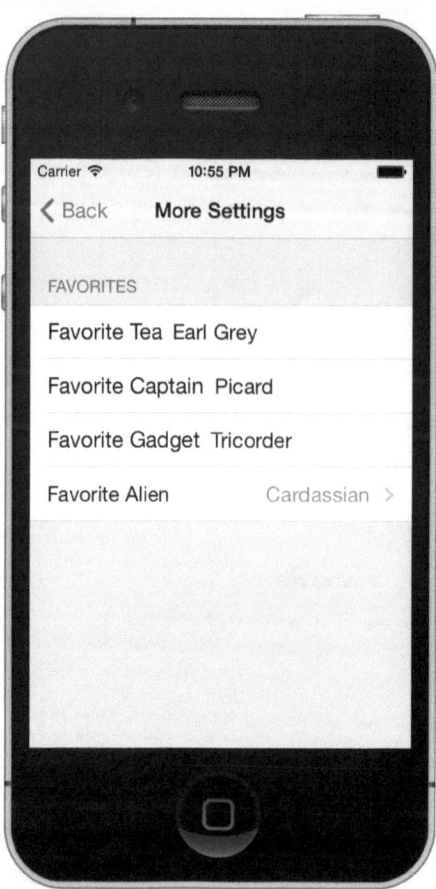

Figure 12-5. A child settings view for our application

When users launch our application, they will be presented with a list of the preferences gathered in the Settings application (see Figure 12-6).

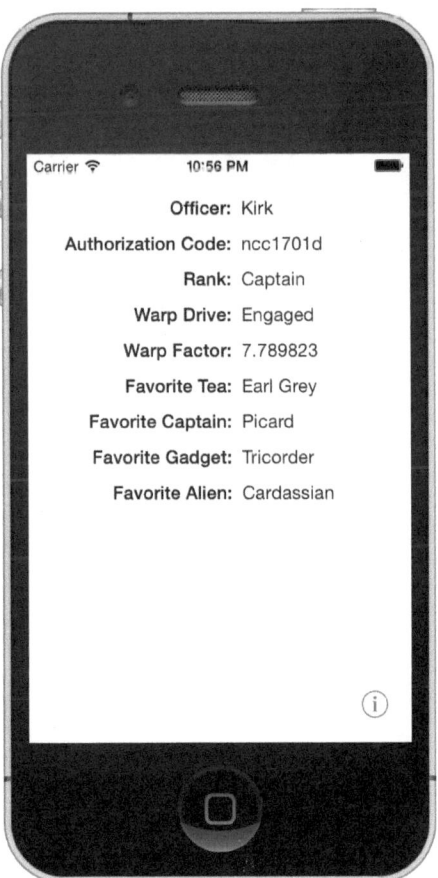

Figure 12-6. Our application's main view

To show how to update preferences from within our application, we also provide a little information button in the lower-right corner. This button takes users to another view where they can change additional preferences directly in our application (see Figure 12-7).

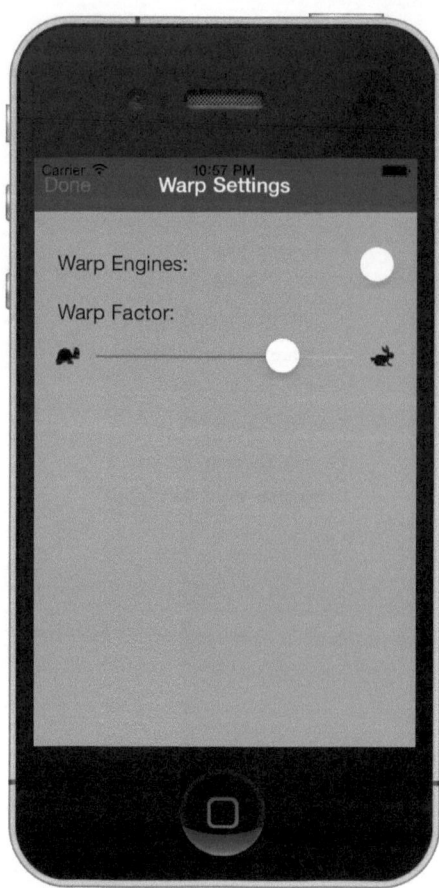

Figure 12-7. Setting some preferences directly in our application

Let's get started building Bridge Control, shall we?

Creating the Project

In Xcode, press ⇧⌘N or select **File ➤ New ➤ Project....** When the new project assistant comes up, select *Application* from under the *iOS* heading in the left pane, click the *Utility Application* icon, and click *Next*. On the next screen, name your project *Bridge Control*. Set *Devices* to *iPhone*. Make sure that *BID* is set as the class prefix and that the *Use Core Data* button is unchecked, and then click the *Next* button. Finally, choose a location for your project and click *Create*.

We haven't used this particular project template before, so let's take a quick look at the project before we proceed. The Utility Application template creates an application similar to the multiview application we built in Chapter 6. The application has a main view and a secondary view called the **flipside view**. Tapping the information button on the main view takes you to the flipside view, and tapping the *Done* button on the flipside view takes you back to the main view.

It takes several controllers and views to implement this type of application. All of these are provided, as stubs, by the template. Expand the *Bridge Control* folder, where you'll find the usual application delegate class, as well as two additional controller classes and a storyboard file to contain the GUI (see Figure 12-8).

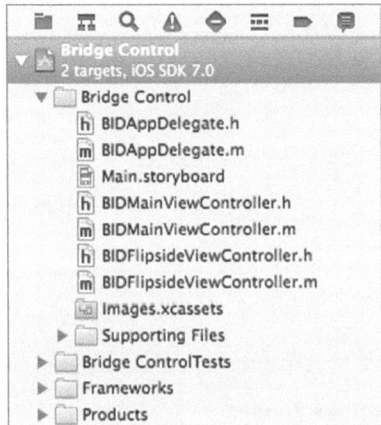

Figure 12-8. Our project created from the Utility Application template. Notice the application delegate, the storyboard, and the main and flipside view controllers

Working with the Settings Bundle

The Settings application uses the contents of each application's settings bundle to construct a settings view for that application. If an application has no settings bundle, then the Settings app doesn't show anything for that application. Each settings bundle must contain a property list called *Root.plist* that defines the root-level preferences view. This property list must follow a very precise format, which we'll talk about when we set up the property list for our app's settings bundle.

When the Settings application starts up, it checks each application for a settings bundle and adds a settings group for each application that includes a settings bundle. If we want our preferences to include any subviews, we need to add property lists to the bundle and add an entry to *Root.plist* for each child view. You'll see exactly how to do that in this chapter.

Adding a Settings Bundle to Our Project

In the project navigator, click the *Bridge Control* folder, and then select **File ➤ New ➤ File…** or press ⌘N. In the left pane, select *Resource* under the *iOS* heading, and then select the *Settings Bundle* icon (see Figure 12-9). Click the *Next* button, leave the default name of *Settings.bundle*, and click *Create*.

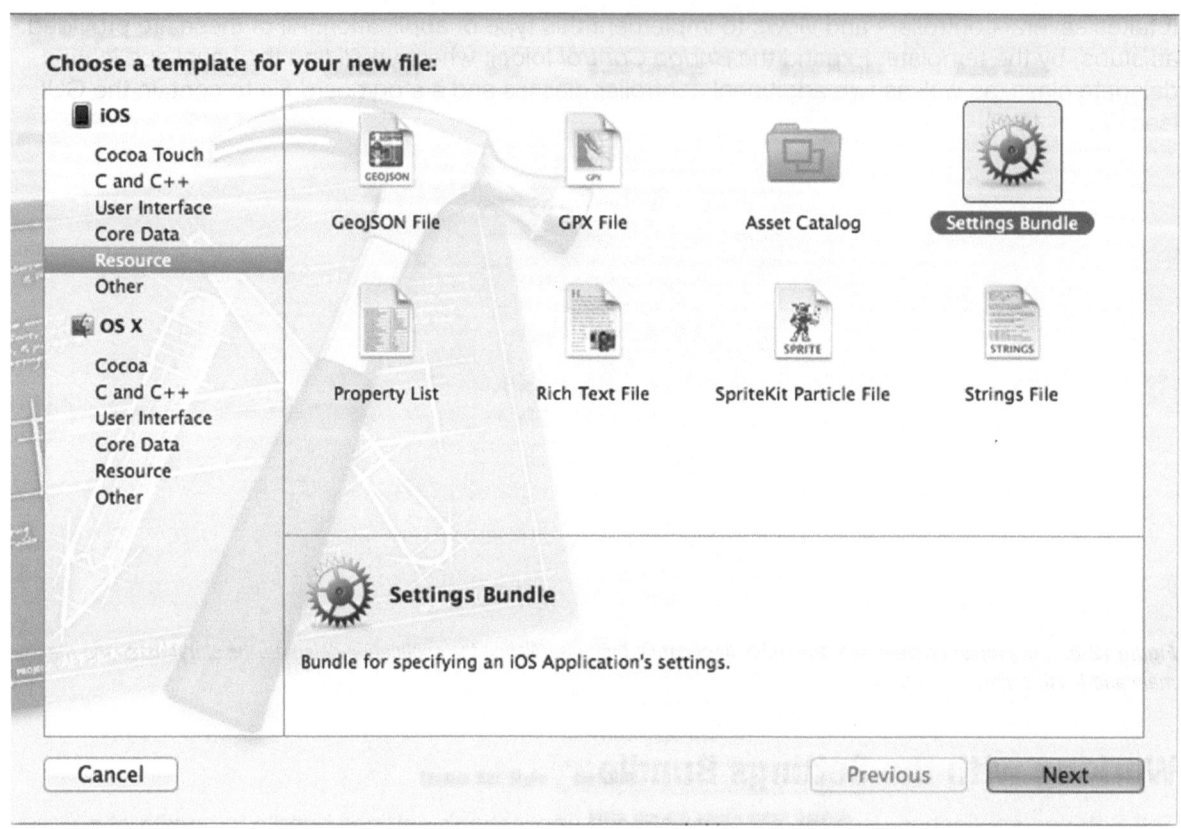

Figure 12-9. Creating a settings bundle in Xcode

You should now see a new item in the project window called *Settings.bundle*. Expand the *Settings.bundle* item, and you should see two subitems: a folder named *en.lproj*, containing a file named *Root.strings*, and an icon named *Root.plist*. We'll discuss *en.lproj* in Chapter 22 when we talk about localizing your application into other languages. Here, we'll concentrate on *Root.plist*.

Setting Up the Property List

Select *Root.plist* and take a look at the editor pane. You're looking at Xcode's property list editor (see Figure 12-10). This editor functions in the same way as the Property List Editor application in */Developer/Applications/Utilities*.

Key	Type	Value
▼ iPhone Settings Schema	Dictionary	(2 items)
▶ Preference Items	Array	(4 items)
Strings Filename	String	Root

Figure 12-10. Root.plist in the property list editor pane. If your editing pane looks slightly different, don't panic. Simply control-click in the editing pane and select Show Raw Keys/Values from the contextual menu that appears

Notice the organization of the items in the property list. Property lists are essentially dictionaries, storing item types and values and using a key to retrieve them, just as an NSDictionary does.

Several different types of nodes can be put into a property list. The *Boolean*, *Data*, *Date*, *Number*, and *String* node types are meant to hold individual pieces of data, but you also have a couple of ways to deal with whole collections of nodes, as well. In addition to *Dictionary* node types, which allow you to store other dictionaries, there are *Array* nodes, which store an ordered list of other nodes similar to an NSArray. The *Dictionary* and *Array* types are the only property list node types that can contain other nodes.

> **Note** Although you can use most kinds of objects as keys in an NSDictionary, keys in property list dictionary nodes must be strings. However, you are free to use any node type for the values.

When creating a settings property list, you need to follow a very specific format. Fortunately, *Root. plist*, the property list that came with the settings bundle you just added to your project, follows this format exactly. Let's take a look.

In the *Root.plist* editor pane, names of keys can either be displayed in their true, "raw" form or in a slightly more human-readable form. We're big fans of seeing things as they truly are whenever possible, so right-click anywhere in the editor and make sure the **Show Raw Keys/Values** option in the contextual menu is checked (see Figure 12-11). The rest of our discussion here uses the real names for all the keys we're going to talk about, so this step is important.

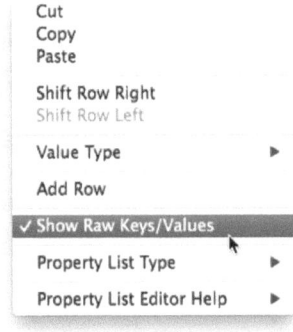

Figure 12-11. Control-click anywhere in the property list editing pane and make sure the Show Raw Keys/Values item is checked. This will ensure that real names are used in the property list editor, which makes your editing experience more precise

Caution At the time of writing, leaving the property list, either by editing a different file or by quitting Xcode, resets the **Show Raw Keys/Values** item to be unchecked. If your text suddenly looks a little different, take another look at that menu item and make sure it is checked.

One of the items in the dictionary is *StringsTable*. A strings table is used in translating your application into another language. We'll cover the use of strings tables in Chapter 22 when we get into localization. We won't be using it in this chapter, but feel free to leave it in your project since it won't do any harm.

In addition to *StringsTable*, the property list contains a node named *PreferenceSpecifiers*, which is an array. This array node is designed to hold a set of dictionary nodes, where each node represents either a single preference item that the user can modify or a single child view that the user can drill down into.

You'll notice that Xcode's template kindly gave us four nodes (see Figure 12-12). Those nodes aren't likely to reflect our actual preferences, so delete *Item 1*, *Item 2*, and *Item 3* (select each one and press the **Delete** key, one after another), leaving just *Item 0* in place.

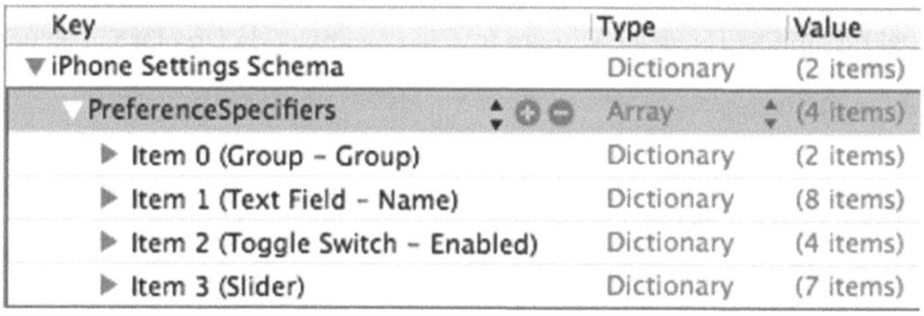

Key	Type	Value
▼ iPhone Settings Schema	Dictionary	(2 items)
▼ PreferenceSpecifiers ↕ ⊕ ⊖	Array ↕ (4 items)
▶ Item 0 (Group – Group)	Dictionary	(2 items)
▶ Item 1 (Text Field – Name)	Dictionary	(8 items)
▶ Item 2 (Toggle Switch – Enabled)	Dictionary	(4 items)
▶ Item 3 (Slider)	Dictionary	(7 items)

Figure 12-12. Root.plist in the editor pane, this time with PreferenceSpecifiers expanded

Note To select an item in the property list, it is best to click on one side or another of the *Key* column to avoid bringing up the *Key* column's dropdown menu.

Single-click *Item 0* but don't expand it. Xcode's property list editor lets you add rows simply by pressing the **Return** key. The current selection state—including which row is selected and whether it's expanded—determines where the new row will be inserted. When an unexpanded array or dictionary is selected, pressing **Return** adds a sibling node after the selected row. In other words, it will add another node at the same level as the current selection. If you were to press **Return** (but don't do that now), you would get a new row called *Item 1* immediately after *Item 0*. Figure 12-13 shows an example of hitting **Return** to create a new row. Notice the dropdown menu that allows you to specify the kind of preference specifier this item represents—more on this in a bit.

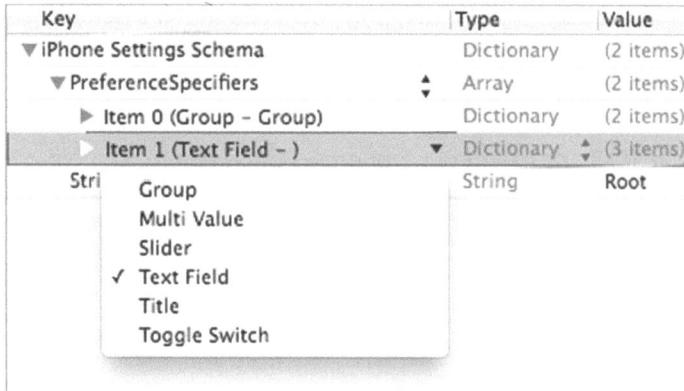

Figure 12-13. *We selected Item 0 and hit return to create a new sibling row. Note the dropdown menu that appears, allowing us to specify the kind of preference specifier this item represents*

Now expand *Item 0* and see what it contains (see Figure 12-14). The editor is now ready to add child nodes to the selected item. If you were to press **Return** at this point (again, don't actually press it now), you would get a new first child row inside *Item 0*.

Key	Type	Value
▼ iPhone Settings Schema	Dictionary	(2 items)
▼ PreferenceSpecifiers	Array	(1 item)
Item 0 (Group – Group)	Dictionary	(2 items)
Title	String	Group
Type	String	PSGroupSpecifier

Figure 12-14. *When you expand Item 0, you'll find a row with a key of Type and a second row with a key of Title. This represents a group with a title of Group*

One of the items inside *Item 0* has a key of *Type*. Every property list node in the *PreferenceSpecifiers* array must have an entry with this key. The *Type* key is typically the second entry, but order doesn't matter in a dictionary, so the *Type* key doesn't need to be second. The *Type* key tells the Settings application what type of data is associated with this item.

In *Item 0*, the *Type* item has a value of *PSGroupSpecifier*. This indicates that the item represents the start of a new group. Each item that follows will be part of this group—until the next item with a *Type* of *PSGroupSpecifier*.

If you look back at Figure 12-3, you'll see that the Settings application presents the application settings in a grouped table. *Item 0* in the *PreferenceSpecifiers* array in a settings bundle property list should always be a *PSGroupSpecifier*, so that the settings start in a new group. This is important because you need at least one group in every Settings table.

The only other entry in *Item 0* has a key of *Title*, and this is used to set an optional header just above the group that is being started.

Now take a closer look at the *Item 0* row itself, and you'll see that it's actually shown as *Item 0 (Group – Group)*. The values in parentheses represent the value of the *Type* item (the first *Group*) and the *Title* item (the second *Group*). This is a nice shortcut that Xcode gives you so that you can visually scan the contents of a settings bundle.

As shown back in Figure 12-3, we called our first group *General Info*. Double-click the value next to *Title*, and change it from *Group* to *General Info* (see Figure 12-15). When you enter the new title, you may notice a slight change to *Item 0*. It's now shown as *Item 0 (Group – General Info)* to reflect the new title.

Key		Type	Value
▼ iPhone Settings Schema		Dictionary	(2 items)
▼ PreferenceSpecifiers	⇕	Array	(1 item)
▼ Item 0 (Group – Group)		Dictionary	(2 items)
Title	⇕ ⊕ ⊖	String	⇕ General Info
Type	⇕	String	PSGroupSpecifier

Figure 12-15. We changed the title of the Item 0 group from Group to General Info

Adding a Text Field Setting

We now need to add a second item in this array, which will represent the first actual preference field. We're going to start with a simple text field.

If you single-click the *PreferenceSpecifiers* row in the editor pane (don't do this, just keep reading) and press **Return** to add a child, the new row will be inserted at the beginning of the list, which is not what we want. We want to add a row at the end of the array.

To add the row, click the disclosure triangle to the left of *Item 0* to close it, and then select *Item 0* and press **Return**. This gives you a new sibling row after the current row (see Figure 12-16). As usual, when the item is added, a dropdown menu appears, showing the default value of *Text Field*.

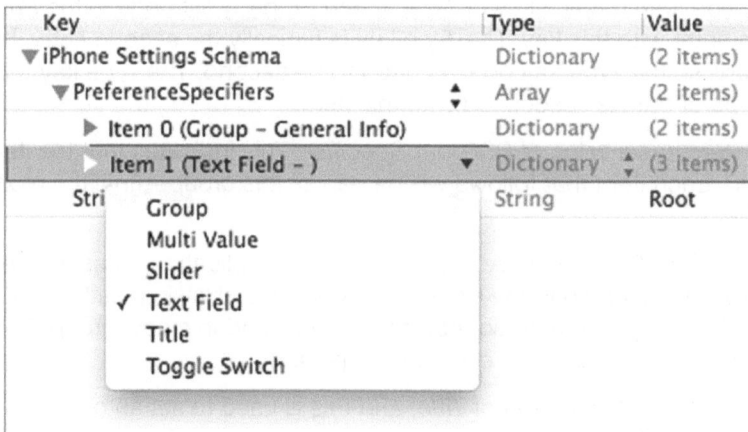

Figure 12-16. Adding a new sibling row to Item 0

Click somewhere outside the dropdown menu to make it go away, and then click the disclosure triangle next to *Item 1* to expand it. You'll see that it contains a *Type* row set to *PSTextFieldSpecifier*. This is the *Type* value used to tell the Settings application that we want the user to edit this setting in a text field. It also contains two empty rows for *Title* and *Key* (see Figure 12-17).

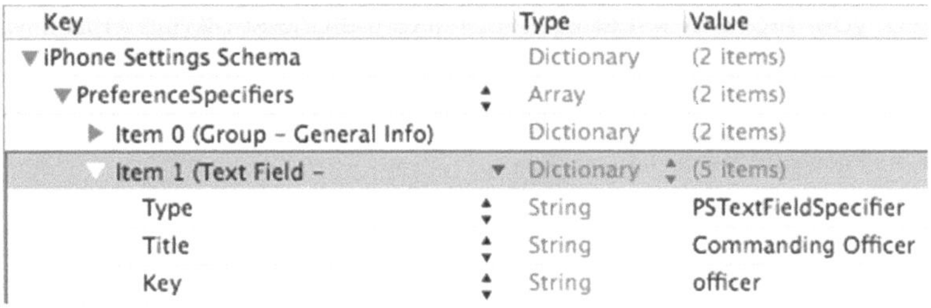

Key	Type	Value
▼ iPhone Settings Schema	Dictionary	(2 items)
▼ PreferenceSpecifiers	Array	(2 items)
▶ Item 0 (Group – General Info)	Dictionary	(2 items)
▼ Item 1 (Text Field –	Dictionary	(5 items)
Type	String	PSTextFieldSpecifier
Title	String	Commanding Officer
Key	String	officer

Figure 12-17. Our text field item, expanded to show the type, title, and key

Select the *Title* row, and then double-click in the whitespace of the *Value* column. Type in *Commanding Officer* to set the *Title* value. This is the text that will appear in the Settings app.

Now do the same for the *Key* row (no, that's not a misprint, you're really looking at a key called *Key*). For a value, type in *officer* (note the lowercase first letter). Remember that user defaults work like a dictionary. This entry tells the Settings application which key to use when it stores the value entered in this text field.

Recall what we said about NSUserDefaults? It lets you store values using a key, similarly to an NSDictionary. Well, the Settings application will do the same thing for each of the preferences it saves on your behalf. If you give it a key value of *foo*, then, later in your application, you can request the value for *foo*, and it will give you the value the user entered for that preference. We will use this same key value later to retrieve this setting from the user defaults in our application.

> **Note**   Our *Title* has a value of *Commanding Officer* and our *Key* has a value of *officer*. This uppercase/lowercase difference will happen frequently, and here we're even compounding the difference by using two words for the displayed title, and a single word for the key. The *Title* is what appears on the screen, so the capital *C* and *O*, and putting a space between the words, all makes sense. The *Key* is a text string we'll use to retrieve preferences from the user defaults, so all lowercase makes sense there. Could we use all lowercase for *Title*? You bet. Could we use all capitals for *Key*? Sure! As long as you capitalize it the same way when you save and when you retrieve, it doesn't matter which convention you use for your preference keys.

Now select the last of the three *Item 1* rows (the one with a *Key* of *Key*) and press **Return** to add another entry to the *Item 1* dictionary, giving this one a key of *AutocapitalizationType*. Note that, as soon as you start typing *AutocapitalizationType*, Xcode presents you with a list of matching choices, so you can simply pick one from the list instead of typing the whole name. After you've entered *AutocapitalizationType*, a popup appears in the *Value* column, where you can select from the available options. Choose *Words*. This specifies that the text field should automatically capitalize each word that the user types in this field.

Create one last new row and give it a key of *AutocorrectionType* and a value of *No*. This will tell the Settings application not to autocorrect values entered into this text field. In any situation where you do want the text field to use autocorrection, you would set the value in this row to *Yes*. Again, Xcode presents you with a list of matching choices as you begin entering *AutocorrectionType*, and it shows you a list of valid options in a popup.

When you're finished, your property list should look like the one shown in Figure 12-18.

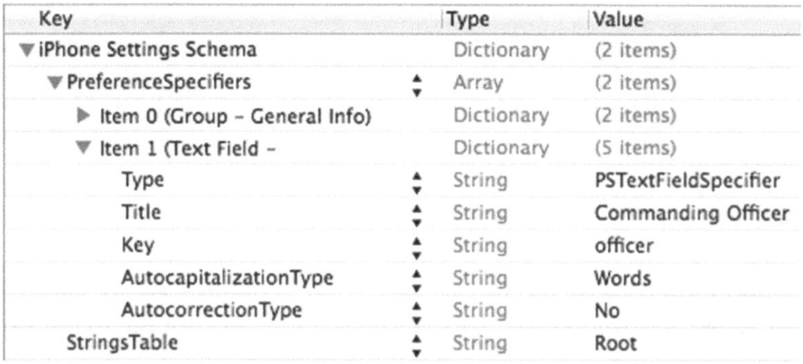

Key		Type	Value
▼ iPhone Settings Schema		Dictionary	(2 items)
▼ PreferenceSpecifiers	⇕	Array	(2 items)
▶ Item 0 (Group – General Info)		Dictionary	(2 items)
▼ Item 1 (Text Field –		Dictionary	(5 items)
Type	⇕	String	PSTextFieldSpecifier
Title	⇕	String	Commanding Officer
Key	⇕	String	officer
AutocapitalizationType	⇕	String	Words
AutocorrectionType	⇕	String	No
StringsTable	⇕	String	Root

Figure 12-18. The finished text field specified in Root.plist

Adding an Application Icon

Before we try our new setting, let's add an application icon to the project. You've done this before.

Save *Root.plist*, the property file you just edited. Next, use the project navigator to select the *Images.xcassets* item, and then select the *AppIcon* item it contains. There, you'll find a set of drop targets where icons can be placed.

In the Finder, navigate first to the source code archive, and then into the 12 – *Bridge Control* folder. Drag the file *Icon.png* into your project's configuration editor, dropping it onto the app icon drop target on the left.

That's it. Now compile and run the application by selecting **Product ➤ Run**. You haven't built any sort of GUI for the app yet, so you'll see a pretty boring start screen consisting of a dark grey background with a small blue info icon in one corner. Press the home button, and then tap the icon for the Settings application. You will find an entry for your application, which uses the application icon added earlier (see Figure 12-2). Click the *Bridge Control* row, and you will be presented with a simple settings view with a single text field, as shown in Figure 12-19.

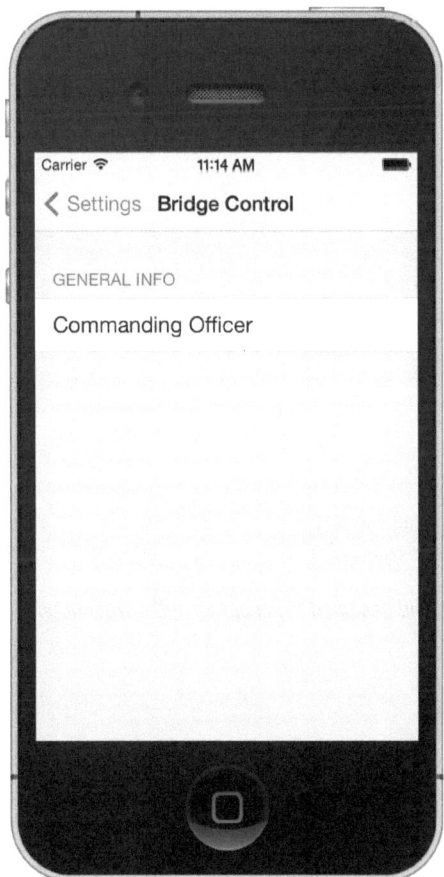

Figure 12-19. Our root view in the Settings application after adding a group and a text field

Quit the simulator and go back to Xcode. We're not finished yet, but you should now have a sense of how easy it is to add preferences to your application. Let's add the rest of the fields for our root settings view. The first one we'll add is a secure text field for the user's authorization code.

Adding a Secure Text Field Setting

Click *Root.plist* to return to your setting specifiers (don't forget to turn on *Show Raw Keys/Values*, assuming Xcode's editing area has reset this). Collapse *Item 0* and *Item 1*, and then select *Item 1*. Press ⌘C to copy it to the clipboard, and then press ⌘V to paste it back. This will create a new *Item 2* that is identical to *Item 1*. Expand the new item and change the *Title* to *Authorization Code* and the *Key* to *authorizationCode*. Remember that the *Title* is what's shown in an on-screen label, and the *Key* is what's used for saving the value.

Next, add one more child to the new item. Remember that the order of items does not matter, so feel free to place it directly below the *Key* item you just edited. To do this, select the *Key/authorizationCode* row, and then hit **Return**.

Give the new item a *Key* of *IsSecure* (note the leading uppercase *I*), and you'll see that Xcode automatically changes the *Type* to *Boolean*. Now change its *Value* from *NO* to *YES*, which tells the Settings application that this field needs to hide the user's input like a password field, rather than behaving like an ordinary text field. Finally, change *AutocapitalizationType* to *None*. Our finished *Item 2* is shown in Figure 12-20.

Key		Type	Value
▼ iPhone Settings Schema	⊕	Dictionary	(2 items)
▼ PreferenceSpecifiers	↕	Array	(3 items)
▶ Item 0 (Group – General Info)		Dictionary	(2 items)
▶ Item 1 (Text Field – Commanding		Dictionary	(5 items)
▼ Item 2 (Text Field – Authorization		Dictionary	(6 items)
Type	↕	String	PSTextFieldSpecifier
Title	↕	String	Authorization Code
Key	↕	String	authorizationCode
IsSecure	↕	Boolean	YES
AutocapitalizationType	↕	String	None
AutocorrectionType	↕	String	No

Figure 12-20. Our finished Item 2, a text field designed to accept an authorizationCode

Adding a Multivalue Field

The next item we're going to add is a **multivalue field**. This type of field will automatically generate a row with a disclosure indicator. Clicking it will let users drill down to another table, where they can select one of several rows.

Collapse *Item 2*, select the row, and then press **Return** to add *Item 3*. Use the pop-up attached to the *Key* field to select *Multi Value,* and then expand *Item 3* by clicking the disclosure triangle.

The expanded *Item 3* already contains a few rows. One of them, the *Type* row, is set to *PSMultiValueSpecifier*. Look for the *Title* row and set its value to *Rank*. Then find the *Key* row and give it a value of *rank*. The next part is a little tricky, so let's talk about it before we do it.

We're going to add two more children to *Item 3*, but they will be *Array* type nodes, not *String* type nodes, as follows:

- One array, called *Titles*, will hold a list of the values from which the user can select.

- The other array, called *Values*, will hold a list of the values that are stored in the user defaults.

So, if the user selects the first item in the list, which corresponds to the first item in the *Titles* array, the Settings application will actually store the first value from the *Values* array. This pairing of *Titles* and *Values* lets you present user-friendly text to the user, but actually stores something else, like a number, date, or different string.

Both of these arrays are required. If you want them to be the same, you can create one array, copy it, paste it back in, and then change the key so that you have two arrays with the same content, but stored under different keys. We'll actually do just that.

Select *Item 3* (leave it open) and press **Return** to add a new child. You'll see that, once again, Xcode is aware of the type of file we're editing and even seems to anticipate what we want to do: the new child row already has its *Key* set to *Titles* and is configured to be an *Array*, which is just what we wanted! Expand the *Titles* row and hit **Return** to add a child node. Repeat this five more times, so you have a total of six child nodes. All six nodes should be *String* type and should be given the following values: *Ensign, Lieutenant, Lieutenant Commander, Commander, Captain,* and *Commodore.*

Once you've created all six nodes and entered their values, collapse *Titles* and select it. Next, press **⌘C** to copy it and press **⌘V** to paste it back. This will create a new item with a key of *Titles - 2*. Double-click *Titles - 2* and change it to *Values*.

We're almost finished with our multivalue field. There's just one more required value in the dictionary, which is the default value. Multivalue fields must have one—and only one—row selected. So, we need to specify the default value to be used if none has yet been selected, and it needs to correspond to one of the items in the *Values* array (not the *Titles* array, if they are different). Xcode already added a *DefaultValue* row when we created this item, so all we need to do now is give it a value of *Ensign*. Figure 12-21 shows our version of *Item 3*.

Key		Type	Value
▼ iPhone Settings Schema		Dictionary	(2 items)
▼ PreferenceSpecifiers	↕	Array	(4 items)
▶ Item 0 (Group – General Info)		Dictionary	(2 items)
▶ Item 1 (Text Field – Commanding		Dictionary	(5 items)
▶ Item 2 (Text Field – Authorization		Dictionary	(6 items)
▼ Item 3 (Multi Value – Rank)		Dictionary	(6 items)
▼ Titles	↕	Array	(6 items)
Item 0		String	Ensign
Item 1		String	Lieutenant
Item 2		String	Lieutenant Commander
Item 3		String	Commander
Item 4		String	Captain
Item 5		String	Commodore
▼ Values	↕ ⊕ ⊖	Array	(6 items)
Item 0		String	Ensign
Item 1		String	Lieutenant
Item 2		String	Lieutenant Commander
Item 3		String	Commander
Item 4		String	Captain
Item 5		String	Commodore
Type	↕	String	PSMultiValueSpecifier
Title	↕	String	Rank
Key	↕	String	rank
DefaultValue	↕	String	Ensign

Figure 12-21. Our finished Item 3, a multivalue field designed to let the user select from one of five possible values

Let's check our work. Save the property list, and build and run the application again. When your application starts, press the home button and launch the Settings application. When you select *Bridge Control*, you should see three fields on your root-level view (see Figure 12-22). Go ahead and play with your creation, and then let's move on.

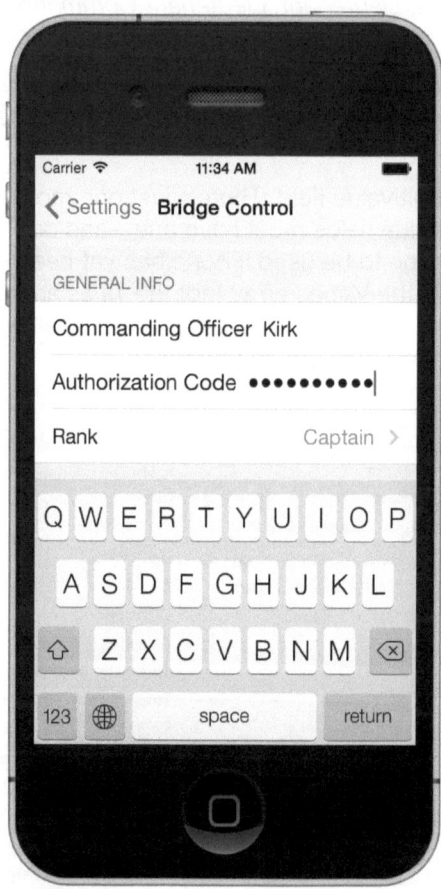

Figure 12-22. Three fields down. Not too shabby!

Adding a Toggle Switch Setting

The next item we need to get from the user is a Boolean value that indicates whether our warp engines are turned on. To capture a Boolean value in our preferences, we are going to tell the Settings application to use a UISwitch by adding another item to our *PreferenceSpecifiers* array with a type of *PSToggleSwitchSpecifier*.

Collapse *Item 3* if it's currently expanded, and then single-click it to select it. Press **Return** to create *Item 4*. Use the dropdown menu to select *Toggle Switch*, and then click the disclosure triangle to expand *Item 4*. You'll see there's already a child row with a *Key* of *Type* and a *Value* of *PSToggleSwitchSpecifier*. Give the empty *Title* row a value of *Warp Drive* and set the value of the *Key* row to *warp*.

We have one more required item in this dictionary, which is the default value. Just as with the *Multi Value* setup, here Xcode has already created a *DefaultValue* row for us. Let's turn on our warp engines by default by giving the *DefaultValue* row a value of *YES*. Figure 12-23 shows our completed *Item 4*.

Key		Type	Value
▼ iPhone Settings Schema		Dictionary	(2 items)
▼ PreferenceSpecifiers	⬍	Array	(5 items)
▶ Item 0 (Group – General Info)		Dictionary	(2 items)
▶ Item 1 (Text Field – Commanding)		Dictionary	(5 items)
▶ Item 2 (Text Field – Authorization)		Dictionary	(6 items)
▶ Item 3 (Multi Value – Rank)		Dictionary	(6 items)
▼ Item 4 (Toggle Switch – Warp)	▼	Dictionary ⬍	(4 items)
Type	⬍	String	PSToggleSwitchSpecifier
Title	⬍	String	Warp Drive
Key	⬍	String	warp
DefaultValue	⬍	Boolean	YES

Figure 12-23. Our finished Item 4, a toggle switch to turn the warp engines on and off. Engage!

Adding the Slider Setting

The next item we need to implement is a slider. In the Settings application, a slider can have a small image at each end, but it can't have a label. Let's put the slider in its own group with a header, so that the user will know what the slider does.

Start by collapsing *Item 4*. Now single-click *Item 4* and press **Return** to create a new row. Use the pop-up to turn the new item into a *Group*, and then click the item's disclosure triangle to expand it. You'll see that *Type* is already set to *PSGroupSpecifier*. This will tell the Settings application to start a new group at this location. Double-click the value in the row labeled *Title* and change the value to *Warp Factor*.

Collapse *Item 5* and select it, and then press **Return** to add a new sibling row. Use the pop-up to change the new item into a *Slider*, which indicates to the Settings application that it should use a `UISlider` to get this information from the user. Expand *Item 6* and set the value of the *Key* row to *warpFactor*, so that the Settings application knows which key to use when storing this value.

We're going to allow the user to enter a value from 1 to 10, and we'll set the default to *warp 5*. Sliders need to have a minimum value, a maximum value, and a starting (or default) value; and all of these need to be stored as numbers, not strings, in your property list. Fortunately, Xcode has already created rows for all these values. Give the *DefaultValue* row a value of *5*, the *MinimumValue* row a value of *1*, and the *MaximumValue* row a value of *10*.

If you want to test the slider, go ahead, but hurry back. We're going to do just a bit more customization.

As noted, sliders can have images. You can place a small 21 × 21-pixel image at each end of the slider. Let's provide little icons to indicate that moving the slider to the left slows us down and moving it to the right speeds us up.

Adding Icons to the Settings Bundle

In the *12 - Bridge Control* folder in the project archive that accompanies this book, you'll find two icons called *rabbit.png* and *turtle.png*. We need to add both of these to our settings bundle. Because these images need to be used by the Settings application, we can't just put them in our *Bridge Control* folder; we need to put them in the settings bundle, so the Settings application can access them.

To do that, find the *Settings.bundle* in the project navigator. We'll need to open this bundle in the Finder. Control-click the *Settings.bundle* icon in the project navigator. When the contextual menu appears, select **Show in Finder** (see Figure 12-24) to show the bundle in the Finder.

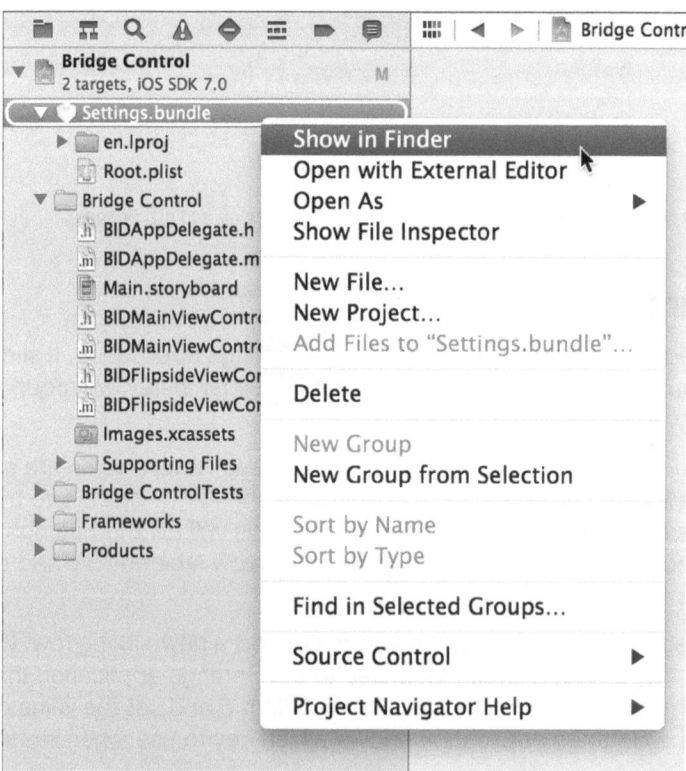

Figure 12-24. The Settings.bundle contextual menu

Remember that bundles look like files in the Finder, but they are really folders. When the Finder window opens to show the *Settings.bundle* file, control-click the file and select **Show Package Contents** from the contextual menu that appears. This will open the settings bundle in a new Finder window, and you should see the same two items that you see in *Settings.bundle* in Xcode. Copy the two icon files, *rabbit.png* and *turtle.png*, from the *12 - Bridge Control* folder into the *Settings.bundle* package contents in the Finder window.

You can leave this window open in the Finder, as we'll need to copy another file here soon. Now we'll return to Xcode and tell the slider to use these two images.

Back in Xcode, return to *Root.plist* and add two more child rows under *Item 6*. Give one a key of *MinimumValueImage* and a value of *turtle*. Give the other a key of *MaximumValueImage* and a value of *rabbit*. Figure 12-25 shows our finished *Item 6*.

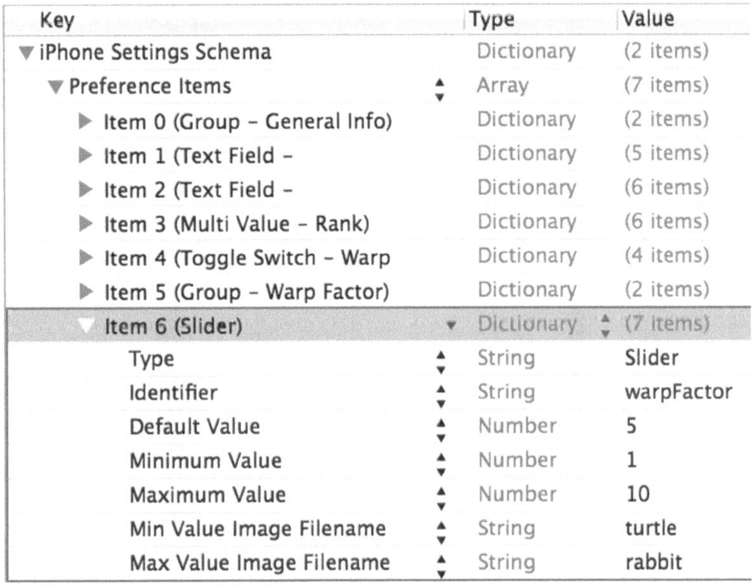

Key	Type	Value
▼ iPhone Settings Schema	Dictionary	(2 items)
▼ Preference Items	Array	(7 items)
▶ Item 0 (Group – General Info)	Dictionary	(2 items)
▶ Item 1 (Text Field –	Dictionary	(5 items)
▶ Item 2 (Text Field –	Dictionary	(6 items)
▶ Item 3 (Multi Value – Rank)	Dictionary	(6 items)
▶ Item 4 (Toggle Switch – Warp)	Dictionary	(4 items)
▶ Item 5 (Group – Warp Factor)	Dictionary	(2 items)
▼ Item 6 (Slider)	Dictionary	(7 items)
Type	String	Slider
Identifier	String	warpFactor
Default Value	Number	5
Minimum Value	Number	1
Maximum Value	Number	10
Min Value Image Filename	String	turtle
Max Value Image Filename	String	rabbit

Figure 12-25. Our finished Item 6: a slider with turtle and rabbit icons to represent slow and fast

Save your property list, and then build and run the app to make sure everything is still hunky-dory. You should be able to navigate to the Settings application and find the slider waiting for you, with the sleepy turtle and the happy rabbit at their respective ends (see Figure 12-26).

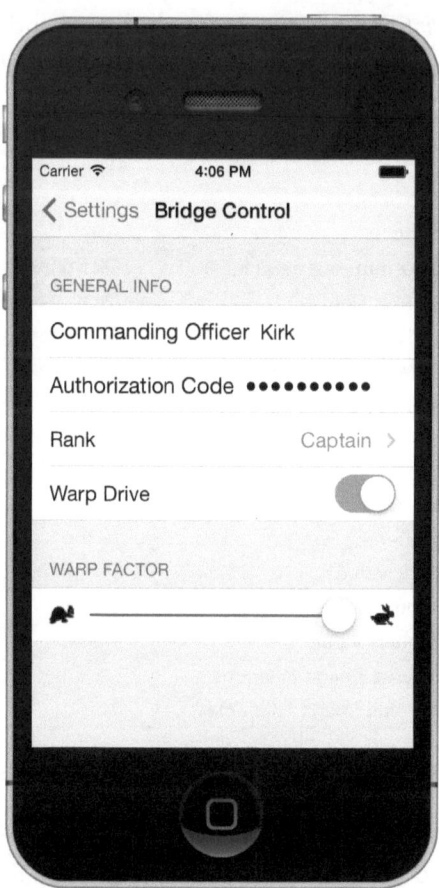

Figure 12-26. We have text fields, multivalue fields, a toggle switch, and a slider. We're almost finished

Adding a Child Settings View

We're going to add another preference specifier to tell the Settings application that we want it to display a child settings view. This specifier will present a row with a disclosure indicator that, when tapped, will take the user down to a whole new view full of preferences. Let's get to it.

Since we don't want this new preference to be grouped with the slider, first we'll copy the group specifier in *Item 0* and paste it at the end of the *PreferenceSpecifiers* array to create a new group for our child settings view.

In *Root.plist*, collapse all open items, and then single-click *Item 0* to select it and press ⌘C to copy it to the clipboard. Next, select *Item 6*, and then press ⌘V to paste in a new *Item 7*. Expand Item 7 and double-click the *Value* column next to the key *Title*, changing it from *General Info* to *Additional Info*.

Now collapse *Item 7* again. Select it and press **Return** to add *Item 8*, which will be our actual child view. Expand it by clicking the disclosure triangle. Find the *Type* row, give it a value of *PSChildPaneSpecifier*, and then set the value of the *Title* row to *More Settings*.

We need to add one final row to *Item 8*, which will tell the Settings application which property list to load for the *More Settings* view. Add another child row, and give it a key of *File* and a value of *More* (see Figure 12-27). The file extension *.plist* is assumed and must not be included (if it is, the Settings application won't find the plist file).

Key	Type	Value
▼ iPhone Settings Schema	Dictionary	(2 items)
▼ PreferenceSpecifiers	Array	(9 items)
▶ Item 0 (Group – General Info)	Dictionary	(2 items)
▶ Item 1 (Text Field –	Dictionary	(5 items)
▶ Item 2 (Text Field –	Dictionary	(6 items)
▶ Item 3 (Multi Value – Rank)	Dictionary	(6 items)
▶ Item 4 (Toggle Switch – Warp	Dictionary	(4 items)
▶ Item 5 (Group – Warp Factor)	Dictionary	(2 items)
▶ Item 6 (Slider)	Dictionary	(7 items)
▼ Item 7 (Group – Additional Info)	Dictionary	(2 items)
Title	String	Additional Info
Type	String	PSGroupSpecifier
▼ Item 8 (Child Pane – More	Dictionary	(3 items)
Type	String	PSChildPaneSpecifier
Title	String	More Settings
File	String	More

Figure 12-27. *Our finished Items 7 and 8, setting up the new Additional Info settings group and providing the child pane link to the file, More.plist*

We are adding a child view to our main preference view. The settings in that child view are specified in the *More.plist* file. We need to copy *More.plist* into the settings bundle. We can't add new files to the bundle in Xcode, and the Property List Editor's Save dialog will not let us save into a bundle. So, we need to create a new property list, save it somewhere else, and then drag it into the *Settings.bundle* window using the Finder.

You've now seen all the different types of preference fields that you can use in a settings bundle plist file. To save yourself some typing, you can grab *More.plist* out of the *12 - Bridge Control* folder in the project archive that accompanies this book, and then drag it into that *Settings.bundle* window we left open earlier.

Tip   When you create your own child settings views, the easiest approach is to make a copy of *Root.plist* and give it a new name. Next, delete all of the existing preference specifiers except the first one and add whatever preference specifiers you need for that new file.

We're finished with our settings bundle. Feel free to compile, run, and test the Settings application. You should be able to reach the child view and set values for all the other fields. Go ahead and play with it, and make changes to the property list if you want.

Tip We've covered almost every configuration option available (at least at the time of this writing). You can find the full documentation of the settings property list format in the document called *Settings Application Schema Reference* in the iOS Dev Center. You can get that document, along with a ton of other useful reference documents, from this page: http://developer.apple.com/library/ios/navigation/.

Before continuing, select the *Image.xcasset* item in Xcode's project navigator, and then copy the *rabbit.png* and *turtle.png* icons from the *12 - Bridge Control* folder in the project archive into the left side of the editor area. This will add these icons to the project as new images resources, ready for use. We'll use them in our application to show the value of the current settings.

You might have noticed that the two icons you just added are exactly the same ones you added to your settings bundle earlier, and you might be wondering why. Remember that iOS applications can't read files out of other applications' sandboxes. The settings bundle doesn't become part of our application's sandbox; it becomes part of the Settings application's sandbox. Since we also want to use those icons in our application, we need to add them separately to our *Bridge Control* folder, so they are copied into our application's sandbox, as well.

Reading Settings in Our Application

We've now solved half of our problem. The user can use the Setting app to declare their preferences, but how do we get to them from within our application? As it turns out, that's the easy part.

Retrieving User Settings

We'll use a class called NSUserDefaults to access the user's settings. NSUserDefaults is implemented as a singleton, which means there is only one instance of NSUserDefaults running in our application. To get access to that one instance, we call the class method standardUserDefaults, like so:

```
NSUserDefaults *defaults = [NSUserDefaults standardUserDefaults];
```

Once we have a pointer to the standard user defaults, we use it much like an NSDictionary. To get a value from it, we can call objectForKey:, which will return an Objective-C object, such as an NSString, NSDate, or NSNumber. If we want to retrieve the value as a scalar—like an int, float, or BOOL—we can use another method, such as intForKey:, floatForKey:, or boolForKey:.

When you were creating the property list for this application, you added an array of *PreferenceSpecifiers* inside a plist file. Within the Settings application, some of those specifiers were used to create groups, while others were used to create interface objects for user interaction. Those are the specifiers we are really interested in because they hold the keys the real settings data. Every specifier that was tied to a user setting has a *Key* named *Key*. Take a minute to go back and check.

For example, the *Key* for our slider has a value of *warpFactor*. The *Key* for our *Authorization Code* field is *authorizationCode*. We'll use those keys to retrieve the user settings.

Instead of using strings for each key directly in our methods, we'll use some precompiler #define statements for the values. That way we can use these makeshift constants in our code instead of inline strings, where we would run the risk of mistyping something. We'll set these up in a header file, since we're going to use some of them in more than just this class later on. So, open up *BIDMainViewController.h* and add these bold lines near the top of the file:

```
#import "BIDFlipsideViewController.h"

#define kOfficerKey                 @"officer"
#define kAuthorizationCodeKey       @"authorizationCode"
#define kRankKey                    @"rank"
#define kWarpDriveKey               @"warp"
#define kWarpFactorKey              @"warpFactor"
#define kFavoriteTeaKey             @"favoriteTea"
#define kFavoriteCaptainKey         @"favoriteCaptain"
#define kFavoriteGadgetKey          @"favoriteGadget"
#define kFavoriteAlienKey           @"favoriteAlien"
```

These constants are the keys that we used in our plist file for the different preference fields. Now that we have a place to display the settings, let's quickly set up our main view with a bunch of labels. Before going over to Interface Builder, let's create outlets for all the labels we'll need. Single-click *BIDMainViewController.m*, and make the following changes:

```
#import "BIDMainViewController.h"

@interface BIDMainViewController ()

@property (weak, nonatomic) IBOutlet UILabel *officerLabel;
@property (weak, nonatomic) IBOutlet UILabel *authorizationCodeLabel;
@property (weak, nonatomic) IBOutlet UILabel *rankLabel;
@property (weak, nonatomic) IBOutlet UILabel *warpDriveLabel;
@property (weak, nonatomic) IBOutlet UILabel *warpFactorLabel;
@property (weak, nonatomic) IBOutlet UILabel *favoriteTeaLabel;
@property (weak, nonatomic) IBOutlet UILabel *favoriteCaptainLabel;
@property (weak, nonatomic) IBOutlet UILabel *favoriteGadgetLabel;
@property (weak, nonatomic) IBOutlet UILabel *favoriteAlienLabel;

@end
```

There's nothing new here. Next, we declare nine properties, all of them labels, and all of them with the IBOutlet keyword to make them connectable in Interface Builder.

Save your changes. Now that we have our outlets declared, let's head over to the storyboard file to create the GUI.

Creating the Main View

Select *MainStoryboard.storyboard* to edit it in Interface Builder. When it comes up, you'll see the main view on the left and the flipside view on the right, connected by a segue. Notice that the background of the main view is dark gray. Let's change it to white.

Single-click the *View* belonging to the *Main View Controller*, and bring up the attributes inspector. Use the color well labeled *Background* to change the background to white. Note that the color well also functions as a pop-up menu if you click on the right edge. If you prefer, use that menu to select *White Color*.

Now we're going to add a bunch of labels to the *View*, so it looks like the one shown in Figure 12-28. We'll need a grand total of 18 labels. Half of them, on the left side of the screen, will be right-aligned and **bold**; the other half, on the right side of the screen, will be used to display the actual values retrieved from the user defaults and will have outlets pointing to them.

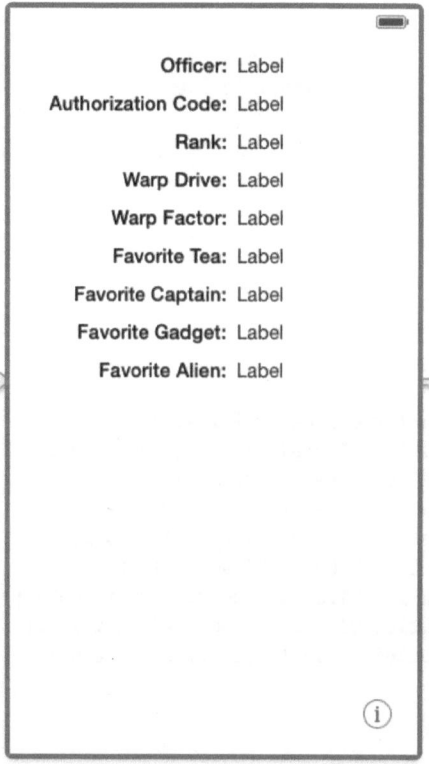

Figure 12-28. The View window in Interface Builder, showing the 18 labels we added

Use Figure 12-28 as your guide to build this view. You don't need to match the appearance exactly, but you must have one label on the view for each of the declared outlets. Go ahead and design the view. You don't need any help for this. When you're finished and have it looking the way you like, come back, and we'll continue. Just so you know, all our labels used 15-point System Font (or System Font Bold), but feel free to go wild with your own design.

The next thing we need to do is control-drag from the *Main View Controller* icon to each of the labels intended to display a settings value. You will control-drag a total of nine times, setting each label to a different outlet. Once you have all nine outlets connected to labels, save your changes.

Updating the Main View Controller

In Xcode, select *BIDMainViewController.m*, and add the following code to the class's @implementation section:

```
@implementation BIDMainViewController

- (void)refreshFields {
    NSUserDefaults *defaults = [NSUserDefaults standardUserDefaults];
    self.officerLabel.text = [defaults objectForKey:kOfficerKey];
    self.authorizationCodeLabel.text = [defaults
                                    objectForKey:kAuthorizationCodeKey];
    self.rankLabel.text = [defaults objectForKey:kRankKey];
    self.warpDriveLabel.text = [defaults boolForKey:kWarpDriveKey]
                           ? @"Engaged" : @"Disabled";
    self.warpFactorLabel.text = [[defaults objectForKey:kWarpFactorKey]
                              stringValue];
    self.favoriteTeaLabel.text = [defaults objectForKey:kFavoriteTeaKey];
    self.favoriteCaptainLabel.text = [defaults
                                    objectForKey:kFavoriteCaptainKey];
    self.favoriteGadgetLabel.text = [defaults objectForKey:kFavoriteGadgetKey];
    self.favoriteAlienLabel.text = [defaults objectForKey:kFavoriteAlienKey];
}

- (void)viewDidAppear:(BOOL)animated {
    [super viewDidAppear:animated];
    [self refreshFields];
}
    .
    .
    .
    .
```

There's not really much here that should throw you. The refreshFields method does two things. First, it grabs the standard user defaults. Second, it sets the text property of all the labels to the appropriate object from the user defaults using the same key values that we put in our plist file. Notice that for warpFactorLabel, we're calling stringValue on the object returned. Most of our other preferences are strings, which come back from the user defaults as NSString objects. The preference stored by the slider, however, comes back as an NSNumber, so we call stringValue on it to get a string representation of the value it holds.

After that, we overrode our superclass's viewDidAppear: method, and there we called our refreshFields method.

What we want to do now is call refreshFields again when we are notified that the flipside controller is being dismissed. Because the flipside view is handled modally, with the main view as its modal parent, the BIDMainViewController's viewDidAppear: method will not be called when the flipside view is dismissed. Fortunately, the Utility Application template we chose has very kindly provided us with a delegate method we can use for exactly that purpose. Add the following line of code to the existing flipsideViewControllerDidFinish: method:

```
- (void)flipsideViewControllerDidFinish:
        (BIDFlipsideViewController *)controller
{
    [self refreshFields];
    [self dismissViewControllerAnimated:YES completion:nil];

}
```

With this in place, our displayed fields will be set to the appropriate preference values both when the view loads and when the flipside view is swapped out.

Changing Defaults from Our Application

Now that we have the main view up and running, let's build the flipside view. As you can see in Figure 12-29, the flipside view features our warp drive switch, as well as the warp factor slider. We'll use the same controls that the Settings application uses for these two items: a switch and a slider. In addition to declaring our outlets, we'll also declare a method called refreshFields, just as we did in BIDMainViewController, and two action methods that will be triggered by the user touching the controls.

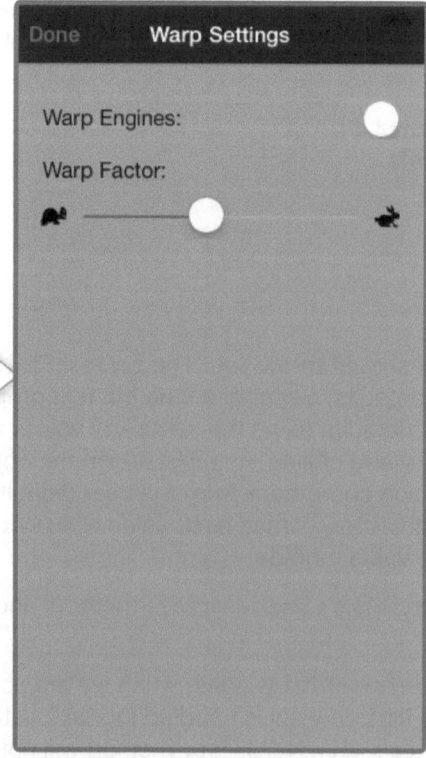

Figure 12-29. Designing the flipside view in Interface Builder

Select *BIDFlipsideViewController.h* and make the following changes:

```
#import <UIKit/UIKit.h>

@class BIDFlipsideViewController;

@protocol BIDFlipsideViewControllerDelegate
- (void)flipsideViewControllerDidFinish:
    (BIDFlipsideViewController *)controller;
@end

@interface BIDFlipsideViewController : UIViewController

@property (weak, nonatomic) id <BIDFlipsideViewControllerDelegate> delegate;
@property (weak, nonatomic) IBOutlet UISwitch *engineSwitch;
@property (weak, nonatomic) IBOutlet UISlider *warpFactorSlider;

- (void)refreshFields;
- (IBAction)engineSwitchTapped;
- (IBAction)warpSliderTouched;
- (IBAction)done:(id)sender;

@end
```

> **Note**   Don't worry too much about the extra code here. As you saw before, the Utility Application template makes BIDMainViewController a delegate of the BIDFlipsideViewController. The extra code here that hasn't been in the other file templates we've used implements that delegate relationship.

Now, save your changes and select *MainStoryboard.storyboard* to edit the GUI in Interface Builder, this time focusing on the *Flipside View Controller Scene* in the document outline. Hold down the **Option** key and click the disclosure triangle to expand *Flipside View Controller* and everything below it. Next, double-click the flipside view title in the title bar and change it from *Title* to *Warp Settings*.

Next, select the *View* in the *Flipside View Controller Scene*, and then bring up the attributes inspector. First, change the background color by using the *Background* popup to select *Light Gray Color*. The default flipside view background color is too dark for black text to look good, but light enough that white text is hard to read.

Next, drag two *Labels* from the library and place them on the *View* window. Double-click one of them, and change it to read *Warp Engines:*. Double-click the other, and call it *Warp Factor:*. You can use Figure 12-29 as a placement guide.

Next, drag over a *Switch* from the library and place it against the right side of the view, across from the label that reads *Warp Engines*. Control-drag from the *Flipside View Controller* icon to the new switch and connect it to the *engineSwitch* outlet. Then control-drag from the switch back to the *Flipside View Controller* icon and connect it to the *engineSwitchTapped* action.

Drag over a *Slider* from the library and place it below the label that reads *Warp Factor:* Resize the slider so that it stretches from the blue guideline on the left margin to the one on the right. Now control-drag from the *Flipside View Controller* icon to the slider, and then connect it to the *warpFactorSlider* outlet. Next, control-drag from the slider to *Flipside View Controller* and select the *warpSliderTouched* action.

Single-click the slider if it's not still selected and bring up the attributes inspector. Set *Minimum* to *1.00*, *Maximum* to *10.00*, and *Current* to *5.00*. Next, select *turtle* for *Min Image* and *rabbit* for *Max Image*. If those don't show up in the pop-up buttons, make sure you dragged the images into the *Images. xcassets* assets catalog.

Now, let's finish the flipside view controller. Select *BIDFlipsideViewController.m*, and add the following import at the top of the file:

```
#import "BIDMainViewController.h"
```

Next, make the following changes within the class's implementation:

```
- (void)viewDidLoad
{
    [super viewDidLoad];
    // Do any additional setup after loading the view, typically from a nib.

    [self refreshFields];
}
.
.
.
- (void)refreshFields {
    NSUserDefaults *defaults = [NSUserDefaults standardUserDefaults];
    self.engineSwitch.on = [defaults boolForKey:kWarpDriveKey];
    self.warpFactorSlider.value = [defaults floatForKey:kWarpFactorKey];

}

- (IBAction)engineSwitchTapped {
    NSUserDefaults *defaults = [NSUserDefaults standardUserDefaults];
    [defaults setBool:self.engineSwitch.on forKey:kWarpDriveKey];
}

- (IBAction)warpSliderTouched {
    NSUserDefaults *defaults = [NSUserDefaults standardUserDefaults];
    [defaults setFloat:self.warpFactorSlider.value forKey:kWarpFactorKey];
}
.
.
.
```

We added a call to our refreshFields method. This method's three lines of code get a reference to the standard user defaults, and then use the outlets for the switch and slider to make them display the values stored in the user defaults. We also implemented the engineSwitchTapped and warpSliderTouched action methods, so that we could stuff the values from our controls back into the user defaults when the user changes them.

Now you should be able to run the app, flip to the flipside, edit the values presented there, and see them reflected in the main view when you flip back.

Registering Default Values

We've created a settings bundle, including some default settings for a few values, to give the Settings app access to our app's preferences. We've also set up our own app to access the same information, with a GUI to let the user see and edit it. However, one piece is missing: our app is completely unaware of the default values specified in the settings bundle. You can see this for yourself by deleting the Bridge Control app from the iOS simulator or the device you're running on (thereby deleting the preferences stored for the app), and then running it from Xcode again. At the start of a fresh launch, the app will show you blank values for all the settings. Even the default values for the warp drive settings, which we defined in the settings bundle, are nowhere to be seen. If you then switch over to the Settings app, you'll see the default values; however, unless you actually change the values there, you'll never see them back in the Bridge Control app!

The reason our default settings disappeared is that our app knows nothing about the settings bundle it contains. So, when it tries to read the value from NSUserDefaults for *warpFactor* and finds nothing saved under that key, it has nothing to show us. Fortunately, NSUserDefaults includes a method called registerDefaults: that lets us specify the default values that we should find if we try to look up a key/value that hasn't been set. To make this work throughout the app, it's best if this is called early during app start-up. Select *BIDAppDelegate.m* and include this header file somewhere at the top of the file, so we can access the key names we defined earlier:

```
#import "BIDMainViewController.h"
```

Next, modify the application:didFinishLaunchingWithOptions: method:

```
- (BOOL)application:(UIApplication *)application
    didFinishLaunchingWithOptions:(NSDictionary *)launchOptions
{
    // Override point for customization after application launch.

    NSDictionary *defaults = @{kWarpDriveKey : @YES,
                               kWarpFactorKey : @5,
                               kFavoriteAlienKey : @"Vulcan"};

    [[NSUserDefaults standardUserDefaults] registerDefaults:defaults];
    return YES;
}
```

The first thing we do here is create a dictionary that contains three key/value pairs, one for each of the keys available in Settings that requires a default value. We're using the same key names we defined earlier to reduce the risk of mistyping a key name. Note that in addition to the new @{} syntax for initializing a dictionary, we're also using the new @*<numeric value>* syntax for creating NSNumber instances wrapping the Boolean value YES and the integer 5.

We pass that entire dictionary to the standard NSUserDefaults instance's registerDefaults: method. From that point on, NSUserDefaults will give us the values we specify here, as long as we haven't set different values either in our app or in the Settings app.

This class is complete. You should be able to compile and run your application. It will look something like Figure 12-6, except yours will be showing whatever values you entered in your Settings application, of course. Couldn't be much easier, could it?

Keeping It Real

Now you should be able to run your app, view the settings, and then press the home button and open the Settings app to tweak some values. Hit the home button again, launch your app again, and you may be in for a surprise. When you go back to your app, you won't see the settings change! They'll remain as they are, showing the old values.

Here's the deal: in iOS, hitting the home button while an app is running doesn't actually quit the app. Instead, the operating system suspends the app in the background, leaving it ready to be quickly fired up again. This is great for switching back and forth between applications, since the amount of time it takes to reawaken a suspended app is much shorter than what it takes to launch it from scratch. However, in our case, we need to do a little more work, so that when our app wakes up, it effectively gets a slap in the face, reloads the user preferences, and redisplays the values they contain.

You'll learn more about background applications in Chapter 15, but we'll give you a sneak peek at the basics of how to make your app notice that it has been brought back to life. To do this, we're going to sign up each of our controller classes to receive a notification that is sent by the application when it wakes up from its state of suspended execution.

A **notification** is a lightweight mechanism that objects can use to communicate with each other. Any object can define one or more notifications that it will publish to the application's **notification center**, which is a singleton object that exists only to pass these notifications between objects. Notifications are usually indications that some event occurred, and objects that publish notifications include a list of notifications in their documentation. The UIApplication class publishes a number of notifications (you can find them in the Xcode documentation viewer, toward the bottom of the *UIApplication* page). The purpose of most notifications is usually pretty obvious from their names, but the documentation contains further information if you're unclear about a given notification's purpose.

Our application needs to refresh its display when the application is about to come to the foreground, so we are interested in the notification called UIApplicationWillEnterForegroundNotification. When we write our viewWillAppear: method, we will subscribe to that notification and tell the notification center to call this method when that notification happens. Add this method to both *BIDMainViewController.m* and *BIDFlipsideViewController.m*:

```
- (void)applicationWillEnterForeground:(NSNotification *)notification {
    NSUserDefaults *defaults = [NSUserDefaults standardUserDefaults];
    [defaults synchronize];
    [self refreshFields];
}
```

The method itself is quite simple. First, it gets a reference to the standard user defaults object and calls its synchronize method, which forces the User Defaults system to save any unsaved changes and also reload any unmodified preferences from storage. In effect, we're forcing it to reread the stored preferences so that we can pick up the changes that were made in the Settings app. Next, the applicationWillEnterForeground: method calls the refreshFields method, which each class uses to update its display.

Now we need to make each of our controllers subscribe to the notification we're interested in by implementing the viewWillAppear: method in both *BIDMainViewController.m* and *BIDFlipsideViewController.m*. Here's the code to add to both classes:

```
- (void)viewWillAppear:(BOOL)animated {
    [super viewWillAppear:animated];

    UIApplication *app = [UIApplication sharedApplication];
    [[NSNotificationCenter defaultCenter] addObserver:self
            selector:@selector(applicationWillEnterForeground:)
            name:UIApplicationWillEnterForegroundNotification
            object:app];
}
```

We start by getting a reference to our application instance, and then use that to subscribe to the UIApplicationWillEnterForegroundNotification, using the default NSNotificationCenter instance and a method called addObserver:selector:name:object:. We then pass the following to this method:

- For an observer, we pass self, which means that our controller class (each of them individually, since this code is going into both of them) is the object that needs to be notified.

- For selector, we pass a selector to the applicationWillEnterForeground: method we just wrote, telling the notification center to call that method when the notification is posted.

- The third parameter, UIApplicationWillEnterForegroundNotification, is the name of the notification that we're interested in receiving.

- The final parameter, app, is the object from which we're interested in getting the notification. If we passed nil for the final parameter, we would get notified any time any method posted the UIApplicationWillEnterForegroundNotification.

That takes care of updating the display, but we also need to consider what happens to the values that are put into the user defaults when the user manipulates the controls in our app. We need to make sure that they are saved to storage before control passes to another app. The easiest way to do that is to call synchronize as soon as the settings are changed, by adding one line to each of our new action methods in *BIDFlipsideViewController.m*:

```
- (IBAction)engineSwitchTapped {
    NSUserDefaults *defaults = [NSUserDefaults standardUserDefaults];
    [defaults setBool:self.engineSwitch.on forKey:kWarpDriveKey];
    [defaults synchronize];
}
```

```
- (IBAction)warpSliderTouched {
    NSUserDefaults *defaults = [NSUserDefaults standardUserDefaults];
    [defaults setFloat:self.warpFactorSlider.value forKey:kWarpFactorKey];
    [defaults synchronize];
}
```

> **Note** Calling the synchronize method is a potentially expensive operation because the entire contents of the user defaults in memory must be compared with what's in storage. When you're dealing with a whole lot of user defaults at once and want to make sure everything is in sync, it's best to try to minimize calls to synchronize, so that this whole comparison isn't performed over and over again. However, calling it once in response to each user action, as we're doing here, won't cause any noticeable performance problems.

There's one more thing to take care of to make this work as cleanly as possible. You already know that you must clean up your memory by setting properties to nil when they're no longer in use, as well as performing other clean-up tasks. The notification system is another place where you need to clean up after yourself by telling the default NSNotificationCenter that you don't want to listen to any more notifications. In our case, where we've registered each view controller to observe this notification in its viewWillAppear: method, we should unregister in the matching viewDidDisappear: method. So, in both *BIDMainViewController.m* and *BIDFlipsideViewController.m*, put the following line at the top of the viewDidDisappear: method:

```
- (void)viewDidDisappear:(BOOL)animated {
    [super viewDidDisappear:(BOOL)animated];
    [[NSNotificationCenter defaultCenter] removeObserver:self];
}
```

Note that it's possible to unregister for specific notifications using the removeObserver:name:object: method by passing in the same values that were used to register your observer in the first place. In any case, the preceding line is a handy way to make sure that the notification center forgets about our observer completely, no matter how many notifications it was registered for.

With that in place, it's time to build and run the app and see what happens when you switch between your app and the Settings app. Changes you make in the Settings app should now be immediately reflected in your app when you switch back to it.

Beam Me Up, Scotty

At this point, you should have a very solid grasp on both the Settings application and the User Defaults mechanism. You know how to add a settings bundle to your application and how to build a hierarchy of views for your application's preferences. You also learned how to read and write preferences using NSUserDefaults, as well as how to let the user change preferences from within your application. You even got a chance to use a new project template in Xcode. There really shouldn't be much in the way of application preferences that you are not equipped to handle now.

In the next chapter, we're going to show you how to keep your application's data around after your application quits. Ready? Let's go!

13

Basic Data Persistence

So far, we've focused on the controller and view aspects of the MVC paradigm. Although several of our applications have read data out of the application bundle, none of them has saved data to any form of persistent storage—nonvolatile storage that survives a restart of the computer or device. So far, with the exception of Application Settings (in Chapter 12), every sample application either did not store data or used volatile (i.e., nonpersistent) storage. Every time one of the sample applications launched, it appeared with exactly the same data it had the first time you launched it.

This approach has worked for us up to this point. But in the real world, your applications will need to persist data. When users make changes, they usually like to find those changes when they launch the program again.

A number of different mechanisms are available for persisting data on an iOS device. If you've programmed in Cocoa for Mac OS X, you've likely used some or all of these techniques.

In this chapter, we're going to look at four different mechanisms for persisting data to the iOS file system:

- ■ Property lists
- ■ Object archives (or archiving)
- ■ SQLite3 (iOS's embedded relational database)
- ■ Core Data (Apple's provided persistence tool)

We will write example applications that use all four approaches.

> **Note** Property lists, object archives, SQLite3, and Core Data are not the only ways you can persist data on iOS; they are just the most common and easiest. You always have the option of using traditional C I/O calls like fopen() to read and write data. You can also use Cocoa's low-level file-management tools. In almost every case, doing so will result in a lot more coding effort and is rarely necessary, but those tools are there if you want them.

Your Application's Sandbox

All four of this chapter's data-persistence mechanisms share an important common element: your application's */Documents* folder. Every application gets its own */Documents* folder, and applications are allowed to read and write from only their own */Documents* directory.

To give you some context, let's take a look at how applications are organized in iOS, by examining the folder layout used by the iPhone simulator. To see this, you'll need to look inside the *Library* directory contained in your home directory. On Mac OS X 10.6 and earlier, this was no problem; however, starting with 10.7, Apple decided to make the *Library* folder hidden by default, so there's a small extra hoop to jump through. Open a Finder window and navigate to your home directory. If you can see your *Library* folder, that's great. If not, hold down the **Alt** key and select **Go ➤ Library**. The Library option is hidden unless you hold down the **Alt** key.

Within the *Library* folder, drill down into *Application Support/iPhone Simulator/*. Within that directory, you'll see a subdirectory for each version of iOS supported by your current Xcode installation. For example, you might see one directory named 7.0 and others named after specific versions of iOS 7 or even iOS 6. Drill down into the directory representing the latest version of iOS supported by your version of Xcode. At this point, you should see several subfolders, including one named *Applications* (see Figure 13-1).

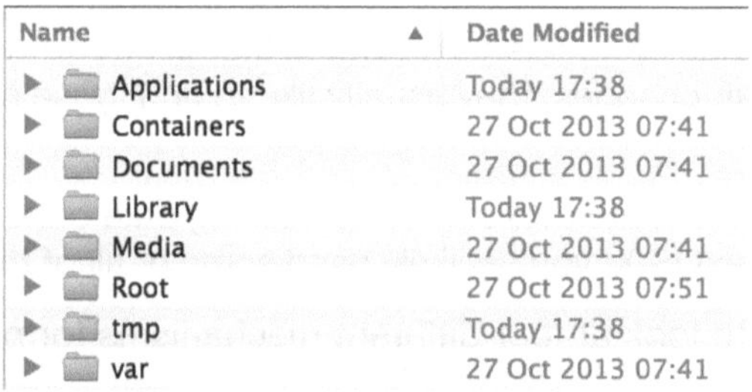

Name	▲	Date Modified
▶ 📁 Applications		Today 17:38
▶ 📁 Containers		27 Oct 2013 07:41
▶ 📁 Documents		27 Oct 2013 07:41
▶ 📁 Library		Today 17:38
▶ 📁 Media		27 Oct 2013 07:41
▶ 📁 Root		27 Oct 2013 07:51
▶ 📁 tmp		Today 17:38
▶ 📁 var		27 Oct 2013 07:41

Figure 13-1. The layout of one user's Library/Application Support/iPhone Simulator/7.0.3/ directory, which shows the Applications folder

> **Note** If you've installed multiple versions of the SDK, you may see a few additional folders inside the *iPhone Simulator* directory, with names indicating the iOS version number they represent. That's perfectly normal.

Although this listing represents the simulator, the file structure is similar to what's on the actual device. As is probably obvious, the *Applications* folder is where iOS stores its applications. If you open the *Applications* folder, you'll see a bunch of folders and files with names that are long strings of characters. These names are globally unique identifiers (GUIDs) that are generated automatically by Xcode. Each of these folders contains one application and its supporting folders.

If you open one of the application subdirectories, you should see something that looks familiar. You'll find one of the iOS applications you've previously built and run in the simulator, along with three support folders:

Documents: Your application stores its data in *Documents*, with the exception of NSUserDefaults–based preference settings.

Library: NSUserDefaults–based preference settings are stored in the *Library/Preferences* folder.

tmp: The *tmp* directory offers a place where your application can store temporary files. Files written into *tmp* will not be backed up by iTunes when your iOS device syncs, but your application does need to take responsibility for deleting the files in *tmp* once they are no longer needed, to avoid filling up the file system.

Getting the Documents Directory

Since our application is in a folder with a seemingly random name, how do we retrieve the full path to the *Documents* directory so that we can read and write our files? It's actually quite easy. The C function NSSearchPathForDirectoriesInDomain() will locate various directories for you. This is a Foundation function, so it is shared with Cocoa for Mac OS X. Many of its available options are designed for OS X and won't return any values on iOS, either because those locations don't exist on iOS (such as the *Downloads* folder) or because your application doesn't have rights to access the location due to iOS's sandboxing mechanism.

Here's some code to retrieve the path to the *Documents* directory:

```
NSArray *paths = NSSearchPathForDirectoriesInDomains(NSDocumentDirectory,
    NSUserDomainMask, YES);
NSString *documentsDirectory = paths[0];
```

The constant NSDocumentDirectory says we are looking for the path to the *Documents* directory. The second constant, NSUserDomainMask, indicates that we want to restrict our search to our application's sandbox. In Mac OS X, this same constant is used to indicate that we want the function to look in the user's home directory, which explains its somewhat odd name.

Though an array of matching paths is returned, we can count on our *Documents* directory residing at index zero in the array. Why? We know that only one directory meets the criteria we've specified since each application has only one *Documents* directory.

We can create a file name by appending another string onto the end of the path we just retrieved. We'll use an NSString method called stringByAppendingPathComponent: that was designed for just that purpose:

```
NSString *filename = [documentsDirectory
    stringByAppendingPathComponent:@"theFile.txt"];
```

After this call, filename would contain the full path to a file called *theFile.txt* in our application's *Documents* directory, and we can use filename to create, read, and write from that file.

Getting the tmp Directory

Getting a reference to your application's temporary directory is even easier than getting a reference to the *Documents* directory. The Foundation function called `NSTemporaryDirectory()` will return a string containing the full path to your application's temporary directory. To create a file name for a file that will be stored in the temporary directory, first find the temporary directory:

```
NSString *tempPath = NSTemporaryDirectory();
```

Next, create a path to a file in that directory by appending a file name to that path, like this:

```
NSString *tempFile = [tempPath
    stringByAppendingPathComponent:@"tempFile.txt"];
```

File-Saving Strategies

All four approaches we're going to look at in this chapter use the iOS file system. In the case of SQLite3, you'll create a single SQLite3 database file and let SQLite3 worry about storing and retrieving your data. In its simplest form, Core Data takes care of all the file system management for you. With the other two persistence mechanisms—property lists and archiving—you need to put some thought into whether you are going to store your data in a single file or in multiple files.

Single-File Persistence

Using a single file for data storage is the easiest approach; and with many applications, it is a perfectly acceptable one. You start by creating a root object, usually an `NSArray` or `NSDictionary` (your root object can also be based on a custom class when using archiving). Next, you populate your root object with all the program data that needs to be persisted. Whenever you need to save, your code rewrites the entire contents of that root object to a single file. When your application launches, it reads the entire contents of that file into memory. When it quits, it writes out the entire contents. This is the approach we'll use in this chapter.

The downside of using a single file is that you need to load all of your application's data into memory, and you must write all of it to the file system for even the smallest changes. But if your application isn't likely to manage more than a few megabytes of data, this approach is probably fine, and its simplicity will certainly make your life easier.

Multiple-File Persistence

Using multiple files for persistence is an alternative approach. For example, an e-mail application might store each e-mail message in its own file.

There are obvious advantages to this method. It allows the application to load only data that the user has requested (another form of lazy loading); and when the user makes a change, only the files that changed need to be saved. This method also gives you the opportunity to free up memory when you receive a low-memory notification. Any memory that is being used to store data that the user is not currently viewing can be flushed and then simply reloaded from the file system the next time it's needed.

The downside of multiple-file persistence is that it adds a fair amount of complexity to your application. For now, we'll stick with single-file persistence.

Next, we'll get into the specifics of each of our persistence methods: property lists, object archives, SQLite3, and Core Data. We'll explore each of these in turn and build an application that uses each mechanism to save some data to the device's file system. We'll start with property lists.

Using Property Lists

Several of our sample applications have used property lists, most recently when we used a property list to specify our application preferences. Property lists are convenient. They can be edited manually using Xcode or the Property List Editor application. Also, both NSDictionary and NSArray instances can be written to and created from property lists, as long as the dictionary or array contains only specific serializable objects.

Property List Serialization

A **serialized object** is one that has been converted into a stream of bytes so it can be stored in a file or transferred over a network. Although any object can be made serializable, only certain objects can be placed into a collection class, such as an NSDictionary or NSArray, and then stored to a property list using the collection class's writeToFile:atomically: or writeToURL:atomically: method. The following Objective-C classes can be serialized this way:

- NSArray
- NSMutableArray
- NSDictionary
- NSMutableDictionary
- NSData
- NSMutableData
- NSString
- NSMutableString
- NSNumber
- NSDate

If you can build your data model from just these objects, you can use property lists to save and load your data.

If you're going to use property lists to persist your application data, you'll use either an NSArray or an NSDictionary to hold the data that needs to be persisted. Assuming that all the objects that you put into the NSArray or NSDictionary are serializable objects from the preceding list, you can write a property list by calling the writeToFile:atomically: method on the dictionary or array instance, like so:

```
[myArray writeToFile:@"/some/file/location/output.plist" atomically:YES];
```

> **Note**   In case you were wondering, the `atomically` parameter tells the method to write the data to an auxiliary file, not to the specified location. Once it has successfully written the file, it will then copy that auxiliary file to the location specified by the first parameter. This is a safer way to write a file because, if the application crashes during the save, the existing file (if there was one) will not be corrupted. It adds a bit of overhead; but in most situations, it's worth the cost.

One problem with the property list approach is that custom objects cannot be serialized into property lists. You also can't use other delivered classes from Cocoa Touch that aren't specified in the previous list of serializable objects, which means that classes like `NSURL`, `UIImage`, and `UIColor` cannot be used directly.

Apart from the serialization issue, keeping all your model data in the form of property lists means that you can't easily create derived or calculated properties (such as a property that is the sum of two other properties), and some of your code that really should be contained in model classes must be moved to your controller classes. Again, these restrictions are OK for simple data models and simple applications. Most of the time, however, your application will be much easier to maintain if you create dedicated model classes.

Simple property lists can still be useful in complex applications. They are a great way to include static data in your application. For example, when your application has a picker, often the best way to include the list of items for it is to create a plist file and place that file in your project's *Resources* folder, which will cause it to be compiled into your application.

Let's a build a simple application that uses property lists to store its data.

The First Version of the Persistence Application

We're going to build a program that lets you enter data into four text fields, saves those fields to a plist file when the application quits, and then reloads the data back from that plist file the next time the application launches (see Figure 13-2).

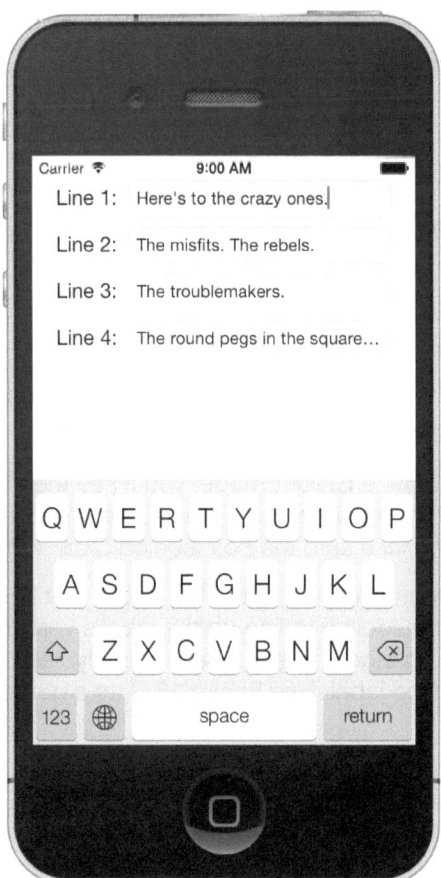

Figure 13-2. The Persistence application

> **Note**   In this chapter's applications, we won't be taking the time to set up all the user interface niceties that
> we have added in previous examples. Tapping the **Return** key, for example, will neither dismiss the keyboard nor
> take you to the next field. If you want to add such polish to the application, doing so would be good
> practice, so we encourage you to do that on your own.

Creating the Persistence Project

In Xcode, create a new project using the *Single View Application* template and name it *Persistence*.
This project contains all the files that we'll need to build our application, so we can dive right in.

Before we build the view with the four text fields, let's create the outlets we need. Expand the *Classes* folder, and then single-click the *BIDViewController.m* file and make the following changes:

```
#import "BIDViewController.h"

@interface BIDViewController ()

@property (strong, nonatomic) IBOutletCollection(UITextField) NSArray *lineFields;

@end
```

Now select *Main.storyboard* to edit the GUI.

Designing the Persistence Application View

Once Xcode switches over to Interface Builder mode, you'll see the *View Controller* scene in the editing pane. Drag a *Text Field* from the library and place it against the top and right blue guidelines. Bring up the attributes inspector. Make sure the box labeled *Clear When Editing Begins* is unchecked.

Now drag a *Label* to the window and place it to the left of the text field using the left blue guideline, and then use the horizontal blue guideline to line up the label's vertical center with that of the text field. Double-click the label and change it to say *Line 1:*. Finally, resize the text field using the left resize handle to bring it close to the label. Use Figure 13-3 as a guide.

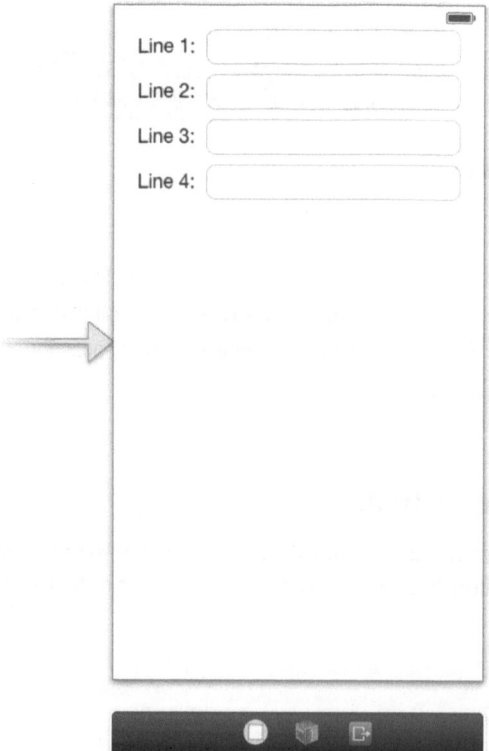

Figure 13-3. Designing the Persistence application's view

Next, select the label and text field, hold down the **Option** key, and drag down to make a copy below the first set. Use the blue guidelines to guide your placement. Now select both labels and both text fields, hold down the **Option** key, and drag down again. You should have four labels next to four text fields. Double-click each of the remaining labels and change their names to *Line 2:*, *Line 3:*, and *Line 4:*. Again, compare your results with Figure 13-3.

Once you have all four text fields and labels placed, control-drag from the *View Controller* icon to each of the four text fields. Connect them all to the lineFields outlet collection, making sure to connect them in order from top to bottom. Save the changes you made to *Main.storyboard*.

Editing the Persistence Classes

In the project navigator, select *BIDViewController.m* and add the following code to the class's @implementation section:

```
@implementation BIDViewController

- (NSString *)dataFilePath
{
    NSArray *paths = NSSearchPathForDirectoriesInDomains(
                        NSDocumentDirectory, NSUserDomainMask, YES);
    NSString *documentsDirectory = [paths objectAtIndex:0];
    return [documentsDirectory stringByAppendingPathComponent:@"data.plist"];
}
.
.
.
```

This first method we added, dataFilePath, returns the full pathname of our data file by finding the *Documents* directory and appending our file name to it. This method will be called from any code that needs to load or save data.

Go down a bit to find the viewDidLoad method. Next, add the following code to it, as well as a new method for receiving notifications named applicationWillResignActive: just below it, like this:

```
- (void)viewDidLoad
{
    [super viewDidLoad];
    // Do any additional setup after loading the view, typically from a nib.
    NSString *filePath = [self dataFilePath];
    if ([[NSFileManager defaultManager] fileExistsAtPath:filePath]) {
        NSArray *array = [[NSArray alloc] initWithContentsOfFile:filePath];
        for (int i = 0; i < 4; i++) {
            UITextField *theField = self.lineFields[i];
            theField.text = array[i];
        }
    }

    UIApplication *app = [UIApplication sharedApplication];
    [[NSNotificationCenter defaultCenter]
     addObserver:self
```

```
            selector:@selector(applicationWillResignActive:)
                name:UIApplicationWillResignActiveNotification
            object:app];
}

- (void)applicationWillResignActive:(NSNotification *)notification
{
    NSString *filePath = [self dataFilePath];
    NSArray *array = [self.lineFields valueForKey:@"text"];
    [array writeToFile:filePath atomically:YES];
}
```

In the viewDidLoad method, we do a few more things. First, we check to see if a data file already exists. If there isn't one, we don't want to bother trying to load it. If the file does exist, we instantiate an array with the contents of that file, and then copy the objects from that array to our four text fields. Because arrays are ordered lists, we copy them in the same order as we save them (the code for which you haven't yet seen), so that we are always sure to get the correct values in the correct fields:

```
NSString *filePath = [self dataFilePath];
if ([[NSFileManager defaultManager] fileExistsAtPath:filePath]) {
    NSArray *array = [[NSArray alloc] initWithContentsOfFile:filePath];
    for (int i = 0; i < 4; i++) {
        UITextField *theField = self.lineFields[i];
        theField.text = array[i];
    }
}
```

After we load the data from the property list, we get a reference to our application instance and use that to subscribe to UIApplicationWillResignActiveNotification, using the default NSNotificationCenter instance and a method called addObserver:selector:name:object:. We pass self as the first parameter, specifying that our BIDViewController instance is the observer that should be notified. For the second parameter, we pass a selector to the applicationWillResignActive: method, telling the notification center to call that method when the notification is posted. The third parameter, UIApplicationWillResignActiveNotification, is the name of the notification that we're interested in receiving. This is a string constant defined by the UIApplication class. The final parameter, app, is the object we're interested in getting the notification from:

```
UIApplication *app = [UIApplication sharedApplication];
[[NSNotificationCenter defaultCenter]
 addObserver:self
    selector:@selector(applicationWillResignActive:)
        name:UIApplicationWillResignActiveNotification
      object:app];
```

The final new method is called applicationWillResignActive:. Notice that it takes a pointer to an NSNotification as an argument. You probably recognize this pattern from Chapter 12. applicationWillResignActive: is a notification method, and all notifications take a single NSNotification instance as their argument.

Our application needs to save its data before the application is terminated or sent to the background, so we are interested in the notification called UIApplicationWillResignActiveNotification. This notification is posted whenever an app is no longer the one with which the user is interacting. This happens when the user taps the home button, as well as when the application is pushed to the background by some other event, such as an incoming phone call. Earlier, in the viewDidLoad method, we used the notification center to subscribe to that particular notification. This method is called when that notification happens:

```
- (void)applicationWillResignActive:(NSNotification *)notification
{
    NSString *filePath = [self dataFilePath];
    NSArray *array = [self.lineFields valueForKey:@"text"];
    [array writeToFile:filePath atomically:YES];
}
```

This method is pretty short, but really does a lot with just a few method calls. We construct an array of strings by calling the text method on each of the text fields in our lineFields array. To accomplish this, we use a clever shortcut: instead of explicitly iterating through our array of text fields, asking each for its text value, and adding that value to a new array, we simply call valueForKey: on our array, passing @"text" as a parameter. The NSArray class's implementation of valueForKey: does the iteration for us, asks each instance it contains for its text value, and returns a new array containing all the values. After that, we write the contents of that array out to a plist file. That's all there is to saving our data using property lists.

That wasn't too bad, was it? When our main view is finished loading, we look for a plist file. If it exists, we copy data from it into our text fields. Next, we register to be notified when the application becomes inactive (either by being quit or pushed to the background). When that happens, we gather the values from our four text fields, stick them in a mutable array, and write that mutable array to a property list.

Why don't you compile and run the application? It should build and then launch in the simulator. Once it comes up, you should be able to type into any of the four text fields. When you've typed something in them, press the home button (the circular button with the rounded square in it at the bottom of the simulator window). It's very important that you press the home button. If you just exit the simulator, that's the equivalent of forcibly quitting your application. In that case, the view controller will never receive the notification that the application is going inactive, and your data will not be saved. After pressing the home button, you may quit the simulator, or stop the app from Xcode and run it again. Your text will be restored the next time the app starts.

> **Note**   It's important to understand that pressing the home button doesn't typically quit the app—at least not at first. The app is put into a background state, ready to be instantly reactivated in case the user switches back to it. We'll dig into the details of these states and their implications for running and quitting apps in Chapter 15. In the meantime, if you want to verify that the data really was saved, you can quit the iOS simulator entirely and then restart your app from Xcode. Quitting the simulator is basically the equivalent of rebooting an iPhone. The next time your app starts, it will give the user a fresh relaunch experience.

Property list serialization is pretty cool and easy to use. However, it's a little limiting, since only a small selection of objects can be stored in property lists. Let's look at a somewhat more robust approach.

Archiving Model Objects

In the last part of Chapter 9, when we built the `Presidents` data model object, we saw an example of the process of loading archived data using `NSCoder`. In the Cocoa world, the term **archiving** refers to another form of serialization, but it's a more generic type that any object can implement. Any model object specifically written to hold data should support archiving. The technique of archiving model objects lets you easily write complex objects to a file and then read them back in.

As long as every property you implement in your class is either a scalar (e.g., `int` or `float`) or an instance of a class that conforms to the `NSCoding` protocol, you can archive your objects completely. Since most Foundation and Cocoa Touch classes capable of storing data do conform to `NSCoding` (though there are a few noteworthy exceptions, such as `UIImage`), archiving is relatively easy to implement for most classes.

Although not strictly required to make archiving work, another protocol should be implemented along with `NSCoding`: the `NSCopying` protocol, which allows your object to be copied. Being able to copy an object gives you a lot more flexibility when using data model objects. For example, think back to the Presidents application in Chapter 9. Instead of that complex code we wrote to store changes the user made so we could handle both the *Cancel* and *Save* buttons, we could have made a copy of the `president` object and stored the changes in that copy. If the user tapped *Save*, we would just copy the changed version over to replace the original version.

Conforming to NSCoding

The `NSCoding` protocol declares two methods, which are both required. One encodes your object into an archive; the other one creates a new object by decoding an archive. Both methods are passed an instance of `NSCoder`, which you work with in very much the same way as `NSUserDefaults`, introduced in the previous chapter. You can encode and decode both objects and native datatypes like `int` and `float` values using key-value coding.

A method to encode an object might look like this:

```
- (void)encodeWithCoder:(NSCoder *)encoder
{
    [encoder encodeObject:foo forKey:kFooKey];
    [encoder encodeObject:bar forKey:kBarKey];
    [encoder encodeInt:someInt forKey:kSomeIntKey];
    [encoder encodeFloat:someFloat forKey:kSomeFloatKey]
}
```

To support archiving in our object, we need to encode each of our instance variables into encoder using the appropriate encoding method. If you are subclassing a class that also conforms to NSCoding, you need to make sure you call encodeWithCoder: on your superclass to ensure that the superclass encodes its data. Therefore, your method would look like this instead:

```
- (void)encodeWithCoder:(NSCoder *)encoder
{
    [super encodeWithCoder:encoder];
    [encoder encodeObject:foo forKey:kFooKey];
    [encoder encodeObject:bar forKey:kBarKey];
    [encoder encodeInt:someInt forKey:kSomeIntKey];
    [encoder encodeFloat:someFloat forKey:kSomeFloatKey]
}
```

We also need to implement a method that initializes an object from an NSCoder, allowing us to restore an object that was previously archived. Implementing the initWithCoder: method is slightly more complex than implementing encodeWithCoder:. If you are subclassing NSObject directly or subclassing some other class that doesn't conform to NSCoding, your method would look something like the following:

```
- (id)initWithCoder:(NSCoder *)decoder
{
    if (self = [super init]) {
        foo = [decoder decodeObjectForKey:kFooKey];
        bar = [decoder decodeObjectForKey:kBarKey];
        someInt = [decoder decodeIntForKey:kSomeIntKey];
        someFloat = [decoder decodeFloatForKey:kAgeKey];
    }
    return self;
}
```

The method initializes an object instance using [super init]. If that's successful, it sets its properties by decoding values from the passed-in instance of NSCoder. When implementing NSCoding for a class with a superclass that also conforms to NSCoding, the initWithCoder: method needs to look slightly different. Instead of calling init on super, it needs to call initWithCoder:, like so:

```
- (id)initWithCoder:(NSCoder *)decoder
{
    if (self = [super initWithCoder:decoder]) {
        foo = [decoder decodeObjectForKey:kFooKey];
        bar = [decoder decodeObjectForKey:kBarKey];
        someInt = [decoder decodeIntForKey:kSomeIntKey];
        someFloat = [decoder decodeFloatForKey:kAgeKey];
    }
    return self;
}
```

And that's basically it. As long as you implement these two methods to encode and decode all your object's properties, your object is archivable and can be written to and read from archives.

Implementing NSCopying

As we mentioned earlier, conforming to NSCopying is a very good idea for any data model objects. NSCopying has one method, called copyWithZone:, which allows objects to be copied. Implementing NSCopying is similar to implementing initWithCoder:. You just need to create a new instance of the same class, and then set all of that new instance's properties to the same values as this object's properties. Here's what a copyWithZone: method might look like:

```
- (id)copyWithZone:(NSZone *)zone
{
    MyClass *copy = [[[self class] allocWithZone:zone] init];
    copy.foo = [self.foo copyWithZone:zone];
    copy.bar = [self.bar copyWithZone:zone];
    copy.someInt = self.someInt;
    copy.someFloat = self.someFloat;
    return copy;
}
```

> **Note**   Don't worry too much about the NSZone parameter. This pointer is to a struct that is used by the system to manage memory. Only in rare circumstances did developers ever need to worry about zones or create their own, and nowadays, it's almost unheard of to have multiple zones. Calling copy on an object is the same as calling copyWithZone: using the default zone, which is always what you want. In fact, on the modern iOS, zones are completely ignored. The fact that NSCopying uses zones at all is a historical oddity for the sake of backwards compatibility.

Archiving and Unarchiving Data Objects

Creating an archive from an object (or objects) that conforms to NSCoding is relatively easy. First, we create an instance of NSMutableData to hold the encoded data, and then we create an NSKeyedArchiver instance to archive objects into that NSMutableData instance:

```
NSMutableData *data = [[NSMutableData alloc] init];
NSKeyedArchiver *archiver = [[NSKeyedArchiver alloc]
    initForWritingWithMutableData:data];
```

After creating both of those, we then use key-value coding to archive any objects we wish to include in the archive, like this:

```
[archiver encodeObject:myObject forKey:@"keyValueString"];
```

Once we've encoded all the objects we want to include, we just tell the archiver we're finished, and then we write the NSMutableData instance to the file system:

```
[archiver finishEncoding];
BOOL success = [data writeToFile:@"/path/to/archive" atomically:YES];
```

If anything went wrong while writing the file, success will be set to NO. If success is YES, the data was successfully written to the specified file. Any objects created from this archive will be exact copies of the objects that were last written into the file.

To reconstitute objects from the archive, we go through a similar process. We create an NSData instance from the archive file and create an NSKeyedUnarchiver to decode the data:

```
NSData *data = [[NSData alloc] initWithContentsOfFile:@"/path/to/archive"];
NSKeyedUnarchiver *unarchiver = [[NSKeyedUnarchiver alloc]
    initForReadingWithData:data];
```

After that, we read our objects from the unarchiver using the same key that we used to archive the object:

```
self.object = [unarchiver decodeObjectForKey:@"keyValueString"];
```

Finally, we tell the archiver we are finished:

```
[unarchiver finishDecoding];
```

If you're feeling a little overwhelmed by archiving, don't worry. It's actually fairly straightforward. We're going to retrofit our Persistence application to use archiving, so you'll get to see it in action. Once you've done it a few times, archiving will become second nature, as all you're really doing is storing and retrieving your object's properties using key-value coding.

The Archiving Application

Let's redo the Persistence application, so it uses archiving instead of property lists. We're going to be making some fairly significant changes to the Persistence source code, so you should make a copy of your entire project folder before continuing.

Implementing the BIDFourLines Class

Once you're ready to proceed and have a copy of your *Persistence* project open in Xcode, select the *Persistence* folder and press ⌘N or select **File ➤ New ➤ File**…. When the new file assistant comes up, select *Cocoa Touch*, select *Objective-C class*, and click *Next*. On the next screen, name the class *BIDFourLines* and select *NSObject* in the *Subclass of* control. Click *Next* again. Now choose the *Persistence* folder to save the files to and click *Create*. This class is going to be our data model. It will hold the data that we're currently storing in a dictionary in the property list application.

Single-click *BIDFourLines.h* and make the following changes:

```
#import <Foundation/Foundation.h>

@interface BIDFourLines : NSObject <NSCoding, NSCopying>

@property (copy, nonatomic) NSArray *lines;

@end
```

This is a very straightforward data model class with an array property of four strings. Notice that we've conformed the class to the NSCoding and NSCopying protocols. Now switch over to *BIDFourLines.m* and add the following code:

```objc
#import "BIDFourLines.h"

static NSString * const kLinesKey = @"kLinesKey";

@implementation BIDFourLines

#pragma mark - Coding

- (id)initWithCoder:(NSCoder *)aDecoder
{
    self = [super init];
    if (self) {
        self.lines = [aDecoder decodeObjectForKey:kLinesKey];
    }
    return self;
}

- (void)encodeWithCoder:(NSCoder *)aCoder;
{
    [aCoder encodeObject:self.lines forKey:kLinesKey];
}

#pragma mark - Copying

- (id)copyWithZone:(NSZone *)zone;
{
    BIDFourLines *copy = [[[self class] allocWithZone:zone] init];
    NSMutableArray *linesCopy = [NSMutableArray array];
    for (id line in self.lines) {
        [linesCopy addObject:[line copyWithZone:zone]];
    }
    copy.lines = linesCopy;
    return copy;
}

@end
```

We just implemented all the methods necessary to conform to NSCoding and NSCopying. We encoded all four of our properties in encodeWithCoder: and decoded all four of them using the same four key values in initWithCoder:. In copyWithZone:, we created a new BIDFourLines object and copied all four strings to it. See? It's not hard at all; just make sure you did not forget to change anything if you did a lot of copying and pasting.

Implementing the BIDViewController Class

Now that we have an archivable data object, let's use it to persist our application data. Select *BIDViewController.m* and make the following changes:

```objc
#import "BIDViewController.h"
#import "BIDFourLines.h"

static NSString * const kRootKey = @"kRootKey";

@interface BIDViewController ()

@property (strong, nonatomic) IBOutletCollection(UITextField) NSArray *lineFields;

@end

@implementation BIDViewController

- (NSString *)dataFilePath
{
    NSArray *paths = NSSearchPathForDirectoriesInDomains(
                        NSDocumentDirectory, NSUserDomainMask, YES);
    NSString *documentsDirectory = [paths objectAtIndex:0];
    return [documentsDirectory stringByAppendingPathComponent:@"data.plist"];
    return [documentsDirectory stringByAppendingPathComponent:@"data.archive"];
}

- (void)viewDidLoad
{
    [super viewDidLoad];
    // Do any additional setup after loading the view, typically from a nib.
    NSString *filePath = [self dataFilePath];
    if ([[NSFileManager defaultManager] fileExistsAtPath:filePath]) {
        NSArray *array = [[NSArray alloc] initWithContentsOfFile:filePath];
        for (int i = 0; i < 4; i++) {
            UITextField *theField = self.lineFields[i];
            theField.text = array[i];
        }
        NSData *data = [[NSMutableData alloc]
                        initWithContentsOfFile:filePath];
        NSKeyedUnarchiver *unarchiver = [[NSKeyedUnarchiver alloc]
                                         initForReadingWithData:data];
        BIDFourLines *fourLines = [unarchiver decodeObjectForKey:kRootKey];
        [unarchiver finishDecoding];

        for (int i = 0; i < 4; i++) {
            UITextField *theField = self.lineFields[i];
            theField.text = fourLines.lines[i];
        }
    }
}
```

```
    UIApplication *app = [UIApplication sharedApplication];
    [[NSNotificationCenter defaultCenter]
     addObserver:self
         selector:@selector(applicationWillResignActive:)
             name:UIApplicationWillResignActiveNotification
           object:app];
}

- (void)applicationWillResignActive:(NSNotification *)notification
{
    NSString *filePath = [self dataFilePath];
    NSArray *array = [self.lineFields valueForKey:@"text"];
    [array writeToFile:filePath atomically:YES];

    BIDFourLines *fourLines = [[BIDFourLines alloc] init];
    fourLines.lines = [self.lineFields valueForKey:@"text"];
    NSMutableData *data = [[NSMutableData alloc] init];
    NSKeyedArchiver *archiver = [[NSKeyedArchiver alloc]
                                    initForWritingWithMutableData:data];
    [archiver encodeObject:fourLines forKey:kRootKey];
    [archiver finishEncoding];
    [data writeToFile:filePath atomically:YES];
}

@end
```

Save your changes and take this version of Persistence for a spin.

Not very much has changed, really. We started off by specifying a new file name so that our program doesn't try to load the old property list as an archive. We also defined a new constant that will be the key value we use to encode and decode our object. Next, we redefined the loading and saving by using BIDFourLines to hold the data and using the NSCoding methods to do the actual loading and saving. The GUI is identical to the previous version.

This new version takes several more lines of code to implement than property list serialization, so you might be wondering if there really is an advantage to using archiving over just serializing property lists. For this application, the answer is simple: no, there really isn't any advantage. But think back to the last example in Chapter 9, where we allowed the user to edit a list of presidents, and each president had four different fields that could be edited. To handle archiving that list of presidents with a property list would involve iterating through the list of presidents, creating an NSDictionary instance for each president, copying the value from each of their fields over to the NSDictionary instance, and then adding that instance to another array, which could then be written to a plist file. And that's assuming that we restricted ourselves to using only serializable properties. If we didn't, using property list serialization wouldn't even be an option without doing a lot of conversion work.

On the other hand, if we had an array of archivable objects, such as the BIDFourLines class that we just built, we could archive the entire array by archiving the array instance itself. Collection classes like NSArray, when archived, archive all of the objects they contain. As long as every object you put into an array or dictionary conforms to NSCoding, you can archive the array or dictionary and restore it so that all the objects that were in it when you archived it will be in the restored array or dictionary.

In other words, this approach scales beautifully (in terms of code size, at least). No matter how many objects you add, the work to write those objects to disk (assuming you're using single-file persistence) is exactly the same. With property lists, the amount of work increases with every object you add.

Using iOS's Embedded SQLite3

The third persistence option we're going to discuss is using iOS's embedded SQL database, called SQLite3. SQLite3 is very efficient at storing and retrieving large amounts of data. It's also capable of doing complex aggregations on your data, with much faster results than you would get doing the same thing using objects.

Consider a couple scenarios. What if your application needs to calculate the sum of a particular field across all the objects in your application? Or, what if you need the sum from just the objects that meet certain criteria? SQLite3 allows you to get this information without loading every object into memory. Getting aggregations from SQLite3 is several orders of magnitude faster than loading all the objects into memory and summing their values. Being a full-fledged embedded database, SQLite3 contains tools to make it even faster by, for example, creating table indexes that can speed up your queries.

> **Note**   There are several schools of thought about the pronunciation of "SQL" and "SQLite." Most official documentation says to pronounce "SQL" as "Ess-Queue-Ell" and "SQLite" as "Ess-Queue-Ell-Light." Many people pronounce them, respectively, as "Sequel" and "Sequel Light." A small cadre of hardened rebels prefer "Squeal" and "Squeal Light." Pick whatever works best for you (and be prepared to be mocked and shunned by the infidels if you choose to join the "Squeal" movement).

SQLite3 uses the Structured Query Language (SQL), the standard language used to interact with relational databases. Whole books have been written on the syntax of SQL (hundreds of them, in fact), as well as on SQLite itself. So if you don't already know SQL and you want to use SQLite3 in your application, you have a little work ahead of you. We'll show you how to set up and interact with the SQLite database from your iOS applications, and we'll also show you some of the basics of the syntax in this chapter. But to really make the most of SQLite3, you'll need to do some additional research and exploration. A couple of good starting points are "An Introduction to the SQLite3 C/C++ Interface" (http://www.sqlite.org/cintro.html) and "SQL As Understood by SQLite" (http://www.sqlite.org/lang.html).

Relational databases (including SQLite3) and object-oriented programming languages use fundamentally different approaches to storing and organizing data. The approaches are different enough that numerous techniques and many libraries and tools for converting between the two have been developed. These different techniques are collectively called **object-relational mapping** (ORM). There are currently several ORM tools available for Cocoa Touch. In fact, we'll look at one ORM solution provided by Apple, called Core Data, later in the chapter.

But before we do that, we're going to focus on the SQLite3 basics, including setting it up, creating a table to hold your data, and using the database in an application. Obviously, in the real world, an application as simple as the one we're working on wouldn't warrant the investment in SQLite3. But this application's simplicity is exactly what makes it a good learning example.

Creating or Opening the Database

Before you can use SQLite3, you must open the database. The function that's used to do that, sqlite3_open(), will open an existing database; or, if none exists at the specified location, the function will create a new one. Here's what the code to open a new database might look like:

```
sqlite3 *database;
int result = sqlite3_open("/path/to/database/file", &database);
```

If result is equal to the constant SQLITE_OK, then the database was successfully opened. Note that the path to the database file must be passed in as a C string, not as an NSString. SQLite3 was written in portable C, not Objective-C, and it has no idea what an NSString is. Fortunately, there is an NSString method that generates a C string from an NSString instance:

```
const char *stringPath = [pathString UTF8String];
```

When you're finished with an SQLite3 database, close it:

```
sqlite3_close(database);
```

Databases store all their data in tables. You can create a new table by crafting an SQL CREATE statement and passing it in to an open database using the function sqlite3_exec, like so:

```
char *errorMsg;
const char *createSQL = "CREATE TABLE IF NOT EXISTS PEOPLE"
    "(ID INTEGER PRIMARY KEY AUTOINCREMENT, FIELD_DATA TEXT)";
int result = sqlite3_exec(database, createSQL, NULL, NULL, &errorMsg);
```

> **Tip** If two inline strings are separated by nothing but whitespace, including line breaks, they are concatenated into a single string.

As before, you need to verify that result is equal to SQLITE_OK to make sure your command ran successfully. If it didn't, errorMsg will contain a description of the problem that occurred.

The function sqlite3_exec is used to run any command against SQLite3 that doesn't return data, including updates, inserts, and deletes. Retrieving data from the database is little more involved. You first need to prepare the statement by feeding it your SQL SELECT command:

```
NSString *query = @"SELECT ID, FIELD_DATA FROM FIELDS ORDER BY ROW";
sqlite3_stmt *statement;
int result = sqlite3_prepare_v2(database, [query UTF8String],
    -1, &statement, nil);
```

> **Note** All of the SQLite3 functions that take strings require an old-fashioned C string. In the example, we
> created and passed a C string. Specifically, we created an NSString and derived a C string by using one of
> NSString's methods called UTF8String. Either method is acceptable. If you need to do manipulation on
> the string, using NSString or NSMutableString will be easier; however, converting from NSString to a C
> string incurs a bit of extra overhead.

If result equals SQLITE_OK, your statement was successfully prepared, and you can start stepping
through the result set. Here is an example of stepping through a result set and retrieving an int and
an NSString from the database:

```
while (sqlite3_step(statement) == SQLITE_ROW) {
    int rowNum = sqlite3_column_int(statement, 0);
    char *rowData = (char *)sqlite3_column_text(statement, 1);
    NSString *fieldValue = [[NSString alloc] initWithUTF8String:rowData];
    // Do something with the data here
}
sqlite3_finalize(statement);
```

Using Bind Variables

Although it's possible to construct SQL strings to insert values, it is common practice to use
something called **bind variables** for this purpose. Handling strings correctly—making sure they
don't have invalid characters and that quotes are inserted properly—can be quite a chore. With bind
variables, those issues are taken care of for us.

To insert a value using a bind variable, you create your SQL statement as normal, but put a question
mark (?) into the SQL string. Each question mark represents one variable that must be bound before
the statement can be executed. Next, you prepare the SQL statement, bind a value to each of the
variables, and execute the command.

Here's an example that prepares an SQL statement with two bind variables, binds an int to the first
variable and a string to the second variable, and then executes and finalizes the statement:

```
char *sql = "insert into foo values (?, ?);";
sqlite3_stmt *stmt;
if (sqlite3_prepare_v2(database, sql, -1, &stmt, nil) == SQLITE_OK) {
    sqlite3_bind_int(stmt, 1, 235);
    sqlite3_bind_text(stmt, 2, "Bar", -1, NULL);
}
if (sqlite3_step(stmt) != SQLITE_DONE)
    NSLog(@"This should be real error checking!");
sqlite3_finalize(stmt);
```

There are multiple bind statements available, depending on the datatype you wish to use. Most bind functions take only three parameters:

- The first parameter to any bind function, regardless of the datatype, is a pointer to the `sqlite3_stmt` used previously in the `sqlite3_prepare_v2()` call.

- The second parameter is the index of the variable to which you're binding. This is a one-indexed value, meaning that the first question mark in the SQL statement has index 1, and each one after it is one higher than the one to its left.

- The third parameter is always the value that should be substituted for the question mark.

A few bind functions, such as those for binding text and binary data, have two additional parameters:

- The first additional parameter is the length of the data being passed in the third parameter. In the case of C strings, you can pass -1 instead of the string's length, and the function will use the entire string. In all other cases, you need to tell it the length of the data being passed in.

- The final parameter is an optional function callback in case you need to do any memory cleanup after the statement is executed. Typically, such a function would be used to free memory allocated using `malloc()`.

The syntax that follows the bind statements may seem a little odd, since we're doing an insert. When using bind variables, the same syntax is used for both queries and updates. If the SQL string had an SQL query, rather than an update, we would need to call `sqlite3_step()` multiple times until it returned `SQLITE_DONE`. Since this is an update, we call it only once.

The SQLite3 Application

In Xcode, create a new project using the *Single View Application* template and name it *SQLite Persistence*. This project will start off identical to the previous project, so begin by opening the *BIDViewController.m* file, and then make the following changes:

```
#import "BIDViewController.h"

@interface BIDViewController ()

@property (strong, nonatomic) IBOutletCollection(UITextField) NSArray *lineFields;

@end
```

Next, select *Main.storyboard*. Design the view and connect the outlet collection by following the instructions in the "Designing the Persistence Application View" section earlier in this chapter. Once your design is complete, save the storyboard file.

We've covered the basics, so let's see how this would work in practice. We're going to retrofit our Persistence application again, this time storing its data using SQLite3. We'll use a single table and store the field values in four different rows of that table. We'll also give each row a row number that corresponds to its field. For example, the value from the first line will get stored in the table with a row number of 0, the next line will be row number 1, and so on. Let's get started.

Linking to the SQLite3 Library

SQLite 3 is accessed through a procedural API that provides interfaces to a number of C function calls. To use this API, we'll need to link our application to a dynamic library called *libsqlite3.dylib*, located in */usr/lib* on both Mac OS X and iOS. The process of linking a dynamic library into your project is exactly the same as that of linking in a framework.

Select the *SQLite Persistence* item at the very top of the project navigator's list (leftmost pane), and then select *SQLite Persistence* from the *TARGETS* section in the main area (see the middle pane of Figure 13-4). Be careful that you have selected *SQLite Persistence* from the *TARGETS* section, not from the *PROJECT* section.

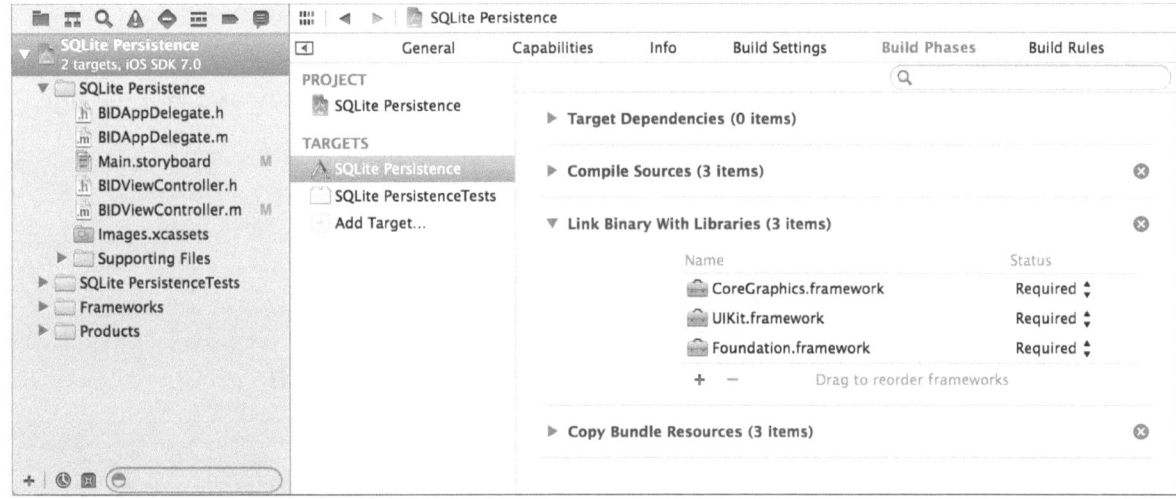

Figure 13-4. *Selecting the SQLite Persistence project in the project navigator; selecting the SQLite Persistence target; and finally, selecting the Build Phases tab*

With the *SQLite Persistence* target selected, click the *Build Phases* tab in the rightmost pane. You'll see a list of items, initially all collapsed, which represent the various steps Xcode goes through to build the application. Expand the item labeled *Link Binary With Libraries*. You'll see the standard frameworks that our application is set up to link with by default: *CoreGraphics.framework*, *UIKit.framework*, and *Foundation.framework*.

Now, let's add the SQLite3 library to our project. Click the + button at the bottom of the linked frameworks list, and you'll be presented with a sheet that lists all available frameworks and libraries. Find *libsqlite3.dylib* in the list (or use the handy search field) and click the *Add* button. Note that there may be several other entries in that directory that start with *libsqlite3*. Be sure you select *libsqlite3.dylib*. It is an alias that always points to the latest version of the SQLite3 library. Adding this to the project puts it into the project's *Frameworks* folder.

Modifying the Persistence View Controller

Now it's time to change things around again. This time, we'll replace the NSCoding code with its SQLite equivalent. Once again, we'll change the file name so that we won't be using the same file that we used in the previous version. We also want to make sure the file name properly reflects the type of data it holds. Finally, we're going to change the methods that save and load the data.

Select *BIDViewController.m* and make the following changes:

```objc
#import "BIDViewController.h"
#import <sqlite3.h>

@interface BIDViewController ()

@property (strong, nonatomic) IBOutletCollection(UITextField) NSArray *lineFields;

@end

@implementation BIDViewController

- (NSString *)dataFilePath
{
    NSArray *paths = NSSearchPathForDirectoriesInDomains(
                        NSDocumentDirectory, NSUserDomainMask, YES);
    NSString *documentsDirectory = [paths objectAtIndex:0];
    return [documentsDirectory stringByAppendingPathComponent:@"data.sqlite"];
}

- (void)viewDidLoad
{
    [super viewDidLoad];
    // Do any additional setup after loading the view, typically from a nib.
    sqlite3 *database;
    if (sqlite3_open([[self dataFilePath] UTF8String], &database)
        != SQLITE_OK) {
        sqlite3_close(database);
        NSAssert(0, @"Failed to open database");
    }

    // Useful C trivia: If two inline strings are separated by nothing
    // but whitespace (including line breaks), they are concatenated into
    // a single string:
    NSString *createSQL = @"CREATE TABLE IF NOT EXISTS FIELDS "
                            "(ROW INTEGER PRIMARY KEY, FIELD_DATA TEXT);";
    char *errorMsg;
    if (sqlite3_exec (database, [createSQL UTF8String],
                    NULL, NULL, &errorMsg) != SQLITE_OK) {
        sqlite3_close(database);
        NSAssert(0, @"Error creating table: %s", errorMsg);
    }
```

```objc
    NSString *query = @"SELECT ROW, FIELD_DATA FROM FIELDS ORDER BY ROW";
    sqlite3_stmt *statement;
    if (sqlite3_prepare_v2(database, [query UTF8String],
                            -1, &statement, nil) == SQLITE_OK) {
        while (sqlite3_step(statement) == SQLITE_ROW) {
            int row = sqlite3_column_int(statement, 0);
            char *rowData = (char *)sqlite3_column_text(statement, 1);

            NSString *fieldValue = [[NSString alloc]
                                    initWithUTF8String:rowData];
            UITextField *field = self.lineFields[row];
            field.text = fieldValue;
        }
        sqlite3_finalize(statement);
    }
    sqlite3_close(database);

    UIApplication *app = [UIApplication sharedApplication];
    [[NSNotificationCenter defaultCenter]
     addObserver:self
        selector:@selector(applicationWillResignActive:)
            name:UIApplicationWillResignActiveNotification
          object:app];
}

- (void)applicationWillResignActive:(NSNotification *)notification
{
    sqlite3 *database;
    if (sqlite3_open([[self dataFilePath] UTF8String], &database)
        != SQLITE_OK) {
        sqlite3_close(database);
        NSAssert(0, @"Failed to open database");
    }
    for (int i = 0; i < 4; i++) {
        UITextField *field = self.lineFields[i];
        // Once again, inline string concatenation to the rescue:
        char *update = "INSERT OR REPLACE INTO FIELDS (ROW, FIELD_DATA) "
                    "VALUES (?, ?);";
        char *errorMsg = NULL;
        sqlite3_stmt *stmt;
        if (sqlite3_prepare_v2(database, update, -1, &stmt, nil)
            == SQLITE_OK) {
            sqlite3_bind_int(stmt, 1, i);
            sqlite3_bind_text(stmt, 2, [field.text UTF8String], -1, NULL);
        }
        if (sqlite3_step(stmt) != SQLITE_DONE)
            NSAssert(0, @"Error updating table: %s", errorMsg);
        sqlite3_finalize(stmt);
    }
    sqlite3_close(database);
}
```

```
- (void)didReceiveMemoryWarning
{
    [super didReceiveMemoryWarning];
    // Dispose of any resources that can be recreated.
}
```

@end

The first piece of new code to look at is in the viewDidLoad method. We begin by opening the database. If we hit a problem with opening the database, we close it and raise an assertion:

```
sqlite3 *database;
if (sqlite3_open([[self dataFilePath] UTF8String], &database)
    != SQLITE_OK) {
    sqlite3_close(database);
    NSAssert(0, @"Failed to open database");
}
```

Next, we need to make sure that we have a table to hold our data. We can use SQL CREATE TABLE to do that. By specifying IF NOT EXISTS, we prevent the database from overwriting existing data. If there is already a table with the same name, this command quietly exits without doing anything, so it's safe to call every time our application launches without explicitly checking to see if a table exists:

```
NSString *createSQL = @"CREATE TABLE IF NOT EXISTS FIELDS "
                       "(ROW INTEGER PRIMARY KEY, FIELD_DATA TEXT);";
char *errorMsg;
if (sqlite3_exec (database, [createSQL UTF8String],
                  NULL, NULL, &errorMsg) != SQLITE_OK) {
    sqlite3_close(database);
    NSAssert(0, @"Error creating table: %s", errorMsg);
}
```

Finally, we need to load our data. We do this using an SQL SELECT statement. In this simple example, we create an SQL SELECT that requests all the rows from the database and ask SQLite3 to prepare our SELECT. We also tell SQLite3 to order the rows by the row number, so that we always get them back in the same order. Absent this, SQLite3 will return the rows in the order in which they are stored internally.

```
NSString *query = @"SELECT ROW, FIELD_DATA FROM FIELDS ORDER BY ROW";
sqlite3_stmt *statement;
if (sqlite3_prepare_v2(database, [query UTF8String],
                       -1, &statement, nil) == SQLITE_OK) {
```

Next, we step through each of the returned rows:

```
while (sqlite3_step(statement) == SQLITE_ROW) {
```

Now we grab the row number, store it in an int, and then grab the field data as a C string:

```
int row = sqlite3_column_int(statement, 0);
char *rowData = (char *)sqlite3_column_text(statement, 1);
```

Next, we set the appropriate field with the value retrieved from the database:

```
NSString *fieldValue = [[NSString alloc]
                        initWithUTF8String:rowData];
UITextField *field = self.lineFields[row];
field.text = fieldValue;
```

Finally, we close the database connection, and we're finished:

```
    }
    sqlite3_finalize(statement);
}
sqlite3_close(database);
```

Note that we close the database connection as soon as we're finished creating the table and loading any data it contains, rather than keeping it open the entire time the application is running. It's the simplest way of managing the connection; and in this little app, we can just open the connection those few times we need it. In a more database-intensive app, you might want to keep the connection open all the time.

The other changes we made are in the applicationWillResignActive: method, where we need to save our application data. Because the data in the database is stored in a table, our application's data will look something like Table 13-1 when stored.

Table 13-1. Data Stored in the FIELDS Table of the Database

ROW	FIELD_DATA
0	Here's to the crazy ones.
1	The misfits. The rebels.
2	The troublemakers.
3	The round pegs in the square holes.

The applicationWillResignActive: method starts by once again opening the database. To save the data, we loop through all four fields and issue a separate command to update each row of the database:

```
for (int i = 0; i < 4; i++) {
    UITextField *field = self.lineFields[i];
```

The first thing we do in the loop is craft a field name, so we can retrieve the correct text field outlet. Remember that valueForKey: allows you to retrieve a property based on its name. We also declare a pointer to be used for the error message if we encounter an error.

We craft an INSERT OR REPLACE SQL statement with two bind variables. The first represents the row that's being stored; the second is for the actual string value to be stored. By using INSERT OR REPLACE instead of the more standard INSERT, we don't need to worry about whether a row already exists:

```
char *update = "INSERT OR REPLACE INTO FIELDS (ROW, FIELD_DATA) "
               "VALUES (?, ?);";
```

Next, we declare a pointer to a statement, prepare our statement with the bind variables, and bind values to both of the bind variables:

```
sqlite3_stmt *stmt;
if (sqlite3_prepare_v2(database, update, -1, &stmt, nil)
    == SQLITE_OK) {
    sqlite3_bind_int(stmt, 1, i);
    sqlite3_bind_text(stmt, 2, [field.text UTF8String], -1, NULL);
}
```

Now we call sqlite3_step to execute the update, check to make sure it worked, and finalize the statement, ending the loop:

```
if (sqlite3_step(stmt) != SQLITE_DONE)
    NSAssert(0, @"Error updating table: %s", errorMsg);
sqlite3_finalize(stmt);
```

Notice that we used an assertion here to check for an error condition. We use assertions rather than exceptions or manual error checking because this condition should happen only if we, the developers, make a mistake. Using this assertion macro will help us debug our code, and it can be stripped out of our final application. If an error condition is one that a user might reasonably experience, you should probably use some other form of error checking.

> **Note**   There is one condition that could cause an error to occur in the preceding SQLite code that is not a programmer error. If the device's storage is completely full—to the extent that SQLite can't save its changes to the database—then an error will occur here, as well. However, this condition is fairly rare and will probably result in deeper problems for the user, outside the scope of our app's data. Our app probably wouldn't even launch successfully if the system were in that state. So we're going to just sidestep the issue entirely.

Once we're finished with the loop, we close the database:

```
sqlite3_close(database);
```

Why don't you compile and run the app? Enter some data and then press the iPhone simulator's home button. Quit the simulator (to force the app to actually quit), and then relaunch the SQLite Persistence application. That data should be right where you left it. As far as the user is concerned, there's absolutely no difference between the various versions of this application; however, each version uses a very different persistence mechanism.

Using Core Data

The final technique we're going to demonstrate in this chapter is how to implement persistence using Apple's Core Data framework. Core Data is a robust, full-featured persistence tool. Here, we will show you how to use Core Data to re-create the same persistence you've seen in our Persistence application so far.

Note For more comprehensive coverage of Core Data, check out *More iOS 7 Development* by Kevin Kim, Alex Horovitz, David Mark, and Jeff LaMarche (Apress, 2014). That book devotes several chapters to Core Data. You might also be interested in *Pro Core Data for iOS* by Michael Privet and Robert Warner (Apress, 2011).

In Xcode, create a new project. This time, select the *Empty Application* template and click *Next*. Name the product *Core Data Persistence* and select *iPhone* from the *Device Family* popup; however, but don't click the *Next* button just yet. If you look just below the *Device Family* popup, you should see a check box labeled *Use Core Data*. There's a certain amount of complexity involved in adding Core Data to an existing project, so Apple has kindly provided an option with some application project templates to do much of the work for you.

Check the *Use Core Data* check box (see Figure 13-5), and then click the *Next* button. When prompted, choose a directory to store your project and click *Create*.

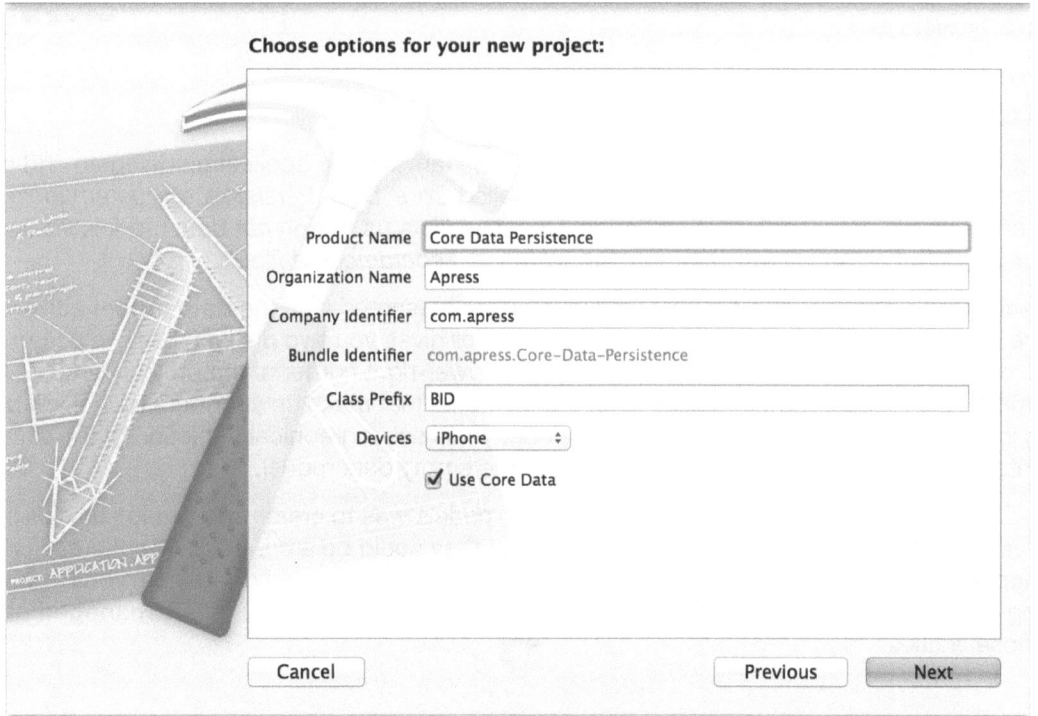

Figure 13-5. Some project templates, including Empty Application, offer the option to use Core Data for persistence

Before we move on to our code, let's take a look at the project window, which contains some new stuff. Expand the *Core Date Persistence* folder if it's closed (see Figure 13-6).

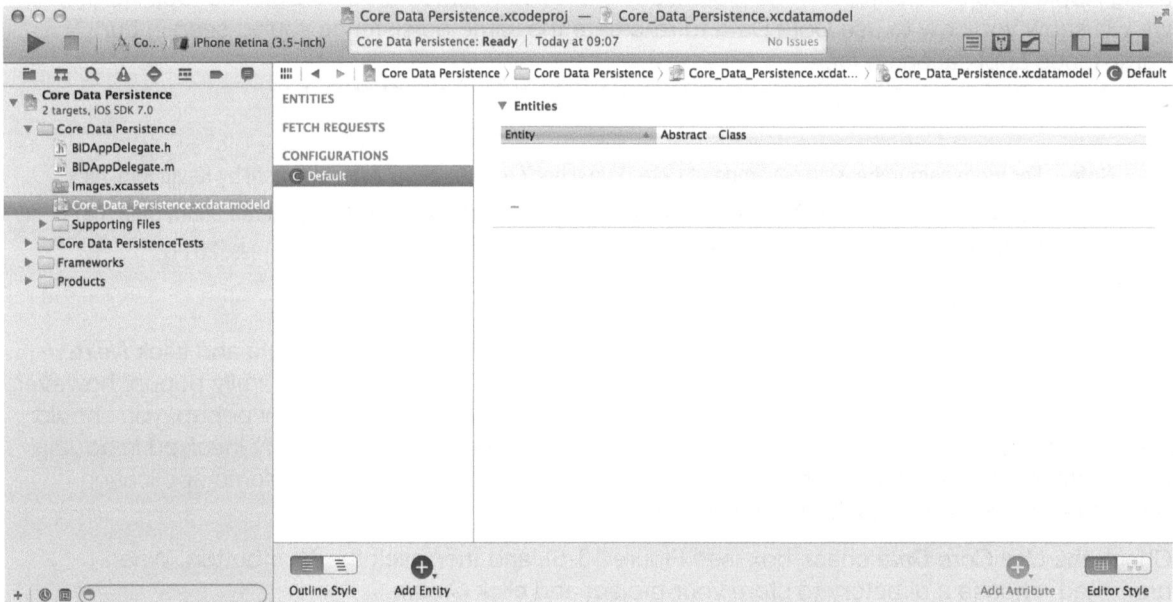

Figure 13-6. Our project template with the files needed for Core Data. The Core Data model is selected, and the data model editor is shown in the editing pane

Entities and Managed Objects

Most of what you see in the project navigator should be familiar: the application delegate and the image assets catalog. In addition, you'll find a file called *Core_Data_Persistence.xcdatamodeld*, which contains our data model. Within Xcode, Core Data lets us design our data models visually, without writing code, and stores that data model in the *.xcdatamodeld* file.

Single-click the *.xcdatamodeld* file now, and you will be presented with the **data model editor** (see the right side of Figure 13-6). The data model editor gives you two distinct views into your data model, depending on the setting of the control in the lower-right corner of the project window. In Table mode, the mode shown in Figure 13-6, the elements that make up your data model will be shown in a series of editable tables. In Graph mode, you'll see a graphical depiction of the same elements. At the moment, both views reflect the same empty data model.

Before Core Data, the traditional way to create data models was to create subclasses of NSObject and conform them to NSCoding and NSCopying so that they could be archived, as we did earlier in this chapter. Core Data uses a fundamentally different approach. Instead of classes, you begin by creating **entities** here in the data model editor; and then, in your code, you create **managed objects** from those entities.

Note   The terms *entity* and *managed object* can be a little confusing, since both refer to data model objects. *Entity* refers to the description of an object. *Managed object* refers to actual concrete instances of that entity created at runtime. So, in the data model editor, you create entities; but in your code, you create and retrieve managed objects. The distinction between entities and managed objects is similar to the distinction between a class and instances of that class.

An entity is made up of properties. There are three types of properties:

Attributes: An attribute serves the same function in a Core Data entity as an instance variable does in an Objective-C class. They both hold the data.

Relationships: As the name implies, a relationship defines the relationship between entities. For example, to create a Person entity, you might start by defining a few attributes such as hairColor, eyeColor, height, and weight. You might also define address attributes, such as state and zipCode, or you might embed them in a separate HomeAddress entity. Using the latter approach, you would then create a relationship between a Person and a HomeAddress. Relationships can be **to-one** and **to-many**. The relationship from Person to HomeAddress is probably to-one, since most people have only a single home address. The relationship from HomeAddress to Person might be to-many, since there may be more than one Person living at that HomeAddress.

Fetched properties: A fetched property is an alternative to a relationship. Fetched properties allow you to create a query that is evaluated at fetch time to see which objects belong to the relationship. To extend our earlier example, a Person object could have a fetched property called Neighbors that finds all HomeAddress objects in the data store that have the same ZIP code as the Person's own HomeAddress. Due to the nature of how fetched properties are constructed and used, they are always one-way relationships. Fetched properties are also the only kind of relationship that lets you traverse multiple data stores.

Typically, attributes, relationships, and fetched properties are defined using Xcode's data model editor. In our Core Data Persistence application, we'll build a simple entity, so you can get a sense of how this all works together.

Key-Value Coding

In your code, instead of using accessors and mutators, you will use **key-value coding** to set properties or retrieve their existing values. Key-value coding may sound intimidating, but you've already used it quite a bit in this book. Every time we used NSDictionary, for example, we were using key-value coding because every object in a dictionary is stored under a unique key value. The key-value coding used by Core Data is a bit more complex than that used by NSDictionary, but the basic concept is the same.

When working with a managed object, the key you will use to set or retrieve a property's value is the name of the attribute you wish to set. So, here's how to retrieve the value stored in the attribute called name from a managed object:

```
NSString *name = [myManagedObject valueForKey:@"name"];
```

Similarly, to set a new value for a managed object's property, do this:

```
[myManagedObject setValue:@"Gregor Overlander" forKey:@"name"];
```

Putting It All in Context

So where do these managed objects live? They live in something called a **persistent store**, also referred to as a **backing store**. Persistent stores can take several different forms. By default, a Core Data application implements a backing store as an SQLite database stored in the application's *Documents* directory. Even though your data is stored via SQLite, classes in the Core Data framework do all the work associated with loading and saving your data. If you use Core Data, you don't need to write any SQL statements. You just work with objects, and Core Data figures out what it needs to do behind the scenes.

SQLite isn't the only option Core Data has for storage. Backing stores can also be implemented as binary flat files or even stored in an XML format. Another option is to create an in-memory store, which you might use if you're writing a caching mechanism; however, it doesn't save data beyond the end of the current session. In almost all situations, you should just leave it as the default and use SQLite as your persistent store.

Although most applications will have only one persistent store, it is possible to have multiple persistent stores within the same application. If you're curious about how the backing store is created and configured, take a look at the file *BIDAppDelegate.m* in your Xcode project. The Xcode project template we chose provided us with all the code needed to set up a single persistent store for our application.

Other than creating it (which is handled for you in your application delegate), you generally won't work with your persistent store directly. Rather, you will use something called a **managed object context**, often referred to as just a **context**. The context manages access to the persistent store and maintains information about which properties have changed since the last time an object was saved. The context also registers all changes with the undo manager, which means that you always have the ability to undo a single change or roll back all the way to the last time data was saved.

> **Note**   You can have multiple contexts pointing to the same persistent store, though most iOS applications will use only one. You can find out more about using multiple contexts and the undo manager in the Apress book, *More iOS 7 Development* (Apress, 2014).

Many Core Data method calls require an NSManagedObjectContext as a parameter or must be executed against a context. With the exception of more complicated, multithreaded iOS applications, you can just use the managedObjectContext property provided by your application delegate, which is a default context that is created for you automatically, also courtesy of the Xcode project template.

You may notice that in addition to a managed object context and a persistent store coordinator, the provided application delegate also contains an instance of NSManagedObjectModel. This class is responsible for loading and representing, at runtime, the data model you will create using the data model editor in Xcode. You generally won't need to interact directly with this class. It's used behind the scenes by the other Core Data classes, so they can identify which entities and properties you've defined in your data model. As long as you create your data model using the provided file, there's no need to worry about this class at all.

Creating New Managed Objects

Creating a new instance of a managed object is pretty easy, though not quite as straightforward as creating a normal object instance using alloc and init. Instead, you use the insertNewObjectFor EntityForName:inManagedObjectContext: factory method in a class called NSEntityDescription. NSEntityDescription's job is to keep track of all the entities defined in the app's data model and to let you create instances of those entities. This method creates and returns an instance representing a single entity in memory. It returns either an instance of NSManagedObject that is set up with the correct properties for that particular entity; or, if you've configured your entity to be implemented with a specific subclass of NSManagedObject, an instance of that class. Remember that entities are like classes. An entity is a description of an object and defines which properties a particular entity has.

To create a new object, do this:

```
NSManagedObject *thing = [NSEntityDescription
                  insertNewObjectForEntityForName:@"Thing"
                          inManagedObjectContext:context];
```

The method is called insertNewObjectForEntityForName:inManagedObjectContext: because, in addition to creating the object, it inserts the newly created object into the context and then returns that object. After this call, the object exists in the context, but is not yet part of the persistent store. The object will be added to the persistent store the next time the managed object context's save: method is called.

Retrieving Managed Objects

To retrieve managed objects from the persistent store, you'll use a **fetch request**, which is Core Data's way of handling a predefined query. For example, you might say, "Give me every Person whose eyeColor is blue."

After first creating a fetch request, you provide it with an NSEntityDescription that specifies the entity of the object or objects you wish to retrieve. Here is an example that creates a fetch request:

```
NSFetchRequest *request = [[NSFetchRequest alloc] init];
NSEntityDescription *entityDescr = [NSEntityDescription
    entityForName:@"Thing" inManagedObjectContext:context];
[request setEntity:entityDescr];
```

Optionally, you can also specify criteria for a fetch request using the NSPredicate class. A **predicate** is similar to the SQL WHERE clause and allows you to define the criteria used to determine the results of your fetch request. Here is a simple example of a predicate:

```
NSPredicate *pred = [NSPredicate predicateWithFormat:@"(name = %@)", nameString];
[request setPredicate: pred];
```

The predicate created by the first line of code tells a fetch request that, instead of retrieving all managed objects for the specified entity, it should retrieve just those where the name property is set to the value currently stored in the nameString variable. So, if nameString is an NSString that holds the value @"Bob", we are telling the fetch request to bring back only managed objects that have a name property set to "Bob". This is a simple example, but predicates can be considerably more complex and can use Boolean logic to specify the precise criteria you might need in most any situation.

> **Note**   Learn Objective-C on the Mac, 2nd Edition, by Scott Knaster, Waqar Maliq, and Mark Dalrymple (Apress 2012) has an entire chapter devoted to the use of NSPredicate.

After you've created your fetch request, provided it with an entity description, and optionally given it a predicate, you **execute** the fetch request using an instance method on NSManagedObjectContext:

```
NSError *error;
NSArray *objects = [context executeFetchRequest:request error:&error];
if (objects == nil) {
    // handle error
}
```

executeFetchRequest:error: will load the specified objects from the persistent store and return them in an array. If an error is encountered, you will get a nil array, and the error pointer you provided will point to an NSError object that describes the specific problem. If no error occurs, you will get a valid array, though it may not have any objects in it since it is possible that none meets the specified criteria. From this point on, any changes you make to the managed objects returned in that array will be tracked by the managed object context you executed the request against, and saved when you send that context a save: message.

The Core Data Application

Let's take Core Data for a spin now. First, we'll return our attention to Xcode and create our data model.

Designing the Data Model

Select *Core_Data_Persistence.xcdatamodel* to open Xcode's data model editor. The data model editing pane shows all the entities, fetch requests, and configurations that are contained within your data model.

> **Note** The Core Data concept of **configurations** lets you define one or more named subsets of the entities contained in your data model, which can be useful in certain situations. For example, if you want to create a suite of apps that shares the same data model, but some apps shouldn't have access to everything (perhaps there's one app for normal users and another for sysadmins), this approach lets you do that. You can also use multiple configurations within a single app as it switches between different modes of operation. In this book, we're not going to deal with configurations at all; but since the list of configurations (including the single default configuration that contains everything in your model) is right there, staring you in the face beneath the entities and fetch requests, we thought it was worth a mention here.

As shown in Figure 13-6, those lists are empty now because we haven't created anything yet. Remedy that by clicking the plus icon labeled *Add Entity* in the lower-left corner of the entity pane. This will create a brand-new entity with the name *Entity* (see Figure 13-7).

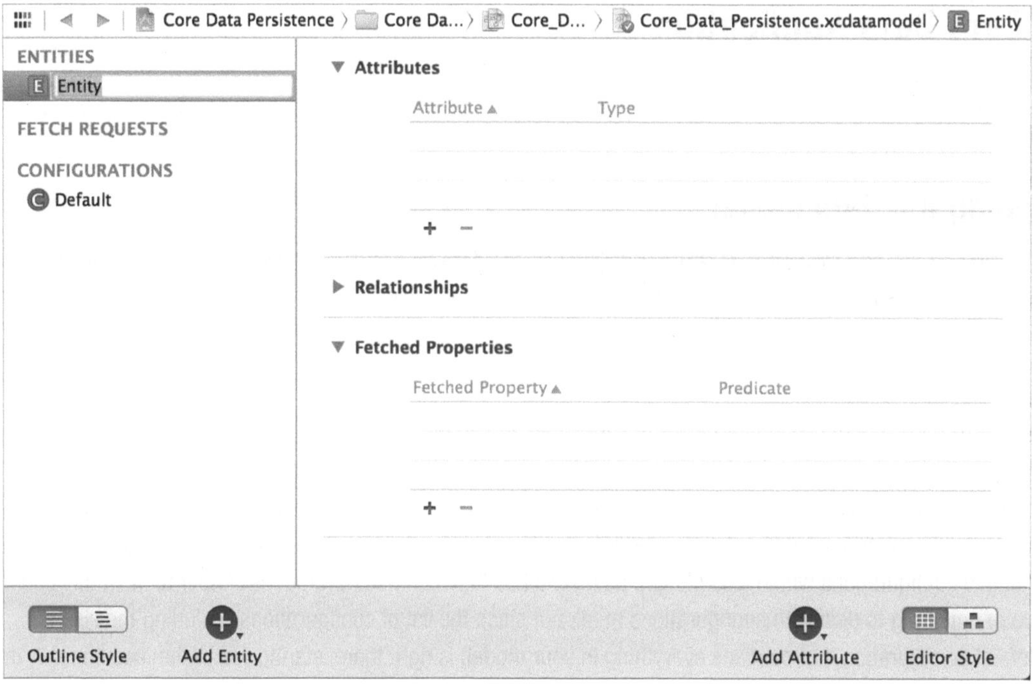

Figure 13-7. The data model editor, showing our newly added entity

As you build your data model, you'll probably find yourself switching between *Table* view and *Graph* view using the *Editor Style* control at the bottom right of the editing area. Switch to *Graph* view now. *Graph* view presents a little box representing our entity, which itself contains sections for showing the entity's attributes and relationships, also currently empty (see Figure 13-8). *Graph* view is really useful if your model contains multiple entities because it shows a graphic representation of all the relationships between your entities.

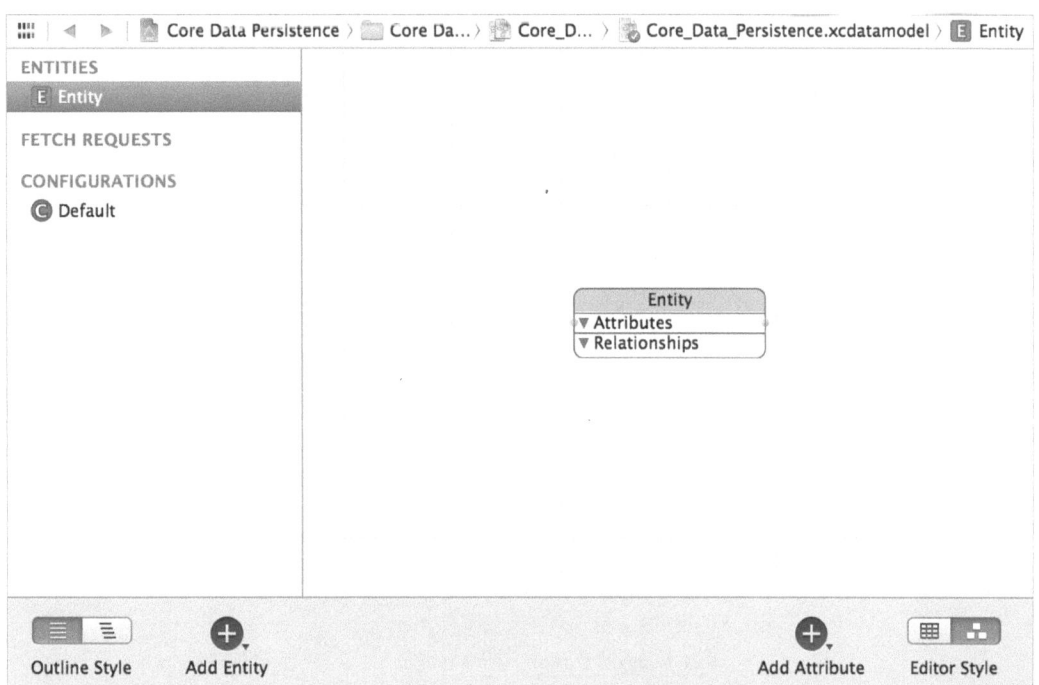

Figure 13-8. Using the control in the lower-right corner, we switched the data model editor into Graph mode. Note that Graph mode shows the same entities as Table mode, just in a graphic form. This is useful if you have multiple entities with relationships between them

Note   If you prefer working graphically, you can actually build your entire model in Graph view. We're going to stick with Table view in this chapter because it's easier to explain. When you're creating your own data models, feel free to work in Graph view if that approach suits you better.

Whether you're using Table view or Graph view for designing your data model, you'll almost always want to bring up the Core Data data model inspector. This inspector lets you view and edit relevant details for whatever item is selected in the data model editor—whether it's an entity, attribute, relationship, or anything else. You can browse an existing model without the data model inspector; but to really work on a model, you'll invariably need to use this inspector, much as you frequently use the attributes inspector when editing nib files.

Press ⌥⌘3 to open the data model inspector. At the moment, the inspector shows information about the entity we just added. Change the *Name* field from *Entity* to *Line* (see Figure 13-9).

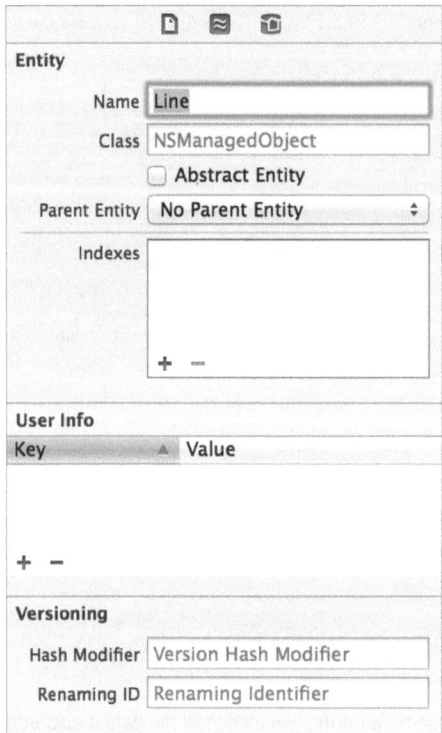

Figure 13-9. Using the data model inspector to change our entity's name to Line

If you're currently in Graph view, switch to Table view now. Table view shows more details for each piece of the entity we're working on, so it's usually more useful than Graph view when creating a new entity. In Table view, most of the data model editor is taken up by the table showing the entity's attributes, relationships, and fetched properties. This is where we'll set up our entity.

Notice that at the lower right of the editing area, there's an icon containing a plus sign, similar to the one at the lower left, which you used to create the entity. If you select your entity and then click the plus sign and hold down the mouse button, a popup menu will appear, allowing you to add an attribute, relationship, or fetched property to your entity (see Figure 13-10).

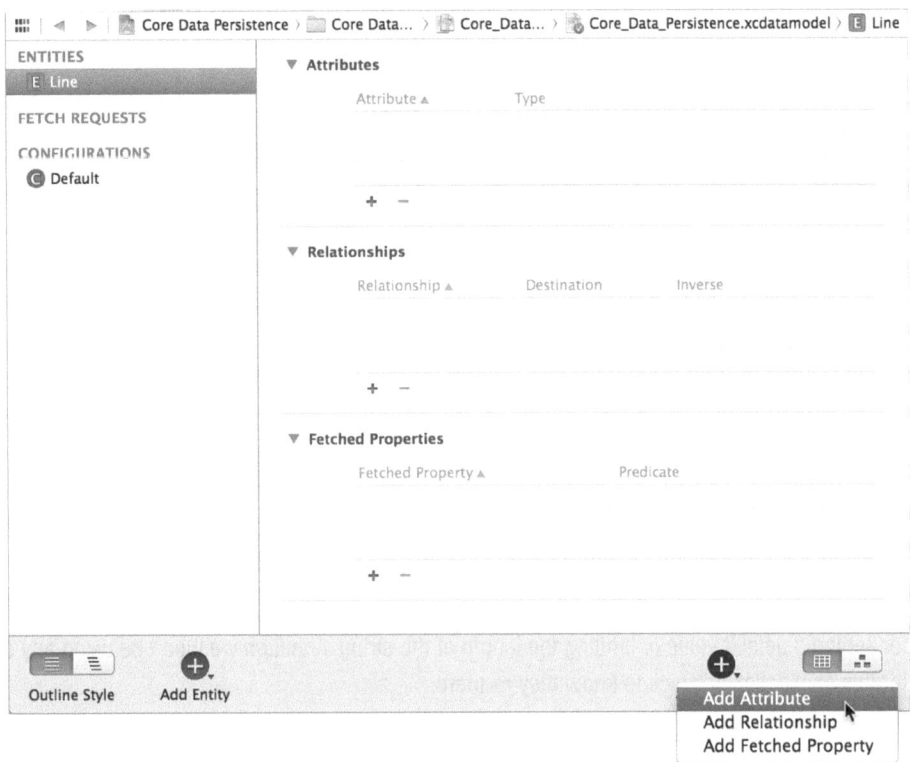

Figure 13-10. With an entity selected, press and hold the right plus sign icon to add an attribute, relationship, or fetched property to your entity

> **Note**   Notice that you don't need to press and hold to add an attribute. You'll get the same result if you just click the plus icon. Shortcut!

Go ahead and use this technique to add an attribute to your *Line* entity. A new attribute, creatively named *attribute*, is added to the *Attributes* section of the table and selected. In the table, you'll see that not only is the row selected, but the attribute's name is selected as well. This means that immediately after clicking the plus sign, you can start typing the name of the new attribute without further clicking.

Change the new attribute's name from *attribute* to *lineNumber* and click the popup next to the name to change its *Type* from *Undefined* to *Integer 16*. Doing so turns this attribute into one that will hold an integer value. We will be using this attribute to identify which of the managed object's four fields holds data. Since we have only four options, we selected the smallest integer type available.

Now direct your attention to the data model inspector, where additional details can be configured. The check box below the *Name* field on the right, *Optional*, is selected by default. Click it to deselect it. We don't want this attribute to be optional—a line that doesn't correspond to a label on our interface is useless.

Selecting the *Transient* check box creates a transient attribute. This attribute is used to specify a value that is held by managed objects while the app is running, but is never saved to the data store. We do want the line number saved to the data store, so leave the *Transient* check box unchecked.

Selecting the *Indexed* check box will cause an index in the underlying SQL database to be created on the column that holds this attribute's data. Leave the *Indexed* check box unchecked. The amount of data is small, and we won't provide the user with a search capability; therefore, there's no need for an index.

Beneath that are more settings that allow us to do some simple data validation by specifying minimum and maximum values for the integer, a default value, and more. We won't be using any of these settings in this example.

Now make sure the *Line* entity is selected and click the plus sign to add a second attribute. Change the name of your new attribute to *lineText* and change its *Type* to *String*. This attribute will hold the actual data from the text field. Leave the *Optional* check box checked for this one; it is altogether possible that the user won't enter a value for a given field.

> **Note**   When you change the *Type* to *String*, you'll notice that the inspector shows a slightly different set of options for setting a default value or limiting the length of the string. Although we won't be using any of those options for this application, it's nice to know they're there.

Guess what? Your data model is complete. That's all there is to it. Core Data lets you point and click your way to an application data model. Let's finish building the application so you can see how to use our data model from our code.

Creating the Persistence View and Controller

Because we selected the *Empty Application* template, we weren't provided with a view controller. Go back to the project navigator, single-click the *Core Data Persistence* folder, and press ⌘N or select **File ➤ New ➤ New File…** to bring up the new file assistant. Select *Objective-C class* from the *Cocoa Touch* heading and click *Next*. On the next sheet, name the class *BIDViewController,* select a *Subclass of UIViewController*, and make sure the box labeled *Targeted for iPad* is unchecked. However, do check the box that says *With XIB for user interface* to have Xcode create a nib file automatically. We've been using storyboards almost exclusively throughout this book; however, nib files still work just fine for simple GUIs, and it's worth knowing how they work, so here we go. Click *Next* and choose the directory in which to save the file. When you're finished, *BIDViewController.h, BIDViewController.m,* and *BIDViewController.xib* will be placed in your *Core Data Persistence* folder.

Select *BIDViewController.m* and make the following changes, which should look very familiar to you:

```
#import "BIDViewController.h"

@interface BIDViewController ()

@property (strong, nonatomic) IBOutletCollection(UITextField) NSArray *lineFields;

@end
```

Save this file. Next, select *BIDViewController.xib* to edit the GUI in Interface Builder. Design the view and connect the outlet collection by following the instructions in the "Designing the Persistence Application View" section earlier in this chapter. You might also find it useful to refer back to Figure 13-3. The biggest difference you'll notice is that there's no *View Controller* icon to represent our view controller; instead, there is a *File's Owner* icon. A nib file differs from a storyboard scene, where a *View Controller* appears beneath each full-screen view. In a nib file, the *File's Owner* icon only appears in the document outline at the left. Once your design is complete, save the nib file.

Now go back to *BIDViewController.m*, and make the following changes:

```
#import "BIDViewController.h"
#import "BIDAppDelegate.h"

static NSString * const kLineEntityName = @"Line";
static NSString * const kLineNumberKey = @"lineNumber";
static NSString * const kLineTextKey = @"lineText";

@interface BIDViewController ()

@property (strong, nonatomic) IBOutletCollection(UITextField) NSArray *lineFields;

@end

@implementation BIDViewController

- (id)initWithNibName:(NSString *)nibNameOrNil bundle:(NSBundle *)nibBundleOrNil
{
    self = [super initWithNibName:nibNameOrNil bundle:nibBundleOrNil];
    if (self) {
        // Custom initialization
    }
    return self;
}

- (void)viewDidLoad
{
    [super viewDidLoad];
    BIDAppDelegate *appDelegate = [UIApplication sharedApplication].delegate;
    NSManagedObjectContext *context = [appDelegate managedObjectContext];
    NSFetchRequest *request = [[NSFetchRequest alloc]
                                    initWithEntityName:kLineEntityName];
```

```
    NSError *error;
    NSArray *objects = [context executeFetchRequest:request error:&error];
    if (objects == nil) {
        NSLog(@"There was an error!");
        // Do whatever error handling is appropriate
    }

    for (NSManagedObject *oneObject in objects) {
        int lineNum = [[oneObject valueForKey:kLineNumberKey] intValue];
        NSString *lineText = [oneObject valueForKey:kLineTextKey];

        UITextField *theField = self.lineFields[lineNum];
        theField.text = lineText;
    }

    UIApplication *app = [UIApplication sharedApplication];
    [[NSNotificationCenter defaultCenter]
     addObserver:self
        selector:@selector(applicationWillResignActive:)
            name:UIApplicationWillResignActiveNotification
          object:app];
}

- (void)applicationWillResignActive:(NSNotification *)notification
{
    BIDAppDelegate *appDelegate = [UIApplication sharedApplication].delegate;
    NSManagedObjectContext *context = [appDelegate managedObjectContext];
    NSError *error;
    for (int i = 0; i < 4; i++) {
        UITextField *theField = self.lineFields[i];

        NSFetchRequest *request = [[NSFetchRequest alloc]
                                   initWithEntityName:kLineEntityName];
        NSPredicate *pred = [NSPredicate
                             predicateWithFormat:@"(%K = %d)", kLineNumberKey, i];
        [request setPredicate:pred];

        NSArray *objects = [context executeFetchRequest:request error:&error];
        if (objects == nil) {
            NSLog(@"There was an error!");
            // Do whatever error handling is appropriate
        }

        NSManagedObject *theLine = nil;
        if ([objects count] > 0) {
            theLine = [objects objectAtIndex:0];
        } else {
            theLine = [NSEntityDescription
                       insertNewObjectForEntityForName:kLineEntityName
                       inManagedObjectContext:context];
        }
```

```
        [theLine setValue:[NSNumber numberWithInt:i] forKey:kLineNumberKey];
        [theLine setValue:theField.text forKey:kLineTextKey];


    }
    [appDelegate saveContext];
}

- (void)didReceiveMemoryWarning
{
    [super didReceiveMemoryWarning];
    // Dispose of any resources that can be recreated.
}

@end
```

Now let's look at the viewDidLoad method, which needs to check whether there is any existing data in the persistent store. If there is, it should load the data and populate the fields with it. The first thing we do in that method is to get a reference to our application delegate, which we then use to get the managed object context that was created for us:

```
BIDAppDelegate *appDelegate = [UIApplication sharedApplication].delegate;
NSManagedObjectContext *context = [appDelegate managedObjectContext];
```

The next order of business is to create a fetch request and pass it the entity name, so it knows which type of objects to retrieve:

```
NSFetchRequest *request = [[NSFetchRequest alloc]
                    initWithEntityName:kLineEntityName];
```

Since we want to retrieve all Line objects in the persistent store, we do not create a predicate. By executing a request without a predicate, we're telling the context to give us every Line object in the store. We make sure we got back a valid array and log it if we didn't.

```
NSError *error;
NSArray *objects = [context executeFetchRequest:request error:&error];
if (objects == nil) {
    NSLog(@"There was an error!");
    // Do whatever error handling is appropriate
}
```

Next, we use fast enumeration to loop through the array of retrieved managed objects, pull the lineNum and lineText values from each managed object, and use that information to update one of the text fields on our user interface:

```
for (NSManagedObject *oneObject in objects) {
    int lineNum = [[oneObject valueForKey:kLineNumberKey] intValue];
    NSString *lineText = [oneObject valueForKey:kLineTextKey];

    UITextField *theField = self.lineFields[lineNum];
    theField.text = lineText;
}
```

Then, just as with all the other applications in this chapter, we register to be notified when the application is about to move out of the active state (either by being shuffled to the background or exited completely), so we can save any changes the user has made to the data:

```
UIApplication *app = [UIApplication sharedApplication];
[[NSNotificationCenter defaultCenter]
 addObserver:self
    selector:@selector(applicationWillResignActive:)
        name:UIApplicationWillResignActiveNotification
      object:app];
```

Let's look at applicationWillResignActive: next. We start out the same way as the previous method: by getting a reference to the application delegate and using that to get a pointer to our application's default context:

```
BIDAppDelegate *appDelegate = [UIApplication sharedApplication].delegate;
NSManagedObjectContext *context = [appDelegate managedObjectContext];
```

After that, we go into a loop that executes four times, one time for each text field, and then get a reference to the correct field:

```
for (int i = 0; i < 4; i++) {
    UITextField *theField = self.lineFields[i];
```

Next, we create our fetch request for our Line entry. We need to find out if there's already a managed object in the persistent store that corresponds to this field, so we create a predicate that identifies the correct object for the field:

```
NSFetchRequest *request = [[NSFetchRequest alloc]
                          initWithEntityName:kLineEntityName];
NSPredicate *pred = [NSPredicate
                    predicateWithFormat:@"(%K = %d)", kLineNumberKey, i];
[request setPredicate:pred];
```

Now we execute the fetch request against the context and check to make sure that objects is not nil. If it is nil, there was an error, and we should do whatever error checking is appropriate for our application. For this simple application, we're just logging the error and moving on:

```
NSArray *objects = [context executeFetchRequest:request error:&error];
if (objects == nil) {
    NSLog(@"There was an error!");
    // Do whatever error handling is appropriate
}
```

After that, we declare a pointer to an NSManagedObject and set it to nil. We do this because we don't know yet whether we're going to get a managed object from the persistent store or create a new one. To know this, we check if an object that matched our criteria was returned. If there is one, we load it. If there isn't one, we create a new managed object to hold this field's text:

```
NSManagedObject *theLine = nil;
if ([objects count] > 0) {
    theLine = [objects objectAtIndex:0];
} else {
    theLine = [NSEntityDescription
                insertNewObjectForEntityForName:kLineEntityName
                inManagedObjectContext:context];
}
```

Next, we use key-value coding to set the line number and text for this managed object:

```
        [theLine setValue:[NSNumber numberWithInt:i] forKey:kLineNumberKey];
        [theLine setValue:theField.text forKey:kLineTextKey];
```

Finally, once we're finished looping, we tell the context to save its changes:

```
        [appDelegate saveContext];
```

Making the Persistence View Controller the Application's Root Controller

Because we used the Empty Application template instead of the Single View Application template, we have one more step to take before our fancy new Core Data application will work. We need to create an instance of BIDViewController to act as our application's root controller and add its view as a subview of our application's main window. Let's do that now.

To make the root controller's view a subview of the application's window so that the user can interact with it, switch to *BIDAppDelegate.m* and make the following changes at the top of that file:

```
#import "BIDAppDelegate.h"
#import "BIDViewController.h"

@implementation BIDAppDelegate

@synthesize managedObjectContext = _managedObjectContext;
@synthesize managedObjectModel = _managedObjectModel;
@synthesize persistentStoreCoordinator = _persistentStoreCoordinator;

- (BOOL)application:(UIApplication *)application
    didFinishLaunchingWithOptions:(NSDictionary *)launchOptions
{
    self.window = [[UIWindow alloc] initWithFrame:[[UIScreen mainScreen] bounds]];
    // Override point for customization after application launch.
    BIDViewController *controller = [[BIDViewController alloc] init];
    self.window.rootViewController = controller;
```

```
    self.window.backgroundColor = [UIColor whiteColor];
    [self.window makeKeyAndVisible];
    return YES;
}
.
.
.
```

That's it! Build and run the app to make sure it works. The Core Data version of your application should behave exactly the same as the previous versions.

It may seem that Core Data entails a lot of work; and, for a simple application like this, it doesn't offer much of an advantage. But in more complex applications, Core Data can substantially decrease the amount of time you spend designing and writing your data model.

Persistence Rewarded

You should now have a solid handle on four different ways of preserving your application data between sessions—five ways if you include the user defaults that you learned how to use in the previous chapter. We built an application that persisted data using property lists and modified the application to save its data using object archives. We then made a change and used the iOS's built-in SQLite3 mechanism to save the application data. Finally, we rebuilt the same application using Core Data. These mechanisms are the basic building blocks for saving and loading data in almost all iOS applications.

Documents and iCloud

One of the biggest new features added to iOS in the past couple of years is Apple's iCloud service, which provides cloud storage services for iOS devices, as well as for computers running OS X. Most iOS users will probably encounter the iCloud device backup option immediately when setting up a new device or upgrading an old device to a more recent version of iOS. And they will quickly discover the advantages of automatic backup that doesn't even require the use of a computer.

Computerless backup is a great feature, but it only scratches the surface of what iCloud can do. What may be even a bigger feature of iCloud is that it provides app developers with a mechanism for transparently saving data to Apple's cloud servers with very little effort. You can make your apps save data to iCloud and have that data automatically transfer to any other devices that are registered to the same iCloud user. Users may create a document on their iPad and later view the same document on their iPhone or Mac without any intervening steps; the document just appears.

A system process takes care of making sure the user has a valid iCloud login and manages the file transfers, so you don't need to worry about networks or authentication. Apart from a small amount of app configuration, just a few small changes to your methods for saving files and locating available files will get you well on your way to having an iCloud–backed app.

One key component of the iCloud filing system is the UIDocument class. UIDocument takes a portion of the work out of creating a document-based app by handling some of the common aspects of reading and writing files. That way, you can spend more of your time focusing on the unique features of your app, instead of building the same plumbing for every app you create.

Whether you're using iCloud or not, UIDocument provides some powerful tools for managing document files in iOS. To demonstrate these features, the first portion of this chapter is dedicated to creating TinyPix, a simple document-based app that saves files to local storage. This is an approach that can work well for all kinds of iOS-based apps.

Later in this chapter, we'll show you how to iCloud-enable TinyPix. For that to work, you'll need to have one or more iCloud-connected iOS devices at hand. You'll also need a paid iOS developer account, so that you can install on devices. This is because apps running in the simulator don't have access to iCloud services.

Managing Document Storage With UIDocument

Anyone who has used a desktop computer for anything besides just surfing the Web has probably worked with a document-based application. From TextEdit to Microsoft Word to GarageBand to Xcode, any piece of software that lets you deal with multiple collections of data, saving each collection to a separate file, could be considered a document-based application. Often, there's a one-to-one correspondence between an on-screen window and the document it contains; however, sometimes (e.g., Xcode) a single window can display multiple documents that are all related in some way.

On iOS devices, we don't have the luxury of multiple windows, but plenty of apps can still benefit from a document-based approach. Now iOS developers have a little boost in making it work thanks to the UIDocument class, which takes care of the most common aspects of document file storage. You won't need to deal with files directly (just URLs), and all the necessary reading and writing happens on a background thread, so your app can remain responsive even while file access is occurring. It also automatically saves edited documents periodically and whenever the app is suspended (such as when the device is shut down, the home button is pressed, and so on), so there's no need for any sort of save button. All of this helps make your apps behave the way users expect their iOS apps to behave.

Building TinyPix

We're going to build an app called TinyPix that lets you edit simple 8 × 8 images, in glorious 1-bit color (see Figure 14-1)! For the user's convenience, each picture is blown up to the full screen size for editing. And, of course, we'll be using UIDocument to represent the data for each image.

Figure 14-1. Editing an extremely low-resolution icon in TinyPix

Start off by creating a new project in Xcode. From the *iOS Application* section, select the *Master-Detail Application* template, and then click *Next*. Name this new app *TinyPix* and set the *Devices* pop-up to *iPhone*. Make sure the *Use Core Data* checkbox is unchecked. Now click *Next* again and choose the location to save your project.

In Xcode's project navigator, you'll see that your project contains files for BIDAppDelegate, BIDMasterViewController, and BIDDetailViewController, as well as the *Main.storyboard* file. We'll make changes to most of these files to some extent, and we will create a few new classes along the way, as well.

Creating BIDTinyPixDocument

The first new class we're going to create is the document class that will contain the data for each TinyPix image that's loaded from file storage. Select the *TinyPix* folder in Xcode and press ⌘N to create a new file. From the *iOS Cocoa Touch* section, select *Objective-C class* and click *Next*. Enter *BIDTinyPixDocument* in the *Class* field, enter *UIDocument* in the *Subclass of* field, and click *Next*. Finally, click *Create* to create the files.

Let's think about the public API of this class before we get into its implementation details. This class is going to represent an 8 × 8 grid of pixels, where each pixel consists of a single on or off value. So, let's give it a method that takes a pair of row and column indexes and returns a BOOL value. Let's also provide a method to set a specific state at a specified row and column and, as a convenience, another method that simply toggles the state at a particular place.

Select *BIDTinyPixDocument.h* to edit the new class's header. Add the following bold lines:

```
#import <UIKit/UIKit.h>

@interface BIDTinyPixDocument : UIDocument

// row and column range from 0 to 7
- (BOOL)stateAtRow:(NSUInteger)row column:(NSUInteger)column;
- (void)setState:(BOOL)state atRow:(NSUInteger)row column:(NSUInteger)column;
- (void)toggleStateAtRow:(NSUInteger)row column:(NSUInteger)column;

@end
```

Now switch over to *BIDTinyPixDocument.m*, where we'll implement storage for our 8 × 8 grid, the methods defined in our public API, and the required UIDocument methods that will enable loading and saving our documents.

Let's start by defining the storage for our 8 × 8 bitmap data. We'll hold this data in an instance of NSMutableData, which lets us work directly with an array of byte data that is still contained inside an object, so that the usual Cocoa memory management will take care of freeing the memory when we're finished with it. Add this class extension to make it happen:

```
#import "BIDTinyPixDocument.h"

@interface BIDTinyPixDocument ()
@property (strong, nonatomic) NSMutableData *bitmap;
@end

@implementation BIDTinyPixDocument
```

The UIDocument class has a designated initializer that all subclasses should use. This is where we'll create our initial bitmap. In true bitmap style, we're going to minimize memory usage by using a single byte to contain each row. Each bit in the byte represents the on/off value of a column index within that row. In total, our document contains just 8 bytes.

Note   This section contains a small amount of bitwise operations, as well as some C pointer and array manipulation. This is all pretty mundane for C developers; but if you don't have much C experience, it may seem puzzling or even impenetrable. In that case, feel free to simply copy and use the code provided (it works just fine). If you really want to understand what's going on, you may want to dig deeper into C itself, perhaps by adding a copy of *Learn C on the Mac* by Dave Mark (Apress, 2009) to your bookshelf.

Add this method to our document's implementation, placing it directly above the @end at the bottom of the file:

```
- (id)initWithFileURL:(NSURL *)url {
    self = [super initWithFileURL:url];
    if (self) {
        unsigned char startPattern[] = {
            0x01,
            0x02,
            0x04,
            0x08,
            0x10,
            0x20,
            0x40,
            0x80
        };

        self.bitmap = [NSMutableData dataWithBytes:startPattern length:8];
    }
    return self;
}
```

This starts off each bitmap with a simple diagonal pattern stretching from one corner to another.

Now, it's time to implement the methods that make up the public API we defined in the header. Let's tackle the method for reading the state of a single bit first. This simply grabs the relevant byte from our array of bytes, and then does a bit shift and an AND operation to determine whether the specified bit was set, returning YES or NO accordingly. Add this method above the @end:

```
- (BOOL)stateAtRow:(NSUInteger)row column:(NSUInteger)column {
    const char *bitmapBytes = [self.bitmap bytes];
    char rowByte = bitmapBytes[row];
    char result = (1 << column) & rowByte;
    if (result != 0) {
        return YES;
    } else {
        return NO;
    }
}
```

Next comes the inverse: a method that sets the value specified at a given row and column. Here, we once again grab a pointer to the relevant byte for the specified row and do a bit shift. But this time, instead of using the shifted bit to examine the contents of the row, we use it to either set or unset a bit in the row. Add this method above the @end:

```
- (void)setState:(BOOL)state atRow:(NSUInteger)row column:(NSUInteger)column {
    char *bitmapBytes = [self.bitmap mutableBytes];
    char *rowByte = &bitmapBytes[row];

    if (state) {
        *rowByte = *rowByte | (1 << column);
```

```
    } else {
        *rowByte = *rowByte & ~(1 << column);
    }
}
```

Now, let's add the convenience method, which lets outside code simply toggle a single cell. Add this method above the @end:

```
- (void)toggleStateAtRow:(NSUInteger)row column:(NSUInteger)column {
    BOOL state = [self stateAtRow:row column:column];
    [self setState:!state atRow:row column:column];
}
```

Our document class requires two final pieces before it fits into the puzzle of a document-based app: methods for reading and writing. As we mentioned earlier, you don't need to deal with files directly. You don't even need to worry about the URL that was passed into the initWithFileURL: method earlier. All that you need to do is implement one method that transforms the document's data structure into an NSData object, ready for saving, and another that takes a freshly loaded NSData object and pulls the object's data structure out of it. Because our document's internal structure is already contained in an NSMutableData object, which is a subclass of NSData, these implementations are pleasingly simple. Add these two methods above the @end:

```
- (id)contentsForType:(NSString *)typeName error:(NSError **)outError {
    NSLog(@"saving document to URL %@", self.fileURL);
    return [self.bitmap copy];
}
```

```
- (BOOL)loadFromContents:(id)contents ofType:(NSString *)typeName
        error:(NSError **)outError {
    NSLog(@"loading document from URL %@", self.fileURL);
    self.bitmap = [contents mutableCopy];
    return true;
}
```

The first of these methods, contentsForType:error:, is called whenever our document is about to be saved to storage. It simply returns an immutable copy of our bitmap data, which the system will take care of storing later.

The second method, loadFromContents:ofType:error:, is called whenever the system has just loaded data from storage and wants to provide this data to an instance of our document class. Here, we just grab a mutable copy of the data that has been passed in. We've included some logging statements, just so you can see what's happening in the Xcode log later on.

Each of these methods allows you to do some things that we're ignoring in this app. They both provide a typeName parameter, which you could use to distinguish between different types of data storage that your document can load from or save to. They also have an outError parameter, which you could use to specify that an error occurred while copying data to or from your document's in-memory data structure. In our case, however, what we're doing is so simple that these aren't important concerns.

That's all we need for our document class. Sticking to MVC principles, our document sits squarely in the model camp, knowing nothing about how it's displayed. And thanks to the UIDocument superclass, the document is even shielded from most of the details about how it's stored.

Code Master

Now that we have our document class ready to go, it's time to address the first view that a user sees when running our app: the list of existing TinyPix documents, which is taken care of by the BIDMasterViewController class. We need to let this class know how to grab the list of available documents, let the user choose an existing document for viewing or editing, and create and name a new document. When a document is created or chosen, it's then passed along to the detail controller for display.

Start by selecting *BIDMasterViewController.m*. This file, generated as part of the Master–Detail application template, contains starter code for displaying an array of items. We're not going to use any of that, but instead do these things all on our own. Therefore, delete all the methods from the @implementation block and all the declarations in the class extension at the top. When you're done, you should have a clean slate that looks something like this:

```
#import "BIDMasterViewController.h"
#import "BIDDetailViewController.h"

@interface BIDMasterViewController ()
@end

@implementation BIDMasterViewController
@end
```

We'll also include a segmented control in our GUI, which will allow the user to choose a tint color that will be used as a highlight color for portions of the TinyPix GUI. Although this is not a particularly useful feature in and of itself, it will help demonstrate the iCloud mechanism, as the highlight color setting makes its way from the device on which you set it to another of your connected devices running the same app. The first version of the app will use the color as a local setting on each device. Later in the chapter, we'll add the code to make the color setting propagate through iCloud to the user's other devices.

To implement the color selection control, we'll add an outlet and an action to our code as well. We'll also add properties for holding onto a list of document filenames and a pointer to the document the user has chosen. Make these changes to *BIDMasterViewController.m*:

```
#import "BIDMasterViewController.h"
#import "BIDDetailViewController.h"
#import "BIDTinyPixDocument.h"

@interface BIDMasterViewController () <UIAlertViewDelegate>

@property (weak, nonatomic) IBOutlet UISegmentedControl *colorControl;
@property (strong, nonatomic) NSArray *documentFilenames;
@property (strong, nonatomic) BIDTinyPixDocument *chosenDocument;

@end
    .
    .
    .
```

Before we implement the table view methods and other standard methods we need to deal with, we are going to write a couple of private utility methods. The first of these takes a file name, combines it with the file path of the app's *Documents* directory, and returns a URL pointing to that specific file. The *Documents* directory is a special location that iOS sets aside, one for each app installed on an iOS device. You can use it to store documents created by your app, and rest assured that those documents will be automatically included whenever users back up their iOS device, whether it's to iTunes or iCloud.

Add this method to the implementation, placing it directly above the @end at the bottom of the file:

```
- (NSURL *)urlForFilename:(NSString *)filename {
    NSFileManager *fm = [NSFileManager defaultManager];
    NSArray *urls = [fm URLsForDirectory:NSDocumentDirectory
                                inDomains:NSUserDomainMask];
    NSURL *directoryURL = urls[0];
    NSURL *fileURL = [directoryURL URLByAppendingPathComponent:filename];
    return fileURL;
}
```

The second private method is a bit longer. It also uses the *Documents* directory, this time to search for files representing existing documents. The method takes the files it finds and sorts them by creation date, so that the user will see the list of documents sorted "blog-style" with the newest items first. The document file names are stashed away in the documentFilenames property, and then the table view (which we admittedly haven't yet dealt with) is reloaded. Add this method above the @end:

```
- (void)reloadFiles {
    NSArray *paths = NSSearchPathForDirectoriesInDomains(NSDocumentDirectory,
        NSUserDomainMask, YES);
    NSString *path = paths[0];
    NSFileManager *fm = [NSFileManager defaultManager];

    NSError *dirError;
    NSArray *files = [fm contentsOfDirectoryAtPath:path error:&dirError];
    if (!files) {
        NSLog(@"Error listing files in directory %@: %@",
            path, dirError);
    }
    NSLog(@"found files: %@", files);

    files = [files sortedArrayUsingComparator:
            ^NSComparisonResult(id filename1, id filename2) {
        NSDictionary *attr1 = [fm attributesOfItemAtPath:
                            [path stringByAppendingPathComponent:filename1]
                                                error:nil];
        NSDictionary *attr2 = [fm attributesOfItemAtPath:
                            [path stringByAppendingPathComponent:filename2]
                                                error:nil];
        return [attr2[NSFileCreationDate] compare: attr1[NSFileCreationDate]];
    }];
    self.documentFilenames = files;
    [self.tableView reloadData];
}
```

Now, let's deal with our dear old friends, the table view data source methods. These should be pretty familiar to you by now. Add the following three methods above the @end:

```
- (NSInteger)numberOfSectionsInTableView:(UITableView *)tableView {
    return 1;
}

- (NSInteger)tableView:(UITableView *)tableView
        numberOfRowsInSection:(NSInteger)section {
    return [self.documentFilenames count];
}

- (UITableViewCell *)tableView:(UITableView *)tableView
        cellForRowAtIndexPath:(NSIndexPath *)indexPath {
    UITableViewCell *cell = [tableView dequeueReusableCellWithIdentifier:
                                @"FileCell"];

    NSString *path = self.documentFilenames[indexPath.row];
    cell.textLabel.text = path.lastPathComponent.stringByDeletingPathExtension;
    return cell;
}
```

These methods are based on the contents of the array stored in the documentFilenames property. The tableView:cellForForAtIndexPath: method relies on the existence of a cell attached to the table view with "FileCell" set as its identifier, so we must be sure to set that up in the storyboard a little later.

If not for the fact that we haven't touched our storyboard yet, the code we have now would almost be something we could run and see in action; however, with no pre-existing TinyPix documents, we would have nothing to display in our table view. And so far, we don't have any way to create new documents, either. Also, we have not yet dealt with the color-selection control we're going to add. So, let's do a bit more work before we try to run our app.

The user's choice of highlight color will be used to immediately set a tint color for the app. This is a new feature of iOS 7 that lets you define the highlight color for portions of your app or the entire app at once. The UIView class has a tintColor property; and when it's set for any view, the value will propagate down to all subviews. That means that, by setting the value on the app's UIWindow (each app has just one), every subview in the app will get the same value.

At the same time, we'll store the value in NSUserDefaults for later retrieval. Here's the action method that will do that by passing along the segmented control's chosen index, along with a method that actually sets the color in the uppermost view. Add these methods above the @end:

```
- (IBAction)chooseColor:(id)sender {
    NSInteger selectedColorIndex = [(UISegmentedControl *)sender
                                    selectedSegmentIndex];
    [self setTintColorForIndex:selectedColorIndex];

    NSUserDefaults *prefs = [NSUserDefaults standardUserDefaults];
    [prefs setInteger:selectedColorIndex forKey:@"selectedColorIndex"];
    [prefs synchronize];
}
```

```
- (void)setTintColorForIndex:(NSInteger)selectedColorIndex {
    switch (selectedColorIndex) {
        case 0:
            self.view.window.tintColor = [UIColor redColor];
            break;
        case 1:
            self.view.window.tintColor = [UIColor colorWithRed:0
                                                          green:0.6
                                                           blue:0
                                                          alpha:1];
            break;
        case 2:
            self.view.window.tintColor = [UIColor blueColor];
            break;
        default:
            break;
    }
}
```

We realize that we haven't yet set this up in the storyboard, but we'll get there! We'll also need a method to make sure that the segmented control in our app's GUI will show the current tint color value from NSUserDefaults as soon as it's about to be displayed. The best place to put this is in viewDidAppear: because, when that method is called, our view is already in its window. This means we can access the top-level object to set the color:

```
- (void)viewDidAppear:(BOOL)animated {
    [super viewDidAppear:animated];

    NSUserDefaults *prefs = [NSUserDefaults standardUserDefaults];
    NSInteger selectedColorIndex = [prefs integerForKey:@"selectedColorIndex"];
    [self setTintColorForIndex:selectedColorIndex];
    [self.colorControl setSelectedSegmentIndex:selectedColorIndex];
}
```

Now let's create a new viewDidLoad method. After calling the superclass's implementation, we'll start by adding a button to the right side of the navigation bar. The user will press this button to create a new TinyPix document. We finish by calling the reloadFiles method that we implemented earlier. Make this change to viewDidLoad:

```
- (void)viewDidLoad
{
    [super viewDidLoad];

    UIBarButtonItem *addButton = [[UIBarButtonItem alloc]
        initWithBarButtonSystemItem:UIBarButtonSystemItemAdd
        target:self
        action:@selector(insertNewObject)];
    self.navigationItem.rightBarButtonItem = addButton;

    [self reloadFiles];
}
```

You may have noticed that, when we created the UIBarButtonItem in this method, we told it to call the insertNewObject method when it's pressed. We haven't written that method yet, so let's do so now. Add this method above the @end:

```
- (void)insertNewObject {
    // get the name
    UIAlertView *alert =
    [[UIAlertView alloc] initWithTitle:@"Filename"
                                message:
     @"Enter a name for your new TinyPix document."
                               delegate:self
                      cancelButtonTitle:@"Cancel"
                      otherButtonTitles:@"Create", nil];
    alert.alertViewStyle = UIAlertViewStylePlainTextInput;
    [alert show];
}
```

This method creates an alert panel that includes a text-input field and displays it. The responsibility of creating a new item instead falls to the delegate method that the alert view calls when it's finished, which we'll also address now. Add this method above the @end:

```
- (void)alertView:(UIAlertView *)alertView
        didDismissWithButtonIndex:(NSInteger)buttonIndex {
    if (buttonIndex == 1) {
        NSString *filename = [NSString stringWithFormat:@"%@.tinypix",
                              [alertView textFieldAtIndex:0].text];
        NSURL *saveUrl = [self urlForFilename:filename];
        self.chosenDocument = [[BIDTinyPixDocument alloc]
                               initWithFileURL:saveUrl];
        [self.chosenDocument saveToURL:saveUrl
                      forSaveOperation:UIDocumentSaveForCreating
                     completionHandler:^(BOOL success) {
                         if (success) {
                             NSLog(@"save OK");
                             [self reloadFiles];
                             [self performSegueWithIdentifier:@"masterToDetail"
                                                       sender:self];
                         } else {
                             NSLog(@"failed to save!");
                         }
                     }];
    }
}
```

This method starts out simply enough. It checks the value of buttonIndex to see which button was pressed (a "0" indicates that the user pressed the *Cancel* button). It then creates a file name based on the user's entry, a URL based on that file name (using the urlForFilename: method we wrote earlier), and a new BIDTinyPixDocument instance using that URL.

What comes next is a little more subtle. It's important to understand here that just creating a new document with a given URL doesn't create the file. In fact, at the time that the `initWithFileURL:` is called, the document doesn't yet know if the given URL refers to an existing file or to a new file that needs to be created. We need to tell it what to do. In this case, we tell it to save a new file at the given URL with this code:

```
[self.chosenDocument saveToURL:saveUrl
            forSaveOperation:UIDocumentSaveForCreating
            completionHandler:^(BOOL success) {
    .
    .
    .

    }];
```

Of interest is the purpose and usage of the block that is passed in as the last argument. The method we're calling, `saveToURL:forSaveOperation:completionHandler:`, doesn't have a return value to tell us how it all worked out. In fact, the method returns immediately after it's called, long before the file is actually saved. Instead, it starts the file-saving work and later, when it's done, calls the block that we gave it, using the `success` parameter to let us know whether it succeeded. To make it all work as smoothly as possible, the file-saving work is actually performed on a background thread. The block we pass in, however, is executed on the thread that called `saveToURL:forSaveOperation:completionHandler:` in the first place. In this particular case, that means that the block is executed on the main thread, so we can safely use any facilities that require the main thread, such as UIKit. With that in mind, take a look again at what happens inside that block:

```
if (success) {
    NSLog(@"save OK");
    [self reloadFiles];
    [self performSegueWithIdentifier:@"masterToDetail" sender:self];
} else {
    NSLog(@"failed to save!");
}
```

This is the content of the block we passed in to the file-saving method, and it's called later, after the file operation is completed. We check to see if it succeeded; if so, we do an immediate file reload, and then initiate a segue to another view controller. This is an aspect of segues that we didn't cover in Chapter 10, but it's pretty straightforward.

The idea is that a segue in a storyboard file can have an identifier, just like a table view cell, and you can use that identifier to trigger a segue programmatically. In this case, we'll just need to remember to configure that segue in the storyboard when we get to it. But before we do that, let's add the last method this class needs, to take care of that segue. Insert this method above the @end:

```
- (void)prepareForSegue:(UIStoryboardSegue *)segue sender:(id)sender {
    if (sender == self) {
        // if sender == self, a new document has just been created,
        // and chosenDocument is already set.
```

```objc
        UIViewController *destination = segue.destinationViewController;
        if ([destination respondsToSelector:@selector(setDetailItem:)]) {
            [destination setValue:self.chosenDocument forKey:@"detailItem"];
        }
    } else {
        // find the chosen document from the tableview
        NSIndexPath *indexPath = [self.tableView indexPathForSelectedRow];
        NSString *filename = self.documentFilenames[indexPath.row];
        NSURL *docUrl = [self urlForFilename:filename];
        self.chosenDocument = [[BIDTinyPixDocument alloc]
                                initWithFileURL:docUrl];
        [self.chosenDocument openWithCompletionHandler:^(BOOL success) {
            if (success) {
                NSLog(@"load OK");
                UIViewController *destination = segue.destinationViewController;
                if ([destination respondsToSelector:@selector(setDetailItem:)]) {
                    [destination setValue:self.chosenDocument
                                   forKey:@"detailItem"];
                }
            } else {
                NSLog(@"failed to load!");
            }
        }];
    }
}
```

This method has two clear paths of execution that are determined by the condition at the top. Remember from our discussion of storyboards in Chapter 10 that this method is called on a view controller whenever a new controller is about to be pushed onto the navigation stack. The sender parameter points out the object that initiated the segue, and we use that to figure out just what to do here. If the segue is initiated by the programmatic method call we performed in the alert view delegate method, then sender will be equal to itself. In that case, we know that the chosenDocument property is already set, and we simply pass its value to the destination view controller.

Otherwise, we know we're responding to the user touching a row in the table view, and that's where things get a little more complicated. That's the time to construct a URL (much as we did when creating a document), create a new instance of our document class, and try to open the file. You'll see that the method we call to open the file, openWithCompletionHandler:, works similarly to the save method we used earlier. We pass it a block that it will save for later execution. Just as with the file-saving method, the loading occurs in the background, and this block will be executed on the main thread when it's complete. At that point, if the loading succeeded, we pass the document along to the detail view controller.

Note that both of these methods use the key-value coding technique that we've used a few times before, letting us set the detailItem property of the segue's destination controller, even though we don't include its header. This will work out just fine for us, since BIDDetailViewController—the detail view controller class created as part of the Xcode project—happens to include a property called detailItem right out of the box.

With the amount of code we now have in place, it's high time we configure the storyboard, so that we can run our app and make something happen. Save your code and continue.

Initial Storyboarding

Select *Main.storyboard* in the Xcode project navigator and take a look at what's already there. You'll find scenes for the navigation controller, the master view controller, and the detail view controller (see Figure 14-2). You can ignore the navigation controller entirely, since all our work will be with the other two.

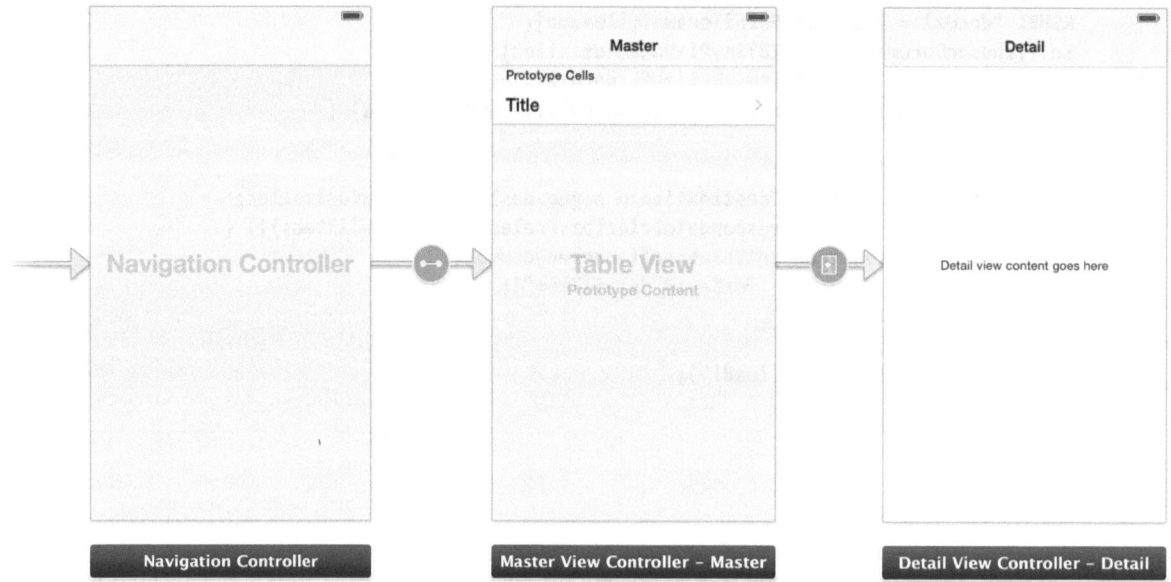

Figure 14-2. The TinyPix storyboard, showing the navigation controller, master view controller, and detail view controller

Let's start by dealing with the master view controller scene. This is where the table view showing the list of all our TinyPix documents is configured. By default, this scene's table view is configured to use dynamic cells instead of static cells (*see* Chapter 10 if you need a refresher on the difference between these two cell types). We want our table view to get its contents from the data source methods we implemented, so this default setting is just what we want. We do need to configure the cell prototype though, so select it and open the attributes inspector. Set the cell's *Identifier* to *FileCell*. This will let the data source code we wrote earlier access the table view cell.

We also need to create the segue that we're triggering in our code. Do this by control-dragging from the master detail view controller's icon (an orange circle at the bottom of its scene or the *Master View Controller - Master* icon in the dock) over to the detail view controller, and then selecting *Push* from the storyboard segues menu.

You'll now see two segues that seem to connect the two scenes. By selecting each of them, you can tell where they're coming from. Selecting one segue highlights the whole master scene; selecting the second one highlights just the table view cell. Select the segue that highlights the whole scene, and use the attributes inspector to set its *Identifier* to *masterToDetail*.

The final touch needed for the master view controller scene is to let the user pick which color will be used to represent an "on" point in the detail view. Instead of implementing some kind of comprehensive color picker, we're just going to add a segmented control that will let the user pick from a set of predefined colors.

Find a *Segmented Control* in the object library, drag it out, and place it in the navigation bar at the top of the master view (see Figure 14-3).

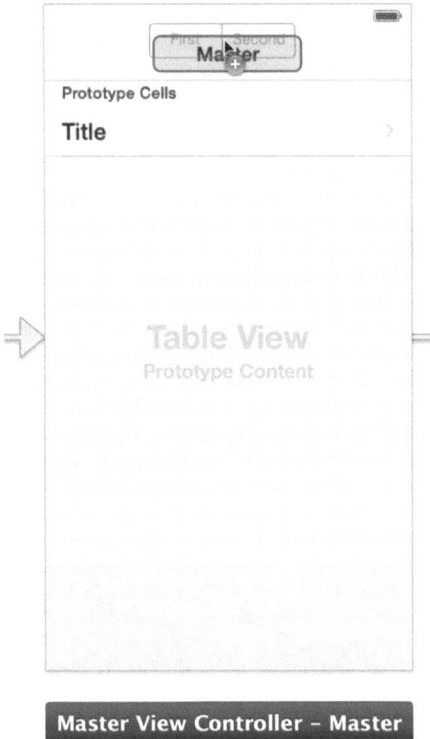

Figure 14-3. *The TinyPix storyboard, showing the master view controller with a segmented control being dropped on the controller's navigation bar*

Make sure the segmented control is selected and open the attributes inspector. In the *Segmented Control* section at the top of the inspector, use the stepper control to change the number of *Segments* from 2 to 3. Next, double-click the title of each segment in turn, changing them to *Red*, *Green*, and *Blue*, respectively. After setting those titles, click one of the resizing handles for the segmented control to make it fill out to the right width.

Next, control-drag from the segmented control to the icon representing the master controller (the orange circle below the controller or the dock icon labeled *Master View Controller – Master*) and select the *chooseColor:* method. Then control-drag from the master controller back to the segmented control, and select the *colorControl* outlet.

We've finally reached a point where we can run the app and see all our hard work brought to life! Run your app. You'll see it start up and display an empty table view with a segmented control at the top and a plus button in the upper-right corner (see Figure 14-4).

Figure 14-4. The TinyPix app when it first appears. Click the plus icon to add a new document. You'll be prompted to name your new TinyPix document. At the moment, all the detail view does is display the document name in a label

Hit the plus button, and the app will ask you to name the new document. Give it a name, tap *Create*, and you'll see the app transition to the detail display, which is, well, under construction right now. All the default implementation of the detail view controller does is display the description of its detailItem in a label. Of course, there's more information in the console pane. It's not much, but it's something!

Tap the back button to return to the master list, where you'll see the item you added. Go ahead and create one or two more items to see that they're correctly added to the list. Finally, head back to Xcode because we've got more work to do!

Creating BIDTinyPixView

Our next order of business is the creation of a view class to display our grid and let the user edit it. Select the *TinyPix* folder in the project navigator, and press ⌘N to create a new file. In the *iOS Cocoa Touch* section, select *Objective C class* and click *Next*. Name the new class *BIDTinyPixView* and choose *UIView* in the *Subclass of* popup. Click *Next*, verify that the save location is OK, and click *Create*.

> **Note** The implementation of our view class includes some drawing and touch handling that we haven't covered yet. Rather than bog down this chapter with too many details about these topics, we're just going to quickly show you the code. We'll cover details about drawing with Core Graphics in Chapter 16 and responding to touches and drags in Chapter 18.

Select *BIDTinyPixView.h* and make the following changes:

```
#import <UIKit/UIKit.h>
@class BIDTinyPixDocument;

@interface BIDTinyPixView : UIView

@property (strong, nonatomic) BIDTinyPixDocument *document;

@end
```

All we're doing here is adding a property, so that the controller can pass along the document.

Now switch over to *BIDTinyPixView.m*, where we have some more substantial work ahead of us. Start by adding this class extension at the top of the file:

```
#import "BIDTinyPixView.h"
#import "BIDTinyPixDocument.h"

typedef struct {
    NSUInteger row;
    NSUInteger column;
} GridIndex;

@interface BIDTinyPixView ()

@property (assign, nonatomic) CGSize blockSize;
@property (assign, nonatomic) CGSize gapSize;
@property (assign, nonatomic) GridIndex selectedBlockIndex;

@end
```

```
@implementation BIDTinyPixView
```
•
•
•

Here, we defined a C struct called GridIndex as a handy way to deal with row/column pairs. We also defined a class extension with some properties that we'll need to use later.

The default empty UIView subclass contains an initWithFrame: method, which is really the default initializer for the UIView class. However, since this class is going to be loaded from a storyboard, it will instead be initialized using the initWithCoder: method. We'll implement both of these, making each call a third method that initializes our properties. Make this change to initWithFrame: and add the code just below it:

```
- (id)initWithFrame:(CGRect)frame
{
    self = [super initWithFrame:frame];
    if (self) {
        // Initialization code
        [self commonInit];
    }
    return self;
}

- (id)initWithCoder:(NSCoder *)aDecoder {
    self = [super initWithCoder:aDecoder];
    if (self) {
        [self commonInit];
    }
    return self;
}

- (void)commonInit{
    _blockSize = CGSizeMake(34, 34);
    _gapSize = CGSizeMake(5, 5);
    _selectedBlockIndex.row = NSNotFound;
    _selectedBlockIndex.column = NSNotFound;
}
```

The _blockSize and _gapSize values are specifically tuned to a view that's 310 points across. If we wanted to be extra clever here, we could have defined them dynamically based on the view's actual frame; however, this is the simplest approach that works for our case, so we're sticking with it!

Now let's take a look at the drawing routines. We override the standard UIView drawRect: method, use that to simply walk through all the blocks in our grid, and then call another method for each block. Add the following bold code and don't forget to remove the comment marks around the drawRect: method:

```
/*
// Only override drawRect: if you perform custom drawing.
// An empty implementation adversely affects performance during animation.
- (void)drawRect:(CGRect)rect
{
    // Drawing code
    if (!_document) return;

    for (NSUInteger row = 0; row < 8; row++) {
        for (NSUInteger column = 0; column < 8; column++) {
            [self drawBlockAtRow:row column:column];
        }
    }
}
*/


- (void)drawBlockAtRow:(NSUInteger)row column:(NSUInteger)column {
    CGFloat startX = (_blockSize.width + _gapSize.width) * (7 - column) + 1;
    CGFloat startY = (_blockSize.height + _gapSize.height) * row + 1;
    CGRect blockFrame = CGRectMake(startX, startY,
                                     _blockSize.width, _blockSize.height);
    UIColor *color = [_document stateAtRow:row column:column] ?
        [UIColor blackColor] : [UIColor whiteColor];
    [color setFill];
    [self.tintColor setStroke];
    UIBezierPath *path = [UIBezierPath bezierPathWithRect:blockFrame];
    [path fill];
    [path stroke];
}
```

Finally, we add a set of methods that respond to touch events by the user. Both touchesBegan:withEvent: and touchesMoved:withEvent: are standard methods that every UIView subclass can implement to capture touch events that happen within the view's frame. These two methods use other methods we're adding here: to calculate a grid location based on a touch location and to toggle a specific value in the document. Add these four methods at the bottom of the file, just above the @end:

```
- (GridIndex)touchedGridIndexFromTouches:(NSSet *)touches {
    GridIndex result;
    UITouch *touch = [touches anyObject];
    CGPoint location = [touch locationInView:self];
    result.column = 8 - (location.x * 8.0 / self.bounds.size.width);
    result.row = location.y * 8.0 / self.bounds.size.height;
    return result;
}


- (void)toggleSelectedBlock {
    [_document toggleStateAtRow:_selectedBlockIndex.row
                         column:_selectedBlockIndex.column];
    [[_document.undoManager prepareWithInvocationTarget:_document]
     toggleStateAtRow:_selectedBlockIndex.row column:_selectedBlockIndex.column];
    [self setNeedsDisplay];
}
```

```
- (void)touchesBegan:(NSSet *)touches withEvent:(UIEvent *)event {
    self.selectedBlockIndex = [self touchedGridIndexFromTouches:touches];
    [self toggleSelectedBlock];
}

- (void)touchesMoved:(NSSet *)touches withEvent:(UIEvent *)event {
    GridIndex touched = [self touchedGridIndexFromTouches:touches];
    if (touched.row != _selectedBlockIndex.row
        || touched.column != _selectedBlockIndex.column) {
        _selectedBlockIndex = touched;
        [self toggleSelectedBlock];
    }
}
```

Sharp-eyed readers may have noticed that the `toggleSelectedBlock` method does something a bit special. After calling the document's `toggleStateAtRow:column:` method to change the value of a particular grid point, it does something more. Let's take another look:

```
- (void)toggleSelectedBlock {
    [_document toggleStateAtRow:_selectedBlockIndex.row
                         column:_selectedBlockIndex.column];
    [[_document.undoManager prepareWithInvocationTarget:_document]
     toggleStateAtRow:_selectedBlockIndex.row column:_selectedBlockIndex.column];
    [self setNeedsDisplay];

}
```

The call to `_document.undoManager` returns an instance of NSUndoManager. We haven't dealt with this directly anywhere else in this book, but NSUndoManager is the structural underpinning for the undo/redo functionality in both iOS and Mac OS X. The idea is that anytime the user performs an action in the GUI, you use NSUndoManager to leave a sort of breadcrumb by "recording" a method call that will undo what the user just did. NSUndoManager will store that method call on a special undo stack, which can be used to backtrack through a document's state whenever the user activates the system's undo functionality.

The way it works is that the `prepareWithInvocationTarget:` method returns a special kind of proxy object to which you can send any message, and the message will be packed up with the target and pushed onto the undo stack. So, while it may look like you're calling `toggleStateAtRow:column:` twice in a row, the second time it's not being called but instead is just being queued up for later potential use. This kind of spectacularly dynamic behavior is an area where Objective-C really stands out in comparison to static languages such as C++, where techniques such as letting one object act as a proxy to another or packing up a method invocation for later use have no language support and are nearly impossible (and therefore many tasks, such as building undo support, can be quite tedious).

So, why are we doing this? We haven't been giving any thought to undo/redo issues up to this point, so why now? The reason is that registering an undoable action with the document's `undoManager` marks the document as "dirty" and ensures that it will be saved automatically at some point in the next few seconds. The fact that the user's actions are also undoable is just icing on the cake, at least in this application. In an app with a more complex document structure, allowing document-wide undo support can be hugely beneficial.

Save your changes. Now that our view class is ready to go, let's head back to the storyboard to configure the GUI for the detail view.

Storyboard Detailing

Select *Main.storyboard*, find the detail scene, and take a look at what's there right now.

All the GUI contains is a label ("Detail view content goes here"), which is the one that contained the document's description when you ran the app earlier. That label isn't particularly useful, so select the label in the detail view controller and press the **Delete** key to remove it.

Use the object library to find a *UIView* and drag it into the detail view. Interface Builder will help you line it up so that it fills the entire area. After dropping it there, use the size inspector to set both its width and height to 310. Finally, drag the view and use the guidelines to center it in its container (see Figure 14-5).

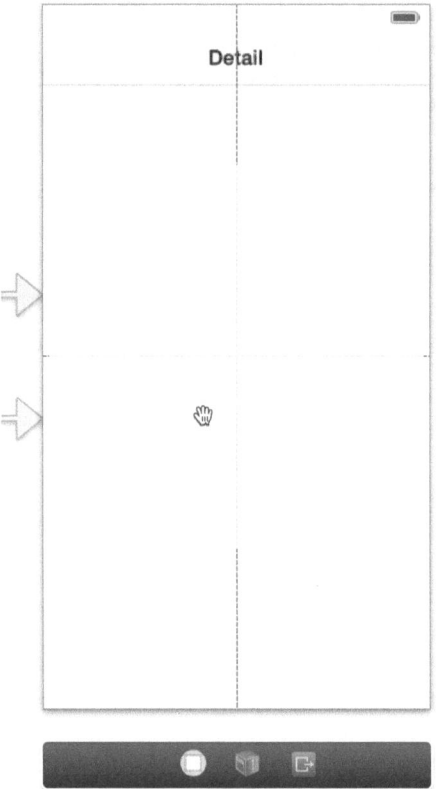

Figure 14-5. We replaced the label in the detail view with another view, 310 × 310 pixels, centered in its containing view. The view becomes somewhat invisible while dragging, but here you can see that it's partly covering the dashed lines that appear when you drag it to the center of the view

Switch over to the identity inspector, so we can change this UIView instance into an instance of our custom class. In the *Custom Class* section at the top of the inspector, select the *Class* pop-up list and choose *BIDTinyPixView*.

Before we go on, we need to adjust the constraints for this new view. We want it to stay centered no matter what the screen size is (so it works well on both the iPhone 4 and iPhone 5 series), but we also want it to maintain its size, as well. So, with the view still selected, click the Align icon at the bottom of the editing area to make its options appear. Click the checkboxes for *Horizontal Center in Container* and *Vertical Center in Container*, and then click the *Add 2 Constraints* button. Next, click the *Pin* icon at the bottom of the editing area to bring up its popup controller. Click the *Width* and *Height* checkboxes, and then click the *Add 2 Constraints* button to make it happen.

Now we need to wire up the custom view to our detail view controller. We haven't prepared an outlet for our custom view yet, but that's OK since Xcode's drag-to-code feature will do that for us.

Activate the assistant editor. A text editor should slide into place alongside the GUI editor, displaying the contents of *BIDDetailViewController.m*. If it's showing you anything else, use the jump bar at the top of the text editor to make *BIDDetailViewController.m* come into view.

To make the connection, control-drag from the *Tiny Pix View* to the code, releasing the drag in the class extension at the top of the file, somewhere around the `configureView` declaration. In the pop-up window that appears, make sure that *Connection* is set to *Outlet*, name the new outlet *pixView*, and click the *Connect* button.

You should see that making those connections has added this line to *BIDDetailViewController.m*:

```
@property (weak, nonatomic) IBOutlet BIDTinyPixView *pixView;
```

One thing it didn't add, however, is any knowledge of our custom view class to the source code. Let's take care of that by adding this line toward the top of *BIDDetailViewController.m*:

```
#import "BIDDetailViewController.h"
#import "BIDTinyPixView.h"

@interface BIDDetailViewController ()
    .
    .
    .
```

Now let's modify the `configureView` method. This isn't a standard `UIViewController` method. It's just a private method that the project template included in this class as a convenient spot to put code that needs to update the view after anything changes. Since we're not using the description label, we delete the line that sets that. Next, we add a bit of code to pass the chosen document along to our custom view and tell it to redraw itself by calling `setNeedsDisplay`:

```
- (void)configureView
{
    // Update the user interface for the detail item.

    if (self.detailItem) {
        self.detailDescriptionLabel.text = [self.detailItem description];
        self.pixView.document = self.detailItem;
        [self.pixView setNeedsDisplay];
    }
}
```

We're nearly finished with this class, but we need to make one more change. Remember when we mentioned the autosaving that takes place when a document is notified that some editing has occurred, triggered by registering an undoable action? The save normally happens within about 10 seconds after the edit occurs. Like the other saving and loading procedures we described earlier in this chapter, it happens in a background thread, so that normally the user won't even notice. However, that works only as long as the document is still around.

With our current set-up, there's a risk that when the user hits the back button to go back to the master list, the document instance will be deallocated without any save operation occurring, and the user's latest changes will be lost. To make sure this doesn't happen, we need to add some code to the viewWillDisappear: method to close the document as soon as the user navigates away from the detail view. Closing a document causes it to be automatically saved, and again, the saving occurs on a background thread. In this particular case, we don't need to do anything when the save is done, so we pass in nil instead of a block:

Add this viewWillDisappear: method:

```
- (void)viewWillDisappear:(BOOL)animated
{
    [super viewWillDisappear:animated];
    UIDocument *doc = self.detailItem;
    [doc closeWithCompletionHandler:nil];
}
```

And with that, this version of our first truly document-based app is ready to try out! Fire it up and bask in the glory. You can create new documents, edit them, flip back to the list, and then select another document (or the same document), and it all just works. If you open the Xcode console while doing this, you'll see some output each time a document is loaded or saved. Using the autosaving system, you don't have direct control over just when saves occur (except for when closing a document), but it can be interesting to watch the logs just to get a feel for when they happen.

Adding iCloud Support

You now have a fully working document-based app, but we're not going to stop here. We promised you iCloud support in this chapter, and it's time to deliver!

Modifying TinyPix to work with iCloud is pretty straightforward. Considering all that's happening behind the scenes, this requires a surprisingly small number of changes. We'll need to make some revisions to the method that loads the list of available files and the method that specifies the URL for loading a new file, but that's about it.

Apart from the code changes, we will also need to deal with some additional administrative details. Apple allows an app to save to iCloud only if it contains an embedded provisioning profile that is configured to allow iCloud usage. This means that to add the iCloud support to our app, you must have a paid iOS developer membership and have installed your developer certificate. It also works only with actual devices, not the simulator, so you'll need to have at least one iOS device registered with iCloud to run the new iCloud-backed TinyPix. With two devices, you'll have even more fun, as you can see how changes made on one device propagate to the other.

Creating a Provisioning Profile

First, you need to create an iCloud-enabled provisioning profile for TinyPix. This used to require a lot of convoluted steps on Apple's developer website, but Xcode 5 makes this easy. In the project navigator, select the TinyPix item at the top, and then click the Capabilities tab in the editing area. You should see something like what's shown in Figure 14-6.

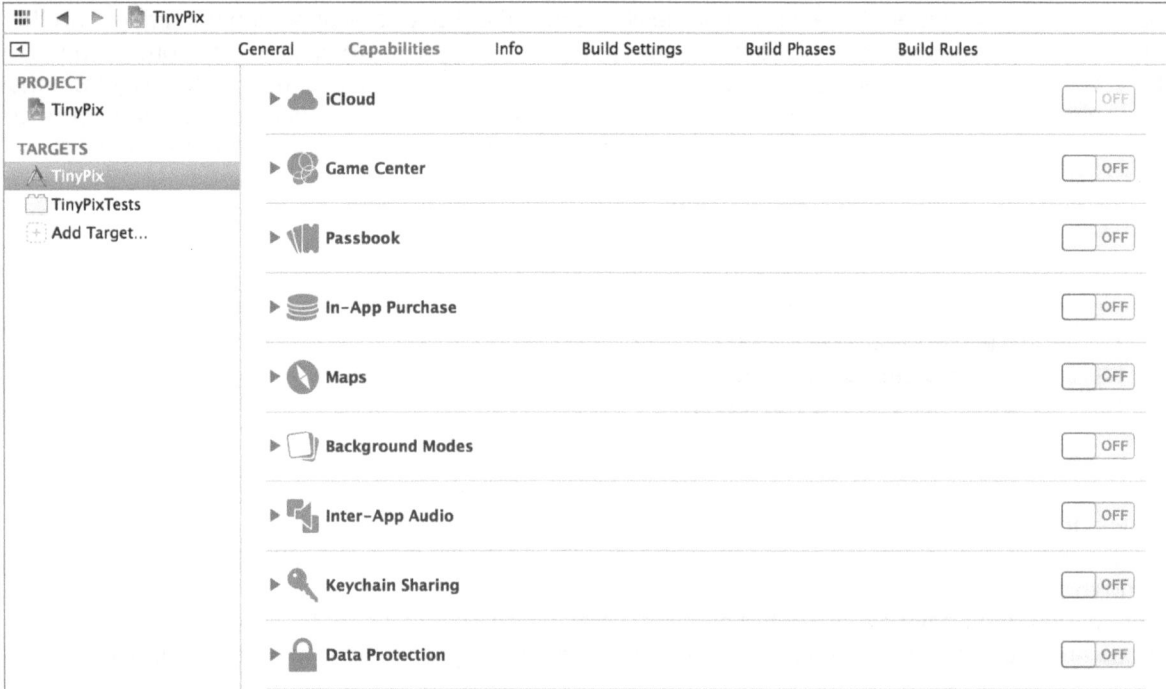

Figure 14-6. Xcode 5's presentation of easily configurable app technologies and services

The list of capabilities shown in Figure 14-6 can all be configured directly in Xcode, all without needing to go to a website, create and download provisioning profiles, and so on. For TinyPix, we want to enable iCloud, the first capability listed, so click the disclosure triangle next to the cloud icon. Here you'll see some information about what this capability is for. Click the switch at the right to turn it on. Xcode will then communicate with Apple's servers to configure the provisioning profile for this app. This will require you to log in with your Apple ID, and it obviously requires you to be connected to the internet. After it's enabled, click to turn on the key-value store checkbox, as shown in Figure 14-7.

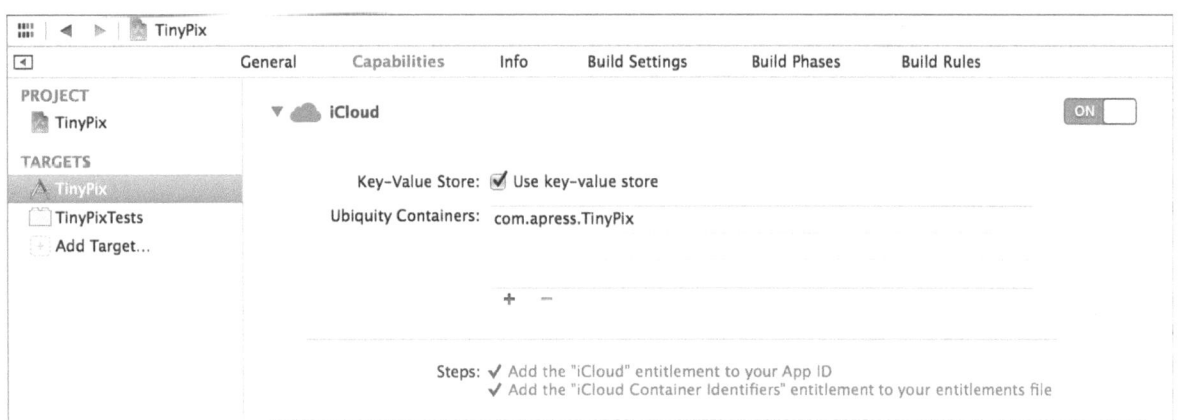

Figure 14-7. The app is now configured to use iCloud. This simple configuration let us remove several pages from this chapter, which probably ends up saving the life of a tree or two. Thanks, Apple!

You're finished! Your app now has the necessary permissions to access iCloud from your code. The rest is a simple matter of programming.

How to Query

Select *BIDMasterViewController.m*, so we can start making changes for iCloud. The biggest change is going to be the way we look for available documents. In the first version of TinyPix, we used NSFileManager to see what's available on the local file system. This time, we're going to do things a little differently. Here, we will fire up a special sort of query to look for documents.

Start by adding a pair of properties in the class extension: one to hold a pointer to an ongoing query and the other to hold the list of all the documents the query finds.

```
@interface BIDMasterViewController () <UIAlertViewDelegate>

@property (weak, nonatomic) IBOutlet UISegmentedControl *colorControl;
@property (strong, nonatomic) NSArray *documentFilenames;
@property (strong, nonatomic) BIDTinyPixDocument *chosenDocument;
@property (strong, nonatomic) NSMetadataQuery *query;
@property (strong, nonatomic) NSMutableArray *documentURLs;
- (NSURL *)urlForFilename:(NSString *)filename;
- (void)reloadFiles;
@end
```

Now, let's look at the new file-listing method. Remove the entire reloadFiles method and replace it with this:

```
- (void)reloadFiles {
    NSFileManager *fileManager = [NSFileManager defaultManager];
    // passing nil is OK here, matches first entitlement
    NSURL *cloudURL = [fileManager URLForUbiquityContainerIdentifier:nil];
    NSLog(@"got cloudURL %@", cloudURL);  // returns nil in simulator
```

```
    self.query = [[NSMetadataQuery alloc] init];
    _query.predicate = [NSPredicate predicateWithFormat:@"%K like '*.tinypix'",
                        NSMetadataItemFSNameKey];
    _query.searchScopes = [NSArray arrayWithObject:
                            NSMetadataQueryUbiquitousDocumentsScope];
    [[NSNotificationCenter defaultCenter]
     addObserver:self
     selector:@selector(updateUbiquitousDocuments:)
     name:NSMetadataQueryDidFinishGatheringNotification
     object:nil];
    [[NSNotificationCenter defaultCenter]
     addObserver:self
     selector:@selector(updateUbiquitousDocuments:)
     name:NSMetadataQueryDidUpdateNotification
     object:nil];
    [_query startQuery];
}
```

There are some new things here that are definitely worth mentioning. The first is seen in this line:

```
NSURL *cloudURL = [fileManager URLForUbiquityContainerIdentifier:nil];
```

That's a mouthful, for sure. Ubiquity? What are we talking about here? When it comes to iCloud, a lot of Apple's terminology for identifying resources in iCloud storage includes words like "ubiquity" and "ubiquitous" to indicate that something is omnipresent—accessible from any device using the same iCloud login credentials.

In this case, we're asking the file manager to give us a base URL that will let us access the iCloud directory associated with a particular container identifier. A container identifier is normally a string containing your company's unique bundle seed ID and the application identifier. The container identifier is used to pick one of the iCloud entitlements contained within your app. Passing nil here is a shortcut that just means "give me the first one in the list." Since our app contains only one item in that list (created in the previous section), that shortcut suits our needs perfectly.

After that, we create and configure an instance of NSMetadataQuery:

```
    self.query = [[NSMetadataQuery alloc] init];
    _query.predicate = [NSPredicate predicateWithFormat:@"%K like '*.tinypix'",
                        NSMetadataItemFSNameKey];
    _query.searchScopes = [NSArray arrayWithObject:
                            NSMetadataQueryUbiquitousDocumentsScope];
```

This class was originally written for use with the Spotlight search facility on Mac OS X, but it's now doing extra duty as a way to let iOS apps search iCloud directories. We give the query a predicate, which limits its search results to include only those with the correct sort of file name, and we give it a search scope that limits it to look just within the *Documents* folder in the app's iCloud storage. Next, we set up some notifications to let us know when the query is complete, so we can fire up the query.

Now we need to implement the method that those notifications call when the query is done. Add this method just below the reloadFiles method:

```
- (void)updateUbiquitousDocuments:(NSNotification *)notification {
    self.documentURLs = [NSMutableArray array];
    self.documentFilenames = [NSMutableArray array];

    NSLog(@"updateUbiquitousDocuments, results = %@", self.query.results);
    NSArray *results = [self.query.results sortedArrayUsingComparator:
        ^NSComparisonResult(id obj1, id obj2) {
        NSMetadataItem *item1 = obj1;
        NSMetadataItem *item2 = obj2;
        return [[item2 valueForAttribute:NSMetadataItemFSCreationDateKey]
                compare:
                [item1 valueForAttribute:NSMetadataItemFSCreationDateKey]];
    }];

    for (NSMetadataItem *item in results) {
        NSURL *url = [item valueForAttribute:NSMetadataItemURLKey];
        [self.documentURLs addObject:url];
        [(NSMutableArray *)_documentFilenames addObject:[url lastPathComponent]];
    }

    [self.tableView reloadData];
}
```

The query's results contain a list of NSMetadataItem objects, from which we can get items like file URLs and creation dates. We use this to sort the items by date, and then grab all the URLs for later use.

Save Where?

The next change is to the urlForFilename: method, which once again is completely different. Here, we're using a ubiquitous URL to create a full path URL for a given file name. We insert "Documents" in the generated path as well, to make sure we're using the app's *Documents* directory. Delete the old method and replace it with this new one:

```
- (NSURL *)urlForFilename:(NSString *)filename {
    // be sure to insert "Documents" into the path
    NSURL *baseURL = [[NSFileManager defaultManager]
                      URLForUbiquityContainerIdentifier:nil];
    NSURL *pathURL = [baseURL URLByAppendingPathComponent:@"Documents"];
    NSURL *destinationURL = [pathURL URLByAppendingPathComponent:filename];
    return destinationURL;
}
```

Now, build and run your app on an actual iOS device (not the simulator). If you've run the previous version of the app on that device, you'll find that any TinyPix masterpieces you created earlier are now nowhere to be seen. This new version ignores the local *Documents* directory for the app and relies completely on iCloud. However, you should be able to create new documents and find that they stick around after quitting and restarting the app. Moreover, you can even delete the

TinyPix app from your device entirely, run it again from Xcode, and find that all your iCloud-saved documents are available at once. If you have an additional iOS device configured with the same iCloud user, use Xcode to run the app on that device, and you'll see all the same documents appear there, as well! It's pretty sweet. You can also find these documents in the iCloud section of your iOS device's Settings app, as well as the iCloud section of your Mac's System Preferences app if you're running OS X 10.8 or later.

Storing Preferences on iCloud

We can "cloudify" one more piece of functionality with just a bit of effort. iOS's iCloud support includes a class called NSUbiquitousKeyValueStore, which works a lot like an NSDictionary (or NSUserDefaults, for that matter); however, its keys and values are stored in the cloud. This is great for application preferences, login tokens, and anything else that doesn't belong in a document, but could be useful when shared among all of a user's devices.

In TinyPix, we'll use this feature to store the user's preferred highlight color. That way, instead of needing to be configured on each device, the user sets the color once, and it shows up everywhere.

Select *BIDMasterViewController.m*, so we can make a couple of small changes. First, find chooseColor: and make the following changes:

```
- (IBAction)chooseColor:(id)sender {
    NSInteger selectedColorIndex = [(UISegmentedControl *)sender selectedSegmentIndex];
    NSUserDefaults *prefs = [NSUserDefaults standardUserDefaults];
    [prefs setInteger:selectedColorIndex forKey:@"selectedColorIndex"];
    [prefs synchronize];
    NSUbiquitousKeyValueStore *prefs = [NSUbiquitousKeyValueStore defaultStore];
    [prefs setLongLong:selectedColorIndex forKey:@"selectedColorIndex"];
}
```

Here, we grab a slightly different object instead of NSUserDefaults. This new class doesn't have a setInteger: method, so we use setLongLong: instead, which will do the same thing.

Next, find the viewDidAppear: method and change it as shown here:

```
- (void)viewDidAppear:(BOOL)animated
{
    [super viewDidAppear:animated];
    NSUserDefaults *prefs = [NSUserDefaults standardUserDefaults];
    NSInteger selectedColorIndex = [prefs integerForKey:@"selectedColorIndex"];
    NSUbiquitousKeyValueStore *prefs = [NSUbiquitousKeyValueStore defaultStore];
    NSInteger selectedColorIndex = (int)[prefs longLongForKey:
                                    @"selectedColorIndex"];
    [self setTintColorForIndex:selectedColorIndex];
    [self.colorControl setSelectedSegmentIndex:selectedColorIndex];

}
```

That's it! You can now run the app on multiple devices configured for the same iCloud user and will see that setting the color on one device results in the new color appearing on the other device the next time a document is opened there. Piece of cake!

What We Didn't Cover

We now have the basics of an iCloud-enabled, document-based application up and running, but there are a few more issues that you may want to consider. We're not going to cover these topics in this book; but if you're serious about making a great iCloud-based app, you'll want to think about these areas:

- Documents stored in iCloud are prone to conflicts. What happens if you edit the same TinyPix file on several devices at once? Fortunately, Apple has already thought of this and provides some ways to deal with these conflicts in your app. It's up to you to decide whether you want to ignore conflicts, try to fix them automatically, or ask the user to help sort out the problem. For full details, search for a document titled "Resolving Document Version Conflicts" in the Xcode documentation viewer.

- Apple recommends that you design your application to work in a completely offline mode in case the user isn't using iCloud for some reason. It also recommends that you provide a way for a user to move files between iCloud storage and local storage. Sadly, Apple doesn't provide or suggest any standard GUI for helping a user manage this, and current apps that provide this functionality, such as Apple's iWork apps, don't seem to handle it in a particularly user-friendly way. See Apple's "Managing the Life Cycle of a Document" in the Xcode documentation for more on this.

- Apple supports using iCloud for Core Data storage and even provides a class called `UIManagedDocument` that you can subclass if you want to make that work. See the `UIManagedDocument` class reference for more information, or take a look at *More iOS 7 Development: Further Explorations of the iOS SDK*, by Kevin Kim, Alex Horowitz, Dave Mark, and Jeff LaMarche (Apress, 2014) for a hands-on guide to building an iCloud-backed Core Data app. We should point out that this architecture is a lot more complex and problematic than normal iCloud document storage. Apple has taken steps to improve things in iOS 7, but it's still not perfectly smooth, so look before you leap.

What's up next? In Chapter 15, we'll take you through the process of making sure your apps work properly in a multithreaded, multitasking environment.

Grand Central Dispatch, Background Processing, and You

If you've ever tried your hand at multithreaded programming, in any environment, chances are you've come away from the experience with a feeling of dread, terror, or worse. Fortunately, technology marches on, and Apple has come up with a new approach that makes multithreaded programming much easier. This approach is called **Grand Central Dispatch**, and we'll get you started using it in this chapter. We'll also dig into the multitasking capabilities of iOS, showing you how to adjust your applications to play nicely in this new world and work even better than before.

Grand Central Dispatch

One of the biggest challenges developers face today is to write software that can perform complex actions in response to user input while remaining responsive, so that the user isn't constantly kept waiting while the processor does some behind-the-scenes task. If you think about it, that challenge has been with us all along; and in spite of the advances in computing technology that bring us faster CPUs, the problem persists. If you want evidence, you need look no further than your nearest computer screen. Chances are that the last time you sat down to work at your computer, at some point, your work flow was interrupted by a spinning mouse cursor of some kind or another.

So why does this continue to vex us, given all the advances in system architecture? One part of the problem is the way that software is typically written: as a sequence of events to be performed in order. Such software can scale up as CPU speeds increase, but only to a certain point. As soon as the program gets stuck waiting for an external resource, such as a file or a network connection, the entire sequence of events is effectively paused. All modern operating systems now allow the use of multiple threads of execution within a program, so that even if a single thread is stuck waiting for a specific event, the other threads can keep going. Even so, many developers see multithreaded programming as something of a black art and shy away from it.

Fortunately, Apple has some good news for anyone who wants to break up their code into simultaneous chunks without too much hands-on intimacy with the system's threading layer. This good news is called Grand Central Dispatch (GCD). It provides an entirely new API for splitting up the work your application needs to do into smaller chunks that can be spread across multiple threads and, with the right hardware, multiple CPUs.

Much of this new API is accessed using **blocks**, another Apple innovation that adds a sort of anonymous in-line function capability to C and Objective-C. Blocks have a lot in common with similar features in languages such as Ruby and Lisp, and they can provide interesting new ways to structure interactions between different objects while keeping related code closer together in your methods.

Introducing SlowWorker

As a platform for demonstrating how GCD works, we'll create an application called SlowWorker, which consists of a simple interface driven by a single button and a text view. Click the button, and a synchronous task is immediately started, locking up the app for about ten seconds. Once the task completes, some text appears in the text view (see Figure 15-1).

Figure 15-1. The SlowWorker application hides its interface behind a single button. Click the button, and the interface hangs for about ten seconds while the application does its work

Start by using the *Single View Application* template to make a new application in Xcode, as you've done many times before. Name this one *SlowWorker*, set *Devices* to *iPhone*, click *Next* to save your project, and so on. Next, make the following additions to *BIDViewController.m*:

```objc
#import "BIDViewController.h"

@interface BIDViewController ()

@property (weak, nonatomic) IBOutlet UIButton *startButton;
@property (weak, nonatomic) IBOutlet UITextView *resultsTextView;

@end
```

This simply defines a couple of outlets to the two objects visible in our GUI.

Now continue by adding the following code in bold inside the @implementation section:

```objc
@implementation BIDViewController

- (NSString *)fetchSomethingFromServer
{
    [NSThread sleepForTimeInterval:1];
    return @"Hi there";
}

- (NSString *)processData:(NSString *)data
{
    [NSThread sleepForTimeInterval:2];
    return [data uppercaseString];
}

- (NSString *)calculateFirstResult:(NSString *)data
{
    [NSThread sleepForTimeInterval:3];
    return [NSString stringWithFormat:@"Number of chars: %d",
            [data length]];
}

- (NSString *)calculateSecondResult:(NSString *)data
{
    [NSThread sleepForTimeInterval:4];
    return [data stringByReplacingOccurrencesOfString:@"E"
                                          withString:@"e"];
}

- (IBAction)doWork:(id)sender
{
    NSDate *startTime = [NSDate date];
    NSString *fetchedData = [self fetchSomethingFromServer];
    NSString *processedData = [self processData:fetchedData];
    NSString *firstResult = [self calculateFirstResult:processedData];
    NSString *secondResult = [self calculateSecondResult:processedData];
```

```
        NSString *resultsSummary = [NSString stringWithFormat:
                                    @"First: [%@]\nSecond: [%@]", firstResult,
                                    secondResult];
        self.resultsTextView.text = resultsSummary;
        NSDate *endTime = [NSDate date];
        NSLog(@"Completed in %f seconds",
            [endTime timeIntervalSinceDate:startTime]);
}
.
.
.
```

As you can see, the work of this class (such as it is) is split up into a number of small chunks. This code is just meant to simulate some slow activities, and none of those methods really do anything time-consuming at all. To make things interesting, each method contains a call to the sleepForTimeInterval: class method in NSThread, which simply makes the program (specifically, the thread from which the method is called) effectively pause and do nothing at all for the given number of seconds. The doWork: method also contains code at the beginning and end to calculate the amount of time it took for all the work to be done.

Now open *Main.storyboard* and drag a *Button* and a *Text View* into the empty *View* window, laying things out as shown in Figure 15-2. Control-drag from *File's Owner* to connect the view controller's two outlets to the button and the text view.

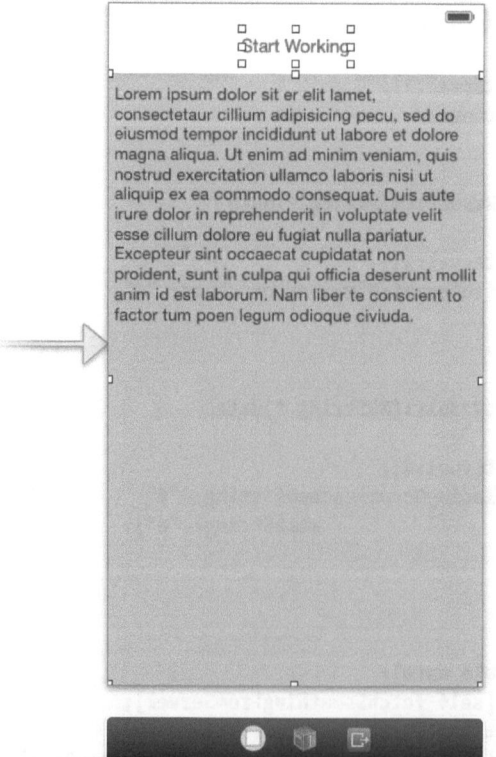

Figure 15-2. The SlowWorker interface consists of a button and a text view. Be sure to uncheck the Editable checkbox for the text view and delete all of its text

Next, select the button and go to the connections inspector to connect the button's *Touch Up Inside* event to *View Controller*, selecting the view controller's doWork: method. Finally, select the text view, use the attributes inspector to uncheck the *Editable* checkbox (it's in the upper-right corner), and delete the default text from the text view.

Save your work, and then select *Run*. Your app should start up, and pressing the button will make it work for about ten seconds (the sum of all those sleep amounts) before showing you the results. During your wait, you'll see that the *Start Working* button fades visibly, never turning back to its normal color until the "work" is done. Also, until the work is complete, the application's view is unresponsive. Tapping anywhere on the screen has no effect. In fact, the only way you can interact with your application during this time is by tapping the home button to switch away from it. This is exactly the state of affairs we want to avoid!

In this particular case, the wait is not too bad, since the application appears to be hung for just a few seconds; however, if your app regularly hangs this way for much longer, using it will be a frustrating experience. In the worst of cases, the operating system may actually kill your app if it's unresponsive for too long. In any case, you'll end up with some unhappy users—and maybe even some ex-users!

Threading Basics

Before we start implementing solutions, let's go over some concurrency basics. This is far from a complete description of threading in iOS or threading in general. We just want to explain enough for you to understand what we're doing in this chapter.

Most modern operating systems (including, of course, iOS) support the notion of threads of execution. Each process can contain multiple threads, which all run concurrently. If there's just one processor core, the operating system will switch between all executing threads, much like it switches between all executing processes. If more than one core is available, the threads will be distributed among them, just as processes are.

All threads in a process share the same executable program code and the same global data. Each thread can also have some data that is exclusive to the thread. Threads can make use of a special structure called a **mutex** (short for mutual exclusion) or a lock, which can ensure that a particular chunk of code can't be run by multiple threads at once. This is useful for ensuring correct outcomes when multiple threads access the same data simultaneously, by locking out other threads when one thread is updating a value (in what's called a **critical section** of your code).

A common concern when dealing with threads is the idea of code being **thread-safe**. Some software libraries are written with thread concurrency in mind and have all their critical sections properly protected with mutexes. Some code libraries aren't thread-safe.

For example, in Cocoa Touch, the Foundation framework (containing basic classes appropriate for all sorts of Objective-C programming, such as NSString, NSArray, and so on) is generally considered to be thread-safe. However, the UIKit framework (containing the classes specific to building GUI applications, such as UIApplication, UIView and all its subclasses, and so on) is, for the most part, not thread-safe. This means that in a running iOS application, all method calls that deal with any UIKit objects should be executed from within the same thread, which is commonly known as the **main thread**. If you access UIKit objects from another thread, all bets are off! You are likely to encounter seemingly inexplicable bugs (or, even worse, you won't experience any problems, but some of your users will be affected by them after you ship your app).

By default, the main thread is where all the action of your iOS app occurs (e.g., dealing with actions triggered by user events). Thus, for simple applications, it's nothing you need to worry about. Action methods triggered by a user are already running in the main thread. Up to this point in the book, our code has been running exclusively on the main thread, but that's about to change.

Tip   A lot has been written about thread safety, and it's well worth your time to dig in and try to digest as much of it as you can. One great place to start is Apple's own documentation. Take a few minutes and read through this page (it will definitely help):

http://developer.apple.com/library/ios/#documentation/Cocoa/Conceptual/Multithreading/ThreadSafetySummary/ThreadSafetySummary.html

---

Units of Work

The problem with the threading model described earlier is that, for the average programmer, writing error-free, multithreaded code is nearly impossible. This is not meant as a critique of our industry or of the average programmer's abilities; it's simply an observation. The complex interactions you must account for in your code when synchronizing data and actions across multiple threads are really just too much for most people to tackle. Imagine that 5% of all people have the capacity to write software at all. Only a small fraction of those 5% are really up to the task of writing heavy-duty multithreaded applications. Even people who have done it successfully will often advise others to not follow their example!

Fortunately, all hope is not lost. It is possible to implement some concurrency without too much low-level thread-twisting. Just as we have the ability to display data on the screen without directly poking bits into video RAM and to read data from disk without interfacing directly with disk controllers, we can also leverage software abstractions that let us run our code on multiple threads without requiring us to do much directly with the threads.

The solutions that Apple encourages us to use are centered on the ideas of splitting up long-running tasks into units of work and putting those units into queues for execution. The system manages the queues for us, executing units of work on multiple threads. We don't need to start and manage the background threads directly, and we are freed from much of the bookkeeping that's usually involved in implementing multithreaded applications; the system takes care of that for us.

GCD: Low-Level Queuing

This idea of putting units of work into queues that can be executed in the background, with the system managing the threads for you, is really powerful and greatly simplifies many development situations where concurrency is needed. GCD made its debut on OS X several years ago, providing the infrastructure to do just that. A couple of years later, this technology came to the iOS platform as well. This technology works not only with Objective-C, but also with C and C++.

GCD puts some great concepts—units of work, painless background processing, and automatic thread management—into a C interface that can be used from all of the C-based languages. To top things off, Apple has made its implementation of GCD open source, so it can be ported to other Unix-like operating systems, as well.

One of the key concepts of GCD is the **queue**. The system provides a number of predefined queues, including a queue that's guaranteed to always do its work on the main thread. It's perfect for the non-thread-safe UIKit! You can also create your own queues—as many as you like. GCD queues are strictly first-in, first-out (FIFO). Units of work added to a GCD queue will always be started in the order they were placed in the queue. That said, they may not always finish in the same order, since a GCD queue will automatically distribute its work among multiple threads, if possible.

GCD has access to a pool of threads that are reused throughout the lifetime of the application, and it will try to maintain a number of threads that's appropriate for the machine's architecture. It will automatically take advantage of a more powerful machine by utilizing more processor cores when it has work to do. Until recently, iOS devices were all single-core, so this wasn't much of an issue. But now that all iOS devices released in the past few years feature dual-core processors, GCD is becoming truly useful.

Becoming a Blockhead

Along with GCD, Apple has added a bit of new syntax to the C language itself (and, by extension, Objective-C and C++) to implement a language feature called **blocks** (also known as **closures** or **lambdas** in some other languages), which are really important for getting the most out of GCD. The idea behind a block is to let a particular chunk of code be treated like any other C-language type. A block can be assigned to a variable, passed as an argument to a function or method, and (unlike most other types) executed. In this way, blocks can be used as an alternative to the delegate pattern in Objective-C or to callback functions in C.

Much like a method or function, a block can take one or more parameters and specify a return value. To declare a block variable, you use the caret (^) symbol along with some additional parenthesized bits to declare parameters and return types. To define the block itself, you do roughly the same, but follow it up with the actual code defining the block wrapped in curly braces:

```
// Declare a block variable "loggerBlock" with no parameters
// and no return value.
void (^loggerBlock)(void);

// Assign a block to the variable declared above.  A block without parameters
// and with no return value, like this one, needs no "decorations" like the use
// of void in the preceding variable declaration.
loggerBlock = ^{ NSLog(@"I'm just glad they didn't call it a lambda"); };

// Execute the block, just like calling a function.
loggerBlock();  // this produces some output in the console
```

If you've done much C programming, you may recognize that this is similar to the concept of a function pointer in C. However, there are a few critical differences. Perhaps the biggest difference—the one that's the most striking when you first see it—is that blocks can be defined in-line in your code. You can define a block right at the point where it's going to be passed to another method or function.

Another big difference is that a block can access all variables available in the scope of its creation. By default, the block "captures" any variable you access this way. It duplicates the value into a new variable with the same name, leaving the original intact. Objective-C objects are automatically sent a `retain` message (and later, when the block is done, a `release`, effectively giving strong semantics to the variable inside the block) while scalar values such as int and float are simply copied. However, you can make an outside variable "read/write" by prepending the storage qualifier __block before its declaration. Note that there are two underscores before block, not just one. Or, if you want to pass in an object pointer with weak semantics, you can preface it with it with __weak:

```
// define a variable that can be changed by a block
__block int a = 0;

// define a block that tries to modify a variable in its scope
void (^sillyBlock)(void) = ^{ a = 47; };

// check the value of our variable before calling the block
NSLog(@"a == %d", a); // outputs "a == 0"

// execute the block
sillyBlock();

// check the values of our variable again, after calling the block
NSLog(@"a == %d", a); // outputs "a == 47"
```

As mentioned previously, blocks really shine when used with GCD, which lets you take a block and add it to a queue in a single step. When you do this with a block that you define immediately at that point, rather than a block stored in a variable, you have the added advantage of being able to see the relevant code directly in the context where it's being used.

Improving SlowWorker

To see how blocks work, let's revisit SlowWorker's doWork: method. It currently looks like this:

```
- (IBAction)doWork:(id)sender
{
    NSDate *startTime = [NSDate date];
    NSString *fetchedData = [self fetchSomethingFromServer];
    NSString *processedData = [self processData:fetchedData];
    NSString *firstResult = [self calculateFirstResult:processedData];
    NSString *secondResult = [self calculateSecondResult:processedData];
    NSString *resultsSummary = [NSString stringWithFormat:
                        @"First: [%@]\nSecond: [%@]", firstResult,
                        secondResult];
    self.resultsTextView.text = resultsSummary;
    NSDate *endTime = [NSDate date];
    NSLog(@"Completed in %f seconds",
        [endTime timeIntervalSinceDate:startTime]);
}
```

We can make this method run entirely in the background by wrapping all the code in a block and passing it to a GCD function called dispatch_async. This function takes two parameters: a GCD queue and a block to assign to the queue. Make these two changes to your copy of doWork:. Be sure to add the closing brace and parenthesis at the end of the method:

```
- (IBAction)doWork:(id)sender
{
    NSDate *startTime = [NSDate date];
    dispatch_queue_t queue =
        dispatch_get_global_queue(DISPATCH_QUEUE_PRIORITY_DEFAULT, 0);
    dispatch_async(queue, ^{
        NSString *fetchedData = [self fetchSomethingFromServer];
        NSString *processedData = [self processData:fetchedData];
        NSString *firstResult = [self calculateFirstResult:processedData];
        NSString *secondResult = [self calculateSecondResult:processedData];
        NSString *resultsSummary = [NSString stringWithFormat:
                                @"First: [%@]\nSecond: [%@]", firstResult,
                                secondResult];
        self.resultsTextView.text = resultsSummary;
        NSDate *endTime = [NSDate date];
        NSLog(@"Completed in %f seconds",
                [endTime timeIntervalSinceDate:startTime]);
    });
}
```

The first line grabs a preexisting global queue that's always available, using the dispatch_get_global_queue() function. That function takes two arguments: the first lets you specify a priority, and the second is currently unused and should always be 0. If you specify a different priority in the first argument, such as DISPATCH_QUEUE_PRIORITY_HIGH or DISPATCH_QUEUE_PRIORITY_LOW, you will actually get a different global queue, which the system will prioritize differently. For now, we'll stick with the default global queue.

The queue is then passed to the dispatch_async() function, along with the block of code that comes after. GCD takes that entire block and passes it to a background thread, where it will be executed one step at a time, just as when it was running in the main thread.

Note that we define a variable called startTime just before the block is created, and then use its value at the end of the block. Intuitively, this doesn't seem to make sense because, by the time the block is executed, the doWork: method has exited, so the NSDate instance that the startTime variable is pointing to should already be released! This is a crucial point of block usage: if a block accesses any variables from "the outside" during its execution, then some special setup happens when the block is created, allowing the block access to those variables. The values contained by such variables will either be duplicated (if they are plain C types such as int or float) or retained (if they are pointers to objects), so that the values they contain can be used inside the block. When dispatch_async is called in the second line of doWork:, and the block shown in the code is created, startTime is actually sent a retain message, the return value of which is assigned to what is essentially a new immutable variable with the same name (startTime) inside the block.

The startTime variable needs to be immutable inside the block, so that code inside the block can't accidentally mess with a variable that's defined outside the block. If that were allowed all the time, it would just be confusing for everyone. Sometimes, however, you actually do want to let a block write to a value defined on the outside, and that's where the __block storage qualifier (which we mentioned a couple of pages ago) comes in handy. If __block is used to define a variable, then it is directly available to any and all blocks that are defined within the same scope. An interesting side effect of this is that __block-qualified variables are not duplicated or retained when used inside a block.

Don't Forget That Main Thread

Getting back to the project at hand, there's one problem here: UIKit thread-safety. Remember that messaging any GUI object from a background thread, including our resultsTextView, is a no-no. Fortunately, GCD provides a way to deal with this, too. Inside the block, we can call another dispatching function, passing work back to the main thread! We do this by once again calling dispatch_async(), this time passing in the queue returned by the dispatch_get_main_queue() function. This always gives us the special queue that lives on the main thread, ready to execute blocks that require the use of the main thread. Make one more change to your version of doWork::

```
- (IBAction)doWork:(id)sender
{
    NSDate *startTime = [NSDate date];
    dispatch_queue_t queue =
        dispatch_get_global_queue(DISPATCH_QUEUE_PRIORITY_DEFAULT, 0);
    dispatch_async(queue, ^{
        NSString *fetchedData = [self fetchSomethingFromServer];
        NSString *processedData = [self processData:fetchedData];
        NSString *firstResult = [self calculateFirstResult:processedData];
        NSString *secondResult = [self calculateSecondResult:processedData];
        NSString *resultsSummary = [NSString stringWithFormat:
                                    @"First: [%@]\nSecond: [%@]", firstResult,
                                    secondResult];
        dispatch_async(dispatch_get_main_queue(), ^{
            self.resultsTextView.text = resultsSummary;
        });
        NSDate *endTime = [NSDate date];
        NSLog(@"Completed in %f seconds",
            [endTime timeIntervalSinceDate:startTime]);
    });
}
```

Giving Some Feedback

If you build and run your app at this point, you'll see that it now seems to work a bit more smoothly, at least in some sense. The button no longer gets stuck in a highlighted position after you touch it, which perhaps leads you to tap again, and again, and so on. If you look in Xcode's console log, you'll see the result of each of those taps, but only the results of the last tap will be shown in the text view.

What we really want to do is enhance the GUI so that, after the user presses the button, the display is immediately updated in a way that indicates that an action is underway. We also want the button disabled while the work is in progress. We'll do this by adding a

UIActivityIndicatorView to our display. This class provides the sort of spinner seen in many applications and web sites. Start by declaring it in the class extension at the top of *BIDViewController.m*:

```
@interface BIDViewController ()

@property (weak, nonatomic) IBOutlet UIButton *startButton;
@property (weak, nonatomic) IBOutlet UITextView *resultsTextView;
@property (weak, nonatomic) IBOutlet UIActivityIndicatorView *spinner;

@end
```

Next, open *Main.Storyboard*, locate an *Activity Indicator View* in the library, and drag it into our view, next to the button (see Figure 15-3).

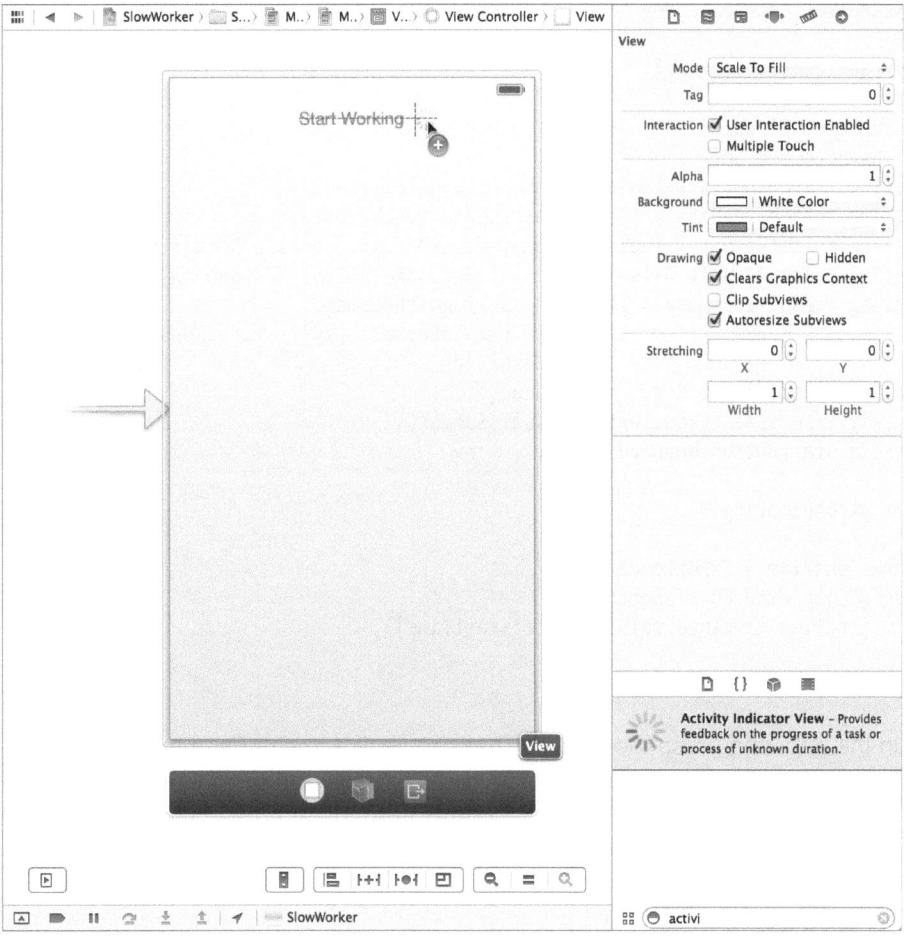

Figure 15-3. Dragging an activity indicator view into our main view in Interface Builder

With the activity indicator spinner selected, use the attributes inspector to check the *Hides When Stopped* checkbox, so that our spinner will appear only when we tell it to start spinning (no one wants an unspinning spinner in their GUI).

Next, control-drag from the *View Controller* icon to the spinner and connect the *spinner* outlet. Save your changes.

Now open *BIDViewController.m*. Here, we'll first work on the doWork: method a bit, adding a few lines to manage the appearance of the button and the spinner when the user clicks and when the work is done. We'll first set the button's enabled property to NO, which prevents it from registering any taps and also shows that the button is disabled by making its text gray and somewhat transparent. Next, we get the spinner moving:

```
- (IBAction)doWork:(id)sender
{
    NSDate *startTime = [NSDate date];
    self.startButton.enabled = NO;

    [self.spinner startAnimating];
    dispatch_queue_t queue =
        dispatch_get_global_queue(DISPATCH_QUEUE_PRIORITY_DEFAULT, 0);
    dispatch_async(queue, ^{
        NSString *fetchedData = [self fetchSomethingFromServer];
        NSString *processedData = [self processData:fetchedData];
        NSString *firstResult = [self calculateFirstResult:processedData];
        NSString *secondResult = [self calculateSecondResult:processedData];
        NSString *resultsSummary = [NSString stringWithFormat:
                                    @"First: [%@]\nSecond: [%@]", firstResult,
                                    secondResult];
        dispatch_async(dispatch_get_main_queue(), ^{
            self.resultsTextView.text = resultsSummary;
            self.startButton.enabled = YES;

[self.spinner stopAnimating];
        });
        NSDate *endTime = [NSDate date];
        NSLog(@"Completed in %f seconds",
            [endTime timeIntervalSinceDate:startTime]);
    });
}
```

Build and run the app, and press the button. That's more like it, eh? Even though the work being done takes a few seconds, the user isn't just left hanging. The button is disabled and looks the part, as well. Also, the animated spinner lets the user know that the app hasn't actually hung and can be expected to return to normal at some point.

Concurrent Blocks

So far, so good, but we're not quite finished yet! The sharp-eyed among you will notice that, after going through these motions, we still haven't really changed the basic sequential layout of our algorithm (if you can even call this simple list of steps an algorithm). All that we're doing is moving a chunk of this method to a background thread and then finishing up in the main thread. The Xcode console output proves it: this work takes ten seconds to run, just as it did at the outset. The 900-pound gorilla in the room is that calculateFirstResult: and calculateSecondResult: don't need to be performed in sequence, and doing them concurrently could give us a substantial speedup.

Fortunately, GCD has a way to accomplish this by using what's called a **dispatch group**. All blocks that are dispatched asynchronously within the context of a group, via the dispatch_group_async() function, are set loose to execute as fast as they can, including being distributed to multiple threads for concurrent execution, if possible. We can also use dispatch_group_notify() to specify an additional block that will be executed when all the blocks in the group have been run to completion.

Make the following changes to your copy of doWork:. Again, make sure you get that trailing bit of curly brace and parenthesis:

```
- (IBAction)doWork:(id)sender
{
    NSDate *startTime = [NSDate date];
    self.startButton.enabled = NO;
    self.startButton.alpha = 0.5f;
    [self.spinner startAnimating];
    dispatch_queue_t queue =
        dispatch_get_global_queue(DISPATCH_QUEUE_PRIORITY_DEFAULT, 0);
    dispatch_async(queue, ^{
        NSString *fetchedData = [self fetchSomethingFromServer];
        NSString *processedData = [self processData:fetchedData];
        NSString *firstResult = [self calculateFirstResult:processedData];
        NSString *secondResult = [self calculateSecondResult:processedData];
        __block NSString *firstResult;
        __block NSString *secondResult;
        dispatch_group_t group = dispatch_group_create();
        dispatch_group_async(group, queue, ^{
            firstResult = [self calculateFirstResult:processedData];
        });
        dispatch_group_async(group, queue, ^{
            secondResult = [self calculateSecondResult:processedData];
        });
        dispatch_group_notify(group, queue, ^{
            NSString *resultsSummary = [NSString stringWithFormat:
                                        @"First: [%@]\nSecond: [%@]",
                                        firstResult,
                                        secondResult];
            dispatch_async(dispatch_get_main_queue(), ^{
                self.resultsTextView.text = resultsSummary;
                self.startButton.enabled = YES;
                self.startButton.alpha = 1;
                [self.spinner stopAnimating];
            });
            NSDate *endTime = [NSDate date];
            NSLog(@"Completed in %f seconds",
                    [endTime timeIntervalSinceDate:startTime]);
        });
    });
}
```

One complication here is that each of the calculate methods returns a value that we want to grab, so we must first create the variables using the __block storage modifier. This ensures the values set inside the blocks are made available to the code that runs later.

With this in place, build and run the app again. You'll see that your efforts have paid off. What was once a ten-second operation now takes just seven seconds, thanks to the fact that we're running both of the calculations simultaneously.

Obviously, our contrived example gets the maximum effect because these two "calculations" don't actually do anything but cause the thread they're running on to sleep. In a real application, the speedup would depend on what sort of work is being done and which resources are available. The performance of CPU-intensive calculations is helped by this technique only if multiple CPU cores are available, and it will get better almost for free as more cores are added to future iOS devices. Other uses, such as fetching data from multiple network connections at once, would see a speed increase even with just one CPU.

As you can see, GCD is not a panacea. Using GCD won't automatically speed up every application. But by carefully applying these techniques at those points in your app where speed is essential, or where you find that your application feels like it's lagging in its responses to the user, you can easily provide a better user experience, even in situations where you can't improve the real performance.

Background Processing

Another important technology for handling concurrency is background processing. This allows your apps to run in the background—in some circumstances, even after the user has pressed the home button.

This functionality should not be confused with the true multitasking that modern desktop operating systems now feature, where all the programs you launch remain resident in the system RAM until you explicitly quit them. iOS devices still have too little RAM to be able to pull that off very well. Instead, this background processing is meant to allow applications that require specific kinds of system functionality to continue to run in a constrained manner. For instance, if you have an app that plays an audio stream from an Internet radio station, iOS will let that app continue to run, even if the user switches to another app. Beyond that, it will even provide standard pause and volume controls in the iOS control center (the translucent control panel that appears when you swipe up from the bottom of the screen) while your app is playing audio.

Assume you're creating an app that does one of the following things: plays audio even when the user is running another app, requests continuous location updates, responds to a special type of push request telling it to load new data from a server, or implements Voice over IP (VoIP) to let users send and receive phone calls on the Internet. In each of these cases, you can declare this situation in your app's *Info.plist* file, and the system will treat your app in a special way. This usage, while interesting, is probably not something that most readers of this book will be tackling, so we're not going to delve into it here.

Besides running apps in the background, iOS also includes the ability to put an app into a suspended state after the user presses the home button. This state of suspended execution is conceptually similar to putting your Mac into sleep mode. The entire working memory of the application is held in RAM; it just isn't executed while suspended. As a result, switching back to such an application is lightning-fast. This isn't limited to special applications. In fact, it is the default behavior of any app you build with Xcode (though this can be disabled by another setting in the

Info.plist file). To see this in action, open your device's Mail application and drill down into a message. Next, press the home button, open the Notes application, and select a note. Now double-tap the home button and switch back to Mail. You'll see that there's no perceptible lag; it just slides into place as if it had been running all along.

For most applications, this sort of automatic suspending and resuming is all you're likely to need. However, in some situations, your app may need to know when it's about to be suspended and when it has just been awakened. The system provides ways of notifying an app about changes to its execution state via the UIApplication class, which has a number of delegate methods and notifications for just this purpose. We'll show you how to use them later in this chapter.

When your application is about to be suspended, one thing it can do, regardless of whether it's one of the special backgroundable application types, is request a bit of additional time to run in the background. The idea is to make sure your app has enough time to close any open files, network resources, and so on. We'll give you an example of this in a bit.

Application Life Cycle

Before we get into the specifics of how to deal with changes to your app's execution state, let's talk a bit about the various states in its life cycle:

- **Not Running**: This is the state that all apps are in on a freshly rebooted device. An application that has been launched at any point after the device is turned on will return to this state only under specific conditions:

    - If its Info.plist includes the UIApplicationExitsOnSuspend key (with its value set to YES)

    - If it was previously Suspended and the system needs to clear out some memory

    - If it crashes while running

- **Active**: This is the normal running state of an application when it's displayed on the screen. It can receive user input and update the display.

- **Background**: In this state, an app is given some time to execute some code, but it can't directly access the screen or get any user input. All apps enter this state briefly when the user presses the home button; most of them quickly move on to the Suspended state. Apps that want to do any sort of background processing stay in this state until they're made Active again.

- **Suspended**: A Suspended app is frozen. This is what happens to normal apps after their brief stint in the Background state. All the memory the app was using while it was active is held just as it was. If the user brings the app back to the Active state, it will pick up right where it left off. On the other hand, if the system needs more memory for whichever app is currently Active, any Suspended apps may be terminated (and placed back into the Not Running state) and their memory freed for other use.

- **Inactive**: An app enters the Inactive state only as a temporary rest stop between two other states. The only way an app can stay Inactive for any length of time is if the user is dealing with a system prompt (such as those shown for an incoming call or SMS message) or if the user has locked the screen. This state is basically a sort of limbo.

State-Change Notifications

To manage changes between these states, UIApplication defines a number of methods that its delegate can implement. In addition to the delegate methods, UIApplication also defines a matching set of notification names (see Table 15-1). This allows other objects besides the app delegate to register for notifications when the application's state changes.

Table 15-1. Delegate Methods for Tracking Your Application's Execution State and Their Corresponding Notification Names

Delegate Method	Notification Name
application:didFinishLaunchingWithOptions:	UIApplicationDidFinishLaunchingNotification
applicationWillResignActive:	UIApplicationWillResignActiveNotification
applicationDidBecomeActive:	UIApplicationDidBecomeActiveNotification
applicationDidEnterBackground:	UIApplicationDidEnterBackgroundNotification
applicationWillEnterForeground:	UIApplicationWillEnterForegroundNotification
applicationWillTerminate:	UIApplicationWillTerminateNotification

Note that each of these methods is directly related to one of the running states: Active, Inactive, and Background. Each delegate method is called (and each notification posted) in only one of those states. The most important state transitions are between Active and other states. Some transitions, like from Background to Suspended, occur without any notice whatsoever. Let's go through these methods and discuss how they're meant to be used.

The first of these, application:didFinishLaunchingWithOptions:, is one you've already seen many times in this book. It's the primary way of doing application-level coding directly after the app has launched.

The next two methods, applicationWillResignActive: and applicationDidBecomeActive:, are both used in a number of circumstances. If the user presses the home button, applicationWillResignActive: will be called. If the user later brings the app back to the foreground, applicationDidBecomeActive: will be called. The same sequence of events occurs if the user receives a phone call. To top it all off, applicationDidBecomeActive: is also called when the application launches for the first time! In general, this pair of methods brackets the movement of an application from the Active state to the Inactive state. They are good places to enable and disable any animations, in-app audio, or other items that deal with the app's presentation to the user. Because of the multiple situations where applicationDidBecomeActive: is used, you may want to put some of your app initialization code there instead of in application:didFinishLaunchingWithO ptions:. Note that you should not assume in applicationWillResignActive: that the application is about to be sent to the background; it may just be a temporary change that ends up with a move back to the Active state.

After those methods come applicationDidEnterBackground: and applicationWillEnterForeground:, which have a slightly different usage area: dealing with an app that is definitely being sent to the background. applicationDidEnterBackground: is where your app should free all resources that can be re-created later, save all user data, close network connections, and so on. This is also the spot where you can request more time to run in the background if you need to, as we'll demonstrate shortly. If you spend too much time doing things in applicationDidEnterBackground:—more than about five seconds—the system will decide that your app is misbehaving and terminate it. You should implement applicationWillEnterForeground: to re-create whatever was torn down in applicationDidEnterBackground:, such as reloading user data, reestablishing network connections, and so on. Note that when applicationDidEnterBackground: is called, you can safely assume that applicationWillResignActive: has also been recently called. Likewise, when applicationWillEnterForeground: is called, you can assume that applicationDidBecomeActive: will soon be called, as well.

Last in the list is applicationWillTerminate:, which you'll probably use seldom, if ever. It is called only if your application is already in the background and the system decides to skip suspension for some reason and simply terminate the app.

Now that you have a basic theoretical understanding of the states an application transitions between, let's put this knowledge to the test with a simple app that does nothing more than write a message to Xcode's console log each time one of these methods is called. We'll then manipulate the running app in a variety of ways, just as a user might, and see which transitions occur.

Creating State Lab

In Xcode, create a new project based on the *Single View Application* template and name it *State Lab*. This app won't display anything but the default gray screen it's born with. All the output it's going to generate will end up in the Xcode console instead. The *BIDAppDelegate.m* file already contains all the methods we're interested in. We just need to add some logging, as shown in bold. Note that we've also removed the comments from these methods, just for the sake of brevity:

```
#import "BIDAppDelegate.h"

#import "BIDViewController.h"

@implementation BIDAppDelegate

- (BOOL)application:(UIApplication *)application didFinishLaunchingWithOptions:(NSDictionary *)
launchOptions
{
    NSLog(@"%@", NSStringFromSelector(_cmd));
    return YES;
}

- (void)applicationWillResignActive:(UIApplication *)application
{
    NSLog(@"%@", NSStringFromSelector(_cmd));
}

- (void)applicationDidEnterBackground:(UIApplication *)application
{
    NSLog(@"%@", NSStringFromSelector(_cmd));
}
```

```
- (void)applicationWillEnterForeground:(UIApplication *)application
{
    NSLog(@"%@", NSStringFromSelector(_cmd));
}

- (void)applicationDidBecomeActive:(UIApplication *)application
{
    NSLog(@"%@", NSStringFromSelector(_cmd));
}

- (void)applicationWillTerminate:(UIApplication *)application
{
    NSLog(@"%@", NSStringFromSelector(_cmd));
}

@end
```

You may be wondering about that NSLog call we're using in all these methods. Objective-C provides a handy built-in variable called _cmd that always contains the selector of the current method. A **selector**, in case you need a refresher, is simply Objective-C's way of referring to a method. The NSStringFromSelector function returns an NSString representation of a given selector. Our usage here simply gives us a shortcut for outputting the current method name without needing to retype it or copy and paste it.

Exploring Execution States

Now build and run the app. The simulator will appear and launch our application. Switch back to Xcode and take a look at the console (**View ➤ Debug Area ➤ Activate Console**), where you should see something like this:

```
2013-11-15 19:12:36.953 State Lab[12751:70b] application:didFinishLaunchingWith
Options:
2013-11-15 19:12:36.957 State Lab[12751:70b] applicationDidBecomeActive:
```

Here, you can see that the application has successfully launched and been moved into the Active state. Now go back to the simulator and press the home button, and you should see the following in the console:

```
2013-11-15 19:13:10.378 State Lab[12751:70b] applicationWillResignActive:
2013-11-15 19:13:10.386 State Lab[12751:70b] applicationDidEnterBackground:
```

These two lines show the app actually transitioning between two states: it first becomes Inactive, and then goes to Background. What you can't see here is that the app also switches to a third state: Suspended. Remember that you do not get any notification that this has happened; it's completely outside your control. Note that the app is still live in some sense, and Xcode is still connected to it, even though it's not actually getting any CPU time. Verify this by tapping the app's icon to relaunch it, which should produce this output:

```
2013-11-15 19:13:55.739 State Lab[12751:70b] applicationWillEnterForeground:
2013-11-15 19:13:55.739 State Lab[12751:70b] applicationDidBecomeActive:
```

There you are, back in business. The app was previously Suspended, is woken up to Inactive, and then ends up Active again. So, what happens when the app is really terminated? Tap the home button again, and you'll see this:

```
2013-11-15 19:14:35.035 State Lab[12751:70b] applicationWillResignActive:
2013-11-15 19:14:35.036 State Lab[12751:70b] applicationDidEnterBackground:
```

Now double-tap the home button. The sideways-scrolling of apps should appear. Press and swipe upwards on the State Lab screenshot until it flies offscreen, killing the application. What happens? You may be surprised to see that none of our NSLog calls print anything to the console. Instead, the app hangs in *main.m* on the call to the UIMainApplication function with the error message *"Thread 1: signal SIGKILL"*. Click the Stop button in the upper-left corner of Xcode, and now State Lab is truly and completely terminated.

As it turns out, the applicationWillTerminate: method isn't normally called when the system is moving an app from the Suspended to Not Running state. When an app is Suspended, whether the system decides to dump it to reclaim memory or you manually force-quit it, the app simply vanishes and doesn't get a chance to do anything. The applicationWillTerminate: method is called only if the app being terminated is in the Background state. This can occur, for instance, if your app is actively running in the Background state, using system resources in one of the predefined ways (audio playback, GPS usage, and so on) and is force-quit either by the user or by the system. In the case we just explored with State Lab, the app was in the Suspended state, not Background, and was therefore terminated immediately without any notification.

There's one more interesting interaction to examine here. It's what happens when the system shows an alert dialog, temporarily taking over the input stream from the app and putting it into an Inactive state. This state can be readily triggered only when running on a real device instead of the simulator, using the built-in Messages app. Messages, like many other apps, can receive messages from the outside and display them in several ways.

To see how these are set up, run the Settings app on your device, choose Notification Center from the list, and then select the Messages app from the list of apps. The hot "new" way to show messages, which debuted way back in iOS 5, is called Banners. This works by showing a small banner overlaid at the top of the screen, which doesn't need to interrupt whatever app is currently running. What we want to show is the bad old Alerts method, which makes a modal panel appear in front of the current app, requiring a user action. Select that, so that the Messages app turns back into the kind of pushy jerk that users of iOS 4 and earlier always had to deal with.

Now back to your computer. In Xcode, use the pop-up at the upper left to switch from the simulator to your device, and then hit the Run button to build and run the app on your device. Now all you need to do is send a message to your device from the outside. If your device is an iPhone, you can send it an SMS message from another phone. If it's an iPod touch or an iPad, you're limited to Apple's own iMessage communication, which works on all iOS devices, as well as OS X in the Messages app. Figure out what works for your setup, and send your device a message via SMS or iMessage. When your device displays the system alert showing the incoming message, this will appear in the Xcode console:

```
2013-11-18 00:04:28.295 State Lab[16571:60b] applicationWillResignActive:
```

Note that our app didn't get sent to the background. It's in the Inactive state and can still be seen behind the system alert. If this app were a game or had any video, audio, or animations running, this is where we would probably want to pause them.

Press the Close button on the alert, and you'll get this:

```
2013-11-18 00:05:23.830 State Lab[16571:60b] applicationDidBecomeActive:
```

Now let's see what happens if you decide to reply to the message instead. Send another message to your device, generating this:

```
2013-11-18 00:05:55.487 State Lab[16571:60b] applicationWillResignActive:
```

This time, hit Reply, which switches you over to the Messages app, and you should see the following flurry of activity:

```
2013-11-18 00:06:10.513 State Lab[16571:60b] applicationDidBecomeActive:
2013-11-18 00:06:11.137 State Lab[16571:60b] applicationWillResignActive:
2013-11-18 00:06:11.140 State Lab[16571:60b] applicationDidEnterBackground:
```

Interesting! Our app quickly becomes Active, becomes Inactive again, and finally goes to Background (and then, silently, Suspended).

Using Execution State Changes

So, what should we make of all this? Based on what we've just demonstrated, it seems like there's a clear strategy to follow when dealing with these state changes:

Active ➤ Inactive

Use applicationWillResignActive:/UIApplicationWillResignActiveNotification to "pause" your app's display. If your app is a game, you probably already have the ability to pause the gameplay in some way. For other kinds of apps, make sure no time-critical demands for user input are in the works because your app won't be getting any user input for a while.

Inactive ➤ Background

Use applicationDidEnterBackground:/UIApplicationDidEnterBackgroundNotification to release any resources that don't need to be kept around when the app is backgrounded (such as cached images or other easily reloadable data) or that wouldn't survive backgrounding anyway (such as active network connections). Getting rid of excess memory usage here will make your app's eventual Suspended snapshot smaller, thereby decreasing the risk that your app will be purged from RAM entirely. You should also use this opportunity to save any application data that will help your users pick up where they left off the next time your app is relaunched. If your app comes back to the Active state, normally this won't matter; however, in case it's purged and must be relaunched, your users will appreciate starting off in the same place.

Background ➤ Inactive

Use `applicationWillEnterForeground:`/`UIApplicationWillEnterForeground` to undo anything you did when switching from Inactive to Background. For example, here you can reestablish persistent network connections.

Inactive ➤ Active

Use `applicationDidBecomeActive:`/`UIApplicationDidBecomeActive` to undo anything you did when switching from Active to Inactive. Note that, if your app is a game, this probably does not mean dropping out of pause straight to the game; you should let your users do that on their own. Also keep in mind that this method and notification are used when an app is freshly launched, so anything you do here must work in that context, as well.

There is one special consideration for the **Inactive ➤ Background** transition. Not only does it have the longest description in the previous list, but it's also probably the most code- and time-intensive transition in applications because of the amount of bookkeeping you may want your app to do. When this transition is underway, the system won't give you the benefit of an unlimited amount of time to save your changes here. It gives you about five seconds. If your app takes longer than that to return from the delegate method (and handle any notifications you've registered for), then your app will be summarily purged from memory and pushed into the Not Running state! If this seems unfair, don't worry because there is a reprieve available. While handling that delegate method or notification, you can ask the system to perform some additional work for you in a background queue, which buys you some extra time. We'll demonstrate that technique in the next section.

Handling the Inactive State

The simplest state change your app is likely to encounter is from Active to Inactive, and then back to Active. You may recall that this is what happens if your iPhone receives an SMS message while your app is running and displays it for the user. In this section, we're going to make State Lab do something visually interesting, so that you can see what happens if you ignore that state change. Next, we'll show you how to fix it.

We'll also add a `UILabel` to our display and make it move using Core Animation, which is a really nice way of animating objects in iOS.

Start by adding a `UILabel` as an instance variable and property in *BIDViewController.m*:

```
#import "BIDViewController.h"

@interface BIDViewController ()

@property (strong, nonatomic) UILabel *label;

@end
```

Now let's set up the label when the view loads. Add the bold lines shown here to the viewDidLoad method:

```
- (void)viewDidLoad
{
    [super viewDidLoad];
    // Do any additional setup after loading the view, typically from a nib.
    CGRect bounds = self.view.bounds;
    CGRect labelFrame = CGRectMake(bounds.origin.x, CGRectGetMidY(bounds) - 50,
                                   bounds.size.width, 100);
    self.label = [[UILabel alloc] initWithFrame:labelFrame];
    self.label.font = [UIFont fontWithName:@"Helvetica" size:70];
    self.label.text = @"Bazinga!";
    self.label.textAlignment = NSTextAlignmentCenter;
    self.label.backgroundColor = [UIColor clearColor];
    [self.view addSubview:self.label];
}
```

It's time to set up some animation. We'll define two methods: one to rotate the label to an upside-down position and one to rotate it back to normal:

```
- (void)rotateLabelDown
{
    [UIView animateWithDuration:0.5
            animations:^{
                self.label.transform = CGAffineTransformMakeRotation(M_PI);
            }
            completion:^(BOOL finished){
                [self rotateLabelUp];
            }];
}

- (void)rotateLabelUp
{
    [UIView animateWithDuration:0.5
            animations:^{
                self.label.transform = CGAffineTransformMakeRotation(0);
            }
            completion:^(BOOL finished){
                [self rotateLabelDown];
            }];
}
```

This deserves a bit of explanation. UIView defines a class method called animateWithDuration:animations:completion:, which sets up an animation. Any animatable attributes that we set within the animations block don't have an immediate effect on the receiver. Instead, Core Animation will smoothly transition that attribute from its current value to the new value we specify. This is what's called an **implicit animation**, and it is one of the main features of Core Animation. The final completion block lets us specify what will happen after the animation is complete.

So, each of these methods sets the label's transform property to a particular rotation, specified in radians. Each also sets up a completion block to just call the other method, so the text will continue to animate back and forth forever.

Finally, we need to set up a way to kick-start the animation. For now, we'll do this by adding this line at the end of viewDidLoad (but we'll change this later, for reasons we'll describe at that time):

```
[self rotateLabelDown];
```

Now, build and run the app. You should see the *Bazinga!* label rotate back and forth (see Figure 15-4).

Figure 15-4. The State Lab application doing its label rotating magic

To test the **Active ➤ Inactive** transition, you really need to once again run this on an actual iPhone and send an SMS message to it from elsewhere. Unfortunately, there's no way to simulate this behavior in any version of the iOS simulator that Apple has released so far. If you don't yet have the ability to build and install on a device or don't have an iPhone, you won't be able to try this for yourself. In that case, please follow along as best you can!

Build and run the app on an iPhone, and see that the animation is running along. Now send an SMS message to the device. When the system alert comes up to show the message, you'll see that the animation keeps on running! That may be slightly comical, but it's probably irritating for a user. We will use transition notifications to stop our animation when this occurs.

Our controller class will need to have some internal state to keep track of whether it should be animating at any given time. For this purpose, let's add an ivar to *BIDViewController.m*. Because this simple BOOL doesn't need to be accessed by any outside classes, we skip the header and add it to the @implementation section:

```
@implementation BIDViewController {
    BOOL animate;
}
```

Since our class isn't the application delegate, we can't just implement the delegate methods and expect them to work. Instead, we sign up to receive notifications from the application when the execution state changes. Do this by adding the following code to the end of the viewDidLoad method in BIDViewController.m:

```
NSNotificationCenter *center = [NSNotificationCenter defaultCenter];
[center addObserver:self
           selector:@selector(applicationWillResignActive)
               name:UIApplicationWillResignActiveNotification
             object:nil];
[center addObserver:self
           selector:@selector(applicationDidBecomeActive)
               name:UIApplicationDidBecomeActiveNotification
             object:nil];
```

This sets up these two notifications, so each will call a method in our class at the appropriate time. Define these methods anywhere you like inside the @implementation block:

```
- (void)applicationWillResignActive
{
    NSLog(@"VC: %@", NSStringFromSelector(_cmd));
    animate = NO;
}

- (void)applicationDidBecomeActive
{
    NSLog(@"VC: %@", NSStringFromSelector(_cmd));
    animate = YES;
    [self rotateLabelDown];
}
```

This snippet includes the same method logging as before, just so you can see where the methods occur in the Xcode console. We added the preface "VC: " to distinguish this call from the NSLog() calls in the delegate (VC is for view controller). The first of these methods just turns off the animate flag. The second turns the flag back on, and then actually starts up the animations again. For that first method to have any effect, we need to add some code to check the animate flag and keep on animating only if it's enabled:

```
- (void)rotateLabelUp
{
    [UIView animateWithDuration:0.5
            animations:^{
                self.label.transform = CGAffineTransformMakeRotation(0);
            }
            completion:^(BOOL finished){
                if (animate) {
                    [self rotateLabelDown];
                }
            }];
}
```

We added this to the completion block of rotateLabelUp (and only there), so that our animation will stop only when the text is right-side up.

Now build and run the app again, and see what happens. Chances are, you'll see some flickery madness, with the label rapidly flipping up and down, not even rotating! The reason for this is simple, but perhaps not obvious (though we did hint at it earlier).

Remember that we started up the animations at the end of viewDidLoad by calling rotateLabelDown? Well, we're now calling rotateLabelDown in applicationDidBecomeActive, as well. And remember that applicationDidBecomeActive will be called, not only when we switch from Inactive back to Active, but also when the app launches and becomes Active in the first place! That means we're starting our animations twice, and Core Animation doesn't seem to deal well with multiple animations—indeed, both animations try to change the same attributes at the same time! The solution is simply to delete the line you previously added at the end of viewDidLoad:

```
    [self rotateLabelDown];
```

Now build and run the app again, and you should see that it's animating properly. Once again, send an SMS message to your iPhone. This time, when the system alert appears, you'll see that the animation in the background stops as soon as the text is right-side up. Tap the Close button, and the animation starts back up.

Now you've seen what to do for the simple case of switching from Active to Inactive and back. The bigger task, and perhaps the more important one, is dealing with a switch to the background and then back to foreground.

Handling the Background State

As mentioned earlier, switching to the Background state is pretty important to ensure the best possible user experience. This is the spot where you'll want to discard any resources that can easily be reacquired (or will be lost anyway when your app goes silent) and save information about your app's current state, all without occupying the main thread for more than five seconds.

To demonstrate some of these behaviors, we're going to extend State Lab in a few ways. First, we're going to add an image to the display, so that we can later show you how to get rid of the in-memory image. Then we're going to show you how to save some information about the app's state, so we can easily restore it later. Finally, we'll show you how to make sure these activities aren't taking up too much main thread time by putting all this work into a background queue.

Removing Resources When Entering the Background

Start by adding *smiley.png* from the book's source archive to your project's *State Lab folder*. Be sure to enable the checkbox that tells Xcode to copy the file to your project directory. Don't add it to the Images.xcassets asset catalog because that would provide automatic caching, which would interfere with the specific resource management we're going to implement.

Now let's add properties for both an image and an image view to *BIDViewController.m*:

```
@interface BIDViewController ()

@property (strong, nonatomic) UILabel *label;
@property (strong, nonatomic) UIImage *smiley;
@property (strong, nonatomic) UIImageView *smileyView;

@end
```

Next, set up the image view and put it on the screen by modifying the viewDidLoad method, as shown here:

```
- (void)viewDidLoad
{
    [super viewDidLoad];
    // Do any additional setup after loading the view, typically from a nib.
    CGRect bounds = self.view.bounds;
    CGRect labelFrame = CGRectMake(bounds.origin.x, CGRectGetMidY(bounds) - 50,
                                   bounds.size.width, 100);
    self.label = [[UILabel alloc] initWithFrame:labelFrame];
    self.label.font = [UIFont fontWithName:@"Helvetica" size:70];
    self.label.text = @"Bazinga!";
    self.label.textAlignment = NSTextAlignmentCenter;
    self.label.backgroundColor = [UIColor clearColor];

    // smiley.png is 84 x 84
    CGRect smileyFrame = CGRectMake(CGRectGetMidX(bounds) - 42,
                                    CGRectGetMidY(bounds)/2 - 42,
                                    84, 84);
    self.smileyView = [[UIImageView alloc] initWithFrame:smileyFrame];
    self.smileyView.contentMode = UIViewContentModeCenter;
    NSString *smileyPath = [[NSBundle mainBundle] pathForResource:@"smiley"
                                                           ofType:@"png"];
    self.smiley = [UIImage imageWithContentsOfFile:smileyPath];
    self.smileyView.image = self.smiley;
```

```
[self.view addSubview:self.smileyView];

[self.view addSubview:self.label];

NSNotificationCenter *center = [NSNotificationCenter defaultCenter];
[center addObserver:self
           selector:@selector(applicationWillResignActive)
               name:UIApplicationWillResignActiveNotification
             object:nil];
[center addObserver:self
           selector:@selector(applicationDidBecomeActive)
               name:UIApplicationDidBecomeActiveNotification
             object:nil];
}
```

Build and run the app, and you'll see the incredibly happy-looking smiley face toward the top of your screen (see Figure 15-5).

Figure 15-5. The State Lab application doing its label-rotating magic with the addition of a smiley icon

Next, press the home button to switch your app to the background, and then tap its icon to launch it again. You'll see that the app starts up right where it left off. That's good for the user, but we're not optimizing system resources as well as we could.

Remember that the fewer resources we use while our app is Suspended, the lower the risk that iOS will terminate our app entirely. By clearing any easily re-created resources from memory when we can, we increase the chance that our app will stick around and therefore relaunch super-quickly.

Let's see what we can do about that smiley face. We would really like to free up that image when going to the Background state and re-create it when coming back from the Background state. To do that, we'll need to add two more notification registrations inside viewDidLoad:

```
[center addObserver:self
           selector:@selector(applicationDidEnterBackground)
               name:UIApplicationDidEnterBackgroundNotification
             object:nil];
[center addObserver:self
           selector:@selector(applicationWillEnterForeground)
               name:UIApplicationWillEnterForegroundNotification
             object:nil];
```

And we want to implement the two new methods:

```
- (void)applicationDidEnterBackground
{
    NSLog(@"VC: %@", NSStringFromSelector(_cmd));
    self.smiley = nil;
    self.smileyView.image = nil;
}

- (void)applicationWillEnterForeground
{
    NSLog(@"VC: %@", NSStringFromSelector(_cmd));
    NSString *smileyPath = [[NSBundle mainBundle] pathForResource:@"smiley"
                                                           ofType:@"png"];
    self.smiley = [UIImage imageWithContentsOfFile:smileyPath];
    self.smileyView.image = self.smiley;
}
```

Build and run the app, and repeat the same steps of backgrounding your app and switching back to it. You should see that, from the user's standpoint, the behavior appears to be about the same. If you want to verify for yourself that this is really happening, comment out the contents of the applicationWillEnterForeground method, and then build and run the app again. You'll see that the image really does disappear.

Saving State When Entering the Background

Now that you've seen an example of how to free up some resources when entering the Background state, it's time to think about saving state. Remember that the idea is to save all information relevant to what the user is doing, so that, if your application is later dumped from memory, users can still pick up right where they left off the next time they return.

The kind of state we're talking about here is really application-specific. You might want to keep track of which document users were looking at, their cursor location in a text field, which application view was open, and so on. In our case, we're just going to keep track of the selection in a segmented control.

Start by adding a new property in *BIDViewController.m*:

```
#import "BIDViewController.h"

@interface BIDViewController ()

@property (strong, nonatomic) UILabel *label;
@property (strong, nonatomic) UIImage *smiley;
@property (strong, nonatomic) UIImageView *smileyView;
@property (strong, nonatomic) UISegmentedControl *segmentedControl;

@end
```

Next, move to the middle of the viewDidLoad method, where you'll create the segmented control and add it to the view:

```
    .
    .
    .

    self.smileyView.image = self.smiley;

    self.segmentedControl = [[UISegmentedControl alloc] initWithItems:
                            [NSArray arrayWithObjects:
                                @"One", @"Two", @"Three", @"Four", nil]] ;
    self.segmentedControl.frame = CGRectMake(bounds.origin.x + 20,
                                            50,
                                            bounds.size.width - 40, 30);

    [self.view addSubview:self.segmentedControl];
    [self.view addSubview:self.smileyView];
    [self.view addSubview:self.label];
    .
    .
    .
```

Build and run the app. You should see the segmented control and be able to click its segments to select them one at a time. Background your app again by clicking the home button, bring up the taskbar (by double-clicking the home button) and kill your app, and then relaunch it. You'll find yourself back at square one, with no segment selected. That's what we need to fix next.

Saving the selection is simple enough; we just need to add a few lines to the end of the applicationDidEnterBackground method in *BIDViewController.m*:

```
- (void)applicationDidEnterBackground
{
    NSLog(@"VC: %@", NSStringFromSelector(_cmd));
    self.smiley = nil;
```

```
    self.smileyView.image = nil;
    NSInteger selectedIndex = self.segmentedControl.selectedSegmentIndex;
    [[NSUserDefaults standardUserDefaults] setInteger:selectedIndex
                                        forKey:@"selectedIndex"];
}
```

But where should we restore this selection index and use it to configure the segmented control? The inverse of this method, applicationWillEnterForeground, isn't what we want. When that method is called, the app has already been running, and the setting is still intact. Instead, we need to access this when things are being set up after a new launch, which brings us back to the viewDidLoad method. Add the bold lines shown here at the end of the method:

```
    .
    .
    .

    [self.view addSubview:self.label];

    NSNumber *indexNumber = [[NSUserDefaults standardUserDefaults]
                            objectForKey:@"selectedIndex"];
    if (indexNumber) {
        NSInteger selectedIndex = [indexNumber intValue];
        self.segmentedControl.selectedSegmentIndex = selectedIndex;
    }

    .
    .
    .
```

We needed to include a little sanity check here to see whether there's a value stored for the selectedIndex key, to cover cases such as the first app launch, where nothing has been selected.

Now build and run the app, touch a segment, and then do the full background-kill-restart dance. There it is—your selection is intact!

Obviously, what we've shown here is pretty minimal, but the concept can be extended to all kinds of application states. It's up to you to decide how far you want to take it in order to maintain the illusion for the users that your app was always there, just waiting for them to come back!

Requesting More Backgrounding Time

Earlier, we mentioned the possibility of your app being dumped from memory if moving to the Background state takes too much time. For example, your app may be in the middle of doing a file transfer that it would really be a shame not to finish; however, trying to hijack the applicationDidEnterBackground method to make it complete the work there, before the application is really backgrounded, isn't really an option. Instead, you should use applicationDidEnterBackground as a platform for telling the system that you have some extra work you would like to do, and then start up a block to actually do it. Assuming that the system has enough available RAM to keep your app in memory while the user does something else, the system will oblige you and keep your app running for a while.

We'll demonstrate this, not with an actual file transfer, but with a simple sleep call. Once again, we'll be using our new acquaintances GCD and blocks to make the contents of our applicationDidEnterBackground method run in a separate queue.

In *BIDViewController.m*, modify the applicationDidEnterBackground method as follows:

```
- (void)applicationDidEnterBackground
{
    NSLog(@"VC: %@", NSStringFromSelector(_cmd));
    UIApplication *app = [UIApplication sharedApplication];

    __block UIBackgroundTaskIdentifier taskId;
    taskId = [app beginBackgroundTaskWithExpirationHandler:^{
        NSLog(@"Background task ran out of time and was terminated.");
        [app endBackgroundTask:taskId];
    }];

    if (taskId == UIBackgroundTaskInvalid) {
        NSLog(@"Failed to start background task!");
        return;
    }

    dispatch_async(dispatch_get_global_queue(DISPATCH_QUEUE_PRIORITY_DEFAULT, 0),
    ^{
        NSLog(@"Starting background task with %f seconds remaining",
            app.backgroundTimeRemaining);
        self.smiley = nil;
        self.smileyView.image = nil;
        NSInteger selectedIndex = self.segmentedControl.selectedSegmentIndex;
        [[NSUserDefaults standardUserDefaults] setInteger:selectedIndex
                                            forKey:@"selectedIndex"];

        // simulate a lengthy (25 seconds) procedure
        [NSThread sleepForTimeInterval:25];

        NSLog(@"Finishing background task with %f seconds remaining",
            app.backgroundTimeRemaining);
        [app endBackgroundTask:taskId];
    });
}
```

Let's look through this code piece by piece. First, we grab the shared UIApplication instance, since we'll be using it several times in this method. And then comes this:

```
    __block UIBackgroundTaskIdentifier taskId;
    taskId = [app beginBackgroundTaskWithExpirationHandler:^{
        NSLog(@"Background task ran out of time and was terminated.");
        [app endBackgroundTask:taskId];
    }];
```

The call to beginBackgroundTaskWithExpirationHandler: returns an identifier that we'll need to keep track of for later use. We've declared the taskId variable it's stored in with the __block storage qualifier, since we want to be sure the identifier returned by the method is shared among any blocks we create in this method.

With the call to beginBackgroundTaskWithExpirationHandler:, we're basically telling the system that we need more time to accomplish something, and we promise to let it know when we're finished. The block we give as a parameter may be called if the system decides that we've been going way too long anyway and decides to stop running.

Note that the block we gave ended with a call to endBackgroundTask:, passing along taskId. That tells the system that we're finished with the work for which we previously requested extra time. It's important to balance each call to beginBackgroundTaskWithExpirationHandler: with a matching call to endBackgroundTask: so that the system knows when we've completed the work.

> **Note**   Depending on your computing background, the use of the word *task* here may evoke associations
> with what we usually call a *process*, consisting of a running program that may contain multiple threads,
> and so on. In this case, try to put that out of your mind. The use of *task* in this context really just means
> "something that needs to get done." Any task you create here is running within your still-executing app.

Next, we do this:

```
if (taskId == UIBackgroundTaskInvalid) {
    NSLog(@"Failed to start background task!");
    return;
}
```

If our earlier call to beginBackgroundTaskWithExpirationHandler: returned the special value UIBackgroundTaskInvalid, that means the system is refusing to grant us any additional time. In that case, you could try to do the quickest part of whatever needs doing anyway and hope that it completes quickly enough that your app won't be terminated before it's finished. This was more likely to be an issue when running on older devices, such as the iPhone 3G, that didn't support multitasking. In this example, however, we're just letting it slide.

Next comes the interesting part where the work itself is actually done:

```
dispatch_async(dispatch_get_global_queue(DISPATCH_QUEUE_PRIORITY_DEFAULT, 0),
^{
    NSLog(@"Starting background task with %f seconds remaining",
          app.backgroundTimeRemaining);
    self.smiley = nil;
    self.smileyView.image = nil;
    NSInteger selectedIndex = self.segmentedControl.selectedSegmentIndex;
    [[NSUserDefaults standardUserDefaults] setInteger:selectedIndex
                                        forKey:@"selectedIndex"];
    // simulate a lengthy (25 seconds) procedure
    [NSThread sleepForTimeInterval:25];
```

```
    NSLog(@"Finishing background task with %f seconds remaining",
        app.backgroundTimeRemaining);
    [app endBackgroundTask:taskId];
});
```

All this does is take the same work our method was doing in the first place and place it in a background queue. At the end of that block, we call endBackgroundTask: to let the system know that we're finished.

With that in place, build and run the app, and then background your app by pressing the home button. Watch the Xcode console as well as the status bar at the bottom of the Xcode window. You'll see that this time, your app stays running (you don't get the "Debugging terminated" message in the status bar), and after 25 seconds, you will see the final log in your output. A complete run of the app up to this point should give you console output along these lines:

```
2013-11-18 01:30:08.194 State Lab[12158:70b] application:didFinishLaunchingWith
Options:
2013-11-18 01:30:08.209 State Lab[12158:70b] applicationDidBecomeActive:
2013-11-18 01:30:08.210 State Lab[12158:70b] VC: applicationDidBecomeActive
2013-11-18 01:30:17.010 State Lab[12158:70b] applicationWillResignActive:
2013-11-18 01:30:17.011 State Lab[12158:70b] VC: applicationWillResignActive
2013-11-18 01:30:17.018 State Lab[12158:70b] applicationDidEnterBackground:
2013-11-18 01:30:17.019 State Lab[12158:70b] VC: applicationDidEnterBackground
2013-11-18 01:30:17.021 State Lab[12158:3a03] Starting background task with
179.988868 seconds remaining
2013-11-18 01:30:42.027 State Lab[12158:3a03] Finishing background task with
154.986797 seconds remaining
```

As you can see, the system is much more generous with time when doing things in the background than it is in the main thread of your app. Following this procedure can really help you out if you have any ongoing tasks to deal with.

Note that we asked for a single background task identifier; but in practice, you can ask for as many as you need. For example, if you have multiple network transfers happening at Background time and you need to complete them, you can ask for an identifier for each and allow them to continue running in a background queue. So, you can easily allow multiple operations to run in parallel during the available time. Also consider that the task identifier you receive is a normal C-language value (not an object). Apart from being stored in a local __block variable, it can also be stored as an instance variable if that better suits your class design.

Grand Central Dispatch, Over and Out

This has been a pretty heavy chapter, with a lot of new concepts thrown your way. Not only have you learned about a complete new feature set Apple added to the C language, but you've also discovered a new conceptual paradigm for dealing with concurrency without worrying about threads. We also demonstrated some techniques for making sure your apps play nicely in the multitasking world of iOS. Now that we've gotten some of this heavy stuff out of the way, let's move on to the next chapter, which focuses on drawing. Pencils out, let's draw!

Chapter 16

Drawing with Core Graphics

Every application we've built so far has been constructed from views and controls that are part of the UIKit framework. You can do a lot with UIKit, and a great many applications can be constructed using only its predefined objects. Some visual elements, however, can't be fully realized without going beyond what the UIKit stock components offer.

For example, sometimes an application needs to be able to do custom drawing. Fortunately, iOS includes the Core Graphics framework which allows us to do a wide array of drawing tasks. In this chapter, we'll explore this powerful graphics environment. We'll also build sample applications that demonstrate key features of Core Graphics and explain its main concepts.

Paint the World

One of the main components of Core Graphics is a set of APIs called **Quartz 2D**. This is a collection of functions, datatypes, and objects designed to let you draw directly into a view or an image in memory. Quartz 2D treats the view or image that is being drawn into as a virtual canvas. It follows what's called a **painter's model**, which is just a fancy way of saying that the drawing commands are applied in much the same way that paint is applied to a canvas.

If a painter paints an entire canvas red, and then paints the bottom half of the canvas blue, the canvas will be half red and half either blue or purple (blue if the paint is opaque; purple if the paint is semitransparent). Quartz 2D's virtual canvas works the same way. If you paint the whole view red, and then paint the bottom half of the view blue, you'll have a view that's half red and half either blue or purple, depending on whether the second drawing action was fully opaque or partially transparent. Each drawing action is applied to the canvas on top of any previous drawing actions.

Quartz 2D provides a variety of line, shape, and image drawing functions. Though easy to use, Quartz 2D is limited to two-dimensional drawing. Although many Quartz 2D functions do result in drawing that takes advantage of hardware acceleration, there is no guarantee that any particular action you take in Quartz 2D will be accelerated.

Now that you have a general idea of Quartz 2D, let's try it out. We'll start with the basics of how Quartz 2D works, and then build a simple drawing application with it.

The Quartz 2D Approach to Drawing

When using Quartz 2D (Quartz for short), you'll usually add the drawing code to the view doing the drawing. For example, you might create a subclass of UIView and add Quartz function calls to that class's drawRect: method. The drawRect: method is part of the UIView class definition and is called every time a view needs to redraw itself. If you insert your Quartz code in drawRect:, that code will be called, and then the view will redraw itself.

Quartz 2D's Graphics Contexts

In Quartz, as in the rest of Core Graphics, drawing happens in a **graphics context**, usually referred to simply as a **context**. Every view has an associated context. You retrieve the current context, use that context to make various Quartz drawing calls, and let the context worry about rendering your drawing onto the view. You can think of this context as a sort of canvas. The system provides you with a default context where the contents will appear on the screen. However, it's also possible to create a context of your own for doing drawing that you don't want to appear immediately, but to save for later or use for something else. We're going to be focusing mainly on the default context, which you can acquire with this line of code:

```
CGContextRef context = UIGraphicsGetCurrentContext();
```

> **Note**   Here we're using Core Graphics C functions, rather than Objective-C objects, to do our drawing. Some of these functions have object-oriented equivalents, which we'll delve into a little later.

Once you've defined your graphics context, you can draw into it by passing the context to a variety of Core Graphics drawing functions. For example, this sequence will create a **path** describing a simple line, and then draw that path:

```
CGContextSetLineWidth(context, 4.0);
CGContextSetStrokeColorWithColor(context, [UIColor redColor].CGColor);
CGContextMoveToPoint(context, 10.0, 10.0);
CGContextAddLineToPoint(context, 20.0, 20.0);
CGContextStrokePath(context);
```

The first call specifies that any subsequent drawing commands that create the current path should be performed with a brush that is 4 points wide. Think of this as selecting the size of the brush you're about to paint with. Until you call this function again with a different number, all lines will have a width of 4 points when drawn. You then specify that the stroke color should be red. In Core Graphics, two colors are associated with drawing actions:

- The **stroke color** is used in drawing lines and for the outline of shapes.
- The **fill color** is used to fill in shapes.

A context has a sort of invisible pen associated with it that does the line drawing. As drawing commands are executed, the movements of this pen form a path. When you call CGContextMoveToPoint(), you lift the virtual pen and move to the location you specify, without actually drawing anything. Whatever operation comes next, it will do its work relative to the point to which you moved the pen. In the earlier example, for instance, we first moved the pen to (10, 10). The next function call drew a line from the current pen location (10, 10) to the specified location (20, 20), which became the new pen location.

When you draw in Core Graphics, you're not drawing anything you can actually see—at least not immediately. You're creating a path, which can be a shape, a line, or some other object; however, it contains no color or other features to make it visible. It's like writing in invisible ink. Until you do something to make it visible, your path can't be seen. So, the next step is to call the CGContextStrokePath() function, which tells Quartz to draw the path you're using. This function will use the line width and the stroke color we set earlier to actually color (or "paint") the path and make it visible.

The Coordinate System

In the previous chunk of code, we passed a pair of floating-point numbers as parameters to CGContextMoveToPoint() and CGContextLineToPoint(). These numbers represent positions in the Core Graphics coordinate system. Locations in this coordinate system are denoted by their x and y coordinates, which we usually represent as (x, y). The upper-left corner of the context is (0, 0). As you move down, y increases. As you move to the right, x increases.

In the previous code snippet, we drew a diagonal line from (10, 10) to (20, 20), which would look like the one shown in Figure 16-1.

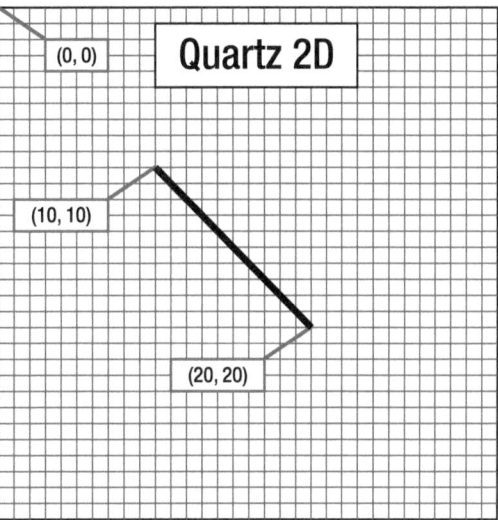

Figure 16-1. Drawing a line using Quartz 2D's coordinate system

The coordinate system is one of the gotchas in drawing with Quartz on iOS because its vertical component is flipped from what many graphics libraries use and from the traditional Cartesian coordinate system (introduced by René Descartes in the 17th century). In other systems such as OpenGL, or even the OS X version of Quartz, (0, 0) is in the lower-left corner; and as the y coordinate increases, you move toward the top of the context or view, as shown in Figure 16-2.

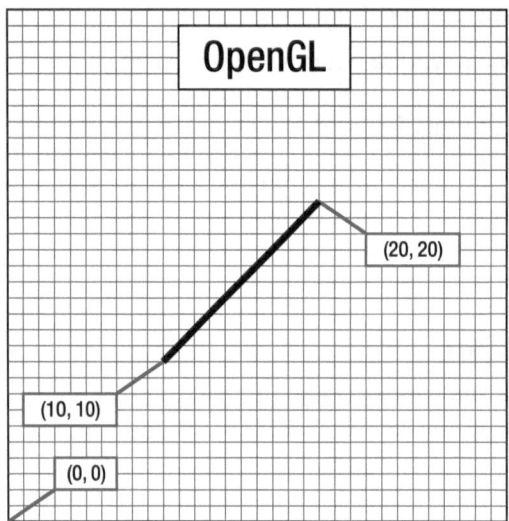

Figure 16-2. *In many graphics libraries, including OpenGL, drawing from (10, 10) to (20, 20) would produce a line that looks like this instead of the line in Figure 16-1*

To specify a point in the coordinate system, some Quartz functions require two floating-point numbers as parameters. Other Quartz functions ask for the point to be embedded in a CGPoint, a struct that holds two floating-point values: x and y. To describe the size of a view or other object, Quartz uses CGSize, a struct that also holds two floating-point values: width and height. Quartz also declares a datatype called CGRect, which is used to define a rectangle in the coordinate system. A CGRect contains two elements: a CGPoint called origin, with x and y values that identify the top left of the rectangle; and a CGSize called size, which identifies the width and height of the rectangle.

Specifying Colors

An important part of drawing is color, so understanding the way colors work on iOS is critical. This is one of the areas where the UIKit does provide an Objective-C class: UIColor. You can't use a UIColor object directly in Core Graphic calls. However, UIColor is just a wrapper around CGColor (which is what the Core Graphic functions require), so you can retrieve a CGColor reference from a UIColor instance by using its CGColor property, as we showed earlier, in this code snippet:

```
CGContextSetStrokeColorWithColor(context, [UIColor redColor].CGColor);
```

We created a UIColor instance using a convenience method called redColor, and then retrieved its CGColor property and passed that into the function.

A Bit of Color Theory for Your iOS Device's Display

In modern computer graphics, any color displayed on the screen has its data stored in some way based on something called a **color model**. A color model (sometimes called a **color space**) is simply a way of representing real-world color as digital values that a computer can use. One common way to represent colors is to use four components: red, green, blue, and alpha. In Quartz, each of these values is represented as CGFloat (which is a 4-byte floating-point value, the same as float). These values should always contain a value between 0.0 and 1.0.

> **Note**   A floating-point value that is expected to be in the range 0.0 to 1.0 is often referred to as a **clamped floating-point variable**, or sometimes just a **clamp**.

The red, green, and blue components are fairly easy to understand, as they represent the **additive primary colors**, or the **RGB color model** (see Figure 16-3). If you add together light of these three colors in equal proportions, the result will appear to the eye as either white or a shade of gray, depending on the intensity of the light mixed. Combining the three additive primaries in different proportions gives you a range of different colors, referred to as a **gamut**.

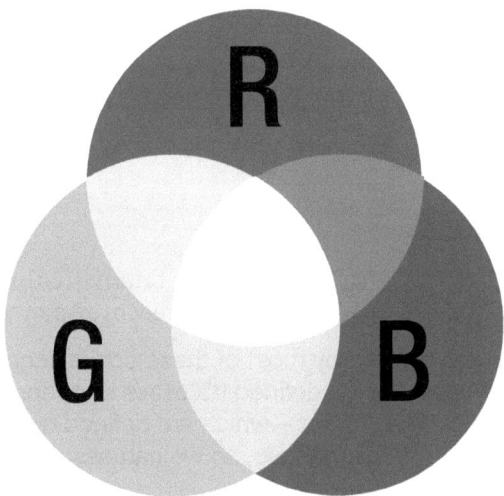

Figure 16-3. A simple representation of the additive primary colors that make up the RGB color model

In grade school, you probably learned that the primary colors are red, yellow, and blue. These primaries, which are known as the **historical subtractive primaries**, or the **RYB color model**, have little application in modern color theory and are almost never used in computer graphics. The color gamut of the RYB color model is much more limited than the RGB color model, and it also doesn't lend itself easily to mathematical definition. As much as we hate to tell you that your wonderful third-grade art teacher, Mrs. Smedlee, was wrong about anything—well, in the context of computer graphics, she was. For our purposes, the primary colors are red, green, and blue, not red, yellow, and blue.

In addition to red, green, and blue, Quartz uses another color component, called **alpha**, which represents how transparent a color is. When drawing one color on top of another color, alpha is used to determine the final color that is drawn. With an alpha of 1.0, the drawn color is 100% opaque and obscures any colors beneath it. With any value less than 1.0, the colors below will show through and mix with the color above. If the alpha is 0.0, then this color will be completely invisible and whatever is behind it will show through completely. When an alpha component is used, the color model is sometimes referred to as the **RGBA color model,** although technically speaking, the alpha isn't really part of the color; it just defines how the color will interact with other colors when it is drawn.

Other Color Models

Although the RGB model is the most commonly used in computer graphics, it is not the only color model. Several others are in use, including the following:

- Hue, saturation, value (HSV)
- Hue, saturation, lightness (HSL)
- Cyan, magenta, yellow, black (CMYK), which is used in four-color offset printing
- Grayscale

To make matters even more confusing, there are different versions of some of these models, including several variants of the RGB color space.

Fortunately, for most operations, we don't need to worry about the color model that is being used. We can just call CGColor on our UIColor objects, and in most cases Core Graphics will handle any necessary conversions.

Color Convenience Methods

UIColor has a large number of convenience methods that return UIColor objects initialized to a specific color. In our previous code sample, we used the redColor method to initialize a color to red.

Fortunately, the UIColor instances created by most of these convenience methods all use the RGBA color model. The only exceptions are the predefined UIColors that represent grayscale values—such as blackColor, whiteColor, and darkGrayColor—which are defined only in terms of white level and alpha. In our examples here, we're not using those, so we can assume RGBA for now.

If you need more control over color, instead of using one of those convenience methods based on the name of the color, you can create a color by specifying all four of the components. Here's an example:

```
UIColor *red = [UIColor colorWithRed:1.0 green:0.0 blue:0.0 alpha:1.0];
```

Drawing Images in Context

Quartz allows you to draw images directly into a context. This is another example of an Objective-C class (UIImage) that you can use as an alternative to working with a Core Graphics data structure

(CGImage). The UIImage class contains methods to draw its image into the current context. You'll need to identify where the image should appear in the context using either of the following techniques:

- By specifying a CGPoint to identify the image's upper-left corner

- By specifying a CGRect to frame the image, resized to fit the frame if necessary

You can draw a UIImage into the current context, like so:

```
UIImage *image; // assuming this exists and points at a UIImage instance
CGPoint drawPoint = CGPointMake(100.0, 100.0);
[image drawAtPoint:drawPoint];
```

Drawing Shapes: Polygons, Lines, and Curves

Quartz provides a number of functions to make it easier to create complex shapes. To draw a rectangle or a polygon, you don't need to calculate angles, draw lines, or do any math at all. You can just call a Quartz function to do the work for you. For example, to draw an ellipse, you define the rectangle into which the ellipse needs to fit and let Core Graphics do the work:

```
CGRect theRect = CGRectMake(0, 0, 100, 100);
CGContextAddEllipseInRect(context, theRect);
CGContextDrawPath(context, kCGPathFillStroke);
```

You use similar methods for rectangles. Quartz also provides methods that let you create more complex shapes, such as arcs and Bezier paths.

> **Note**   We won't be working with complex shapes in this chapter's examples. To learn more about arcs and Bezier paths in Quartz, check out the *Quartz 2D Programming Guide* in the iOS Dev Center at `http://developer.apple.com/documentation/GraphicsImaging/Conceptual/drawingwithquartz2d/` or in Xcode's online documentation.

Quartz 2D Tool Sampler: Patterns, Gradients, and Dash Patterns

Quartz offers quite an impressive array of tools. For example, Quartz supports filling polygons not only with solid colors, but also with gradients. And in addition to drawing solid lines, it can also use an assortment of dash patterns. Take a look at the screenshots in Figure 16-4, which are from Apple's QuartzDemo sample code, to see a sampling of what Quartz can do for you.

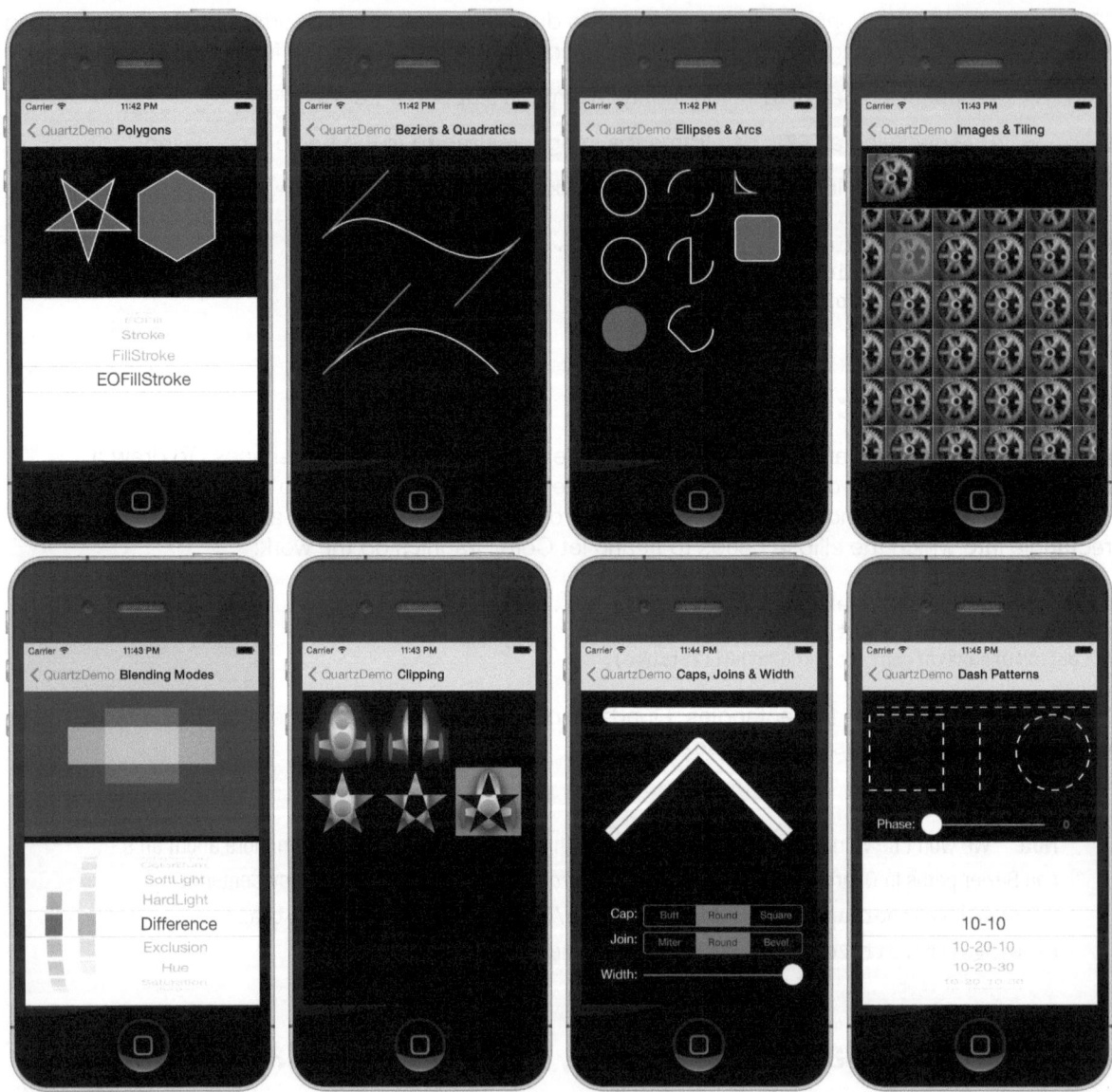

Figure 16-4. Some examples of what Quartz 2D can do, from the QuartzDemo sample project provided by Apple

Now that you have a basic understanding of how Quartz works and what it is capable of doing, let's try it out.

The QuartzFun Application

Our next application is a simple drawing program (see Figure 16-5). We're going to build this application using Quartz to give you a real feel for how the concepts we've been describing fit together.

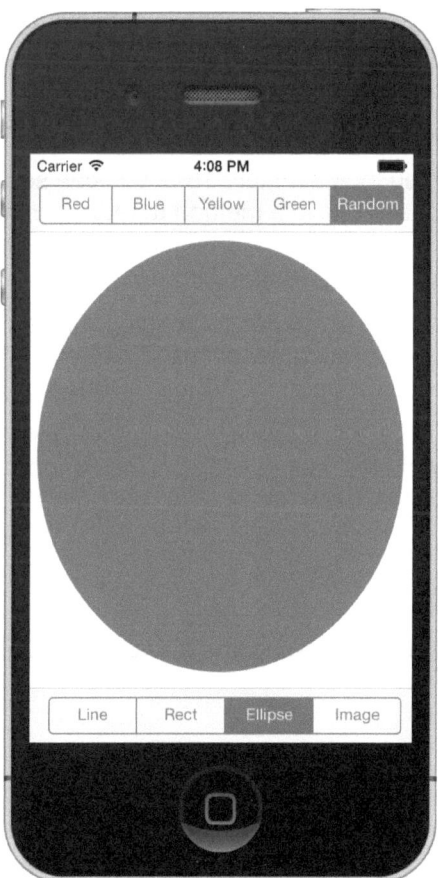

Figure 16-5. Our chapter's simple drawing application in action

The application features a bar across the top and one across the bottom, each with a segmented control. The control at the top lets you change the drawing color, and the one at the bottom lets you change the shape to be drawn. When you touch and drag, the selected shape will be drawn in the selected color. To minimize the application's complexity, only one shape will be drawn at a time.

Setting Up the QuartzFun Application

In Xcode, create a new iPhone project using the *Single View Application* template and call it *QuartzFun*. The template has already provided us with an application delegate and a view controller. We're going to be executing our custom drawing in a custom view, so we need to also create a subclass of UIView where we'll do the drawing by overriding the drawRect: method.

With the *QuartzFun* folder selected (the folder that currently contains the app delegate and view controller files), press ⌘N to bring up the new file assistant, and then select *Objective-C class* from the *Cocoa Touch* section. Name the new class *BIDQuartzFunView* and make it a subclass of *UIView*.

We're going to define some constants, as we've done in previous projects; but this time, our constants will be needed by more than one class. We'll create a header file just for the constants.

Select the *QuartzFun* group again and press ⌘**N** to bring up the new file assistant. Select the *Header File* template from the *C and C++* heading, and name the file *BIDConstants.h*.

We have two more files to go. If you look at Figure 16-5, you can see that we offer an option to select a random color. UIColor doesn't have a method to return a random color, so we'll need to write code to do that. We could put that code into our controller class, but because we're savvy Objective-C programmers, we'll put it into a category on UIColor.

Again, select the *QuartzFun* folder and press ⌘**N** to bring up the new file assistant. Select the *Objective-C category* from the *Cocoa Touch* heading and hit *Next*. When prompted, name the category *BIDRandom* and make it a *Category on UIColor*. Click *Next*, and then save the file into your project folder.

You should now have a new pair of files named *UIColor+BIDRandom.h* and *UIColor+BIDRandom.m* for your category.

Creating a Random Color

Let's tackle the category first. Add the following line to *UIColor+BIDRandom.h*:

```
#import <UIKit/UIKit.h>

@interface UIColor (BIDRandom)
+ (UIColor *)randomColor;
@end
```

Now, switch over to *UIColor+BIDRandom.m*, and add this code:

```
#import "UIColor+BIDRandom.h"

#define ARC4RANDOM_MAX 0x100000000LL

@implementation UIColor (BIDRandom)
+ (UIColor *)randomColor {
    CGFloat red = (CGFloat)arc4random() / (CGFloat)ARC4RANDOM_MAX;
    CGFloat blue = (CGFloat)arc4random() / (CGFloat)ARC4RANDOM_MAX;
    CGFloat green = (CGFloat)arc4random() / (CGFloat)ARC4RANDOM_MAX;
    return [UIColor colorWithRed:red green:green blue:blue alpha:1.0];
}
@end
```

This is fairly straightforward. For each color component, we use the arc4random() function to generate a random floating point number, which we then divide by a constant representing the maximum value that arc4random() can return. That way, each component ends up with a random number between 0.0 and 1.0. We then use those three components to create a new color. We set the alpha value to 1.0 so that all generated colors will be opaque.

Defining Application Constants

Next, we'll define constants for each of the options that the user can select using the segmented controllers. Single-click *BIDConstants.h* and add the following code:

```
#ifndef QuartzFun_BIDConstants_h
#define QuartzFun_BIDConstants_h

typedef NS_ENUM(NSInteger, ShapeType) {
    kLineShape = 0,
    kRectShape,
    kEllipseShape,
    kImageShape
};

typedef NS_ENUM(NSInteger, ColorTabIndex) {
    kRedColorTab = 0,
    kBlueColorTab,
    kYellowColorTab,
    kGreenColorTab,
    kRandomColorTab
};

#define degreesToRadian(x) (M_PI * (x) / 180.0)

#endif
```

To make our code more readable, we've declared two enumerated types using `typedef` and the `NS_ENUM` macro. One will represent the shape options available in our application; the other will represent the various color options available. The values these constants hold will correspond to segments on the two segmented controllers we'll create in our application.

> **Note**   Just in case you haven't seen this form before, the purpose of the `#ifndef` compiler directive is to first test if `QuartzFun_BIDConstants_h` is defined and, if not, to define it. Why not just put in the `#define`? This way, if a *.h* file is included more than once, either directly or via other *.h* files, the directive won't be duplicated. This normally isn't needed when compiling Objective-C code using the `#import` directive, but it is a pretty common pattern when developing in C and using the older `#include` directive, which isn't smart enough to avoid pulling in the same header multiple times.

Implementing the QuartzFunView Skeleton

Since we're going to do our drawing in a subclass of UIView, let's set up that class with everything it needs, except for the actual code to do the drawing, which we'll add later. Single-click *BIDQuartzFunView.h* and add the following code at the top:

```
#import <UIKit/UIKit.h>
#import "BIDConstants.h"

@interface BIDQuartzFunView : UIView
@property (assign, nonatomic) CGPoint firstTouchLocation;
@property (assign, nonatomic) CGPoint lastTouchLocation;
@property (assign, nonatomic) ShapeType shapeType;
@property (assign, nonatomic) BOOL useRandomColor;
@property (strong, nonatomic) UIColor *currentColor;
@property (strong, nonatomic) UIImage *drawImage;
@end
```

First, we import the *BIDConstants.h* header we just created so we can use our enumeration values. We then declare our properties. The first two will track the user's finger as it drags across the screen. We'll store the location where the user first touches the screen in firstTouchLocation. We'll store the location of the user's finger while dragging and when the drag ends in lastTouchLocation. Our drawing code will use these two variables to determine where to draw the requested shape.

Next, we define a ShapeType to keep track of the shape the user wants to draw, as well as a Boolean that will be used to keep track of whether the user is requesting a random color. Next, we use a UIColor property to keep track of the currently chosen color. Finally, we define a UIImage property that will hold the image to be drawn on the screen when the user selects the rightmost toolbar item on the bottom toolbar (see Figure 16-6). Note the first four properties are all low-level C types and are therefore declared with assign keyword, while the last two are objects declared using the strong keyword.

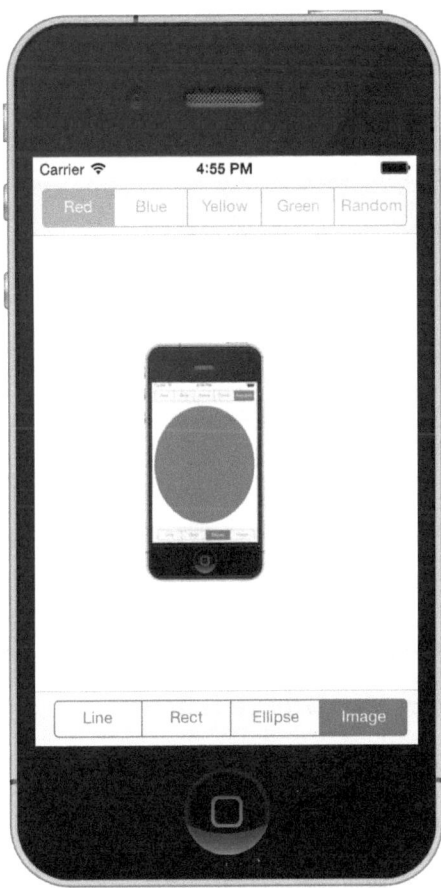

Figure 16-6. When drawing a UIImage to the screen, notice that the color control is disabled. Can you tell which app is running on the tiny iPhone?

Switch over to *BIDQuartzFunView.m*; we have several changes we need to make in this file. For starters, import the *UIColor+BIDRandom.h* header so that we can generate random colors by adding this line near the top, just below the other import:

```
#import "UIColor+BIDRandom.h"
```

And now onward to the implementation itself. The template gave us a method called initWithFrame:, but we won't be using that. Keep in mind that object instances in nibs and storyboards are stored as archived objects, which is the same mechanism we used in Chapter 13 to archive and load our objects to disk. As a result, when an object instance is loaded from a nib or a storyboard, neither init nor initWithFrame: is ever called. Instead, initWithCoder: is used, so this is where we need to add any initialization code. In our case, we'll set the initial color value to red, initialize useRandomColor to NO, and load the image file that we're going to draw later in the chapter. Delete the existing stub implementation of initWithFrame: and replace it with the following method:

```
- (id)initWithCoder:(NSCoder*)coder {
    if (self = [super initWithCoder:coder]) {
        _currentColor = [UIColor redColor];
        _useRandomColor = NO;
        _drawImage = [UIImage imageNamed:@"iphone.png"] ;
    }
    return self;
}
```

After initWithCoder:, we need to add a few more methods to respond to the user's touches. After initWithCoder:, insert the following three methods:

```
#pragma mark - Touch Handling

- (void)touchesBegan:(NSSet *)touches withEvent:(UIEvent *)event {
    if (self.useRandomColor) {
        self.currentColor = [UIColor randomColor];
    }
    UITouch *touch = [touches anyObject];
    self.firstTouchLocation = [touch locationInView:self];
    self.lastTouchLocation = [touch locationInView:self];
    [self setNeedsDisplay];
}

- (void)touchesEnded:(NSSet *)touches withEvent:(UIEvent *)event {
    UITouch *touch = [touches anyObject];
    self.lastTouchLocation = [touch locationInView:self];
    [self setNeedsDisplay];
}

- (void)touchesMoved:(NSSet *)touches withEvent:(UIEvent *)event {
    UITouch *touch = [touches anyObject];
    self.lastTouchLocation = [touch locationInView:self];
    [self setNeedsDisplay];
}
```

These three methods are inherited from UIView, which in turn inherits them from UIView's parent, UIResponder. They can be overridden to find out where the user is touching the screen. They work as follows:

- touchesBegan:withEvent: is called when the user's finger first touches the screen. In that method, we change the color if the user has selected a random color using the new randomColor method we added to UIColor earlier. After that, we store the current location so that we know where the user first touched the screen, and we indicate that our view needs to be redrawn by calling setNeedsDisplay on self.

- touchesMoved:withEvent: is continuously called while the user is dragging a finger on the screen. All we do here is store the new location in lastTouchLocation and indicate that the screen needs to be redrawn.

- touchesEnded:withEvent: is called when the user lifts the finger off the screen. Just as in the touchesMoved:withEvent: method, all we do is store the final location in the lastTouchLocation variable and indicate that the view needs to be redrawn.

Don't worry if you don't fully grok the rest of the code here. We'll get into the details of working with touches and the specifics of the touchesBegan:withEvent:, touchesMoved:withEvent:, and touchesEnded:withEvent: methods in Chapter 17.

We'll come back to this class once we have our application skeleton up and running. That drawRect: method, which is currently commented out, is where we will do this application's real work, and we haven't written that yet. Let's finish setting up the application before we add our drawing code.

Creating and Connecting Outlets and Actions

Before we can start drawing, we need to add the segmented controls to our GUI, and then hook up the actions and outlets. Single-click *Main.storyboard* to set these things up.

The first order of business is to change the class of the view. In the document outline, expand the items for the scene and for the view controller it contains, and then single-click the *View* icon. Press ⌘3 to bring up the identity inspector and change the class from *UIView* to *BIDQuartzFunView*.

Now use the object library to find a *Navigation Bar* in the library. Make sure you are grabbing a *Navigation Bar*, not a *Navigation Controller.* We want the bar that goes at the top of the view. Place the navigation bar near the top of the view, just beneath the status bar. Note that you can't actually see where the status bar ends, so use the *Size Inspector* to set its *y* value to 20.

Next, look for a *Segmented Control* in the library and drag that directly on top of the navigation bar. Drop it in the center of the navigation bar, not on the left or right side (see Figure 16-7).

Figure 16-7. Dragging out a segmented control, being sure to drop it on top of the navigation bar

Once you drop the control, it should stay selected. Grab one of the resize dots on either side of the segmented control and resize it so that it takes up the entire width of the navigation bar. You don't get any blue guidelines, but Interface Builder won't let you make the bar any bigger than you want it in this case, so just drag until it won't expand any farther.

With the segmented control still selected, bring up the attributes inspector and change the number of segments from *2* to *5*. Double-click each segment in turn, changing its label to (from left to right) *Red*, *Blue*, *Yellow*, *Green*, and *Random*, in that order. At this point, your view should look like Figure 16-8.

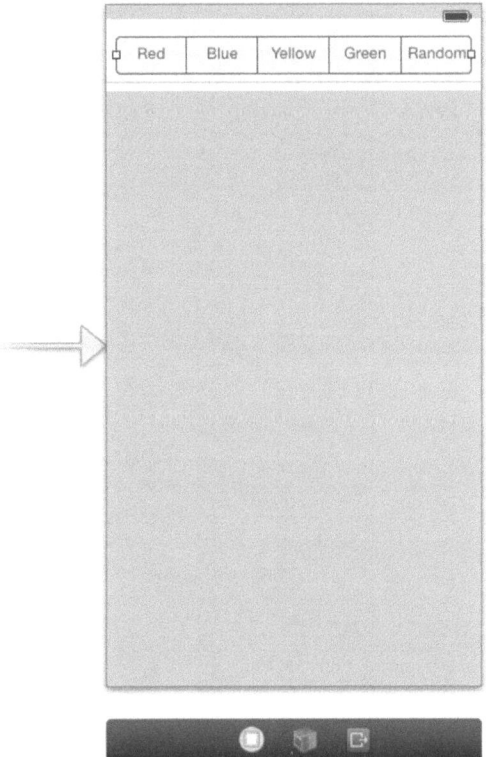

Figure 16-8. The completed navigation bar

Bring up the assistant editor, if it's not already open, and select *BIDViewController.m* from the jump bar. Now control-drag from the segmented control in the dock to the *BIDViewController.m* file on the right, into the space between the @interface and @end lines near the top that delineate the class extension. When your cursor is between the @interface and @end declarations, release the mouse to create a new outlet. Name the new outlet *colorControl*, and leave all the other options at their default values. Make sure you are dragging from the segmented control, not from the navigation bar or navigation item.

Next, let's add an action. Control-drag once again from the same segmented control over to the header file, directly above the @end declaration at the bottom of the file. This time, insert an action called changeColor:. The popup should default to using the *Value Changed* event, which is what we want. You should also set the *Type* to *UISegmentedControl*.

Now look for a *Toolbar* in the library (*not* a *Navigation Bar*) and drag one of those over, snug to the bottom of the view window. The toolbar from the library has a button on it that we don't need, so select the button and press the **Delete** key on your keyboard. The button should disappear, leaving a blank toolbar in its stead.

With the toolbar in place, grab another *Segmented Control* and drop it onto the toolbar (see Figure 16-9).

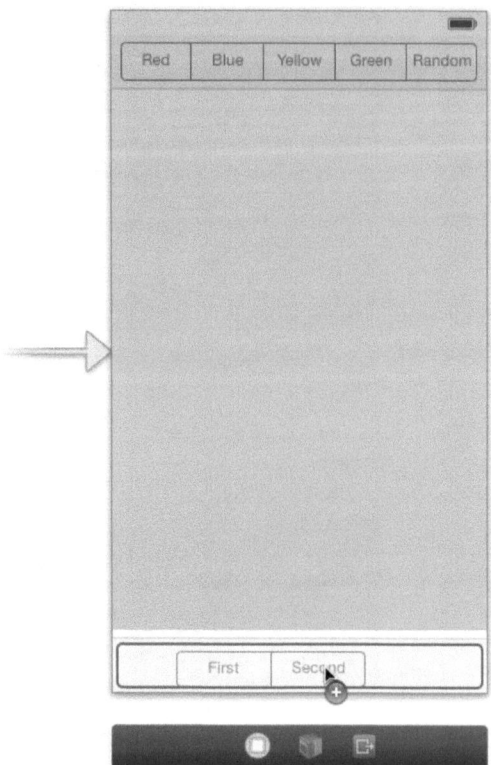

Figure 16-9. The view, showing a toolbar at the bottom of the window with a segmented control dropped onto the toolbar

It's time to resize the segmented control. In the dock, select the *Bar Button Item* that contains the *Segmented Control* as a subitem. A resize handle should appear on the right side of the segmented control in the editing area. Drag that handle to resize the segmented control and resize it so it fills the toolbar, leaving just a bit of space on each side. Interface Builder won't give you guidelines or prevent you from making the segmented control wider than the toolbar, as it did with the navigation bar, so you'll need to be a little careful to resize the segmented control to the correct size.

Next, select the *Segmented Control* in the dock, bring up the attributes inspector, and change the number of segments from *2* to *4*. Now double-click each segment and change the titles of the four segments to *Line*, *Rect*, *Ellipse*, and *Image*, in that order.

Once you've done that, be sure the *Segmented Control* is selected, and then control-drag from the segmented control over to *BIDViewController.m* to create another action. Change the connection type to *Action* and name this new action *changeShape:*.

The last bit of GUI configuration we'll need to do here is to create some constraints. The navigation bar at the top is fine, since the default constraints created by Xcode when we build our app will keep it in place at the top. However, the toolbar at the bottom needs some help. Select the toolbar and use the Pin button at the bottom of the editing area to add constraints for the toolbar's left, right, and bottom edges (see Figure 16-10).

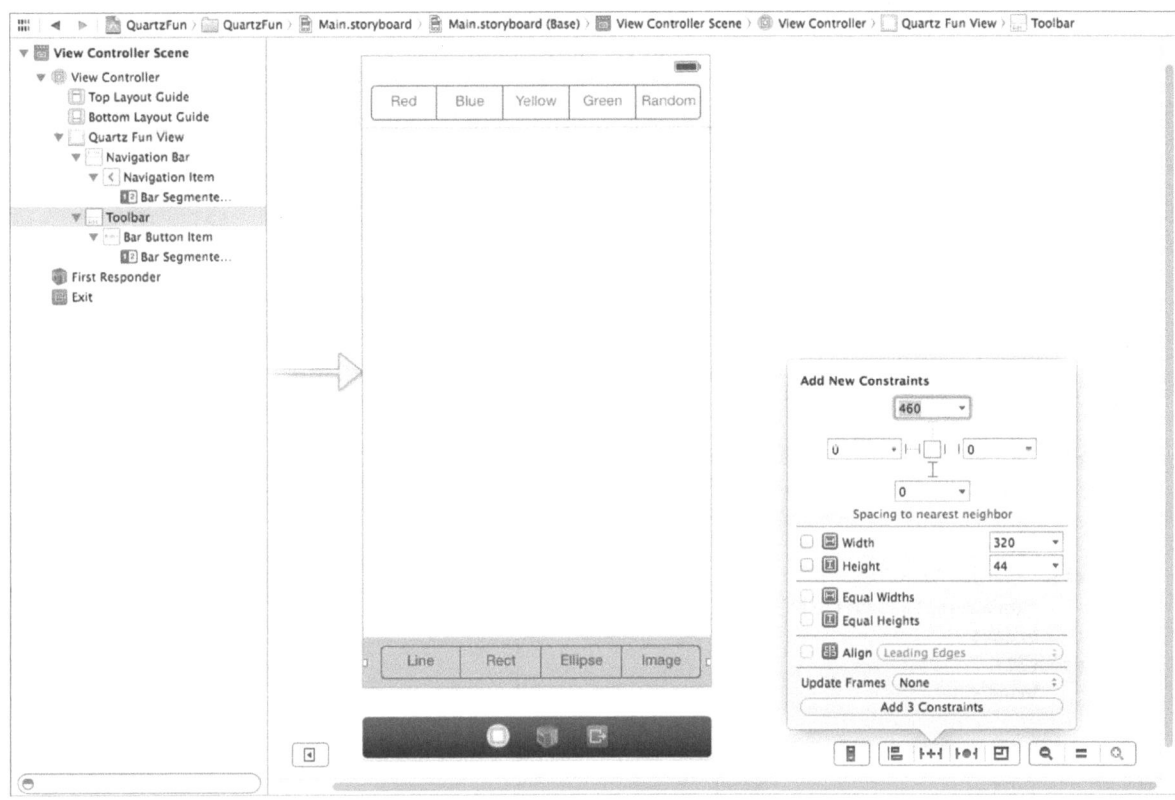

Figure 16-10. *Note that the popup window includes a numeric setting for the toolbar's distance from the top. We're ignoring that, and instead adding constraints for the other three sides*

Our next task is to implement our action methods.

Implementing the Action Methods

Save the storyboard and feel free to close the assistant editor. Now select *BIDViewController.m*. The first thing we need to do is to import our constants file, so that we have access to our enumeration values. We'll also be interacting with our custom view, so we need to import its header as well. At the top of the file, immediately below the existing import statement, add the following lines of code:

```
#import "BIDConstants.h"
#import "BIDQuartzFunView.h"
```

Next, look for the stub implementation of changeColor: that Xcode created for you and add the following code to it:

```
- (IBAction)changeColor:(id)sender {
    UISegmentedControl *control = sender;
    ColorTabIndex index = [control selectedSegmentIndex];
```

```
        BIDQuartzFunView *funView = (BIDQuartzFunView *)self.view;

    switch (index) {
        case kRedColorTab:
            funView.currentColor = [UIColor redColor];
            funView.useRandomColor = NO;
            break;
        case kBlueColorTab:
            funView.currentColor = [UIColor blueColor];
            funView.useRandomColor = NO;
            break;
        case kYellowColorTab:
            funView.currentColor = [UIColor yellowColor];
            funView.useRandomColor = NO;
            break;
        case kGreenColorTab:
            funView.currentColor = [UIColor greenColor];
            funView.useRandomColor = NO;
            break;
        case kRandomColorTab:
            funView.useRandomColor = YES;
            break;
        default:
            break;
    }
}
```

This is pretty straightforward. We simply look at which segment was selected and create a new color based on that selection to serve as our current drawing color. In order to keep the compiler happy, we cast view, which is declared as an instance of UIView in our superclass, to QuartzFunView. After that, we set the currentColor property so that our class knows which color to use when drawing, except when a random color is selected. When a random color is chosen, it will look at the useRandomColor property, so we also set that to the appropriate value for each selection. Since all the drawing code will be in the view itself, we don't need to do anything else in this method.

Next, look for the existing implementation of changeShape: and add the following code to it:

```
- (IBAction)changeShape:(id)sender {
    UISegmentedControl *control = sender;
    [(BIDQuartzFunView *)self.view setShapeType:[control
                                        selectedSegmentIndex]];

    if ([control selectedSegmentIndex] == kImageShape) {
        self.colorControl.enabled = NO;
    } else {
        self.colorControl.enabled = YES;
    }
}
```

In this method, all we do is set the shape type based on the selected segment of the control. Do you recall the ShapeType enum? The four elements of the enum correspond to the four toolbar segments at the bottom of the application view. We set the shape to be the same as the currently selected segment, and we enable or disable the colorControl based on whether the *Image* segment was selected.

> **Note**   You may have wondered why we put a navigation bar at the top of the view and a toolbar at the
> bottom of the view. According to the *Human Interface Guidelines* published by Apple, navigation bars were
> specifically designed to be placed at the top of the screen and toolbars are designed for the bottom. If you
> read the descriptions of the *Toolbar* and *Navigation Bar* in Interface Builder's library window, you'll see this
> design intention spelled out.

Make sure that everything is in order by compiling and running your app. You won't be able to draw
shapes on the screen yet, but the segmented controls should work; and when you tap the *Image*
segment in the bottom control, the color controls should disappear.

Now that we have everything working, let's do some drawing.

Adding Quartz 2D Drawing Code

We're ready to add the code that does the drawing. We'll draw a line, some shapes, and an image.
We're going to work incrementally, adding a small amount of code and then running the app to see
what that code does.

Drawing the Line

Let's do the simplest drawing option first: drawing a single line. Select *BIDQuartzFunView.m* and
replace the commented-out `drawRect:` method with this one:

```
- (void)drawRect:(CGRect)rect {
    CGContextRef context = UIGraphicsGetCurrentContext();

    CGContextSetLineWidth(context, 2.0);
    CGContextSetStrokeColorWithColor(context, self.currentColor.CGColor);

    switch (self.shapeType) {
        case kLineShape:
            CGContextMoveToPoint(context,
                                  self.firstTouchLocation.x,
                                  self.firstTouchLocation.y);
            CGContextAddLineToPoint(context,
                                      self.lastTouchLocation.x,
                                      self.lastTouchLocation.y);
            CGContextStrokePath(context);
            break;
        case kRectShape:
            break;
        case kEllipseShape:
            break;
```

```
        case kImageShape:
            break;
        default:
            break;
    }
}
```

We start things off by retrieving a reference to the current context, so we know where to draw:

```
CGContextRef context = UIGraphicsGetCurrentContext();
```

Next, we set the line width to `2.0`, which means that any line that we stroke will be 2 points wide:

```
CGContextSetLineWidth(context, 2.0);
```

After that, we set the color for stroking lines. Since `UIColor` has a `CGColor` property, which is what this function needs, we use that property of our `currentColor` property to pass the correct color on to this function.

```
CGContextSetStrokeColorWithColor(context, self.currentColor.CGColor);
```

We use a `switch` to jump to the appropriate code for each shape type. As we mentioned earlier, we'll start off with the code to handle `kLineShape`, get that working, and then we'll add code for each shape in turn as we make our way through this example:

```
switch (self.shapeType) {
    case kLineShape:
```

To draw a line, we tell the graphics context to create a path starting at the first place the user touched. Remember that we stored that value in the `touchesBegan:` method, so it will always reflect the starting point of the most recent touch or drag:

```
CGContextMoveToPoint(context,
                self.firstTouchLocation.x,
                self.firstTouchLocation.y);
```

Next, we draw a line from that spot to the last spot the user touched. If the user's finger is still in contact with the screen, `lastTouch` contains the finger's current location. If the user is no longer touching the screen, `lastTouch` contains the location of the user's finger when it was lifted off the screen:

```
CGContextAddLineToPoint(context,
                self.lastTouchLocation.x,
                self.lastTouchLocation.y);
```

Next, we stroke the path. This function will stroke the line we just drew, using the color and width we set earlier:

```
CGContextStrokePath(context);
```

After that, we finish the switch statement:

```
    break;
case kRectShape:
    break;
case kEllipseShape:
    break;
case kImageShape:
    break;
default:
    break;
}
```

And that's it for now. At this point, you should be able to compile and run the app once more. The *Rect*, *Ellipse*, and *Shape* options won't work, but you should be able to draw lines just fine using any of the color choices (see Figure 16-11).

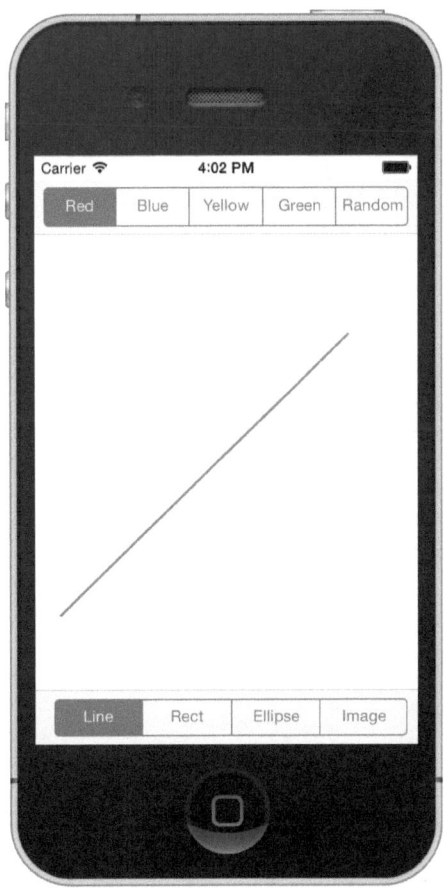

Figure 16-11. The line-drawing part of our application is now complete. Here, we are drawing using the color red

Drawing the Rectangle and Ellipse

Let's write the code to draw the rectangle and the ellipse at the same time, since Quartz implements both of these objects in basically the same way. Add the following bold code to your existing drawRect: method:

```
- (void)drawRect:(CGRect)rect {
    CGContextRef context = UIGraphicsGetCurrentContext();

    CGContextSetLineWidth(context, 2.0);
    CGContextSetStrokeColorWithColor(context, self.currentColor.CGColor);

    CGContextSetFillColorWithColor(context, self.currentColor.CGColor);
    CGRect currentRect = CGRectMake(self.firstTouchLocation.x,
                                    self.firstTouchLocation.y,
                                    self.lastTouchLocation.x -
                                        self.firstTouchLocation.x,
                                    self.lastTouchLocation.y -
                                        self.firstTouchLocation.y);

    switch (self.shapeType) {
        case kLineShape:
            CGContextMoveToPoint(context,
                                    self.firstTouchLocation.x,
                                    self.firstTouchLocation.y);
            CGContextAddLineToPoint(context,
                                    self.lastTouchLocation.x,
                                    self.lastTouchLocation.y);
            CGContextStrokePath(context);
            break;
        case kRectShape:
            CGContextAddRect(context, currentRect);
            CGContextDrawPath(context, kCGPathFillStroke);
            break;
        case kEllipseShape:
            CGContextAddEllipseInRect(context, currentRect);
            CGContextDrawPath(context, kCGPathFillStroke);
            break;
        case kImageShape:
            break;
        default:
            break;
    }
}
```

Because we want to paint both the ellipse and the rectangle in a solid color, we add a call to set the fill color using currentColor:

```
CGContextSetFillColorWithColor(context, self.currentColor.CGColor);
```

Next, we declare a CGRect variable. We do this here because both the rectangle and ellipse are drawn based on a rectangle. We'll use currentRect to hold the rectangle described by the user's drag. Remember that a CGRect has two members: size and origin. A function called CGRectMake() lets us create a CGRect by specifying the x, y, width, and height values, so we use that to make our rectangle.

The code to create the rectangle is pretty straightforward. We use the point stored in firstTouch to create the origin. Next, we figure out the size by getting the difference between the two x values and the two y values. Note that, depending on the direction of the drag, one or both size values may end up with negative numbers, but that's OK. A CGRect with a negative size will simply be rendered in the opposite direction of its origin point (to the left for a negative width; upward for a negative height):

```
CGRect currentRect = CGRectMake(self.firstTouchLocation.x,
                                self.firstTouchLocation.y,
                                self.lastTouchLocation.x -
                                    self.firstTouchLocation.x,
                                self.lastTouchLocation.y -
                                    self.firstTouchLocation.y);
```

Once we have this rectangle defined, drawing either a rectangle or an ellipse is as easy as calling two functions: one to draw the rectangle or ellipse in the CGRect we defined, and the other to stroke and fill it:

```
case kRectShape:
    CGContextAddRect(context, currentRect);
    CGContextDrawPath(context, kCGPathFillStroke);
    break;
case kEllipseShape:
    CGContextAddEllipseInRect(context, currentRect);
    CGContextDrawPath(context, kCGPathFillStroke);
    break;
```

Compile and run your application. Try out the *Rect* and *Ellipse* tools to see how you like them. Don't forget to change colors, including using a random color.

Drawing the Image

For our last trick, let's draw an image. The *16 - QuartzFun* folder contains an image named *iphone. png* that you can add to your project's *Images.xcassets* item. Or, you can use any *.png* file you prefer, as long as you remember to change the file name in the following code to point to that image.

Add the following code to your drawRect: method:

```
- (void)drawRect:(CGRect)rect {
    CGContextRef context = UIGraphicsGetCurrentContext();

    CGContextSetLineWidth(context, 2.0);
    CGContextSetStrokeColorWithColor(context, self.currentColor.CGColor);

    CGContextSetFillColorWithColor(context, _currentColor.CGColor);
    CGRect currentRect = CGRectMake(self.firstTouchLocation.x,
```

```
                                            self.firstTouchLocation.y,
                                            self.lastTouchLocation.x -
                                                self.firstTouchLocation.x,
                                            self.lastTouchLocation.y -
                                                self.firstTouchLocation.y);

    switch (self.shapeType) {
        case kLineShape:
            CGContextMoveToPoint(context,
                                    self.firstTouchLocation.x,
                                    self.firstTouchLocation.y);
            CGContextAddLineToPoint(context,
                                    self.lastTouchLocation.x,
                                    self.lastTouchLocation.y);
            CGContextStrokePath(context);
            break;
        case kRectShape:
            CGContextAddRect(context, currentRect);
            CGContextDrawPath(context, kCGPathFillStroke);
            break;
        case kEllipseShape:
            CGContextAddEllipseInRect(context, currentRect);
            CGContextDrawPath(context, kCGPathFillStroke);
            break;
        case kImageShape: {
            CGFloat horizontalOffset = self.drawImage.size.width / 2;
            CGFloat verticalOffset = self.drawImage.size.height / 2;
            CGPoint drawPoint = CGPointMake(self.lastTouchLocation.x -
                                                horizontalOffset,
                                            self.lastTouchLocation.y -
                                                verticalOffset);
            [self.drawImage drawAtPoint:drawPoint];
            break;
        }
        default:
            break;
    }
}
```

> **Note** Notice that, in the `switch` statement, we added curly braces around the code following
> `case kImageShape:`. That's because the compiler has a problem with variables declared in the
> first line after a `case` statement. These curly braces are our way of telling the compiler to stop
> complaining. We could also have declared `horizontalOffset` before the `switch` statement, but
> our chosen approach keeps the related code together.

First, we calculate the center of the image, since we want the image drawn centered on the point where the user last touched. Without this adjustment, the image would be drawn with the upper-left corner at the user's finger, also a valid option. We then make a new CGPoint by subtracting these offsets from the x and y values in lastTouchLocation:

```
CGFloat horizontalOffset = self.drawImage.size.width / 2;
CGFloat verticalOffset = self.drawImage.size.height / 2;
CGPoint drawPoint = CGPointMake(self.lastTouchLocation.x -
                               horizontalOffset,
                           self.lastTouchLocation.y -
                               verticalOffset);
```

Now we tell the image to draw itself. This line of code will do the trick:

```
[self.drawImage drawAtPoint:drawPoint];
```

Optimizing the QuartzFun Application

Our application does what we want, but we should consider a bit of optimization. In our little application, you won't notice a slowdown; however, in a more complex application that is running on a slower processor, you might see some lag.

The problem occurs in *BIDQuartzFunView.m*, in the methods touchesMoved: and touchesEnded:. Both methods include this line of code:

```
[self setNeedsDisplay];
```

Obviously, this is how we tell our view that something has changed and that it needs to redraw itself. This code works, but it causes the entire view to be erased and redrawn, even if only a tiny bit has changed. We do want to erase the screen when we get ready to drag out a new shape, but we don't want to clear the screen several times a second as we drag out our shape.

Rather than forcing the entire view to be redrawn many times during our drag, we can use setNeedsDisplayInRect: instead. setNeedsDisplayInRect: is a UIView method that marks just one rectangular portion of a view's region as needing redisplay. By using this method, we can be more efficient by marking only the part of the view that is affected by the current drawing operation as needing to be redrawn.

We need to redraw, not just the rectangle between firstTouch and lastTouch, but any part of the screen encompassed by the current drag. If the user touched the screen and then scribbled all over, but we redrew only the section between firstTouch and lastTouch, then we would leave a lot of stuff drawn on the screen by the previous redraw that we don't want to remain.

The solution is to keep track of the entire area that has been affected by a particular drag in a CGRect instance variable. In touchesBegan:, we reset that instance variable to just the point where the user touched. Then, in touchesMoved: and touchesEnded:, we use a Core Graphics function to get the union of the current rectangle and the stored rectangle, and we store the resulting rectangle. We also use it to specify which part of the view needs to be redrawn. This approach gives us a running total of the area impacted by the current drag.

Now we'll calculate the current rectangle in the drawRect: method for use in drawing the ellipse and rectangle shapes. We'll move that calculation into a new method, so that it can be used in all three places without repeating code. Ready? Let's do it.

Make the following changes to *BIDQuartzFunView.h*:

```
#import <UIKit/UIKit.h>
#import "BIDConstants.h"

@interface BIDQuartzFunView : UIView
@property (assign, nonatomic) CGPoint firstTouchLocation;
@property (assign, nonatomic) CGPoint lastTouchLocation;
@property (assign, nonatomic) ShapeType shapeType;
@property (assign, nonatomic) BOOL useRandomColor;
@property (strong, nonatomic) UIColor *currentColor;
@property (strong, nonatomic) UIImage *drawImage;
@property (readonly, nonatomic) CGRect currentRect;
@property (assign, nonatomic) CGRect redrawRect;
@end
```

We declare a CGRect called redrawRect that we will use to keep track of the area that needs to be redrawn. We also declare a read-only property called currentRect, which will return the rectangle that we were previously calculating in drawRect:.

Switch over to *BIDQuartzFunView.m* and insert the following code at the top of the file, after the existing @implementation line:

```
- (CGRect)currentRect {
    return CGRectMake (self.firstTouchLocation.x,
                       self.firstTouchLocation.y,
                       self.lastTouchLocation.x - self.firstTouchLocation.x,
                       self.lastTouchLocation.y - self.firstTouchLocation.y);
}
```

Now, in the drawRect: method, change all references to currentRect to self.currentRect, so that the code uses that new accessor we just created. Next, delete the lines of code where we calculated currentRect:

```
- (void)drawRect:(CGRect)rect {
    CGContextRef context = UIGraphicsGetCurrentContext();

    CGContextSetLineWidth(context, 2.0);
    CGContextSetStrokeColorWithColor(context, self.currentColor.CGColor);

    CGContextSetFillColorWithColor(context, self.currentColor.CGColor);

    CGRect currentRect = CGRectMake(self.firstTouchLocation.x,
                                    self.firstTouchLocation.y,
                                    self.lastTouchLocation.x -
                                        self.firstTouchLocation.x,
                                    self.lastTouchLocation.y -
                                        self.firstTouchLocation.y);
```

```
    switch (self.shapeType) {
        case kLineShape:
            CGContextMoveToPoint(context,
                                    self.firstTouchLocation.x,
                                    self.firstTouchLocation.y);
            CGContextAddLineToPoint(context,
                                    self.lastTouchLocation.x,
                                    self.lastTouchLocation.y);
            CGContextStrokePath(context);
            break;
        case kRectShape:
            CGContextAddRect(context, self.currentRect);
            CGContextDrawPath(context, kCGPathFillStroke);
            break;
        case kEllipseShape:
            CGContextAddEllipseInRect(context, self.currentRect);
            CGContextDrawPath(context, kCGPathFillStroke);
            break;
        case kImageShape: {
            CGFloat horizontalOffset = self.drawImage.size.width / 2;
            CGFloat verticalOffset = self.drawImage.size.height / 2;
            CGPoint drawPoint = CGPointMake(self.lastTouchLocation.x -
                                            horizontalOffset,
                                            self.lastTouchLocation.y -
                                            verticalOffset);
            [self.drawImage drawAtPoint:drawPoint];
            break;
        }
        default:
            break;
    }
}
```

We also need to make some changes to touchesEnded:withEvent: and touchesMoved:withEvent:.
We will recalculate the space impacted by the current operation and use that to indicate that only
a portion of our view needs to be redrawn. Replace the existing touchesEnded: and touchesMoved:
methods with these new versions:

```
- (void)touchesEnded:(NSSet *)touches withEvent:(UIEvent *)event {
    UITouch *touch = [touches anyObject];
    self.lastTouchLocation = [touch locationInView:self];

    if (self.shapeType == kImageShape) {
        CGFloat horizontalOffset = self.drawImage.size.width / 2;
        CGFloat verticalOffset = self.drawImage.size.height / 2;
        self.redrawRect = CGRectUnion(self.redrawRect,
                                CGRectMake(self.lastTouchLocation.x -
                                            horizontalOffset,
                                            self.lastTouchLocation.y -
                                            verticalOffset,
                                            self.drawImage.size.width,
                                            self.drawImage.size.height));
```

```
    } else {
        self.redrawRect = CGRectUnion(self.redrawRect, self.currentRect);
    }
    self.redrawRect = CGRectInset(self.redrawRect, -2.0, -2.0);
    [self setNeedsDisplayInRect:self.redrawRect];
}

- (void)touchesMoved:(NSSet *)touches withEvent:(UIEvent *)event {
    UITouch *touch = [touches anyObject];
    self.lastTouchLocation = [touch locationInView:self];

    if (self.shapeType == kImageShape) {
        CGFloat horizontalOffset = self.drawImage.size.width / 2;
        CGFloat verticalOffset = self.drawImage.size.height / 2;
        self.redrawRect = CGRectUnion(self.redrawRect,
                                      CGRectMake(self.lastTouchLocation.x -
                                                  horizontalOffset,
                                                  self.lastTouchLocation.y -
                                                  verticalOffset,
                                                  self.drawImage.size.width,
                                                  self.drawImage.size.height));
    }
    self.redrawRect = CGRectUnion(_redrawRect, self.currentRect);
    [self setNeedsDisplayInRect:self.redrawRect];
}
```

With only a few additional lines of code, we reduced the amount of work necessary to redraw our view by getting rid of the need to erase and redraw any portion of the view that hasn't been affected by the current drag. Being kind to your iOS device's precious processor cycles like this can make a big difference in the performance of your applications, especially as they get more complex.

> **Note**   If you're interested in a more in-depth exploration of Quartz 2D topics, you might want to take a look at *Beginning iPad Development for iPhone Developers: Mastering the iPad SDK* by Jack Nutting, Dave Wooldridge, and David Mark (Apress, 2010). This book covers a lot of Quartz 2D drawing. All the drawing code and explanations in that book apply to the iPhone as well as the iPad.

Drawing to a Close

In this chapter, we've really just scratched the surface of the drawing capabilities built into iOS. You should feel pretty comfortable with Quartz 2D now; and with some occasional references to Apple's documentation, you can probably handle most any drawing requirement that comes your way.

Now it's time to level up your graphics skills even further! Chapter 17 will introduce you to the new Sprite Kit framework in iOS 7, which lets you do blazingly-fast bitmap rendering for creating games or other fast-moving, interactive content.

Getting Started with Sprite Kit

In iOS 7, Apple introduced Sprite Kit, a framework for the high-performance rendering of 2D graphics. That sounds a bit like Core Graphics and Core Animation, so what's new here? Well, unlike Core Graphics (which is focused on drawing graphics using a painter's model) or Core Animation (which is focused on animating attributes of GUI elements), Sprite Kit is focused on a different area entirely: video games! Sprite Kit is built on top of OpenGL, a technology present in many computing platforms that allows modern graphics hardware to write graphics bitmaps into a video buffer at incredible speeds. With Sprite Kit, you get the great performance characteristics of OpenGL, but without needing to dig into the depths of OpenGL coding.

This is Apple's first foray into the graphical side of game programming in the iOS era. It was released for iOS 7 and OS X 10.9 (Mavericks) at the same time and provides the same API on both platforms, so that apps written for one can be easily ported to the other. Although Apple has never before supplied a framework quite like Sprite Kit, it has clear similarities to various open-source libraries such as Cocos2D. If you've used Cocos2D or something similar in the past, you'll feel right at home.

Sprite Kit does not implement a flexible, general-purpose drawing system like Core Graphics; There are no methods for drawing paths, gradients, or filling spaces with color. Instead, what you get is a **scene graph** (analogous to UIKit's view hierarchy); the ability to transform each graph node's position, scale, and rotation; and the ability for each node to draw itself. Most drawing occurs in an instance of the SKSprite class (or one of its subclasses), which represents a single graphical image ready for putting on the screen.

In this chapter, we're going to use Sprite Kit build a simple shooting game call **TextShooter**. Instead of using premade graphics, we're going to build our game objects with pieces of text, using a subclass of SKSprite that is specialized for just this purpose. Using this approach, you won't need to pull graphics out of a project library or anything like that. The app we make will be simple in appearance, but easy to modify and play with.

Simple Beginnings

Let's get the ball rolling. In Xcode, create a new application using the SpriteKit Game application template from the iOS Application section. Name your new project *TextShooter*, leave the other settings in their typical positions, and save it alongside your other projects.

Now take a look at the project Xcode created. You'll see it has a pretty standard-looking BIDAppDelegate class and a small BIDViewController class that does some initial configuration of an SKView object. The SKView object, which is loaded from the application's storyboard, is the view that will display all our Sprite Kit content. After configuring the SKView to make it show us some performance characteristics while running, the viewDidLoad method creates a new instance of BIDMyScene and tells the SKView to display the scene.

In a way, this has some parallels to the UIViewController classes we've been using throughout this book. The SKView class acts a bit like UINavigationController, in the sense that it is sort of a blank slate that simply manages access to the display for other controllers. At this point, things start to diverge, however. Unlike UINavigationController, the top-level objects managed by SKView aren't UIViewController subclasses. Instead, they're subclasses of SKScene, which in turn knows how to manage a graph of objects that can be displayed, acted upon by the physics engine, and so on. When developing with Sprite Kit, you'll probably make a new SKScene subclass for each visually distinct portion of your app. A scene can represent a fast-paced game display with dozens of objects animating around the screen or something as simple as a start menu. We'll see multiple uses of SKScene in this chapter.

You should also take a look at the BIDMyScene class created by the template. It has just two methods: an initializer that creates an on-screen label and a touch-event handler that creates a new bitmap-based sprite every time the user touches the screen. Go ahead and run this app to see what it does (the results are shown in Figure 17-1).

Figure 17-1. *The default Sprite Kit app in action. Some text is displayed in the center of the screen, and each tap on the screen puts a rotating graphic of a fighter jet at that location*

Initial Scene Customization

Well that's something, but we're going to take our app in a different direction entirely. Let's start by gutting the two methods that are set up for us by Xcode. First, delete the initWithSize: method entirely (we'll write a whole new one later). Next, take away most of the touchesBegan:withEvent: method, leaving just the for loop and the first line of code it contains, like this:

```
- (void)touchesBegan:(NSSet *)touches withEvent:(UIEvent *)event {
    /* Called when a touch begins */

    for (UITouch *touch in touches) {
        CGPoint location = [touch locationInNode:self];
    }
}
```

The next thing we're going to do is fix a minor stylistic problem with this template: the name of the BIDMyScene class itself. Each scene in a Sprite Kit game represents a particular chunk of the player's gaming experience, and it really should be named to match. Calling something "my" scene really doesn't tell us anything, so we're going to rename it. Xcode actually has a handy piece of functionality that will help us here. Hold your mouse pointer over the word BIDMyScene in either the *.h* or *.m* file for the class, right-click (or **Ctrl**-click if you're using a trackpad) to bring up the context menu, and select Refactor ➤ Rename… to get started. In the panel that appears at the top of the window, type *BIDLevelScene* as the new class name, make sure the *Rename related files* checkbox is selected, and then click *Preview*. A new panel will slide out, showing you all the changes that Xcode is about to make on your behalf, as shown in Figure 17-2.

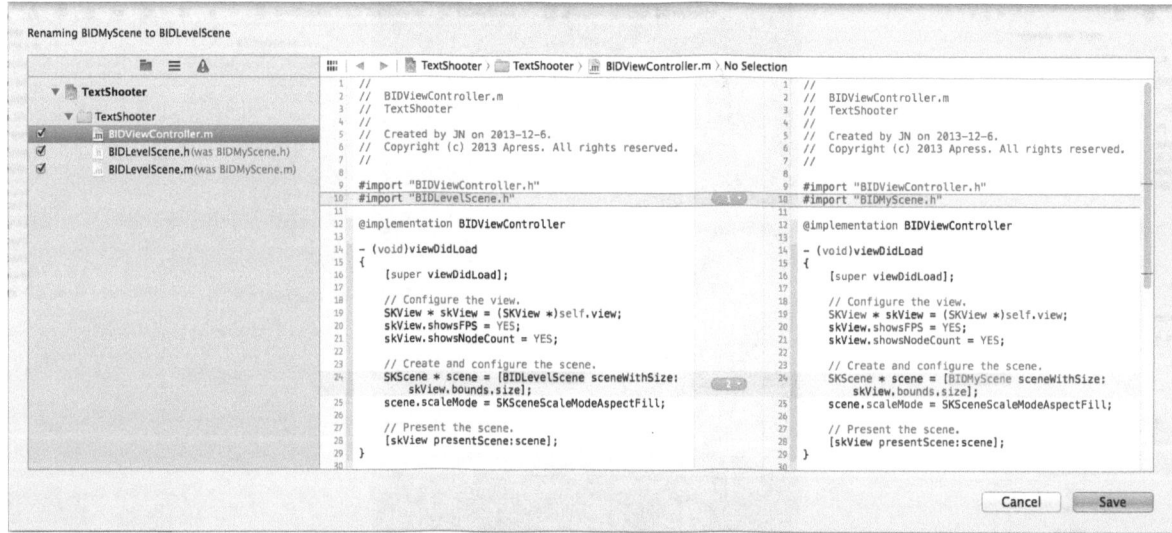

Figure 17-2. Side-by-side comparisons of files we're about to change

Click the *Save* button, which triggers yet another sliding panel from the top of the window. This one is offering to turn on an Xcode feature called *snapshots* that you should feel free to *Disable*. You'll see that Xcode changes the name of the class in its source files, renames the source code files themselves, and also changes all references to the class in *BIDViewController.m*. Nice!

Hiding the Status Bar

While you're poking around in *BIDViewController.m*, make one more change: disable the iOS status bar. Just add this method anywhere inside the @implementation section:

```
- (BOOL)prefersStatusBarHidden {
    return YES;
}
```

That change will make the iOS status bar disappear while our game is running, which is usually what you want for action games like this.

Scene Setup

Now switch over to *BIDLevelScene.h*. This class can override the `initWithSize:` method from its parent class as its default initializer, but we're going to create two new methods around creating instances, allowing us to include a level number. At the same time, we're going to add properties for the level number, the number of lives the player has, and a flag to let us know whether the level is finished. Add the bold lines shown below:

```
@interface BIDLevelScene : SKScene

@property (assign, nonatomic) NSUInteger levelNumber;
@property (assign, nonatomic) NSUInteger playerLives;
@property (assign, nonatomic) BOOL finished;

+ (instancetype)sceneWithSize:(CGSize)size levelNumber:(NSUInteger)levelNumber;
- (instancetype)initWithSize:(CGSize)size levelNumber:(NSUInteger)levelNumber;

@end
```

Now switch over to *BIDLevelScene.m*, where we'll lay down some more infrastructure. Earlier, we asked you to remove the `initWithSize:` method created by the application template. Now it's time to add the following methods instead:

```
+ (instancetype)sceneWithSize:(CGSize)size levelNumber:(NSUInteger)levelNumber {
    return [[self alloc] initWithSize:size levelNumber:levelNumber];
}

- (instancetype)initWithSize:(CGSize)size {
    return [self initWithSize:size levelNumber:1];
}

- (instancetype)initWithSize:(CGSize)size levelNumber:(NSUInteger)levelNumber {
    if (self = [super initWithSize:size]) {
        _levelNumber = levelNumber;
        _playerLives = 5;

        self.backgroundColor = [SKColor whiteColor];

        SKLabelNode *lives = [SKLabelNode labelNodeWithFontNamed:@"Courier"];
        lives.fontSize = 16;
        lives.fontColor = [SKColor blackColor];
        lives.name = @"LivesLabel";
        lives.text = [NSString stringWithFormat:@"Lives: %lu",
                      (unsigned long)_playerLives];
        lives.verticalAlignmentMode = SKLabelVerticalAlignmentModeTop;
        lives.horizontalAlignmentMode = SKLabelHorizontalAlignmentModeRight;
        lives.position = CGPointMake(self.frame.size.width,
                                     self.frame.size.height);
        [self addChild:lives];
```

```
        SKLabelNode *level = [SKLabelNode labelNodeWithFontNamed:@"Courier"];
        level.fontSize = 16;
        level.fontColor = [SKColor blackColor];
        level.name = @"LevelLabel";
        level.text = [NSString stringWithFormat:@"Level: %lu",
                      (unsigned long)_levelNumber];
        level.verticalAlignmentMode = SKLabelVerticalAlignmentModeTop;
        level.horizontalAlignmentMode = SKLabelHorizontalAlignmentModeLeft;
        level.position = CGPointMake(0, self.frame.size.height);
        [self addChild:level];
    }
    return self;
}
```

That first method, sceneWithSize:levelNumber:, gives us a factory method that will work as a shorthand for creating a level and setting its level number at once. In the second method, initWithSize:, we override the class's default initializer, passing control to the third method (and passing along a default value for the level number). That third method in turn calls the designated initializer from its superclass's implementation. This may seem like a roundabout way of doing things, but it's a common pattern when you want to add new initializers to a class while still using the class's designated initializer.

The third method we added, initWithSize:levelNumber:, is where we set up the basic configuration of our level scene. First, we set the values of a couple of instance variables to point at the parameters that were passed in. Second, we set the scene's background color. Note that we're using a class called SKColor instead of UIColor here. In fact, SKColor isn't really a class at all; it's a sort of alias that can be used in place of either UIColor for an iOS app or NSColor for an OS X app. This allows us to port games between iOS and OS X a little more easily.

After that, we create two instances of a class called SKLabelNode. This is a handy class that works somewhat like a UILabel, letting us choose a font, set a text value, and specify some alignments. We create one label for displaying the number of lives at the upper right of the screen and another that will show the level number at the upper left of the screen.

If you think about the points we're passing in as positions for each of those labels, you may be surprised to see that we're passing in the scene's height. In UIKit, positioning anything at the height of a UIView would put it at the bottom of that view; but in Scene Kit, the y-axis is flipped, so the maximum value of the scene's height is a position at the top of the screen instead.

You'll also see that we gave each label a name. This works similar to a tag or identifier in other parts of UIKit, and it will let us retrieve those labels later by asking for them by name.

Run the game now, and you'll see that we have a very basic structure in place, as shown in Figure 17-3.

Figure 17-3. Our game doesn't have much fun factor right now, but at least it has a high framerate!

Player Movement

Now it's time to add a little interactivity. We're going to make a new class that represents a player. It will know how to draw itself using internal components, as well as how to move to a new location in a nicely animated way. Next, we'll insert an instance of the new class into the scene and write some code to let the player move the object around by touching the screen.

Every object that's going to be part of our scene must be a subclass of SKNode. Thus, you'll use Xcode's File menu to create a new Objective-C class named BIDPlayerNode that's a subclass of SKNode. In the nearly-empty *BidPlayerNode.m* file that's created, add the following methods:

```
- (instancetype)init {
    if (self = [super init]) {
        self.name = [NSString stringWithFormat:@"Player %p", self];
        [self initNodeGraph];
    }
}
```

```
    return self;
}

- (void)initNodeGraph {
    SKLabelNode *label = [SKLabelNode labelNodeWithFontNamed:@"Courier"];
    label.fontColor = [SKColor darkGrayColor];
    label.fontSize = 40;
    label.text = @"v";
    label.zRotation = M_PI;
    label.name = @"label";

    [self addChild:label];

}
```

Our BIDPlayerNode doesn't display anything itself. Instead, the init method sets up a subnode that will do the actual drawing. This subnode is another instance of SKLabelNode, just like the one we created for displaying the level number and the number of lives remaining. We're not setting a position for the label, which means that its position is coordinate (0, 0). Just like views, each node lives in a coordinate system that is inherited from its parent object. Giving this node a zero position means that it will appear on-screen at the BIDPlayerNode instance's position. Any non-zero values would effectively be an offset from that point.

We also set a rotation value for the label, so that the lowercase letter "v" it contains will be shown upside-down. The name of the rotation property, zRotation, may seem a bit surprising; however, it simply refers to the z-axis of the coordinate space in use with Sprite Kit. You only see the x- and y-axes on screen, but the z-axis is useful for ordering items for display purposes, as well as for rotating things around. The values assigned to zRotation need to be in radians instead of degrees, so we assign the value M_PI, which is equivalent to the mathematical value *pi*. Since pi radians are equal to 180 degrees, this is just what we want.

Adding the Player to the Scene

Now switch back to *BIDLevelScene.m*. Here, we're going to add an instance of SKPlayerNode to the scene. Start off by importing the new class's header and adding a property inside a new class extension:

```
#import "BIDLevelScene.h"
#import "BIDPlayerNode.h"

@interface BIDLevelScene ()

@property (strong, nonatomic) BIDPlayerNode *playerNode;

@end
```

Continue by adding the following bold code near the end of the initWithSize:levelNumber: method. Be sure to put it before the return self and before the right-curly-brace above it:

```
        _playerNode = [BIDPlayerNode node];
        _playerNode.position = CGPointMake(CGRectGetMidX(self.frame),
                                    CGRectGetHeight(self.frame) * 0.1);

        [self addChild:_playerNode];
    }
    return self;
}
```

If you build and run the app now, you should see that the player appears near the lower middle of the screen, as shown in Figure 17-4.

Figure 17-4. An upside-down "v" to the rescue!

Handling Touches

Next, we're going to put some logic back into the touchesBegan:withEvent: method, which we earlier left nearly empty. Insert the bold lines shown here:

```
- (void)touchesBegan:(NSSet *)touches withEvent:(UIEvent *)event {
    /* Called when a touch begins */

    for (UITouch *touch in touches) {
        CGPoint location = [touch locationInNode:self];
        if (location.y < CGRectGetHeight(self.frame) * 0.2 ) {
            CGPoint target = CGPointMake(location.x,
                                        self.playerNode.position.y);
            CGFloat duration = [self.playerNode moveToward:target];
        }
    }
}
```

The preceding snippet uses any touch location in the lower fifth of the screen as the basis of a new location toward which you want the player node to move. It also tells the player node to move toward it. In its current state, this will give you a compiler error since we haven't defined the player node's moveToward: method yet. So, start by declaring the method in *BIDPlayerNode.h*, like this:

```
#import <SpriteKit/SpriteKit.h>

@interface BIDPlayerNode : SKNode

// returns duration of future movement
- (CGFloat)moveToward:(CGPoint)location;

@end
```

Player Movement

Next, switch over to *BIDPlayerNode.m* and add the following implementation:

```
- (CGFloat)moveToward:(CGPoint)location {
    [self removeActionForKey:@"movement"];

    CGFloat distance = BIDPointDistance(self.position, location);
    CGFloat pixels = [UIScreen mainScreen].bounds.size.width;
    CGFloat duration = 2.0 * distance / pixels;

    [self runAction:[SKAction moveTo:location duration:duration]
            withKey:@"movement"];

    return duration;
}
```

We'll skip the first line for now, returning to it shortly. This method compares the new location to the current position and figures out the distance and the number of pixels to move. Next, it figures out how much time the movement should take, using a numeric constant to set the speed of the overall movement. Finally it creates an SKAction to make the move happen. SKAction is a part of Sprite Kit that knows how to make changes to nodes over time, letting you easily animate a node's position, size, rotation, transparency, and more. In this case, we are telling the player node to run a simple movement action over a particular duration, and then assigning that action to the key @"movement". As you see, this key is the same as the key used in the first line of this method to remove an action. We started off this method by removing any existing action with the same key, so that the user can tap several locations in quick succession without spawning a lot of competing actions trying to move in different ways!

Geometry Calculations

Now you'll notice that we've introduced another compiler error, since Xcode can't find any function called BIDPointDistance(). This is one of several simple geometric functions that our app will use to perform calculations using points, vectors, and floats. Let's put this in place now. Use Xcode to make a new file, this time a *Header File* from the *C and C++* section. Name it *BIDGeometry.h* and give it the following content:

```
#ifndef TextShooter_BIDGeometry_h
#define TextShooter_BIDGeometry_h

// Takes a CGVector and a CGFLoat.
// Returns a new CGFloat where each component of v has been multiplied by m.
static inline CGVector BIDVectorMultiply(CGVector v, CGFLoat m) {
    return CGVectorMake(v.dx * m, v.dy * m);
}

// Takes two CGPoints.
// Returns a CGVector representing a direction from p1 to p2.
static inline CGVector BIDVectorBetweenPoints(CGPoint p1, CGPoint p2) {
    return CGVectorMake(p2.x - p1.x, p2.y - p1.y);
}

// Takes a CGVector.
// Returns a CGFloat containing the length of the vector, calculated using
// Pythagoras' theorem.
static inline CGFloat BIDVectorLength(CGVector v) {
    return sqrtf(powf(v.dx, 2) + powf(v.dy, 2));
}

// Takes two CGPoints. Returns a CGFloat containing the distance between them,
// calculated with Pythagoras' theorem.
static inline CGFloat BIDPointDistance(CGPoint p1, CGPoint p2) {
    return sqrtf(powf(p2.x - p1.x, 2) + powf(p2.y - p1.y, 2));
}

#endif
```

These are simple implementations of some common operations that are useful in many games: multiplying vectors, creating vectors pointing from one point to another, and calculating distances. To let the code use these, just add the following import near the top of *BIDPlayerNode.m*:

```
#import "BIDGeometry.h"
```

Now build and run the app. After the player ship appears, tap anywhere in the bottom portion of the screen to see that the ship slides left or right to reach the point you tapped. You can tap again before the ship reaches its destination, and it will immediately begin a new animation to move toward the new spot. That's fine, but wouldn't it be nice if the player's ship were a bit livelier in its motion?

Wobbly Bits

Let's give the ship a bit of a wobble as it moves by adding another animation. Add the bold lines to BIDPlayerNode's moveToward: method.

```
- (CGFloat)moveToward:(CGPoint)location {
    [self removeActionForKey:@"movement"];
    [self removeActionForKey:@"wobbling"];

    CGFloat distance = BIDPointDistance(self.position, location);
    CGFloat pixels = [UIScreen mainScreen].bounds.size.width;
    CGFloat duration = 2.0 * distance / pixels;

    [self runAction:[SKAction moveTo:location duration:duration]
           withKey:@"movement"];

    CGFloat wobbleTime = 0.3;
    CGFloat halfWobbleTime = wobbleTime * 0.5;
    SKAction *wobbling = [SKAction
                          sequence:@[[SKAction scaleXTo:0.2
                                               duration:halfWobbleTime],
                                      [SKAction scaleXTo:1.0
                                               duration:halfWobbleTime]
                          ]];
    NSUInteger wobbleCount = duration / wobbleTime;

    [self runAction:[SKAction repeatAction:wobbling count:wobbleCount]
           withKey:@"wobbling"];

    return duration;
}
```

What we just did is similar to the movement action we created earlier, but it differs in some important ways. For the basic movement, we simply calculated the movement duration, and then created and ran a movement action in a single step. This time, it's a little more complicated. First, we define the time for a single "wobble" (the ship may wobble multiple times while moving, but will wobble at a consistent rate throughout). The wobble itself consists of first scaling the ship along the x-axis (i.e., its width) to 2/10ths of its normal size, and then scaling it back to it to its full size. Each of these is a single action that is packed together into another kind of action called a sequence, which performs all the actions it contains one after another. Next, we figure out how many times this wobble can happen during the duration of the ship's travel and wrap the wobbling sequence inside a repeat action, telling it how many complete wobble cycles it should execute. And, as before, we start the method by canceling any previous wobbling action, since we wouldn't want competing wobblers.

Now run the app, and you'll see that the ship wobbles pleasantly when moving back and forth. It kind of looks like it's walking!

Creating Your Enemies

So far so good, but this game is going to need some enemies for our players to shoot at. We'll use Xcode to make a new Objective-C class called BIDEnemyNode, using SKNode as the parent class. We're not going to give the enemy class any real behavior just yet, but we will give it an appearance. We'll use the same technique that we used for the player, using text to build the enemy's body. Surely, there's no text character more intimidating than the letter X, so our enemy will be a letter X... made of lowercase Xs! Try not to be scared just thinking about that as you add these methods:

```
- (instancetype)init {
    if (self = [super init]) {
        self.name = [NSString stringWithFormat:@"Enemy %p", self];
        [self initNodeGraph];
    }
    return self;
}

- (void)initNodeGraph {
    SKLabelNode *topRow = [SKLabelNode
                               labelNodeWithFontNamed:@"Courier-Bold"];
    topRow.fontColor = [SKColor brownColor];
    topRow.fontSize = 20;
    topRow.text = @"x x";
    topRow.position = CGPointMake(0, 15);
    [self addChild:topRow];

    SKLabelNode *middleRow = [SKLabelNode
                                 labelNodeWithFontNamed:@"Courier-Bold"];
    middleRow.fontColor = [SKColor brownColor];
    middleRow.fontSize = 20;
    middleRow.text = @"x";
    [self addChild:middleRow];

    SKLabelNode *bottomRow = [SKLabelNode
                                 labelNodeWithFontNamed:@"Courier-Bold"];
    bottomRow.fontColor = [SKColor brownColor];
    bottomRow.fontSize = 20;
    bottomRow.text = @"x x";
    bottomRow.position = CGPointMake(0, -15);
    [self addChild:bottomRow];
}
```

There's nothing much new there; we're just adding multiple "rows" of text by shifting the y value for each of their positions.

Putting Enemies in the Scene

Now let's make some enemies appear in the scene by making some changes to *BIDLevelScene.m*. First, add the bold lines shown here, near the top:

```
#import "BIDLevelScene.h"
#import "BIDPlayerNode.h"
#import "BIDEnemyNode.h"

#define ARC4RANDOM_MAX        0x100000000

@interface BIDLevelScene ()

@property (strong, nonatomic) BIDPlayerNode *playerNode;
@property (strong, nonatomic) SKNode *enemies;

@end
```

We imported the header for our new enemy class. We also defined the maximum return value of the arc4random() function, which we're going to use a bit later. Random number generators can be really useful for making game levels that are different every time, and arc4random() is about as random as they come. Finally, we added a new property for holding all the enemies that will be added to the level. You might think that we'd use an NSMutableArray for this, but it turns out that using a plain SKNode is perfect for the job. SKNode can hold any number of child nodes. And since we need to add all the enemies to the scene anyway, we may as well hold them all in an SKNode for easy access.

The next step is to create the spawnEnemies method, as shown here:

```
- (void)spawnEnemies {
    NSUInteger count = log(self.levelNumber) + self.levelNumber;
    for (NSUInteger i = 0; i < count; i++) {
        BIDEnemyNode *enemy = [BIDEnemyNode node];
        CGSize size = self.frame.size;
        CGFloat x = (size.width * 0.8 * arc4random() / ARC4RANDOM_MAX) +
                    (size.width * 0.1);
        CGFloat y = (size.height * 0.5 * arc4random() / ARC4RANDOM_MAX) +
                    (size.height * 0.5);
        enemy.position = CGPointMake(x, y);
        [self.enemies addChild:enemy];
    }
}
```

Finally, add these lines near the end of the initWithSize:levelNumber: method to create an empty enemies node, and then call the spawnEnemies method:

```
[self addChild: playerNode];
_enemies = [SKNode node];
[self addChild:_enemies];
[self spawnEnemies];
```

Now run the app, and you'll see a dreadful enemy placed randomly in the upper portion of the screen (see Figure 17-5). Don't you wish you could shoot it?

Figure 17-5. I'm sure you'll agree that the X made of Xs just needs to be shot

Start Shooting

It's time to implement the next logical step in the development of this game: letting the player attack the enemies. We want the player to be able to tap anywhere in the upper 80% of the screen to shoot a bullet at the enemies. We're going to use the **physics engine** included in Sprite Kit both to move our player's bullets and to let us know when a bullet collides with an enemy.

But first, what is this thing we call a physics engine? Basically, a physics engine is a software component that keeps track of multiple physical objects (commonly referred to as **bodies**) in a world, along with the forces that are acting upon them. It also makes sure that everything moves in a realistic way. It can take into account the force of gravity, handle collisions between objects (so that objects don't occupy the same space simultaneously), and even simulate physical characteristics like friction and bounciness.

It's important to understand that a physics engine is typically separate from a graphics engine. Apple provides convenient APIs to let us work with both, but they are essentially separate. It's common to have objects in your display, such as our labels that show the current level number and remaining lives, that are completely separate from the physics engine. And it's possible to create objects that have a physics body, but don't actually display anything at all.

Defining Your Physics Categories

One of the things that the Sprite Kit physics engine lets us do is to assign objects to several distinct **physics categories**. A physics category has nothing to do with Objective-C categories. Instead, a physics category is a way to group related objects so that the physics engine can handle collisions between them in different ways. In this game, for example, we'll create three categories: one for enemies, one for the player, and one for player missiles. We definitely want the physics engine to concern itself with collisions between enemies and player missiles, but we probably want it to ignore collisions between player missiles and the player itself. This is easy to set up using physics categories.

So, let's create the categories we're going to need. Use Xcode to make a new C header file called *BIDPhysicsCategories.h* and give it the following contents:

```
#ifndef TextShooter_BIDPhysicsCategories_h
#define TextShooter_BIDPhysicsCategories_h

typedef NS_OPTIONS(uint32_t, BIDPhysicsCategory) {
    PlayerCategory        = 1 << 1,
    EnemyCategory         = 1 << 2,
    PlayerMissileCategory = 1 << 3
};

#endif
```

Here we declared three category constants. Note that the categories work as a bitmask, so each of them must be a power of two. We can easily do this by bit-shifting. These are set up as a bitmask in order to simplify the physics engine's API a little bit. With bitmasks, we can logically *OR* several values together. This enables us to use a single API call to tell the physics engine how to deal with collisions between many different layers. We'll see this in action soon.

Creating the BIDBulletNode class

Now that we've laid some groundwork, let's create some bullets so we can start shooting.

Create a new class called BIDBulletNode, once again using SKNode as its superclass. Start in the header file, where you'll declare the two public methods this class will have:

```
#import <SpriteKit/SpriteKit.h>

@interface BIDBulletNode : SKNode

+ (instancetype)bulletFrom:(CGPoint)start toward:(CGPoint)destination;
- (void)applyRecurringForce;

@end
```

The first method is a factory method for creating new instances of the class. The second is one that you'll need to call from your scene each frame, to tell the bullet to move. Now switch over to *BIDBulletNode.m* to start implementing this class.

The first thing we're going to do is import header for our special geometry functions and physics categories. The second step is to add a class extension with a single property, which will contain this bullet's thrust vector:

```
#import "BIDBulletNode.h"
#import "BIDPhysicsCategories.h"
#import "BIDGeometry.h"

@interface BIDBulletNode ()

@property (assign, nonatomic) CGVector thrust;

@end
```

Next, we implement an init method. Like other init methods in this application, this is where we create the partial object graph for our bullet. This will consist of a single dot. While we're at it, let's also configure physics for this class by creating and configuring an SKPhysicsBody instance and attaching it to self. In the process, we tell the new body what category it belongs to and which categories should be checked for collisions with this object.

```
@implementation BIDBulletNode

- (instancetype)init {
    if (self = [super init]) {
        SKLabelNode *dot = [SKLabelNode labelNodeWithFontNamed:@"Courier"];
        dot.fontColor = [SKColor blackColor];
        dot.fontSize = 40;
        dot.text = @".";
        [self addChild:dot];
```

```
        SKPhysicsBody *body = [SKPhysicsBody bodyWithCircleOfRadius:1];
        body.dynamic = YES;
        body.categoryBitMask = PlayerMissileCategory;
        body.contactTestBitMask = EnemyCategory;
        body.collisionBitMask = EnemyCategory;
        body.mass = 0.01;

        self.physicsBody = body;
        self.name = [NSString stringWithFormat:@"Bullet %p", self];
    }
    return self;
}
```

Applying Physics

Next, we'll create the factory method that creates a new bullet and gives it a thrust vector that the physics engine will use to propel the bullet towards its target:

```
+ (instancetype)bulletFrom:(CGPoint)start toward:(CGPoint)destination {
    BIDBulletNode *bullet = [[self alloc] init];

    bullet.position = start;

    CGVector movement = BIDVectorBetweenPoints(start, destination);
    CGFloat magnitude = BIDVectorLength(movement);
    if (magnitude == 0.0f) return nil;

    CGVector scaledMovement = BIDVectorMultiply(movement, 1 / magnitude);

    CGFloat thrustMagnitude = 100.0;
    bullet.thrust = BIDVectorMultiply(scaledMovement, thrustMagnitude);

    return bullet;
}
```

The basic calculations are pretty simple. We first determine a movement vector that points from the start location to the destination, and then we determine its magnitude (length). Dividing the movement vector by its magnitude produces a normalized **unit vector**, a vector that points in the same direction as the original, but is exactly one unit long (a unit, in this case, is the same as a "point" on the screen—e.g., two pixels on a Retina device, one pixel on older devices). Creating a unit vector is very useful because we can multiply that by a fixed magnitude (in this case, 100) to determine a uniformly powerful thrust vector, no matter how far away the user tapped the screen.

The final piece of code we need to add to this class is this method, which applies thrust to the physics body. We'll call this once per frame, from inside the scene:

```
- (void)applyRecurringForce {
    [self.physicsBody applyForce:self.thrust];
}
```

Adding Bullets to the Scene

Now switch over to *BIDLevelScene.m* to add bullets to the scene itself. For starters, import the header for the new class near the top. Next, add another property to contain all bullets in a single SKNode, just as you did earlier for enemies:

```
#import "BIDLevelScene.h"
#import "BIDPlayerNode.h"
#import "BIDEnemyNode.h"
#import "BIDBulletNode.h"

#define ARC4RANDOM_MAX      0x100000000

@interface BIDLevelScene ()

@property (strong, nonatomic) BIDPlayerNode *playerNode;
@property (strong, nonatomic) SKNode *enemies;
@property (strong, nonatomic) SKNode *playerBullets;

@end
```

Find the section of the initWithSize:levelNumber: method where you previously added the enemies. That's the place to set up the playerBullets node, too.

```
_playerBullets = [SKNode node];
[self addChild:_playerBullets];
```

Now we're ready to code the actual missile launches. Add this else clause to the touchesBegan:withEvent: method, so that all taps in the upper part of the screen shoot a bullet instead of moving the ship:

```
- (void)touchesBegan:(NSSet *)touches withEvent:(UIEvent *)event {
    for (UITouch *touch in touches) {
        CGPoint location = [touch locationInNode:self];
        if (location.y < CGRectGetHeight(self.frame) * 0.2 ) {
            CGPoint target = CGPointMake(location.x,
                                         self.playerNode.position.y);
            [self.playerNode moveToward:target];

        } else {
            BIDBulletNode *bullet = [BIDBulletNode
                                     bulletFrom:self.playerNode.position
                                     toward:location];
            if (bullet) {
                [self.playerBullets addChild:bullet];
            }
        }
    }
}
```

That adds the bullet, but none of the bullets we add will actually move unless we tell them to by applying thrust every frame. Our scene already contains an empty method called update:. This method is called each frame, and that's the perfect place to do any game logic that needs to occur each frame. Rather than updating all our bullets right in that method, however, we put that code in a separate method that we call from the update: method:

```
- (void)update:(CFTimeInterval)currentTime {
    [self updateBullets];
}

- (void)updateBullets {
    NSMutableArray *bulletsToRemove = [NSMutableArray array];
    for (BIDBulletNode *bullet in self.playerBullets.children) {
        // Remove any bullets that have moved off-screen
        if (!CGRectContainsPoint(self.frame, bullet.position)) {
            // mark bullet for removal
            [bulletsToRemove addObject:bullet];
            continue;
        }
        // Apply thrust to remaining bullets
        [bullet applyRecurringForce];
    }
    [self.playerBullets removeChildrenInArray:bulletsToRemove];
}
```

Before telling each bullet to apply its recurring force, we also check whether each bullet is still on-screen. Any bullet that's gone off-screen is put into a temporary array; and then, at the end, those are swept out of the playerBullets node. Note that this two-stage process is necessary because the for loop at work in this method is iterating over all children in the playerBullets node. Making changes to a collection while you're iterating over it is never a good idea, and it can easily lead to a crash.

Now build and run the app, and you'll see that, in addition to moving the player's ship, you can make it shoot missiles upwards by tapping on the screen (see Figure 17-6). Neat!

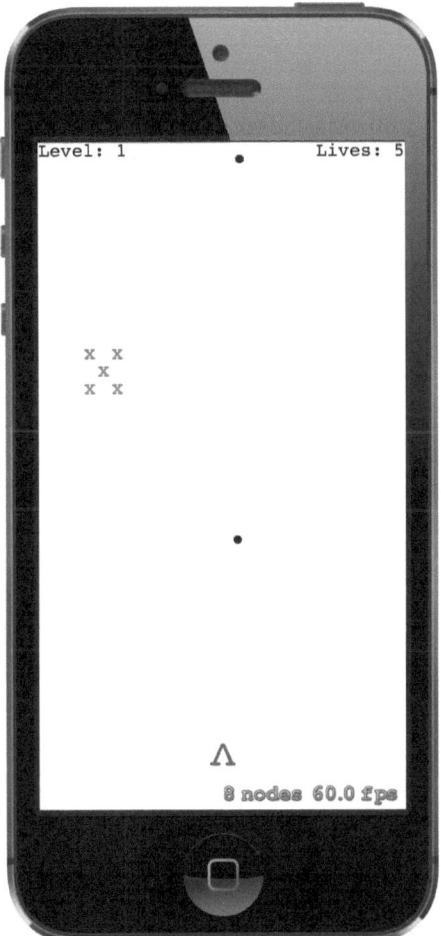

Figure 17-6. Shooting up a storm!

Attacking Enemies with Physics

A couple of important gameplay elements are still missing from our game. The enemies never attack us, and we can't yet get rid of the enemies by shooting them. Let's take care of the latter right now. We're going to set things up so that shooting an enemy has the effect of dislodging it from the spot where it's currently fixed on the screen. This feature will use the physics engine for all the heavy lifting, and it will involve making changes to BIDPlayerNode, BIDEnemyNode, and BIDLevelScene.

For starters, let's add physics bodies to our nodes that don't already have them. Start with *BIDEnemyNode.m*, adding these #import statements near the top:

```
#import "BIDPhysicsCategories.h"
#import "BIDGeometry.h"
```

Next, add the following line to the init method:

```
- (instancetype)init {
    if (self = [super init]) {
        self.name = [NSString stringWithFormat:@"Enemy %p", self];
        [self initNodeGraph];
        [self initPhysicsBody];
    }
    return self;
}
```

Now add the code to really set up the physics body. This is pretty similar to what you did earlier for the BIDPlayerBullet class:

```
- (void)initPhysicsBody {
    SKPhysicsBody *body = [SKPhysicsBody bodyWithRectangleOfSize:
                            CGSizeMake(40, 40)];
    body.affectedByGravity = NO;
    body.categoryBitMask = EnemyCategory;
    body.contactTestBitMask = PlayerCategory|EnemyCategory;
    body.mass = 0.2;
    body.angularDamping = 0.0f;
    body.linearDamping = 0.0f;
    self.physicsBody = body;
}
```

Then select *BIDPlayerNode.m*, where you're going to do a pretty similar set of things. First, add the following #import near the top:

```
#import "BIDPhysicsCategories.h"
```

Follow up by adding the bold line shown here to the init method:

```
- (instancetype)init {
    if (self = [super init]) {
        self.name = [NSString stringWithFormat:@"Player %p", self];
        [self initNodeGraph];
        [self initPhysicsBody];
    }
    return self;
}
```

Finally, add the new initPhysicsBody method:

```
- (void)initPhysicsBody {
    SKPhysicsBody *body = [SKPhysicsBody bodyWithRectangleOfSize:
                            CGSizeMake(20, 20)];
    body.affectedByGravity = NO;
    body.categoryBitMask = PlayerCategory;
```

```
    body.contactTestBitMask = EnemyCategory;
    body.collisionBitMask = 0;

    self.physicsBody = body;
}
```

At this point, you can run the app and see that your bullets now have the ability to knock enemies into space. However, you'll also see there's a problem here. When you start the game and then send the lone enemy hurtling into space, you're stuck! This is probably a good time to add level management to the game.

Finishing Levels

We need to enhance BIDLevelScene so that it knows when it's time to move to the next level. It can figure this out simply enough by looking at the number of available enemies. If it finds that there aren't any on-screen, then the level is over, and the game should transition to the next.

Keeping Tabs on the Enemies

Begin by adding this updateEnemies method. It works a lot like the updateBullets method added earlier:

```
- (void)updateEnemies {
    NSMutableArray *enemiesToRemove = [NSMutableArray array];
    for (SKNode *node in self.enemies.children) {
        // Remove any enemies that have moved off-screen
        if (!CGRectContainsPoint(self.frame, node.position)) {
            // mark enemy for removal
            [enemiesToRemove addObject:node];
            continue;
        }
    }
    if ([enemiesToRemove count] > 0) {
        [self.enemies removeChildrenInArray:enemiesToRemove];
    }
}
```

That takes care of removing each enemy from the level's enemies array each time one goes off-screen. Now let's modify the update: method, telling it to call updateEnemies, as well as a new method we haven't yet implemented:

```
- (void)update:(CFTimeInterval)currentTime {
    /* Called before each frame is rendered */
    if (self.finished) return;

    [self updateBullets];
    [self updateEnemies];
    [self checkForNextLevel];
}
```

We started out that method by checking the finished property. Since we're about to add code that can officially end a level, we want to be sure that we don't keep doing additional processing after the level is complete! Then, just as we're checking each frame to see if any bullets or enemies have gone off-screen, we're going to call checkForNextLevel each frame to see if the current level is complete. Let's add this method:

```
- (void)checkForNextLevel {
    if ([self.enemies.children count] == 0) {
        [self goToNextLevel];
    }
}
```

Transitioning to the Next Levels

The checkForNextLevel method in turn calls another method we haven't yet implemented. The goToNextLevel method marks this level as finished, displays some text on the screen to let the player know, then starts the next level:

```
- (void)goToNextLevel {
    self.finished = YES;

    SKLabelNode *label = [SKLabelNode labelNodeWithFontNamed:@"Courier"];
    label.text = @"Level Complete!";
    label.fontColor = [SKColor blueColor];
    label.fontSize = 32;
    label.position = CGPointMake(self.frame.size.width * 0.5,
                                 self.frame.size.height * 0.5);
    [self addChild:label];

    BIDLevelScene *nextLevel = [[BIDLevelScene alloc]
                                initWithSize:self.frame.size
                                levelNumber:self.levelNumber + 1];
    nextLevel.playerLives = self.playerLives;
    [self.view presentScene:nextLevel
                transition:[SKTransition flipHorizontalWithDuration:1.0]];
}
```

The second half of the goToNextLevel method creates a new instance of BIDLevelScene and gives it all the start values it needs. It then tells the view to present the new scene, using a transition to smooth things over. The SKTransition class lets us pick from a variety of transition styles. Run the app and complete a level to see what this one looks like (see Figure 17-7).

Figure 17-7. Here you see a snapshot taken during the end-of-level screen-flipping transition

The transition in use here makes it looks like we're flipping a card over its horizontal axis, but there are plenty more to choose from! See the documentation or header file for SKTransition to see more possibilities. We'll use a couple more variations later in this chapter.

Customizing Collisions

Now we've got a game that you can really play. You can clear level after level by knocking enemies upward off the screen. That's OK, but there's really not much challenge! We mentioned earlier that having enemies attack the player is one piece of missing gameplay, and now it's time to make that happen. We're going to make things a little harder by making the enemies fall down when they're bumped, either from being hit by a bullet or from being touched by another enemy. We also want to make it so that being hit by a falling enemy takes a life away from the player. You also may have noticed that after a bullet hits an enemy, the bullet squiggles its way around the enemy and continues on its upward trajectory, which is pretty weird. We're going to tackle all these things by implementing a collision-handling routine in *BIDLevelScene.m*.

The method for handling detected collisions is a delegate method for the SKPhysicsWorld class. Our scene has a physics world by default, but we need to set it up a little bit before it will tell us anything. For starters, it's good to let the compiler know that we're going to implement a delegate protocol, so let's add this declaration to the class extension declaration near the top of the file:

```
@interface BIDLevelScene () <SKPhysicsContactDelegate>
```

We still need to configure the world a bit (giving it a slightly less cruel amount of gravity) and tell it who its delegate is. To do so, we add these bold lines near the end of the init method, at the same place we've been adding all our other setup:

```
self.physicsWorld.gravity = CGVectorMake(0, -1);
self.physicsWorld.contactDelegate = self;
```

Now that we've set the physics world's contactDelegate to be the BIDLevelScene, we can implement the relevant delegate method. The core of the method looks like this:

```
- (void)didBeginContact:(SKPhysicsContact *)contact {
    if (contact.bodyA.categoryBitMask == contact.bodyB.categoryBitMask) {
        // Both bodies are in the same category
        SKNode *nodeA = contact.bodyA.node;
        SKNode *nodeB = contact.bodyB.node;

        // What do we do with these nodes?
    } else {
        SKNode *attacker = nil;
        SKNode *attackee = nil;

        if (contact.bodyA.categoryBitMask > contact.bodyB.categoryBitMask) {
            // Body A is attacking Body B
            attacker = contact.bodyA.node;
            attackee = contact.bodyB.node;
        } else {
            // Body B is attacking Body A
            attacker = contact.bodyB.node;
            attackee = contact.bodyA.node;
        }
        if ([attackee isKindOfClass:[BIDPlayerNode class]]) {
            self.playerLives--;
        }
        // What do we do with the attacker and the attackee?
    }
}
```

Go ahead and add that method, but if you look at it right now, you'll see that it doesn't really do much yet. In fact, the only concrete result of that method is to reduce the number of player lives each time a falling enemy hits the player's ship. But the enemies aren't falling yet!

The idea behind this implementation is to look at the two colliding objects and to figure out whether they are of the same category (in which case, they are "friends" to one another) or if they are of different categories. If they are of different categories, we have to determine who is attacking whom.

If you look at the order of the categories declared in *BIDPhysicsCategories.h*, you'll see that they are specified in order of increased "attackyness": Player nodes can be attacked by Enemy nodes, which in turn can be attacked by PlayerMissile nodes. That means that we can use a simple greater-than comparison to figure out who is the "attacker" in this scenario.

For the sake of simplicity and modularity, we don't really want the scene to decide how each object should react to being attacked by an enemy or bumped by another object. It's much better to build those details into the affected node classes themselves. But, as you see in the method we've got, the only thing we're sure of is that each side has an SKNode instance. Rather than coding up a big chain of if-else statements to ask each node which SKNode subclass it belongs to, we can use regular polymorphism to let each of our node classes handle things in its own way. In order for that to work, we have to add methods to SKNode, with default implementations that do nothing and let our subclasses override them where appropriate. This calls for a category! Not a Sprite Kit physics category this time, but a genuine Objective-C @category definition.

Adding a Category to SKNode

To add a category to SKNode, right-click the *TextShooter* folder in Xcode's project navigator and choose **New File...** from the popup menu. From the assistant's *iOS/Cocoa Touch* section, choose *Objective-C category*, and then click *Next*. Give it a *Category* name of *Extra* and type in *SKNode* in the *Category on* field. Now click *Next* again and create the files. Select *SKNode+Extra.h* and add the bold method declarations shown here:

```
#import <SpriteKit/SpriteKit.h>

@interface SKNode (Extra)

- (void)receiveAttacker:(SKNode *)attacker contact:(SKPhysicsContact *)contact;
- (void)friendlyBumpFrom:(SKNode *)node;

@end
```

Switch over to the matching *.m* file and enter the following empty definitions:

```
#import "SKNode+Extra.h"

@implementation SKNode (Extra)

- (void)receiveAttacker:(SKNode *)attacker contact:(SKPhysicsContact *)contact {
    // default implementation does nothing
}

- (void)friendlyBumpFrom:(SKNode *)node {
    // default implementation does nothing
}

@end
```

Now head back over to *BIDLevelScene.m* to finish up its part of the collision handling. Start by adding a new header at the top:

```
#import "BIDLevelScene.h"
#import "BIDPlayerNode.h"
#import "BIDEnemyNode.h"
#import "BIDBulletNode.h"
#import "SKNode+Extra.h"
```

Next, go back to the didBeginContact: method, where you'll add the bits that actually do some work:

```
- (void)didBeginContact:(SKPhysicsContact *)contact {
    if (contact.bodyA.categoryBitMask == contact.bodyB.categoryBitMask) {
        // Both bodies are in the same category
        SKNode *nodeA = contact.bodyA.node;
        SKNode *nodeB = contact.bodyB.node;

        // What do we do with these nodes?
        [nodeA friendlyBumpFrom:nodeB];
        [nodeB friendlyBumpFrom:nodeA];
    } else {
        SKNode *attacker = nil;
        SKNode *attackee = nil;

        if (contact.bodyA.categoryBitMask > contact.bodyB.categoryBitMask) {
            // Body A is attacking Body B
            attacker = contact.bodyA.node;
            attackee = contact.bodyB.node;
        } else {
            // Body B is attacking Body A
            attacker = contact.bodyB.node;
            attackee = contact.bodyA.node;
        }
        if ([attackee isKindOfClass:[BIDPlayerNode class]]) {
            self.playerLives--;
        }
        // What do we do with the attacker and the attackee?
        if (attacker) {
            [attackee receiveAttacker:attacker contact:contact];
            [self.playerBullets removeChildrenInArray:@[attacker]];
            [self.enemies removeChildrenInArray:@[attacker]];
        }
    }
}
```

All we added here were a few calls to our new methods. If the collision is "friendly fire," such as two enemies bumping into each other, we'll tell each of them that it received a friendly bump from the other. Otherwise, after figuring out who attacked whom, we tell the attackee that it's come under attack from another object. Finally, we remove the attacker from whichever of the playerBullets or enemies nodes it may be in. We tell each of those nodes to remove the attacker, even though it can only be in one of them, but that's OK. Telling a node to remove a child it doesn't have isn't an error—it just has no effect.

Adding Custom Collision Behavior to Enemies

Now that all that's in place, we can implement some specific behaviors for our nodes by overriding the category we added to SKNode.

Select *BIDEnemyNode.m* and add the following two methods:

```
- (void)friendlyBumpFrom:(SKNode *)node {
    self.physicsBody.affectedByGravity = YES;
}

- (void)receiveAttacker:(SKNode *)attacker contact:(SKPhysicsContact *)contact {
    self.physicsBody.affectedByGravity = YES;
    CGVector force = BIDVectorMultiply(attacker.physicsBody.velocity,
                                       contact.collisionImpulse);
    CGPoint myContact = [self.scene convertPoint:contact.contactPoint
                                          toNode:self];
    [self.physicsBody applyForce:force
                         atPoint:myContact];
}
```

The first of those, friendlyBumpFrom:, simply turns on gravity for the affected enemy. So, if one enemy is in motion and bumps into another, the second enemy will suddenly notice gravity and start falling downward.

The receiveAttacker:contact: method, which is called if the enemy is hit by a bullet, first turns on gravity for the enemy. However, it also uses the contact data that was passed in to figure out just where the contact occurred and applies a force to that point, giving it an extra push in the direction that the bullet was fired.

Showing Accurate Player Lives

Run the game, and you'll see that you can shoot at enemies to knock them down. You'll also see that any other enemies bumped into by a falling enemy will fall, as well.

> **Note** At the start of each level, the world performs one step of its physics simulation to make sure that there aren't physics bodies overlapping each other. This will produce an interesting side effect at higher levels, since there will be an increasing chance that multiple randomly placed enemies will occupy overlapping spaces. Whenever that happens, the enemies will be immediately shifted so they no longer overlap, and our collision-handling code will be triggered, which subsequently turns on gravity and lets them fall! This behavior wasn't anything we planned on when we started building this game, but it turns out to be a happy accident that makes higher levels progressively more difficult, so we're letting physics run its course!

If you let enemies hit you as they fall, the number of player lives decreases, but... hey wait, it just shows *5* all the time! The *Lives* display is set up when the level is created, but it's never updated after that. Fortunately this is easily fixed by implementing the setPlayerLives: setter instead of using the automatically synthesized setter, like this:

```
- (void)setPlayerLives:(NSUInteger)playerLives  {
    _playerLives = playerLives;
    SKLabelNode *lives = (id)[self childNodeWithName:@"LivesLabel"];
    lives.text = [NSString stringWithFormat:@"Lives: %lu",
                        (unsigned long)_playerLives];
}
```

The preceding snippet uses the name we previously associated with the label (in the init method) to find the label again and set a new text value. Play the game again, and you'll see that, as you let enemies rain down on your player, the number of lives will decrease to zero. And then the game doesn't end. After the next hit, you end up with a very large number of lives indeed, as you can see in Figure 17-8.

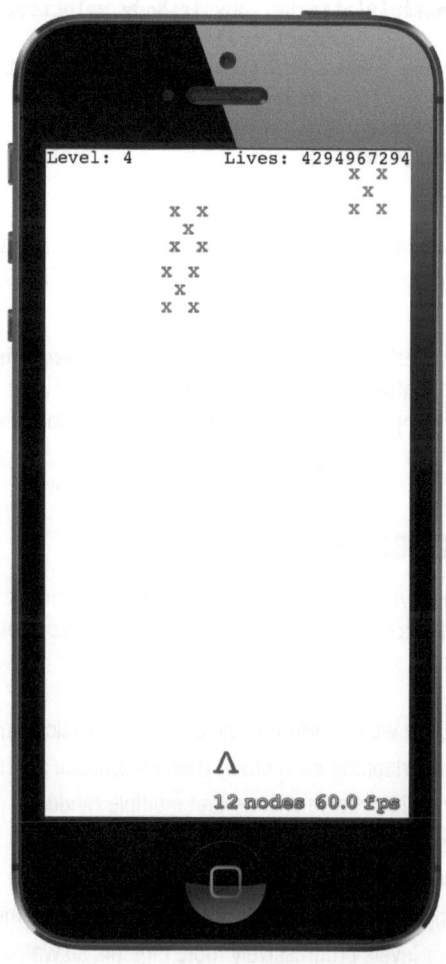

Figure 17-8. That's a lot of lives

So what's going on here? Well, we are using an unsigned integer to hold the number of lives. And when you're using unsigned integers and dip below zero, you sort of wrap around that zero boundary and end up with the maximum allowed unsigned integer value instead!

The reason this problem appears is really because we haven't written any code to detect the end of the game; that is, the point in time when the number of player lives hits zero. We'll do that soon, but first let's make our on-screen collisions a bit more stimulating.

Spicing Things up with Particles

One of the nice features of Sprite Kit is the inclusion of a particle system. Particle systems are used in games to create visual effects simulating smoke, fire, explosions, and more. Right now, whenever our bullets hit an enemy or an enemy hits the player, the attacking object simply blinks out of existence. Let's make a couple of particle systems to improve this situation!

Start out by pressing **Cmd-N** to make a new file. Select the *iOS/Resource* section on the left, and then choose *SpriteKit Particle File* on the right. Click *Next*, and on the following screen choose the *Spark* particle template. Click *Next* again and name this file *MissileExplosion.sks*.

Your First Particle

You'll see that Xcode creates the particle file and also adds a new resource called *spark.png* to the project. At the same time, the entire Xcode editing area switches over to the new particle file, showing you a huge, animated exploding thing.

We don't want something quite this extravagant and enormous when our bullets hit enemies, so let's reconfigure this thing. All the properties that define this particle's animation are available in the *SKNode Inspector*, which you can bring up by pressing **Opt-Cmd-7**. Figure 17-9 shows both the massive explosion and the inspector.

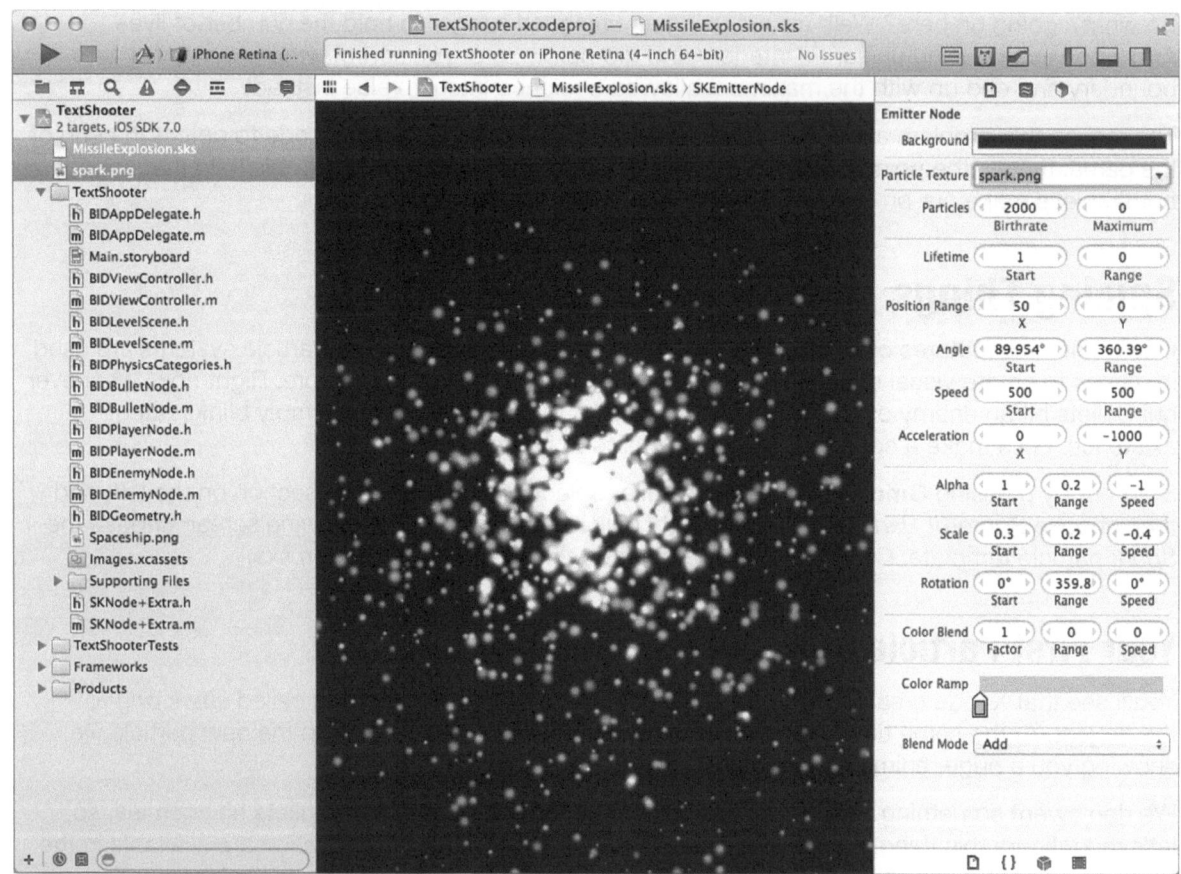

Figure 17-9. Explosion city! The parameters shown on the right define how the default particle looks

Now, for our bullet hit, let's make it a much smaller explosion. It will have a whole different set of parameters, all of which you configure right in the inspector. First, fix the colors to match what our game looks like by clicking the *Background* color well and setting it to white. Next, click the small color well in the *Color Ramp* at the bottom and set it to black. Also, change the *Blend Mode* to *Alpha*, and now you'll see that the flaming fountain has turned all inky.

The rest of the parameters are all numeric. Change them one at a time, setting them all as shown in Figure 17-10. At each step of the way, you'll see the particle effect change until it eventually reaches its target appearance (see Figure 17-10).

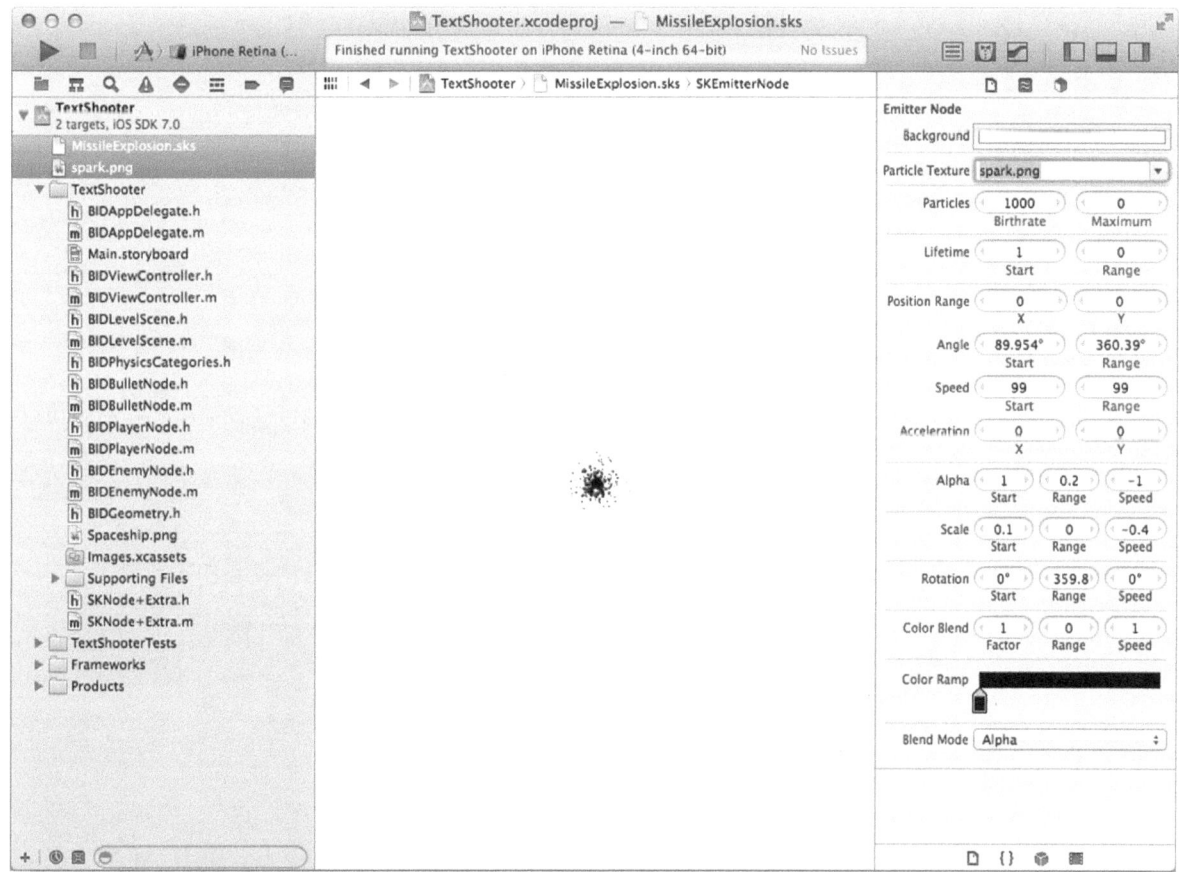

Figure 17-10. *This is the final missile explosion particle effect we want*

Now make another particle system, once again using the *Spark* template. Name this one *EnemyExplosion.sks* and set its parameters as shown in Figure 17-11.

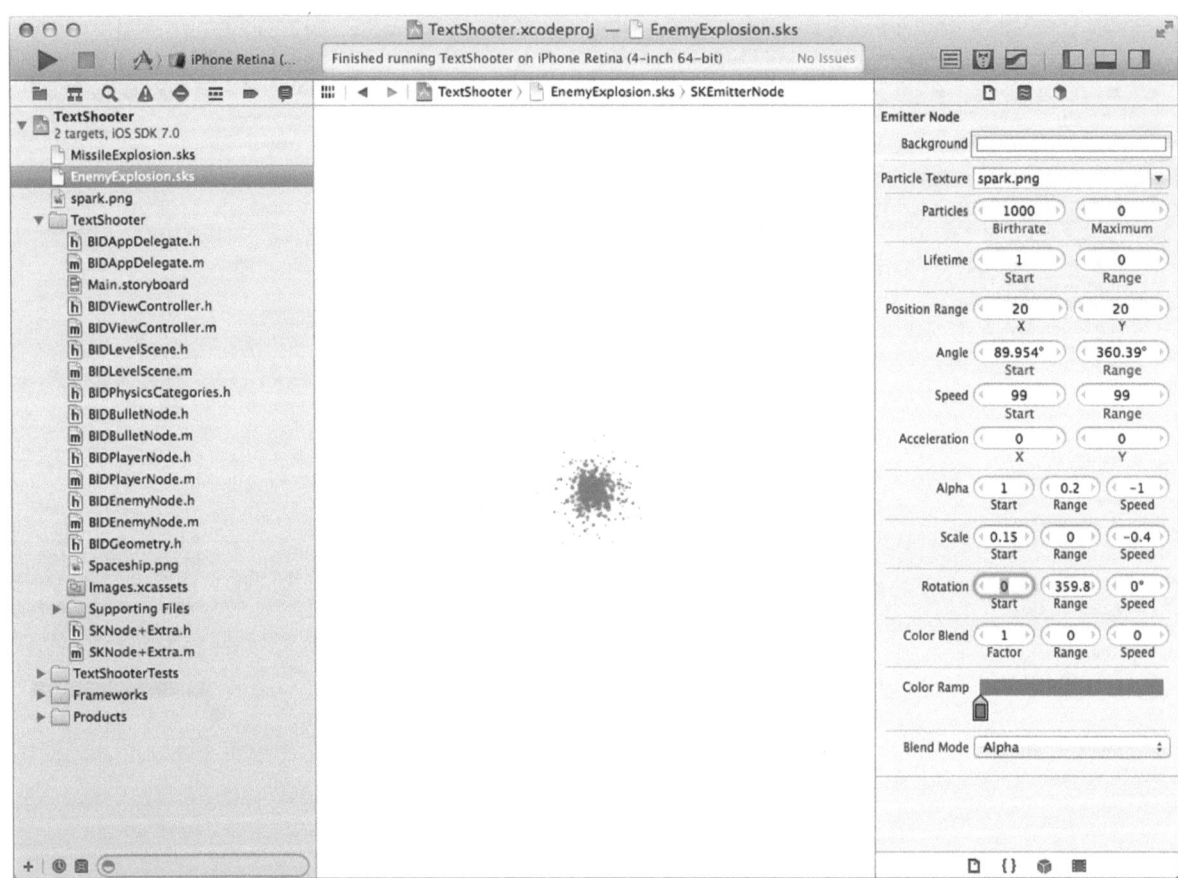

Figure 17-11. Here's the enemy explosion we want to create. In case you're seeing this book in black and white, the color we've chosen in the Color Ramp at the bottom is deep red

Putting Particles into the Scene

Now let's start putting these particles to use. Switch over to *BIDEnemyNode.m* and add the bold code shown here to the bottom of the receiveAttacker:contact: method:

```
- (void)receiveAttacker:(SKNode *)attacker contact:(SKPhysicsContact *)contact {
    self.physicsBody.affectedByGravity = YES;
    CGVector force = BIDVectorMultiply(attacker.physicsBody.velocity,
                                       contact.collisionImpulse);
    CGPoint myContact = [self.scene convertPoint:contact.contactPoint
                                         toNode:self];
    [self.physicsBody applyForce:force
                         atPoint:myContact];

    NSString *path = [[NSBundle mainBundle] pathForResource:@"MissileExplosion"
                                                     ofType:@"sks"];
    SKEmitterNode *explosion = [NSKeyedUnarchiver unarchiveObjectWithFile:path];
```

```
    explosion.numParticlesToEmit = 20;
    explosion.position = contact.contactPoint;
    [self.scene addChild:explosion];
}
```

Run the game, shoot some enemies, and you'll see a nice little explosion where each bullet hits an enemy, as shown in Figure 17-12.

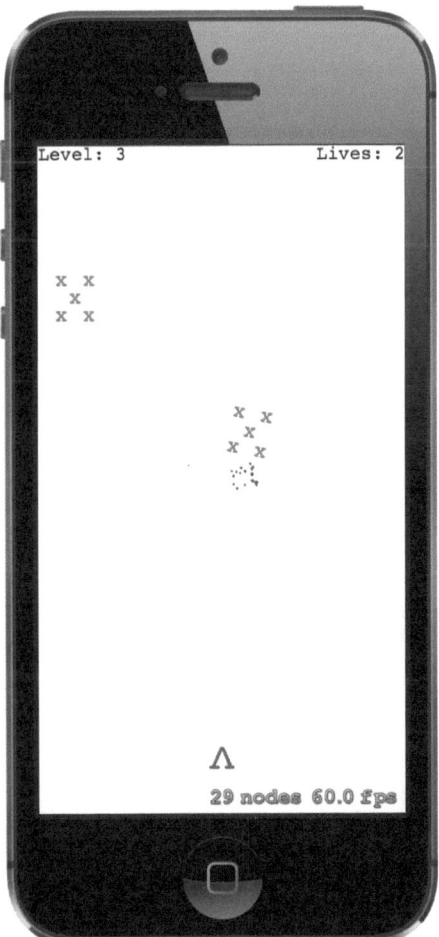

Figure 17-12. Bullets smash nicely after impact

Nice! Now let's do something similar for those times an enemy smashes into a player's ship. Select *BIDPlayerNode.m* and add this method:

```
- (void)receiveAttacker:(SKNode *)attacker contact:(SKPhysicsContact *)contact {
    NSString *path = [[NSBundle mainBundle] pathForResource:@"EnemyExplosion"
                                                     ofType:@"sks"];
    SKEmitterNode *explosion = [NSKeyedUnarchiver unarchiveObjectWithFile:path];
```

```
        explosion.numParticlesToEmit = 50;
        explosion.position = contact.contactPoint;
        [self.scene addChild:explosion];
}
```

Play again, and you'll see a nice red splat every time an enemy hits the player, as shown in Figure 17-13.

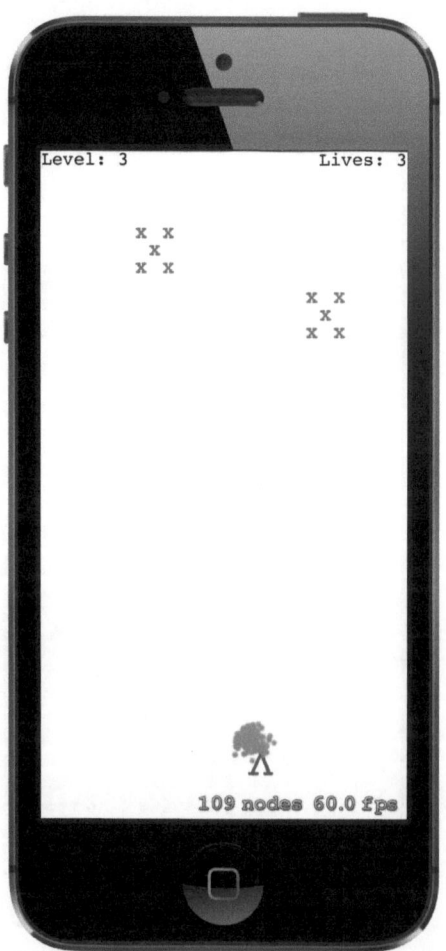

Figure 17-13. Ouch!

These changes are pretty simple, but they improve the feel of the game substantially. Now when things collide, you have visual consequences and can see that something happened.

The End Game

As we mentioned before, we currently have a small problem in the game. When the number of lives hits zero, we need to end the game. What we'll do is create a new scene class to transition to when the game is over. You've seen us do a scene transition before, when moving from one level to the next. This will be similar, but with a new class.

So, create a new Objective-C class. Use SKScene as the parent class and name the new class BIDGameOverScene.

We'll start with a very simple implementation that just displays "Game Over" text and does nothing more. We'll accomplish this by adding this code to the @implementation in *BIDGameOverScene.m*:

```
- (instancetype)initWithSize:(CGSize)size {
    if (self = [super initWithSize:size]) {
        self.backgroundColor = [SKColor purpleColor];
        SKLabelNode *text = [SKLabelNode labelNodeWithFontNamed:@"Courier"];
        text.text = @"Game Over";
        text.fontColor = [SKColor whiteColor];
        text.fontSize = 50;
        text.position = CGPointMake(self.frame.size.width * 0.5,
                                    self.frame.size.height * 0.5);
        [self addChild:text];
    }
    return self;
}
```

Now let's switch back to *BIDLevelScene.m*. We'll need to import the header for the new scene at the top:

```
#import "BIDLevelScene.h"
#import "BIDPlayerNode.h"
#import "BIDEnemyNode.h"
#import "BIDBulletNode.h"
#import "SKNode+Extra.h"
#import "BIDGameOverScene.h"
```

The basic action of what to do when the game ends is defined by this new method. Here, we both show an extra explosion and kick off a transition to the new scene we just created:

```
- (void)triggerGameOver {
    self.finished = YES;

    NSString *path = [[NSBundle mainBundle] pathForResource:@"EnemyExplosion"
                                                     ofType:@"sks"];
    SKEmitterNode *explosion = [NSKeyedUnarchiver unarchiveObjectWithFile:path];
    explosion.numParticlesToEmit = 200;
    explosion.position = _playerNode.position;
    [self addChild:explosion];
    [_playerNode removeFromParent];
```

```
    SKTransition *transition = [SKTransition doorsOpenVerticalWithDuration:1.0];
    SKScene *gameOver = [[BIDGameOverScene alloc] initWithSize:self.frame.size];
    [self.view presentScene:gameOver transition:transition];
}
```

Next, create this new method that will check for the end of the game, call triggerGameOver if it's time, and return either YES to indicate the game ended or NO to indicate that it's still on:

```
- (BOOL)checkForGameOver {
    if (self.playerLives == 0) {
        [self triggerGameOver];
        return YES;
    }
    return NO;
}
```

Finally, add a check to the existing update: method. It checks for the game over state and only checks for a potential next level transition if the game is still going. Otherwise, there's a risk that the final enemy on a level could take the player's final life and trigger two scene transitions at once!

```
- (void)update:(CFTimeInterval)currentTime {
    if (self.finished) return;

    [self updateBullets];
    [self updateEnemies];
    if (![self checkForGameOver]) {
        [self checkForNextLevel];
    }
}
```

Now run the game again, let falling enemies damage your ship five times, and you'll see the Game Over screen, as shown in Figure 17-14.

Figure 17-14. *That's it, man. Game over, man—game over*

At last, a Beginning (Create a StartScene)

This leads us to another problem: What do we do after the game is over? We could allow the player to tap to restart the game; but while thinking of that, a thought crossed my mind. Shouldn't this game have some sort of start screen, so the player isn't immediately thrust into a game at launch time? And shouldn't the game over screen lead you back there? Of course the answer to both questions is yes! Go ahead and create another new Objective-C class, once again using SKScene as the superclass, and this time naming it BIDStartScene.

We're going to make a super-simple start scene here. All it will do is display some text and start the game when the user taps anywhere. Add all the bold code shown here to complete this class:

```objc
#import "BIDStartScene.h"
#import "BIDLevelScene.h"

@implementation BIDStartScene

- (instancetype)initWithSize:(CGSize)size {
    if (self = [super initWithSize:size]) {
        self.backgroundColor = [SKColor greenColor];

        SKLabelNode *topLabel = [SKLabelNode labelNodeWithFontNamed:@"Courier"];
        topLabel.text = @"TextShooter";
        topLabel.fontColor = [SKColor blackColor];
        topLabel.fontSize = 48;
        topLabel.position = CGPointMake(self.frame.size.width * 0.5,
                                self.frame.size.height * 0.7);
        [self addChild:topLabel];

        SKLabelNode *bottomLabel = [SKLabelNode labelNodeWithFontNamed:
                                @"Courier"];
        bottomLabel.text = @"Touch anywhere to start";
        bottomLabel.fontColor = [SKColor blackColor];
        bottomLabel.fontSize = 20;
        bottomLabel.position = CGPointMake(self.frame.size.width * 0.5,
                                self.frame.size.height * 0.3);
        [self addChild:bottomLabel];

    }
    return self;
}

- (void)touchesBegan:(NSSet *)touches withEvent:(UIEvent *)event {
    SKTransition *transition = [SKTransition doorwayWithDuration:1.0];
    SKScene *game = [[BIDLevelScene alloc] initWithSize:self.frame.size];
    [self.view presentScene:game transition:transition];
}

@end
```

Now go back to *BIDGameOverScene.m*, so we can make the game over scene perform a transition to the start scene. Add this header import:

```objc
#import "BIDGameOverScene.h"
#import "BIDStartScene.h"
```

And then add these two methods:

```
- (void)didMoveToView:(SKView *)view {
    [self performSelector:@selector(goToStart) withObject:nil afterDelay:3.0];
}

- (void)goToStart {
    SKTransition *transition = [SKTransition flipVerticalWithDuration:1.0];
    SKScene *start = [[BIDStartScene alloc] initWithSize:self.frame.size];
    [self.view presentScene:start transition:transition];
}
```

The didMoveToView: method is called on any scene after it's been put in place in a view. Here, we simply trigger a three second pause, followed by a transition back to the start scene.

There's just one more piece of the puzzle to make all our scenes transition to each other as they should. We need to change the app startup procedure so that, instead of jumping right into the game, it shows us the start screen instead. This takes us back to *BIDViewController.m*, where we first import the header for our start scene:

```
#import "BIDViewController.h"
#import "BIDLevelScene.h"
#import "BIDStartScene.h"
```

Then, in the viewDidLoad method, we just replace one scene class name with another:

```
    // Create and configure the scene.
    SKScene * scene = [BIDLevelScene sceneWithSize:skView.bounds.size];
    SKScene * scene = [BIDStartScene sceneWithSize:skView.bounds.size];
```

Now give it a whirl! Launch the app, and you'll be greeted by the start scene. Touch the screen, play the game, die a lot, and you'll get to the game over scene. Wait a few seconds, and you're back to the start screen, as shown in Figure 17-15.

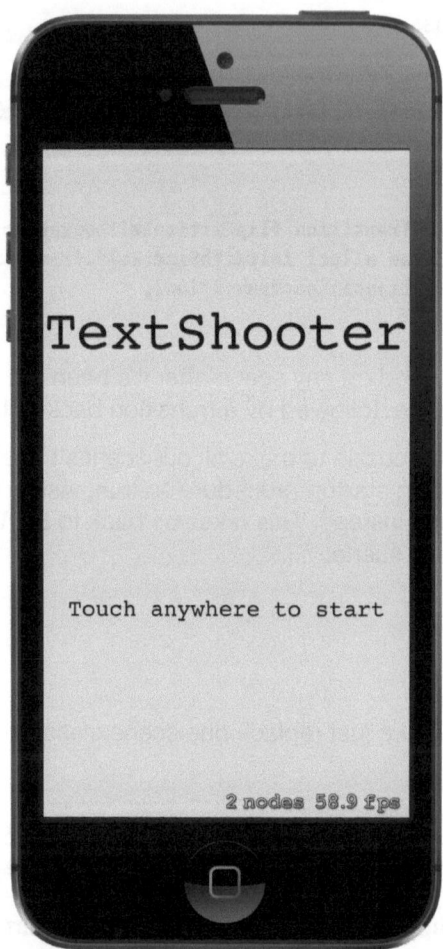

Figure 17-15. Finally, we made it to the start screen!

A Sound is Worth a Thousand Pictures

OK, just one more thing. We've been working on a video game, and video games are known for being noisy, but ours is completely silent! Fortunately, Sprite Kit contains audio playback code that's extremely easy to use. Start by digging into the code archive for this chapter and finding the prepared audio files: *enemyHit.wav*, *gameOver.wav*, *gameStart.wav*, *playerHit.wav*, and *shoot.wav*. Drag all of them into Xcode's project navigator.

> **Note**   These sound effects were created using the excellent, open source CFXR application (available from
> `https://github.com/nevyn/cfxr`). If you need quirky little sound effects, CFXR is hard to beat!

Now we'll bake in easy playback for each of these sound effects. Start with *BIDBulletNode.m*, adding the bold code to the end of the `bulletFrom:toward:` method, just before the `return` line:

```
[bullet runAction:[SKAction playSoundFileNamed:@"shoot.wav"
                            waitForCompletion:NO]];
```

Next, switch over *to BIDEnemyNode.m*, adding these lines to the end of the `receiveAttacker:contact:` method:

```
[self runAction:[SKAction playSoundFileNamed:@"enemyHit.wav"
                          waitForCompletion:NO]];
```

Now do something extremely similar in *BIDPlayerNode.m*, adding these lines to the end of the `receiveAttacker:contact:` method:

```
[self runAction:[SKAction playSoundFileNamed:@"playerHit.wav"
                          waitForCompletion:NO]];
```

Those are enough in-game sounds to satisfy for the moment. Go ahead and run the game at this point, to try them out. I think you'll agree that the simple addition of particles and sounds gives the game a much better feel.

Now let's just add some effects for starting the game and ending the game. In *BIDStartScene.m*, add these lines at the end of the `touchesBegan:withEvent:` method:

```
[self runAction:[SKAction playSoundFileNamed:@"gameStart.wav"
                          waitForCompletion:NO]];
```

And finally, add these lines to the end of the `triggerGameOver` method in *BIDLevelScene.m*:

```
[self runAction:[SKAction playSoundFileNamed:@"gameOver.wav"
                          waitForCompletion:NO]];
```

Now when you play the game, you'll be inundated by comforting bleeps and bloops, just like when you were a kid! Or maybe when your parents were kids. Or your grandparents! Just trust me, all the games used to sound pretty much like this.

Game On

Although TextShooter may be simple in appearance, the techniques you've learned in this chapter form the basis for all sorts of game development using Sprite Kit. You've learned how to organize your code across multiple node classes, group objects together using the node graph, and more. You've also been given a taste of what it's like to build this sort of game one feature at a time, discovering each step along the way. Of course we're not showing you all of our own missteps made along the way—this book is already about 700 pages long without that—but even counting those, this app really was built from scratch, in roughly the order shown in this chapter, in just a few short hours.

Once you get going, Sprite Kit allows you to build up a lot of structure in a short amount of time. As you've seen, you can use text-based sprites if you don't have images handy. And if you want to swap them out for real graphics later, it's no problem. One early reader even pointed out a middle path: Instead of plain old ASCII text in the strings in your source code, you can insert emoji characters by using Apple's Character Viewer input source. Accomplishing this is left as an exercise to the reader!

Chapter 18

Taps, Touches, and Gestures

The screens of the iPhone, iPod touch, and iPad—with their crisp, bright, touch-sensitive display—are truly things of beauty and masterpieces of engineering. The multitouch screen common to all iOS devices is one of the key factors in the platform's tremendous usability. Because the screen can detect multiple touches at the same time and track them independently, applications are able to detect a wide range of gestures, giving the user power that goes beyond the interface.

Suppose you are in the Mail application staring at a long list of junk e-mail that you want to delete. You can tap each one individually, tap the trash icon to delete it, and then wait for the next message to download, deleting each one in turn. This method is best if you want to read each message before you delete it.

Alternatively, from the list of messages, you can tap the *Edit* button in the upper-right corner, tap each e-mail row to mark it, and then hit the *Trash* button to delete all marked messages. This method is best if you don't need to read each message before deleting it. Another alternative is to swipe across a message in the list from right to left. That gesture produces a *More* button and a *Trash* button for that message. Tap the *Trash* button, and the message is deleted.

This example is just one of the countless gestures that are made possible by the multitouch display. You can pinch your fingers together to zoom out while viewing a picture or reverse-pinch to zoom in. On the home screen, you can long-press an icon to turn on "jiggly mode," which allows you to delete applications from your iOS device.

In this chapter, we're going to look at the underlying architecture that lets you detect gestures. You'll learn how to detect the most common gestures, as well as how to create and detect a completely new gesture.

Multitouch Terminology

Before we dive into the architecture, let's go over some basic vocabulary. First, a **gesture** is any sequence of events that happens from the time you touch the screen with one or more fingers until you lift your fingers off the screen. No matter how long it takes, as long as one or more fingers remain against the screen, you are still within a gesture (unless a system event, such as an incoming phone call, interrupts it). Note that Cocoa Touch doesn't expose any class or structure that represents a gesture. In some sense, a gesture is a verb, and a running app can watch the user input stream to see if one is happening.

A gesture is passed through the system inside a series of **events**. Events are generated when you interact with the device's multitouch screen. They contain information about the touch or touches that occurred.

The term **touch** refers to a finger being placed on the screen, dragging across the screen, or being lifted from the screen. The number of touches involved in a gesture is equal to the number of fingers on the screen at the same time. You can actually put all five fingers on the screen, and as long as they aren't too close to each other, iOS can recognize and track them all. Now there aren't many useful five-finger gestures, but it's nice to know the iOS can handle one if necessary. In fact, experimentation has shown that the iPad can handle up to 11 simultaneous touches! This may seem excessive, but could be useful if you're working on a multiplayer game, in which several players are interacting with the screen at the same time.

A **tap** happens when you touch the screen with a finger and then immediately lift your finger off the screen without moving it around. The iOS device keeps track of the number of taps and can tell you if the user double-tapped, triple-tapped, or even 20-tapped. It handles all the timing and other work necessary to differentiate between two single-taps and a double-tap, for example.

A **gesture recognizer** is an object that knows how to watch the stream of events generated by a user and recognize when the user is touching and dragging in a way that matches a predefined gesture. The UIGestureRecognizer class and its various subclasses can help take a lot of work off your hands when you want to watch for common gestures. This class nicely encapsulates the work of looking for a gesture and can be easily applied to any view in your application.

The Responder Chain

Since gestures are passed through the system inside events, and events are passed through the **responder chain**, you need to have an understanding of how the responder chain works in order to handle gestures properly. If you've worked with Cocoa for Mac OS X, you're probably familiar with the concept of a responder chain, as the same basic mechanism is used in both Cocoa and Cocoa Touch. If this is new material, don't worry; we'll explain how it works.

Responding to Events

Several times in this book, we've mentioned the first responder, which is usually the object with which the user is currently interacting. The first responder is the start of the responder chain, but it's not alone. There are always other responders in the chain as well. In a running application, the responder chain is a changing set of objects that are able to respond to user events. Any class that has UIResponder as one of its superclasses is a **responder**. UIView is a subclass of UIResponder, and UIControl is a subclass of UIView, so all views and all controls are responders. UIViewController is also a subclass of UIResponder, meaning that it is a responder, as are all of its subclasses, such as UINavigationController and UITabBarController. Responders, then, are so named because they respond to system-generated events, such as screen touches.

If the first responder doesn't handle a particular event, such as a gesture, it passes that event up the responder chain. If the next object in the chain responds to that particular event, it will usually consume the event, which stops the event's progression through the responder chain. In some cases, if a responder only partially handles an event, that responder will take an action and forward the event to the next responder in the chain. That's not usually what happens, though. Normally, when an object responds to an event, that's the end of the line for the event. If the event goes through the entire responder chain and no object handles the event, the event is then discarded.

Let's take a more specific look at the responder chain. The first responder is almost always a view or control and gets the first shot at responding to an event. If the first responder doesn't handle the event, it passes the event to its view controller. If the view controller doesn't consume the event, the event is then passed to the first responder's parent view. If the parent view doesn't respond, the event will go to the parent view's controller, if it has one.

The event will proceed up the view hierarchy, with each view and then that view's controller getting a chance to handle the event. If the event makes it all the way up through the view hierarchy without being handled by a view or a controller, the event is passed to the application's window. If the window doesn't handle the event, it passes that event to the application's UIApplication object instance.

If UIApplication doesn't respond to the event, there's one more spot where you can build a global catchall as the end of the responder chain: the app delegate. If the app delegate is a subclass of UIResponder (which it normally is if you create your project from one of Apple's application templates), the app will try to pass it any unhandled events. Finally, if the app delegate isn't a subclass of UIResponder or doesn't handle the event, then the event goes gently into the good night.

This process is important for a number of reasons. First, it controls the way gestures can be handled. Let's say a user is looking at a table and swipes a finger across a row of that table. What object handles that gesture?

If the swipe is within a view or control that's a subview of the table view cell, that view or control will get a chance to respond. If it doesn't respond, the table view cell gets a chance. In an application like Mail, in which a swipe can be used to delete a message, the table view cell probably needs to look at that event to see if it contains a swipe gesture. Most table view cells don't respond to gestures, however. If they don't respond, the event proceeds up to the table view, and then up the rest of the responder chain until something responds to that event or it reaches the end of the line.

Forwarding an Event: Keeping the Responder Chain Alive

Let's take a step back to that table view cell in the Mail application. We don't know the internal details of the Apple Mail application; however, let's assume, for the nonce, that the table view cell handles the delete swipe and only the delete swipe. That table view cell must implement the methods related to receiving touch events (discussed shortly) so that it can check to see if that event could be interpreted as part of a swipe gesture. If the event matches a swipe that the table view is looking for, then the table view cell takes an action, and that's that; the event goes no further.

If the event doesn't match the table view cell's swipe gesture, the table view cell is responsible for forwarding that event manually to the next object in the responder chain. If it doesn't do its forwarding job, the table and other objects up the chain will never get a chance to respond, and the application may not function as the user expects. That table view cell could prevent other views from recognizing a gesture.

Whenever you respond to a touch event, you need to keep in mind that your code doesn't work in a vacuum. If an object intercepts an event that it doesn't handle, it needs to pass it along manually, by calling the same method on the next responder. Here's a bit of fictional code:

```
- (void)respondToFictionalEvent:(UIEvent *)event
{
    if ([self shouldHandleEvent:event]) {
        [self handleEvent:event];
    } else {
        [[self nextResponder] respondToFictionalEvent:event];
    }
}
```

Notice that we call the same method on the next responder. That's how to be a good responder-chain citizen. Fortunately, most of the time, methods that respond to an event also consume the event. However, it's important to know that if that's not the case, you need to make sure the event is passed along to the next link in the responder chain.

The Multitouch Architecture

Now that you know a little about the responder chain, let's look at the process of handling gestures. As we've indicated, gestures are passed along the responder chain, embedded in events. This means that the code to handle any kind of interaction with the multitouch screen needs to be contained in an object in the responder chain. Generally, that means we can choose to either embed that code in a subclass of UIView or embed the code in a UIViewController.

So, does this code belong in the view or in the view controller?

If the view needs to do something to itself based on the user's touches, the code probably belongs in the class that defines that view. For example, many control classes, such as UISwitch and UISlider, respond to touch-related events. A UISwitch might want to turn itself on or off based on a touch. The folks who created the UISwitch class embedded gesture-handling code in the class so the UISwitch can respond to a touch.

Often, however, when the gesture being processed affects more than the object being touched, the gesture code really belongs in the relevant view controller class. For example, if the user makes a gesture touching one row that indicates that all rows should be deleted, the gesture should be handled by code in the view controller. The way you respond to touches and gestures in both situations is exactly the same, regardless of the class to which the code belongs.

The Four Touch Notification Methods

Four methods are used to notify a responder about touches. When the user first touches the screen, the system looks for a responder that has a method called `touchesBegan:withEvent:`. To find out when the user first begins a gesture or taps the screen, implement this method in your view or your view controller. Here's an example of what that method might look like:

```
- (void)touchesBegan:(NSSet *)touches withEvent:(UIEvent *)event
{
    NSUInteger numTaps = [[touches anyObject] tapCount];
    NSUInteger numTouches = [touches count];

    // Do something here.
}
```

This method (and each of the touch-related methods) is passed an `NSSet` instance called `touches` and an instance of `UIEvent`. You can determine the number of fingers currently pressed against the screen by getting a count of the objects in `touches`. Every object in `touches` is a `UITouch` event that represents one finger touching the screen. If this touch is part of a series of taps, you can find out the tap count by asking any of the `UITouch` objects. In the preceding example, a `numTaps` value of 2 tells you that the screen was tapped twice in quick succession. Similarly, a `numTouches` value of 2 tells you the user tapped the screen with two fingers at once. If both have a value of 2, then the user double-tapped with two fingers.

All the objects in `touches` may not be relevant to the view or view controller in which you've implemented this method. A table view cell, for example, probably doesn't care about touches that are in other rows or that are in the navigation bar. You can get a subset of `touches` that has only those touches that fall within a particular view from the event:

```
NSSet *myTouches = [event touchesForView:self.view];
```

Every `UITouch` represents a different finger, and each finger is located at a different position on the screen. You can find out the position of a specific finger using the `UITouch` object. It will even translate the point into the view's local coordinate system if you ask it to:

```
CGPoint point = [touch locationInView:self];
```

You can get notified while the user is moving fingers across the screen by implementing `touchesMoved:withEvent:`. This method is called multiple times during a long drag, and each time it is called, you will get another set of touches and another event. In addition to being able to find out each finger's current position from the `UITouch` objects, you can also discover the previous location of that touch, which is the finger's position the last time either `touchesMoved:withEvent:` or `touchesBegan:withEvent:` was called.

When the user's fingers are removed from the screen, another event, `touchesEnded:withEvent:`, is invoked. When this method is called, you know that the user is finished with a gesture.

There's one final touch-related method that responders might implement. It's called touchesCancelled:withEvent:, and it is called if the user is in the middle of a gesture when something happens to interrupt it, like the phone ringing. This is where you can do any cleanup you might need so you can start fresh with a new gesture. When this method is called, touchesEnded:withEvent: will not be called for the current gesture.

OK, enough theory—let's see some of this in action.

The TouchExplorer Application

We're going to build a little application that will give you a better feel for when the four touch-related responder methods are called. In Xcode, create a new project using the *Single View Application* template. Enter *TouchExplorer* as the *Product Name* and select *iPhone* for the *Devices* pop-up.

TouchExplorer will print messages to the screen that indicate the touch and tap count every time a touch-related method is called (see Figure 18-1).

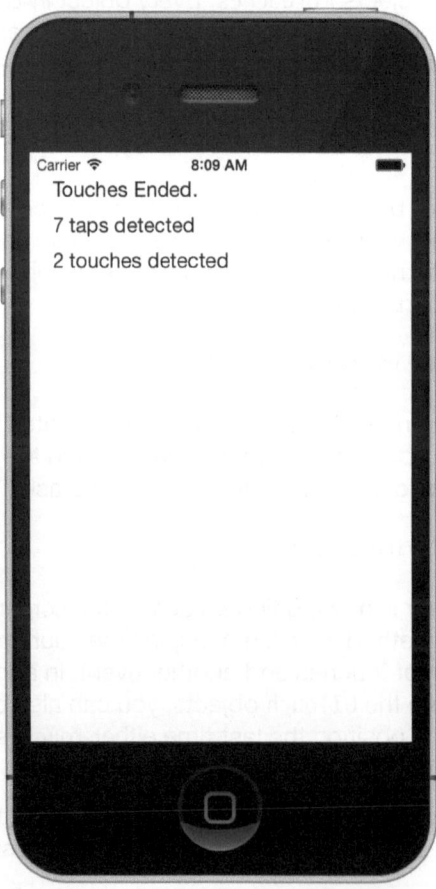

Figure 18-1. *The TouchExplorer application*

Note   Although the applications in this chapter will run on the simulator, you won't be able to see all the available multitouch functionality unless you run them on a real iOS device. If you have a paid membership in Apple's iOS Developer Program, you have the ability to run the programs you write on your device of choice. The Apple web site does a great job of walking you through the process of getting everything you need to prepare to connect Xcode to your device.

We need three labels for this application: one to indicate which method was last called, another to report the current tap count, and a third to report the number of touches. Single-click *BIDViewController.m* and add three outlets to the class extension at the top of the file:

```
#import "BIDViewController.h"

@interface BIDViewController ()

@property (weak, nonatomic) IBOutlet UILabel *messageLabel;
@property (weak, nonatomic) IBOutlet UILabel *tapsLabel;
@property (weak, nonatomic) IBOutlet UILabel *touchesLabel;

@end
```

Now select *Main.storyboard* to edit the GUI. You'll see the usual empty view contained in all new projects of this kind. Drag a label onto the view, using the blue guidelines to place the label toward the upper-left corner of the view. Use the resize handle on the right edge of the label to resize the label over to the right-hand blue guideline. Next, use the attribute inspector to set the label alignment to centered. Finally, hold down the **Option** key and drag two more labels out from the original, spacing them one below the other. This leaves you with three labels (see Figure 18-1).

Next, control-drag from the *View Controller* icon to each of the three labels, connecting the top one to the *messageLabel* outlet, the middle one to the *tapsLabel* outlet, and the last one to the *touchesLabel* outlet.

Feel free to play with the fonts and colors if you're feeling a bit like Picasso. When you're finished placing the labels, double-click each one and press the **Delete** key to get rid of the text that's in them.

Next, single-click either the background of the view you've been working on or the *View* icon in the document outline, and then bring up the attributes inspector (see Figure 18-2). On the inspector, go to the *View* section and make sure that both *User Interaction Enabled* and *Multiple Touch* are checked. If *Multiple Touch* is not checked, your controller class's touch methods will always receive one and only one touch, no matter how many fingers are actually touching the phone's screen.

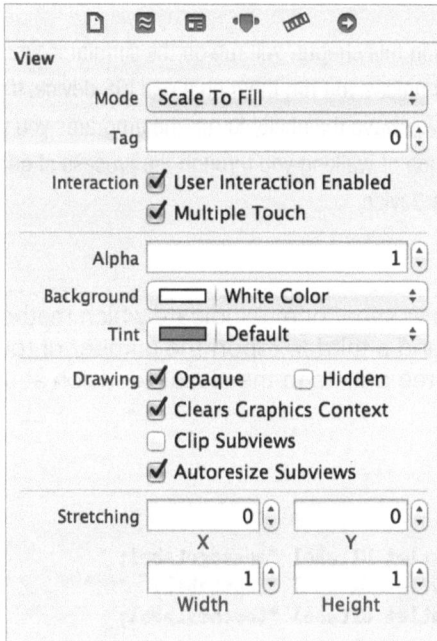

Figure 18-2. *In the View attributes, make sure both User Interaction Enabled and Multiple Touch are checked*

When you're finished, switch back *BIDViewController.m* and add the following code to the class's @implementation section:

```
@implementation BIDViewController

- (void)viewDidLoad
{
    [super viewDidLoad];
    // Do any additional setup after loading the view, typically from a nib.
}

- (void)didReceiveMemoryWarning
{
    [super didReceiveMemoryWarning];
    // Dispose of any resources that can be recreated.
}

- (void)updateLabelsFromTouches:(NSSet *)touches
{
    NSUInteger numTaps = [[touches anyObject] tapCount];
    NSString *tapsMessage = [[NSString alloc]
                            initWithFormat:@"%d taps detected", numTaps];
    self.tapsLabel.text = tapsMessage;
```

```
    NSUInteger numTouches = [touches count];
    NSString *touchMsg = [[NSString alloc] initWithFormat:
                            @"%d touches detected", numTouches];
    self.touchesLabel.text = touchMsg;
}

#pragma mark - Touch Event Methods
- (void)touchesBegan:(NSSet *)touches withEvent:(UIEvent *)event
{
    self.messageLabel.text = @"Touches Began";
    [self updateLabelsFromTouches:touches];
}

- (void)touchesCancelled:(NSSet *)touches withEvent:(UIEvent *)event
{
    self.messageLabel.text = @"Touches Cancelled";
    [self updateLabelsFromTouches:touches];
}

- (void)touchesEnded:(NSSet *)touches withEvent:(UIEvent *)event
{
    self.messageLabel.text = @"Touches Ended.";
    [self updateLabelsFromTouches:touches];
}

- (void)touchesMoved:(NSSet *)touches withEvent:(UIEvent *)event
{
    self.messageLabel.text = @"Drag Detected";
    [self updateLabelsFromTouches:touches];
}

@end
```

In this controller class, we implement all four of the touch-related methods we discussed earlier. Each one sets messageLabel so the user can see when each method is called. Next, all four of them call updateLabelsFromTouches: to update the other two labels. The updateLabelsFromTouches: method gets the tap count from one of the touches, figures out the number of touches by looking at the count of the touches set, and updates the labels with that information.

Compile and run the application. If you're running in the simulator, try repeatedly clicking the screen to drive up the tap count. You should also try clicking and holding down the mouse button while dragging around the view to simulate a touch and drag. Note that a drag is not the same as a tap; therefore, once you start your drag, the app will report zero taps.

You can emulate a two-finger pinch in the iOS simulator by holding down the **Option** key while you click with the mouse and drag. You can also simulate two-finger swipes by first holding down the **Option** key to simulate a pinch, moving the mouse so the two dots representing virtual fingers are next to each other, and then holding down the **Shift** key (while still holding down the **Option** key). Pressing the **Shift** key will lock the position of the two fingers relative to each other, enabling you to do swipes and other two-finger gestures. You won't be able to do gestures that require three or more fingers, but you can do most two-finger gestures on the simulator using combinations of the **Option** and **Shift** keys.

If you're able to run this program on a device, see how many touches you can get to register at the same time. Try dragging with one finger, then two fingers, and then three. Try double- and triple-tapping the screen, and see if you can get the tap count to go up by tapping with two fingers.

Play around with the TouchExplorer application until you feel comfortable with what's happening and with the way that the four touch methods work. When you're ready, continue on to see how to detect one of the most common gestures: the swipe.

The Swipes Application

The application we're about to build does nothing more than detect swipes, both horizontal and vertical. If you swipe your finger across the screen from left to right, right to left, top to bottom, or bottom to top, the app will display a message across the top of the screen for a few seconds informing you that a swipe was detected (see Figure 18-3).

Figure 18-3. The Swipes application will detect both vertical and horizontal swipes

Detecting swipes is relatively easy. We're going to define a minimum gesture length in pixels, which is how far the user needs to swipe before the gesture counts as a swipe. We'll also define a variance, which is how far from a straight line our user can veer and still have the gesture count as a horizontal or vertical swipe. A diagonal line generally won't count as a swipe, but one that's just a little off from horizontal or vertical will.

When the user touches the screen, we'll save the location of the first touch in a variable. We'll then check as the user's finger moves across the screen to see if it reaches a point where it has gone far enough and straight enough to count as a swipe. Let's build it.

Create a new project in Xcode using the *Single View Application* template, set *Devices* to *iPhone*, and name the project *Swipes*.

Single-click *BIDViewController.m* and add the following code to the class extension near the top:

```
#import "BIDViewController.h"

@interface BIDViewController ()

@property (weak, nonatomic) IBOutlet UILabel *label;
@property (nonatomic) CGPoint gestureStartPoint;

@end
```

We start by declaring an outlet for our one label and a variable to hold the first spot the user touches. Next, we declare a method that will be used to erase the text after a few seconds.

Select *Main.storyboard* to open it for editing. Make sure that the view is set so *User Interaction Enabled* and *Multiple Touch* are both checked using the attributes inspector, and drag a *Label* from the library and drop it in the upper portion of the *View* window. Set up the label so it takes the entire width of the view from blue guideline to blue guideline, and its alignment is centered. Feel free to play with the text attributes to make the label easier to read. Control-drag from the *View Controller* icon to the label and connect it to the *label* outlet. Finally, double-click the label and delete its text.

Then switch over to *BIDViewController.m* and add the bold code shown here:

```
static CGFloat const kMinimumGestureLength = 25;
static CGFloat const kMaximumVariance      =  5;

@implementation BIDViewController

- (void)viewDidLoad
{
    [super viewDidLoad];
    // Do any additional setup after loading the view, typically from a nib.
}

- (void)didReceiveMemoryWarning
{
    [super didReceiveMemoryWarning];
    // Dispose of any resources that can be recreated.
}
```

```
- (void)eraseText
{
    self.label.text = @"";
}

#pragma mark - Touch Handling

- (void)touchesBegan:(NSSet *)touches withEvent:(UIEvent *)event
{
    UITouch *touch = [touches anyObject];
    self.gestureStartPoint = [touch locationInView:self.view];
}

- (void)touchesMoved:(NSSet *)touches withEvent:(UIEvent *)event
{
    UITouch *touch = [touches anyObject];
    CGPoint currentPosition = [touch locationInView:self.view];

    CGFloat deltaX = fabsf(self.gestureStartPoint.x - currentPosition.x);
    CGFloat deltaY = fabsf(self.gestureStartPoint.y - currentPosition.y);

    if (deltaX >= kMinimumGestureLength && deltaY <= kMaximumVariance) {
        self.label.text = @"Horizontal swipe detected";
        [self performSelector:@selector(eraseText)
                    withObject:nil afterDelay:2];
    } else if (deltaY >= kMinimumGestureLength &&
                deltaX <= kMaximumVariance){
        self.label.text = @"Vertical swipe detected";
        [self performSelector:@selector(eraseText) withObject:nil
                    afterDelay:2];
    }
}
}
@end
```

Let's start with the touchesBegan:withEvent: method. All we do there is grab any touch from the touches set and store its point. We're primarily interested in single-finger swipes right now, so we don't worry about how many touches there are; we just grab one of them:

```
UITouch *touch = [touches anyObject];
self.gestureStartPoint = [touch locationInView:self.view];
```

In the next method, touchesMoved:withEvent:, we do the real work. First, we get the current position of the user's finger:

```
UITouch *touch = [touches anyObject];
CGPoint currentPosition = [touch locationInView:self.view];
```

After that, we calculate how far the user's finger has moved both horizontally and vertically from its starting position. The function fabsf() is from the standard C math library that returns the absolute value of a float. This allows us to subtract one from the other without needing to worry about which is the higher value:

```
CGFloat deltaX = fabsf(self.gestureStartPoint.x - currentPosition.x);
CGFloat deltaY = fabsf(self.gestureStartPoint.y - currentPosition.y);
```

Once we have the two deltas, we check to see if the user has moved far enough in one direction without having moved too far in the other to constitute a swipe. If that's true, we set the label's text to indicate whether a horizontal or vertical swipe was detected. We also use performSelector:wit hObject:afterDelay: to erase the text after it has been on the screen for 2 seconds. That way, the user can practice multiple swipes without needing to worry whether the label is referring to an earlier attempt or the most recent one:

```
if (deltaX >= kMinimumGestureLength && deltaY <= kMaximumVariance) {
    self.label.text = @"Horizontal swipe detected";
    [self performSelector:@selector(eraseText)
                withObject:nil afterDelay:2];
} else if (deltaY >= kMinimumGestureLength &&
            deltaX <= kMaximumVariance){
    self.label.text = @"Vertical swipe detected";
    [self performSelector:@selector(eraseText) withObject:nil
                afterDelay:2];
}
```

Go ahead and compile and run the application. If you find yourself clicking and dragging with no visible results, be patient. Click and drag straight down or straight across until you get the hang of swiping.

Automatic Gesture Recognition

The procedure we just used for detecting a swipe wasn't too bad. All the complexity is in the touchesMoved:withEvent: method, and even that wasn't all that complicated. But there's an even easier way to do this. iOS includes a class called UIGestureRecognizer, which eliminates the need for watching all the events to see how fingers are moving. You don't use UIGestureRecognizer directly, but instead create an instance of one of its subclasses, each of which is designed to look for a particular type of gesture, such as a swipe, pinch, double-tap, triple-tap, and so on.

Let's see how to modify the Swipes app to use a gesture recognizer instead of our hand-rolled procedure. As always, you might want to make a copy of your *Swipes* project folder and start from there.

Start by selecting *BIDViewController.m* and deleting both the touchesBegan:withEvent: and touchesMoved:withEvent: methods. That's right, you won't need them. Next, add a couple of new methods in their place:

```
- (void)reportHorizontalSwipe:(UIGestureRecognizer *)recognizer
{
    self.label.text = @"Horizontal swipe detected";
    [self performSelector:@selector(eraseText) withObject:nil afterDelay:2];
}
```

```
- (void)reportVerticalSwipe:(UIGestureRecognizer *)recognizer
{
    self.label.text = @"Vertical swipe detected";
    [self performSelector:@selector(eraseText) withObject:nil afterDelay:2];
}
```

These methods implement the actual "functionality" (if you can call it that) that's provided by the swipe gestures, just as the touchesMoved:withEvent: did previously. Now add the new code shown here to the viewDidLoad method:

```
- (void)viewDidLoad
{
    [super viewDidLoad];
    // Do any additional setup after loading the view, typically from a nib.
    UISwipeGestureRecognizer *vertical =
        [[UISwipeGestureRecognizer alloc]
          initWithTarget:self action:@selector(reportVerticalSwipe:)];
    vertical.direction = UISwipeGestureRecognizerDirectionUp|
                         UISwipeGestureRecognizerDirectionDown;
    [self.view addGestureRecognizer:vertical];

    UISwipeGestureRecognizer *horizontal =
        [[UISwipeGestureRecognizer alloc]
          initWithTarget:self action:@selector(reportHorizontalSwipe:)];
    horizontal.direction = UISwipeGestureRecognizerDirectionLeft|
                         UISwipeGestureRecognizerDirectionRight;
    [self.view addGestureRecognizer:horizontal];
}
```

There you have it! To sanitize things even further, you can also delete the lines referring to gestureStartPoint from *BIDViewController.h* and *BIDViewController.m*, as well (but leaving them there won't harm anything). Thanks to UIGestureRecognizer, all we needed to do here was create and configure some gesture recognizers and add them to our view. When the user interacts with the screen in a way that one of the recognizers recognizes, the action method we specified is called.

In terms of total lines of code, there's not much difference between these two approaches for a simple case like this. But the code that uses gesture recognizers is undeniably simpler to understand and easier to write. You don't need to give even a moment's thought to the issue of calculating a finger's movement over time because that's already done for you by the UISwipeGestureRecognizer. And better yet, Apple's gesture recognition system is extendable, which means that if your application requires really complex gestures that aren't covered by any of Apple's recognizers, you can make your own, and keep the complex code (along the lines of what we saw earlier) tucked away in the recognizer class instead of polluting your view controller code. We'll build an example of just such a thing later in this chapter.

Implementing Multiple Swipes

In the Swipes application, we worried about only single-finger swipes, so we just grabbed any object out of the touches set to figure out where the user's finger was during the swipe. This approach is fine if you're interested in only single-finger swipes, the most common type of swipe used.

But what if you want to handle two- or three-finger swipes? In the earliest versions of this book, we dedicated about 50 lines of code, and a fair amount of explanation, to achieving this by tracking multiple UITouch instances across multiple touch events. Now that we have gesture recognizers, this is a solved problem. A UISwipeGestureRecognizer can be configured to recognize any number of simultaneous touches. By default, each instance expects a single finger, but you can configure it to look for any number of fingers pressing the screen at once. Each instance responds only to the exact number of touches you specify, so what we'll do is create a whole bunch of gesture recognizers in a loop.

Make a copy of your *Swipes* project folder.

Edit *BIDViewController.m* and modify the viewDidLoad method, replacing it with the one shown here:

```objectivec
- (void)viewDidLoad
{
    [super viewDidLoad];
    // Do any additional setup after loading the
    // view, typically from a nib.
    for (NSUInteger touchCount = 1; touchCount <= 5; touchCount++) {
        UISwipeGestureRecognizer *vertical;
        vertical = [[UISwipeGestureRecognizer alloc]
                    initWithTarget:self action:@selector(reportVerticalSwipe:)];
        vertical.direction = UISwipeGestureRecognizerDirectionUp
        | UISwipeGestureRecognizerDirectionDown;
        vertical.numberOfTouchesRequired = touchCount;
        [self.view addGestureRecognizer:vertical];

        UISwipeGestureRecognizer *horizontal;
        horizontal = [[UISwipeGestureRecognizer alloc]
                      initWithTarget:self action:@selector(reportHorizontalSwipe:)];
        horizontal.direction = UISwipeGestureRecognizerDirectionLeft
        | UISwipeGestureRecognizerDirectionRight;
        horizontal.numberOfTouchesRequired = touchCount;
        [self.view addGestureRecognizer:horizontal];
    }
}
```

Note that in a real application, you might want different numbers of fingers swiping across the screen to trigger different behaviors. You can easily do that using gesture recognizers, simply by having each of them call a different action method.

Now all we need to do is change the logging by adding a method that gives us a handy description of the number of touches, and then using that in the reporting methods, as shown here. Add this method toward the bottom of the BIDViewController class, just above the two swipe-reporting methods:

```objectivec
- (NSString *)descriptionForTouchCount:(NSUInteger)touchCount
{
    switch (touchCount) {
        case 1:
            return @"Single";
        case 2:
            return @"Double ";
```

```
        case 3:
            return @"Triple ";
        case 4:
            return @"Quadruple ";
        case 5:
            return @"Quintuple ";
        default:
            return @"";
    }
}
```

Next, modify the two swipe-reporting methods as shown:

```
- (void)reportHorizontalSwipe:(UIGestureRecognizer *)recognizer
{
    self.label.text = @"Horizontal swipe detected";
    self.label.text = [NSString stringWithFormat:@"%@Horizontal swipe detected",
                         [self descriptionForTouchCount:
                             [recognizer numberOfTouches]]];
    [self performSelector:@selector(eraseText) withObject:nil afterDelay:2];
}

- (void)reportVerticalSwipe:(UIGestureRecognizer *)recognizer
{
    self.label.text = @"Vertical swipe detected";
    self.label.text = [NSString stringWithFormat:@"%@Vertical swipe detected",
                         [self descriptionForTouchCount:
                             [recognizer numberOfTouches]]];
    [self performSelector:@selector(eraseText) withObject:nil afterDelay:2];
}
```

Compile and run the app. You should be able to trigger double- and triple-swipes in both directions, yet still be able to trigger single-swipes. If you have small fingers, you might even be able to trigger a quadruple- or quintuple-swipe.

> **Tip**   In the simulator, if you hold down the **Option** key, a pair of dots, representing a pair of fingers, will appear. Get them close together, and then hold down the **Shift** key. This will keep the dots in the same position relative to each other, allowing you to move the pair of fingers around the screen. Now click and drag down the screen to simulate a double-swipe. Cool!

With a multiple-finger swipe, one thing to be careful of is that your fingers aren't too close to each other. If two fingers are very close to each other, they may register as only a single touch. Because of this, you shouldn't rely on quadruple- or quintuple-swipes for any important gestures because many people will have fingers that are too big to do those swipes effectively. Also, on the iPad some four- and five-finger gestures are turned on by default at the system level for switching between apps and going to the home screen. These can be turned off in the Settings app, but you're probably better off just not using such gestures in your own apps.

Detecting Multiple Taps

In the TouchExplorer application, we printed the tap count to the screen, so you've already seen how easy it is to detect multiple taps. It's not quite as straightforward as it seems, however, because often you will want to take different actions based on the number of taps. If the user triple-taps, you get notified three separate times. You get a single-tap, a double-tap, and finally a triple-tap. If you want to do something on a double-tap but something completely different on a triple-tap, having three separate notifications could cause a problem.

Fortunately, the engineers at Apple anticipated this situation, and they provided a mechanism to let multiple gesture recognizers play nicely together, even when they're faced with ambiguous inputs that could seemingly trigger any of them. The basic idea is that you place a restriction on a gesture recognizer, telling it to not trigger its associated method unless some other gesture recognizer fails to trigger its own method.

That seems a bit abstract, so let's make it real. One commonly used gesture recognizer is represented by the UITapGestureRecognizer class. A tap recognizer can be configured to do its thing when a particular number of taps occur. Imagine that we have a view for which we want to define distinct actions that occur when the user taps once or double-taps. You might start off with something like the following:

```
UITapGestureRecognizer *singleTap = [[UITapGestureRecognizer alloc]
                                    initWithTarget:self
                                    action:@selector(doSingleTap)];
singleTap.numberOfTapsRequired = 1;
[self.view addGestureRecognizer:singleTap];

UITapGestureRecognizer *doubleTap = [[UITapGestureRecognizer alloc]
                                    initWithTarget:self
                                    action:@selector(doDoubleTap)];
doubleTap.numberOfTapsRequired = 2;
[self.view addGestureRecognizer:doubleTap];
```

The problem with this piece of code is that the two recognizers are unaware of each other, and they have no way of knowing that the user's actions may be better suited to another recognizer. If the user double-taps the view in the preceding code, the doDoubleTap method will be called, but the doSingleMethod will also be called—twice!—once for each tap.

The way around this is to create a failure requirement. We tell singleTap that it should trigger its action only if doubleTap doesn't recognize and respond to the user input by adding this single line:

```
[singleTap requireGestureRecognizerToFail:doubleTap];
```

This means that, when the user taps once, singleTap doesn't do its work immediately. Instead, singleTap waits until it knows that doubleTap has decided to stop paying attention to the current gesture (that is, the user didn't tap twice). We're going to build on this further with our next project.

In Xcode, create a new project with the *Single View Application* template. Call this new project *TapTaps* and use the *Devices* popup to choose *iPhone*.

This application will have four labels: one each that informs us when it has detected a single-tap, double-tap, triple-tap, and quadruple-tap (see Figure 18-4).

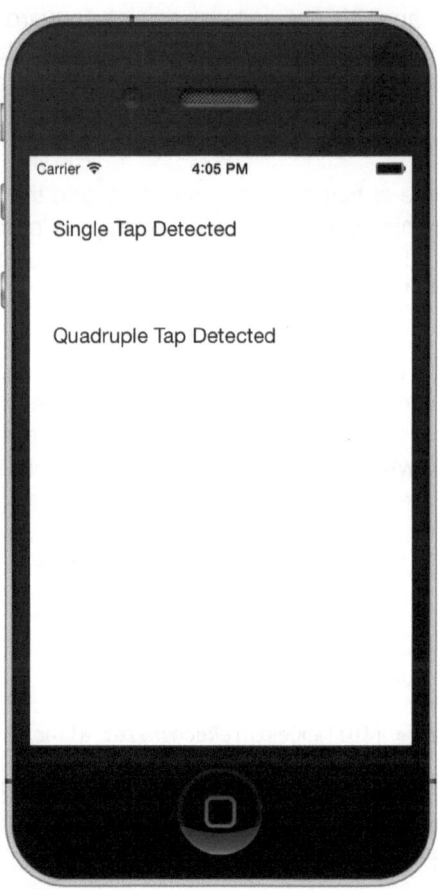

Figure 18-4. The TapTaps application detects up to four sequential taps

We need outlets for the four labels, and we also need separate methods for each tap scenario to simulate what we would have in a real application. We'll also include a method for erasing the text fields. Open *BIDViewController.m* and make the following changes to the class interface near the top:

```
#import "BIDViewController.h"

@interface BIDViewController ()

@property (weak, nonatomic) IBOutlet UILabel *singleLabel;
@property (weak, nonatomic) IBOutlet UILabel *doubleLabel;
@property (weak, nonatomic) IBOutlet UILabel *tripleLabel;
@property (weak, nonatomic) IBOutlet UILabel *quadrupleLabel;

@end
```

Save the file and select *Main.storyboard* to edit the GUI. Once you're there, add four *Labels* to the view from the library. Make all four labels stretch from blue guideline to blue guideline, set their alignment to centered, and then format them however you see fit. Feel free to make each label a different color, but that is by no means necessary. When you're finished, control-drag from the *View Controller* icon to each label and connect each one to *singleLabel*, *doubleLabel*, *tripleLabel*, and *quadrupleLabel*, respectively. Finally, make sure you double-click each label and press the **Delete** key to get rid of any text.

Now select *BIDViewController.m* and add the following code changes:

```
@implementation BIDViewController

- (void)viewDidLoad
{
    [super viewDidLoad];
    // Do any additional setup after loading the view, typically from a nib.
    UITapGestureRecognizer *singleTap =
    [[UITapGestureRecognizer alloc] initWithTarget:self
                                            action:@selector(singleTap)];
    singleTap.numberOfTapsRequired = 1;
    singleTap.numberOfTouchesRequired = 1;
    [self.view addGestureRecognizer:singleTap];

    UITapGestureRecognizer *doubleTap =
    [[UITapGestureRecognizer alloc] initWithTarget:self
                                            action:@selector(doubleTap)];
    doubleTap.numberOfTapsRequired = 2;
    doubleTap.numberOfTouchesRequired = 1;
    [self.view addGestureRecognizer:doubleTap];
    [singleTap requireGestureRecognizerToFail:doubleTap];

    UITapGestureRecognizer *tripleTap =
    [[UITapGestureRecognizer alloc] initWithTarget:self
                                            action:@selector(tripleTap)];
    tripleTap.numberOfTapsRequired = 3;
    tripleTap.numberOfTouchesRequired = 1;
    [self.view addGestureRecognizer:tripleTap];
    [doubleTap requireGestureRecognizerToFail:tripleTap];

    UITapGestureRecognizer *quadrupleTap =
    [[UITapGestureRecognizer alloc] initWithTarget:self
                                            action:@selector(quadrupleTap)];
    quadrupleTap.numberOfTapsRequired = 4;
    quadrupleTap.numberOfTouchesRequired = 1;
    [self.view addGestureRecognizer:quadrupleTap];
    [tripleTap requireGestureRecognizerToFail:quadrupleTap];
}
```

```
- (void)didReceiveMemoryWarning
{
    [super didReceiveMemoryWarning];
    // Dispose of any resources that can be recreated.
}

- (void)singleTap
{
    self.singleLabel.text = @"Single Tap Detected";
    [self performSelector:@selector(clearLabel:)
                withObject:self.singleLabel
                afterDelay:1.6f];
}

- (void)doubleTap
{
    self.doubleLabel.text = @"Double Tap Detected";
    [self performSelector:@selector(clearLabel:)
                withObject:self.doubleLabel
                afterDelay:1.6f];
}

- (void)tripleTap
{
    self.tripleLabel.text = @"Triple Tap Detected";
    [self performSelector:@selector(clearLabel:)
                withObject:self.tripleLabel
                afterDelay:1.6f];
}

- (void)quadrupleTap
{
    self.quadrupleLabel.text = @"Quadruple Tap Detected";
    [self performSelector:@selector(clearLabel:)
                withObject:self.quadrupleLabel
                afterDelay:1.6f];
}

- (void)clearLabel:(UILabel *)label
{
    label.text = @"";
}

@end
```

The four tap methods do nothing more in this application than set one of the four labels and use per
formSelector:withObject:afterDelay: to erase that same label after 1.6 seconds. The clearLabel:
method erases the text from any label that is passed into it.

The interesting part of this is what occurs in the viewDidLoad method. We start off simply enough, by setting up a tap gesture recognizer and attaching it to our view:

```
UITapGestureRecognizer *singleTap =
[[UITapGestureRecognizer alloc] initWithTarget:sclf
                                    action:@selector(singleTap)];
singleTap.numberOfTapsRequired = 1;
singleTap.numberOfTouchesRequired = 1;
[self.view addGestureRecognizer:singleTap];
```

Note that we set both the number of taps (touches in the same position, one after another) required to trigger the action and touches (number of fingers touching the screen at the same time) to 1. After that, we set another tap gesture recognizer to handle a double-tap:

```
UITapGestureRecognizer *doubleTap =
[[UITapGestureRecognizer alloc] initWithTarget:self
                                    action:@selector(doubleTap)];
doubleTap.numberOfTapsRequired = 2;
doubleTap.numberOfTouchesRequired = 1;
[self.view addGestureRecognizer:doubleTap];
[singleTap requireGestureRecognizerToFail:doubleTap];
```

This is pretty similar to the previous code, right up until that last line, in which we give singleTap some additional context. We are effectively telling singleTap that it should trigger its action only in case some other gesture recognizer—in this case, doubleTap—decides that the current user input isn't what it's looking for.

Let's think about what this means. With those two tap gesture recognizers in place, a single tap in the view will immediately make singleTap think, "Hey, this looks like it's for me." At the same time, doubleTap will think, "Hey, this looks like it *might* be for me, but I'll need to wait for one more tap." Because singleTap is set to wait for doubleTap's "failure," it doesn't send its action method right away; instead, it waits to see what happens with doubleTap.

After that first tap, if another tap occurs immediately, doubleTap says, "Hey, that's mine all right," and it fires its action. At that point, singleTap will realize what happened and give up on that gesture. On the other hand, if a particular amount of time goes by (the amount of time that the system considers to be the maximum length of time between taps in a double-tap), doubleTap will give up, and singleTap will see the failure and finally trigger its event.

The rest of the method goes on to define gesture recognizers for three and four taps, and at each point it configures one gesture to be dependent on the failure of the next:

```
UITapGestureRecognizer *tripleTap =
[[UITapGestureRecognizer alloc] initWithTarget:self
                                    action:@selector(tripleTap)];
tripleTap.numberOfTapsRequired = 3;
tripleTap.numberOfTouchesRequired = 1;
[self.view addGestureRecognizer:tripleTap];
[doubleTap requireGestureRecognizerToFail:tripleTap];
```

```
UITapGestureRecognizer *quadrupleTap =
[[UITapGestureRecognizer alloc] initWithTarget:self
                                   action:@selector(quadrupleTap)];
quadrupleTap.numberOfTapsRequired = 4;
quadrupleTap.numberOfTouchesRequired = 1;
[self.view addGestureRecognizer:quadrupleTap];
[tripleTap requireGestureRecognizerToFail:quadrupleTap];
```

Note that we don't need to explicitly configure every gesture to be dependent on the failure of each of the higher tap-numbered gestures. That multiple dependency comes about naturally as a result of the chain of failure established in our code. Since `singleTap` requires the failure of `doubleTap`, `doubleTap` requires the failure of `tripleTap`, and `tripleTap` requires the failure of `quadrupleTap`. By extension, `singleTap` requires that all of the others fail.

Compile and run the app. Whether you single-, double-, triple-, or quadruple-tap, you should see only one label displayed.

Detecting Pinch and Rotation

Another common gesture is the two-finger pinch. It's used in a number of applications (e.g., Mobile Safari, Mail, and Photos) to let you zoom in (if you pinch apart) or zoom out (if you pinch together).

Detecting pinches is really easy, thanks to `UIPinchGestureRecognizer`. This one is referred to as a continuous gesture recognizer because it calls its action method over and over again during the pinch. While the gesture is underway, the recognizer goes through a number of states. The only one we want to watch for is `UIGestureRecognizerStateBegan`, which is the state that the recognizer is in when it first calls the action method after detecting that a pinch is happening. At that moment, the pinch gesture recognizer's `scale` property is set to an initial value of `1.0`; for the rest of the gesture, that number goes up and down, relative to how far the user's fingers move from the start. We're going to use the `scale` value to resize the text in a label.

Another common gesture is the two-finger rotation. This is also a continuous gesture recognizer and is named `UIRotationGestureRecognizer`. It has a rotation property that is `0.0` by default when the gesture begins, and then changes from `0.0` to `2.0*PI` as the user rotates her fingers.

Create a new project in Xcode, again using the *Single View Application* template, and call this one *PinchMe*. First, drag and drop the beautiful *yosemite-meadows.png* image from *07 PinchMe* (or some other favorite photo of yours) into your project. Don't forget to select *Copy items into the destination groups folder (if needed)*. Expand the *PinchMe* folder, single-click *BIDViewController.h*, and make the following change:

```
#import <UIKit/UIKit.h>

@interface BIDViewController : UIViewController <UIGestureRecognizerDelegate>

@end
```

The big change here is that we let `BIDViewController` conform to the `UIGestureRecognizerDelegate` protocol in order to allow several gesture recognizers to recognize gestures simultaneously.

Now bounce over to *BIDViewController.m* and add the following code changes:

```objc
#import "BIDViewController.h"

@interface BIDViewController ()

@property (strong, nonatomic) UIImageView *imageView;

@end

@implementation BIDViewController {
    CGFloat scale, previousScale;
    CGFloat rotation, previousRotation;
}

- (void)viewDidLoad
{
    [super viewDidLoad];
    // Do any additional setup after loading the view, typically from a nib.
    previousScale = 1;

    UIImage *image = [UIImage imageNamed:@"yosemite-meadows.png"];
    self.imageView = [[UIImageView alloc] initWithImage:image];
    self.imageView.userInteractionEnabled = YES;
    self.imageView.center = self.view.center;
    [self.view addSubview:self.imageView];

    UIPinchGestureRecognizer *pinchGesture =
    [[UIPinchGestureRecognizer alloc]
      initWithTarget:self action:@selector(doPinch:)];
    pinchGesture.delegate = self;
    [self.imageView addGestureRecognizer:pinchGesture];

    UIRotationGestureRecognizer *rotationGesture =
    [[UIRotationGestureRecognizer alloc]
      initWithTarget:self action:@selector(doRotate:)];
    rotationGesture.delegate = self;
    [self.imageView addGestureRecognizer:rotationGesture];
}

- (BOOL)gestureRecognizer:(UIGestureRecognizer *)gestureRecognizer
shouldRecognizeSimultaneouslyWithGestureRecognizer:
(UIGestureRecognizer *)otherGestureRecognizer
{
    return YES;
}
```

```objectivec
- (void)transformImageView
{
    CGAffineTransform t = CGAffineTransformMakeScale(scale * previousScale,
                                                     scale * previousScale);
    t = CGAffineTransformRotate(t, rotation + previousRotation);
    self.imageView.transform = t;
}

- (void)doPinch:(UIPinchGestureRecognizer *)gesture
{
    scale = gesture.scale;
    [self transformImageView];
    if (gesture.state == UIGestureRecognizerStateEnded) {
        previousScale = scale * previousScale;
        scale = 1;
    }
}

- (void)doRotate:(UIRotationGestureRecognizer *)gesture
{
    rotation = gesture.rotation;
    [self transformImageView];
    if (gesture.state == UIGestureRecognizerStateEnded) {
        previousRotation = rotation + previousRotation;
        rotation = 0;
    }
}

- (void)didReceiveMemoryWarning
{
    [super didReceiveMemoryWarning];
    // Dispose of any resources that can be recreated.
}

@end
```

First, we define four instance variables for the current and previous scale and rotation. The previous values are the values from a previously triggered and ended gesture recognizer; we need to keep track of these values as well because both the UIPinchGestureRecognizer for scaling and UIRotationGestureRecognizer for rotation will always start at the default positions of 1.0 scale and 0.0 rotation:

```objectivec
@implementation BIDViewController {
    CGFloat scale, previousScale;
    CGFloat rotation, previousRotation;
}
```

Next, in `viewDidLoad`, we begin by creating a `UIImageView` to pinch and rotate. We must remember to enable user interaction on the image view because `UIImageView` is one of the few UIKit classes that have user interaction disabled by default.

```
UIImage *image = [UIImage imageNamed:@"yosemite-meadows.png"];
self.imageView = [[UIImageView alloc] initWithImage:image];
self.imageView.userInteractionEnabled = YES;
self.imageView.center = self.view.center;
[self.view addSubview:self.imageView];
```

Next, we set up a pinch gesture recognizer and a rotation gesture recognizer, and we tell them to notify us via the doPinch: method and doRotation: methods, respectively. We tell both to use self as their delegate:

```
UIPinchGestureRecognizer *pinchGesture =
[[UIPinchGestureRecognizer alloc]
  initWithTarget:self action:@selector(doPinch:)];
pinchGesture.delegate = self;
[self.imageView addGestureRecognizer:pinchGesture];

UIRotationGestureRecognizer *rotationGesture =
[[UIRotationGestureRecognizer alloc]
  initWithTarget:self action:@selector(doRotate:)];
rotationGesture.delegate = self;
[self.imageView addGestureRecognizer:rotationGesture];
```

In the gestureRecognizer:shouldRecognizeSimultaneoslyWithGestureRecognizer:, we always return YES to allow our pinch and rotation gestures to work together; otherwise, the gesture recognizer that starts first would always block the other:

```
- (BOOL)gestureRecognizer:(UIGestureRecognizer *)gestureRecognizer
shouldRecognizeSimultaneouslyWithGestureRecognizer:
(UIGestureRecognizer *)otherGestureRecognizer
{
    return YES;
}
```

Next, we implement a helper method for transforming the image view according to the current scaling and rotation from the gesture recognizers. Notice that we multiply the scale by the previous scale. We also add to the rotation with the previous rotation. This allows us to adjust for pinch and rotation that has been done previously when a new gesture starts from the default 1.0 scale and 0.0 rotation.

```
- (void)transformImageView
{
    CGAffineTransform t = CGAffineTransformMakeScale(scale * previousScale,
                                                     scale * previousScale);
    t = CGAffineTransformRotate(t, rotation + previousRotation);
    self.imageView.transform = t;
}
```

Finally we implement the action methods that take the input from the gesture recognizers and update the transformation of the image view. In both doPinch: and doRotate:, we first extract the new scale or rotation values. Next, we update the transformation for the image view. And finally, if the gesture reports it is ending by having a state equal to UIGestureRecognizerStateEnded, we store the current correct scale or rotation values, and then reset the current scale or rotation values to the default 1.0 scale or 0.0 rotation:

```
- (void)doPinch:(UIPinchGestureRecognizer *)gesture
{
    scale = gesture.scale;
    [self transformImageView];
    if (gesture.state == UIGestureRecognizerStateEnded) {
        previousScale = scale * previousScale;
        scale = 1;
    }
}

- (void)doRotate:(UIRotationGestureRecognizer *)gesture
{
    rotation = gesture.rotation;
    [self transformImageView];
    if (gesture.state == UIGestureRecognizerStateEnded) {
        previousRotation = rotation + previousRotation;
        rotation = 0;
    }
}
```

And that's all there is to pinch and rotation detection. Compile and run the app to give it a try. As you do some pinching and rotation, you'll see the image change in response (see Figure 18-5). If you're on the simulator, remember that you can simulate a pinch by holding down the **Option** key and clicking and dragging in the simulator window using your mouse.

Figure 18-5. The PinchMe application detects the pinch and rotation gesture

Defining Custom Gestures

You've now seen how to detect the most commonly used iPhone gestures. The real fun begins when you start defining your own custom gestures! You've already learned how to use a few of UIGestureRecognizer's subclasses, so now it's time to learn how to create your own gestures, which can be easily attached to any view you like.

Defining a custom gesture is tricky. You've already mastered the basic mechanism, and that wasn't too difficult. The tricky part is being flexible when defining what constitutes a gesture.

Most people are not precise when they use gestures. Remember the variance we used when we implemented the swipe, so that even a swipe that wasn't perfectly horizontal or vertical still counted? That's a perfect example of the subtlety you need to add to your own gesture definitions. If you define your gesture too strictly, it will be useless. If you define it too generically, you'll get too many false positives, which will frustrate the user. In a sense, defining a custom gesture can be hard because you must be precise about a gesture's imprecision. If you try to capture a complex gesture like, say, a figure eight, the math behind detecting the gesture is also going to get quite complex.

The CheckPlease Application

In our sample, we're going to define a gesture shaped like a check mark (see Figure 18-6).

Figure 18-6. *An illustration of our check-mark gesture*

What are the defining properties of this check-mark gesture? Well, the principal one is that sharp change in angle between the two lines. We also want to make sure that the user's finger has traveled a little distance in a straight line before it makes that sharp angle. In Figure 18-6, the legs of the check mark meet at an acute angle, just under 90 degrees. A gesture that required exactly an 85-degree angle would be awfully hard to get right, so we'll define a range of acceptable angles.

Create a new project in Xcode using the *Single View Application* template and call the project *CheckPlease*. In this project, we're going to need to do some fairly standard analytic geometry to calculate such things as the distance between two points and the angle between two lines. Don't worry if you don't remember much geometry; we've provided you with functions that will do the calculations for you.

Look In the *17 - CheckPlease* folder for two files: *CGPointUtils.h* and *CGPointUtils.c*. Drag both of these files to the *CheckPlease* folder of your project. Feel free to use these utility functions in your own applications.

In Xcode, control-click in the *CheckPlease* folder and add a new file to the project. Use the file-creation assistant to create a new Objective-C class called BIDCheckMarkRecognizer. In the *Subclass of* control, type *UIGestureRecognizer*. Now select *BIDCheckMarkRecognizer.m* and make the following changes:

```
#import "BIDCheckMarkRecognizer.h"
#import "CGPointUtils.h"
#import <UIKit/UIGestureRecognizerSubclass.h>

static CGFloat const kMinimumCheckMarkAngle  =   50;
static CGFloat const kMaximumCheckMarkAngle  =  135;
static CGFloat const kMinimumCheckMarkLength =   10;

@implementation BIDCheckMarkRecognizer {
    CGPoint lastPreviousPoint;
    CGPoint lastCurrentPoint;
    CGFloat lineLengthSoFar;
}

@end
```

After importing *CGPointUtils.h*, the file we mentioned earlier, we import a special header file called *UIGestureRecognizerSubclass.h*, which contains declarations that are intended for use only by a subclass. The important thing this does is to make the gesture recognizer's state property writable. That's the mechanism our subclass will use to affirm that the gesture we're watching was successfully completed.

Next, we define the parameters that we use to decide whether the user's finger-squiggling matches our definition of a check mark. You can see that we've defined a minimum angle of 50 degrees and a maximum angle of 135 degrees. This is a pretty broad range; depending on your needs, you might decide to restrict the angle. We experimented a bit with this and found that our practice check mark gestures fell into a fairly broad range, which is why we chose a relatively large tolerance here. We were somewhat sloppy with our check mark gestures, and so we expect that at least some of our users will be, as well. As a wise man once said, "Be rigorous in what you produce and tolerant in what you accept."

Now we declare three instance variables: lastPreviousPoint, lastCurrentPoint, and lineLengthSoFar. Each time we're notified of a touch, we're given the previous touch point and the current touch point. Those two points define a line segment. The next touch adds another segment. We store the previous touch's previous and current points in lastPreviousPoint and lastCurrentPoint, which gives us the previous line segment. We can then compare that line segment to the current touch's line segment. Comparing these two line segments can tell us whether we're still drawing a single line or if there's a sharp enough angle between the two segments that we're actually drawing a check mark.

Remember that every UITouch object knows its current position in the view, as well as its previous position in the view. In order to compare angles, however, we need to know the line that the previous two points made, so we need to store the current and previous points from the last time the user touched the screen. We'll use these two variables to store those two values each time this method is called, so that we have the ability to compare the current line to the previous line and check the angle.

We also declare an instance variable to keep a running count of how far the user has dragged the finger. If the finger hasn't traveled at least 10 pixels (the value defined in kMinimumCheckMarkLength), it doesn't matter whether the angle falls in the correct range. If we didn't require this distance, we would receive a lot of false positives.

The CheckPlease Touch Methods

Next, add these two methods to handle touch events sent to the gesture recognizer:

```
- (void)touchesBegan:(NSSet *)touches withEvent:(UIEvent *)event
{
    [super touchesBegan:touches withEvent:event];
    UITouch *touch = [touches anyObject];
    CGPoint point = [touch locationInView:self.view];
    lastPreviousPoint = point;
    lastCurrentPoint = point;
    lineLengthSoFar = 0.0;
}
```

```
- (void)touchesMoved:(NSSet *)touches withEvent:(UIEvent *)event
{
    [super touchesMoved:touches withEvent:event];
    UITouch *touch = [touches anyObject];
    CGPoint previousPoint = [touch previousLocationInView:self.view];
    CGPoint currentPoint = [touch locationInView:self.view];
    CGFloat angle = angleBetweenLines(lastPreviousPoint,
                                      lastCurrentPoint,
                                      previousPoint,
                                      currentPoint);
    if (angle >= kMinimumCheckMarkAngle && angle <= kMaximumCheckMarkAngle
        && lineLengthSoFar > kMinimumCheckMarkLength) {
        self.state = UIGestureRecognizerStateEnded;
    }
    lineLengthSoFar += distanceBetweenPoints(previousPoint, currentPoint);
    lastPreviousPoint = previousPoint;
    lastCurrentPoint = currentPoint;
}
```

You'll notice that each of these methods first calls the superclass's implementation—something we haven't previously done in any of our touch methods. We need to do this in a UIGestureRecognizer subclass so that our superclass can have the same amount of knowledge about the events as we do. Now let's move on to the code itself.

In `touchesBegan:withEvent:`, we determine the point that the user is currently touching and store that value in `lastPreviousPoint` and `lastCurrentPoint`. Since this method is called when a gesture begins, we know there is no previous point to worry about, so we store the current point in both. We also reset the length of the line we're tracking to 0.

In `touchesMoved:withEvent:`, we calculate the angle between the line from the current touch's previous position to its current position and the line between the two points stored in the `lastPreviousPoint` and `lastCurrentPoint` instance variables. Once we have that angle, we check to see if it falls within our range of acceptable angles and check to make sure that the user's finger has traveled far enough before making that sharp turn. If both of those are true, we set the label to show that we've identified a check mark gesture. Next, we calculate the distance between the touch's position and its previous position, add that to `lineLengthSoFar`, and replace the values in `lastPreviousPoint` and `lastCurrentPoint` with the two points from the current touch, so we'll have them next time through this method.

Now that we have a gesture recognizer of our own to try out, it's time to connect it to a view, just as we did with the others we used. Switch over to *BIDViewController.m* and add the following bold code to the top of the file:

```
#import "BIDViewController.h"
#import "BIDCheckMarkRecognizer.h"

@interface BIDViewController ()

@property (weak, nonatomic) IBOutlet UILabel *label;

@end
```

Here, we simply import the header for the gesture recognizer we defined, and then add an outlet to a label that we'll use to inform the user when we've detected a check mark gesture.

Select *Main.storyboard* to edit the GUI. Add a *Label* from the library to the view, pushed up against the upper and left blue guidelines. Resize it so it spans from the left blue guideline to the right blue guideline, and set its alignment to centered. Next, control-drag from the *View Controller* icon to that label to connect it to the *label* outlet, and then double-click the label to delete its text.

Now switch back to *BIDViewController.m* and add the following code to the @implementation section:

```
@implementation BIDViewController

- (void)doCheck:(BIDCheckMarkRecognizer *)check
{
    self.label.text = @"Checkmark";
    [self performSelector:@selector(eraseLabel)
                withObject:nil afterDelay:1.6];
}

- (void)eraseLabel
{
    self.label.text = @"";
}
```

This gives us an action method to connect our recognizer to, which in turn triggers the familiar-looking eraseLabel method. Next, edit the viewDidLoad method, adding the following lines, which connect an instance of our new recognizer to the view:

```
- (void)viewDidLoad
{
    [super viewDidLoad];
        // Do any additional setup after loading the view, typically from a nib.
    BIDCheckMarkRecognizer *check = [[BIDCheckMarkRecognizer alloc]
                                initWithTarget:self
                                action:@selector(doCheck:)];
    [self.view addGestureRecognizer:check];
}
```

Compile and run the app, and try out the gesture.

When defining new gestures for your own applications, make sure you test them thoroughly. If you can, also have other people test them for you, as well. You want to make sure that your gesture is easy for the user to do, but not so easy that it gets triggered unintentionally. You also need to make sure that you don't conflict with other gestures used in your application. A single gesture should not count, for example, as both a custom gesture and a pinch.

Garçon? Check, Please!

You should now understand the mechanism iOS uses to tell your application about touches, taps, and gestures. You also learned how to detect the most commonly used iOS gestures and even got a taste of how you might go about defining your own custom gestures. The iPhone's interface relies on gestures for much of its ease of use, so you'll want to have these techniques at the ready for most of your iOS development.

When you're ready to move on, turn the page, and we'll tell you how to figure out where in the world you are using Core Location.

Chapter 19

Where Am I? Finding Your Way with Core Location and Map Kit

Every iOS device has the ability to determine where in the world it is using a framework called Core Location. iOS also includes a framework called Map Kit that lets you easily create a live interactive map showing any locations you like, including of course the user's location. In this chapter we'll get you started using both of these frameworks.

Core Location can actually leverage three technologies to do this: GPS, cell ID location, and Wi-Fi Positioning Service (WPS). GPS is the most accurate of the three technologies, but it is not available on first-generation iPhones, iPod touches, or Wi-Fi-only iPads. In short, any device with at least a 3G data connection also contains a GPS unit. GPS reads microwave signals from multiple satellites to determine the current location.

> **Note** Technically, Apple uses a version of GPS called **Assisted GPS**, also known as A-GPS. A-GPS uses network resources to help improve the performance of stand-alone GPS. The basic idea is that the telephony provider deploys services on its network that mobile devices will automatically find and collect some data from. This allows a mobile device to determine its starting location much more quickly than if it were relying on the GPS satellites alone.

Cell ID location lookup gives a rough approximation of the current location based on the physical location of the cellular base station that the device is currently in contact with. Since each base station can cover a fairly large area, there is a fairly large margin of error here. Cell ID location lookup requires a cell radio connection, so it works only on the iPhone (all models, including the very first) and any iPad with a 3G data connection.

The WPS option uses the MAC addresses from nearby Wi-Fi access points to make a guess at your location by referencing a large database of known service providers and the areas they service. WPS is imprecise and can be off by many miles.

All three methods put a noticeable drain on the battery, so keep that in mind when using Core Location. Your application shouldn't poll for location any more often than is absolutely necessary. When using Core Location, you have the option of specifying a desired accuracy. By carefully specifying the absolute minimum accuracy level you need, you can prevent unnecessary battery drain.

The technologies that Core Location depends on are hidden from your application. We don't tell Core Location whether to use GPS, triangulation, or WPS. We just tell it how accurate we would like it to be, and it will decide from the technologies available to it which is best for fulfilling our request.

The Location Manager

The Core Location API is actually fairly easy to use. The main class we'll work with is `CLLocationManager`, usually referred to as the **location manager**. To interact with Core Location, you need to create an instance of the location manager, like this:

```
CLLocationManager *locationManager = [[CLLocationManager alloc] init];
```

This creates an instance of the location manager, but it doesn't actually start polling for your location. You must create an object that conforms to the `CLLocationManagerDelegate` protocol and assign it as the location manager's delegate. The location manager will call delegate methods when location information becomes available or changes. The process of determining location may take some time—even a few seconds.

Setting the Desired Accuracy

After you set the delegate, you also want to set the desired accuracy. As we mentioned, don't specify a degree of accuracy any greater than you absolutely need. If you're writing an application that just needs to know which state or country the phone is in, don't specify a high level of precision. Remember that the more accuracy you demand of Core Location, the more juice you're likely to use. Also, keep in mind that there is no guarantee that you will get the level of accuracy you have requested.

Here's an example of setting the delegate and requesting a specific level of accuracy:

```
locationManager.delegate = self;
locationManager.desiredAccuracy = kCLLocationAccuracyBest;
```

The accuracy is set using a `CLLocationAccuracy` value, a type that's defined as a `double`. The value is in meters, so if you specify a `desiredAccuracy` of 10, you're telling Core Location that you want it to try to determine the current location within 10 meters, if possible. Specifying `kCLLocationAccuracyBest` (as we did previously) or specifying `kCLLocationAccuracyBestForNavigation` (where it uses other sensor data as well) tells Core Location to use the most accurate method that's currently available. In addition, you can also use kCLLocationAccuracyNearestTenMeters, kCLLocationAccuracyHundredMeters, kCLLocationAccuracyKilometer, and kCLLocationAccuracyThreeKilometers.

Setting the Distance Filter

By default, the location manager will notify the delegate of any detected change in the device's location. By specifying a **distance filter**, you are telling the location manager not to notify you of every change, but instead to notify you only when the location changes by more than a certain amount. Setting up a distance filter can reduce the amount of polling your application does.

Distance filters are also set in meters. Specifying a distance filter of 1000 tells the location manager not to notify its delegate until the iPhone has moved at least 1,000 meters from its previously reported position. Here's an example:

```
locationManager.distanceFilter = 1000;
```

If you ever want to return the location manager to the default setting, which applies no filter, you can use the constant kCLDistanceFilterNone, like this:

```
locationManager.distanceFilter = kCLDistanceFilterNone;
```

Just as when specifying the desired accuracy, you should take care to avoid getting updates any more frequently than you really need them; otherwise, you waste battery power. A speedometer app that's calculating the user's velocity based on the user's location will probably want to have updates as quickly as possible, but an app that's going to show the nearest fast-food restaurant can get by with a lot fewer updates.

Starting the Location Manager

When you're ready to start polling for location, you tell the location manager to start. It will go off and do its thing and then call a delegate method when it has determined the current location. Until you tell it to stop, it will continue to call your delegate method whenever it senses a change that exceeds the current distance filter.

Here's how you start the location manager:

```
[locationManager startUpdatingLocation];
```

Using the Location Manager Wisely

If you need to determine the current location only and have no need to continuously poll for location, you should have your location delegate stop the location manager as soon as it gets the information your application requires. If you need to continuously poll, make sure you stop polling as soon as you possibly can. Remember that as long as you are getting updates from the location manager, you are putting a strain on the user's battery.

To tell the location manager to stop sending updates to its delegate, call stopUpdatingLocation, like this:

```
[locationManager stopUpdatingLocation];
```

The Location Manager Delegate

The location manager delegate must conform to the CLLocationManagerDelegate protocol, which defines several methods, all of them optional. One of these methods is called by the location manager when it has determined the current location or when it detects a change in location. Another method is called when the location manager encounters an error. We'll implement both of these in our app.

Getting Location Updates

When the location manager wants to inform its delegate of the current location, it calls the locationManager:didUpdateLocations: method. This method takes two parameters:

- The first parameter is the location manager that called the method.

- The second parameter is an array of CLLocation objects that describe the current location of the device and perhaps a few previous locations. If several location updates occur in a short period of time, they may be reported all at once with a single call to this method. In any case, the most recent location is always the last item in this array.

Getting Latitude and Longitude Using CLLocation

Location information is passed from the location manager using instances of the CLLocation class. This class has five properties that might be of interest to your application:

- coordinate

- horizontalAccuracy

- altitude

- verticalAccuracy

- timestamp

The latitude and longitude are stored in a property called coordinate. To get the latitude and longitude in degrees, do this:

```
CLLocationDegrees latitude = theLocation.coordinate.latitude;
CLLocationDegrees longitude = theLocation.coordinate.longitude;
```

The CLLocation object can also tell you how confident the location manager is in its latitude and longitude calculations. The horizontalAccuracy property describes the radius of a circle with the coordinate as its center. The larger the value in horizontalAccuracy, the less certain Core Location is of the location. A very small radius indicates a high level of confidence in the determined location.

You can see a graphic representation of horizontalAccuracy in the Maps application (see Figure 19-1). The circle shown in Maps uses horizontalAccuracy for its radius when it detects your location. The location manager thinks you are at the center of that circle. If you're not, you're almost certainly somewhere inside the circle. A negative value in horizontalAccuracy is an indication that you cannot rely on the values in coordinate for some reason.

Figure 19-1. *The Maps application uses Core Location to determine your current location. The outer circle is a visual representation of the horizontal accuracy*

The CLLocation object also has a property called altitude that can tell you how many meters above (or below) sea level you are:

```
CLLocationDistance altitude = theLocation.altitude;
```

Each CLLocation object maintains a property called verticalAccuracy that is an indication of how confident Core Location is in its determination of altitude. The value in altitude could be off by as many meters as the value in verticalAccuracy. If the verticalAccuracy value is negative, Core Location is telling you it could not determine a valid altitude.

CLLocation objects also have a timestamp that tells when the location manager made the location determination.

In addition to these properties, `CLLocation` has a useful instance method that will let you determine the distance between two `CLLocation` objects. The method is called `distanceFromLocation:` and it works like this:

```
CLLocationDistance distance = [fromLocation distanceFromLocation:toLocation];
```

The preceding line of code will return the distance between two `CLLocation` objects: `fromLocation` and `toLocation`. This `distance` value returned will be the result of a great-circle distance calculation that ignores the `altitude` property and calculates the distance as if both points were at sea level. For most purposes, a great-circle calculation will be more than sufficient; however, if you do want to take altitude into account when calculating distances, you'll need to write your own code to do it.

> **Note**   If you're not sure what's meant by *great-circle distance*, you might want to think back to geography class and the notion of a *great-circle route*. The idea is that the shortest distance between any two points on the earth's surface will be found along a path that would, if extended, go the entire way around the earth: a "great circle." The most obvious great circles are perhaps the ones you've seen on maps: The equator, and the longitudinal lines. However, such a circle can be found for any two points on the surface of the earth. The calculation performed by `CLLocation` determines the distance between two points along such a route, taking the curvature of the earth into account. Without accounting for that curvature, you would end up with the length of a straight line connecting the two points, which isn't much use, since that line would invariably go straight through some amount of the earth itself!

Error Notifications

If Core Location is not able to determine your current location, it will call a second delegate method named `locationManager:didFailWithError:`. The most likely cause of an error is that the user denies access. The user must authorize use of the location manager, so the first time your application wants to determine the location, an alert will pop up on the screen asking if it's OK for the current program to access your location (see Figure 19-2).

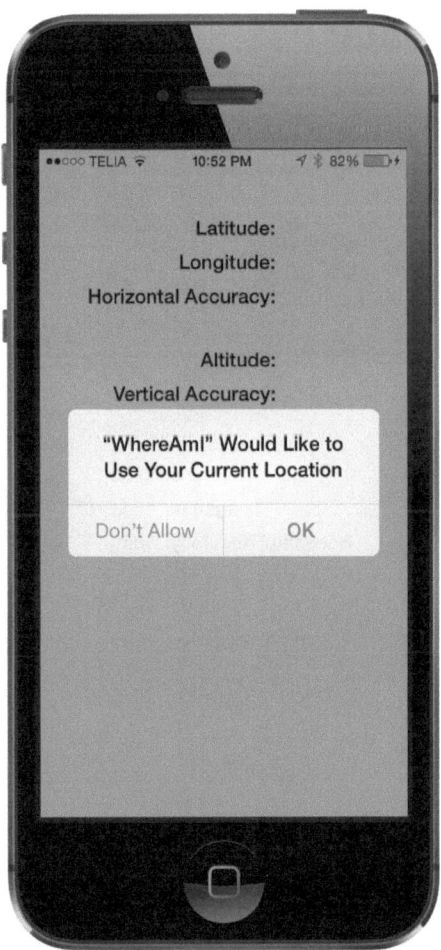

Figure 19-2. *Location manager access must be approved by the user*

If the user taps the *Don't Allow* button, your delegate will be notified of the fact by the location manager using the locationManager:didFailWithError: with an error code of kCLErrorDenied. Another commonly encountered error code supported by the location manager is kCLErrorLocationUnknown, which indicates that Core Location was unable to determine the location but that it will keep trying. While a kCLErrorLocationUnknown error indicates a problem that may be temporary, kCLErrorDenied and other errors generally indicate that your application will not be able to access Core Location any time during the remainder of the current session.

Note   When working in the simulator, a dialog will appear outside the simulator window, asking to use your current location. In that case, your location will be determined using a super-secret algorithm kept in a locked vault buried deep beneath Apple headquarters in Cupertino.

Trying Out Core Location

Let's build a small application to detect the iPhone's current location and the total distance traveled while the program has been running. You can see what the first version of our application will look like in Figure 19-3.

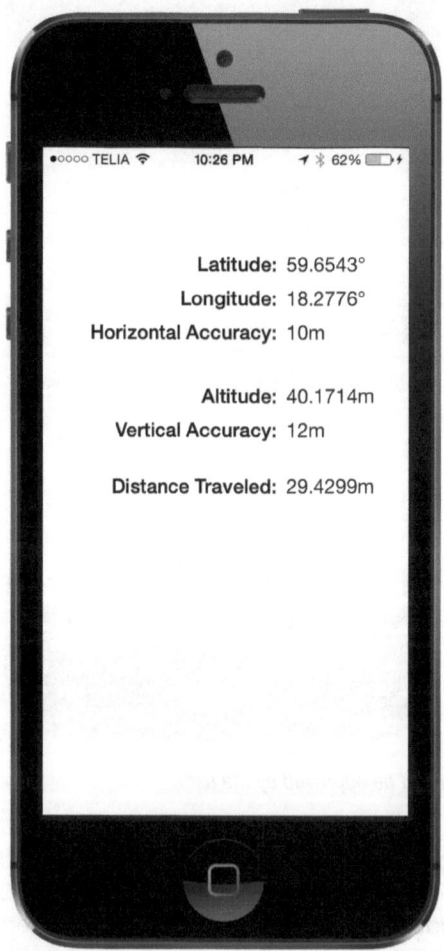

Figure 19-3. The WhereAmI application in action

In Xcode, create a new project using the *Single View Application* template and call it *WhereAmI*. Next, set *Device Family* to *iPhone*, select *BIDViewController.h*, and make the following changes:

```
#import <UIKit/UIKit.h>
#import <CoreLocation/CoreLocation.h>

@interface BIDViewController :
    UIViewController <CLLocationManagerDelegate>

@end
```

First, notice that we've included the Core Location header files. Core Location is not part of either UIKit or Foundation, so we need to include the header files manually. Next, we conform this class to the `CLLocationManagerDelegate` method, so that we can receive location information from the location manager.

Now select *BIDViewController.m* and add these property declarations to the class extension near the top of the file:

```
#import "BIDViewController.h"

@interface BIDViewController ()

@property (strong, nonatomic) CLLocationManager *locationManager;
@property (strong, nonatomic) CLLocation *previousPoint;
@property (assign, nonatomic) CLLocationDistance totalMovementDistance;
@property (weak, nonatomic) IBOutlet UILabel *latitudeLabel;
@property (weak, nonatomic) IBOutlet UILabel *longitudeLabel;
@property (weak, nonatomic) IBOutlet UILabel *horizontalAccuracyLabel;
@property (weak, nonatomic) IBOutlet UILabel *altitudeLabel;
@property (weak, nonatomic) IBOutlet UILabel *verticalAccuracyLabel;
@property (weak, nonatomic) IBOutlet UILabel *distanceTraveledLabel;

@end
```

First, we declare a `CLLocationManager` pointer, which will be used to hold a pointer to the instance of the Core Location Manager we're going create. We also declare a pointer to a `CLLocation`, which we will set to the location of the last update we received from the location manager. This way, each time the user moves far enough to trigger update, we'll be able to add the latest movement distance to our running total.

The remaining properties are all outlets that will be used to update labels on the user interface.

Select *Main.storyboard* to create the GUI. Using Figure 19-3 as your guide, drag 12 *Labels* from the library to the *View* window. Six of them should be placed on the left side of the screen, right-justified, and made bold. Give the six bold labels the values *Latitude:*, *Longitude:*, *Horizontal Accuracy:*, *Altitude:*, *Vertical Accuracy:*, and *Distance Traveled:*. Since the *Horizontal Accuracy:* label is the longest, you might place that one first, and then **Option**-drag copies of that label to create the other five left-side labels. The six right-side labels should be left-justified and placed next to each of the bold labels.

Each of the labels on the right side should be connected to the appropriate outlet we defined in the header file earlier. Once you have all six attached to outlets, double-click each one in turn, and delete the text it holds. Save your changes.

Next, select *BIDViewController.m* and insert the following lines in `viewDidLoad` to configure the location manager:

```
- (void)viewDidLoad
{
    [super viewDidLoad];
    // Do any additional setup after loading the view, typically from a nib.
    self.locationManager = [[CLLocationManager alloc] init];
    self.locationManager.delegate = self;
```

```
    self.locationManager.desiredAccuracy = kCLLocationAccuracyBest;
    [self.locationManager startUpdatingLocation];
}
```

In the viewDidLoad method, we allocate and initialize a CLLocationManager instance, assign our controller class as the delegate, set the desired accuracy to the best available, and then tell our location manager instance to start giving us location updates.

Now insert the following new delegate methods at the end of the @implementation block to handle information received from the location manager:

```
#pragma mark - CLLocationManagerDelegate Methods
- (void)locationManager:(CLLocationManager *)manager
    didUpdateLocations:(NSArray *)locations {
    CLLocation *newLocation = [locations lastObject];
    NSString *latitudeString = [NSString stringWithFormat:@"%g\u00B0",
                                newLocation.coordinate.latitude];
    self.latitudeLabel.text = latitudeString;

    NSString *longitudeString = [NSString stringWithFormat:@"%g\u00B0",
                                 newLocation.coordinate.longitude];
    self.longitudeLabel.text = longitudeString;

    NSString *horizontalAccuracyString = [NSString stringWithFormat:@"%gm",
                                          newLocation.horizontalAccuracy];
    self.horizontalAccuracyLabel.text = horizontalAccuracyString;

    NSString *altitudeString = [NSString stringWithFormat:@"%gm",
                                newLocation.altitude];
    self.altitudeLabel.text = altitudeString;

    NSString *verticalAccuracyString = [NSString stringWithFormat:@"%gm",
                                        newLocation.verticalAccuracy];
    self.verticalAccuracyLabel.text = verticalAccuracyString;

    if (newLocation.verticalAccuracy < 0 ||
        newLocation.horizontalAccuracy < 0) {
        // invalid accuracy
        return;
    }

    if (newLocation.horizontalAccuracy > 100 ||
        newLocation.verticalAccuracy > 50) {
        // accuracy radius is so large, we don't want to use it
        return;
    }

    if (self.previousPoint == nil) {
        self.totalMovementDistance = 0;
```

```
    } else {
        self.totalMovementDistance += [newLocation
                                distanceFromLocation:self.previousPoint];
    }
    self.previousPoint = newLocation;

    NSString *distanceString = [NSString stringWithFormat:@"%gm",
                                self.totalMovementDistance];
    self.distanceTraveledLabel.text = distanceString;

}

- (void)locationManager:(CLLocationManager *)manager
      didFailWithError:(NSError *)error {
    NSString *errorType = (error.code == kCLErrorDenied) ?
    @"Access Denied" : @"Unknown Error";
    UIAlertView *alert = [[UIAlertView alloc]
                         initWithTitle:@"Error getting Location"
                         message:errorType
                         delegate:nil
                         cancelButtonTitle:@"Okay"
                         otherButtonTitles:nil];
    [alert show];
}
```

Updating Location Manager

Since this class designated itself as the location manager's delegate, we know that location updates will come into this class if we implement the delegate method locationManager:didUpdateLocations:. Now, let's look at our implementation of that method.

The first thing we do in the delegate method is update the first five labels with values from the CLLocation object passed in the newLocation argument:

```
NSString *latitudeString = [NSString stringWithFormat:@"%g\u00B0",
                                newLocation.coordinate.latitude];
self.latitudeLabel.text = latitudeString;

NSString *longitudeString = [NSString stringWithFormat:@"%g\u00B0",
                                newLocation.coordinate.longitude];
self.longitudeLabel.text = longitudeString;

NSString *horizontalAccuracyString = [NSString stringWithFormat:@"%gm",
                                    newLocation.horizontalAccuracy];
self.horizontalAccuracyLabel.text = horizontalAccuracyString;

NSString *altitudeString = [NSString stringWithFormat:@"%gm",
                                newLocation.altitude];
self.altitudeLabel.text = altitudeString;

NSString *verticalAccuracyString = [NSString stringWithFormat:@"%gm",
                                    newLocation.verticalAccuracy];
self.verticalAccuracyLabel.text = verticalAccuracyString;
```

> **Note**   Both the longitude and latitude are displayed in formatting strings containing the cryptic-looking
> \u00B0. This is the hexadecimal value of the Unicode representation of the degree symbol (°). It's never a
> good idea to put anything other than ASCII characters directly in a source code file, but including the hex
> value in a string is just fine, and that's what we've done here.

Next, we check the accuracy of the values that the location manager gives us. Negative accuracy values indicate that the location is actually invalid, while high accuracy values indicate that the location manager isn't quite sure about the location. These accuracy values are in meters and indicate the radius of a circle from the location we're given, meaning that the true location could be anywhere in that circle. Our code checks to see whether these values are acceptably accurate; if not, it simply returns from this method rather than doing anything more with garbage data:

```
if (newLocation.verticalAccuracy < 0 ||
    newLocation.horizontalAccuracy < 0) {
    // invalid accuracy
    return;
}

if (newLocation.horizontalAccuracy > 100 ||
    newLocation.verticalAccuracy > 50) {
    // accuracy radius is so large, we don't want to use it
    return;
}
```

Next, we check whether previousPoint is nil. If it is, then this update is the first valid one we've gotten from the location manager, so we zero out the distanceFromStart property. Otherwise, we add the latest location's distance from the previous point to the total distance. In either case, we update previousPoint to contain the current location:

```
if (self.previousPoint == nil) {
    self.totalMovementDistance = 0;
} else {
    self.totalMovementDistance += [newLocation
                        distanceFromLocation:self.previousPoint];
}
self.previousPoint = newLocation;
```

After that, we populate the final label with the total distance that we've traveled from the start point. While this application runs, if the user moves far enough for the location manager to detect the change, the *Distance Traveled:* field will be continually updated with the distance the user has moved since the application started:

```
NSString *distanceString = [NSString stringWithFormat:@"%gm",
                        self.totalMovementDistance];
self.distanceTraveledLabel.text = distanceString;
```

And there you have it. Core Location is fairly straightforward and easy to use.

Compile and run the application, and then try it. If you have the ability to run the application on your iPhone or iPad, try going for a drive with the application running and watch the values change as you drive. Um, actually, it's better to have someone else do the driving!

Visualizing your Movement on a Map

What we've done so far is pretty neat, but wouldn't it be nice if we could visualize our travel on a map? Fortunately, iOS includes the Map Kit framework to help us out here. Map Kit utilizes the same back-end services that Apple's Maps app uses, which means it's fairly robust and improving all the time. It contains one primary view class representing a map display, and it responds to user gestures just as you'd expect of any modern mapping app. This view also lets us insert annotations for any locations we want to show up on our map, which by default show up as "pins" that can be touched to reveal some more info. We're going to extend our WhereAmI app to display the user's starting position and current position on a map.

Start off by selecting *BIDViewController.h* in Xcode. Add the following near the top to import the mapping framework headers:

```
#import <UIKit/UIKit.h>
#import <CoreLocation/CoreLocation.h>
#import <MapKit/MapKit.h>
```

Next, switch to *BIDViewController.m* and add a new property declaration below the others in the class extension:

```
@property (weak, nonatomic) IBOutlet MKMapView *mapView;
```

Now select *Main.storyboard* to edit the view. We'd like to keep all of our labels as they are, but we need to make them pop out from the backdrop of the map view in some way. A semitransparent box in the form of a UIView will do nicely. So, select all the labels, and then choose **Editor ➤ Embed In ➤ View** from the menu.

Make sure the new view is selected, and then use the attributes inspector to disable the *User Interaction Enabled* checkbox (so that touching anything in this view will be ignored, passing all touch events to the map view instead) and to set its background color to something partly transparent. Drag the view to the bottom of its superview. Now we need to create some constraints so that this box will keep both its position at the bottom and its vertical size, no matter how the screen size changes. So, click the *Pin* button at the bottom of the editor area to bring up the constraint creation panel. In the upper section of this panel, click the checkboxes to the left, right, and bottom of the small square. In the middle part, click the *Height* checkbox. When you find yourself looking at something like Figure *19-4*, click the *Add 4 Constraints* button at the bottom:

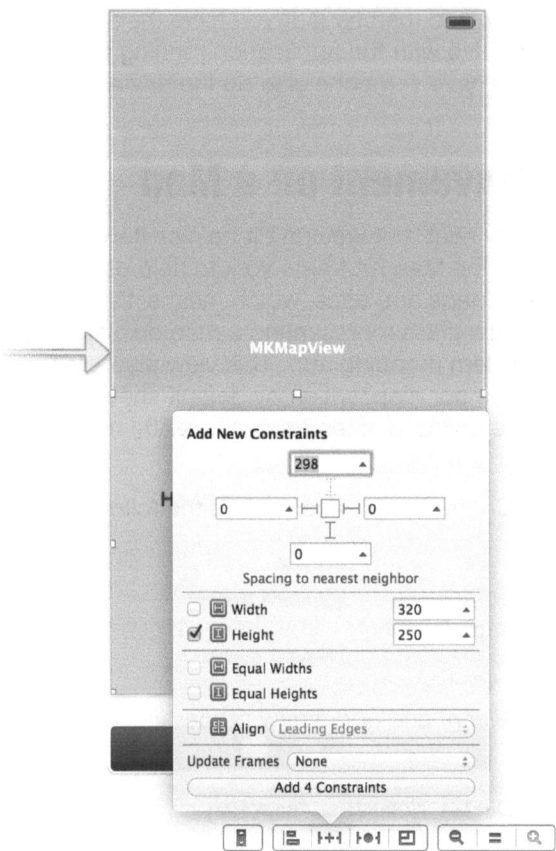

Figure 19-4. All our labels are now boxed in and shifted down. Setting these constraints will make this view stay put

Now find an *MKMapView* in the object library and drag it into your main view. Use the resize handles to make it fill the entire view, and then select **Editor ➤ Arrange ➤ Send to Back** to make it appear behind the pre-existing labels. Hook up the map view by control-dragging from the *View Controller* to the map view and selecting the *mapView* outlet. Create constraints for the map view using the *Pin* panel again, this time clicking all four checkboxes surrounding the small box in the upper portion before clicking the *Add 4 Constraints* button.

Now that these preliminaries are in place, it's time to write a little code that will make this map do some work for us. Before dealing with the controller, we need to set up a sort of model class to represent our starting point. *MKMapView* is built as the View part of an MVC architecture, and it works best if we have distinct classes to represent markers on the map. We can pass model objects off to the map view, and it will query them for coordinates, a title, and so on using a protocol defined in the Map Kit framework.

Make a new Objective-C class in Xcode by subclassing from NSObject and naming it *BIDPlace*. Select *BIDPlace.h* and modify it as shown here. You need to import the Map Kit header, specify a protocol the new class conforms to, and add some properties:

```
#import <Foundation/Foundation.h>
#import <MapKit/MapKit.h>
```

```
@interface BIDPlace : NSObject <MKAnnotation>

@property (copy, nonatomic) NSString *title;
@property (copy, nonatomic) NSString *subtitle;
@property (assign, nonatomic) CLLocationCoordinate2D coordinate;

@end
```

This is a fairly "dumb" class that acts solely as a holder for these properties. We don't even need to touch the .m file here! In a real-world example, you may have real model classes that need to be shown on a map as an annotation, and the MKAnnotation framework lets you add this capability to any class of your own without messing up any existing class hierarchies.

Select *BIDViewController.m* and get started by importing the header for the new class:

```
#import "BIDPlace.h"
```

Now find the viewDidLoad method and add this line to the end of it:

```
self.mapView.showsUserLocation = YES;
```

That does just what you probably imagine: it saves us the hassle of manually moving a marker around as the user moves by automatically drawing one for us.

Now let's revisit the locationManager:didUpdateLocations: method. We've already got some code in there that notices the first valid location data we receive and establishes our start point. We're also going to allocate a new instance of our *BIDPlace* class. We set its properties, giving it a location. We also add a title and subtitle that we want to appear when a marker for this location is displayed. Finally, we pass this object off to the map view.

We also create a new MKCoordinateRegion, a special struct included in Map Kit that lets us tell the view which section of the map we want it to display. MKCoordinateRegion uses our new location's coordinates and a pair of distances in meters (100, 100) that specify how wide and tall the displayed map portion should be. We pass this off to the map view as well, telling it to animate the change. All of this is done by adding the bold lines shown here:

```
if (self.previousPoint == nil) {
    self.totalMovementDistance = 0;

    BIDPlace *start = [[BIDPlace alloc] init];
    start.coordinate = newLocation.coordinate;
    start.title = @"Start Point";
    start.subtitle = @"This is where we started!";

    [self.mapView addAnnotation:start];
    MKCoordinateRegion region;
    region = MKCoordinateRegionMakeWithDistance(newLocation.coordinate,
                                                100, 100);
    [self.mapView setRegion:region animated:YES];
```

```
} else {
    self.totalMovementDistance += [newLocation
                            distanceFromLocation:self.previousPoint];
}
self.previousPoint = newLocation;
```

So now we've told the map view that we have an annotation (i.e., a visible place-marker) that we want the user to see. But how should it be displayed? Well, the map view figures out what sort of view to display for each annotation by asking its delegate. In a more complex app, that would work for us. But in this example we haven't made ourselves a delegate, simply because it's not necessary for our simple use case. Unlike `UITableView`, which requires its data source to supply cells for display, `MKMapView` has a different strategy: if it's not provided with annotation views by a delegate, it simply displays a default sort of view represented by a red "pin" on the map that reveals some more info when touched. Neat!

Now build and run your app, and you'll see the map view load. As soon as it gets valid position data, you'll see it scroll to the right location, drop a pin at your starting point, and mark your current location with a glowing blue dot (see Figure 19-5). Not bad for a few dozen lines of code!

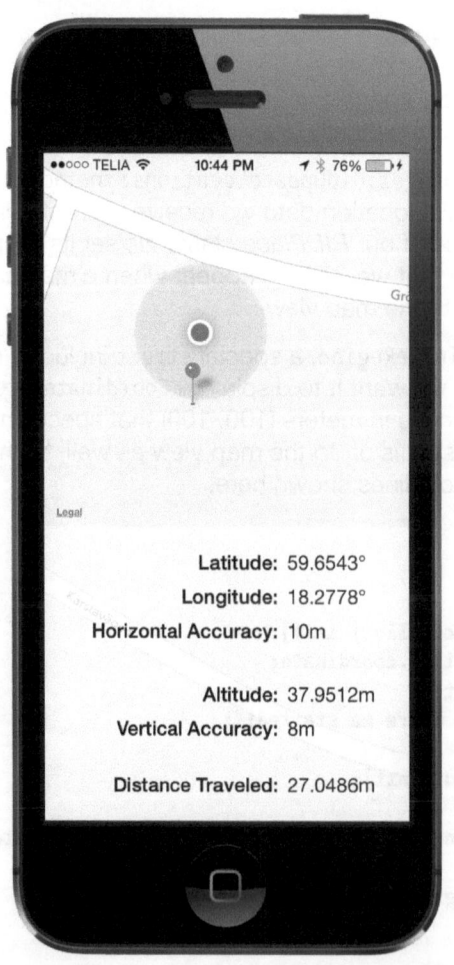

Figure 19-5. The red pin marks our starting location, and the blue dot shows how far we've gotten

Wherever You Go, There You Are

You've now seen pretty much all there is to Core Location. You've also seen the basic operation of Map Kit, as well. Although the underlying technologies are quite complex, Apple has provided simple interfaces that hide most of the complexity, making it quite easy to add location-related and mapping features to your applications so you can tell where the users are, notice when they move, and mark their location (and any other locations) on a map.

And speaking of moving, when you're ready proceed directly to the next chapter, so we can play with the iPhone's built-in accelerometer.

Chapter 20

Whee! Gyro and Accelerometer!

One of the coolest features of the iPhone, iPad, and iPod touch is the built-in accelerometer—the tiny device that lets iOS know how the device is being held and if it's being moved. iOS uses the accelerometer to handle autorotation, and many games use it as a control mechanism. The accelerometer can also be used to detect shakes and other sudden movement. This capability was extended even further with the introduction of the iPhone 4, which was the first iPhone to include a built-in gyroscope to let developers determine the angle at which the device is positioned around each axis. The gyro and accelerometer are now standard fare on all new iPads and iPod touches. In this chapter, we're going to introduce you to the use of the Core Motion framework to access the gyro and accelerometer values in your application.

Accelerometer Physics

An **accelerometer** measures both acceleration and gravity by sensing the amount of inertial force in a given direction. The accelerometer inside your iOS device is a three-axis accelerometer. This means that it is capable of detecting either movement or the pull of gravity in three-dimensional space. In other words, you can use the accelerometer to discover not only how the device is currently being held (as autorotation does), but also to learn if it's laying on a table and even whether it's face down or face up.

Accelerometers give measurements in g-forces (*g* for gravity), so a value of 1.0 returned by the accelerometer means that 1 g is sensed in a particular direction, as in these examples:

- If the device is being held still with no movement, there will be approximately 1 g of force exerted on it by the pull of the earth.

- If the device is being held perfectly upright, in portrait orientation, it will detect and report about 1 g of force exerted on its y-axis.

- If the device is being held at an angle, that 1 g of force will be distributed along different axes depending on how it is being held. When held at a 45-degree angle, the 1 g of force will be split roughly equally between two of the axes.

Sudden movement can be detected by looking for accelerometer values considerably larger than 1 g. In normal usage, the accelerometer does not detect significantly more than 1 g on any axis. If you shake, drop, or throw your device, the accelerometer will detect a greater amount of force on one or more axes. (Please do not drop or throw your own iOS device to test this theory, unless you are looking for an excuse to upgrade to the newest model!)

Figure 20-1 shows a graphic representation of the three axes used by the accelerometer. Notice that the accelerometer uses the more standard convention for the y coordinate, with increases in y indicating upward force, which is the opposite of Quartz 2D's coordinate system (discussed in Chapter 16). When you are using the accelerometer as a control mechanism with Quartz 2D, you need to translate the y-coordinate. When working with Sprite Kit, which is more likely when you are using the accelerometer to control animation, no translation is required.

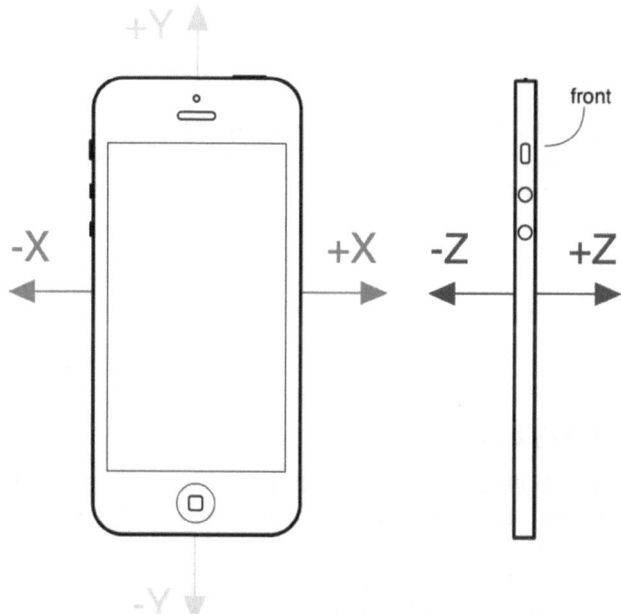

Figure 20-1. The iPhone accelerometer's axes in three dimensions. The front view of an iPhone on the left shows the x- and y-axes. The side view on the right shows the z-axis

Don't Forget Rotation

We mentioned earlier that all current devices include a gyroscope sensor, allowing you to read values describing the device's rotation around its axes.

If the difference between the gyroscope and the accelerometer seems unclear, consider an iPhone lying flat on a table. If you begin to turn the phone around while it's lying flat, the accelerometer values won't change. That's because the forces bent on moving the phone—in this case, just the force of gravity pulling straight down the z-axis—aren't changing. (In reality, things are a bit fuzzier than that, and the action of your hand bumping the phone will surely trigger a small amount of accelerometer action.) During that same movement, however, the device's rotation values will change—particularly the z-axis rotation value. Turning the device clockwise will generate a negative value, and turning it counterclockwise gives a positive value. Stop turning, and the z-axis rotation value will go back to zero.

Rather than registering an absolute rotation value, the gyroscope tells you about changes to the device's rotation as they happen. You'll see how this works in this chapter's first example, coming up shortly.

Core Motion and the Motion Manager

Accelerometer and gyroscope values are accessed using the Core Motion framework. This framework provides, among other things, the CMMotionManager class, which acts as a gateway for all the values describing how the device is being moved by its user. Your application creates an instance of CMMotionManager and then puts it to use in one of two modes:

- It can execute some code for you whenever motion occurs.

- It can hang on to a perpetually updated structure that lets you access the latest values at any time.

The latter method is ideal for games and other highly interactive applications that need to be able to poll the device's current state during each pass through the game loop. We'll show you how to implement both approaches.

Note that the CMMotionManager class isn't actually a singleton, but your application should treat it like one. You should create only one of these per app, using the normal alloc and init methods. So, if you need to access the motion manager from several places in your app, you should probably create it in your application delegate and provide access to it from there.

Besides the CMMotionManager class, Core Motion also provides a few other classes, such as CMAccelerometerData and CMGyroData, which are simple containers through which your application can access motion data. We'll touch on these classes as we get to them.

Event-Based Motion

We mentioned that the motion manager can operate in a mode where it executes some code for you each time the motion data changes. Most other Cocoa Touch classes offer this sort of functionality by letting you connect to a delegate that gets a message when the time comes, but Core Motion does things a little differently.

Instead of using a set of delegate methods to let us know what happens, CMMotionManager lets you pass in a block to execute whenever motion occurs. We've already used blocks a couple of times in this book, and now you're going to see another application of this technique.

Use Xcode to create a new *Single View Application* project named *MotionMonitor*. This will be a simple app that reads both accelerometer data and gyroscope data (if available), and then displays the information on the screen.

> **Note**   The applications in this chapter do not function on the simulator because the simulator has no accelerometer. Aw, shucks.

Now select the *BIDViewController.m* file and make the following changes:

```
#import "BIDViewController.h"

@interface BIDViewController ()

@property (weak, nonatomic) IBOutlet UILabel *accelerometerLabel;
@property (weak, nonatomic) IBOutlet UILabel *gyroscopeLabel;

@end
```

This provides us with outlets to a pair of labels where we'll display the information. Nothing much needs to be explained here, so just go ahead and save your changes.

Next, open *Main.storyboard* in Interface Builder and drag out a *Label* from the library into the view. Resize the label to make it run from the left blue guideline to the right blue guideline, resize it to be about half the height of the entire view, and then align the top of the label to the top blue guideline.

Now open the attributes inspector and change the *Lines* field from 1 to 0. The *Lines* attribute is used to specify just how many lines of text may appear in the label and provides a hard upper limit. If you set it to 0, no limit is applied, and the label can contain as many lines as you like.

Next, **Option**-drag the label to create a copy and align the copy with the blue guidelines in the bottom half of the view.

Now **Control**-drag from the *File's Owner* icon to each of the labels, connecting *accelerometerLabel* to the upper one and *gyroscopeLabel* to the lower one.

Finally, double-click each of the labels and delete the existing text.

This simple GUI is complete, so save your work and get ready for some coding.

Next, select *BIDViewController.m*. Now comes the interesting part. Add following content:

```
#import "BIDViewController.h"
#import <CoreMotion/CoreMotion.h>

@interface BIDViewController ()

@property (weak, nonatomic) IBOutlet UILabel *accelerometerLabel;
@property (weak, nonatomic) IBOutlet UILabel *gyroscopeLabel;

@property (strong, nonatomic) CMMotionManager *motionManager;
@property (strong, nonatomic) NSOperationQueue *queue;

@end
```

```
@implementation BIDViewController

- (NSUInteger)supportedInterfaceOrientations
{
    return UIInterfaceOrientationMaskPortrait;
}

- (void)viewDidLoad
{
    [super viewDidLoad];
    // Do any additional setup after loading the view, typically from a nib.
    self.motionManager = [[CMMotionManager alloc] init];
    self.queue = [[NSOperationQueue alloc] init];
    if (self.motionManager.accelerometerAvailable) {
        self.motionManager.accelerometerUpdateInterval = 1.0 / 10.0;
        [self.motionManager startAccelerometerUpdatesToQueue:self.queue
                                            withHandler:
         ^(CMAccelerometerData *accelerometerData, NSError *error) {
             NSString *labelText;
             if (error) {
                 [self.motionManager stopAccelerometerUpdates];
                 labelText = [NSString stringWithFormat:
                             @"Accelerometer encountered error: %@", error];
             } else {
                 labelText = [NSString stringWithFormat:
                             @"Accelerometer\n---\n"
                             "x: %+.2f\ny: %+.2f\nz: %+.2f",
                             accelerometerData.acceleration.x,
                             accelerometerData.acceleration.y,
                             accelerometerData.acceleration.z];
             }
             dispatch_async(dispatch_get_main_queue(), ^{
                 self.accelerometerLabel.text = labelText;
             });
         }];
    } else {
        self.accelerometerLabel.text = @"This device has no accelerometer.";
    }
    if (self.motionManager.gyroAvailable) {
        self.motionManager.gyroUpdateInterval = 1.0 / 10.0;
        [self.motionManager startGyroUpdatesToQueue:self.queue withHandler:
         ^(CMGyroData *gyroData, NSError *error) {
             NSString *labelText;
             if (error) {
                 [self.motionManager stopGyroUpdates];
                 labelText = [NSString stringWithFormat:
                             @"Gyroscope encountered error: %@", error];
             } else {
                 labelText = [NSString stringWithFormat:
                             @"Gyroscope\n---\n"
                             "x: %+.2f\ny: %+.2f\nz: %+.2f",
                             gyroData.rotationRate.x,
```

```
                            gyroData.rotationRate.y,
                            gyroData.rotationRate.z];
            }
            dispatch_async(dispatch_get_main_queue(), ^{
                self.gyroscopeLabel.text = labelText;
            });
        }];
    } else {
        self.gyroscopeLabel.text = @"This device has no gyroscope";
    }
}

- (void)didReceiveMemoryWarning
{
    [super didReceiveMemoryWarning];
    // Dispose of any resources that can be recreated.
}

@end
```

First, we import the header file for working with the Core Motion framework and add two additional properties to the class extension:

```
@interface BIDViewController ()

@property (weak, nonatomic) IBOutlet UILabel *accelerometerLabel;
@property (weak, nonatomic) IBOutlet UILabel *gyroscopeLabel;

@property (strong, nonatomic) CMMotionManager *motionManager;
@property (strong, nonatomic) NSOperationQueue *queue;

@end
```

Next, we override the supportedInterfaceOrientations method to avoid having the screen be rotated as we try out our motion sensors:

```
- (NSUInteger)supportedInterfaceOrientations
{
    return UIInterfaceOrientationMaskPortrait;
}
```

Then, in the viewDidLoad method, we add all the code we need to fire up the sensors, tell the sensors to report to us every 1/10 second, and update the screen when they do so.

Thanks to the power of blocks, it's all really simple and cohesive. Instead of putting parts of the functionality in delegate methods, you can define behaviors in blocks to see a behavior in the same method where it's being configured. Let's take this apart a bit. We start off with this:

```
self.motionManager = [[CMMotionManager alloc] init];
self.queue = [[NSOperationQueue alloc] init];
```

This code first creates an instance of `CMMotionManager`, which we'll use to monitor motion events. The code then creates an operation queue, which is simply a container for a pile of work that needs to be done, as you may recall from Chapter 15.

> **Caution**   The motion manager wants to have a queue in which it will put the bits of work to be done, as specified by the blocks you will give it, each time an event occurs. It would be tempting to use the system's default queue for this purpose, but the documentation for `CMMotionManager` explicitly warns not to do this! The concern is that the default queue could end up chock-full of these events and have a hard time processing other crucial system events as a result.

The next step is to configure the accelerometer. We first check to make sure the device actually has an accelerometer. All handheld iOS devices released so far do have one, but it's worth checking in case some future device doesn't. Next, we set the time interval we want between updates, specified in seconds. Here, we're asking for 1/10 second. Note that setting this doesn't guarantee that we'll receive updates at precisely that speed. In fact, that setting is really a cap, specifying the best rate the motion manager will be allowed to give us. In reality, it may update less frequently than that:

```
if (self.motionManager.accelerometerAvailable) {
    self.motionManager.accelerometerUpdateInterval = 1.0 / 10.0;
```

Next, we tell the motion manager to start reporting accelerometer updates. We pass in the queue where it will put its work and the block that defines the work that will be done each time an update occurs. Remember that a block always starts off with a caret (^), followed by a parentheses-wrapped list of arguments that the block expects to be populated when it's executed (in this case, the accelerometer data and potentially an error to alert us of trouble), and finishes with a curly brace section that contains the code to be executed:

```
[self.motionManager startAccelerometerUpdatesToQueue:self.queue
                                withHandler:
 ^(CMAccelerometerData *accelerometerData, NSError *error) {
```

What follows is the content of the block. It creates a string based on the current accelerometer values, or it generates an error message if there's a problem. Next, it pushes that string value into the `accelerometerLabel`. We can't do that directly here because UIKit classes like `UILabel` usually work well only when accessed from the main thread. Due to the way this code will be executed, from within an `NSOperationQueue`, we simply don't know the specific thread in which we'll be executing. So, we use the `dispatch_async()` function to pass control to the main thread before setting the label's `text` property.

Note that the accelerometer values are accessed through the `acceleration` property of the `accelerometerData` that was passed into it. The `acceleration` property is of type `CMAcceleration`, which is just a simple `struct` containing three `float` values. `accelerometerData` itself is an instance of the `CMAccelerometerData` class, which is really just a wrapper for `CMAcceleration`! If you think this seems like an unnecessary profusion of classes and types for simply passing three floats around, well, you're not alone. Regardless, here's how to use it:

```
NSString *labelText;
if (error) {
    [self.motionManager stopAccelerometerUpdates];
    labelText = [NSString stringWithFormat:
                @"Accelerometer encountered error: %@", error];
} else {
    labelText = [NSString stringWithFormat:
                @"Accelerometer\n---\n"
                 "x: %+.2f\ny: %+.2f\nz: %+.2f",
                accelerometerData.acceleration.x,
                accelerometerData.acceleration.y,
                accelerometerData.acceleration.z];
}
dispatch_async(dispatch_get_main_queue(), ^{
    self.accelerometerLabel.text = labelText;
});
}];
```

Next, we finish the block and complete the square-bracketed method call where we were passing that block in the first place. Finally, we provide a different code path entirely, in case the device doesn't have an accelerometer:

```
} else {
    self.accelerometerLabel.text = @"This device has no accelerometer.";
}
```

As mentioned earlier, all iOS devices so far have an accelerometer, but it's still wise to check for one because who knows what the future holds in store?

The code for the gyroscope is, as you surely noticed, structurally identical, differing only in the particulars of which methods are called and how reported values are accessed. It's similar enough that there's no need to walk you through it here.

Now build and run your app on whatever iOS device you have, and then try it out (see Figure 20-2). As you tilt your device around in different ways, you'll see how the accelerometer values adjust to each new position and will hold steady as long as you hold the device steady.

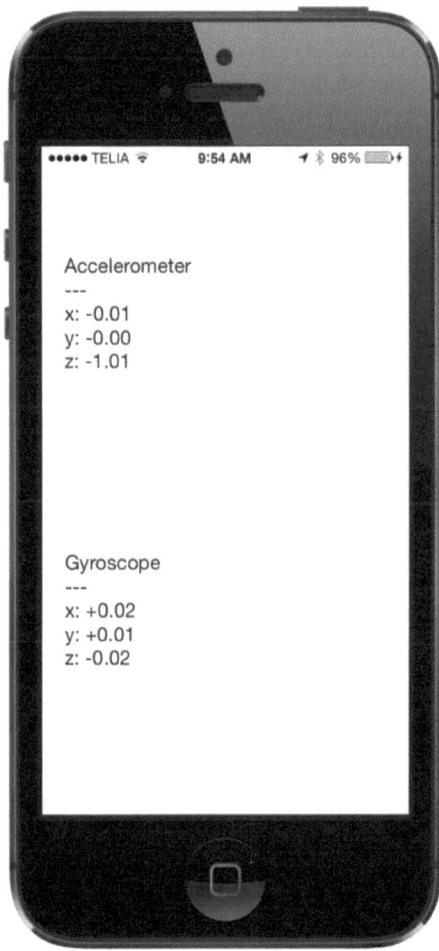

Figure 20-2. MotionMonitor running on an iPhone. Unfortunately, you'll get only a pair of error messages if you run this app in the simulator

If you run this on a device with a gyroscope, you'll see how those values change, as well. Whenever the device is standing still, no matter which orientation it is in, the gyroscope values will hover around zero. As you rotate the device, you'll see that the gyroscope values change, depending on how you rotate it on its various axes. The values will always move back to zero when you stop moving the device.

Proactive Motion Access

You've seen how to access motion data by passing CMMotionManager blocks to be called as motion occurs. This kind of event-driven motion handling can work well enough for the average Cocoa app, but sometimes it doesn't quite fit an application's particular needs. Interactive games, for example, typically have a perpetually running loop that processes user input, updates the state of the game, and redraws the screen. In such a case, the event-driven approach isn't such a good fit, since you would need to implement an object that waits for motion events, remembers the latest positions from each sensor as they're reported, and is ready to report the data back to the main game loop when necessary.

Fortunately, `CMMotionManager` has a built-in solution. Instead of passing in blocks, we can just tell it to activate the sensors using the `startAccelerometerUpdates` and `startGyroUpdates` methods. Once we do so, we can simply read the values any time we want, directly from the motion manager!

Let's change our MotionMonitor app to use this approach, just so you can see how it works. Start by making a copy of your *MotionMonitor* project folder. Close the open Xcode project and open the one from the new copy instead, heading straight to *BIDViewController.m*. The first step is to remove the queue property and add a new property, a pointer to an `NSTimer` that will trigger all our display updates:

```
#import "BIDViewController.h"
#import <CoreMotion/CoreMotion.h>

@interface BIDViewController ()

@property (weak, nonatomic) IBOutlet UILabel *accelerometerLabel;
@property (weak, nonatomic) IBOutlet UILabel *gyroscopeLabel;

@property (strong, nonatomic) CMMotionManager *motionManager;
@property (strong, nonatomic) NSOperationQueue *queue;
@property (strong, nonatomic) NSTimer *updateTimer;

@end
```
.
.
.

Next, get rid of the entire `viewDidLoad` method we had before and replace it with this simpler version, which just sets up the motion manager and provides informational labels for devices lacking sensors:

```
- (void)viewDidLoad
{
    [super viewDidLoad];
    // Do any additional setup after loading the view, typically from a nib.
    self.motionManager = [[CMMotionManager alloc] init];
    if (self.motionManager.accelerometerAvailable) {
        self.motionManager.accelerometerUpdateInterval = 1.0 / 10.0;
    } else {
        self.accelerometerLabel.text = @"This device has no accelerometer.";
    }
    if (self.motionManager.gyroAvailable) {
        self.motionManager.gyroUpdateInterval = 1.0/10.0;
    } else {
        self.gyroscopeLabel.text = @"This device has no gyroscope.";
    }
}
```

We want our timer—and the motion manager itself—to be active only during a small window of time, when the view is actually being displayed. That way, we keep the usage of our main game loop to a bare minimum. We can accomplish this by implementing viewWillAppear: and viewDidDisappear:, as shown here:

```
- (void)viewWillAppear:(BOOL)animated {
    [super viewWillAppear:animated];
    [self.motionManager startAccelerometerUpdates];
    [self.motionManager startGyroUpdates];
    self.updateTimer = [NSTimer
                            scheduledTimerWithTimeInterval:1.0 / 10.0
                            target:self
                            selector:@selector(updateDisplay)
                            userInfo:nil
                            repeats:YES];
}

- (void)viewDidDisappear:(BOOL)animated {
    [super viewDidDisappear:animated];
    [self.motionManager stopAccelerometerUpdates];
    [self.motionManager stopGyroUpdates];
    [self.updateTimer invalidate];
    self.updateTimer = nil;
}
```

The code in viewWillAppear: creates a new timer and schedules it to fire once every 1/10 second, calling the updateDisplay method, which we haven't created yet. Add this method just below viewDidDisappear:

```
- (void)updateDisplay {
    if (self.motionManager.accelerometerAvailable) {
        CMAccelerometerData *accelerometerData =
                            self.motionManager.accelerometerData;
        self.accelerometerLabel.text = [NSString stringWithFormat:
                            @"Accelerometer\n---\n"
                            "x: %+.2f\ny: %+.2f\nz: %+.2f",
                            accelerometerData.acceleration.x,
                            accelerometerData.acceleration.y,
                            accelerometerData.acceleration.z];
    }
    if (self.motionManager.gyroAvailable) {
        CMGyroData *gyroData = self.motionManager.gyroData;
        self.gyroscopeLabel.text = [NSString stringWithFormat:
                            @"Gyroscope\n---\n"
                            "x: %+.2f\ny: %+.2f\nz: %+.2f",
                            gyroData.rotationRate.x,
                            gyroData.rotationRate.y,
                            gyroData.rotationRate.z];
    }
}
```

Build and run the app on your device, and you should see that it behaves exactly like the first version. Now you've seen two ways of accessing motion data. Use whichever suits your application best.

Accelerometer Results

We mentioned earlier that the iPhone's accelerometer detects acceleration along three axes, and it provides this information using the CMAcceleration struct. Each CMAcceleration has an x, y, and z field, each of which holds a floating-point value. A value of 0 means that the accelerometer detects no movement on that particular axis. A positive or negative value indicates force in one direction. For example, a negative value for y indicates that a downward pull is sensed, which is probably an indication that the phone is being held upright in portrait orientation. A positive value for y indicates some force is being exerted in the opposite direction, which could mean the phone is being held upside down or that the phone is being moved in a downward direction.

Keeping the diagram in Figure 20-1 in mind, let's look at some accelerometer results (see Figure 20-3). Note that in real life you will almost never get values this precise, as the accelerometer is sensitive enough to sense even tiny amounts of motion, and you will usually pick up at least some tiny amount of force on all three axes. This is real-world physics, not high-school physics.

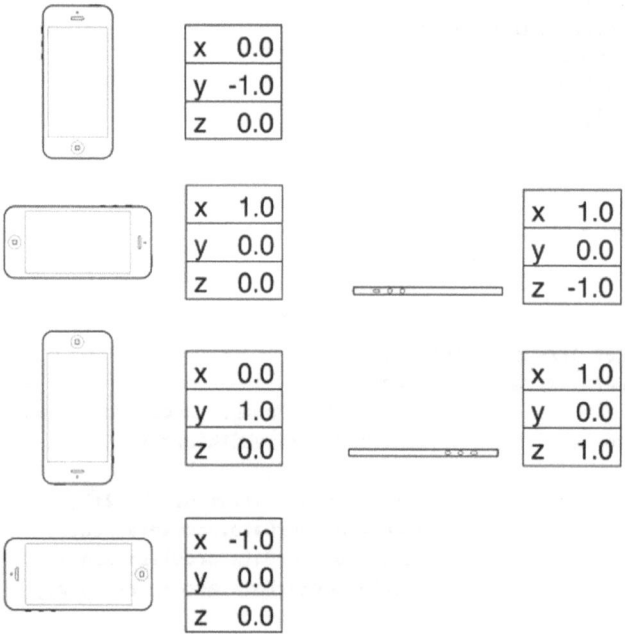

Figure 20-3. *Idealized acceleration values for different device orientations*

The most common usage of the accelerometer in third-party applications is probably as a controller for games. We'll create a program that uses the accelerometer for input a little later in the chapter, but first we'll look at another common accelerometer use: detecting shakes.

Detecting Shakes

Like a gesture, a shake can be used as a form of input to your application. For example, the drawing program GLPaint, which is one of Apple's iOS sample code projects, lets users erase drawings by shaking their iOS device, sort of like an Etch A Sketch.

Detecting shakes is relatively trivial. All it requires is checking for an absolute value on one of the axes that is greater than a set threshold. During normal usage, it's not uncommon for one of the three axes to register values up to around 1.3 g, but getting values much higher than that generally requires intentional force. The accelerometer seems to be unable to register values higher than around 2.3 g (at least in our experience), so you don't want to set your threshold any higher than that.

To detect a shake, you could check for an absolute value greater than 1.5 for a slight shake and 2.0 for a strong shake, like this:

```
CMAccelerometerData *accelerometerData =
    self.motionManager.accelerometerData;
if (fabsf(accelerometerData.acceleration.x) > 2.0
    || fabsf(accelerometerData.acceleration.y) > 2.0
    || fabsf(accelerometerData.acceleration.z) > 2.0) {
    // Do something here...
}
```

This code would detect any movement on any axis that exceeded two g-forces.

You could implement more sophisticated shake detection by requiring the user to shake back and forth a certain number of times to register as a shake, like so:

```
static NSInteger shakeCount = 0;
static NSDate *shakeStart;

NSDate *now = [[NSDate alloc] init];
NSDate *checkDate = [[NSDate alloc] initWithTimeInterval:1.5f
                                              sinceDate:shakeStart];
if ([now compare:checkDate] == NSOrderedDescending
    || shakeStart == nil) {
    shakeCount = 0;
    shakeStart = [[NSDate alloc] init];
}

CMAccelerometerData *accelerometerData =
    self.motionManager.accelerometerData;
if (fabsf(accelerometerData.acceleration.x) > 2.0
    || fabsf(accelerometerData.acceleration.y) > 2.0
    || fabsf(accelerometerData.acceleration.z) > 2.0) {
    shakeCount++;
    if (shakeCount > 4) {
        // Do something
        shakeCount = 0;
        shakeStart = [[NSDate alloc] init];
    }
}
```

This method keeps track of the number of times the accelerometer reports a value above 2.0. If it happens four times within a 1.5-second span of time, it registers as a shake.

Baked-In Shaking

There's actually another way to check for shakes—one that's baked right into the responder chain. Remember back in Chapter 18 when we implemented methods like `touchesBegan:withEvent:` to detect touches? Well, iOS also provides three similar responder methods for detecting motion:

- When motion begins, the `motionBegan:withEvent:` method is sent to the first responder and then on through the responder chain, as discussed in Chapter 17.

- When the motion ends, the `motionEnded:withEvent:` method is sent to the first responder.

- If the phone rings, or some other interrupting action happens during the shake, the `motionCancelled:withEvent:` message is sent to the first responder.

This means that you can actually detect a shake without using `CMMotionManager` directly. All you need to do is override the appropriate motion-sensing methods in your view or view controller, and they will be called automatically when the user shakes the phone. Unless you specifically need more control over the shake gesture, you should use the baked-in motion detection rather than the manual method described previously. However, we thought we would show you the basics of the manual method in case you ever do need more control.

Now that you have the basic idea of how to detect shakes, we're going to break your phone.

Shake and Break

Okay, we're not really going to break your phone, but we'll write an application that detects shakes, and then makes your phone look and sound as if it broke as a result of the shake.

When you launch the application, the program will display a picture that looks like the iPhone home screen (see Figure 20-4). Shake the phone hard enough, though, and your poor phone will make a sound that you never want to hear coming out of a consumer electronics device. What's more, your screen will look like the one shown in Figure 20-5. Why do we do these evil things? Not to worry. You can reset the iPhone to its previously pristine state by touching the screen.

Figure 20-4. The ShakeAndBreak application looks innocuous enough…

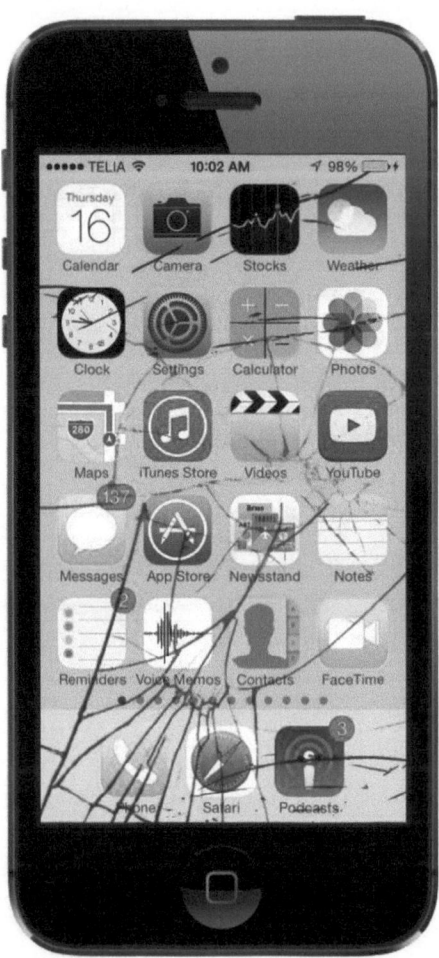

Figure 20-5. ...but handle it too roughly and—oh no!

Create a new project in Xcode using the *Single View Application* template. Call the new project *ShakeAndBreak*. In the *20 - ShakeAndBreak* folder of the project archive, we've provided the two images and the sound file you need for this application. Drag *home.png*, *homebroken.png*, and *glass.wav* to your project.

Now let's start creating our view controller. We're going to need to create an outlet to point to an image view so that we can change the displayed image. Single-click *BIDViewController.m* and add the following property declaration to the class extension:

```
#import "BIDViewController.h"

@interface BIDViewController ()

@property (weak, nonatomic) IBOutlet UIImageView *imageView;

@end
```

Save the file. Now select *Main.storyboard* to edit the file in Interface Builder. Click the *View Controller* to select it, and then bring up the attributes inspector and change the *Status Bar* popup under *Simulated Metrics* from *Inferred* to *None*. Next, drag an *Image View* over from the library to the view in the layout area. The image view should automatically resize to take up the full window, so just place it so that it sits perfectly within the window.

Control-drag from the *View Controller* icon to the image view and select the *imageView* outlet, and then save the storyboard.

Next, go back to the *BIDViewController.m* file.

We're going to add some additional properties for both of the images we're going to display, to track whether we're showing the broken image. We're also adding an audio player object that we'll use to play our breaking glass sound. The following bold lines go near the top of the file:

```
#import "BIDViewController.h"
#import <AVFoundation/AVFoundation.h>

@interface BIDViewController ()

@property (weak, nonatomic) IBOutlet UIImageView *imageView;
@property (strong, nonatomic) UIImage *fixed;
@property (strong, nonatomic) UIImage *broken;
@property (assign, nonatomic) BOOL brokenScreenShowing;
@property (strong, nonatomic) AVAudioPlayer *crashPlayer;

@end
```

Give the viewDidLoad method the following implementation:

```
@implementation BIDViewController

- (void)viewDidLoad
{
    [super viewDidLoad];
    // Do any additional setup after loading the view, typically from a nib.

    NSURL *url = [[NSBundle mainBundle] URLForResource:@"glass"
                                        withExtension:@"wav"];

    NSError *error = nil;
    self.crashPlayer = [[AVAudioPlayer alloc] initWithContentsOfURL:url
                                                    error:&error];
    if (!self.crashPlayer) {
        NSLog(@"Audio Error! %@", error.localizedDescription);
    }

    self.fixed = [UIImage imageNamed:@"home.png"];
    self.broken = [UIImage imageNamed:@"homebroken.png"];

    self.imageView.image = self.fixed;
}
```

At this point, we've created an NSURL object pointing to our sound file and initialized an instance of AVAudioPlayer, a class that will simply play the sound. After a quick sanity check to make sure the audio player was set up correctly, we loaded both images we need to use and put the first one in place.

Next, add the following new method:

```
- (void)motionEnded:(UIEventSubtype)motion withEvent:(UIEvent *)event;
{
    if (!self.brokenScreenShowing && motion == UIEventSubtypeMotionShake) {
        self.imageView.image = self.broken;
        [self.crashPlayer play];
        self.brokenScreenShowing = YES;
    }
}
```

This method will be called whenever a shake happens. After checking to make sure the broken screen isn't already showing and that the event we're looking at really is a shake event, the method shows the broken image and plays our shattering noise.

The last method is one you should already be familiar with by now. It's called when the screen is touched. All we to do in that method is to set the image back to the unbroken screen and to set brokenScreenShowing back to NO:

```
- (void)touchesBegan:(NSSet *)touches withEvent:(UIEvent *)event
{
    self.imageView.image = self.fixed;
    self.brokenScreenShowing = NO;
}
```

Compile and run the application, and take it for a test shake. For those of you who don't have the ability to run this application on your iOS device, you can still give this a try. The simulator does not simulate the accelerometer hardware, but it does include a menu item that simulates the shake event, so this will work with the simulator, too.

Go have some fun with it. When you're finished, come on back, and you'll see how to use the accelerometer as a controller for games and other programs.

Accelerometer As Directional Controller

Instead of using buttons to control the movement of a character or object in a game, developers often use an accelerometer to accomplish this task. In a car-racing game, for example, twisting the iOS device like a steering wheel might steer your car, while tipping it forward might accelerate, and tipping it back might brake.

Exactly how you use the accelerometer as a controller will vary greatly, depending on the specific mechanics of the game. In the simplest cases, you might just take the value from one of the axes, multiply it by a number, and add that to one of the coordinates of the controlled objects. In more complex games where physics are modeled more realistically, you would need to make adjustments to the velocity of the controlled object based on the values returned from the accelerometer.

The one tricky aspect of using the accelerometer as a controller is that the delegate method is not guaranteed to call back at the interval you specify. If you tell the motion manager to read the accelerometer 60 times a second, all that you can say for sure is that it won't update more than 60 times a second. You're not guaranteed to get 60 evenly spaced updates every second. So, if you're doing animation based on input from the accelerometer, you must keep track of the time that passes between updates and factor that into your equations to determine how far objects have moved.

Rolling Marbles

For our next trick, we're going to let you move a sprite around the iPhone's screen by tilting the phone. This is a very simple example of using the accelerometer to receive input. We'll use Quartz 2D to handle our animation.

> **Note**   As a general rule, when you're working with games and other programs that need smooth animation, you'll probably want to use Sprite Kit or OpenGL ES. We're using Quartz 2D in this application for the sake of simplicity and to reduce the amount of code that's unrelated to using the accelerometer.

In this application, as you tilt your iPhone, the marble will roll around as if it were on the surface of a table (see Figure 20-6). Tip it to the left, and the ball will roll to the left. Tip it farther, and it will move faster. Tip it back, and it will slow down, and then start going in the other direction.

Figure 20-6. The Ball application lets you roll a marble around the screen. You'll see a black screen, but for printing purposes we changed it to light gray here. Think of all the ink we're saving! The squid will thank us

In Xcode, create a new project using the *Single View Application* template and call this one *Ball*. In the *20 - Ball* folder in the project archive, you'll find an image called *ball.png*. Drag that to your project.

Next, select the *Ball* project in the *Project Navigator*, and then the *General* tab of the *Ball* target. In the *Deployment Info* section, deselect all *Device Orientation* checkboxes except *Portrait* (see Figure 20-7). This disables the default interface orientation changes; we want to roll our ball and not change interface orientation as we move our device around.

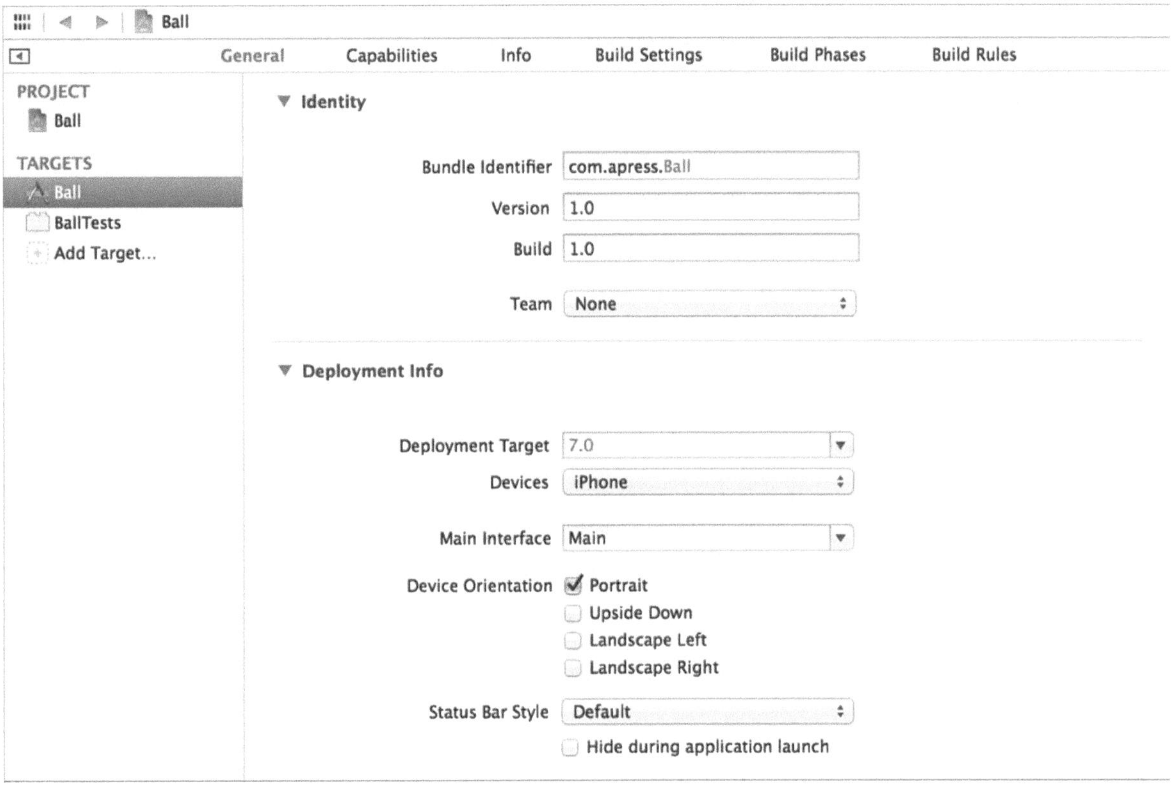

Figure 20-7. Disabling all interface orientation except Portrait on the Summary tab of the target

Now single-click the *Ball* folder and select File ➤ New ➤ File.... Select *Objective-C class* from the *Cocoa Touch* category, click Next, and name the new class *BIDBallView*. Select *UIView* in the *Subclass of* pop-up, click *Next*, and then click *Create* to save the class files. We'll get back to editing this class a little later.

Select *Main.storyboard* to edit the file in Interface Builder. Single-click the *View* icon and use the identity inspector to change the view's class from *UIView* to *BIDBallView*. Next, switch to the attributes inspector and change the view's *Background* to *Black Color*. Finally, save the storyboard.

Now it's time to edit *BIDViewController.m*. Add the following lines toward the top of the file:

```
#import "BIDViewController.h"
#import "BIDBallView.h"
#import <CoreMotion/CoreMotion.h>

#define kUpdateInterval    (1.0f / 60.0f)

@interface BIDViewController ()
@property (strong, nonatomic) CMMotionManager *motionManager;
@property (strong, nonatomic) NSOperationQueue *queue;
@end
```

@implementation BIDViewController

.

.

.

Next, populate viewDidLoad with this code:

```
- (void)viewDidLoad
{
    [super viewDidLoad];
    // Do any additional setup after loading the view, typically from a nib.
    self.motionManager = [[CMMotionManager alloc] init];
    self.queue = [[NSOperationQueue alloc] init];
    self.motionManager.accelerometerUpdateInterval = kUpdateInterval;
    [self.motionManager startAccelerometerUpdatesToQueue:self.queue
                                    withHandler:
     ^(CMAccelerometerData *accelerometerData, NSError *error) {
         [(id)self.view setAcceleration:accelerometerData.acceleration];
         [self.view performSelectorOnMainThread:@selector(update)
                            withObject:nil
                         waitUntilDone:NO];
    }];
}
```

> **Note** After entering this code, you will see an error as a result of BIDBallView not being complete. We're
> doing the bulk of our work in the BIDBallView class, and it's up next.

The viewDidLoad method here is similar to some of what we've done elsewhere in this chapter. The
main difference is that we are declaring a much higher update interval of 60 times per second. In the
block that we tell the motion manager to execute when there are accelerometer updates to report,
we pass the acceleration object along to our view. We then call a method named update, which
updates the position of the ball in the view based on acceleration and the amount of time that has
passed since the last update. Since that block can be executed on any thread, and the methods
belonging to UIKit objects (including UIView) can be safely used only from the main thread, we once
again force the update method to be called in the main thread.

Writing the Ball View

Select *BIDBallView.h*. Here, you'll need to import the Core Motion header file and add the property
that our controller will use to pass along an acceleration value:

```
#import <UIKit/UIKit.h>
#import <CoreMotion/CoreMotion.h>

@interface BIDBallView : UIView
```

@property (assign, nonatomic) CMAcceleration acceleration;

@end

Switch over to *BIDBallView.m* and make the following changes to the class extension near the top:

```
#import "BIDBallView.h"

@interface BIDBallView ()

@property (strong, nonatomic) UIImage *image;
@property (assign, nonatomic) CGPoint currentPoint;
@property (assign, nonatomic) CGPoint previousPoint;
@property (assign, nonatomic) CGFloat ballXVelocity;
@property (assign, nonatomic) CGFloat ballYVelocity;

@end
```

Let's look at the properties and talk about what we're doing with each of them. The first is a UIImage that will point to the sprite that we'll be moving around the screen:

```
UIImage *image;
```

After that, we keep track of two CGPoint variables. The currentPoint property will hold the current position of the ball. We'll also keep track of the last point where we drew the sprite. That way, we can build an update rectangle that encompasses both the new and old positions of the ball, so that it is drawn at the new spot and erased at the old one:

```
CGPoint    currentPoint;
CGPoint    previousPoint;
```

We also have two variables to keep track of the ball's current velocity in two dimensions. Although this isn't going to be a very complex simulation, we do want the ball to move in a manner similar to a real ball. We'll calculate the ball movement in the next section. We'll get acceleration from the accelerometer and keep track of velocity on two axes with these variables.

```
CGFloat ballXVelocity;
CGFloat ballYVelocity;
```

Now let's write the code to draw and move the ball around the screen. First, add the following methods at the beginning of the @implementation section in *BIDBallView.m*:

```
@implementation BIDBallView

- (void)commonInit
{
    self.image = [UIImage imageNamed:@"ball.png"];
    self.currentPoint = CGPointMake((self.bounds.size.width / 2.0f) +
                                    (self.image.size.width / 2.0f),
                                    (self.bounds.size.height / 2.0f) +
                                    (self.image.size.height / 2.0f));
}
```

```objc
- (id)initWithCoder:(NSCoder *)coder
{
    self = [super initWithCoder:coder];
    if (self) {
        [self commonInit];
    }
    return self;
}

- (id)initWithFrame:(CGRect)frame
{
    self = [super initWithFrame:frame];
    if (self) {
        [self commonInit];
    }
    return self;
}
    .
    .
    .
```

Both the initWithCoder: and the initWithFrame: methods call our commonInit method. Our view that is created in a storyboard file will be initialized with the initWithCoder: method. We call the commonInit method from both initializer methods so that our view class can safely be created both from code and from a nib file. This is a nice thing to do for any view class that may be reused, such as this fancy ball rolling view.

Now uncomment the commented-out drawRect: method and give it this simple implementation:

```objc
- (void)drawRect:(CGRect)rect
{
    // Drawing code
    [self.image drawAtPoint:self.currentPoint];
}
```

Next, add these methods to the end of the class:

```objc
    .
    .
    .
#pragma mark -

- (void)setCurrentPoint:(CGPoint)newPoint
{
    self.previousPoint = self.currentPoint;
    _currentPoint = newPoint;

    if (self.currentPoint.x < 0) {
        _currentPoint.x = 0;
        self.ballXVelocity = 0;
    }
```

```objc
    if (self.currentPoint.y < 0){
        _currentPoint.y = 0;
        self.ballYVelocity = 0;
    }
    if (self.currentPoint.x > self.bounds.size.width - self.image.size.width) {
        _currentPoint.x = self.bounds.size.width - self.image.size.width;
        self.ballXVelocity = 0;
    }
    if (self.currentPoint.y >
        self.bounds.size.height - self.image.size.height) {
        _currentPoint.y = self.bounds.size.height - self.image.size.height;
        self.ballYVelocity = 0;
    }

    CGRect currentRect =
    CGRectMake(self.currentPoint.x, self.currentPoint.y,
               self.currentPoint.x + self.image.size.width,
               self.currentPoint.y + self.image.size.height);
    CGRect previousRect =
    CGRectMake(self.previousPoint.x, self.previousPoint.y,
               self.previousPoint.x + self.image.size.width,
               self.currentPoint.y + self.image.size.width);
    [self setNeedsDisplayInRect:CGRectUnion(currentRect, previousRect)];
}

- (void)update
{
    static NSDate *lastUpdateTime = nil;

    if (lastUpdateTime != nil) {
        NSTimeInterval secondsSinceLastDraw =
        [[NSDate date] timeIntervalSinceDate:lastUpdateTime];

        self.ballYVelocity = self.ballYVelocity -
                             (self.acceleration.y * secondsSinceLastDraw);
        self.ballXVelocity = self.ballXVelocity +
                             (self.acceleration.x * secondsSinceLastDraw);

        CGFloat xAccel = secondsSinceLastDraw * self.ballXVelocity * 500;
        CGFloat yAccel = secondsSinceLastDraw * self.ballYVelocity * 500;

        self.currentPoint = CGPointMake(self.currentPoint.x + xAccel,
                                        self.currentPoint.y + yAccel);
    }
    // Update last time with current time
    lastUpdateTime = [[NSDate alloc] init];
}

@end
```

Calculating Ball Movement

Our drawRect: method couldn't be much simpler. We just draw the image we loaded in commonInit: at the position stored in currentPoint. The currentPoint accessor is a standard accessor method. The setCurrentPoint: mutator is another story, however.

The first things we do in setCurrentPoint: are to store the old currentPoint value in previousPoint and assign the new value to currentPoint:

```
self.previousPoint = self.currentPoint;
self.currentPoint = newPoint;
```

Next, we do a boundary check. If either the x or y position of the ball is less than 0 or greater than the width or height of the screen (accounting for the width and height of the image), then the acceleration in that direction is stopped:

```
if (self.currentPoint.x < 0) {
    _currentPoint.x = 0;
    self.ballXVelocity = 0;
}
if (self.currentPoint.y < 0){
    _currentPoint.y = 0;
    self.ballYVelocity = 0;
}
if (self.currentPoint.x > self.bounds.size.width - self.image.size.width) {
    _currentPoint.x = self.bounds.size.width - self.image.size.width;
    self.ballXVelocity = 0;
}
if (self.currentPoint.y >
    self.bounds.size.height - self.image.size.height) {
    _currentPoint.y = self.bounds.size.height - self.image.size.height;
    self.ballYVelocity = 0;
}
```

Tip   Do you want to make the ball bounce off the walls more naturally, instead of just stopping? It's easy enough to do. Just change the two lines in setCurrentPoint: that currently read self.ballXVelocity = 0; to **self.ballXVelocity = - (self.ballXVelocity / 2.0);**. And change the two lines that currently read self.ballYVelocity = 0; to **self.ballYVelocity = - (self.ballYVelocity / 2.0);**. With these changes, instead of killing the ball's velocity, we reduce it in half and set it to the inverse. Now the ball has half the velocity in the opposite direction.

After that, we calculate two CGRects based on the size of the image. One rectangle encompasses the area where the new image will be drawn, and the other encompasses the area where it was last drawn. We'll use these two rectangles to ensure that the old ball is erased at the same time the new one is drawn:

```
CGRect currentRect =
CGRectMake(self.currentPoint.x, self.currentPoint.y,
            self.currentPoint.x + self.image.size.width,
            self.currentPoint.y + self.image.size.height);
CGRect previousRect =
CGRectMake(self.previousPoint.x, self.previousPoint.y,
            self.previousPoint.x + self.image.size.width,
            self.currentPoint.y + self.image.size.width);
```

Finally, we create a new rectangle that is the union of the two rectangles we just calculated and feed that to setNeedsDisplayInRect: to indicate the part of our view that needs to be redrawn:

```
[self setNeedsDisplayInRect:CGRectUnion(currentRect, previousRect)];
```

The last substantive method in our class is update, which is used to figure out the correct new location of the ball. This method is called in the accelerometer method of its controller class after it feeds the view the new acceleration object. The first thing this method does is to declare a static NSDate variable that will be used to keep track of how long it has been since the last time the update method was called. The first time through this method, when lastUpdateTime is nil, we don't do anything because there's no point of reference. Because the updates are happening about 60 times a second, no one will ever notice a single missing frame:

```
static NSDate *lastUpdateTime = nil;

if (lastUpdateTime != nil) {
```

Every other time through this method, we calculate how long it has been since the last time this method was called. The NSDate instance returned by [NSDate date] represents the current time. By asking it for the time interval since lastUpdateDate, we get a number representing the number of seconds between the current time and lastUpdateTime:

```
NSTimeInterval secondsSinceLastDraw =
[[NSDate date] timeIntervalSinceDate:lastUpdateTime];
```

Next, we calculate the new velocity in both directions by adding the current acceleration to the current velocity. We multiply acceleration by secondsSinceLastDraw so that our acceleration is consistent across time. Tipping the phone at the same angle will always cause the same amount of acceleration:

```
self.ballYVelocity = self.ballYVelocity -
                    (self.acceleration.y * secondsSinceLastDraw);
self.ballXVelocity = self.ballXVelocity +
                    (self.acceleration.x * secondsSinceLastDraw);
```

After that, we figure out the actual change in pixels since the last time the method was called based on the velocity. The product of velocity and elapsed time is multiplied by 500 to create movement that looks natural. If we didn't multiply it by some value, the acceleration would be extraordinarily slow, as if the ball were stuck in molasses:

```
CGFloat xAccel = secondsSinceLastDraw * self.ballXVelocity * 500;
CGFloat yAccel = secondsSinceLastDraw * self.ballYVelocity * 500;
```

Once we know the change in pixels, we create a new point by adding the current location to the calculated acceleration and assign that to currentPoint. By using self.currentPoint, we use that accessor method we wrote earlier, rather than assigning the value directly to the instance variable:

```
self.currentPoint = CGPointMake(self.currentPoint.x + xAccel,
                                self.currentPoint.y + yAccel);
```

That ends our calculations, so all that's left is to update lastUpdateTime with the current time:

```
lastUpdateTime = [[NSDate alloc] init];
```

Before you build the app, add the Core Motion framework using the technique mentioned earlier. Once it's added, go ahead and build and run the app.

If all went well, the application will launch, and you should be able to control the movement of the ball by tilting the phone. When the ball gets to an edge of the screen, it should stop. Tip the phone back the other way, and it should start rolling in the other direction. Whee!

Rolling On

Well, we've certainly had some fun in this chapter with physics and the amazing iOS accelerometer and gyro. We created a great April Fools' prank, and you got to see the basics of using the accelerometer as a control device. The possibilities for applications using the accelerometer and gyro are nearly as endless as the universe. So now that you have the basics down, go create something cool and surprise us!

When you feel up to it, we're going to get into using another bit of iOS hardware: the built-in camera.

Chapter 21

The Camera and Photo Library

By now, it should come as no surprise to you that the iPhone, iPad, and iPod touch have a built-in camera and a nifty application called Photos to help you manage all those awesome pictures and videos you've taken. What you may not know is that your programs can use the built-in camera to take pictures. Your applications can also allow the user to select from among the media already stored on the device. We'll look at both of these abilities in this chapter.

Using the Image Picker and UIImagePickerController

Because of the way iOS applications are sandboxed, applications ordinarily can't get to photographs or other data that live outside their own sandboxes. Fortunately, both the camera and the media library are made available to your application by way of an **image picker**.

As the name implies, an image picker is a mechanism that lets you select an image from a specified source. When this class first appeared in iOS, it was used only for images. Nowadays, you can use it to capture video as well.

Typically, an image picker will use a list of images and/or videos as its source (see the left side of Figure 21-1). You can, however, specify that the picker use the camera as its source (see the right side of Figure 21-1).

Figure 21-1. An image picker in action. Users are presented with a list of images (left). Once an image is selected, it can be moved and scaled (right). And, yeah, sometimes my camera roll is just pictures of Clumsy Ninja. I blame my children for this

The image picker interface is implemented by way of a modal controller class called `UIImagePickerController`. You create an instance of this class, specify a delegate (as if you didn't see that coming), specify its image source and whether you want the user to pick an image or a video, and then launch it modally. The image picker will take control of the device to let the user select a picture or video from the existing media library. Or, the user can take a new picture or video with the camera. Once the user makes a selection, you can give the user an opportunity to do some basic editing, such as scaling or cropping an image or trimming away a bit of a video clip. All of that behavior is implemented by the `UIImagePickerController`, so you really don't need to do much heavy lifting here.

Assuming the user doesn't press cancel, the image or video that the user either captures or selects from the library will be delivered to your delegate. Regardless of whether the user selects a media file or cancels, your delegate is responsible for dismissing the `UIImagePickerController` so that the user can return to your application.

Creating a UIImagePickerController is extremely straightforward. You just allocate and initialize an instance the way you would with most classes. There is one catch, however: not every iOS device has a camera. Older iPod touches were the first examples of this, and the first-generation iPad is the latest. However, more such devices may roll off Apple's assembly lines in the future. Before you create an instance of UIImagePickerController, you need to check to see whether the device your program is currently running on supports the image source you want to use. For example, before letting the user take a picture with the camera, you should make sure the program is running on a device that has a camera. You can check that by using a class method on UIImagePickerController, like this:

```
if ([UIImagePickerController isSourceTypeAvailable:
        UIImagePickerControllerSourceTypeCamera]) {
```

In this example, we're passing UIImagePickerControllerSourceTypeCamera to indicate that we want to let the user take a picture or shoot a video using the built-in camera. The method isSourceTypeAvailable: returns YES if the specified source is currently available. We can specify two other values in addition to UIImagePickerControllerSourceTypeCamera:

- UIImagePickerControllerSourceTypePhotoLibrary specifies that the user should pick an image or video from the existing media library. That image will be returned to your delegate.

- UIImagePickerControllerSourceTypeSavedPhotosAlbum specifies that the user will select the image from the library of existing photographs, but that the selection will be limited to the camera roll. This option will run on a device without a camera, where it is less useful but still allows you to select any screenshots you have taken.

After making sure that the device your program is running on supports the image source you want to use, launching the image picker is relatively easy:

```
UIImagePickerController *picker = [[UIImagePickerController alloc] init];
picker.delegate = self;
picker.sourceType = UIImagePickerControllerSourceTypeCamera;
[self presentViewController:picker animated:YES completion:nil];
```

After we have created and configured the UIImagePickerController, we use a method that our class inherited from UIView called presentViewController:animated:completion: to present the image picker to the user.

> **Tip**   The presentViewController:animated:completion: method is not limited to just presenting image pickers. You can present any view controller to the user, modally, by calling this method on the view controller for a currently visible view.

Implementing the Image Picker Controller Delegate

To find out when the user has finished using the image picker, you need to implement the UIImagePickerControllerDelegate protocol. This protocol defines two methods: imagePickerContro ller:didFinishPickingMediaWithInfo: and imagePickerControllerDidCancel:.

The imagePickerController:didFinishPickingMediaWithInfo: method is called when the user has successfully captured a photo or video, or selected an item from the media library. The first argument is a pointer to the UIImagePickerController that you created earlier. The second argument is an NSDictionary instance that will contain the chosen photo or the URL of the chosen video, as well as optional editing information if you enabled editing in the image picker controller (and if and the user actually did some editing). That dictionary will also contain the original, unedited image stored under the key UIImagePickerControllerOriginalImage. Here's an example of a delegate method that retrieves the original image:

```
- (void)imagePickerController:(UIImagePickerController *)picker
didFinishPickingMediaWithInfo:(NSDictionary *)info
{
    UIImage *selectedImage = info[UIImagePickerControllerEditedImage];
    UIImage *originalImage = info[UIImagePickerControllerOriginalImage];

    // do something with selectedImage and originalImage

    [picker dismissViewControllerAnimated:YES completion:nil];
}
```

The editingInfo dictionary will also tell you which portion of the entire image was chosen during editing by way of an NSValue object stored under the key UIImagePickerControllerCropRect. You can convert this NSValue instance into a CGRect, like so:

```
    NSValue *cropValue = info[UIImagePickerControllerCropRect];
    CGRect cropRect = [cropValue CGRectValue];
```

After this conversion, cropRect will specify the portion of the original image that was selected during the editing process. If you do not need this information, you can just ignore it.

> **Caution** If the image returned to your delegate comes from the camera, that image will not be stored in the photo library automatically. It is your application's responsibility to save the image, if necessary.

The other delegate method, imagePickerControllerDidCancel:, is called if the user decides to cancel the process without capturing or selecting any media. When the image picker calls this delegate method, it's just notifying you that the user is finished with the picker and didn't choose anything.

Both of the methods in the UIImagePickerControllerDelegate protocol are marked as optional, but they really aren't, and here is why: modal views like the image picker must be told to dismiss themselves. As a result, even if you don't need to take any application-specific actions when the user cancels an image picker, you still need to dismiss the picker. At a bare minimum, your imagePickerControllerDidCancel: method will need to look like this for your program to function correctly:

```
- (void)imagePickerControllerDidCancel:(UIImagePickerController *)picker
{
    [picker dismissViewControllerAnimated:YES completion:NULL];
}
```

Road Testing the Camera and Library

In this chapter, we're going to build an application that lets the user take a picture or shoot some video with the camera. Or, the user can select something from the photo library, and then display the selection on the screen (see Figure 21-2). If the user is on a device without a camera, we will hide the *New Photo or Video* button and allow only selection from the photo library.

Figure 21-2. The Camera application in action

Create a new project in Xcode using the *Single View Application* template, naming the application *Camera*. The first order of business is to add a couple of outlets to this application's view controller. We need one to point to the image view, so that we can update it with the image returned from the image picker. We'll also need an outlet to point to the *New Photo or Video* button, so we can hide the button if the device doesn't have a camera.

We also need two action methods: one for the *New Photo or Video* button and one that lets the user select an existing picture from the photo library.

Expand the *Camera* folder so that you can get to all the relevant files. Select *BIDViewController.m* and add the following protocol conformance declarations and properties to the class extension:

```
#import "BIDViewController.h"

@interface BIDViewController ()
<UIImagePickerControllerDelegate, UINavigationControllerDelegate>

@property (weak, nonatomic) IBOutlet UIImageView *imageView;
@property (weak, nonatomic) IBOutlet UIButton *takePictureButton;

@end
```

The first thing you might notice is that we've actually conformed our class to two different protocols: UIImagePickerControllerDelegate and UINavigationControllerDelegate. Because UIImagePickerController is a subclass of UINavigationController, we must conform our class to both of these protocols. The methods in UINavigationControllerDelegate are optional, and we don't need either of them to use the image picker; however, we do need to conform to the protocol, or the compiler will give us a warning later on.

The other thing you might notice is that, while we'll be dealing with an instance of UIImageView for displaying a chosen image, we don't have anything similar for displaying a chosen video. UIKit doesn't include any publicly available class like UIImageView that works for showing video content, so we'll have to show video using another technique instead. When we get to that point, we will use an instance of MPMoviePlayerController, grabbing its view property and inserting it into our view hierarchy. This is a highly unusual way of using any view controller, but it's actually an Apple-approved technique to show video inside a view hierarchy.

We're also going to add two action methods that we want to connect our buttons to. For now, we'll just create empty implementations so that Interface Builder can see them. We'll fill in the actual code later:

```
- (IBAction)shootPictureOrVideo:(id)sender {
}

- (IBAction)selectExistingPictureOrVideo:(id)sender {
}
```

Save your changes and select *Main.storyboard* to edit the GUI in Interface Builder.

Designing the Interface

Drag two *Buttons* from the library to the window labeled *View*. Place them one above the other, aligning the bottom button with the bottom blue guideline. Double-click the top button and give it a title of *New Photo or Video*. Now double-click the bottom button and give it a title of *Pick from Library*. Next, drag an *Image View* from the library and place it above the buttons. Expand the image view to take up the entire space of the view above the buttons, as shown earlier in Figure 21-2.

Now **Control**-drag from the *View Controller* icon to the image view and select the *imageView* outlet. Drag again from *View Controller* to the *New Photo or Video* button and select the *takePictureButton* outlet.

Next, select the *New Photo or Video* button and bring up the connections inspector. Drag from the *Touch Up Inside* event to *View Controller* and select the *shootPictureOrVideo:* action. Now click the *Pick from Library* button, drag from the *Touch Up Inside* event in the connections inspector to *View Controller*, and select the *selectExistingPictureOrVideo:* action.

Once you've made these connections, save your changes.

Implementing the Camera View Controller

Select *BIDViewController.m*, where we have some more changes to make. Since we're going to allow users to optionally capture a video, we need a property for an MPMoviePlayerController instance. Two more properties keep track of the last selected image and video, along with a string to determine whether a video or image was the last thing chosen. We also need to import a few additional headers to make this all work. Add the bold lines shown here:

```
#import "BIDViewController.h"
#import <MediaPlayer/MediaPlayer.h>
#import <MobileCoreServices/UTCoreTypes.h>

@interface BIDViewController ()
<UIImagePickerControllerDelegate, UINavigationControllerDelegate>

@property (weak, nonatomic) IBOutlet UIImageView *imageView;
@property (weak, nonatomic) IBOutlet UIButton *takePictureButton;

@property (strong, nonatomic) MPMoviePlayerController *moviePlayerController;
@property (strong, nonatomic) UIImage *image;
@property (strong, nonatomic) NSURL *movieURL;
@property (copy, nonatomic) NSString *lastChosenMediaType;

@end
```

Now let's enhance the viewDidLoad method, hiding the takePictureButton if the device we're running on does not have a camera. We also implement the viewDidAppear: method, having it call the updateDisplay method, which we'll implement soon. First, make these changes:

```
@implementation BIDViewController

- (void)viewDidLoad
{
    [super viewDidLoad];
    // Do any additional setup after loading the view, typically from a nib.
    if (![UIImagePickerController isSourceTypeAvailable:
        UIImagePickerControllerSourceTypeCamera])
    {
        self.takePictureButton.hidden = YES;
    }
}

- (void)viewDidAppear:(BOOL)animated
{
    [super viewDidAppear:animated];
    [self updateDisplay];
}

- (void)didReceiveMemoryWarning
{
    [super didReceiveMemoryWarning];
    // Dispose of any resources that can be recreated.
}
```

It's important to understand the distinction between the viewDidLoad and viewDidAppear: methods. The former is called only when the view has just been loaded into memory. The latter is called every time the view is displayed, which happens both at launch and whenever we return to our controller after showing another full-screen view, such as the image picker.

Next up are three utility methods, the first of which is the updateDisplay method. It is called from the viewDidAppear: method, which is called both when the view is first created and again after the user picks an image or video and dismisses the image picker. Because of this dual usage, it needs to make a few checks to see what's what and set up the GUI accordingly. The MPMoviePlayerController doesn't let us change the URL it reads from, so each time we want to display a movie, we'll need to make a new controller. We handle all of that here by adding this code toward the bottom of the file:

```
- (void)updateDisplay
{
    if ([self.lastChosenMediaType isEqual:(NSString *)kUTTypeImage]) {
        self.imageView.image = self.image;
        self.imageView.hidden = NO;
        self.moviePlayerController.view.hidden = YES;
```

```
    } else if ([self.lastChosenMediaType isEqual:(NSString *)kUTTypeMovie]) {
        [self.moviePlayerController.view removeFromSuperview];
        self.moviePlayerController = [[MPMoviePlayerController alloc]
                                        initWithContentURL:self.movieURL];
        [self.moviePlayerController play];
        UIView *movieView = self.moviePlayerController.view;
        movieView.frame = self.imageView.frame;
        movieView.clipsToBounds = YES;
        [self.view addSubview:movieView];
        self.imageView.hidden = YES;
    }
}
```

The second utility method, pickMediaFromSource:, is the one that both of our action methods call. This method is pretty simple. It just creates and configures an image picker, using the passed-in sourceType to determine whether to bring up the camera or the media library. We do so by adding this code toward the bottom of the file:

```
- (void)pickMediaFromSource:(UIImagePickerControllerSourceType)sourceType
{
    NSArray *mediaTypes = [UIImagePickerController
                            availableMediaTypesForSourceType:sourceType];
    if ([UIImagePickerController
        isSourceTypeAvailable:sourceType] && [mediaTypes count] > 0) {
        NSArray *mediaTypes = [UIImagePickerController
                                availableMediaTypesForSourceType:sourceType];
        UIImagePickerController *picker = [[UIImagePickerController alloc] init];
        picker.mediaTypes = mediaTypes;
        picker.delegate = self;
        picker.allowsEditing = YES;
        picker.sourceType = sourceType;
        [self presentViewController:picker animated:YES completion:NULL];
    } else {
        UIAlertView *alert =
        [[UIAlertView alloc] initWithTitle:@"Error accessing media"
                                    message:@"Unsupported media source."
                                    delegate:nil
                            cancelButtonTitle:@"Drat!"
                            otherButtonTitles:nil];
        [alert show];
    }
}
```

The third and final utility method is shrinkImage:toSize:, which we use to shrink our image down to the size of the view in which we're going to show it. Doing so reduces the size of the UIImage we're dealing with, as well as the amount of memory that imageView needs in order to display it. Since we don't want our images to get all weirdly stretched out, we adjust the target size so that what we're drawing matches the original image's aspect ratio. To do this, we add this code toward the end of the file:

```
- (UIImage *)shrinkImage:(UIImage *)original toSize:(CGSize)size
{
    UIGraphicsBeginImageContextWithOptions(size, YES, 0);

    CGFloat originalAspect = original.size.width / original.size.height;
    CGFloat targetAspect = size.width / size.height;
    CGRect targetRect;

    if (originalAspect > targetAspect) {
        // original is wider than target
        targetRect.size.width = size.width;
        targetRect.size.height = size.height * targetAspect / originalAspect;
        targetRect.origin.x = 0;
        targetRect.origin.y = (size.height - targetRect.size.height) * 0.5;
    } else if (originalAspect < targetAspect) {
        // original is narrower than target
        targetRect.size.width = size.width * originalAspect / targetAspect;
        targetRect.size.height = size.height;
        targetRect.origin.x = (size.width - targetRect.size.width) * 0.5;
        targetRect.origin.y = 0;
    } else {
        // original and target have same aspect ratio
        targetRect = CGRectMake(0, 0, size.width, size.height);
    }

    [original drawInRect:targetRect];
    UIImage *final = UIGraphicsGetImageFromCurrentImageContext();
    UIGraphicsEndImageContext();

    return final;
}
```

What you're seeing here is a series of calls that create a new image based on the specified size and render the old image into the new one.

Next, implement the following action methods that we declared in the header:

```
- (IBAction)shootPictureOrVideo:(id)sender {
    [self pickMediaFromSource:UIImagePickerControllerSourceTypeCamera];
}

- (IBAction)selectExistingPictureOrVideo:(id)sender {
    [self pickMediaFromSource:UIImagePickerControllerSourceTypePhotoLibrary];
}
```

Each of these simply calls out to one of the utility methods we defined earlier, passing in a value defined by UIImagePickerController to specify where the picture or video should come from.

Now it's finally time implement the delegate methods for the picker view:

```
#pragma mark - Image Picker Controller delegate methods
- (void)imagePickerController:(UIImagePickerController *)picker
didFinishPickingMediaWithInfo:(NSDictionary *)info
{
    self.lastChosenMediaType = info[UIImagePickerControllerMediaType];
    if ([self.lastChosenMediaType isEqual:(NSString *)kUTTypeImage]) {
        UIImage *chosenImage = info[UIImagePickerControllerEditedImage];
        self.image = [self shrinkImage:chosenImage
                                 toSize:self.imageView.bounds.size];
    } else if ([self.lastChosenMediaType isEqual:(NSString *)kUTTypeMovie]) {
        self.movieURL = info[UIImagePickerControllerMediaURL];
    }
    [picker dismissViewControllerAnimated:YES completion:NULL];
}

- (void)imagePickerControllerDidCancel:(UIImagePickerController *)picker
{
    [picker dismissViewControllerAnimated:YES completion:NULL];
}
```

The first delegate method checks to see whether a picture or video was chosen, makes note of the selection (shrinking the chosen image, if any, to precisely fit the display size along the way), and then dismisses the modal image picker. The second one just dismisses the image picker.

That's all you need to do. Compile and run the app. If you're running on the simulator, you won't have the option to take a new picture, but will only be able to choose from the photo library — as if you had any photos in your simulator's photo library! If you have the opportunity to run the application on a real device, go ahead and try it. You should be able to take a new picture, and zoom in and out of the picture using the pinch gestures. The first time the app needs to access the user's photos on iOS, the user will be asked to allow this access; this is privacy feature that was added back in iOS 6 to make sure that apps aren't sneakily grabbing photos without users' consent.

After choosing a photo, if you zoom in and pan around before hitting the *Use Photo* button, the cropped image will be the one returned to the application in the delegate method.

It's a Snap!

Believe it or not, that's all there is to letting your users take pictures with the camera so that the pictures can be used by your application. You can even let the user do a small amount of editing on that image if you so choose.

In the next chapter, we're going to look at reaching a larger audience for your iOS applications by making them oh-so-easy to translate into other languages. *Êtes-vous prêt? Tournez la page et allez directement. Allez, allez!*

Chapter 22

Application Localization

At the time of this writing, the iPhone is available in more than 90 different countries, and that number will continue to increase over time. You can now buy and use an iPhone on every continent except Antarctica. The iPad and iPod touch are also sold all over the world and are nearly as ubiquitous as the iPhone.

If you plan on releasing applications through the App Store, your potential market is considerably larger than just people in your own country who speak your own language. Fortunately, iOS has a robust **localization** architecture that lets you easily translate your application (or have it translated by others) into, not only multiple languages, but even into multiple dialects of the same language. Do you want to provide different terminology to English speakers in the United Kingdom than you do to English speakers in the United States? No problem.

That is, localization is no problem if you've written your code correctly. Retrofitting an existing application to support localization is much harder than writing your application that way from the start. In this chapter, we'll show you how to write your code so it is easy to localize, and then we'll go about localizing a sample application.

Localization Architecture

When a nonlocalized application is run, all of the application's text will be presented in the developer's own language, also known as the **development base language**.

When developers decide to localize their applications, they create a subdirectory in their application bundle for each supported language. Each language's subdirectory contains a subset of the application's resources that were translated into that language. Each subdirectory is called a **localization project**, or **localization folder**. Localization folder names always end with the *.lproj* extension.

In the iOS Settings application, the user has the ability to set the device's preferred language and region format. For example, if the user's language is English, available regions might be the United States, Australia, and Hong Kong—all regions in which English is spoken.

When a localized application needs to load a resource—such as an image, property list, or nib—the application checks the user's language and region, and then looks for a localization folder that matches that setting. If it finds one, it will load the localized version of the resource instead of the base version.

For users who select French as their iOS language and France as their region, the application will look first for a localization folder named *fr_FR.lproj*. The first two letters of the folder name are the ISO country code that represents the French language. The two letters following the underscore are the ISO code that represents France.

If the application cannot find a match using the two-letter code, it will look for a match using the language's three-letter ISO code. In our example, if the application is unable to find a folder named *fr_FR.lproj*, it will look for a localization folder named *fre_FR or fra_FR*.

All languages have at least one three-letter code. Some have two three-letter codes: one for the English spelling of the language and another for the native spelling. Some languages have only two-letter codes. When a language has both a two-letter code and a three-letter code, the two-letter code is preferred.

> **Note**   You can find a list of the current ISO country codes on the ISO web site
> (http://www.iso.org/iso/country_codes.htm). Both the two- and three-letter codes are part of the
> ISO 3166 standard.

If the application cannot find a folder that is an exact match, it will then look for a localization folder in the application bundle that matches just the language code without the region code. So, staying with our French-speaking person from France, the application next looks for a localization project called *fr.lproj*. If it doesn't find a language project with that name, it will look for *fre.lproj* and then *fra. lproj*. If none of those is found, it checks for *French.lproj*. The last construct exists to support legacy Mac OS X applications; generally speaking, you should avoid it.

If the application doesn't find a language project that matches either the language/region combination or just the language, it will use the resources from the development base language. If it does find an appropriate localization project, it will always look there first for any resources that it needs. If you load a UIImage using imageNamed:, for example, the application will look first for an image with the specified name in the localization project. If it finds one, it will use that image. If it doesn't, it will fall back to the base language resource.

If an application has more than one localization project that matches—for example, a project called *fr_FR.lproj* and one called *fr.lproj*—it will look first in the more specific match, which is *fr_FR.lproj* in this case. If it doesn't find the resource there, it will look in *fr.lproj*. This gives you the ability to provide resources common to all speakers of a language in one language project, localizing only those resources that are impacted by differences in dialect or geographic region.

You should choose to localize only those resources that are affected by language or country. For example, if an image in your application has no words and its meaning is universal, there's no need to localize that image.

Strings Files

What do you do about string literals and string constants in your source code? Consider this source code from the previous chapter:

```
UIAlertView *alert = [[UIAlertView alloc]
    initWithTitle:@"Error accessing photo library"
          message:@"Device does not support a photo library"
         delegate:nil
cancelButtonTitle:@"Drat!"
otherButtonTitles:nil];
[alert show];
```

If you've gone through the effort of localizing your application for a particular audience, you certainly don't want to be presenting alerts written in the development base language. The answer is to store these strings in special text files called **strings files**.

What's in a Strings File?

Strings files are nothing more than Unicode text files that contain a list of string pairs, each identified by a comment. Here is an example of what a strings file might look like in your application:

```
/* Used to ask the user his/her first name */
"LABEL_FIRST_NAME" = "First Name";

/* Used to get the user's last name */
"LABEL_LAST_NAME" = "Last Name";

/* Used to ask the user's birth date */
"LABEL_BIRTHDAY" = "Birthday";
```

The values between the /* and the */ characters are just comments for the translator. They are not used in the application, and you could skip adding them, though they're a good idea. The comments give context, showing how a particular string is being used in the application.

You'll notice that each line lists the same string twice. The string on the left side of the equal sign acts as a key, and it will always contain the same value, regardless of language. The value on the right side of the equal sign is the one that is translated to the local language. So, the preceding strings file, localized into French, might look like this:

```
/* Used to ask the user his/her first name */
"LABEL_FIRST_NAME " = "Prénom";

/* Used to get the user's last name */
"LABEL_LAST_NAME" = "Nom de famille";

/* Used to ask the user's birth date */
"LABEL_BIRTHDAY" = "Anniversaire";
```

The Localized String Macro

You won't actually create the strings file by hand. Instead, you'll embed each localizable text string in a special macro in your code. Once your source code is final and ready for localization, you'll run a command-line program named genstrings. This program will search all your code files for occurrences of the macro, pulling out all the unique strings and embedding them in a localizable strings file.

Let's see how the macro works. First, here's a traditional string declaration:

```
NSString *myString = @"First Name";
```

To make this string localizable, do this instead:

```
NSString *myString = NSLocalizedString(@"LABEL_FIRST_NAME",
    @"Used to ask the user his/her first name");
```

The NSLocalizedString macro takes two parameters:

- The first parameter is the string value in the base language. If there is no localization, the application will use this string.

- The second parameter is used as a comment in the strings file.

NSLocalizedString looks in the application bundle inside the appropriate localization project for a strings file named *localizable.strings*. If it does not find the file, it returns its first parameter, and the string will appear in the development base language. Strings are typically displayed only in the base language during development, since the application will not yet be localized.

If NSLocalizedString finds the strings file, it searches the file for a line that matches the first parameter. In the preceding example, NSLocalizedString will search the strings file for the string "LABEL_FIRST_NAME". If it doesn't find a match in the localization project that matches the user's language settings, it will then look for a strings file in the base language and use the value there. If there is no strings file, it will just use the first parameter you passed to the NSLocalizedString macro.

You could use the base language text as the key for the NSLocalizedString macro because it returns the first key argument if no matching localized text can be found. This would make the preceding example look like this:

```
NSString *myString = NSLocalizedString(@"First Name",
    @"Used to ask the user his/her first name");
```

However, this approach is not recommended for two reasons. First, it is unlikely that you will come up with the perfect text for your app on your first try. Going back and changing all keys in the strings files is cumbersome and error-prone, which means that you will most likely end up with keys that do not match what is used in the app, anyway. The second reason is that, by clearly using uppercase keys, you can immediately notice if you have forgotten to localize any text when you run the app just by looking at it.

Now that you have an idea of how the localization architecture and the strings file work, let's take a look at localization in action.

Real-World iOS: Localizing Your Application

We're going to create a small application that displays the user's current **locale**. A locale (an instance of NSLocale) represents both the user's language and region. It is used by the system to determine which language to use when interacting with the user, as well as how to display dates, currency, and time information, among other things. After we create the application, we will then localize it into other languages. You'll learn how to localize storyboard files, strings files, images, and even your application's display name.

You can see what our application is going to look like in Figure 22-1. The name across the top comes from the user's locale. The ordinals down the left side of the view are static labels, and their values will be set by localizing the storyboard file. The words down the right side, and the flag image at the bottom of the screen, will all chosen in our app's code at runtime based on the user's locale.

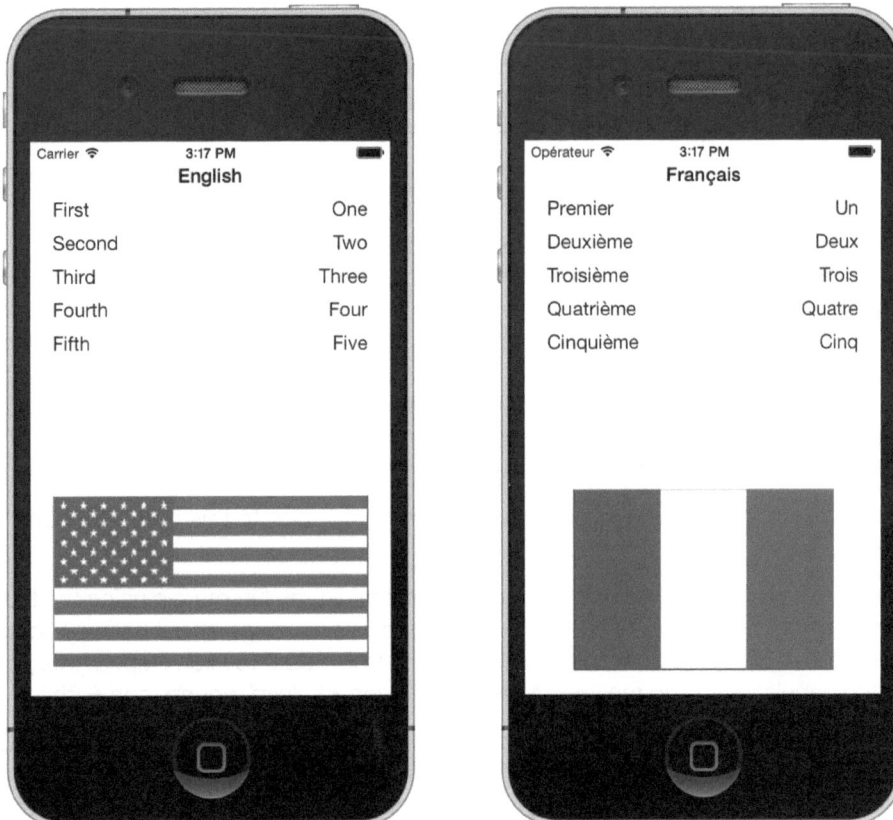

Figure 22-1. The LocalizeMe application shown with two different language/region settings

Let's hop right into it.

Setting Up LocalizeMe

Create a new project in Xcode using the *Single View Application* template and call it *LocalizeMe*.

If you look in the source code archive (in the *22 - LocalizeMe* folder), you'll see a folder named *Images*. Inside that folder, you'll find a pair of images, one named *flag_usa.png* and one named *flag_france.png*. In Xcode, select the *Images.xcassets* item, and then drag both *flag_usa.png* and *flag_france.png* into it.

Now let's add some label outlets to the project's view controller. We need to create one outlet for the blue label across the top of the view, another for the image view that will show a flag, and an outlet collection for all the words down the right-hand side (see Figure 22-1). Select *BIDViewController.m* and make the following changes:

```
#import "BIDViewController.h"

@interface BIDViewController ()

@property (weak, nonatomic) IBOutlet UILabel *localeLabel;
@property (weak, nonatomic) IBOutlet UIImageView *flagImageView;
@property (strong, nonatomic) IBOutletCollection(UILabel) NSArray *labels;

@end
```

Now select *Main.storyboard* to edit the GUI in Interface Builder. Drag a *Label* from the library, dropping it at the top of the view, aligned with the top blue guideline. Resize the label so that it takes the entire width of the view, from blue guideline to blue guideline. With the label selected, open the attributes inspector. Look for the *Font* control and click the small *T* icon it contains to bring up a small font-selection popup. Click *System Bold* to let this title label stand out a bit from the rest. Next, use the attributes inspector to set the text alignment to centered and to set the text color to a bright blue. You can also use the font selector to make the font size larger if you wish. As long as *Autoshrink* is selected in the object attributes inspector, the text will be resized if it gets too long to fit.

With your label in place, control-drag from the *View Controller* icon to this new label, and then select the *localeLabel* outlet.

Next, drag five more *Labels* from the library and put them against the left margin using the blue guideline, one above the other (again, see Figure 22-1). Resize the labels so they go about halfway across the view, or a little less. Double-click the top one and change its text from *Label* to *First*. Repeat this procedure with the other four labels, changing the text to the words *Second*, *Third*, *Fourth*, and *Fifth*.

Drag five more *Labels* from the library, this time placing them against the right margin. Change the text alignment using the object attributes inspector so that they are right-aligned, and then increase the width of the labels so that they stretch from the right blue guideline to about the middle of the view. Control-drag from *View Controller* to each of the five new labels, connecting each one to the labels outlet collection, and making sure to connect them in the right order from top to bottom. Now, double-click each one of the new labels and delete its text. We will be setting these values programmatically.

Finally, drag an *Image View* from the library over to the bottom part of the view, so it touches the bottom and left blue guidelines. In the attributes inspector, select *flag_usa* for the view's *Image* attribute and resize the image to stretch from blue guideline to blue guideline. In the attributes inspector, change the *Mode* attribute from its current value to *Aspect Fit*. Not all flags have the same aspect ratio, and we want to make sure the localized versions of the image look right. Selecting this option will cause the image view to resize any other images put in this image view so they fit, but it will also maintain the correct aspect ratio (ratio of height to width). Next, make the flag bigger until it hits the right-side blue guideline. Finally, control-drag from the view controller to this image view and select the *flagImageView* outlet.

Save your storyboard, and then switch to *BIDViewController.m* and add the following code to the viewDidLoad method:

```
- (void)viewDidLoad
{
    [super viewDidLoad];
    // Do any additional setup after loading the view, typically from a nib.
    NSLocale *locale = [NSLocale currentLocale];
    NSString *currentLangID = [[NSLocale preferredLanguages] objectAtIndex:0];
    NSString *displayLang = [locale displayNameForKey:NSLocaleLanguageCode
                                            value:currentLangID];
    NSString *capitalized = [displayLang capitalizedStringWithLocale:locale];
    self.localeLabel.text = capitalized;

    [self.labels[0] setText:NSLocalizedString(@"LABEL_ONE", @"The number 1")];
    [self.labels[1] setText:NSLocalizedString(@"LABEL_TWO", @"The number 2")];
    [self.labels[2] setText:NSLocalizedString(@"LABEL_THREE",
                                            @"The number 3")];
    [self.labels[3] setText:NSLocalizedString(@"LABEL_FOUR", @"The number 4")];
    [self.labels[4] setText:NSLocalizedString(@"LABEL_FIVE", @"The number 5")];

    NSString *flagFile = NSLocalizedString(@"FLAG_FILE", @"Name of the flag");
    self.flagImageView.image = [UIImage imageNamed:flagFile];
}
```

The first thing we do in this code is get an NSLocale instance that represents the user's current locale. This instance can tell us both the user's language and region preferences, as set in the iPhone's Settings application:

```
NSLocale *locale = [NSLocale currentLocale];
```

Next, we grab the user's preferred language. This gives us a two-character code, such as "en" or "fr":

```
NSString *currentLangID = [[NSLocale preferredLanguages] objectAtIndex:0];
```

The next line of code might need a bit of explanation. NSLocale works somewhat like a dictionary. It can give you a whole bunch of information about the current user's preferences, including the name of the currency and the expected date format. You can find a complete list of the information that you can retrieve in the NSLocale API reference.

In this next line of code, we're using a method called displayNameForKey:value: to retrieve the actual name of the chosen language, translated into the language of the current locale itself. The purpose of this method is to return the value of the item we've requested in a specific language.

The display name for the French language, for example, is *français* in French, but *French* in English. This method gives you the ability to retrieve data about any locale, so that it can be displayed appropriately for all users. In this case, we want the display name of the user's preferred language in the language currently being used, which is why we pass currentLangID as the second argument. This string is a two-letter language code, similar to the one we used earlier to create our language projects. For an English speaker, it would be *en*; and for a French speaker, it would be *fr*:

```
NSString *displayLang = [locale displayNameForKey:NSLocaleLanguageCode
                                            value:currentLangID];
```

The name we get back from this is going to be something like "English" or "français"—and it will only capitalized if language names are always capitalized in the user's preferred language. That's the case in English, but not so in French. We want the name capitalized for displaying as a title, however. Fortunately, NSString has methods for capitalizing strings, including one that will capitalize a string according to the rules of a given locale! Let's use that to turn "français" into "Français":

```
NSString *capitalized = [displayLang capitalizedStringWithLocale:locale];
```

Once we have the display name, we use it to set the top label in the view:

```
self.localeLabel.text = capitalized;
```

Next, we set the five other labels to the numbers 1 through 5, spelled out in our development base language. We also provide a comment indicating what each word is. You can just pass an empty string if the words are obvious, as they are here; however, any string you pass in the second argument will be turned into a comment in the strings file, so you can use this comment to communicate with the person doing your translations:

```
[self.labels[0] setText:NSLocalizedString(@"LABEL_ONE", @"The number 1")];
[self.labels[1] setText:NSLocalizedString(@"LABEL_TWO", @"The number 2")];
[self.labels[2] setText:NSLocalizedString(@"LABEL_THREE",
                                          @"The number 3")];
[self.labels[3] setText:NSLocalizedString(@"LABEL_FOUR", @"The number 4")];
[self.labels[4] setText:NSLocalizedString(@"LABEL_FIVE", @"The number 5")];
```

Finally, we do another string lookup to find the name of the flag image to use and populate our image view with the named image:

```
NSString *flagFile = NSLocalizedString(@"FLAG_FILE", @"Name of the flag");
self.flagImageView.image = [UIImage imageNamed:flagFile];
```

Let's run our application now.

Trying Out LocalizeMe

You can use either the simulator or a device to test *LocalizeMe*. The simulator does seem to cache some language and region settings, so you may want to run the application on the device if you have that option. Once the application launches, it should look like Figure 22-2.

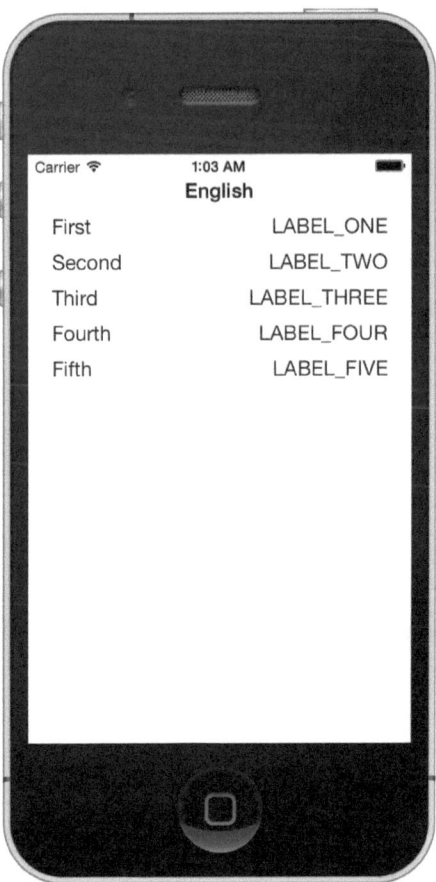

Figure 22-2. *The language running under the authors' base language. Our application is set up for localization, but it is not yet localized*

By using the NSLocalizedString macros instead of static strings, we are ready for localization. However, we are not localized yet, as is glaringly obvious from the uppercase labels in the right column and the lack of a flag image at the bottom. If you use the Settings application on the simulator or on your iPhone to change to another language or region, the results look essentially the same, except for the label at the top of the view (see Figure 22-3).

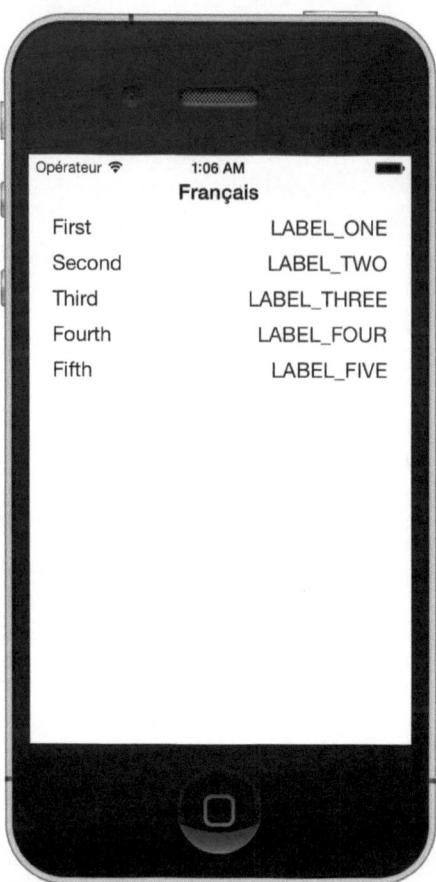

Figure 22-3. The nonlocalized application running on an iPhone and set to use the French language

Localizing the Project

Now let's localize the project. In Xcode's project navigator, single-click *LocalizeMe*, click the *LocalizeMe* project (not one of the targets) in the editing area, and then select the *Info* tab for the project.

Look for the *Localizations* section in the *Info* tab. You'll see that it shows two localizations: *Base* and *English*. When creating a new project, Xcode creates an unspecified default localization called Base, along with a specific localization for the developer's language. We want to add French, so click the plus (+) button at the bottom of the *Localizations* section and select *French (fr)* from the popup list that appears (see Figure 22-4).

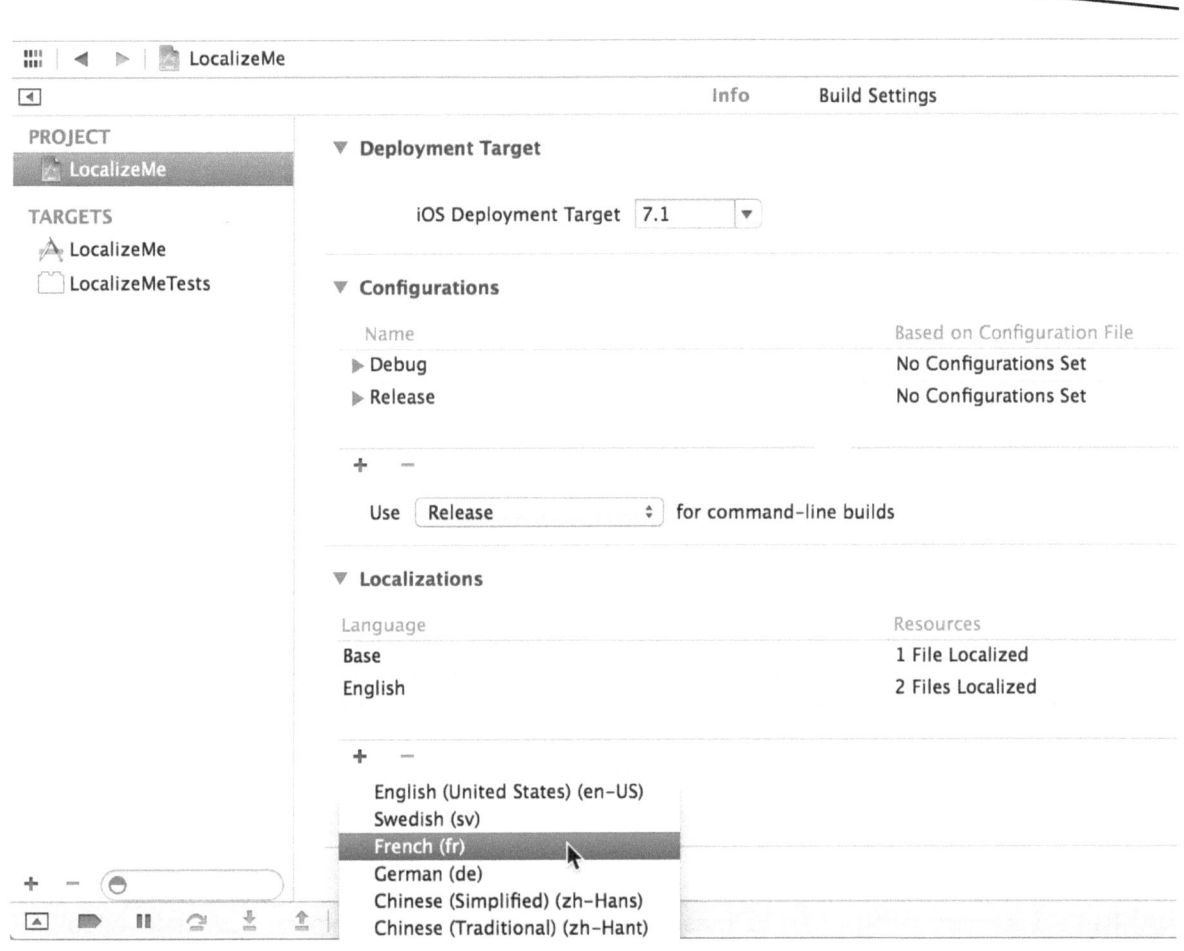

Figure 22-4. The project info settings showing localizations and other information

Next, you will be asked to choose all existing localizable files that you want to localize and what base language you want the new French localization to start from (see Figure 22-5). Right now, each of these popup buttons lets us choose only what it's already showing (either Base or English), so just leave all files checked and select Finish.

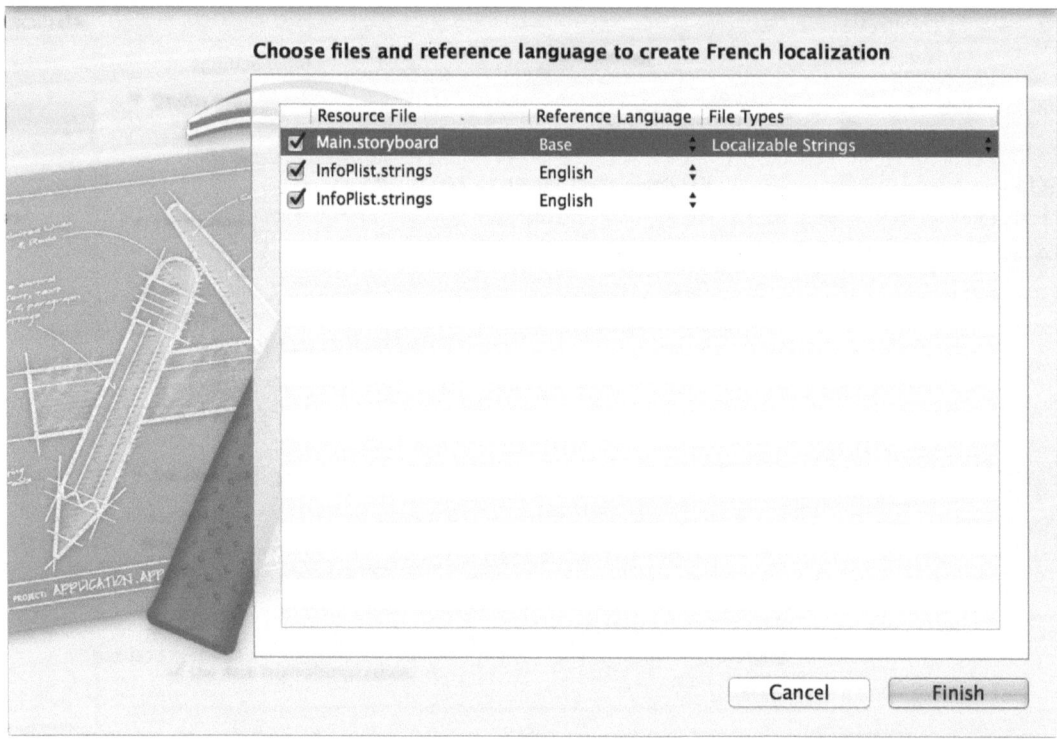

Figure 22-5. Choosing the files for localization

After adding a localization, take a look at the project navigator. Notice that the *Main.storyboard* file now has a disclosure triangle next to it, as if it were a group or folder. Expand it and take a look (see Figure 22-6).

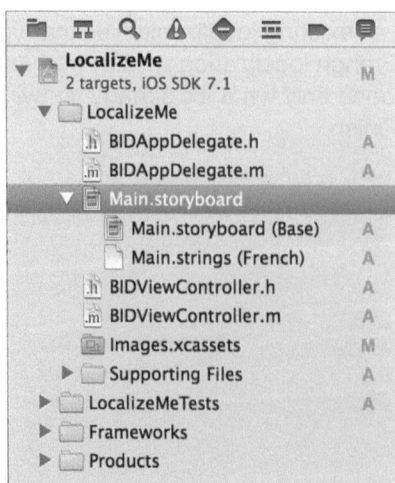

Figure 22-6. Localizable files have a disclosure triangle and a child value for each language or region you add

In our project, *Main.storyboard* is now shown as a group containing two children. The first is called *Main.Storyboard* and tagged as *Base*; the second is called *Main.strings* and tagged as *French*. The *Base* version was created automatically when you created the project, and it represents your development base language.

Each of these files lives in a separate folder, one called *Base.lproj* and one called *fr.lproj*. Go to the Finder and open the *LocalizeMe* folder within your *LocalizeMe* project folder. In addition to all your project files, you should see folders named *Base.lproj* and *fr.lproj*; for that matter, you should see one named *en.lproj*, as well (see Figure 22-7).

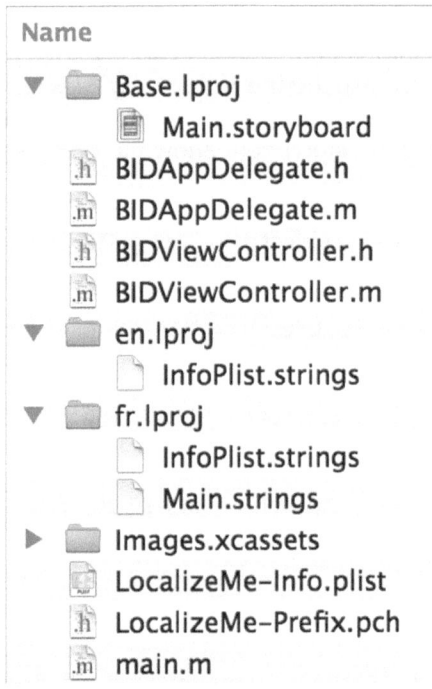

Figure 22-7. From the outset, our Xcode project included an unspecified Base language project folder (Base.lproj), as well as a specific one for our current language (in this case, en.lproj). When we chose to make a file localizable, Xcode created a language project folder (fr.lproj) for the language we selected, as well

Note that the *Base.lproj* folder was there all along, with its copy of *Main.storyboard* inside it. The *en.lproj* folder was also there all the while, holding onto an empty strings file. When Xcode finds a resource that has exactly one localized version, it displays it as a single item. As soon as a file has two or more localized versions, Xcode displays them as a group.

Tip   When dealing with locales, language codes are lowercase, but country codes are uppercase. So, the correct name for the French language project is *fr.lproj*, but the project for Parisian French (French as spoken by people in France) is *fr_FR.lproj*, not *fr_fr.lproj* or *FR_fr.lproj*. The iOS file system is case-sensitive, so it is important to match the case correctly.

When you asked Xcode to create the French localization, Xcode created a new localization project in your project folder called *fr.lproj* and placed two strings files in it. One is a direct copy of *InfoPlist. strings* from the *en.lproj* folder, and the other is a new strings file that contains values extracted from *Base.lproj/Main.storyboard*. Instead of duplicating the entire storyboard file, Xcode just extracts every text string from the storyboard and creates a strings file ready for localization. When the app is compiled and runs later, the values in the strings file are pulled in to replace the values in the storyboard.

Localizing the Storyboard

In Xcode's project navigator, *Main.storyboard* should now have two children: *Main.storyboard (Base)* and *Main.strings (French)*. And if you expand the *Supporting Files* group, you will see a similar arrangement for the *InfoPlist.strings* file. Select *Main.strings (French)* to open the strings file, the values of which will be injected into the storyboard shown to French speakers. You'll see something like the following text:

```
/* Class = "IBUILabel"; text = "Second"; ObjectID = "Agv-gm-Tho"; */
"Agv-gm-Tho.text" = "Second";

/* Class = "IBUILabel"; text = "Fourth"; ObjectID = "HiM-7A-r08"; */
"HiM-7A-r08.text" = "Fourth";

/* Class = "IBUILabel"; text = "Label"; ObjectID = "JHX-Zt-53a"; */
"JHX-Zt-53a.text" = "Label";

/* Class = "IBUILabel"; text = "Label"; ObjectID = "KVR-sO-2C5"; */
"KVR-sO-2C5.text" = "Label";
.
.
.
```

Each of these line-pairs represents a string that was found in the storyboard. The comment tells you the class of the object that contained the string, the original string itself, and a unique `ObjectID` for each object. The line after the comment is where you actually want to change the value on the right-hand side. You'll see that some of these contain ordinals such as *First*; those are the labels on the left, all of which were given names in the storyboard. Others contain just the word *Label*, and these correspond to those labels on the right that kept their default title value. Locate each label text that contains any of the ordinal numbers *First*, *Second*, *Third*, *Fourth*, and *Fifth*; and then change the string to the right of the equal sign to *Premier*, *Deuxième*, *Troisième*, *Quatrième*, and *Cinquième*, respectively. Finally, save the file.

Your storyboard is now localized in French. Compile and run the program. If you're already changed your Settings to the French language, you should see your translated labels on the left. Otherwise, go into the Settings app, switch to French, and then launch the app from Xcode again. For those folks who are a bit unsure about how to make those changes, we'll walk you through it.

In the simulator, go to the Settings application, select the *General* row, and then select the row labeled *International*. From here, you'll be able to change your language and region preferences (see Figure 22-8).

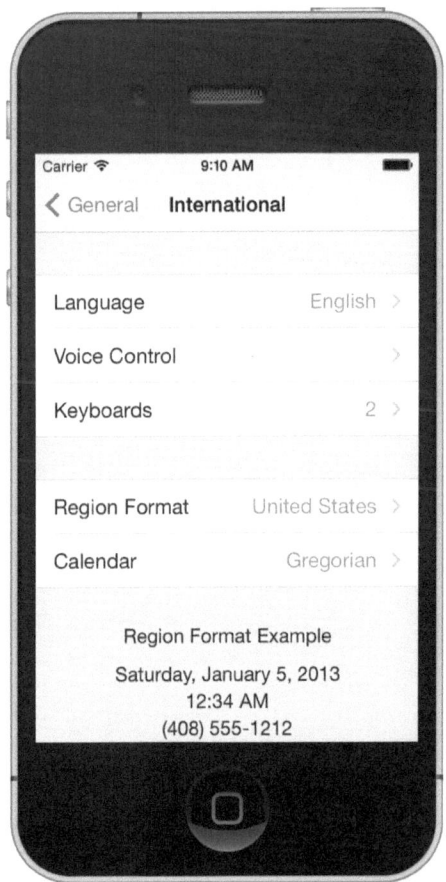

Figure 22-8. Changing the language and region—the two settings that affect the user's locale

You want to change the *Region Format* first because, once you change the language, iOS will reset and return to the home screen. Change the *Region Format* from *United States* to *France* (first select *French*, and then select *France* from the new table that appears), and then change *Language* from *English* to *Français*. Press the *Done* button, and the simulator will reset its language. Now your phone is set to use French.

Run your app again. This time, the words down the left-hand side should show up in French (see Figure 22-9). Unfortunately, the flag and right column of text are still wrong. We'll take care of those in the next section.

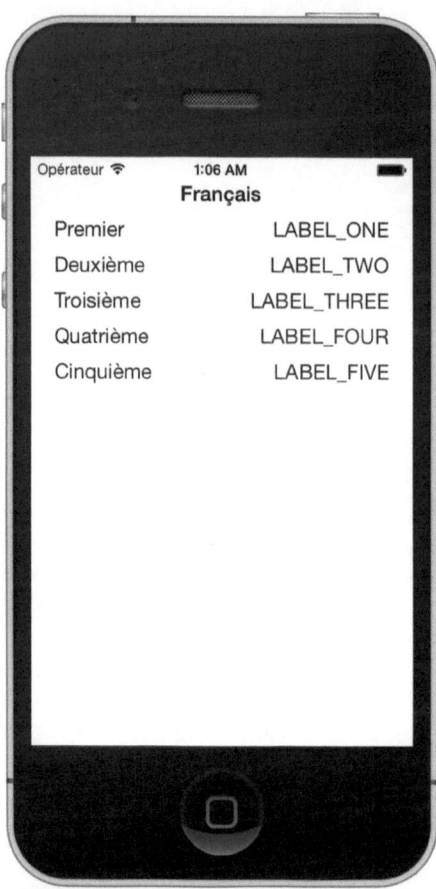

Figure 22-9. The application is partially translated into French now

Generating and Localizing a Strings File

In Figure 22-9, notice that the words on the right side of the view are still in SHOUT_ALL_CAPS style. In order to translate those, we need to generate our base language strings file and then localize that. To accomplish this, we'll need to leave the comfy confines of Xcode for a few minutes.

Launch *Terminal.app*, which is in */Applications/Utilities/*. When the terminal window opens, type cd and follow it with a space. Don't press **Return**.

Now go to the Finder and drag the folder where you've saved your *LocalizeMe* project to the terminal window. As soon as you drop the folder onto the terminal window, the path to the project folder should appear on the command line. Now press **Return**. The cd command is Unix-speak for "change directory," so what you've just done is steer your terminal session from its default directory over to your project directory.

Our next step is to run the program genstrings and tell it to find all the occurrences of NSLocalizedString in your *.m* files in the *LocalizeMe* folder. To do this, type the following command and press **Return**:

```
genstrings ./LocalizeMe/*.m
```

When the command is finished executing (it just takes a fraction of a second on a project this small), you'll be returned to the command line. In the Finder, look in the project folder for a new file called *Localizable.strings*. Drag that to the *LocalizeMe* folder in Xcode's project navigator; however, when it prompts you, *don't* click the *Add* button just yet. Instead, uncheck the box that says *Copy items into destination group's folder (if needed)* because the file is already in your project folder. Click *Finish* to import the file.

> **Caution**   You can rerun `genstrings` at any time to re-create your base language file; however, once you have localized your strings file into another language, it's important that you avoid changing the text used in any of the `NSLocalizedString()` macros. That base-language version of the string is used as a key to retrieve the translations; if you change that text, the translated version will no longer be found, and you will need to either update the localized strings file or have it retranslated.

Once the file is imported, single-click *Localizable.strings* and take a look at it. It contains six entries because we use `NSLocalizableString` six times with five distinct values. The values that we passed in as the second argument have become the comments for each of the strings.

The strings were generated in alphabetical order. In this case, since we're dealing with numbers, alphabetical order is not the most intuitive way to present them. In most cases, however, having them in alphabetical order will be helpful:

```
/* Name of the flag */
"FLAG_FILE" = "FLAG_FILE";

/* The number 5 */
"LABEL_FIVE" = "LABEL_FIVE";

/* The number 4 */
"LABEL_FOUR" = "LABEL_FOUR";

/* The number 1 */
"LABEL_ONE" = "LABEL_ONE";

/* The number 3 */
"LABEL_THREE" = "LABEL_THREE";

/* The number 2 */
"LABEL_TWO" = "LABEL_TWO";
```

Let's localize this sucker.

Make sure *Localizable.strings* is selected, and then repeat the same steps we've performed for the other localizations:

1. Open the file inspector if it's not already visible.

2. In the *Localizations* section, click the *Localize...* button, which brings up a small panel where you can select the original localization to move the existing file to. You should leave this set to *Base*, then click the *Localize* button on the panel.

3. Back in the file inspector's *Localization* section, check the French and English items to make localizations for each of those languages.

Due to a bug in Xcode, you may find that you cant execute those steps exactly as described. It seems that, after the second step, Xcode loses track of the selected file, and you'll have to click *Localizable.strings* again in the project navigator. No biggie!

Back in the project navigator, click the disclosure triangle next to *Localizable.strings* and select the English localization of the file. In the editor, make the following changes:

```
/* Name of the flag */
"FLAG_FILE" = "flag_usa";

/* The number 5 */
"LABEL_FIVE" = "Five";

/* The number 4 */
"LABEL_FOUR" = "Four";

/* The number 1 */
"LABEL_ONE" = "One";

/* The number 3 */
"LABEL_THREE" = "Three";

/* The number 2 */
"LABEL_TWO" = "Two";
```

Next, select the French localization of the file. In the editor, make the following changes:

```
/* Name of the flag */
"FLAG_FILE" = "flag_france";

/* The number 5 */
"LABEL_FIVE" = "Cinq";

/* The number 4 */
"LABEL_FOUR" = "Quatre";

/* The number 1 */
"LABEL_ONE" = "Un";
```

```
/* The number 3 */
"LABEL_THREE" = "Trois";

/* The number 2 */
"LABEL_TWO" = "Deux";
```

In real life (unless you're multilingual), you would ordinarily send this file out to a translation service to translate the values to the right of the equal signs. In this simple example, armed with knowledge that came from years of watching *Sesame Street*, we can do the translation ourselves.

Now save, compile, and run the app. You should see the labels on the right-hand side translated into French (see Figure 22-10); and at the bottom of the screen, you should now see the French flag.

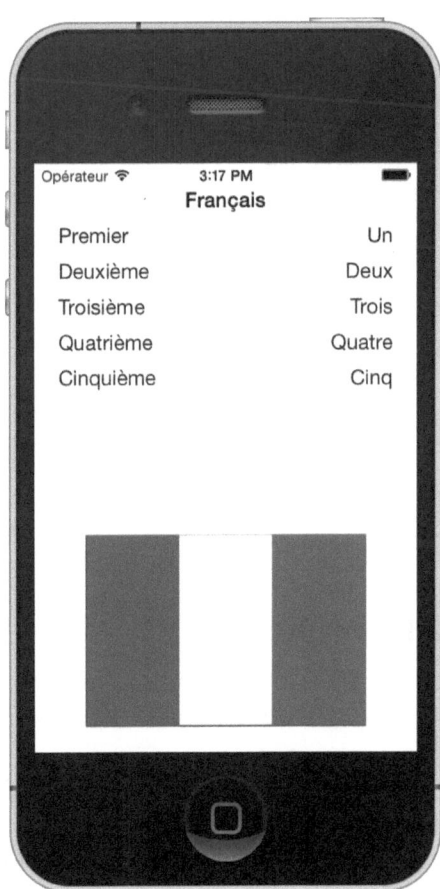

Figure 22-10. At long last, the fully localized app

Use the Settings app to switch back to English and rerun the app, and you'll now see the English text everywhere and the U.S. flag at the bottom.

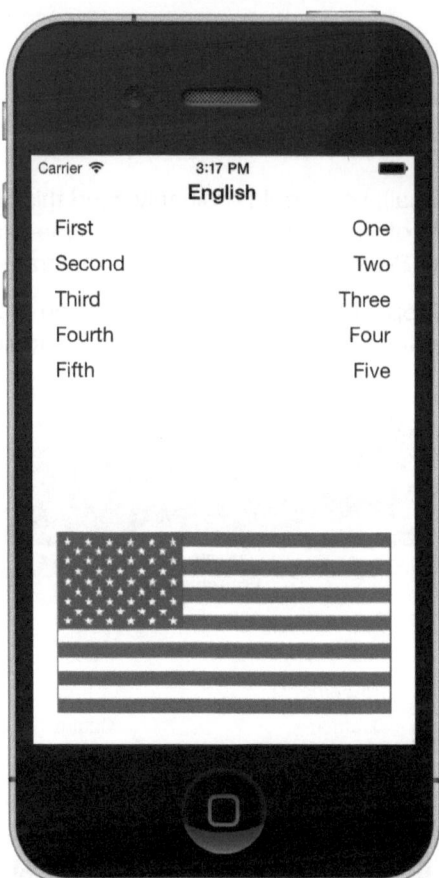

Figure 22-11. And back to the English translation, now equipped with a flag

Localizing the App Display Name

We want to show you one final piece of localization that is commonly used: localizing the app name that's visible on the home screen and elsewhere. Apple does this for several of the built-in apps, and you might want to do so, as well.

The app name used for display is stored in your app's *Info.plist* file, which, in our case, is actually named *LocalizeMe-Info.plist*. You'll find it in the *Supporting Files* folder. Select this file for editing, and you'll see that one of the items it contains, *Bundle display name*, is currently set to *${PRODUCT_NAME}*.

In the syntax used by *Info.plist* files, anything starting with a dollar sign is subject to variable substitution. In this case, it means that when Xcode compiles the app, the value of this item will be replaced with the name of the product in this Xcode project, which is the name of the app itself. This is where we want to do some localization, replacing *${PRODUCT_NAME}* with the localized name for each language. However, as it turns out, this doesn't quite work out as simply as you might expect.

The *Info.plist* file is sort of a special case, and it isn't meant to be localized. Instead, if you want to localize the content of *Info.plist*, you need to make localized versions of a file named *InfoPlist.strings*. Fortunately, that file is already included in every project Xcode creates.

Look in the *Supporting Files* folder and find the *InfoPlist.strings* file. Use the file inspector's *Localizations* section to create a French localization using the same steps you did for the previous localizations (it starts off with an English version located in the *en.lproj* folder).

Now we want to add a line to define the display name for the app. In the *LocalizeMe-Info.plist* file, we were shown the display name associated with a dictionary key called *Bundle display name*; however, that's not the real key name! It's merely an Xcode nicety, trying to give us a more friendly and readable name. The real name is *CFBundleDisplayName*, which you can verify by selecting *LocalizeMe-Info.plist*, right-clicking anywhere in the view, and then selecting Show Raw Keys/Values. This shows you the true names of the keys in use.

So, select the English localization of *InfoPlist.strings* and add the following line:

```
CFBundleDisplayName = "Localize Me";
```

Now select the French localization of the *InfoPlist.strings* file. Edit the file to give the app a proper French name:

```
CFBundleDisplayName = "Localisez Moi";
```

Build and run the app, and then press the Home button to get back to the launch screen. And of course, switch the device or simulator you're using to French if it's currently running in English. You should see the localized name just underneath the app's icon, but sometimes it may not appear immediately. iOS seems to cache this information when a new app is added, but it doesn't necessarily change it when an existing app is replaced by a new version—at least not when Xcode is doing the replacing. So, if you're running in French and you don't see the new name—don't worry. Just delete the app from the launch screen, go back to Xcode, and then build and run the app again.

Now our application is fully localized for the French language.

Auf Wiedersehen

If you want to maximize sales of your iOS application, you'll probably want to localize it as much as possible. Fortunately, the iOS localization architecture makes easy work of supporting multiple languages, and even multiple dialects of the same language, within your application. As you saw in this chapter, nearly any type of file that you add to your application can be localized.

Even if you don't plan on localizing your application, you should get in the habit of using `NSLocalizedString` instead of just using static strings in your code. With Xcode's Code Sense feature, the difference in typing time is negligible. And, should you ever want to translate your application, your life will be much, much easier. Going back late in the project to find all text strings that should be localized is a boring and error-prone process, which you can avoid with a little effort in advance.

And on that note, we have now reached the end of our travels together, so it's time for us to say *sayonara*, *au revoir*, *auf wiedersehen*, *avtío*, *arrivederci*, *hej då*, and *adiós*.

The programming language and frameworks we've worked within this book are the end result of more than 25 years of evolution. And Apple engineers are feverishly working round the clock, thinking of that next, cool, new thing. The iOS platform has just begun to blossom. There is so much more to come.

By making it through this book, you've built yourself a sturdy foundation. You have a solid knowledge of Objective-C, Cocoa Touch, and the tools that bring these technologies together to create incredible new iPhone, iPod touch, and iPad applications. You understand the iOS software architecture—the design patterns that make Cocoa Touch sing. In short, you're ready to chart your own course. We are so proud!

We sure are glad you came along on this journey with us. We wish you the best of luck and hope that you enjoy programming iOS as much as we do.

Index

F

Fabsf() function, 575
Flipside view, 350, 372

G, H

Gestures
    custom gesture, 589
        CheckPlease application
           (see CheckPlease application)
        CheckPlease touch methods, 592
    definition, 563
    events, 564
    gesture recognizer, 564
    handling process, 566
    multitouch architecture, 566
    pinch and rotation detection (see Pinch
        and rotation detection)
    responder chain
        app delegate, 565
        swipe gesture, 565
        UIView, 564
        view/control, 565
        working principle, 564
    swipes application (see Swipes application)
    taps, 564, 579
    touch, 564
    TouchExplorerApplication, 568
        attributes inspector, 569
        BIDViewController.m, 569–570
        option key, 571
        shift key, 571
        view controller icon, 569
    touch notification methods, 567
Globally unique identifiers (GUIDs), 380
GPS, 595
Grand central dispatch (GCD), 455
    future aspects, 487
    queue
        blocks (closures/lambdas) (see Blocks)
        concepts, 460
        first-in, first-out (FIFO), 461
        threads, 461
    SlowWorker, 456
        BIDViewController.m, 457
        doWork: method, 458–459
        implementation, 457
        interface, 458
        sleepForTimeInterval: class method, 458
Gyro and accelerometer, 613
    accelerometer results, 624
    approaches, 622
    axes, graphic representation, 614
    BIDViewController, 633–634
    checkboxes, 632
    core motion and motion manager
        alloc and init methods, 615
        BIDViewController, 616–618
        blocks, 615
        dispatch_async() function, 619
        event-based motion, 615
        MotionMonitor, 615
        square-bracketed method, 620
    detecting shakes, 625
        application, 630
        backed-in shaking, 626
        NSURL object, 630
        shake and break, 626
        viewDidLoad method, 629
    directional controller, 630
        ball movement calculation, 638
        BIDBallView, 635
        CGRects, 639
        drawRect, 636–637
        drew sprite, 635
        implementation, 635
        pixels, velocity, 640
        rolling marbles, 631
        rolling on, 640
        substantive method, 639
    g-force measurement, 613
    proactive motion access, 621
    rotation value, 614
    viewDidDisappear, 623
    viewDidLoad method, 622, 634

I, J

iCloud
    adding support, 447
        NSMetadataQuery, 450
        ongoing query, 449
        provisioning profile, 448
        query, 449
        reloadFiles method, 449, 451

K

Get the eBook for only $10!

Now you can take the weightless companion with you anywhere, anytime. Your purchase of this book entitles you to 3 electronic versions for only $10.

This Apress title will prove so indispensible that you'll want to carry it with you everywhere, which is why we are offering the eBook in 3 formats for only $10 if you have already purchased the print book.

Convenient and fully searchable, the PDF version enables you to easily find and copy code—or perform examples by quickly toggling between instructions and applications. The MOBI format is ideal for your Kindle, while the ePUB can be utilized on a variety of mobile devices.

Go to www.apress.com/promo/tendollars to purchase your companion eBook.